The System of Industrial Relations in Canada

Third Edition

Alton W.J. Craig
Faculty of Administration
University of Ottawa

Prentice-Hall Canada Inc., Scarborough, Ontario

Canadian Cataloguing in Publication Data

Craig, Alton W.J. (Alton Westwood Joseph), 1931–
The system of industrial relations in Canada

3rd ed.
ISBN 0–13–880212–2

1. Industrial relations – Canada. I. Title.

HD8106.5.C7 1990   331′.0971   C89–095212–4

Prentice-Hall, Inc., Englewood Cliffs, New Jersey
Prentice-Hall International, Inc., London
Prentice-Hall of Australia, Pty., Ltd., Sydney
Prentice-Hall of India Pvt., Ltd., New Delhi
Prentice-Hall of Japan, Inc., Tokyo
Prentice-Hall of Southeast Asia (Pte.) Ltd., Singapore
Editora Prentice-Hall do Brasil Ltda., Rio de Janeiro
Prentice-Hall Hispanoamericana, S.A., Mexico

ISBN 0–13–880212–2

Production editors: Chelsea Donaldson/Maryrose O'Neill
Cover image: Stanislaw Fernandes/The Image Bank Canada
Cover designer: Bruce Farquhar
Manufacturing buyer: Sandra Paige
Typesetter: Colborne, Cox & Burns Typographers Inc.

Printed and bound in Canada by John Deyell Company

1 2 3 4 5 JD 94 93 92 91 90

To Dorothy

Contents

3 Theories of the Labour Movement 41

4 The History and Philosophy of the Canadian Labour Movement 61

5 The Structure and Functions of the Canadian Labour Movement 85

6 Legislation Governing Industrial Relations in the Private Sector 111

7 The Negotiation Process   149

8   Forms of Third-Party Assistance in the Negotiation Process   181

9 Administration of the Collective Agreement 206

10 Collective Bargaining in the Public and Parapublic Sectors 228

11 The Outputs of the Canadian Industrial Relations System 261

Preface

Organized into an open-systems framework, the discussions presented in this edition fulfill the need of introductory undergraduate and graduate courses for a detailed, integrated analysis of the industrial relations system in Canada. Cases on certification, contract negotiations, unfair labour practices, and arbitration supplement the major issues brought to light within the text. The short cases have been chosen for their suitability to first-level study, the long cases for their suitability to advanced study.

Open-systems theory is a particularly useful approach to understanding the multidisciplinary nature of industrial relations. It concerns itself with the actors in an industrial relations system and with the way they translate both the constraints imposed by the environment and their own goals, values, and power into system outputs. The three actors in an industrial relations system — unions, management, and third parties — affect and are affected in turn by other actors and by the environment. I have conceptualized these interrelationships in the form of a feedback loop.

There are critics of open-systems theory. These writers attribute to the theory an inappropriate emphasis on stability, harmony, and the collective regulation of industrial relations behaviour.[1] The truth is that open-systems theory presupposes neither cooperation nor conflict as the essential determinant of the union-management relationship. Indeed, this theory avoids generalizations about the attitudes and behaviour of unions and management altogether, leaving these topics wholly problematic.

Action-theory, on the other hand, makes the collective regulation of industrial relations its central focus. Problems common to workers and management, its proponents claim, may inspire various solutions, which are agreed upon through collective bargaining. Action-theory addresses not industrial relations, therefore, but negotiation — one part only of industrial relations — and fails entirely "to acknowledge that which takes place beyond the bargaining table."[2]

Marxism, another analytical approach to the study of industrial relations, views industrial relations as an arena of conflict between classes, more specifically between capital and labour.[3] According to the Marxist, the capitalist seeks to buy labour at the lowest possible price and then to combine it with other factors of production to produce the highest possible profit. The worker, on the other hand, seeks to sell labour at the highest possible price — at least an amount which the worker considers commensurate with the value to production of that particular labour. The union functions to pool power in favour of the workers.

Kark Marx, however, failed to predict the tremendous effect of state power over conditions in the workplace. Since the time of Marx, governments in the industrialized world have legislated hours of work, minimum wages, health and safety, and human rights protection. This state intervention had eradicated the extremes of exploitation which Marx believed would spark the overthrow of the capitalist society and usher in a classless society.

To my mind, familiarity with the psychology and objectives of North American workers and unions diminishes the appeal of Marxist theory to industrial relations analysis in this country. To begin with, the notion and practice of the mixed economy — the combination of private and public enterprise — is strongly entrenched here. Canadian workers and unions, moreover, appear to be neither particularly class conscious nor amenable to revolutionary doctrine. In fact, our unions have proven to be among our most conservative institutions.

Given the limitations of Marxism, action-theory, and other partially developed alternatives too numerous to discuss here, I believe open-systems theory to be the most suitable framework available. In response to some of its critics, however, I have modified the open-systems framework somewhat. In Chapter 1, I define my version of the open-systems industrial relations framework, describing the complex interrelationships between the industrial relations system and environmental subsystems. In Chapter 2, I discuss the characteristics and effects of the environment (the economic, ecological, political, legal, and social subsystems) on the actors, and the inputs and outputs of the industrial relations system.

In the next three chapters, I deal with the labour movement. Chapter 3 sets out major labour theories in the context of four questions central to any analysis of the labour movement: (1) How do we explain the origin or emergence of labour organizations? (2) How do we explain the pattern of growth and development of labour organizations? (3) What are the ultimate goals of labour organizations? and (4) Why do workers join labour organizations? Chapter 4 discusses the history and philosophy of the Canadian labour movement, emphasizes central labour organizations in Canada, and shows how American events have influenced them. Chapter 5 analyzes the general structure and statistical parameters of the movement, discusses the Canadian Labour Congress and its components, and proceeds to a freshly expanded treatment of union governance, including union conventions, democracy, officers and their tenure, leadership, and the growing importance of women in all these areas. The chapter closes by examining some of the relationships between American unions and their Canadian branches, particularly as manifested in the establishment of autonomous Canadian unions.

Chapter 6 compares private-sector labour legislation in jurisdictions from one end of the country to the other. After presenting a historical overview of the legislation, the chapter proceeds to show how different jurisdictions deal with recognition disputes, mandatory third-party assistance in interest and rights disputes, jurisdictional disputes between unions, and public policy questions, drawing attention to philosophical issues where pertinent.

Chapter 7 discusses the negotiation process — the mechanism for converting input into outputs — and includes such topics as the structure of negotiating units, the preparation of demands and counter-demands, and the strategy and tactics used by the parties at different stages of negotiations. The chapter also points out the importance of bargaining power in determining specific outcomes of negotiations and examines the factors contributing to bargaining power. Discussions of good-faith bargaining and concession bargaining are also included in this edition.

Chapter 8 considers the forms of third-party assistance provided by government agencies or private individuals in the event that the parties fail to settle through bilateral negotiations. Using the latest research findings, forms of third-party assistance — both voluntary and mandatory — are compared among eleven jurisdictions. Once a collective agreement is entered into, the problem arises of living with it for its duration: that is, of making it work for the union, management, and workers. Chapter 9 examines grievance procedures and the arbitration of contract interpretation disputes, drawing heavily on the jurisprudence which has been accumulating rapidly from recent arbitration and court decisions.

Chapter 10 sets out problems peculiar to labour relations in the public and parapublic sectors. I include in this chapter discussions on the history and structure of public-sector unions, the controversy surrounding comparisons of wages between public and private sectors, and work stoppages. A comprehensive diagrammatic comparison of legislative provisions among the jurisdictions supplements this part of the book.

Chapter 11 describes three outputs of the Canadian industrial relations system: (1) organizational outputs; (2) worker outputs; and (3) industrial conflict. Representative collective agreement clauses are clearly set out and their effects on both the industrial relations system and the environmental subsystems are discussed. The postscript closes the book by raising crucial questions about the future roles and interrelationships of unions, management, and government. Legal decisions arising from cases under the Charter of Rights and Freedoms, many of which will likely alter the nature of Canadian industrial relations, are also brought to the reader's attention. Finally, in response to Shirley Carr's 1986 ascendancy to CLC leadership, I point out the expanding future for women in the Canadian labour movement.

Notes

1 For one of the more recent critiques of theory in industrial relations, see G. Shien-stock, "Towards a Theory of Industrial Relations," Vol. XIX, No. 2, *British Journal of Industrial Relations* (July 1981), pp. 170–89, and particularly pp. 171–73 for a critique of "the systems model."

2 Ibid., p. 180.

3 For a good summary of the Marxist approach, see Schienstock's article, pp. 180–84.

Acknowledgements

The Humanities and Social Science Research Council (formerly the Canada Council) provided much appreciated financial assistance in the preparation of Chapters 6 and 10 of the first edition of this book, which deal with legislation in the private, public, and parapublic sectors respectively. Special thanks are also extended to Warren Stroud, Phillip Brazeau, and Dick Van Wyck — former students in the Faculty of Law of the University of Ottawa — for their assistance on these two chapters for the first edition. Industrial relations practitioners and government officials interviewed from Victoria to St. John's provided many insights which helped in the preparation of these two chapters for all three editions.

Former colleagues and more recently acquired ones in Labour Canada were extremely helpful and readily provided assistance when it was needed. Gratitude is due to Dr. Garfield Clack, Barry Maloney, Bernie Fortin, Ken Ross, Michael Legault, Denise Roussin, Aline Helmes, Michel Gauvin, J.C. Roy, and Nicole Marchand for providing very useful and timely information and informed suggestions. Very special thanks are due to Fred Longley of the Labour Canada Library for his extensive and generous assistance.

Miss Mary Kehoe, Assistant Editor, Public Relations Department of the Canadian Labour Congress, provided very constructive comments on drafts of the three chapters on the labour movement for the first edition. Professor Bryan Downie of Queen's University provided very helpful advice on Chapters 6 and 8 of the first edition. I am particularly grateful to Professor Joseph B. Rose of McMaster University who provided extensive comments on all chapters of the first edition of the book and to Professor Roy J. Adams of McMaster University who made me more aware than I had been of the role of the Canadian trade union movement in politics, particularly during its early years. My gratitude is also extended to Professor S. Muthuchidambaram of the University of Regina for helpful suggestions on a number of chapters and to Professor Allan Patterson of the University of Manitoba for keeping me abreast of legislative changes which took place in that province. I am extremely grateful to Professor Norman Solomon of the University of Windsor who sent me extensive comments that he made in preparing his review of the second edition for *Relations Industrielles/Industrial Relations*. Kathy Solomon made a number of suggestions to make the book more "student friendly," and many of them are incorporated in this edition. The idea of using newspaper articles was suggested by a number of people, including professors across the country who use the book.

The reviewers selected by Prentice-Hall Canada for the first and second editions of the book provided many constructive and useful suggestions. I am grateful to my associates at the Faculty of Administration, University of Ottawa, especially Professor A. V. Subbarao. In addition, I am deeply indebted to the many students in my third and fourth year undergraduate courses and to my second-year M.B.A. students over a good many years now for their thoughtful and highly constructive comments. I am more than grateful to the late Frank Hintenberger, Associate Editor of Prentice-Hall Canada who persuaded me about 15 years ago to begin the writing of this book — a dream that I had harboured since obtaining my Ph.D. from Cornell University in 1964. His replacement, Executive Editor and Vice-President, Cliff Newman, and Special Projects Editor Marta Tomins were extremely helpful in finalizing the manuscript for the first edition, and Charles Macli did an excellent job of eating it. Elynor Kagan greatly assisted me in finalizing the second edition, and Maureen Chill did an excellent job of editing it.

I am particularly indebted to David Jolliffe, Senior Project Editor, for getting the second edition put on computer disks for me (which made the preparation of this edition so much easier), and for his many suggestions throughout the entire preparation of this edition. Chelsea Donaldson did an outstanding job of tightening up the sentence structure, eliminating much of the unnecessary detail, and strengthening the logical construction of this edition, as well as making many requests for "updates." Maryrose O'Neill did a super job in coordinating the editing and production of this edition. I have been very fortunate in having had excellent people to work with on all three editions of this book.

The typing and retyping of most chapters of the first edition of this book was very capably done by Donna Curtis. Donna's dedication to this project and her penchant for excellence were very much appreciated. Thanks are also extended to Mrs. Louise Moreau and the secretarial staff of the Faculty of Administration, University of Ottawa, for their generous assistance. I would like to make a special dedication of Chapter Six to the memory of Jerry Friedman, an M.B.A. student at the University of Ottawa who assisted me with that chapter in the first edition. I am also extremely indebted to my many friends and colleagues across Canada who have used this book for a number of years now and who volunteered many very constructive suggestions for the second and third editions. Finally, my sincere thanks and continuing gratitude are extended to a dear friend and very wise counsellor, Dr. A. G. Catterson, for helping me over the many frustrating hurdles that usually accompany the writing of a textbook.

This book serves in part as a tribute to my mother, Mrs. Jane Craig, and my late father, Glenson Craig, whose generous financial and moral support during the early years of my university education I shall always appreciate.

Very special thanks are reserved for my dear wife, Dorothy, for all the encouragement and support she has given me over the past thirty years and for her help in the preparation of all three editions of this book. I dedicate it to her as an expression of my utmost and continuing gratitude. My thanks are also extended to our three children — Michael, Ann Marie (Ph.D., Biochemistry) and Robert — for their encouragement and support. I am particularly indebted to Robert for showing me how to use my word processor, and for getting me out of trouble many times in the preparation of the second and third editions. (In May 1989, Michael and Francesca blessed us with our first grandchild, Alexander, who is a constant source of joy and pride to all of us!)

James C. Fish, *The Financial Post*

1

A Framework for the Analysis of Industrial Relations Systems

Introduction

This chapter presents a systems framework for the study of industrial relations.[1] It is based on the belief that an analysis of industrial relations systems should seek not only to explain the many events which occur in the workplace, but also to show how these events influence and are influenced by society at large.

Until recently, research in this area has been characterized by conceptual vagueness and a seeming inability to relate findings to any broad and coherent system of knowledge.[2] If industrial relations is to develop into a respected and

intellectually challenging discipline, more serious attempts must be made to define its essential factors, and show how they fit into a wider system of interdependent variables and propositions. (J.T. Dunlop made a significant contribution in this regard with his book, *Industrial Relations Systems*.)[3] Since then, there have been only scattered attempts to develop more systematic approaches.[4] This chapter is set forth as an analytical tool for the purpose of this book, but it by no means constitutes a theory of industrial relations.[5] I hope, however, that it will someday serve as the basis for attempts to develop such a theory.

It has long been my view that the most promising approach for analyzing industrial relations is open-systems theory, in which the subject matter consists of a set of interrelated factors operating in a larger environment.[6] This approach implies that the system under study receives, in addition to its own internal inputs, external inputs from its environment. It then transforms these inputs into outputs for itself, which flow into pertinent environmental subsystems — legal, political, economic, etc.

Using this simplified explanation of open-systems theory, we can define industrial relations as comprising *a complex of private and public activities, operating in a specified environment, which is concerned with the allocation of rewards to workers for their services and the conditions under which these services are rendered.* The "complex of private and public activities" includes all structural arrangements and processes related to the field of study. "Operating in a specified environment" implies that an industrial relations system functions dynamically in relation to the environmental subsystems of a given society. "Rewards to employees for their services" are the material, social, and psychological rewards that workers receive for the performance of their work. Some of these rewards, such as the monetary ones, may become costs to the employer or to the economy, depending on whether a firm is analyzed as a micro unit or the economy is analyzed as a macro unit. The "conditions under which services are rendered" are the physical and other contingencies under which work is performed.

The second half of our definition is very close to the concepts of "efficiency" and "equity" that Meltz sees as the complementary core concepts of industrial relations.[7] We can think of the "services" offered by employees as the "efficiency" sought by employers, and of "equity" as the wages and other benefits that unions seek for workers as "rewards" for their services. Meltz states that

> . . . the prescriptions which an industrial relationist would apply to a particular employment

relations problem would implicitly recognize that efficiency and equity considerations are primarily complementary. It is the uniqueness of this viewpoint in the context of the employment relationship which sets industrial relations apart as a separate discipline.[8]

The Main Components of the Framework

As we have seen, the main concerns of any industrial relations system are the allocation of rewards to employees and the physical and other conditions under which work is performed. These concerns and the processes by which they are obtained form the foundation for the framework outlined in Figure 1.1.[9] Subsequent chapters will lead us into a more detailed discussion of these outputs in Chapter 11.

The analytical system presented here consists of four basic components: (1) internal inputs expressed as the goals, values, and power of the participants in the system, which are conditioned by external inputs that flow from various environmental subsystems: (2) the complex of private and public processes for converting the inputs into outputs; (3) the outputs, comprising the material, social, and psychological rewards workers receive in exchange for services; and (4) a feedback loop through which the outputs flow not only directly into the industrial relations system itself but also into the environmental subsystems. Through the feedback loop, outputs can shape the subsequent goals, values, and power of the actors in the industrial relations system and influence actors in the environmental subsystems as well.

Before we discuss the four components in more detail, we will need to define the major actors in the system.

The Actors Within the System

The principal actors in an industrial relations system are unions and corporations. Third parties may also be involved. We will examine each of these in turn.

Figure 1.1

A Framework for Analyzing Industrial Relations Systems
(A Structural-Functional Approach)

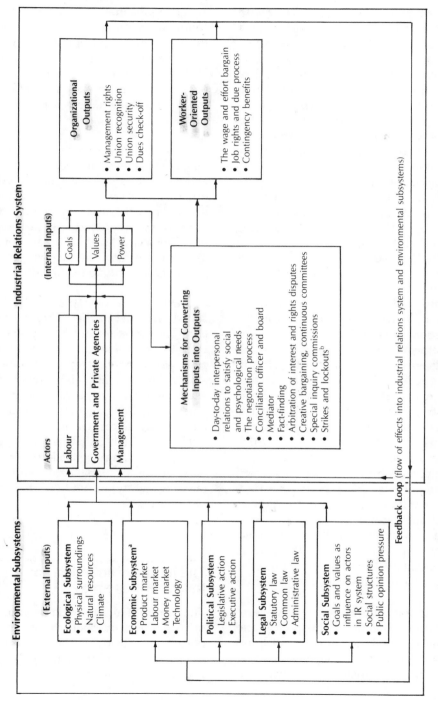

aThis model presupposes but does not explicitly show the interrelationship between the various societal subsystems.

bA work stoppage may also be considered an outcome or output of the industrial relations system.

Unions   Unions are voluntary associations formed to protect workers in their relations with their employers and to express the concerns of workers who might otherwise be powerless when confronting a large corporation or government bureaucracy. Although unions, like other organizations, seem to have a life of their own, they are far from monolithic institutions, and in fact each contains a variety of subgroups whose needs vary and whose expectations must be met, at least to a minimal degree, if the union is to remain credible. Subgroups within unions may be classified by skill level, age, gender, ethnic background, and degree of participation in union activities. Union leaders are, or should be, aware of the demands of competing subgroups so that they can make trade-offs in negotiations which serve all their members adequately.

Corporations and Non-Profit Organizations In the highly industrialized societies of North America, corporations as legal entities are by and large the means by which labour, capital, and other factor-inputs are brought together to produce the goods and services which society wants. To a great degree, ownership of capital and other resources has been divorced from the management of the organization. Thus, a corps of professional managers has evolved which makes the major corporate decisions subject only to loose control by a large and dispersed group of shareholders. Like unions, management cadres contain different subgroups with divergent demands and orientations, and senior management may be called upon to effect trade-offs between, for example, staff members (such as industrial relations experts) and operating managers (in marketing, production, finance, etc.).

Non-profit organizations such as governments, government agencies, hospitals, and schools operate in much the same way as profit-seeking corporations. The objectives of these organizations are to deliver their services as effectively and efficiently as possible, be it pension benefits, mail delivery, health care, or educational programs. Cadres of managers exist in these organizations who do not own the means of producing or delivering the services to the community. Those managers with competing objectives must make trade-offs before they meet union negotiators across the bargaining table.

Industrial relations in the unionized sector take place largely between the first two organizational forms we have described. However, organizations *per se* do not interact. It is individuals at various levels whose interactions constitute the relationships between formal organizations. As we shall see later, collective agreements contain provisions concerning these organizational relationships.

Third Parties   At times, third parties are called on to act in the industrial relations system. They may assume both public and private roles to assist one or the other (or both) of the principal actors. Examples of public actors are labour departments, labour relations boards, or similar government agencies established to designate bargaining agents for specified groups of workers and to resolve any difficulties that may arise as a result. Private actors include law firms, consulting agencies, or private individuals, who assist management and unions (separately or jointly) in their efforts to resolve their differences.

The Inputs of an Industrial Relations System

The inputs of an industrial relations system are of two types: internal (the goals, values, and power of the actors in the system) and external (the effects of environmental subsystems on the goals, values, power of these actors).

Inputs from Within the System The interrelationships among the goals, values, and power of the actors in an industrial relations system determine the system's internal inputs, and in part its outputs. Therefore, in order to discuss internal inputs, we need to look at these three concepts in relation to each of the actors in the system.

Goals Goals are the objectives or needs which an individual or group seeks to achieve or satisfy. The goals of a group are normally defined through agreement. However, specific individuals within a group may dissent from the group's goals; analysis of industrial relations systems must be sensitive to the goals of these individuals.

According to Maslow, there is a hierarchy of basic needs which motivate individual behaviour. These include physiological (life-sustaining) needs as well as the need for safety, love (social acceptance), esteem (recognition), and self-actualization.[10] When one need is satisfied it no longer serves as a motivator and is supplanted by the next higher one. Most of the literature in the field of organizational behaviour seems to suggest that, in North America today, most people have satisfied their physiological and safety needs, and now high-level needs (social acceptance, esteem, self-actualization) motivate individuals.

Although other writers have treated motivation in slightly different ways, they all stress the importance of organizational climate and quality of work in the satisfaction of these high-level needs. For this reason, psychological and social rewards are now taking on a new significance in the workplace, particularly among young members of the labour force.

Values Values refer to the norms or standards which an actor observes in establishing the relative importance of objectives and the means of obtaining them. Faced with a variety of solutions to any given problem, an actor will choose the one that gives the greatest satisfaction, provided it is consistent with his or her (or its) established values.

Power Power refers to the ability to achieve goals despite the resistance of others, and is made up of at least two elements: (1) a strong attachment to a desired object or to one already possessed but threatened; and (2) an ability to impose sanctions. Thus, power begins with a commitment to an issue or a series of issues. If there is no commitment, the ability to impose sanctions is meaningless, since it will not be used. Sanctions may be of three types: (1) moral, such as the use of public opinion; (2) economic, such as strikes, work-to-rule, and lockouts; and (3) physical, such as intimidation or actual violence.[11]

Goals, Values, and Power of the Actors Unions, corporations, and third parties all espouse specific goals, values, and power. It is relatively easy to measure their goals, but often difficult to evaluate their values and power. Over time certain qualitative assessments are possible; for example, changes may occur in the relative importance of some goals or in one party's commitment to them, or the factors which influence the power of a given party may change. But these judgements only reveal whether or not a specific input has increased or decreased in strength or importance. They do not give us precise quantitative evaluations of goals, values, and power.

Generally, organized labour in North America has the very pragmatic objective of obtaining "more, more, and more now," as stated by Samuel Gompers, first president of the American Federation of Labor (AFL). However, this is not to suggest that labour is concerned only with its own needs. To varying degrees, unions embrace an egalitarian norm which manifests itself as a concern for the welfare of all workers. Unions often support social initiatives, such as higher wages for non-union workers in small establishments. R.B. Freeman and J.L. Medoff, two Harvard economists, have recently analyzed a large computerized data base and have concluded that unionism raises productivity in the United States. While reducing wage inequities, however, unionism also reduces profits. Unions have had more success with initiatives directed toward legislation of broad social importance than with those concerned only with special-interest groups.[12]

Even when unions seem guided by Gomper's formula, they recognize that certain goals may take precedence over increased wages and benefits. For example, in 1984 Alberta's electricians agreed to a wage and benefit freeze in favour of greater job security. The agreement contained a novel clause whereby the union and contractors could mutually agree to cut the basic hourly wage before bidding on a job in order to compete with cheaper, non-unionized contractors.[13] Unionized employers had been having difficulty in competing for jobs in the construction industry for a number of years because non-unionized wages were lower than those in the unionized sector of the industry.

The objective of obtaining more — more profits, a greater share of the market, increased growth and greater control over the workplace — is also attributed to private-sector management, which has traditionally been guided by the competitive norm (although oligopolistic and monopolistic industries exert a fair amount of control over the market). In the public sector management attempts to provide reliable services for the lowest possible cost: these are referred to respectively as effectiveness and efficiency. At the same time, both the private and public sectors have come to recognize the mutual benefits to be obtained by satisfying workers' needs: increased productivity, decreased absenteeism, lower worker turnover, greater occupational health and safety, and improved morale.

In North America, government and private agencies acting as third parties in the collective bargaining process are guided by the goal of maintaining industrial peace between labour and management. They help to resolve disputes without work stoppages, or to end work stoppages once they have begun. Governments, for their part, have been involved for some time in labour standards legislation covering employment issues such as minimum wages, hours of work, and statutory holidays. In recent years some government-sponsored agencies have also attempted to regulate bargaining outcomes using compulsory wage-and-price controls. These existed in the United States from 1971 to 1973 and in Canada under the Anti-Inflation Program from 1975 to 1978. In addition, the Government of Canada imposed restraint programs for federal public-sector workers of 6% and 5% in 1983 and 1984 respectively; restraint programs were also implemented in certain provincial sectors. In addition to these monetary programs, government interest in health and safety, equal pay for work of equal value, equal employment opportunities and the quality of work life is increasing.

While all three actors work within the same social environment, and thus share a core of common values, each of them represents a different subgroup within society. As a result, particular goals and values may differ. And where different goals and values clash, conflict often occurs.

Systems theory is often criticized because it assumes harmony among the actors. However our analytical framework presupposes neither conflict (as does that of Marx), nor harmony (as does, for example, Dunlop's). It enables both analyst and practitioner to observe given situations and to determine for themselves whether these situations are characterized by conflict or harmony, stability or instability. Jack Barbash, writing on collective bargaining in the United States, observes that

> [it] is . . . a *co-operative* form of conflict in which the parties — or for that matter the *partners* — seek to exchange what they want from each other. Unlike *competitors* who seek to oust one another, bargainers seek a mutually agreeable exchange.[14]

Barbash contends that collective bargaining is perceived by the actors as an adversary game, the outcome of which determines the way available funds are distributed between wages and profits. "Conflict," he writes, "latent or manifest, is the essence of industrial relations, but it is almost invariably followed by the *resolution* of conflict."[15]

Keep in mind that conflict does not always express itself overtly. In many cases conflicting parties will adopt an accommodative approach to negotiations, whereby both sides gain. This is what Walton and McKersie refer to as "integrative bargaining."[16]

The power of any one actor, as we have seen, lies in the ability of that actor to attain objectives despite the resistance of others. The power of any one actor also varies according to conditions in the environment and in the industrial relations system. For example, a very buoyant economy increases labour's power, whereas a slack economy increases the power of management. The recession of the late 1970s and early 1980s has proven this. A very militant union membership, moreover, will support a labour leader at the bargaining table more than an apathetic union membership will. Likewise, a government may or may not exercise some degree of power, depending on how much economic, political, or social clout it perceives itself to have. For example, the United States government exerted considerable power over both labour and management in a number of industries in 1966 when it released stockpiles of basic materials, thus maintaining or lowering the prices for these commodities.

How important, then, is power in contract negotiations? A recent book by two American authors goes so far as to assume that "bargaining power is the pivotal construct for a general theory of bargaining."[17] Bacharach and Lawler further content that power "pervades all aspects of bargaining and is the key to an integrative analysis of context, process, and outcome."[18] This view accords notably with the ideas presented in this book, and furthermore is consistent with the idea of a contract zone — that area in which the positions of the two principal actors overlap and in which bargaining power helps to define a specific settlement point. As a general rule, both unions and management prefer to reach a settlement within this zone, rather than initiate a work stoppage. The contract zone will be discussed in greater detail in Chapter 7.

So far, our discussion has illustrated how the goals, values, and power of the actors in the industrial relations system create its internal input variables. The following section will examine the external inputs from environmental subsystems into the industrial relations system.

External Conditioning Inputs into the Industrial Relations System

Environmental inputs impose a range within which the internal inputs and outputs will fall. Within that range, however, outputs are determined by the goals, values and, in particular, by the power of the actors in the system. This suggests that the outputs are not deterministic in the Marxist sense but that the actors have some degree of control over both inputs and outputs. The following environmental subsystems have significant conditioning effects on the industrial relations system: (1) the ecological subsystem; (2) the economic subsystem; (3) the political subsystem; (4) the legal subsystem; and (5) the social or cultural subsystem. Each of these will be discussed briefly.

Ecological Subsystem The ecological subsystem is a society's physical surroundings and the way it adjusts to them. For example, the climate of Canada has an influence on several industries: it closes many of our inland ports for a good part of the year and it slows down construction activities. Consequently, the seasonal nature of these and other industries will have a bearing on the timing of negotiations and the level of rewards granted to workers. Furthermore, the availability of key resources in a region has serious consequences for the inputs and outputs of its industrial relations system, and the concentration of key resources in particular areas of the world can have a significant impact on the economies and industrial relations systems of dependent countries. In the winter of 1973, for example, the energy crisis forced many industries in the United Kingdom to operate only three or four days a week.

Although ecology can influence an industrial relations system, it is unable to respond to the outputs from that system. In this respect, the ecological subsystem differs from the other societal subsystems, in which decision-making mechanisms exist to analyze industrial relations outputs and to modify subsequent system inputs.

Economic Subsystem The economic subsystem, comprising the product, labour, and money markets as well as the rate of technological change, also conditions the inputs and outputs of the industrial relations system. We have

already seen that a period of high economic activity promotes high rates of inputs and outputs, and a period of slow economic activity produces the opposite effect. Other macroeconomic conditions, such as inflation, unemployment, and interest rates, can also exert a strong influence on industrial relations.

The product market acts to establish a ceiling on outputs, since consumer demand for a given product influences the producer's (manager's) willingness and ability to provide increased wages and benefits. The labour market, by contrast, acts to establish the minimum inputs and outputs (e.g., wage rates) in order to attract sufficient numbers of workers into the labour force of a specific firm. The money market is affected by monetary and fiscal policies, as well as the interest rate structure. These in turn operate to accelerate or decelerate economic activity, and thus act indirectly as conditioning factors.

It is not always easy for countries to manage monetary and fiscal policies so as to keep prices

Courtesy of Chrysler Canada Ltd.

and wages from rising too rapidly. This fact has given rise to various governmental and other institutional structures to cope with rising wage demands as workers attempt to maintain or increase their real wages. Wage and price controls and increasing demands for escalator or cost-of-living clauses in North American collective agreements in the 1970s are evidence of the many ways in which governments and unions tried to cope with the high rate of inflation at the time.

Technological change, by affecting the capital-labour ratio, job structure, requisite skills, and productivity, has a widespread impact on industrial relations. The Canadian federal government and a number of provincial governments have gone so far as to pass legislation to protect workers from the adverse consequences, in human terms, of technological change. Other countries have tried to cope with the problem by using a variety of "redundancy schemes," whereby all employers contribute to a benefit fund for workers who are made redundant by technological changes. The workers receive lump-sum payments, subsidized retraining, and relocation grants to assist them in moving to areas where there is a demand for labour.

Political Subsystem The political system influences the industrial relations system in many ways. We will mention only a few.

The political structure itself can affect the nature of worker-management negotiations. The formation of centralized systems of collective bargaining is easier in unitary states than it is in decentralized systems. In a number of European countries highly-structured systems allow the parties to view the outputs of their industrial relations systems in relation to the economy of the country as a whole. Canada has one of the world's most decentralized industrial relations systems. Such a system leaves members of small negotiating units with the feeling that their outputs have little effect on the national scene.

For this reason, the executive branch of the political subsystem may intervene to play a direct role in protecting what it perceives to be the public interest. Such intervention has been used frequently in both Canada and the United States in an attempt to obtain settlements between unions and management without work stoppages. In addition, the political subsystem often operates through its legislative branch, enacting or modifying labour relations legislation to establish general "rules of the game" or *ad hoc* measures to cope with particular disputes. On several occasions, the Canadian Parliament has used acts of Parliament to order railway, postal, and other workers back to work with minimum settlements, although these have sometimes been subject to change by further negotiations or arbitration.

Legal Subsystem The legal subsystem includes statutory, common, and administrative law. This subsystem legislates procedural rules determining how unions and management are to conduct themselves in everyday activities and in negotiations. It also legislates labour standards, such as minimum wages, maximum hours, health and safety standards, and pay equity, and thus conditions internal inputs by describing a society's idea of acceptable working standards. Common law, both that which predates statutory law and that which flows from a legal interpretation of statutory law, also has a significant bearing on what the actors in the system may or may not do. Finally, administrative law issuing from bodies such as labour relations boards established by various statutes plays a very decisive role in the industrial relations system. The various administrative tribunals help to fill gaps in the general provisions of statute law. (Much more will be said about this topic in Chapter 6.)

Social or Cultural Subsystem Since all the actors in the industrial relations system are part of society, they have at least some common goals and values. These constitute the social or cultural subsystem. This minimal consensus on goals and values keeps industrial relations systems functioning at both the micro and macro levels.

Even when this consensus breaks down, social pressure may have a strong impact on the process. For example, if the dispute appears to be disruptive to society, the public may put pressure on political, social, or economic leaders to intervene. The political system may then try to resolve the dispute by legislating or otherwise imposing guidelines. At times the involvement of the political subsystem is extensive enough to transform a bipartite system into a tripartite one, in which government wields substantial influence on labour and management. For example, when the unions bargaining in the public sector in Quebec in both 1972 and 1982 formed a common front and organized strikes that disrupted essential services such as schools and hospitals, the Quebec government legislated the workers back to work. Some labour leaders were imprisoned for encouraging workers to violate the back-to-work injunctions. Other provinces have also, on occasion, ordered striking teachers and other essential workers back to work, but Quebec has used this type of special legislation much more often than any other jurisdiction in Canada.[19]

So far, we have described each of the subsystems separately. However, none of them operate in a vacuum. For example, there is, as the preceding section has pointed out, an articulation between the social or cultural subsystem and the political subsystem. Articulations among the other subsystems may also develop, depending upon the problem to be resolved.

One of the major tasks to be accomplished in the study of industrial relations is to define precisely the inputs from within the system (the internal inputs) and the exact role of environmental subsystems in conditioning these inputs. The development of quantitative measure that would allow us to assess the individual impact of each variable, or to combine these measures into some kind of composite index would be ideal. Some interesting approaches have been suggested, but much remains to be done.[20]

Procedures for Converting Inputs into Outputs

Unilateral Decisions Procedures for converting the inputs into outputs may take various forms. Sometimes the outputs may be determined by one party alone, be it the employer or the state. In the non-unionized sectors of North America, it is the employer, in both the private and public sectors, who establishes the levels of rewards offered to workers and who regulates the conditions and sets the standards under which they work. In making these determinations and in attempting to recruit and maintain labour of a suitable quality, the employer is guided by general societal conditions.

Bipartite Negotiations Alternatively, inputs may be converted into outputs through bipartite negotiations between labour unions (or worker associations) and management. In the United States and Canada, this method predominates among organized sectors of the economy where most agreements are reached by the two private parties themselves.

Within the bipartite system, three sets of negotiations are possible. First, competing groups within a union may debate and agree upon the goals to be pursued. Second, a similar process may take place within management: for example, a sales manager may be most concerned with the delivery dates of products or services, whereas the production manager may be chiefly interested in keeping costs down. Some compromises may have to be made. Third, following these two sets of intraorganizational negotiations, bilateral negotiations take place in an attempt to reach a settlement.[21]

Third-Party Negotiations If the two parties fail to reach a settlement, third-party assistance may be necessary. In Canada, we have a compulsory, two-stage conciliation process in most of our political jurisdictions, to which both unions and management must submit before a strike or lockout is legal. (In some provinces this system is now giving way to a one-stage process in which the emphasis is on mediation, and the conciliation board is eliminated.) In the United States, parties wishing to renew a collective agreement must, under federal law, notify the Federal Mediation and Conciliation Service before the expiration of an existing agreement. While mediation is often used in the United States, it is not compulsory except under the eighty-day injunction issued when the President declares a dispute to involve national health and safety.

Compulsory arbitration exists as a final means of resolving contract negotiation disputes in some provinces' public and parapublic sectors. Where arbitration is compulsory, strikes or lockouts are prohibited. Voluntary arbitration is an optional route, however, for disputes among workers who are covered by the federal Public Service Staff Relations Act.

If these or other forms of third-party assistance fail to produce a settlement (that is, convert inputs into outputs), then a settlement is usually determined by a trial of strength. This may take the form of a strike by workers or a lockout by management. Eventually, however, one or more forms of third-party assistance will be used to reach an agreement satisfactory to both sides. It is important to recognize that a strike or lockout is also an output of the system, and one that can have serious consequences for both environmental subsystems and for the actors in the industrial relations system itself.

Industrial relations consist not only of periodic negotitations, but also of the day-to-day relationships among individuals in the workplace. Collective agreements cannot anticipate every action taken by management or unions on a daily basis. Hence all political jurisdictions in Canada require that collective agreements provide for the ongoing resolution of conflicts over the interpretation or application of clauses in collective agreements. This provision takes the form of a grievance procedure, the final stage of

which usually results in third-party binding arbitration. Some 90% or more of collective agreements in the United States also contain such clauses, although they are not required to by law. The grievance procedure and its resulting arbitral decisions have resulted in an elaborate jurisprudence which helps to regulate daily behaviour in the workplace.

Non-unionized Sector

So far we have been discussing the processes used in the unionized sectors of the economy, where the collective bargaining model prevails. Since only about 37% of the Canadian labour force participates in collective bargaining,[22] we should now give some attention to the systems which apply to the non-unionized sector. An American scholar, J.W. Gabarino, has recently identified three major worker relations systems within the non-unionized sector of the American economy, in addition to the collective bargaining model. He has named these the administrative model, the civil service model, and the legal model.[23] These models are pure types, but there may be articulations among them: for example, the collective bargaining model is supported in part by the legal model.

Administrative Model The administrative model, unilaterally established by the employer, is implemented through the hierarchy of an organization. Many of the rules and procedures take written form as personnel policies and handbooks, while others take the form of custom. This model is characterized by an implicit contract expressing a whole set of expectations which management and workers have regarding wages and working conditions. In times of financial hardship, it is understood that the employer has the right to make changes unilaterally. The items included under this model bear a striking resemblance to those in the collective bargaining model, primarily because employers have followed the standards set in the unionized sector, often in the hope of keeping their organizations union-free.

Civil Service Model   The civil service model combines collective bargaining with the administrative model: administration is by a government agency acting under specific laws, procedures for grievances comprise a many-tiered hierarchy, final review is by a public service commission, and representation may be chosen from among external experts including workers associations. There are explicit, detailed, and legally binding procedures for discipline, reduction in workforce, and other personnel functions. Most of the regulations are internally generated, setting them apart from those of the collective bargaining model.

Since workers at all levels of government in Canada are unionized and act in many ways like their counterparts in the collective bargaining model of the private sector, the civil service model does not apply as well to the Canadian public sector as it does to the American public sector.

Legal Model   The legal model emphasizes employment relations law, a body of regulations that deals with compensation and working conditions.[24]

Under common law, workers had few rights attached to their jobs. Employment could be terminated provided the employer gave reasonable notice, and many conditions of employment had no legal support. This situation caused much controversy and, in response, a body of labour standards legislation was developed, which can now be brought to bear in setting minimum or maximum conditions. These standards, however, usually lag behind practices developed in the unionized sector.

In Canada, laws exist which govern unemployment insurance, minimum wages, maximum hours, paid holidays, paid vacations, and occupational health and safety. Workers in some Canadian jurisdictions may refuse to perform duties which they consider hazardous to their health or safety. Laws also exist which prohibit discrimination on the basis of race, creed, colour, sex, and national ancestry, among other

things. Some jurisdictions require equal pay for work of equal value, and practically all jurisdictions have provisions for maternity leave. Federal, Québec, and Nova Scotia laws permit non-unionized workers to appeal dismissals which they feel have not been for "just cause." Their cases may go to impartial third-party arbitration. Human rights legislation in a number of provinces prohibits sexual harassment, and in 1984 the federal government also enacted legislation requiring employers in industries under federal jurisdiction to develop and publicize sexual harassment policies.

While protection for individuals has been growing, so has support for group action, particularly in the area of health and safety. Joint union-management and worker-management committees in Saskatchewan accomplished much in the field of health and safety during the 1970s. One of the major reasons for their success was the assurance felt by both workers and management that they themselves, and not the government, would be the prime agents for ensuring compliance.[25] The Ontario Occupational Health and Safety Act requires the establishment of similar committees. Worker members are selected by workers where no union exists, and by union members where unions operate.

The idea of universal committees in non-unionized as well as unionized sectors was introduced under the Federal Labour Adjustment Benefits Act of 1982. When an employer plans to terminate the employment of 50 or more workers within a four-week period, a joint planning committee of not less than four members must be established. In non-unionized sectors, workers are entitled to select the members of such a committee, just as union members are in the unionized sector. These joint committees are charged with developing adjustment programs to eliminate the need for layoffs or firings, to minimize the impact of job losses, and to help workers find other employment. In attempting to reach its objectives, a joint planning committee may choose to deal with matters normally pertaining to collective agreements. The mandate of these committees — that "the members shall cooperate and make every reasonable effort to develop an adjustment program as expeditiously as possible"[26] — reflects the obligation of parties in the unionized sector to bargain in good faith.

As workers become involved in labour-adjustment-benefit committees and learn what it is like to deal with employers as a united front rather than individually, the likelihood of their forming unions may increase. At the same time, the scope of these committees, according to R.J. Adams, may grow to include not only job losses but technological change, health and safety, training, and possibly the joint management of pension plans.[27] Furthermore, he predicts that the idea of dividing responsibility for these matters among separate committees will be superseded by the idea of a general-purpose committee responsible for coordinating all of these different matters, the boundaries of which to a large extent overlap. As a result, the term "unorganized" may become archaic: "Should collective employment decision making become as widespread as the current trend suggests it might, the term will cease to have any real meaning. Everyone will be organized."[28] C.R. Brookbank, however, sees these initiatives as obstacles to the formation of unions since governments may appear to be doing so much that little will remain for unions to do.[29]

We need hardly take sides with one or the other of these two views. It is useful to note, though, that non-unionized workers in some jurisdictions already have some say about how their rewards and working conditions are determined. They are protected by a large number of laws and regulations, many of which mirror those obtained through the collective bargaining process. New measures deal with just cause for dismissal from non-unionized firms in three jurisdictions. In addition, the setting up of joint committees gives workers a chance to have an input into policies that affect them. Whether these workers remain satisfied with what they have or opt for the advantages (and disadvantages) of collective bargaining in a bid to improve their lot is a crucial question.

Informal Relationships In the preceding sections, we have discussed the formalized procedures for converting inputs into outputs. Equally important, however, are the host of informal relationships among managers, among workers, between the two groups, and between workers and their union leaders. Organizational behaviourists have studied these informal relations among the actors at length, and industrial relations has a lot to learn from their work.

Many individual and group needs are satisfied more through informal relationships than through formal organizational structures and activities. Organizational needs, too, are often best met informally, as numerous studies have shown. Behaviourists are paying close attention to issues such as boredom on the assembly line or in routine jobs; turnover; absenteeism; the quality of work life; and quality circles. Researchers are looking for ways of overcoming the malaise that plagues many organizations.

The Outputs of an Industrial Relations System

The main function of industrial relations systems is the allocation of rewards to employees for their services and the determination of the conditions under which they are to work. Since collective bargaining first began, collective agreements have grown from small documents into fairly large ones. This increase in size reflects the growing number of items that have been added through negotiations over the years and the refinements and elaborations of what were once simple provisions.

The outputs of industrial relations systems are of two major types: those oriented toward organizations and those oriented toward workers. (The former do not exist in non-unionized organizations.)

Collective agreement clauses oriented toward organizations are concerned with (1) management's rights; (2) union recognition; (3) union security; and (4) dues check-off. These clauses represent both the relations between organizational entities and the relations between these entities and their members.

Clauses oriented toward workers are concerned with (1) the wage and effort bargain; (2) job rights and due process; and (3) contingency-oriented benefits. The wage and effort bargain is concerned with reconciling the services workers provide for an organization with returns in the form of wages, cost-of-living (COLA) clauses, hours of work, etc. Job rights and due process involve such things as the role of seniority in promotions, layoffs, and recalls, as well as various aspects of the grievance procedure. Contingency benefits include supplementary unemployment benefits, pension plans, hospital and medical plans, etc. Some of these will be covered in Chapter 11.

In addition to outputs oriented toward organizations and workers, there is a third type of output: conversion mechanisms. Conversion mechanisms — particularly strikes and lockouts — can have an impact not only on the organization and workers, but also on the public, which is not a direct participant in the industrial relations system.

Industrial relations concerns itself with changes in outputs in particular instances, as well as with the relative levels of outputs in the occupational and industrial sectors. Good comparative studies examine industrial, national, and international trends. Analysts are also interested in both the overall rate of change in any one output, and the emphasis placed on different types of outputs under different circumstances. For example, during periods of high unemployment or rapid technological change, emphasis is generally placed on various job and income security provisions; whereas during periods of high employment, more emphasis is placed on wages and other direct and immediate forms of benefits.

A number of questions arise from these observations. To what extent do variations in wages for the same types of jobs act as an allocative mechanism in the labour market? How does one account for variations in wages among industries, and the stability of inter-industry wage differentials over substantial periods of time? To what extent do fringe benefits, which in North America vary from firm to firm, impede labour mobility? How can workers be trained for the new jobs arising from technological change? What keeps some workers in low-income areas despite the visible material advantages of moving to higher-income areas? Labour economists have written a fair amount on these questions; many of the topics could also be incorporated into the study of industrial relations.

Because industrial relations is concerned not only with substantive or material rewards for employment, but also with various types of social and psychological rewards (which are often as critical as material rewards in determining the satisfaction or dissatisfaction of workers), several questions arise. How can informal relationships enhance the needs of the individual and at the same time meet the needs of the organization? What types of communication channels most satisfy the individual and at the same time best serve the organization? What types of problems lend themselves to individual or group decision-making? Under what circumstances can the individual and the organization gain more from participatory than directive management? What conditions allow the individual to achieve his or her potential and at the same time meet the needs of the organization? What types of organizational structures best respond to the need of both the organization and the individual? What kind of job redesign — horizontal or vertical — motivates workers to produce more and better products and services for the organization and its clients? (Horizontal job redesign adds a greater variety of duties at the same level of difficulty. Vertical job redesign adds more challenging duties and opportunities for decision-making.) Does satisfaction lead to higher productivity, as we once thought, or does higher productivity lead to greater satisfaction? These are but a few of the many social and psychological questions for which some answers are beginning to appear. Yet the recent glut of books and articles on organizational behaviour has *not* resulted in a systematic inventory of findings in these critical areas.

The Feedback Loop

As we have seen, environmental subsystems influence outputs. Conversely, however, outputs can influence the unit under analysis (be it a plant, hospital, industry, company, or country), as well as other subsystems of society. The feedback loop in Figure 1.1 reflects this mutual relationship. The loop also reflects the direct, unmediated influence that the outputs of the system can have on the actors within it. A good example of this internal conditioning is the beneficial effect on workers' morale and productivity of satisfactory wages, fringe benefits, and working conditions.

There are a number of reasons why the feedback loop is part of the present framework. From a scientific point of view, observing how the outputs of the industrial relations system return to it in the form of external conditioning inputs to sustain or transform the system itself incorporates a dynamic dimension into the framework. From the point of view of public or private policy, we need to investigate the consequences of the outputs of the industrial relations system for other societal subsystems. For example, what is the impact of strikes on the economic, legal, political and social subsystems? How do wages and other outputs affect costs, prices, and employment at both the organizational and societal level? How do the outputs of the industrial relations system influence community attitudes toward unions and management, and what part do these attitudes play in helping shape public policy in areas such as incomes policies, the right to strike, and other questions which affect the outputs of the industrial relations system? How do outputs affect a country's ability to compete with other countries? It is difficult to establish objective measures with which to assess such effects; nevertheless, we must continue to develop means of analyzing and predicting the behaviour of unions and management and of assessing the outputs of industrial relations systems on society as a whole.

The Analytical, Explanatory, and Predictive Power of the Framework

This section will illustrate at micro and macro levels the problems of analysis, explanation, and control. At the micro level, the closer the goals, values, and power of the actors in the system are to each other, the less likelihood there is of any major internal conflict — unless one of the actors demands concessions that the other is not prepared to make. Under the Canadian system, where conciliation or mediation is compulsory in most jurisdictions before a work stoppage is legal, a government agency is likely to become involved as a third party to resolve such disputes. Thus, a bipartite system can be transformed into a tripartite one.

At the macro level, if the political authorities perceive the outputs of the industrial relations system to be important factors in causing such problems as excess inflation, balance of payment deficits, etc., they are likely to take substantive steps, such as imposing wage and price guidelines or controls. These controls are based on the assumption that the collective bargaining process enables unions to push wages and prices higher than they would be under free competition in labour and product markets. The imposition of government wage and price guidelines resembles arbitration in that it changes the bipartite system into a tripartite system, at least for as long as the government controls are in force.

Another example of the transformation of a bipartite system into a tripartite one may occur during a major strike in an essential industry or service. As mentioned above, Parliament has on several occasions passed special *ad hoc* legislation ordering striking railway, postal, and other workers back to work. Similar legislation has also been used by provincial authorities to end strikes. Whether this is the best way to handle these kinds of disputes is the subject of much debate.[30] Undoubtedly, such measures are taken only when political authorities feel that they have strong support and when it appears that the legislation will be adhered to by the actors in the system. Not only is the feedback loop a useful tool for explaining and predicting the behaviour of actors in the industrial relations system but, by applying it to the analysis of the consequences of a strike and the degree to which the public supports the strike, it enables political authorities to legitimize their intervention in disputes.

Conclusion

This chapter has proposed a framework for the analysis of industrial relations systems and has shown how the framework can be used to explain, analyze and predict events. With more

---

Figure 1.2   **Dunlop's Framework in Diagram Form**

Actors
Labour
Management
Specialized government and/or
private agencies

Ideology
A set of ideas and beliefs held by
the actors that legitimizes the
role of each and that serves to
bind the system together.

Contexts
1 Technological Characteristics
  — Skill levels
  — Variable or fixed workplace
  — Size of work group
  — Job content
  — Relation of workplace to
    residence
  — Stable or variable workforce
  — Etc.

2 Market
  — Labour and product
  — Competitive to monopolistic
  — Local to international
  — Size of enterprise
  — Scope of market
  — Secular expansion or
    contraction
  — Ratio of labour costs to total
    costs
  — Labour market stringency
  — Etc.

3 Budgetary
  — Funds available (very important
    for public sector)

4 Distribution of power in the larger
  society
  — which of the actors has more
    access to the sources of power?

Rules
1 Procedures for determining
  substantive rules (such as
  negotiations)

2 Substantive rules (such as
  wages, hours, fringe benefits)

3 Procedures for applying
  substantive rules to specific
  situations (such as grievances)

work, this framework could serve as a foundation for a theory of industrial relations systems that could explain the relations among the variables. However, that kind of elaboration is the subject of another book — a more generic book than this one. The intent of this chapter has been to lay down the rudiments of the framework and to show the kinds of analyses and explanations that can be done with it, to anticipate the sequence of chapters, and to make some predictions where these seemed appropriate.

For those wishing to use another framework, either as an alternative to the one presented here or for comparative purposes, I suggest Dunlop's work[31], which in large measure inspired me to write this chapter. A schematic presentation of Dunlop's framework is shown in Figure 1.2.

Questions

1 Discuss and explain in detail the main components of the systems approach presented in this chapter.

2 Discuss the major similarities and differences between Dunlop's framework and the one presented in this chapter.

3 What impact, if any, might a major wage increase have on the price of a firm's products or services? What other factors would you include in discussing the impact of a wage increase?

4 In what ways, if any, do the provincial deficit and budgeted expenditures affect labour-management relations in the public sector?

5 Does the systems framework presented in this chapter give you any idea of what you will be studying in this course? Be specific about your expectations and give examples where possible.

6 Do you think that the systems framework presented here takes into account all of the factors present in any industrial relations system, particularly that of your province? Elaborate and give examples.

7 Take a firm or industry with which you are familiar and analyze its industrial relations system using the framework presented in this chapter. What problems, if any, are inherent in the methodology?

8 What modifications to the present framework do you think are necessary to make it more useful in analyzing industrial relations problems?

9 Do you consider this systems framework applicable at the firm, industry, and national levels?

10 Does the systems framework apply equally well to both unionized and non-unionized sectors of the economy? Elaborate.

Notes

1 The present chapter is a refinement of two previous articles by the author: Alton W. J. Craig, "A Model for the Analysis of Industrial Relations Systems," a paper first presented at the 1967 meeting of the Canadian Political Science Association and published in *Canadian Labour and Industrial Relations: Private and Public Sectors*, H.C. Jain, ed. (Toronto: McGraw-Hill Ryerson Limited, 1975), pp. 2-12; and, "A Framework for the Analysis of Industrial Relations Systems," a paper given to the Third World Congress of the International Industrial Relations Association in London, England, in September 1973 and published in *Industrial Relations and the Wider Society: Aspects of Interaction*, B. Barrett, E. Rhodes and J. Beishon, eds. (London: Collier Macmillan, 1975), pp. 8-20. The diagram shown at the beginning of this chapter, which summarizes my conception of the industrial relations system, is not comparable to the one contained in *Canadian Industrial Relations: The Report of the Task Force on Labour Relations* (Ottawa: Privy Council Office, December 1968), p.10. The latter has been erroneously attributed to me, but is not appropriate to any analysis of industrial relations. A similar misattribution, incidentally, is made on page 7 of the first edition of Union-Management Relations in Canada, J. Anderson and M. Gunderson, eds., (Don Mills: Addison-Wesley, 1982).

2 For a good critique of the current status of industrial relations research, see G. Strauss and P. Feuille, "Industrial Relations Research: A Critical Analysis," Vol. 17, No 3, *Industrial Relations* (October 1978), pp. 259-277.

3 J.T. Dunlop, *Industrial Relations Systems* (New York: Holt, 1958).

4 Probably the most noteworthy of these recent attempts is T.A. Kochan, H.C. Katz, and R.B. McKersie, *The Transformation of American Industrial Relations* (New York: Basic Books, 1986), Chapter 1. They use the concept of strategic choice as the central variable in their analysis. However, given that unions now account for only about 17% of the non-agricultural labour force in the US, whereas in Canada this figure is closer to 36%, many Canadian writers feel that the situation here is not close enough to that in the United States to warrant adopting this position to analyze the Canadian scene. See, for example, J.C. Anderson, M. Gunderson, and A. Ponak, eds., *Union-Management Relations in Canada*, 2nd ed. (Don Mills, Ontario: Addison-Wesley Publishers, 1989), p. 18; See also A. Verma and M. Thompson, "Managerial Strategies in Canada and the U.S. in the 1980s," proceedings of the forty-first annual meeting of the Industrial Relations Association B.A. Dennis, ed. (Madison, Wis.: IRRA, 1989), pp. 257-264.

5 For those interested in other attempts to develop industrial relations theory, see J.T. Dunlop, *Industrial Relations Systems*; C. Kerr, J.T. Dunlop, F.H. Harbison, and C.A. Myers, *Industrialism and Industrial Man* (Cambridge, Mass.: Harvard University Press, 1966). See also some more recent attempts, such as S.M.A. Hameed, "A Critique of Industrial Relations Theory," Vol. 37, No. 1, *Relations Industrielles/Industrial Relations*, (1982), pp. 15-31; V. Larouche et E. Deom, "L'approche systematique en relations industrielles," Vol. 39, No. 1, *Relations Industrielles/Industrial Relations* (1984), pp. 114-143; G. Schienstock, "Towards a Theory of Industrial Relations," Vol. XIX, No. 2, *British Journal of Industrial Relations*, (July 1981), pp. 170-189; R. J. Adams, "Competing Paradigms in Industrial Relations," Vol. 38, No. 3, *Relations Industrielles/Industrial Relations*, pp. 508-529; J. Sen and S. Hameed, *Theories of Industrial Relations* (Littleton, Mass.: Copley Publishing Group, 1988); J. Barbash and K. Barbash, eds., *Theories of Comparative Industrial Relations* (Columbia, S.C.: University of Southern California Press, 1989); G. Murray and T. Giles, "Towards an Historical Understanding of Industrial Relations in Canada," Vol. 43, No. 4, *Relations Industrielles/Industrial Relations*, pp. 780-889; A.S. Sethi and S.J. Dimmock, "Collective Bargaining and Industrial Relations Theory," in A.J. Sethi, ed., *Collective Bargaining in Canada* (Scarborough, Ontario: Nelson, 1989), pp. 2-41; G. Hébert, H.C. Jain and N.M. Meltz, eds., *The State of the Art in Industrial Relations* (A project of the Canadian Industrial Relations Association and Published by the Industrial Relations Centre, Queen's University and the Centre for Industrial Relations, University of Toronto, June 1988), Chapters 1 and 2.

6 For a detailed statement of my position, see Alton W.J. Craig, "Mainstream Industrial Relations in Canada," in G. Hébert, H.C. Jain, and N.M. Meltz, eds., *The State of the Art in Industrial Relations*, pp. 9-43, and particularly pp. 9-12. For a brief summary of a number of other paradigms that may be used, see J.C. Anderson, M. Gunderson, and A. Ponak, eds., *Union-Management Relations in Canada*, Chapter 1.

7 N.M. Meltz, "Industrial Relations: Balancing Efficiency with Equity," in *Theories and Concepts in Comparative Industrial Relations*, J. Barbash and K. Barbash, eds., pp. 190-113.

8 Ibid., p. 112.

9 The framework shown in Figure 1.1 and elaborated in the text is derived at least in part from D. Easton's input-output model. See David Easton, *A Systems Analysis of Political Life* (New York: John Wiley and Son, Inc., 1955), particularly Part 1.

10 See Abraham H. Maslow, *Motivation and Personality*, 2nd ed. (New York: Harper and Row, 1970), particularly Chapter 4.

11 J.R. Commons, *The Economics of Collective Action* (New York: Macmillan Co., 1950), pp. 76-77.

12 R.B. Freeman and J.L. Medoff, What Do Unions Do? (New York: Basic Books, 1984), p. 247.

13 "Alberta's Electricians Accept Three-year Freeze on Wages," *Globe and Mail* (September 28, 1984), p. 4.

14 Jack Barbash, "Collective Bargaining and the Theory of Conflict," Vol. XVIII, No. 1, *British Journal of Industrial Relations* (March 1980), p. 87.

15 Ibid., p. 86.

16 R.E. Walton and R.B. McKersie, *A Behavioral Theory of Labor Negotiations* (New York: McGraw-Hill, 1965), p. 5.

17 S. Bacharach and E.J. Lawler, *Bargaining: Power, Tactics and Outcomes* (San Francisco: Jossey-Bass, 1981), p. 43.

18 Ibid.

19 G. Dion, Annexe 6, "Lois spéciales en relations du travail au Canada et dans les provinces (1950-1985)," in *Dictionnaire Canadien des relations du travail* (Quebec: Les Presses de l'Université Laval, 1986), pp. 939-943.

20 See, for example, S.M.A. Hameed, "Theory and Research in the Field of Industrial Relations," *British Journal of Industrial Relations* (July, 1967); J.C. Anderson, "Bargaining Outcomes: An IR Systems Approach," Vol. 19, No. 2, *Industrial Relations* (1979), pp. 126-143.

21 See R.E. Walton and R.B. McKersie, *A Behavioral Theory of Labor Negotiations* for a good analysis of what they consider as the four subprocesses of contract negotiations. This significant book received a great deal of attention shortly after its publication, but there has been little follow-up work along the same lines.

22 P. Kumar, "Estimates of Unionism and Collective Bargaining Coverage in Canada," Vol. 43, No. 4, *Relations Industrielles/Industrial Relations* (1988), pp. 757-779.

23 J.W. Gabarino, "Unions Without Unions: The New Industrial Relations," Vol. 23, No. 1, *Industrial Relations* (Winter 1984), pp. 40-51.

24 For an analysis of these laws in Canada, see R.J. Adams, "The Unorganized: A Rising Force?" No. 201, Faculty of Business, McMaster University, Research and Working Paper Series (Hamilton: April, 1983).

25 Ibid., pp. 10-11.

26 *The Labour Adjustment Benefits Act* (Bill C-78, 1982), s. 60.13(3).

27 R.J. Adams, "The Unorganized: A Rising Force?" p. 15.

28 Ibid., p. 19.

29 C.R. Brookbank, "The Adversary System in Canadian Industrial Relations: Blight or Blessing?" Vol. 35, No. 1, *Relations Industrielles/Industrial Relations* (1980), p. 34.

30 For a good discussion of political involvement in essential services, see Morley Gunderson, ed., *Collective Bargaining in the Essential and Public Service Sectors* (Toronto: University of Toronto Press, 1975). This book resulted from a conference in which a small group of academics and practitioners discussed various ways of dealing with disputes in the essential and public service sectors.

31 For the major components of Dunlop's framework, see J.T. Dunlop, *Industrial Relations Systems* (New York: Holt, 1958), particularly the first four chapters. For an abbreviated form of Dunlop's framework, see E.W. Bakke, C. Kerr and C.W. Anrod, *Unions, Management and the Public*, 3rd ed. (New York: Harcourt, Brace and World, 1967), pp. 3-9.

2

The Environment of the Canadian Industrial Relations System

Dick Hemingway

Introduction

Chapter one established that the industrial relations system operates within the larger environment of society, and that other societal subsystems — ecological, economic, political, legal, and social — influence its outputs. The outputs of the industrial relations system in turn feed back into the environmental subsystems and quite frequently bring about changes in one or more of them.

To deal with the various components of the Canadian environmental subsystems in detail would be an enormous undertaking, and a complete analysis of them simply cannot be given here. Rather, this chapter will attempt a brief outline of the major components of each subsystem. I will also, where possible, include some historical data and explore their implications for the evolution of the system of industrial relations in Canada.

20

The Ecological Subsystem

The ecological subsystem differs from other external inputs in that it has no decision-making mechanism to respond to the outputs of the industrial relations system.

Canada is the world's second largest country in area (next to the Soviet Union), with a total land and fresh-water area of almost 10 million square kilometres. Over 55% of the land area, however, is not suitable for producing forest or vegetable products. In addition, about 97% of Canada's population lives on 24% of its total land area.[1] The vast majority of people live along its southern perimeter; often we interact more with Americans in bordering states than with people in other regions of Canada. The proximity of Canadians and Americans makes for a good deal of cultural commonality and in many cases for close ties in the North American labour movement. These close labour links between the two countries are extremely important since many Canadian union leaders, until recently, took their cue from what was happening in the American industrial relations system. Some writers have referred to this as the "demonstration effect." (We shall show in Chapter 4 why this is no longer the case.)

The severe weather patterns in Canada also have a substantial influence on industrial relations in industries, such as construction and shipping, that are particularly sensitive to climatic variations. In the construction industry, workers try to negotiate generous wage increases during the peak employment season so that their incomes can tide them over the cold winter months when there is little work. The same is true of workers who operate ships on the Great Lakes and the St. Lawrence River, since these waterways are frozen over during the winter.

Seasonal variations can also influence the timing of negotiations in seasonal industries. A union's bargaining power is highest at the beginning of the active season; the employer's bargaining power is greatest during the closed season. Unions on the St. Lawrence Seaway try to bring their negotiations to a head either in the early part of the shipping season or before the end of the season, when companies are trying to complete their shipments before the Seaway freezes over.

The Economic Subsystem

In this section we will start with a discussion of Canadian inflation and incomes policies. This will be followed by a look at the product market, the labour market, the capital and technological market, and the money market. A brief description of each of these markets will outline their significance for the operation of the Canadian industrial relations system.

Inflation

Inflation erodes real income and therefore has a significant impact on the industrial relations system of a country. Negotiated wage settlements, and wages and salaries in general, are very sensitive to changes in the rate of inflation. In times of high inflation, both unionized and non-unionized workers normally seek to retain, or increase, their real wages, the former often by means of cost-of-living allowance (COLA) clauses tied to changes in the Consumer Price Index (CPI). (We will discuss COLA clauses in more detail in Chapter 11.)

The Canadian economy has undergone two recent periods of rapid inflation. The first occurred between 1972 and 1974, and the next between 1977 and 1981. In both cases there was a generally positive relation between the CPI and wage settlements. Real wages increased in tandem with the CPI, except during the 1975–78 period, when wage-and-price controls were in effect.

During the latter half of the 1980s, both wage increases and the CPI levelled out to about 4.5%. However, by the end of the decade many

Mulroney defends high interest rates to fight inflation

BY RICHARD CLEROUX
MARIAN STINSON
and DREW FAGAN
The Globe and Mail

Prime Minister Brian Mulroney defended his high-interest-rate policy yesterday telling reporters he wanted to "crush inflation, smother inflation, before it extends to all areas of the economy."

Mr. Mulroney said Finance Minister Michael Wilson and the governor of the Bank of Canada have a deliberate policy to fight inflation using interest rates.

"You've got to crush it, smother it, before it gets out of command," Mr. Mulroney said. He was visiting his home town of Baie Comeau in his riding of Charlevoix yesterday.

Mr. Mulroney's comments came after the key Bank of Canada rate moved another giant step higher, rising by one-quarter of a percentage point to 12.12 per cent, its loftiest point in 4½ years.

The central bank rate reflects the cost of money to chartered banks and affects the cost of loans. The market is still digesting the banks' last prime rate increase, which came only two weeks ago. Market watchers are already placing their bets on the timing of the next rise; odds seem to favor a move within two weeks.

The last rise in the cost of blue-chip loans was one-half of a percentage point, to 12.75 per cent.

Meanwhile, upward pressure on interest rates gave the Canadian dollar a boost yesterday. It rose by one-third of a cent to close at 83.70 cents (U.S.).

This week's rise in the trend-setting central bank rate came as a surprise to no one, and was in line with money-market rates, which had been moving higher all week. It was the fifth consecutive increase in the bank rate, which is set each Thursday following the auction of treasury bills, at 25 basis points above the average yield.

Mr. Mulroney's comments hark back to former prime minister Pierre Trudeau, who once promised he would "wrestle inflation to the ground."

Mr. Mulroney said inflation has to be beaten "before it extends to all areas of the economy and the country." He lectured reporters for daring to ask him how high he is prepared to let interest rates go. He told them he did not think that was a proper question.

He turned aside recent criticism by Western Canadian premiers that the use of high interest rates to fight inflation is damaging to the west. Saskatchewan Premier Grant Devine brought up the issue at the first ministers' conference luncheon in Ottawa on Monday.

"I've taken note of the comments of the provincial premiers," Mr. Mulroney said. "But it's a federal government decision. It's a responsibility for us and the governor of the Bank of Canada.

"We are acting in a way we sincerely believe to be in the national interest."

Mr. Devine had criticized using high interest rates, which affect the whole country, to deal with inflation, which he sees as mainly an Ontario problem caused by the province's overheated economy.

Alberta Premier Donald Getty has made opposition to the Bank of Canada's interest-rate policy a major plank in his election campaign, arguing that Alberta's economic growth is being unfairly constrained by high interest rates forged to dampen inflation in southern Ontario's overcharged economy.

To protect Albertans from rising rates, Mr. Getty unveiled a policy this week sheltering homeowners from mortgage rates above 12 per cent, and protecting small-business operators from rates above 14 per cent.

The program, which Mr. Getty acknowledged had been forged virtually overnight, is expected to cost about $75-million in the first year of operation.

But the initiative was met with criticism from the opposition parties, which argued that Mr. Getty's action simply lets the federal government off the hook.

Throughout Alberta and Saskatchewan, high interest rates are generally perceived as threatening to choke off economic recovery.

Saskatchewan Finance Minister Gary Lane said yesterday that his ministry is "starting to get indications" that capital investment decisions are being delayed because of the burden of higher interest rates.

"We were starting to turn the corner in this province after last year's drought," Mr. Lane said. "We believe that high interest rates are wrong because they are due to inflation in one province (Ontario) . . . .

Why penalize the rest of the country?"

Wheat farmers in Saskatchewan are now going to their bankers looking for funds to plant spring crops, and Mr. Lane noted that the increase in interest rates will hurt them too. "They have no choice. They have to borrow the money."

Money-market traders said yesterday the Bank of Canada has been holding down the cost of day-to-day loans at 11.25 per cent, to stem the pressure on interest rates.

"There is a widespread feeling that inflation is grabbing hold," said Carl Beigie, chief economist at investment dealer McLean McCarthy Ltd. "The economy in North America remains very strong, and we have to settle it down a bit," and make efforts to take the heat out of consumer spending.

He said analysts are desperate for signs of declining consumption. "At the moment, we're being glutonous." At the same time, investment in productive capacity that will generate goods for export is essential. But business spending is a function of long-term interest rates, which are remaining stable, Mr. Beigie said.

The *Globe and Mail*, March 3, 1989, pp. A1, A2.

analysts, including the Conference Board of Canada, were predicting an economic recession and higher inflation in the 1990s.[2] The determination of the Mulroney government to reduce the deficit led to increases in both business and personal taxes, as well as the proposed introduction of a goods and services tax.

Incomes Policies and their Impact During periods of inflation, the government usually tries to discourage spending by means of monetary and fiscal policies. These attempts are not always successful, however. Indeed, some claim that high interest rates and other fiscal measures may actually contribute to inflationary expectations and cause a wage-and-price spiral.

One alternative to monetary and fiscal restraints is the imposition of an incomes policy, in which wages and/or prices are restricted to minimal increases, by either mandatory or voluntary means. Over the past twenty years, Canadians have experienced both of these approaches.

During 1969 and 1970, Canada had a Prices and Incomes Commission whose mandate was

to enquire into and report upon the causes, processes and consequences of inflation and to inform those making current policy and income decisions, the general public and the Government on how price stability may best be achieved.[3]

Although it had no specific mandate to propose a voluntary wage guideline, the Commission unilaterally announced in June 1970 an upper limit of 6% for annual wage and salary adjustments with provision for exceptions. In fact, increases averaging from 8% to 9% were negotiated by unions and management during the time that this voluntary program was in effect. According to the Commission's final report, the guideline was strongly opposed by worker groups and did not gain the necessary support of the general public and government. When the informal restraint program was terminated at the end of 1970, the common view was that although the 6% upper limit may have had a positive influence in reducing wage and salary increases, any such effect had been quite small.[4]

Five years later, the government was ready to try again. In October 1975, after months of trying unsuccessfully to develop a voluntary wage-and-price controls program in consultation with labour, management, and the provinces, the federal government announced the immediate implementation of measures to provide for "the restraint of profit margins, prices, dividends, and compensation in Canada." The Anti-Inflation Act, which was passed by the House of Commons two months later, was to last for three years. Besides the mandatory wage and price guidelines established in October, an Anti-Inflation Board was set up and mandated to implement further guidelines as necessary. Analysis of wage settlements during this period shows that actual settlements were about 4.5% lower than predicted; factors other than the controls program, however, may have been partially responsible for these results.[5]

During the winter and spring of 1982, Prime Minister Trudeau tried once again to get the provinces to agree to some form of voluntary restraint program. He also met with high-ranking individuals from the business community and held several meetings with representatives from the labour movement. Labour support, however, was not forthcoming.

In August, the government implemented an incomes restraint program aimed at federal public servants. The Public Sector Compensation Restraint Act (Bill C–124) subjected federal public servants to a 6% increase in the first year and 5% in the second year of a two-year program, during which time existing agreements with public sector unions were automatically extended. The government indicated that it would be applying the 6 and 5 program to all ministers of the Crown, members of the Senate and House of Commons, and federal public servants as an example for other governments and private groups to follow.

While unions, and particularly public-sector unions, were very hostile to the program, they did not cause major disruptions to services. Since many unions in the private sector were not only hit hard by layoffs but had to deal with companies in financial difficulties, these unions did not engage in illegal action on behalf of public-sector unions as some people had speculated they would. Employers generally favoured the federal government's move to restrain wages in the public sector and while many business leaders doubted the effectiveness of the 6 and 5 program, they too supported the restraint on wages.

Provincial reactions to the federal program were initially negative. However, it was not long before most of them initiated programs of their own. The British Columbia restraint program was probably the most controversial, since many social services were substantially reduced. Many union rallies were organized to protest cutbacks in government expenditures.

The Product Market

About 25% of the total production of goods and services in Canada is destined for export, most of it to the United States. As a rule, we export raw materials and unfinished goods, and import finished goods, mostly from the United States.

The development of a manufacturing base represents the best prospects for long-term economic stability. Therefore, it is important for Canadian industry to expand both domestic and foreign markets for its finished goods. To accomplish this, it must maintain high levels of productivity and low labour costs per unit of output relative to other trading partners — especially the United States. For this reason it is often in the interests of both employers and unions to assess the possible effects of wage increases on the competitive position of a given industry or firm.

An example of what can happen when our costs get out of line with those in the United States occurred during 1974 and 1975. At that time, not only did the average hourly wage rate in Canada surpass that of the US, but our unit labour costs also increased at a higher rate. As the chief economist for the Canadian Manufacturers Association noted, the result was that (with wage settlements going as high as 15% and 20%) "manufacturing fell apart, imports flooded in and exports fell off."[6] One might also add that wage and price controls were imposed in October 1975.

Declining productivity is also of great concern to both employers and unions; it puts employers at a competitive disadvantage in international markets and this, in turn, can cause layoffs. In fact, the 1981–82 recession saw the introduction of what is now termed "concession bargaining" in which unions gave up some of the benefits which they had earlier won. Concession bargaining was more prevalent in the United States than in Canada and reflected the fact that workers were more concerned with job security than with real income gains at that time. In 1982 American workers gave up eight paid holidays and reportedly conceded $3.5 million in wages and other benefits.[7]

However, unions did make demands of their own in exchange for these concessions. The US auto industry is a case in point. During the recession, Ford and GM workers agreed to take voluntary wages cuts. But when, in 1983 and 1984, the automakers registered record-breaking profits, the union demanded that Ford and GM establish "job banks" to maintain income and provide retraining for workers who might lose their jobs due to subcontracting, automation, or productivity gains. The Ford agreement included a four-year ban on closing any of its 17 plants or 48 parts factories.[8] Both collective agreements provided for a wage increase of 15 cents per hour in the first year of the three-year agreements. It was estimated that the raises, plus lump-sum payments, profit-sharing, and cost-of-living adjustments would provide GM workers with about $12,000 over three years.[9]

Despite the 1984 prosperity, officials of both companies expressed concern over high labour rates, and problems in competing with the Japanese auto industry. Nevertheless, the Ford and GM settlements may have influenced other negotiations in which concesssions had been granted by workers in the depth of the recession.

The Free Trade Agreement between Canada and the United States The signing of the Free Trade Agreement between Canada and the United States in 1988 raised all kinds of speculation about its impact on employment in Canada. It was generally agreed that in the short run a number of industries would be seriously affected. The International Lady Garment Workers Union suggested that free trade would cost 20,000 to 25,000 jobs in Ontario alone, and the Prime Minister promised a $63-million a

year program to ease the transition for the clothing industry.[10] The Canadian Council of Furniture Manufacturers predicted that at least 3,500 workers in Canada's furniture industry would lose their jobs over the first five years of the Agreement.[11] The textile industry, which has always been protected by high tariffs, was expected to be affected not only because of free trade, but also because of the probability that tariffs on textiles — which range as high as 25% — would be cut as a result of a special study ordered by the Minister of Finance, Michael Wilson. There has been a running feud between the textile and clothing industries, with the textile industry's high tariffs being blamed for difficulties in the clothing industry, which of course uses textiles as a raw material.[12]

In addition, studies by the federal Department of Industry, Science and Technology forecasted that printing, home furniture, plastics, and wood products would experience difficulties under the free trade deal. However, copper smelting, petrochemicals, steel, aluminum, the massive retail sector, and sporting goods would likely benefit, they claimed. A wide range of other industries including nickel mining, shipbuilding, brewing, dairy, publishing, lumber, and newsprint were expected to see little or no change.[13]

While "mega-mergers" had been taking place with increasing frequency for several years prior to the signing of the Agreement, many analysts considered some of the takeovers that occurred subsequently to be partly free trade driven.[14] One economist has argued that 85% of the projected gains from free-trade will come from restructuring and rationalizing Canadian industry through mergers and greater economies of scale.[15]

The long-term effects of the deal are the subject of much speculation, and it is too early to predict with any precision what they are likely to be. However, Canadian companies will certainly have to become more efficient in order to compete in the new North American market, and this drive for efficiency is bound to have serious repercussions for workers in a number of industries.

How can we minimize the negative effects of the deal on the industrial relations system? A task force of union leaders and business representatives, in conjunction with the Canadian Labour Market and Productivity Centre, suggested in 1989 that a number of employment adjustment programs be put in place to cushion the impact of free trade on affected employees. It recommended, among other things, tax incentives to encourage individual firms to finance special training programs and additional government aid for individual laid-off workers.[16] In the same year, the Advisory Council on Adjustment, set up by the government to ensure that Canadians took advantage of the Free Trade Agreement, also submitted its report. Instead of focusing on dislocations caused only by the Free Trade Agreement, the Council took a broader view. Its recommendations were applicable to all workers who lost their jobs, regardless of whether the loss was due to free trade, technological obsolescence, or simply poor management.[17] The Council acknowledged the primary role of the government in training the unemployed, but insisted that the responsibility for most of Canada's training effort must rest with the private sector. It proposed the establishment of a flexible corporate tax liability for firms, which could be completely offset by a firm's expenditure for training, up to the full amount of the tax. The Council acknowledged, however, that there could be difficulties in ensuring that firms gave meaningful training and that the tax was not used as a way to raise their revenues.[18] It also recommended that the federal government increase funding for programs such as Skill Shortage and Skill Investment. In addition, it recommended improved severance pay, longer notice prior to layoffs, the implementation of a protection fund to compensate workers for lost pay and benefits when companies go bankrupt, and the provision of monetary and other assistance to unions that implement training schemes.[19]

This brief discussion indicates the importance of the product market to the industrial relations system. It is important for both management and unions to cooperate, particularly when competing in international markets. In domestic markets, too, where the demand for goods or services is elastic, prices and wages must not be pushed up so high that sales, and hence jobs, are reduced.

The Labour Market

Ostry and Zaidi define the supply of labour at any given time as "a *schedule or function* relating the quantity of man-hours (of standard efficiency) offered in response to varying levels of wage-rates per hour."[20] While this definition refers to person-hours of standard efficiency, the fact is that labour is not homogeneous. Workers are endowed with various degrees of ability, education, and training (termed "human capital" by labour economists), which to some extent determine the various categories of labour known as occupations. These range from the most highly skilled and trained occupational categories to the lowest, commonly called the unskilled level. Fortunately, there are many functions to be performed in industry and commerce which require the full range of skills workers bring to the labour market.

The labour force can be broken down into three major industry groups. These are (1) primary industries such as agriculture, forestry, fishing, and mining; (2) secondary industries such as manufacturing and construction; and (3) tertiary industries such as utilities (electricity, gas, waterworks, and transportation and communication), trade, finance, and a variety of community, personal, and government services. Figure 2.1 illustrates the percentage of the labour force employed in each of the three industry groups in 1911, 1951, and 1988, and indicates the evolution of the Canadian labour market. One of the more dramatic changes indicated in Figure 2.1 is the pronounced reduction in agriculture since 1911. Since 1951, the sec-

Figure 2.1   **Labour Force by Major Industry Group**
1911, 1951, 1988

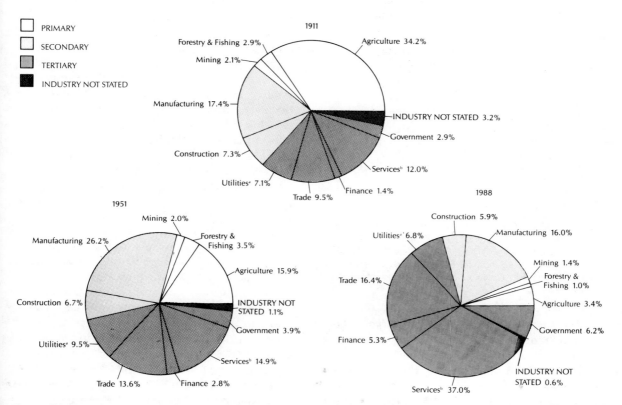

PRIMARY

SECONDARY

TERTIARY

INDUSTRY NOT STATED

Source: For the years 1911 to 1981, Sylvia Ostry and Mahmood A. Zaidi, *Labour Economics in Canada*, 3rd ed. (Toronto: Macmillan of Canada, 1979), p. 109. Copyright © Sylvia Ostry and Mahmood A. Zaidi, 1979. Reprinted by permission of Macmillan of Canada, a division of Gage Publishing Ltd. **1988 percentages are based on statistics from Statistics Canada,** *Labour Force Annual Average* 1981– 88. Labour Force Survey.

[a]"Utilities" includes transportation, communications, electricity, gas, and waterworks.

[b]"Services" includes occupations in which a service is provided but no goods are produced.

[c]The 1988 figures for "forestry and fishing" also include trapping.

ondary sector has been decreasing as well. Tertiary industries, on the other hand, have expanded greatly. This growth in the tertiary industries has had a significant impact on the labour market in all industrialized nations.

As Table 2.1 illustrates, about a third of primary sector workers, with the exception of agricultural workers, are unionized. In the secondary sector, the rate of unionization is almost as high. The service sector, however, has seen the most rapid increase in union recruitment in recent years. Government employees are now the most organized group of workers in Canada, and workers in transportation and other utilities are not far behind. In years to come, the remaining tertiary industries, particularly services and trade, will offer the most potential for union expansion.

Table 2.1   Workers Organized by Industry 1986

Industry group	[%] Workers unionized
Agriculture	1.2
Forestry	48.9
Fishing & Trapping	60.2
Mines, quarries, and oil wells	28.1
Manufacturing	38.2
Construction	53.9
Transportation, Communications, and other utilities	56.7
Trade	9.8
Finance	2.8
Services	34.8
Public Administration	76.3

Source: Statistics Canada, *Annual Report of the Minister of Supply and Services Canada under the Corporations Labour and Unions Returns Act, Part 11 — Labour Unions 1986,* Catalogue No. 71–202 (Ottawa: Supply and Services Canada, August 1986), p. 39. Reproduced by permission of the Minister of Supply and Services Canada.

The Changing Demographics of the Labour Force   Figure 2.2 illustrates some of the major demographic trends in the Canadian labour force since 1966. It shows that the participation rate for the 15–24 age group increased for both men and women between 1966 and 1986. These increases have potentially serious conse-quences for the industrial relations system, as the young workers bring new expectations to the workplace. Their levels of education are generally higher than those of previous groups, and they are not as predisposed as older people to accept the discipline which is characteristic of many types of employment.

Because it appears that younger workers are looking for pleasant jobs with relatively good pay, a high degree of challenge, and not too much supervision, employers and unions may have to include greater experimentation with quality-of-work-life projects and job enrich-ment in order to build more satisfaction into the jobs of the future. Some of the more senior

management and union representatives may have a difficult time adjusting to the attitudes of young, highly educated workers. However, if these representatives do not respond in a posi-tive way, young workers may attempt to gain greater control within unions and management and try themselves to exercise more influence on the structure of jobs.

Figure 2.2 also shows that while the partici-pation rate of male workers 25 years and older decreased over the 20-year period, the rate for female workers in the same age group increased substantially. The significant number of women in the labour force has a number of implications for trade unions and industrial relations. On the trade union side, in order to expand into the predominantly female service industries, orga-nized labour will have to exert greater effort to organize women in the labour force.

From an industrial relations point of view, the higher proportion of women in organized workplaces has already begun to change the nature of union bargaining demands. This became very evident during the 1981 postal strike in Canada when the Canadian Union of Postal Workers (whose membership was about 40% female) struck in order to acquire paid maternity leave. Not only have unions had to respond to the needs of women, but women are also starting to play a much more effective and continuing role in the operations of unions. Already there are a number of high-profile women in some of the larger unions in Canada, and their number is likely to increase in the near future.

Unemployment Patterns   Since the peak of the world recession in the early eighties, Cana-da's unemployment rate has declined steadily. The "boom" years, from 1984–1989, meant a high demand for labour, and many unions were able to bargain from a position of power.

However, there is still a good deal of regional variation in Canada's employment pattern. The Atlantic provinces usually suffer from high unemployment, while the Prairies and Ontario

Figure 2.2   **Employment Participation Rates by Sex and Age Groups
1966, 1976, 1986**

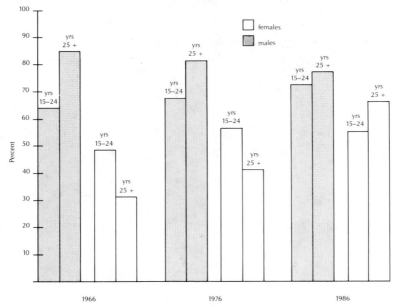

Source: 1966 and 1976 data are from Canada Department of Finance, *Economic Review: April 1985*, Reference Table 28
(Ottawa: Supply and Services Canada, 1989).

maintain the lowest rates overall. Table 2.2 traces these variations since 1966. In the late 1980s, Ontario's unemployment rate fell to the lowest rate since 1970 in that province. By contrast, Atlantic Canada's rate has remained consistently higher.

According to classical and neoclassical economic theory, labour in regions with a high unemployment rate will migrate to those parts of the country where the unemployment rate is low and where wages are high. People from the Atlantic region, for example, would move to Ontario or the Prairies, thereby creating a greater supply of labour in these regions. This, in turn, would reduce wage rates and increase overall employment in Ontario and on the Prairies, while reducing the unemployment rate in the Atlantic provinces.

However, the labour market does not operate the way that neoclassical economics suggests it should. Social and psychological ties often outweigh material advantages. For this reason, unions and management, along with government, often attempt to attract industry to areas of high unemployment in order to stimulate the economy in these areas.

The diversity of Canada's regions gives rise to yet another issue for industrial relations: that of wage differentials. There is a large gap between per capita income levels in the Atlantic provinces on the one hand, and more affluent provinces like Ontario and British Columbia on the other. In industries that bargain on a multi-provincial basis, such as pulp and paper, the question often arises as to whether or not wages should vary according to local labour market conditions, or be pegged at the same rate across the country. The Irving Pulp and Paper Com-

Table 2.2   **Unemployment, Canada and by Region**
1966–1986

			Unemployment rate			
Year	Canada	Atlantic region	Quebec	Ontario	Prairie region	British Columbia
			[%]			
1966	3.4	5.2	4.1	2.6	2.3	4.6
1967	3.8	5.3	4.6	3.2	2.6	5.1
1968	4.5	5.8	5.6	3.6	3.2	5.9
1969	4.4	6.2	6.1	3.2	3.3	5.0
1970	5.7	6.0	7.0	4.4	5.0	7.7
1971	6.2	7.0	7.3	5.4	5.2	7.2
1972	6.2	7.6	7.5	5.0	5.3	7.8
1973	5.5	7.7	6.8	4.3	4.6	6.7
1974	5.3	8.3	6.6	4.4	3.4	6.2
1975	6.9	9.8	8.1	6.3	4.0	8.5
1976	7.1	10.8	8.7	6.2	4.1	8.6
1977	8.1	12.5	10.3	7.0	4.8	8.5
1978	8.3	12.5	10.9	7.2	5.2	8.3
1979	7.4	11.6	9.6	6.5	4.3	7.6
1980	7.5	11.1	9.8	6.8	4.3	6.8
1981	7.5	11.5	10.3	6.6	4.5	6.7
1982	11.0	14.3	13.8	9.8	7.6	12.1
1983	11.9	15.0	13.9	10.4	9.7	13.8
1984	11.3	15.4	12.8	9.1	9.8	14.7
1985	10.5	15.7	11.8	8.0	9.2	14.1
1986	9.5	14.9	11.0	7.0	8.9	12.5

Source: Canada Department of Finance, *Economic Review: April 1985* (Ottawa: Supply and Services Canada, 1985), Reference Table 33, p. 108. Figures for 1985 and 1986 are from the *Labour Force Survey*, Statistics Canada. Reproduced by permission of the Minister of Supply and Services Canada.

pany is a good example of a company which insists on keeping its rates in line with local levels of income. On the other hand, companies such as International Paper and Abitibi have collective agreements which provide the same pay levels for workers in their plants in Ontario, Quebec, and the Atlantic provinces. The higher rates paid by large companies make it difficult for companies based in low-income areas to attract a sufficient quantity and quality of labour.

Another more or less constant factor in the Canadian employment picture is the fact that unemployment among young workers is con-

sistently much higher than among older workers (see Table 2.3). During the recessionary years of the early eighties, unemployment in the 15–24 age group soared as high as 22.3% for males, and 17% for females. In times of soft demand for goods and services, the first to be laid off are usually the younger, less experienced workers.

The problem of youth unemployment is of concern to both industry and government. Not only is it a significant waste of human resources, but it places a heavy financial burden on unemployment insurance and welfare programs. One can argue, as well, that both industry and

Table 2.3 **Unemployment Rates by Sex and Age Groups 1966–1988**

	Male			Female			
	Total	15–24	25 +	Total	15–24	25 +	Total
				[%]			
1966	3.3	6.3	2.6	3.4	4.8	2.7	3.4
1967	3.9	7.2	3.0	3.7	5.5	2.8	3.8
1968	4.6	8.7	3.5	4.4	6.5	3.3	4.5
1969	4.3	8.3	3.2	4.7	6.5	3.7	4.4
1970	5.6	11.2	4.1	5.8	8.6	4.4	5.7
1971	6.0	12.0	4.3	6.6	9.8	5.0	6.2
1972	5.8	11.9	4.1	7.0	9.6	5.7	6.2
1973	4.9	10.0	3.4	6.7	9.2	5.4	5.5
1974	4.8	9.6	3.3	6.4	8.9	5.1	5.3
1975	6.2	12.5	4.3	8.1	11.4	6.5	6.9
1976	6.3	13.2	4.2	8.4	12.1	6.6	7.1
1977	7.3	14.9	4.9	9.4	13.8	7.4	8.1
1978	7.5	15.0	5.2	9.6	13.8	7.7	8.3
1979	6.6	13.2	4.5	8.8	12.7	7.0	7.4
1980	6.9	13.7	4.8	8.4	12.6	6.5	7.5
1981	7.0	14.1	4.8	8.3	12.3	6.7	7.5
1982	11.0	21.1	8.2	10.9	16.1	8.8	11.0
1983	12.0	22.3	9.2	11.6	17.0	9.6	11.8
1984	11.2	19.3	9.0	11.3	16.1	9.7	11.2
1985	10.3	18.1	8.3	10.7	14.5	9.4	10.5
1986	9.3	16.4	7.6	9.8	13.6	8.6	9.5
1987	8.5	14.8	7.0	9.3	12.4	8.3	8.8
1988	7.4	12.9	6.0	8.3	11.0	7.5	7.8

Source: 1966–1980 figures are from Canada Department of Finance, *Economic Review: April 1985* (Ottawa: Supply and Services Canada, 1985), Reference Table 28. p. 103. 1981–1988 figures are from Statistics Canada, *The Labour Force Survey* (Ottawa: Supply and Services Canada, 1989). Reproduced by permission of the Minister of Supply and Services Canada.

government have a social responsibility to help people in this age group grow into productive members of society.[21]

One proposed solution to this problem is the implementation of apprenticeship and training programs, financed jointly by management, unions, and perhaps government. An example was the Critical Trades Skill Training Program, which was inaugurated in 1978. Under this program, substantially increased federal funds were allocated to assist the private sector in training workers or prospective workers for certain highly skilled trades. The scheme provided an excellent opportunity for unions and management to cooperate to increase the supply of skilled labour, and to tackle the often intractable problem of unemployment among youth.

In 1985, however, the Conservative government replaced the skill training plan with six new programs, under the title "Canadian Jobs Strategy." These programs were designed (1) to help workers whose jobs are threatened due to changing technology and economic conditions; (2) to assist young people and women facing difficulties entering the labour market by providing them with a combination of training and

Peter Redman, *The Financial Post*

work experience; (3) to provide meaningful assistance for the long-term unemployed; (4) to offer help to workers in communities facing chronic high unemployment, plant closures, mass layoffs, or severe economic decline; and (6) to stimulate the search for innovative solutions to labour market problems. Some of these objectives were new; others combined existing programs while giving them new directions.[22] Overall, federal spending on job training in 1988 was only $1.5 billion, compared with $1.7 billion in 1984.[23]

Capital and Technology

We will discuss capital and technology together since capital does not mean very much until it is converted into the technological structures needed to produce goods and services.

Until recently, Canadian industry was not as capital intensive as industry in the United States. Since Canada operated behind high tariff walls in some industries, there was little incentive for employers in these industries to increase their capital investment. One had merely to walk through a number of Canadian and American automobile parts producers to notice the different levels of technology in the two countries. In addition, relatively high tariff walls did not push Canadian companies to try to achieve economies of scale, and hence make more effective use of their technological resources to produce goods at lower cost. A

1978 Royal Commission had the following to say about Canadian industry:

> That Canadian firms are scale-inefficient has become a cliché both in the literature of industrial organizations in Canada and among businessmen. Until 1975 relatively lower wages in Canada as compared with the United States partially masked the effect of low productivity in Canada. When the wage relationship reversed in 1975, the future of the manufacturing sector in Canada looked bleak indeed: low productivity, compounded by high costs of both labour and capital, was rapidly making large segments of Canadian industry uncompetitive internationally. One proposed solution to this predicament was the Economic Council of Canada's recommendation, in its study *Looking Outward*, that Canada move towards multilateral free trade since then all firms would be open to international competition and would have free access to world markets. They would then be forced to move towards their most efficient scale of operation at product, plant and firm levels.[24]

Over the decade that followed, tariffs did begin to fall, and as foreign investment increased, so did Canadian productivity. By 1985, one Canadian authority on productivity claimed that Canada had become more capital intensive than the United States, "which makes Canada the most capital intensive country in the world."[25]

However, the increasing levels of investment did not reflect a more competitive stance on the part of existing Canadian companies, but rather an increase in the level of foreign, and particularly US, investment in Canada. For years past, many Canadians had argued that Canada relied too heavily on foreign investment and a branch plant economy, and that it should somehow acquire more control over its own investment. The 1978 Royal Commission whose report we quote from above had the following to say about foreign ownership in Canada:

> Canadian industry features a higher proportion of foreign ownership than does any other developed country, and the presence of foreign ownership and foreign subsidiaries in Canada contributes to Canada's dependence on capital and technology

from abroad. Repatriation of dividends and interest charges at the rate of $2.5 billion per year reduces the growth of domestic pools of capital. Because of their backing by their parent firms, multinational subsidiaries are often able to obtain capital in Canada on more favourable terms than domestic companies of the same size. Technology is often imported rather than developed in Canada because it is cheaper and less risky to buy or license from foreign firms than to maintain indigenous research and development.[26]

The high degree of foreign ownership of Canadian industry was the major reason the Trudeau government set up the Foreign Investment Review Agency (FIRA) in 1974, to exercise some restraint on the rate of foreign investment and acquisitions in Canada. The Mulroney government renamed the agency the Bureau of Competition Policy (or Competition Tribunal) in 1984. Its new name reflects its more permissive stance toward foreign investment.

Foreign control of Canadian industry can have serious implications for industrial relations policies and practices. In some cases, foreign-based companies try to import their industrial relations policies and practices from the parent company into Canada. Even worse, should Canadian subsidiaries become unprofitable, they can close and move their assets to other countries. Such plant closures became a serious problem in Ontario in the early 1980s, and the provincial government was forced to set guidelines protecting workers. For example, Part XII, section 40(2) of the Ontario Employment Standards Act requires an employer to give specified notice of layoff ranging from 8 to 16 weeks depending on the number of workers to be laid off.[27] In addition, section 40(a) provides that where the employment of 50 or more workers is terminated, severance pay must be given to each worker who has been employed for five or more years at the rate of his or her regular pay per week multiplied by the number of years that the worker has been with the firm, up to a maximum of 26 years. Heavy fines have been given to employers who have failed to comply with these provisions.

Canadian industry probably would not be as highly developed as it is today if it had not been for foreign investment. However, this development does not preclude a certain vigilance concerning the effects of foreign-controlled organizations on industrial relations and workers in this country.

The Money Market

The money market is an important aspect of the economic system that may have an impact on industrial relations in Canada. It is defined as capital available for investment of different types, and interest rates payable on bank loans or long-term securities.

High interest rates seriously curtail purchases of houses, cars, and other durable goods and, as a consequence, affect employment and capital investment in these industries. Unionized workers in a number of industries in the United States, including airlines, trucking, meat packing, rubber, and steel, have negotiated wage cuts, wage freezes, or improved arrangements to help protect their jobs and income. These were negotiated in addition to the Ford and GM agreements mentioned previously.[28]

While the union rhetoric in Canada has been against taking wage cuts or wage freezes, the fact is that they did occur — in 1982, 1983, and 1984. As Kumar points out,

> . . . in 1983 wage freezes or cuts were a feature of 65 settlements (10 percent of the total) affecting more than 200 thousand workers . . . The number of settlements providing a wage freeze or cuts in 1984 increased to 139 agreements (25 percent of the total) involving close to 300 thousand workers (one quarter of the total). While the incidence of the freeze dropped off substantially in 1985, there were still 78 settlements (16 percent of the total) affecting 168 thousand workers where wage rates in the first year of the contract were either frozen or cut.[29]

Wage freezes have been particularly marked in western Canada and in the construction industry.[30]

Money markets are of particular concern to those involved in industries which rely heavily on export markets, and in particular on exports of manufactured products. Exports are higher when the Canadian dollar is trading low on world markets. They drop, however, when the dollar rises in value, as it did during the latter half of the 1980s. What the present monetary system may do with respect to the long-term development of Canadian industry is very difficult to predict, but should the Canadian dollar approach par with the American dollar, many companies would be in difficulty, especially if they wish to operate in international markets. On the other hand, a devalued dollar means higher import prices. Since we import many manufactured goods, the higher prices can lead to inflation and a higher cost of living, which may be reflected in increased wage demands.

Some Concluding Comments on the Economic Subsystem

In this section we have discussed the implications of various aspects of the Canadian economic system for industrial relations policy and practice. We first commented on the roles that projected inflation and real income losses are likely to have on our industrial relations system. We also discussed the impact of previous incomes policies. We have commented on the Canadian import and export situation and the extent to which the Free Trade Agreement with the United States may affect our industrial relations system. We also commented briefly on patterns and trends in the labour market, and on the potential implications of foreign ownership of Canadian assets for our economic development, and for industrial relations policies and practices in particular. Finally, we commented on the money market and how shifts here may have serious implications not only for domestic developments but also for the country's foreign trade. All of these factors act as important conditioning inputs and outputs of the industrial relations system.

The Political Subsystem

As Canadians are well aware, we live in a federal state with a central government and ten provincial governments, along with two territories. The powers of the two levels of government vary, the federal government having more control during wartime and the provincial governments having more control during times of peace. The federal government is bicameral, with an elected House of Commons and a Senate to which members are appointed. At the provincial level, there is only one level of legislature, which is usually referred to as the Legislative Assembly. Ours is a parliamentary system, with members of the governing party voting along party lines rather than as individuals. The same voting pattern is also true of the two major opposition parties. Our prime minister is the leader of the party which has enough seats to form the government.

Canada now has three major political parties at the federal level — the Liberal, Conservative, and New Democratic parties. At the provincial level there are usually two parties (in some cases three) which generally correspond to the parties at the federal level. (The parties in British Columbia and Quebec, however, do not correspond to federal parties.)

The nature of the Canadian system was first set forth in the British North America (BNA) Act of 1867 (now renamed the Constitution Act). Sections 91 and 92 of the Act spelled out the powers of the federal government and provincial legislatures. The most important provisions relating to federal power regarding industrial relations include the preamble of section 91, which gives the federal government the right to make laws for the "Peace, Order and good Government in Canada." There are also 31 items in section 91 itself, of which the following may be considered pertinent to the constitutionality of labour relations:

> The Regulation of Trade and Commerce (2); Unemployment Insurance (2A); Postal Service (5); Navigation and Shipping (10); Sea Coast and Inland Fisheries (12); Ferries between a Province and any British or Foreign Country or between two Provinces (13); Banking, Incorporation of Banks and the Issue of Paper Money (15); Savings Banks (16); The Criminal Law, except the Constitution of Courts of Criminal Jurisdiction, but including the Procedure in Criminal Matters (27); and Such Clauses of Subjects by this Act assigned exclusively to the Legislatures of the Provinces.[31]

Section 92 lists those areas which are within the exclusive domain of the provincial legislatures. There are 16 headings altogether. The most important with respect to the constitutionality of labour legislation are the following:

> Municipal Institutions in the Province (13); Generally all Matters of a merely local or private Nature in the Province (16); and Local Works and Undertakings other than such as are of the following Classes: (a) Lines of Steam or other Ships, Railways, Canals, Telegraphs, and other Works and Undertakings connnecting the Province with any other or others of the Provinces, or extending beyond the Limits of the Province; (b) Lines of Steam Ships between the Province and any British or Foreign Country; (c) Such Works as, although wholly situate within the Province, are before or after their Execution declared by the Parliament of Canada to be for the general Advantage of Canada or for the Advantage of Two or more of the Provinces (10)[32]

Early judicial decisions on the Canadian Constitution were largely in favour of extensive federal jurisdiction. However, the Judicial Committee of the British Privy Council (the court of last resort in Canada until 1949 when it was replaced by the Supreme Court of Canada) soon began to make decisions which favoured increased provincial jurisdiction. The most celebrated case in the industrial relations field was the Snider case, in which a federal statute was overturned, the Judicial Committee deciding that it was beyond the powers of the federal government. John Porter, in his classic book, *The Vertical Mosaic*, has the following to say about the Judicial Committee:

> Gradually through the decisions of judges in the United Kingdom, whose knowledge of Canada

could at the most be slight, the relative weight of responsibility went to the provinces and away from the central government. The federalism which resulted from the decisions of the Judicial Committee left Canada after the 1930's politically and socially incapacitated.[33]

The interpretation of the Constitution Act by judicial authorities has had a significant impact on the Canadian industrial relations system. (This will be spelled out in more detail in Chapter 6.) Today the federal government has jurisdiction over only about 10% of the labour force while the provinces have jurisdiction over the remaining 90%. There is therefore more potential for divergences in labour policy. This makes it difficult for employers and unions operating across provincial boundaries to be consistent in their policies and programs. The federal government may, in the future, begin to assume more responsibility in the industrial relations field. Much will depend on what amendments, if any, are made to the newly repatriated Constitution, and especially on any new division of powers between the federal and provincial governments.

The partisan nature of the Canadian political system makes it difficult to determine how individual members of the parties feel about labour relations and labour policies generally. Internal differences among members are usually ironed out in caucuses after which members vote along party lines. This is different from the American system in which each senator or member of Congress votes as an individual and it is possible to see how an elected member voted on labour issues. In fact, the American Federation of Labor–Congress for Industrial Organization (AFL–CIO) keeps a running record of how each senator and member of Congress votes on issues of importance to the labour movement. The American labour movement is able to "reward its friends and punish its enemies," an ability that the first AFL president, Samuel Gompers, recommended be used by labour in politics. Under the Canadian system, labour has no such power. While lobbying politicians takes place on both sides of the border, it is much more common in the United States, since individual senators and members of Congress play a more important role in shaping government policy in that country. Although party bosses play an important role in American politics, they do not have the control over government policy that party leaders, particularly the leader of the governing party, have in Canada.

These facts are important for Canadian unions and employers to understand, especially while commenting on white papers or presenting their cases before parliamentary committees studying labour issues. The same is true at the provincial level, and this is one reason why we have provincial federations of labour in Canada, as well as provincial arms of the Chamber of Commerce and the Canadian Manufacturers Association. Hence, both unions and employers must understand the political system if they hope to play a role in the formulation of government policies, either by supporting political parties or by spending money lobbying at the senior levels of government.

The Legal Subsystem

Canada's legal system consists not only of the Constitution, but also of the statutory law passed by the federal government and the provincial legislatures, as well as court interpretation of such law. In addition, much common or case law has been built up over the years out of which general legal principles have emerged.

It is noteworthy that, under the Combines Act, unions were illegal until 1872. Up to that time, trade unions were presumed to be against the common good. This supposition also existed in the United States, where it was known as the "criminal conspiracy doctrine." Following the Toronto printers' strike in 1871, the criminal law was amended and a Trades

Union Act was passed which freed trade unions from being prosecuted as criminal conspiracies.

After the Snider case of 1925 (which was mentioned in the section on the political subsystem), federal jurisdiction was limited to only about one tenth of the labour force. As a consequence, legal developments vary from one jurisdiction to another, making it very difficult to keep up with the many amendments that are taking place across Canada in the industrial relations field. Nevertheless, unions and management are expected to keep abreast of and adhere to these changes in regulations. In recent years, moreover, various jurisdictions have been passing increasingly more substantive legislation concerning compulsory collection of union dues and advance notice of technological changes.

As well as laws relating to industrial relations *per se*, all Canadian jurisdictions have employment standards legislation covering, for example, hours of work per day and per week, overtime pay beyond normal hours, and minimum wages for adults and young people. Any industrial relations practitioner or student must be aware of these employment standards because they usually set limits (maximums or minimums) on the outputs of collective bargaining.

A number of jurisdictions in recent years have also passed human rights acts, or their equivalent, which forbid discrimination in employment on the basis of race, colour, religion, age, and sex, among other factors. As a result, an important articulation is developing between industrial relations and human rights legislation. In a couple of cases, for example, provincial human rights commissions have ruled that compulsory retirement at a given age contravenes human rights legislation. All jurisdictions have also passed legislation relating to health and safety in the workplace. The appointment of joint committees on safety and the use of improved work methods to avoid accidents are two outcomes of such legislation which affect the industrial relations system.

Moreover, there is now legislation enabling persons subjected to unwanted sexual harassment to be heard before independent tribunals.

In industrial relations, legislation is implemented through tribunals and agencies. For example, labour relations boards are charged with applying statute law to a specific set of facts, and in this process they develop important jurisprudence referred to as administrative law. In addition, the executive branch of government sometimes acts to resolve disputes when the regular administrative machinery appears incapable of doing so in specific cases.

As we shall see in Chapter 9, arbitration boards are now handing down very important decisions, and a substantial body of arbitrable jurisprudence is building up. Again, people involved in industrial relations should be aware of the general principles which are emerging from arbitration decisions and analyze these principles to ensure that they do not violate them in the provisions of their collective agreements. If any of these administrative tribunals exceed their jurisdiction or act against generally accepted legal principles, the courts often intervene at the request of either unions or management and may make rulings which override the tribunals' decisions.

The Social Subsystem

The social subsystem of any country consists of a set of values and beliefs which serve to guide interaction between individuals and groups and to provide norms for individual and group behaviour. These values and beliefs provide cohesion and unity within a country. However, there may be secondary systems within a country. For example, managers may have a different set of beliefs and values from those who work under them, particularly workers at the lower level of the occupational hierarchy. To the extent that there are differences among the goals and values of the people at the top and bottom of organizations, there is likely to be a certain amount of conflict inherent in such organizational settings.

A person born into a specific society normally acquires in the course of growing up the values and beliefs of that society. This is what sociologists call "the socialization process." However, younger generations may adopt value systems which differ from those of their parents or grandparents and, in the course of a society's development, they may change the basic value and belief systems of their society. The men and women in Canada and other countries who went through the Great Depression and World War II may find their values and beliefs at odds with those of the generations born in the 1950s, 1960s, and 1970s, who have grown up in a more permissive and affluent society.

The important role that values play in every society is succinctly stated by John Porter:

> Besides providing cohesion and unity, value systems give a sense of rightness to the social order and legitimacy for particular practices and usages, including class and power structures, within a given society. For individuals, the value system with which they have been indoctrinated provides a view of the world and an explanation of life in society.[34]

Porter goes on to state that certain social mechanisms are necessary for restating and generalizing values so that they do not become so vague as to cease to perform the function of social cohesion. In particular, he places great emphasis on the role of the mass media in translating particular value systems into a meaningful and coherent whole which serves to guide behaviour.[35]

Every society has certain powerful groups that give it direction, usually through the political system and the formulation of national policy. Corporations and trade unions are two power blocs which try to influence the political process. In some European countries, for example, the Labour parties which form the government have close ties to the labour movement.

But, as John Porter points out, "In Canada there has been throughout the present century a close coalition between political leadership, the mass media, and the corporate world."[36] He also points out that the power of labour leaders does not extend beyond their institutional roles, inasmuch as labour leaders rarely share in the informal aspects of the confraternity of power. In Porter's analysis of Canadian society, people involved in industrial relations need to be aware that the political system is influenced to a considerable degree by large corporations (including the corporate mass media) and not by labour.

Another interesting and increasing power bloc in Canada is that of recently formed interest or pressure groups. Among such groups we could include the women's movement, Native peoples, and consumers. These interest groups are beginning to exercise their power by influencing political decision-making. Organized labour is one such interest group, and because of its long history, it may play a more important role than many of the newer groups.

During the 1970s there was some debate about the extent to which Canadians still embraced the work ethic. A 1973 Department of Manpower and Immigration work ethic study and job satisfaction survey confirmed that Canadians were indeed strongly committed to work. The resulting report had the following to say:

> Work was named by more respondents to the Work Ethic Survey than any other option, including family and friends, as a way [of] achieving one's goals. Canadians see themselves as industrious people to whom work contributes a feeling of success, and for a large proportion, of personal fulfillment. It is not surprising, therefore, that the vast majority of respondents ... expected to get satisfaction from their work, and satisfaction, or more precisely the behaviour that it engenders, has social consequences.[37]

Respondents stressed that work should be interesting, that there should be enough information and authority to do the job, and that it should allow them the opportunity to develop special abilities. Things that were considered to be less important included job security, promotional considerations, pay, hours of work, and fringe benefits.[38] This type of information is important to both business (if it wishes to increase productivity and reduce absenteeism and staff turnover) and labour (if it wishes to increase participation in trade-union activity, particularly at the local level). Managers and union leaders should monitor the extent to which the attitudes of Canadian workers remain constant or change in the coming years.

Conclusion

This chapter has attempted to develop more fully the nature and role of conditioning inputs in the industrial relations system. Following chapters will view specific topics in terms of the broader social framework discussed here; and, in some cases, it will be useful to analyze the way in which societal constraints shape the various aspects of the industrial relations system.

Questions

1 What are the advantages of viewing the industrial relations system within a broader environmental context? Elaborate.

2 How do the various environmental subsystems affect the inputs and outputs of the industrial relations system?

3 Given the specific environmental constraints operating on an organization and the goals, values, and power of its actors, is it possible to predict the specific outputs of contract negotiations for the workers and employers of a particular organization? Choose an organization and explain.

4 Do you think the present constitutional division of powers between the federal and provincial governments in Canada contributes to or detracts from collective bargaining in Canada? Elaborate.

5 Do environmental constraints operate on government, private industry, and parapublic institutions in Canada? Explain.

6 Speculate on whether it is possible to combine environmental influences into some quantitative form in order to make the outputs of an industrial relations system fairly predictable.

7 Specify and give examples of the different constraints operating on the private and public sector collective bargaining systems in your province.

8 Describe the role that public opinion plays in labour–management relations in your province.

9 What are some of the more important constraints under which private employers operate in your province? Do they vary by industry? Be specific.

10 Do economic conditions in the United States affect the industrial relations climate in your province? Elaborate.

Notes

1 *Perspectives Canada 111*, Supply and Services Canada (Ottawa: 1980), p. 243.

2 C. Waddell, "Canada Facing Recession Risk, Board Believes," *Globe and Mail* (May 8, 1989), pp. 16–21.

3 Quoted in Prices and Incomes Commission, *Inflation, Unemployment and Incomes Policies —*

Summary Report (Ottawa: Information Canada, 1972), Preface.

4 Ibid., p. 51.

5 F. Reid, "Wage-and-Price Controls in Canada," *Union-Management Relations in Canada*, eds. J. Anderson and M. Gunderson (Don Mills: Addison-Wesley Publishers, 1982), pp. 493–95.

6 V. Galt, "Labour Turmoil Worsens as Leaders Dig In," *Globe and Mail* (July 20, 1982), p. 1.

7 "Auto Pacts Aid Laid-Off Workers," *Globe and Mail* (October 16, 1984), p. B4.

8 Ibid.

9 Ibid.

10 "Garment Industry Fears Trade Pact Will Hurt It," *The Ottawa Citizen* (December 30, 1988), p. D13.

11 "Trade Deal Will Cost at Least 3,500 Jobs, Furniture Makers Say," *The Ottawa Citizen* (January 5, 1989), p. B9.

12 "Wilson Orders Study of Textile Trade Policy," *Globe and Mail* (February 11, 1989), p. B4.

13 "Federal Studies Show Trade Deal's Winners and Losers," *The Ottawa Citizen* (January 14, 1989), p. F10.

14 Examples include the merger of the Molson and Carling-O'Keefe breweries and the sale of Wardair to Canadian Airlines International.

15 R. Sheppard, "Takeover in Oil, Beer, and Airlines Part of a Trend," pp. A1–A2.

16 D. Dowling, "Task Force Says Bosses Should Pay for Retraining," *The Ottawa Citizen* (January 27, 1989), p. A4.

17 *Adjusting to Win* (Report of the Advisory Council on Adjustment, Supply and Services Canada, March 1989), p. xvii.

18 Ibid., pp. 42–45.

19 Ibid., pp. 56–57, and 60.

20 S. Ostry and M.A. Zaidi, *Labour Economics in Canada*, 3rd ed. (Toronto: Macmillan of Canada, 1979), p. 1.

21 A. Craig, "Report on Manpower Development and Planning — Mechanical Contracting Association," *Manpower Needs in the Mechanical Construction Industry: 1975–1980*, joint study of the Department of Manpower and Immigration, the United Association of the Plumbing and Pipefitting Industry of the USA and Canada, and the Mechanical Contractors Association of Canada

(Spring 1975), p. 25.

22 Employment and Immigration Canada, *Canadian Job Strategies* (Ottawa: June 1985).

23 J. Ferguson, "Business, Labor Aim for Consensus on Foreign Trade," *The Ottawa Citizen* (January 12, 1989), p. E9.

24 *Report of the Royal Commission on Corporate Concentration* (Ottawa: Supply and Services Canada, March 1978), pp. 45–46.

25 D.J. Daly, "Remedies for Increasing Productivity Growth Levels in Canada," Ch. 7, *Lagging Productivity Growth, Causes and Remedies*, eds. S. Maital and N.M. Meltz (Cambridge: Ballinges, 1985), p. 226.

26 *Report of the Royal Commission on Corporate Concentration*, p. 4.

27 *Employment Standards Act*, R.S.O. (1980), s. 40; Regulations 286, s. 4, R.R.O. (1980).

28 W. List, "Canadian Unions' Hard Line Product of Complex Factors," *Globe and Mail* (March 1, 1982), p. B14.

29 P. Kumar, "Recent Wage Deceleration in Canada: Short-Run Response or Structural Change," Vol. 42, No. 4, *Relations Industrielles/Industrial Relations* (1987), p. 690.

30 Ibid., pp. 690–691.

31 Vol. 1, *Decisions of the Judicial Committee of the Privy Council Relating to the British North America Act 1867 and the Canadian Constitution 1867–1954* (Ottawa: Queen's Printer, 1954), pp. xxxvi–xxxviii; and the 1940 and 1949 amendments thereto.

32 Ibid.

33 J. Porter, *The Vertical Mosaic* (Toronto: University of Toronto Press, 1965), p. 380.

34 Ibid., p. 459.

35 Ibid.

36 Ibid., p. 539.

37 Canada Department of Manpower and Immigration, *Canadian Work Values* (Ottawa: Information Canada, 1975), p. 60.

38 Ibid.

With Godsell, *The Financial Post*

3

Theories of the Labour Movement

Introduction

As I pointed out in the Preface, three chapters of this book are devoted to the labour movement. This chapter summarizes the major factors accounting for the emergence and development of labour movements, Chapter 4 discusses the history and philosophy of the Canadian labour movement, and Chapter 5 discusses its structure. In speaking of trade unions today, we seem to take for granted that they have always existed, and do not consider the factors which

gave rise to them or which explain their continued growth. A number of early and well respected scholars in the field of industrial relations put forth various theories that attempted to explain the emergence of trade unions, their patterns of growth, and their structure. However, in recent years, there has been little serious inquiry into trade union theory. One exception has been a study by Kerr, Harbison, Dunlop, and Myers, entitled *Industrialism and Industrial Man*.[1]

41

Dunlop, in an article on the development of trade unions published some years ago, suggested that theorists of the labour movement have posed at least four important questions:

1 How do we explain the origin or emergence of labour organizations?
2 How do we explain the pattern of growth and development of labour organizations?
3 What are the ultimate goals of the labour movement?
4 Why do workers join labour organizations?[2]

The writers whose works Dunlop examined were concerned solely with unionism among blue-collar workers, since white-collar unions did not then exist. Among the early commentators whom Dunlop discussed were Fabian socialist writers Sidney and Beatrice Webb.

The Webbs[3]

Back in the 1890s, the Webbs defined a trade union as "a continuous association of wage-earners for the purpose of maintaining or improving the conditions of their working lives."[4] Their meticulous and detailed research led them to conclude that, in all cases in which trade unions arose, wage-earners (currently referred to as workers) had ceased to be independent producers who owned both the means of production and the goods they created.[5]

The Webbs attributed the development of trade unionism largely to the divorce of capital from labour — a development outlined in the following terms:

> It has, indeed, become a commonplace of modern Trade Unionism that only in those industries in which the worker has ceased to be concerned in the profits of buying and selling — that inseparable characteristic of the ownership and management of the means of production — can effective and stable trade organizations be established.[6]

In effect, stable trade unions came into being, according to the Webbs, only when workers lost control of the ownership and management of the means of production — a situation characteristic of capitalism. Capitalism brought with it not only competition in the product market but also in the labour market. Hence, it is not surprising that the Webbs should have considered the fundamental objective of trade unionism to be "the deliberate regulation of the conditions of employment in such a way as to ward off from the manual-working producers the evil effects of industrial competition."[7] As long as the law protected workers from the evil effects of competition there was little need for unionism. However, the introduction by government of a policy removing such protection provided strong incentive for workers to form unions to protect their interests. The Webbs attributed the formation of British unions to three factors: (1) the divorce of labour from capital; (2) the need to regulate competition; and (3) the lack of government protection.

The Webbs were also interested in union structure and how it evolved. Leaders of early unions had to combat a trend toward what the Webbs referred to as "local monopoly," the tendency of workers to look out for themselves or their fellows in the local community rather than their trade or their fellows in the larger community of that trade.

> The natural selfishness of the local branches is accordingly always being combated by the central executives and national delegate meetings, in the wider interests of the whole body of the members wherever they may be working.[8]

Nonetheless, they note that there seemed to be optimism about the movement from local to national unionism:

> The Trade Union world has, throughout its whole history, manifested an overpowering impulse to the amalgamation of local trade clubs into national unions, with centralised funds and centralised administration.[9]

The process of amalgamation described by the Webbs applies equally well to the modern trade union movement.

Trade Union Methods

Unions enforced their regulations, according to the Webbs, by means of three distinct instruments: "the Method of Mutual Insurance, the Method of Collective Bargaining, and the Method of Legal Enactment."[10]

Method of Mutual Insurance

The method of mutual insurance was used by unions to accumulate funds out of which benefits were paid to workers deprived of their livelihood by causes over which they had no control. These benefits were divided into two categories: "benevolent or friendly" on the one hand and "out-of-work" on the other. The benevolent fund provided sick pay, accident benefits, superannuation allowances, and burial money. The out-of-work pay or trade fund provided money to replace tools lost by theft or fire, or to compensate for unemployment caused by temporary breakdowns of machinery, employer bankruptcy, or depression in a trade.[11] As far as the Webbs were concerned, the out-of-work benefits were the important part of mutual insurance.

Mutual insurance was practised largely during the first quarter of the twentieth century when combination laws in Britain prevented the legal formation of workers into trade unions. Similar provisions in Canada's Criminal Code inhibited union activity in this country. It was only when the combination laws were amended in 1871 that British unions were able to engage actively in collective bargaining. Similar legislative action followed in Canada one year later.

Method of Collective Bargaining

The method of collective bargaining, as discussed by the Webbs, corresponds roughly to the type of collective bargaining that is currently practised in North America and most other industrially advanced countries. "The most obvious form of permanent machinery for Collective Bargaining," the Webbs claimed, "is a joint committee, consisting of equal numbers of representatives of the employers and workmen respectively."[12]

Method of Legal Enactment

The method of legal enactment referred to attempts by trade union leaders and other prominent thinkers of the time to petition Parliament to enact guarantees of basic minimum conditions of employment. The Webbs saw a doctrine of a national minimum emerging which encompassed such items as terms of apprenticeship, sanitation, job safety, working hours, and minimum wages for all grades of labour. This national minimum would be enforced through an elaborate labour code. In their view, trade union officials could have a substantial input in helping government to develop the national minimum. In addition, they saw the possibility of certain unions negotiating for more than the national minimum, where these unions represented groups of workers possessing specialized skills.

The Webbs argued that trade union regulations could be reduced to two economic devices: "the Device of the Common Rule" and "the Device of Restriction of Numbers." They found the device of the common rule to be a universal feature of trade unionism. Its aim was to continuously upgrade the minimum conditions of employment applicable to all types of workers. The Webbs strongly recommended that trade-union leaders use this device.[13] By contrast, the device of the restriction of numbers (usually enforced by limiting admission to a trade through apprenticeship regulations) was seriously questioned by the Webbs, particularly if it caused injustices in the selection of apprentices by preventing many young, underprivileged boys from gaining access to apprenticeship, or by limiting the employer's freedom of choice in hiring, or both.[14]

The Webbs predicted the popularity of the method of legal enactment over mutual insurance or collective bargaining in this statement:

> Whether for good or for evil, it appears inevitable that the growing participation of the wage-earners in political life, and the rising influence of their organisations, must necessarily bring about an increasing use of the Method of Legal Enactment.[15]

Legal enactment, the Webbs noted, appeared to be characterized by peaceful conditions in industry and by an absence of friction between unions and management. Moreover, since it also set minimum standards, it approached universal coverage more closely than mutual insurance or collective bargaining did. The Webbs acknowledged, however, that the regulations established under the legal enactment method were slow to adapt to changing circumstances.[16] Like many other observers, they came to view legal enactment not as a tool for progressive reform but as a rote determined by prevailing custom.

For altering regulations and attaining objectives quickly, the Webbs suggested that the method of collective bargaining was more effective than the other two methods. It also permitted the most powerful groups to obtain benefits beyond those provided by legislation. Despite these perceived advantages, the Webbs expressed a preference for the method of legal enactment, particularly if all regulations were based on the doctrine of a living wage. For them, it was a question of the labour movement's place in society and its role in working toward social justice: "Trade Unionism is not merely an incident of the present phase of capitalistic industry, but has a permanent function to fulfill in the democratic state."[17]

Although the Webbs did not develop a complete theory of the labour movement, they developed one of the most comprehensive treatises of the labour movement. Probably more than any other writers, they have answered the four questions posed by Dunlop. They explained that (1) unions emerged as a result of the divorce of labour from capital and of the need to protect workers from the evils of competition while guaranteeing certain levels of wages and benefits; (2) that unions grew from closely knit community trade organizations, overcoming an initial tendency toward local monopolies, to emerge as national unions; (3) that the ultimate goals of the labour movement were not only to obtain for their members benefits equal to those enjoyed by workers performing equivalent duties, but to establish a national minimum for all workers; and (4) that workers joined unions to improve or protect their wages and working conditions.

Commons[18]

Although John R. Commons, who wrote after World War I, did not consider himself a theorist of the labour movement, there are ideas in a number of his writings which help to explain the formation and development of trade unions. Commons, who confined his analysis to the United States, claimed that trade unions could only be explained by recognizing "the interaction of economic, industrial, and political conditions, with many varieties of individualistic, socialistic, and protectionistic philosophies."[19] He also treated labour history in the United States as part of its industrial and political history. Commons saw two conditions in America that made trade union development in that country different from the development of unions in other countries: the wide expanse of free land in the United States and the early granting of universal suffrage.[20]

The main explanation offered by Commons for the emergence of the American labour movement was the expansion of competitive markets. He set out his explanation, after exhaustive study, in an article entitled "American Shoemakers, 1648-1895."[21] In this article, Commons described the divorce of craftspeople from the ownership and from the sale of their products; but he also described the growth of many intermediary market links between the original production unit and the retailer. In order to protect themselves in this specialized distribution system among local markets, workers would unionize to ensure that competition would be based on product quality and not on the difference in wages between unionized and non-unionized labour.

Commons went on to explain that those workers who were organized into unions to great advantage in one community should help to organize unions in other communities where people worked under non-union conditions. He saw both the desirability and the possibility of workers organizing local unions in nearly all communities where workers in the same trade produced the same kind of goods. This city-by-city type of organizing explains, in large part, the rise of national unions. Hence, for Commons, the broadening of markets was the basic concept underlying the emergence and growth of the trade union movement in the United States. While he recognized the importance of changes in the methods of production, he gave primary emphasis to the expansion of markets:

> The vast area of the United States, coupled with free trade within that area and a spreading network of transportation, has developed an unparalleled extension of the competitive area of markets, and thereby has strikingly distinguished American [labour] movements from those of other countries.[22]

Commons differentiated several periods of trade union growth and decline and identified the factors which were instrumental in these changes.

To summarize, Commons explained the emergence and development of the American labour movement as being a result of the extension of competitive markets. It was left to one of his students, Selig Perlman, to develop a theory of the trade union movement in the United States.

Commons' theme of competitive markets can be used to explain the rise of unions not only in the United States but also in Canada. Many American companies established plants in Canada and it was only logical for unions to try to organize these companies as well. Also, many Canadian companies were producing goods for import into the United States. In order to take "labour out of competition" it was only natural for international unions to organize workers in these companies. For example,

American-based unions organized coal-producing companies in Canada with which American firms did business.

Perlman[23]

In the preface to his classic study, *A Theory of the Labor Movement*, Selig Perlman indicates that he was born in Russia and first embraced the theory of the labour movement in Marxist readings. He later immigrated to North America and joined the research staff of John R. Commons at the University of Wisconsin. As a result of his studies in America, Perlman radically revised his Marxist outlook. In defining his new theory, he noted that three factors appeared to be basic to any modern labour situation:

> First, the resistance power of capitalism, determined by its own historical development; second, the degree of dominance over the labor movements by the intellectual's "mentality," which regularly underestimates capitalism's resistance power and overestimates labor's will to radical change; and third, the degree of maturity of a trade union "mentality."[24]

With respect to capitalism and its resistance power, Perlman insisted that for labour unions to develop and exist in the United States, they would need the support of the middle class. Moreover, they would have to respect the institution of private property upon which capitalism is based since, as Perlman points out, "any suspicion that labor might harbor a design to do away altogether with private property, instead of merely regulating its use, immediately throws the public into an alliance with the anti-union employers."[25]

Furthermore, the dominance of the intellectual mentality, Perlman contended, was not appropriate to the labour movement because socialist or idealist intellectualism detracted from the manualist mentality which produces and sustains a genuine trade union movement. The manualist mentality in Perlman's theory is characterized by the workers' consciousness of the scarcity of job opportunities:

> Manual groups . . . have had their economic attitudes basically determined by a consciousness of scarcity of opportunity, which is characteristic of these groups, and stands out in contrast with the business men's "abundance consciousness," or consciousness of unlimited opportunity.[26]

Perlman proposed, therefore, that a theory of the labour movement should include a theory of the psychology of the labourer.[27] Like Commons, Perlman pointed out that the United States, with its vast regions of uninhabited land, created in the mind of the worker an abundance of opportunity. Hence, unionism could take hold in the United States only when the abundance consciousness of the worker had been replaced by the consciousness of job scarcity.[28]

Although Perlman discussed the socialist leanings of some of the American unions, he rejected it, indicating that trade unionism of the American Federation of Labor type (craft unionism) was a necessary counterbalance to the inevitability of big business. In Perlman's words,

> the province of the union is, therefore, to assert labor's collective mastery over job opportunities and employment bargains, leaving the ownership of the business to the employer, and creating for its members an ever-increasing sphere of economic security and opportunity.[29]

Perlman's theory, then (like that of the Webbs), seems to answer all of the questions posed by Dunlop. He claims that (1) in the United States, unions emerged only when the consciousness of abundance was replaced by the consciousness of job scarcity; (2) that labour organizations grew out of the resistance power of capitalism and the dominance of the manualist mentality; (3) that the ultimate goals of the labour movement are to ensure worker control of job opportunities within the confines of the capitalist system; and (4) that workers join unions because they see them as controlling access to scarce jobs and as providing a degree of job security. Perlman's development of the idea of a manualist mentality, his pragmatism and realistic appraisal of how American labour might survive within a capitalist system, marks him as one of the most important early labour writers.

Hoxie[30]

Robert F. Hoxie's interpretation of the trade union movement in the United States is complex. Writing around the same time as Commons, he discussed not only the different structural types of unions but, more importantly, a number of functional types. Hoxie saw unions emerging as a result of a social or group consciousness which is marked by a fairly unified and well-developed viewpoint and which is translated into group action. However, his group consciousness is not of the job-scarcity type characteristic of Perlman's theory, but much broader in scope. Unionism, according to Hoxie,

> appears primarily as a group interpretation of the social situation in which the workers find themselves, and a remedial program in the form of aims, policies, and methods; the organization and the specific form or structure which it takes are merely the instruments which the group adopts for propagating its viewpoint and putting its program into effect.[31]

Functional Unionism

Hoxie claimed that the essential character of unionism is functional, and went on to develop a typology of unions. Each functional type is determined through an interpretation of the group situation by the group itself and contains a remedial action program developed by this same group. To Hoxie, the functional types may be very narrow or very broad in their orientations:

> The only essential point is that the viewpoint and program, whatever their scope and character, shall command the adherence of the membership of the group so as to constitute an effective motive and guide to group action. If this condition is met the type exists.[32]

In leading up to his general characterization of types, Hoxie states that the master key to the real character of unionism is to be found in the existence of distinct sorts of unions. He felt that unionism was so pragmatic, so much a response to particular situations, that it was impossible to characterize and judge it as a whole. However, he perceived it to have developed along lines distinct enough to allow one to generalize about the different types.[33]

Hoxie's four functional types are as follows: business unionism, friendly or uplift unionism, revolutionary unionism, and predatory unionism.[34]

Business Unionism Business unionism is essentially trade-conscious rather than class-conscious. It is more concerned with the working conditions in a craft or industry than with the working class as a whole. Conservative in its orientation, it is conceived of as a negotiating institution which seeks its ends primarily through the process of collective bargaining. This type is by far the most typical type of union operating in Canada today.

Friendly or Uplift Unionism Friendly or uplift unionism is idealistic, trade- or class-conscious, and sometimes inspires workers to act in the interests of society as a whole. It aspires to elevate the moral, intellectual, and social life of the worker, as well as the worker's standard of living. The major method of friendly or uplift unionism is collective bargaining but it also uses the method of mutual insurance and, on occasion, political action and cooperative enterprise. The labour organization most demonstrating the principles of uplift unionism, according to Hoxie, was the Knights of Labour.[35] The same could probably be said of the early Catholic unions formed in Quebec. As we shall see in the next chapter, these unions were founded on the principles set forth in Papal Encyclicals, and the early unions were very much dominated by the Catholic clergy in Quebec.

Revolutionary Unionism Revolutionary unionism is extremely radical, both in its viewpoints and its actions. Unlike the two previous trade-conscious types, it is clearly class-conscious in nature. There are two variants of the revolutionary unionism type. The first one is socialist and seeks its ultimate ends by invoking class political action. "In short, it looks upon unionism and socialism as the two wings of the working class movement."[36] Hoxie calls these two variants socialist unionism and quasi-anarchistic unionism respectively. A number of unions in Canada in the early post-World War II years were of this nature. The United Mine, Mill and Smelter Workers Union which operated in Sudbury, Ontario and on the West Coast was of this type. It engaged in bitter struggles with the United Steel Workers Union for the allegiance of workers in Sudbury and surrounding areas. The Steel Workers soon replaced it, and the two subsequently merged.

The second variant of revolutionary unionism stays away from socialism and collective bargaining, and focuses its energies on direct action, sabotage, and violence. The International Workers of the World (IWW), which thrived during the early union period in the United States, was of this type. Employers who refused to negotiate with it would soon find their property burned to the ground. Its major stronghold was in the western part of the United States, but it made a number of forays into the eastern states as well.

Predatory Unionism Predatory unionism may be conservative or radical, trade-conscious or class-conscious, but it appears to concern itself solely with immediate ends and is conceived of as ruthless, holding little regard for ethical or legal codes of conduct. There are two variants of this particular type, the first of which is hold-up unionism. While hold-up unionism appears similar to business unionism, it is in essence primarily exclusive and monopolistic. Generally boss-ridden and corrupt, hold-up unionism may engage in "sweetheart" collective agreements in which negotiators accept bribes in exchange for agreeing to settlements which serve employers well and workers badly. For much of its duration the Teamsters Union exhibited many of these characteristics, particularly in its use of "sweetheart" agreements and the use of gangsters to protect its leaders.

Guerilla unionism is similar to hold-up unionism inasmuch as it avoids or lacks principle and uses violent methods. It operates, however, directly against employers rather than in combination with them and, unlike hold-up unionism, cannot be bought off by sweetheart agreements. The International Workers of the World (IWW) would also fit into this category.

Group Consciousness

According to Hoxie, all four of the above are ideal types and no one union may be characterized strictly in terms of any one of them. He contended that the membership of any union could include representatives of all types of unionism. Hoxie's business unionism, however, is what is often called today "bread and butter" unionism, in which members merely pay dues and receive whatever benefits the union may obtain for them. Business unionism is by far the most prevalent type in North American society.

Like Perlman, Hoxie saw unions emerging to a large extent as a result of a unified group consciousness which developed within a particular environmental setting; Perlman's group consciousness was universal only insofar as it concerned itself with scarcity of job opportunities. Hoxie went further and indicated that unionism is not something which is found only among wage-earners, but that "it may exist wherever in society there is a group of men with consciousness of common needs and interests apart from the rest of society."[37]

Implicit in this quotation is the idea that trade unionism could spread to any group of individuals within society who are in close proximity and thus may develop a sense of "groupness." Hence, Hoxie's analysis applies equally well to

unions of professional, technical, and clerical workers as to blue-collar workers.

Although Hoxie did an excellent job of developing a topology of unionism, he did not construct a full-blown theory of the labour movement and answered only three of Dunlop's questions: (1) He explained the origins of trade unions as resulting from the emergence of a group psychology, the scope of which was much broader than that proposed by Perlman, and which could explain the emergence and increasing unionization of both blue-collar and white-collar workers. (2) Since Hoxie concentrated primarily on functional types, he did not really give an explanation for the growth of the trade union movement. (3) Hoxie's functional types differed in their objectives and methods, but did point to a relationship between unionism and capitalism. (4) The involvement of individuals in a group consciousness explained in part why workers join unions.

Tannenbaum[38]

To Frank Tannenbaum, the insecurity of the industrial worker was the critical variable in the explanation of the origin of trade unionism, and the main reason for this insecurity was the machine: "The labor movement is the result, and the machine is the major cause."[39] When Tannenbaum was writing his first book in 1921, the machine seemed to be the centre of gravity in the industrial community. Machines led to increasing urbanization, reduced the skills of workers and their income, made their jobs less secure, and determined the nature of the activities, contact, outlook, and way of life for all those people who were gathered around a machine in the conduct of their daily work. The labour movement had become, therefore, the primary instrument of self-defence for the worker, and it was the hope for greater security that drove the average worker into labour organizations.[40]

Workers joined trade unions in order to improve their bargaining power as they attempted to gain some control over the application of the machine. Also, many unions provided unemployment insurance for workers, sick benefits, disability benefits, and in many cases, death provisions for families.[41] To Tannenbaum, the labour union was the means of holding onto a fleeting and changing world:

> The labor movement serves as a means of stabilizing a dynamic world. To state it in other words, the labor movement serves to make possible the continuance of the dynamic character of our industrial organization within a social organization secure for the individual.[42]

In his second book, *Philosophy of Labor*, Tannenbaum discussed the various ways in which industry can be run, including the method used in various socialist countries, a notable example of which was the Soviet Union. He concluded that government ownership is not appropriate or effective and that

> the corporation and the union will ultimately merge in common ownership and cease to be a house divided. It is only thus that a common identity may once again come to rule the lives of men and endow each one with rights and duties recognized by all.[43]

Tannenbaum provided at least partial answers to three of Dunlop's questions. (1) He saw the quest for security not only as an explanation for why individuals joined trade unions, but also as the basis for the formation of the trade union movement itself. (2) He predicted the increasing unionization of professional and white-collar workers. While noting that the labour movement showed no sign of abatement, Tannenbaum indicated that it "tends to include more and more the professional and the civil-service people of the community, each of whom is interested in stability and security, each of whom operates in terms of service rather than of profit."[44] But while Tannenbaum's writing provided a rudimentary explanation of the growth and development of unionization among professional, technical, and clerical workers, nowhere in his works does he trace out the historical development of the trade union movement, or predict the historical evolution of the future development of trade unions. (3) Tannenbaum perceived the emergence of a new type of society in which labour and management would play a much more cooperative role. This growing cooperation reflected labour's ultimate objective of achieving stability and security in the workplace. (4) He claimed that individual workers joined trade unions to protect themselves from the insecurity caused by the increasing use of machines in the workplace.

Marx[45]

No discussion of unions and the reasons workers join them would be complete without some comment on the contribution of Karl Marx. Marx did much of his writing in England where he deplored the poverty, poor working conditions, and child labour which characterized nineteenth-century European industrial society.

In keeping with his philosophy of the overthrow of the capitalistic system and the establishment of a communist system, Marx regarded unions as one of the more important weapons in waging the class struggle. They were conceived of as class-conscious organizations which came into existence mainly to protect the worker against exploitation by the employer. They were a response to workers' needs to protect their day-to-day interests and, as Taft points out, they could only deal with short-term, day-to-day problems.[46] According to Lozovsky,

> the trade union developed originally out of the spontaneous attempts of the workers to do away with . . . competition, or at least to restrict it for the purpose of obtaining at least such contractual conditions as would raise them above the status of bare slaves.[47]

Young Communist League convention, 1929   NAC-Communist Party of Canada Collection/PA–124365

Labour organizations were viewed as an attempt to support revolts made inevitable by capitalist exploitation, but while labour might have been able to gain temporary concessions, it could not gain permanent relief through trade union action alone. Hence, the isolated revolts that did occur had to build continually until they culminated in a "living embodiment of the struggle between classes."[48]

In the Marxist view, if trade unions were to obtain a high degree of control over conditions in the workplace, and if they were able to satisfy the needs of workers to a high degree, then they would lose their raison d'être. Hence, as far as Marx (and later Engels) was concerned, trade unions engaged in trade union activity *per se* were phenomena of a temporary nature intended primarily to be a political vehicle in a revolution which would overturn the ruling capitalist class and establish a classless society.

The influence of the Communist party on Canadian society and on the Canadian labour movement is described by Norman Penner:

> The greatest impact of the Communist Party on Canadian society was during the thirties when no other organized force was prepared to give expression to the discontent of the Depression and to initiate imaginative, militant, and effective extra-parliamentary activity on the whole host of domestic and foreign policy questions ... Its members took an active and leading part in building the trade-union movement and were partly responsible for making this period the most momentous in Canadian labor history.[49]

While it could be argued that Penner's chapter "The Communist party, the Trade Unions, and CCF" overstates the case somewhat, it is true that Communists did play an important role in trade unionism in Canada during the 1930s.

Marx provided at least partial answers to

three of Dunlop's questions: (1) The search for short-term gains and protection from competition provided a partial reason for the rise of trade unions. (2) With respect to the patterns of growth of trade unions, Marx had nothing to say. (3) Marx saw unions as being in the forefront in the overthrow of the capitalist class and in the formation of a classless society. (4) Workers joined trade unions to seek relief from the evil effects of capitalism and to maintain a level of subsistence above that of slaves.

Bakke[50]

In a classic article written in 1945 and fostered by the Division of Labour Studies at the Yale Institute of Human Relations, E. Wight Bakke tried to discover why people join or do not join unions. By interviewing a cross-section of workers, he isolated the fact that people were more willing to become union members if they thought such action would enhance opportunities for successful living:

> The worker reacts favorably to union membership in proportion to the strength of his belief that this step will reduce his frustrations and anxieties and will further his opportunities relevant to the achievement of his standards of successful living.[51]

A worker, therefore, would react unfavourably if he or she felt that joining a union would have the opposite effect.

Bakke and his associates found that workers believed themselves to be living successfully if they were making progress toward the experience and assurance of:

1 The respect of society and respect of other people;
2 The degree of creature comforts and economic security possessed by the most favored of his customary associates;
3 Independence in and control over his own affairs;
4 Understanding of the forces and factors at work in his world; [and]
5 Integrity.[52]

Bakke refers to these as the workers' goals and then examines the effect that union membership may have on the desire of workers to achieve these goals.

Social Status Unions elevate the social status of some workers by providing them with opportunities to gain union office and thereby to earn the respect of their fellow workers. One example of this would be the ability of a shop steward, union official, or member of a grievance committee to talk with management about workers' problems. Holders of union office also often become members of associations involved in community projects. Furthermore, a worker who starts off as a shop steward may end up being the president of a national union. The presidents of the Canadian Labour Congress, for example, all started fairly low in the union hierarchy and were able to rise progressively to national status. Although all workers cannot achieve this kind of status, some people at least who belong to a union can advance to elected or appointed office, and in this manner acquire the respect of others.

Creature Comforts Concern over the creature comforts and economic security possessed by the most favoured of one's customary associates relates to the "bread and butter" unionism referred to earlier. Bakke and his associates found that when workers looked at creature comforts, they did not compare themselves with the rich or most wealthy people, but rather with people in similar states of life. Hence, if unions could enable workers to enjoy creature comforts comparable to those of their usual associates, then workers would be more likely to join. The converse held if the union was seen as a hindrance to the attainment of such creature comforts.

Control Another important factor in the minds of workers is that of independence in and control over their own affairs. Prior to the advent of unions, workers had very little bargaining power before employers; if workers approached employers with demands for more money or better working conditions, employers could very well dismiss them without any recourse to grievance procedures. Hence, unions helped to provide workers with some degree of control over the conditions of their employment, and also, through the collective bargaining process, gave them some influence within their society. In some cases, however, workers may choose to substitute union control for management control, particularly in unions which are autocratically run. Thus, merely joining a union does not automatically ensure workers control, for control involves participation in union decisions on the part of union members and responsiveness on the part of union officers.

Information To some extent, unions are able to help workers understand the forces at work in their world through their various educational programs and publications. Most unions of any size publish a monthly newspaper in which they explain in clear, direct language developments in their industry and in the economy generally. Workers who read their union's newspaper are thus kept generally well informed of what the union is doing to improve the lot of workers in their industry and elsewhere. In addition, a number of unions conduct educational programs for workers to help them understand the nature and administration of the collective agreements affecting them.

Integrity Bakke uses the word integrity to describe a sense of wholeness, self-respect, justice, and fairness. When workers think about whether or not they should join a union, they probably ask themselves whether or not joining a union will help promote their sense of integrity. If the answer is yes, then they are likely to join, but if the answer is no, then they are likely not to join unless compelled by a union-shop

security clause to do so. Bakke concludes his article with the following statement:

> The contribution of unionism at its best is its provision of a pattern of life which offers chances of successful adjustment and goal realization, not for the few who get out of the working class but for the great majority who must stay there.[53]

The Growth of Unionism

Most of the authors whose writings we have discussed have dealt primarily with the unionization of industrial workers. In recent years, however, there has been a growing amount of research into the reasons why various groups of white-collar workers are turning to unions. Many of the reasons that apply to white-collar workers apply equally well to blue-collar workers. We will look at the factors that apply to both blue- and white-collar workers first, and then at those that apply to white-collar workers only. Our discussion of these factors will refer to the theories discussed earlier in this chapter.

Major Factors Which Determine the Growth of Unionism Among White-Collar and Blue-Collar Workers

Concentration in Large Groups The extent to which workers are concentrated in large groups determines, in great measure, the degree to which they are unionized. In general, the more highly concentrated workers are in large organizations, the more likely they are to turn to unionization.[54] (Bureaucratization is the administrative answer to the problem of governing large numbers of workers.) When workers are highly concentrated, they realize that they are no longer able to strike their own bargains with their employers and thus conclude that the most effective way to improve their employment conditions under these circumstances is by forming unions and dealing collectively with them. The Webbs deal with this fact in their reference to the separation between labour and capital and Hoxie deals with it in terms of group consciousness.

Concern with Job Security Workers are concerned with job security, which can be threatened by the introduction of new technology or by a lesser demand for the services of certain groups. Both of these factors can, and have, affected both blue-collar and white-collar workers.

For many years blue-collar workers have been negotiating clauses in their collective agreements which provide for notice of lay-off, severance pay, continuation of company-paid health and life-insurance plans, company assistance in locating new employment, and other provisions which attempt to cushion the impact of technology. Granted, unions are unable to guarantee employment, but they are at least able to negotiate provisions that make the problem of redundancy or job insecurity less frightening to workers.

A cursory examination of many collective agreements between school boards and teacher groups in Ontario shows clearly that teachers have in many cases negotiated clauses in their collective agreements that attempt to maintain some degree of job security in light of the declining enrollment of students in elementary and secondary schools. University professors often have clauses which provide for recycling in cases where the demand for a university program has declined substantially. Recycling provisions enable professors to undergo retraining in programs where the demand is stable or increasing.

Perlman's preoccupation with the control of scarce jobs, the Webbs' concern with the separation of the worker from the means of production, and Tannenbaum's emphasis on the machine as the centre of gravity of a worker's life are all ways of expressing workers' concern for job security in the context of technological growth.

Legislative Policy The legislative policy of governments can either help or hinder unionization among both blue-collar and white-collar groups. Favourable public policy is, and has been, of crucial importance for the development of unionism and collective bargaining, particularly in the United States and Canada. Following the passage of the Wagner Act of 1935 in the United States — an Act which encouraged unionization and collective bargaining — there was a tremendous growth of unions and collectives among blue-collar workers in mass-production industries. A similar growth took place in Canada following the issuance of Order-in-Council PC 1003 in 1944, an order which was modelled largely on the principles of the Wagner Act.

Since 1967, there has been a phenomenal expansion of unionization among white-collar and other workers in government services, both at the federal and provincial levels. This expansion has been due in large measure to the fact that both the federal government and all the provincial governments have now given collective bargaining rights to their workers. In addition, all provinces have accorded collective bargaining rights to worker in the parapublic sector, which includes professional and white-collar workers in hospitals and in the educational sector. This protective legislation has fostered increasing unionization among various groups within these sectors.[55] The parapublic sector will be dealt with in Chapter 10.)

Neither Perlman nor Tannenbaum recognized the importance of favourable public policy; the Webbs, however, did draw attention to employment standards legislation, as it is called today.

Growth of the Service Sector The economic shift away from primary and manufacturing industries to the service or tertiary industries has influenced the development of unionism among both blue- and white-collar workers. The development of the primary and secondary sectors of the economy, especially manufacturing, brought a rapid rise in the unionized proportion of the labour force. Recently, however, as employment in secondary industries has declined, so has the number of unionized workers (primarily blue-collar workers) in these industries. In Canada, this decline has been offset by an increase in the number of unionized white-collar workers. In the United States, however, the decline in the number of unionized blue-collar workers has been dramatic, and has not been compensated for in the public and parapublic sectors.

The substantial increase of the labour force in the service sector (which employs large numbers of white-collar workers) has not been a complete blessing for unions because this increase has to some extent inhibited the unionization of white-collar and professional workers. Of particular significance is the fact that an increasing proportion of service-sector workers are employed in small establishments. Small establishments are the most difficult to unionize; the degree of unionization in the service sector would probably be higher if its establishments were larger. Because women are more apt than men to be employed in small service establishments, they appear to be less susceptible to unionization, even though both women and men have remarkably similar attitudes toward unions.[56]

In the retail sector, a potentially significant development in unionization occurred in May 1985 when the T. Eaton Company and the Retail, Wholesale, and Department Store Union concluded an agreement covering about 1,000 workers in six southern Ontario stores in Toronto, Bramalea, and St. Catharines, and in a small warehouse in London, Ontario. The workers were certified in 14 separate bargaining units, including separate units for full- and part-time workers and for office workers. A strike against the company began on November 30, 1984 and a country-wide campaign to boycott Eaton's stores was organized by the Canadian Labour Congress. Since a large number of the strikers were women, women's groups also organized boycotts against the company. About a week to ten days before the settlement, the Social Affairs Commission of the Canadian Conference of Catholic Bishops and high-ranking authorities of the United Church urged the T. Eaton Company to conclude agreements with its striking workers.

The major issues in dispute were wages and pensions. The union also wanted a master agreement covering the 14 bargaining units. However, since in Ontario workers lose their employment status after being on strike for six months, there was an incentive for the union to lower its sights and accept an agreement which was only slightly better than the one it rejected in January 1985. The signing of this agreement was seen by the labour movement as a major achievement in its own right, and as a major breakthrough in the retail sector.[57]

Among the theorists we have discussed, only Hoxie makes reference to unionization among both white- and blue-collar workers.

Inadequate Grievance Procedure White-collar groups often have no recourse to an adequate grievance procedure. In the absence of unions, workers may be required to work overtime with neither monetary compensation nor time off, and may have no means of airing their grievance over this and other objectionable practices. Early on in union-management relations, collective agreements guaranteed blue-collar workers recourse to grievance procedures. If agreement cannot be reached between various levels in the union-management hierarchy over controversial issues in the collective agreement, workers may have their grievances heard by impartial third parties whose decisions are binding.

> [T]he complaint may be very serious to the individual involved ... [b]ut, whatever the nature of the specific dispute, a modern organization is not set up to deal directly with individuals. Authority for settling disputes is usually much higher up in the hierarchy than the immediate supervisor or personnel person with whom the complainant tries to bargain.[58]

White-collar workers often regard unions as instruments to resolve their grievances without fear of reprisal from bosses. Bakke is the only theorist to have referred to the grievance procedure. He did so because he recognized that this procedure allows individual workers to retain their self-respect.

Concern with Policy-Making All workers like to have an input into the formulation of policies, especially those policies which affect their daily work life. Blue-collar workers, for example, like to have a say in the way overtime work is allocated, and usually their collective agreements will reflect this concern. Also, they may be concerned that layoffs and recall be subject to systematic procedures rather than to the whims of superiors. For this reason collective agreements contain provisions that require supervisors to consider both a worker's senior-

Plan for Solidarity government could succeed, observers say

Reuter

WARSAW

Solidarity publicly proposed yesterday to form Poland's first non-Communist government since the 1940s and political sources said the suggestion might be accepted under certain conditions.

The official Solidarity newspaper Gazeta Wyborcza made the proposal as efforts continued behind the scenes to resolve a political impasse over this week's election for the powerful new post of president of Poland.

"Your president — our premier," the newspaper said in a front-page headline.

In a separate development, U.S. President George Bush told Gazeta Wyborcza and other Polish papers that the estimated 45,000 Soviet troops in Poland should be withdrawn. Mr. Bush begins a three-day visit to Poland on Sunday.

Solidarity has emerged as king-maker in the presidential election, in which the ruling Communist-dominated coalition is deeply divided and has so far failed to

agree on a candidate who could win a majority in the 560-seat National Assembly.

The independent trade union has 260 seats in the assembly which is expected to vote on the presidency on Thursday or Friday. Its leader Lech Walesa has said he will back Interior Minister Czeslaw Kiszczak.

Gen. Kiszczak was proposed by Communist leader Wojciech Jaruzelski who announced he would not run last Friday. But Gen. Jaruzelski is being urged by powerful forces in the party and the army to change his mind.

Adam Michnik, Gazeta Wyborcza's editor and a top Solidarity strategist, wrote that a Solidarity prime minister and a Communist president would give Poland stability as it faced rapid political change and an economic catastrophe that is threatening to cause a popular "explosion."

Poland needed an alliance of the democratic opposition and the reformist wing of the establishment to give it a "strong and credible system of power," Mr. Michnik said. "Such a setup could be an agree-

ment under which the president will be a candidate of the PZPR (Communist Party) and the premier's portfolio and the mission of forming a government would be given to a candidate of Solidarity," he wrote.

It was the latest in a dramatic series of developments in Poland this year that have included Solidarity's re-legalization in April and its victory over the Communists in partly free parliamentary elections last month.

A senior politician in the ruling coalition said the idea had been sympathetically discussed by some coalition leaders.

He said they suggested Professor Bronislaw Geremek, Solidarity's top political strategist and leader of its parliamentary caucus, for prime minister.

In Paris, a top Soviet official said Moscow had no objections to a Solidarity government in Poland, its neighbor and biggest Warsaw Pact ally.

The *Globe and Mail*, July 4, 1989, p. A14.

ity and ability when making decisions about layoffs and recalls.

Among white-collar workers, teachers are very concerned about class size, and nurses are concerned about the type of care patients receive. Engineers and other professional groups have similar concerns about the nature of the work they do and the control they have over the formulation of policy. Commenting on the American situation, Dennis Chamot points out that

> Discussion with representatives of several unions that are active in organizing professionals confirms that dissatisfaction with policies relating to authority and decision-making is a major issue. For example, at most campuses where faculties have unionized in recent years, the primary concerns were job security and the somewhat related but much broader subject of university governance.[59]

One of the major ways in which professional groups and quasi-professional groups obtain control over the formulation of policy is through collective bargaining. Individually, professionals have very little impact on the formulation of policy but collectively, through their unions or associations, they may be able to bargain with their employers over policy issues relating to authority and decision-making.

Perlman's thesis that workers want to control scarce jobs, Tannenbaum's idea that workers want something to hold onto in a changing world, and Bakke's idea that workers want some control over their affairs reflect the importance of control to all workers.

Poor Personnel Policies The relatively poor personnel policies practised by many managers in organizations where workers are highly concentrated is contributing to unionism. Poor personnel policies lead to dissatisfaction among workers who turn to unions as a means of forcing managers to develop better policies. Bank-

ing, until relatively recently, has been well known as an industry with relatively poor personnel policies and practices. Although some banks have maintained poor personnel policies despite attempts by their workers to unionize (see the decisions of the Canada Labour Relations Board in some of the bank cases), most banks seem to be improving in an attempt to stay union-free. In the depths of the recession in the early 1980s, some retail stores fired long-service workers who considered their income and benefits adequate. Subsequent to the firing, these same long-service workers were rehired as part-time workers with greatly reduced wages and very few benefits. This abuse of economic power facilitated the unionization of these workers and, in general, is such a short-sighted practice that no theorist need comment on it. Practically all the theories discussed here, however, would predict the same outcome: the introduction of a union.

Changes in Family Structure The emergence of the single-parent family is making unionization an economic necessity for many workers. Secondary wage-earners have now become primary wage-earners in many households, partly because of the increasing divorce rates in recent years. In the nursing profession, for example, many nurses are the sole wage-earners for their families and for them the economic benefits of employment are very significant. Nurses agonized over whether or not they should unionize, for many nurses have traditionally seen themselves as highly dedicated, devoted more to service than to income. However, after years of soul-searching, a vast majority of nurses have turned to unions in the hope of improving both their workload and their financial and job security.

None of the theorists discussed mentioned single-parent families, because the divorce rates in their times were not nearly as high as they are today.

Factors Unique to the Development of White-Collar Unionism

A number of factors are unique to the development of unionism among white-collar workers.

Changes in Skill Levels Changes in skill levels may lead to unionism. G.W. Adams points out that the bureaucratization of intellectual work and the explosion of knowledge in both new and existing fields has led to the specialization of intellectual work into minute parts. As this happens, skills are inevitably broken down and routinized to the point where professionals may be unable to practise the skills for which they are trained. Given these conditions, Adams claims that professionals may turn to collective bargaining, and implicitly to unionism, as a method of preserving or recovering what they believe to be an exclusive work jurisdiction.[60] This pattern is also emerging among other white-collar groups.

Inadequate Labour Standards Legislation Canadian labour standards legislation does not apply to professionals. These workers may be required to work very long hours, but are not protected by laws which give other workers time-and-a-half for working over eight hours a day or over 40 hours a week. This is one reason resident doctors completing their internship in hospitals have frequently gone on strike in recent years. Economists, statisticians, and sociologists employed in the Federal Public Service, however, successfully negotiated a time-and-a-half agreement and thus avoided a strike. If these people had not belonged to a union or an association with collective bargaining rights, they probably would not have obtained the overtime benefits. As it stands, this particular group has set an example for others who are not protected by labour standards legislation to form unions and catch up with organized labour.

Changes in Union Image The changing image of unions makes the idea of unionization more acceptable to professionals. No longer are unions considered radical organizations out to destroy the basic fibre of our social and economic systems. In part, this change in image has come about as a result of more people belonging to unions and the families of unionized workers becoming more aware of what unions and collective bargaining are all about.

To counteract the growing appeal of unionism, a number of groups now provide training programs for managers on how to keep their organizations union-free. Membership lists of professional associations are often used by these groups to advertise their programs. They sponsor courses for managers in a number of important sectors of the economy. In the early 1970s when the CLC launched a major campaign to organize office workers in the financial institutions in Toronto, a program was being sponsored for employers in the same sector on how to keep their companies free of unionization.

Conclusion

This chapter has described different viewpoints on why workers join unions, which are summarized in Figure 3.1. In some cases the discussion has included the ultimate objective of unions and their emergence and development. We began with the Webbs, who claimed unions arose largely because workers wanted to protect themselves as members of a wage-earning class who had lost control of the means of production and distribution of goods. We also discussed the work of John R. Commons, who viewed the extension of competitive markets as the major factor in the formation of unions. Then we looked at the ideas of Selig Perlman, one of Commons' former students and colleagues; he saw unions emerging primarily from a con-

Figure 3.1

**A Matrix of
Labour Movement Theorists**

	Labour movement			Why workers join unions
	Origin	Patterns of growth	Ultimate goal	
The Webbs	Divorce of labour and capital	Local to national	To establish national minimum standards	To improve wages and conditions
Commons	Expansion of competitive markets	Local to international	To take labour out of competition	To protect wages and conditions
Perlman	Consciousness of job insecurity	Resistance power of capitalism	To ensure worker control of scarce jobs	To gain systematic access to scarce jobs
Hoxie	Unified group psychology	n/a	Relation of unions & capitalism	Involvement of individuals in group consciousness
Tannenbaum	Insecurity caused by the machine	Increasing unionization of white-collar workers	Union-management cooperation	Quest for security
Marx	Quest for short-term gains	n/a	Overthrow of capitalism	Short-term gains
Bakke	To reduce frustrations and provide for greater security	n/a	n/a	To achieve standards of successful living

sciousness of job-scarcity. Robert Hoxie thought that unions emerged as a result of a group's interpretation of the social situation in which it found itself. Robert Tannenbaum saw the labour movement springing from the rise of machines which threatened job security and other conditions of employment. Karl Marx's ideas regarding trade unions became influential in Canada during the thirties. He saw unions as the vanguard of the movement to overthrow the capitalist system.

Among the more modern writers, we discussed the work of Bakke who, along with his associates, conducted a large number of interviews with workers and attempted to make some sense out of their reasons for joining unions. Bakke indicated that workers would be apt to join unions if they saw unionism as a means of reducing their frustrations and helping them enrich their lives. The final part of this chapter described the growth of unionization among white-collar workers in professional, quasi-professional, technical, and clerical groups. Apart from the works of a few British writers (the most notable of whom is George Bain, a Canadian teaching and conducting research in the United Kingdom) there are very few prominent writers who are trying to articulate any kind of theory which would explain the emergence of unionism among white-collar groups. We did see, however, that many of the factors which explain the rise of unionism among blue-collar workers also explain the rise of unionism among white-collar workers.

Questions

1 Explain how an examination of historical theories of the labour movement can help you to understand how unions operate today.

2 Give a summary of the major ideas of each of the theorists discussed in this chapter. How well do they answer the questions posed by Dunlop?

3 Does John R. Commons' idea of the expansion of markets help to explain the operation of American-based unions in Canada? Elaborate.

4 Provide Canadian examples of the four major types of unions that Hoxie developed. Explain how each union falls into one of the four major categories.

5 Using a graph with Dunlop's four questions on one axis and the name of each theorist on the other axis, develop a detailed analysis of the similarities and differences of the major theorists discussed in this chapter.

6 Is a theory of the labour movement which would apply to both blue-collar and white-collar workers possible? Why or why not?

7 What is the level of unionization in your province? How do the theories discussed in this chapter help you to answer this question?

8 How do you account for the fact that British Columbia is the most highly unionized province in Canada? What are the major factors at work in that province that are not as prevalent in the other provinces?

9 Why was it predictable that the first union to apply to represent workers in Canadian banks was a B.C. union? Why was it predictable that this union was led by women?

10 Explain the rise of unionism in your province.

Notes

1 C. Kerr, F.H. Harbison, J.T. Dunlop, and C.A. Myers, *Industrialism and Industrial Man* (Cambridge: Harvard University Press, 1960). For an attempt to convene the writings of many American trade union theorists, see M. Perlman, *Labour Union Theories in America* (Evanston: Row, Peterson and Company, 1958).

2 J.T. Dunlop, "The Development of Labor Organizations: A Theoretical Framework," *Insights into Labor Issues*, eds. R.A. Lester and J. Shister (New York: The MacMillan Company, 1948). This article has been reprinted in *Readings in Labor Economics and Labor Relations*, 3rd. ed., ed. R.L. Rowan (Homewood, Ill.: Richard D. Irwin, 1976), pp. 63-76.

3 Sidney and Beatrice Webb produced two classic books toward the end of the nineteenth century: *The History of Trade Unionism* (New York: Longmans, Green and Co., 1894) and *Industrial Democracy* (New York: Longmans, Green and Co., 1897). The revised 1920 editions of both books were used as the source reference for this chapter.

4 Webb, *History of Trade Unionism*, p. 1.

5 Ibid., pp. 25-26.

6 Ibid., p. 41.

7 Webb, *Industrial Democracy*, p. 807.

8 Ibid., p. 79.

9 Ibid., p. 833.

10 Ibid., p. 150.

11 Ibid., p. 152 ff.

12 Ibid., p. 185.

13 Ibid., pp. 791-92.

14 Ibid., pp. 704-15.

15 Ibid., p. 253.

16 Ibid., p. 803.

17 Ibid., p. 823.

18 J.R. Commons et al., *History of Labor in the United States*, 2 vols. (New York: The Macmillan Company, 1918). See in particular Vol. 1 and the section by John R. Commons entitled "American Labor History — Introduction," pp. 3-21. See also, L.G. Harter, Jr., *John R. Commons: His Assault on Laissez-Faire* (Corvallis, Oregon: Oregon State University Press, 1962), in particular Ch. 7 "John R. Commons, Student of the Labor Movement," pp. 163-204.

19 Commons, Vol. 1, *History of Labor*, p. 3.

20 Ibid., pp. 4-5.

21 J.R. Commons, "American Shoemakers, 1648-1895," Vol. XXIV, *The Quarterly Journal of Economics* (November, 1909). This article has been reproduced in *Readings in Labor Economics and*

Labor Relations, rev. ed., ed. R.L. Rowan (Homewood, Ill.: Richard D. Irwin, 1972), pp. 93-108.

22 Commons, *History of Labor*, pp. 5-6.

23 S. Perlman, *A Theory of the Labor Movement* (New York: Augustus M. Kelly, 1949). (The book was first published and copyrighted in Perlman's name in 1928. The book was reprinted and published in 1949 by Augustus M. Kelly of New York. It is the 1949 edition to which reference will be made in this chapter.)

24 Ibid., p. x.

25 Ibid., p. 161.

26 Ibid., p. 6.

27 Ibid., p. 237.

28 Ibid., p. 8.

29 Ibid., p. 253.

30 R.F. Hoxie, *Trade Unionism in the United States* (New York: D. Appleton and Co., 1919 or 1921). The version used here is entitled Robert F. Hoxie, *Trade Unionism in the United States*, reproduced from the second revised edition of 1923, and reissued in 1966 by Russell and Russell, a division of Atheneum House Inc. The reader is advised to read the excellent introduction by E.H. Downey.

31 Ibid., p. 60.

32 Ibid., p. 69.

33 Ibid., pp. 37-38.

34 Ibid., pp. 45-52.

35 Ibid., p. 47.

36 Ibid., p. 48.

37 Ibid., p. 59, n. 3.

38 Tannenbaum's contribution to an analysis of the labour movement is included in two of his books. They are *The Labor Movement: Its Conservative Functions and Social Consequences* (New York: G.P. Putnam's Sons, 1921) and *A Philosophy of Labor* (New York: Alfred A. Knopf, 1951).

39 Tannenbaum, *Labor Movement*, p. 29.

40 Ibid., pp. 25-31.

41 Ibid., p. 34.

42 Ibid., pp. 35-36.

43 Tannenbaum, *Philosophy of Labor*, p. 199.

44 Tannenbaum, *Labor Movement*, p. 40.

45 The Marxist analysis of unions comes primarily from Philip Taft, "Theories of the Labor Movement," *Readings in Labor Economics and Labor Relations*, 2nd ed., eds. L.G. Reynolds, S.H. Masters, and C.H. Moser (Englewood Cliffs,

N.J.: Prentice-Hall, 1978), pp. 246-55; and J. Dunlop, "Development of Labor Organizations," pp. 67-68.

46 Taft, "Theories of the Labor Movement," p. 248.

47 A. Lozovsky, *Marx and the Trade Unions* (New York: International Publishing Company, 1935), p. 15; and quoted in Dunlop, "Development of Labor Organizations," p. 67.

48 Taft, "Theories of the Labor Movement," p. 249.

49 N. Penner, *The Canadian Left: A Critical Analysis* (Scarborough: Prentice-Hall Canada Inc., 1977) and particularly Ch. 5, "The Communist Party, the Trade Unions, and CCF", p. 170.

50 The material for this section is taken from E.W. Bakke, "Why Workers Join Unions," Vol. 22, No. 1, *Personnel* (July 1945), pp. 2-11; and reprinted in E.W. Bakke, C. Kerr, and C.W. Anrod, *Unions, Management and the Public*, 3rd ed. (New York: Harcourt, Brace, and World Incorporated, 1967), pp. 85-92.

51 E.W. Bakke, "To Join or Not to Join," *Unions, Management and the Public*, p. 85.

52 Ibid., p. 86.

53 Ibid., p. 92.

54 G.S. Bain, "The Growth of White-Collar Unionism and Public Policy in Canada," Vol. 24, No. 2, *Relations Industrielles/Industrial Relations* (1969), p. 247.

55 For an interesting discussion of the increase in unionization among government workers, see R. Brookbank, "The Adversary System in Canadian Industrial Relations: Blight or Blessing?" Vol. 35, No. 1, *Relations Industrielles/Industrial Relations*, (1980), pp. 20-40.

56 G. Bain, *Union Growth and Public Policy in Canada* (Ottawa: Labour Canada, October 1978), p. 19.

57 L. Slotnick, "Symbol of First Eaton's Pact Outweighs Contents for Union," and "Landmark Agreement Awaits Ratification," *Globe and Mail* (May 9, 1985). For statements on church support for Eaton's workers see L. Slotnick, "United Church Backs Striking Eaton's Clerks," *Globe and Mail* (May 2, 1985); and "Bishops Supporting Workers in Canadian Retail Industry," *The Catholic Register* (May 11, 1985), p. 8.

58 D. Chamot, "Professional Employees Turn to Unions," *Harvard Business Review* (May-June 1976), p. 124.

59 Ibid., p. 122.

60 G.W. Adams, "Collective Bargaining by Salaried Professionals," Vol. 32, No. 2, *Relations Industrielles/Industrial Relations* (1977), p. 189.

R. Norman Matheny, *The Financial Post*

4

The History and Philosophy of the Canadian Labour Movement

Introduction

Before we begin our discussion, we should define our subject, the labour movement, more precisely. The term *labour movement* refers only to the unionized segment of the labour force; those workers and union leaders who have made a conscious decision to join trade unions and to foster their formation and development. A.E. Kovacs describes it as

> a dynamic organizational instrument created by workers and emerging as an institutional force independent of the state and the employers ... Since the movement is an evolutionary force, its philosophy is also subject to alteration with the times.[1]

While Kovacs implies that the labour movement is comprised of one central organization, it is important to note that in Canada it has historically been characterized by several central labour federations, with affiliates made up of various national unions or Canadian branches of international unions, or both, along with directly-chartered locals, provincial and territorial federations of labour, and local labour councils. Its general purpose is to represent workers who belong to these bodies at the national level.

(The national unions and Canadian branches of international unions, provincial and territorial federations, and local labour councils will be dealt with in more detail in Chapter 5.) The complexity of our trade union structure, however, does not invalidate Kovacs' description, it merely makes an analysis of the movement more difficult, since many different forces must be taken into account.

Within the Canadian labour movement, the primary building block is the local union at the plant or establishment level. Workers elect their own officers and pay dues directly to the local. At a higher level, a local union may be part of a national union which organizes workers in a particular industry or occupation for all, or part, of the country. An example is the Canadian Union of Public Employees (CUPE) which in 1988 had 2,086 local unions across Canada representing some 342,000 members, mostly at the municipal level.[2] CUPE is part of the Canadian Labour Congress, which is a federation of national unions and Canadian branches of international unions as well as directly chartered locals. (International unions have their headquarters in the United States with a branch, district, or lodge in Canada; they organize workers in both countries.)

Unions may also be differentiated in terms of the nature of their membership. *Craft* (or horizontal) unions organize strictly on the basis of a specific craft or skill. An example would be the United Brotherhood of Carpenters and Joiners of America, which organizes carpenters only. An *industrial* union, on the other hand, organizes on a vertical basis and includes everyone in an enterprise, unskilled and skilled workers alike. The United Steelworkers of America is an example of this type of union.

Two major themes form the focus of this chapter: (1) the unity and diversity that has, and still does, permeate the Canadian labour movement; and (2) the North-South relationship between Canadian and American unions. While some reference will be made to the development of local unions in Canada, the major focus of our discussion will be on the development of central labour federations. Some of these federations have endured; others, though short-lived, still deserve our attention. Since international unions have played an important role in the evolution of the Canadian labour movement, parallels will be drawn between the Canadian and American federations where appropriate.

Origins

A distinguished Canadian author, Senator Eugene Forsey, has noted that we usually think of trade unions as part of an advanced industrial society, and that we are often shocked to realize that unions existed in Canada as early as the War of 1812. Forsey suggests that we should not be surprised, since at that time

> there were towns and cities. They had to have construction workers. They had to have tools, and stoves, therefore foundries and foundry workers. They had to have boots and shoes and clothes, therefore tailors and shoemakers. They had to have printers. And even in that simple society there were employers and employed, and their interests were not identical. The employed soon found that out, by experience; found out also the employer's strength and their own weakness in individual bargaining on terms and conditions of employment, and so started organizing to prevent their employers from taking advantage of them.[3]

Local unions began in Canada between 1812 and 1859. They probably first emerged in New Brunswick and Nova Scotia. Saint John was the chief centre of union activity between the late 1830s and the late 1850s, since "in the 1850's, [Saint] John (with the adjacent town of Portland) was bigger than Toronto, twice the size of Hamilton, and more than half as big as Montreal. It was the centre of flourishing shipping, shipbuilding, and lumber industries."[4] In Quebec City, too, there was a printers' union in 1827 and, although this particular union did not last long, there were several reorganizations of it that culminated in 1872 in the formation of two locals of the International Typographical Union.[5] Unions of printers, shoemakers, and tailors, among others, sprang up in Montreal, Toronto, and Hamilton. These unions emerged largely as a result of competitive markets (as Commons suggested was the case in the United States). They reflected an attempt on the part of labour organizations to make employers compete on quality and not on the basis of cheap labour.

Despite this early activity, the labour movement in Canada developed relatively slowly until the 1900s. Specialization in agriculture and primary industries, the dominance of domestic production in many industries, the lack of industrial development, the small and scattered population, and inadequate transportation and communication facilities all account for this slow growth.[6] Forsey characterizes early unions and the young Canadian labour movement in the following statement:

> From this sketchy and scattered information, several things seem clear. First, by 1859, there must have been at least 30 to 36 unions, in almost every settled part of the country. Second, except for the . . . ASE [Amalgamated Society of Engineers, a British-based union] branches, all seem to have been purely local, and very few seem to have had any relations with other unions. Third, there seems to have been a fairly high mortality. Fourth, certain crafts predominated, notably printers, engineers, waterfront workers, a few construction trades, moulders and foundrymen, shoemakers, and tailors. Fifth, the only organizations of the unskilled were . . . two longshoremen's unions.[7]

International unionism made its appearance in Canada in the 1850s. The first internationals were British organizations, of which the most important were the Amalgamated Society of Carpenters and Joiners and the Amalgamated Society of Engineers.[8] These two organizations, the only British ones that operated in Canada, had Canadian members as late as the 1920s. American international unions began to appear in Canada during the early 1860s and were soon to become the dominant force on the Canadian trade union scene.[9] The Journeymen Shoe-makers was the first American international union to enter Canada. Its first locals were in Hamilton and Toronto. The Second American international union to enter Canada was the National Union of Iron Moulders with locals in Montreal, Hamilton, Toronto, and Brantford. Both the Shoemakers and Iron Moulders conducted a number of strikes in their early years.[10]

In subsequent decades, a large number of American international unions were to have a significant impact on the development of Canadian unionism. International unions supplanted local, regional, and national unions "because of the mobility of labour across the border . . . and because the international unions had more money, more experience, more organizers, and more skilled negotiators and so could do a more effective job of representing the workers concerned."[11]

Prior to the formation of central federations in Canada, a number of attempts were made to combine the various unions at the local level to further their common objectives. Probably the most significant of these attempts was the formation of the Toronto Trades Assembly in 1871 which comprised 15 local unions. This organization played a leading role in the movement for a nine-hour work day — an objective that preoccupied both Canadian and American unions at that time. It is also credited with contributing to the establishment of the Trade Unions Act and the Criminal Law Amendment Act of 1872 which freed unions from charges of criminal conspiracy (i.e., the accusation that unions worked against the interest of the state). These enactments were fundamental to the continued existence and formation of Canadian unions.

The Toronto Trades Assembly undertook to form a central federation of all labour organizations in Canada during the 1870s and led the call for a general convention, which was held in Toronto on September 23, 1873. The forty delegates who attended this meeting, all from Ontario, decided to form a permanent national organization to be known as the Canadian Labour Union (CLU). Although its organizers had hoped to form a national body, the CLU never did expand to include workers outside of Ontario, and succumbed in the late 1870s to the effects of economic depression.[12]

The Emergence and Development of Central Labour Federations

The rest of this chapter presents a fairly detailed discussion of various Canadian labour federations. Those who would prefer a briefer summary of the dates and objectives of these organizations may turn to Figure 4.1, at the end of the chapter.

Knights of Labor 1869-1910

The Knights of Labor, founded in Philadelphia in 1869, was the first major trade union federation in the United States. It welcomed members from all walks of life: blue-collar workers, white-collar office workers, sales representatives, and others. It conformed to the type of unionism that Hoxie referred to as "uplift unionism." In fact, its first two presidents were clergymen. The Knights were organized in craft or mixed locals, which combined to form district assemblies of craft or mixed memberships. For example, in some cases a local might be composed of carpenters only, whereas in other cases there might be a mixed local composed of carpenters, printers, and other trades. These mixed locals and district assemblies made it difficult for the Knights of Labor to serve their members well, for if the president was a cigarmaker — as Samuel Gompers was — he could be of little use to a carpenter who sought help with problems in his trade.

Not long after their formation in the United States, the Knights of Labor came into Canada. The first Canadian local assembly of the Knights was established in Hamilton in 1875 and by the end of the 1880s it had some 250 local assemblies organized into seven district assemblies.[13] The federation made particularly rapid progress in the Province of Quebec, partly because its structure suited the then rural society of Quebec and partly because the organization had agreed to forego one of its rituals, which required the taking of a secret oath, a practice outlawed by the Catholic Church. Its establishment at an early stage in Quebec laid the groundwork for the development of Catholic unions at a later period in the province's history.

The federation has sometimes been likened to a train station, inasmuch as people were coming in and leaving so rapidly that it was very difficult to get a true idea of its membership. However, for a while the Knights of Labor played a dominant role on the Canadian labour scene, and continued to be active in Canada even after its demise in the United States.

Trades and Labour Congress of Canada 1886-1956

The first permanent national federation was the Trades and Labour Congress of Canada (TLC), established in 1886. This body included both traditional craft unions and assemblies of the Knights of Labor, and remained in existence until the Canadian Labour Congress was formed in 1956. Although it suffered membership losses during certain periods, it maintained continuity in its organization and policies throughout its history.

The Trades and Labour Congress (TLC) was in large measure influenced by, and similar to, the American Federation of Labor (AFL) which was formed in the United States in the same year. The AFL, like the TLC, was a loosely knit federation of autonomous national and international trade unions representing cigarmakers, carpenters, and other unions of craft workers. Each union chartered by the AFL was to have exclusive jurisdiction over its trade, and no other union was to organize workers within that trade. This proscription on dual unionism made it impossible for the American Knights of Labor to belong to the AFL.

Each trade union within the AFL was an autonomous organization in the sense that it had control over most of its own activities. The

AFL was primarily a clearing house that disseminated information to its members, helped coordinate their activities, and acted to resolve problems of overlapping jurisdictions among its affiliated unions.

The AFL was a pragmatic federation which reflected the philosophy of its first president, Samuel Gompers, who led the organization from 1886 to 1924 (with the exception of one three-year term). Although Gompers had been a socialist while he worked in the east end of London, he concluded soon after his arrival in the United States that socialism would not take root in American soil and that a practical approach unfettered by ideology represented labour's best strategy. He came to this conclusion after witnessing strikers being run over by policy officers on horseback in a strike in New York City.

A close link soon developed between the AFL in the United States and the TLC in Canada. Many of the international unions that formed the AFL also had Canadian districts which helped form the TLC. The TLC, however, included not only Canadian branches of international unions associated with the AFL but also district councils or assemblies of the Knights of Labor, as well as strictly Canadian unions. The leadership of the TLC soon came to be dominated by the Canadian directors of international unions affiliated with the AFL. Thus, the AFL indirectly exercised a fair degree of control over the TLC, and this perceived "foreign control" was sometimes a source of conflict within the latter body.

One conflict centred around the TLC's acceptance of the Knights of Labor. The Knights could not belong to the AFL in the United States. The AFL, moreover, frowned on the TLC for accepting the practice of dual unionism among its membership, and tried to have the TLC expel the Knights of Labor. Finally, in 1902, the TLC acceded to the wishes of the AFL, changed its constitution to bar dual unionism, and expelled the Knights and all Canadian national unions whose jurisdictions conflicted with those of TLC affiliates. Hence, the AFL exerted a significant impact on the TLC by effectively limiting its membership to Canadian branches of international unions affiliated with the AFL.

The Canadian labour movement grew rapidly from 1902 to 1920, and particularly from 1913 onward. In 1919 union membership was over 378,000, a figure that was not exceeded until 1937. Unions affiliated with the TLC accounted for the greatest proportion of Canadian union membership and, during this period, the TLC was the main central labour federation in Canada.[14]

According to S. Jamieson, one of Canada's outstanding industrial relations scholars, the following factors were mainly responsible for trade union growth from 1902 to 1920: a favourable economic climate, support in the form of funds and personnel from the headquarters of international unions, unprecedented population growth and economic expansion, settlement of the Prairie provinces, and large-scale railway construction. In addition, labour shortages, inflation, and serious wage-price lags during and immediately after World War I created conditions favourable to organized labour.[15] The 1920s, by contrast, were a period of slow growth for unions in both Canada and the United States. The horizontal (craft) structure of the TLC-affiliated unions did not suit the mass production industries that had begun to emerge in Canada. Nor were these unions easily adaptable to the western Canadian economy, which was characterized largely by primary industries such as mining, forestry, and logging.

During this period, employers in the United States launched what was known as the "American plan," emphasizing the primacy of individualism and discouraging collectivism. This philosophy of individualism impeded the growth of unionism in the United States, and undoubtedly had a similar influence on Canadian branches of American firms.

These factors counteracted the effects of the decade's prosperity, which normally would have encouraged union growth. In this respect, the unionism of the 1920s was quite unique.

The TLC experienced an uneven pattern of growth during the 1930s and 1940s. In the early thirties the Depression caused a decline in membership. Then, from about 1935 to 1945, unionization of the mass production industries led to significant increases, and by 1938 membership was close to the previous high reached in 1920-21.[16]

In 1938, a split within the AFL led to the expulsion of a group of unions calling themselves the Congress of Industrial Organization, or CIO. The TLC followed suit rather reluctantly the following year, and this purge resulted in a substantial loss of membership. Not until well into World War II did it regain its 1938 peak membership levels.

The passage of legislation during the war had a lot to do with its return to full strength. We noted in a previous chapter that favourable legislation is crucial in promoting unions and collective bargaining. The Wagner Act was passed in the United States in 1935, giving unions the right to organize and requiring employers to bargain in good faith with them. However, it was not until 1944 that the Canadian government enacted similar legislation. Order-in-Council P.C. 1003 — the Wartime Labour Relations Regulations — gave workers across Canada the right to choose a union as their bargaining agent, made provisions for the certification of a bargaining agent by the Canadian Wartime Labour Relations Board (CWLRB), required employers and unions to bargain in good faith, prohibited unfair labour practices by unions and employers, and provided for conciliation of contract negotiation disputes. The Order further specified that collective agreements were to contain no-strike and no-lockout clauses and that agreements were to make provision for handling grievances, the final step of which was binding arbitration.

While the TLC professed in principle to be an autonomous labour body having no direct connection with the AFL, it soon became apparent

that the TLC had become firmly committed to the policy of working in close conjunction with the AFL. Purely Canadian national or local organizations formed part of the TLC only when their jurisdictions did not conflict with those of the international unions affiliated with the AFL in the United States. Given this connection between the AFL and the TLC,

> it is hardly surprising that Gompers, in November 1902, asserted that relations between the AFL and the [TLC] were now substantially the same as between the AFL and its state federations. There were in fact important differences, notably the congress's power to charter trades and labour councils ... which it continued to exercise, though within limitations subsequently worked out with the AFL executive council.[17]

The TLC played a significant role in the development of organized labour in Canada. Part of its strength derived from its affiliation with the American Federation of Labor, although this association is judged by some to have been a mixed blessing. The AFL-affiliated unions had financial resources and organizing experience. There were, however, other strictly Canadian federations established after 1886 which operated along nationalistic lines and in opposition to the TLC. In the following sections, some of these major indigenous or national organizations will be discussed. It is these indigenous organizations that made for a great deal of diversity in the historical evolution of the Canadian labour movement.

Canadian Federation of Labour 1908-1927

The first of these indigenous federations was the National Trades and Labour Congress, which existed under that title from 1902 until 1908 when it changed its name to the Canadian Federation of Labour (CFL). Its membership comprised mainly the Knights of Labor which had been expelled from the TLC in 1902, the Provincial Workmen's Association of Nova Scotia,[18] which affiliated with the CFL in 1910, and a number of other strictly Canadian unions.

Its areas of major strength were in Quebec and Nova Scotia. Like some of its purely Canadian successors, the CFL had a predominantly nationalistic outlook and was opposed to what it considered the rigid and AFL-influenced policies of the TLC.

That the CFL failed is in part attributable to the fact that it lacked funds to compete with the organizational abilities of the international unions. The CFL also lost support among unions in Quebec, many of which chose to become part of that province's Catholic trade union movement which was born around 1900. In addition, the alliance between workers in Quebec and Nova Scotia was never more than a tenuous one, with the Nova Scotia section (PWA) seeking a degree of industrial strength against employers that the Quebec section, rural and locally based, could not provide.

Thus, although it lingered on for some time, the CFL never became a major force in the history of the Canadian labour movement. However, its formation and existence reflected a nationalistic preoccupation that was to characterize the Canadian labour movement up to the formation of the Canadian Labour Congress in 1956. Nationalism continues to dominate the thinking of many Canadian trade unionists today.

One Big Union 1919-1956

In the early 1900s western Canada and the western part of the United States were influenced by a number of socialist labour organizations, such as the American Labor Union, the American Federation of Miners and, a little later, the Industrial Workers of the World (IWW, or Wobblies). These organizations won many adherents, particularly in British Columbia and Alberta, in part because there was a feeling among important union leaders in the West that the TLC was controlled primarily by people in eastern Canada. This combination of factors, among others, led to the formation of the One Big Union, which "sprang suddenly into prominence during the Spring and Summer of

1919."[19] The OBU proclaimed a doctrine of revolutionary unionism and was an avowedly class-conscious movement. It sought to organize on an industrial rather than a craft basis, thus appealing to the tastes of western workers, and was composed mainly of western labour unions. Many of these unions were locals of international unions. Western labour councils, including the important Vancouver Trades and Labour Council, also were part of the OBU. At the end of 1919, the OBU had a membership of over 40,000 members, representing 101 local unions with eight central labour councils and two district boards.[20] Its radicalism, however, aroused the opposition of both federal and provincial authorities and this, combined with internal dissension, led to a rapid decline in its fortunes. The OBU is best known for the part it played in the Winnipeg General Strike of 1919, although it did not initiate the strike. It is not known for any lasting contribution to the Canadian labour movement, and what remained of it became part of the Canadian Labour Congress when that body was formed in 1956.

All-Canadian Congress of Labour 1927-1940

During the early 1920s there was an attempt to revive the Canadian Federation of Labour (CFL) as a nationalistic movement. However, the new organization lacked leadership, an attractive philosophy, and a creative purpose. Nevertheless, dissatisfaction continued, with the conservatism of the international craft unions. The militancy of the OBU was scarcely more attractive, and so a real incentive existed to form another indigenous Canadian federation, in this case the All-Canadian Congress of Labour (ACCL).

The initiative for the formation of the ACCL came from the Canadian Brotherhood of Railway Employees (CBRE), founded as a national union in 1908 and affiliated with the TLC between 1917 and 1921. (The CBRE was expelled from the TLC in 1921 because its jurisdiction conflicted with that of an international union.) The ACCL was also composed of

Winnipeg General Strike, 1919   NAC

recruits from the CFL and the OBU of 1919, and a few unaffiliated organizations.

The main objective of the All-Canadian Congress of Labour was to organize workers on an industrial rather than a craft basis, the latter being characteristic of the TLC. A critic of the TLC's conservative philosophy, the ACCL sought to free the Canadian labour movement from any form of American control. While it did not survive the Depression of the 1930s, its members eventually helped form another major federation in 1940, the Canadian Congress of Labour.

Canadian Congress of Labour 1940-1956

As is often the case with events in Canadian labour history, the founding of the Canadian Congress of Labour was in large measure the result of actions initiated in the American arena. In 1935, a split developed within the American Federation of Labor between the craft-oriented leadership and a group of union presidents, led by United Mine Workers president John L. Lewis, which favoured the establishment of industry-oriented unions. The latter group formed the Committee for Industrial Organization (CIO) within the AFL and fought for the industrial union approach and a greater political emphasis until the Federation's leadership expelled the CIO unions in 1938.[21] Thereafter, the group changed its name to the Congress of Industrial Organization, and formed a separate labour federation.

Following the expulsion of the CIO unions in the United States, the AFL pressured the TLC to follow suit and expel the CIO-affiliates from its membership. This the TLC reluctantly did in 1939. These Canadian branches of the CIO and the remnants of the All-Canadian Congress of Labour combined in 1940 to form the Canadian Congress of Labour (CCL), which remained a rival of the TLC until the two federations merged in 1956.[22] There were many battles between the TLC- and CCL-affiliates in Canada from 1940 to 1956, just as there were battles between the AFL- and CIO-affiliated unions from 1938 to 1955 in the United States.

The CCL was founded on the same principle as the CIO; i.e., to organize workers by industry rather than by craft, and to concentrate its efforts primarily on mass production industries. The philosophy of the CCL was political action. It endorsed, for example, the Co-operative Commonwealth Federation (CCF) as the political arm of labour in Canada. (The CCF was a socialist party and the forerunner of the New Democratic Party.) Inasmuch as it was committed to an interventionist philosophy toward the role of government in union-management relations, the CCL differed from the TLC.

An early problem to be overcome by the CCL was the opposition of some former ACCL members to a merger of the CCL with the Canadian branches of international unions represented by the CIO. According to Canadian labour historian I. Abella, the period from 1940 to 1950 was marked by almost constant turmoil over who would control the CCL. This difficulty was temporarily resolved when the CIO agreed that the Canadian sections of international unions and the CCL should be completely autonomous. Nonetheless, as time went on and the number of Canadian branches of international unions in the CCL grew larger, conflicts arose again as to who would control the CCL — the Canadian nationalists, the Canadian directors of international unions, or the CIO itself.

The CLC also had to contend with the spread of Communism within its ranks. With the expulsion of three major left-wing unions, however, and the diminution of Communism in another, this issue soon disappeared as a major concern.[23] Other internal difficulties survived. One such difficulty concerned the payment of dues by international unions directly to the CCL. Another involved the question of whether or not the CCL was empowered to settle jurisdictional disputes involving all of its affiliates, including the Canadian branches of international unions. A third major dilemma was whether or not the CCL leadership could be compelled to accept into membership all CIO unions operating in Canada. In spite of the failure of the CIO to force the CCL to accept a CIO union as an affiliate,[24] the status of CIO unions with respect to CCL membership remained a contentious issue.

In 1952, these problems came to a head at the CCL convention and resulted in a clear defeat for the CCL nationalist wing. As a result, "the international unions were now clearly in control."[25] Policies of the CCL would henceforth align with those agreed to by the international unions. However, while the CCL was controlled by Canadian branches of international unions affiliated with the CIO, all decisions made by the CCL were binding on those affiliates in Canada. In this way the CCL maintained its autonomy from the American organization.

Despite its stormy history, the CCL demonstrated that even with the presence of international unions in Canada, a Canadian trade union federation which was both independent from and the beneficiary of American resources was possible. Moreover, taking industrial unionism as a basis for organizing, the CCL was able to attract many workers to unions who had previously been neglected by the TLC in Canada. The CCL is a good example of a federation that had to struggle with the North-South connections of the labour movement and the diversity that existed among unions within Canada.

Mergers of the Central Federations in Canada and the United States

In 1956, the TLC and the CCL merged to form the Canadian Labour Congress. Although there had been previous attempts to unite the two bodies in Canada, it is undoubtedly true that such an event would not have taken place, at least not as early as 1956, if the AFL and CIO had not merged in the United States the year before.

A number of factors account for the US merger. First, the passage of the Taft-Hartley Act in 1947, which significantly amended the Wagner Act, was seen by both central federations as increasing management's power at the expense of labour. For a number of years the two federations cooperated in trying to get the American Congress to amend the Taft-Hartley Act, but to no avail. Second, the AFL had always dealt severely with Communists, while the CIO accepted Communists as members of its executive bodies. In 1949, the CIO amended its constitution to eliminate all Communist leadership within its ranks, and in so doing removed a major point of contention with the AFL. Around the same time, both federations began to engage in political activities that supported the Democratic Party and improvements in minimum wages and social security. Thus, merging political philosophies drew the AFL and CIO closer together.

There were also conflicts between and within the two federations, which required practical, conciliatory resolutions. Trade-union membership failed to grow much during the early 1950s. There were big changes occurring in the economy, with declining employment in some sectors where unions were established. Of particular note was the growth of the service sector,

where unions were unsuccessful in organizing. Large sums of money were being wasted by both groups as their affiliates fought to organize the same workers.

Even more important than this competition were the deaths of the presidents of both the AFL and the CIO in November 1953, which meant that neither federation had a chief executive officer. George Meany, then secretary-treasurer of the AFL, was easily elected its president. A bitter battle for the leadership took place within the CIO, however; a battle narrowly won by the brilliant Walter Reuther, then president of the UAW. Reuther's control over the CIO was much weaker than Meany's control over the AFL. A merger of the CIO and AFL, therefore, was facilitated by the lack of rivalry for leadership of the merged body.[26]

Before the merger, a two-year no-raiding agreement had been signed by the affiliates of the two organizations, and a unity committee of the AFL and CIO was formed, with the president of each federation playing a key role. The merged federation — American Federation of Labour-Congress of Industrial Organization (AFL-CIO) — named George Meany as its first president.

One of the major reasons for hyphenating the names of the two previous national federations was to maintain the identity of the CIO so as to permit it to control a large sum of money which had been gathered from its affiliates since 1938. This money was largely to organize non-unionized workers. A second and unofficial reason for the hybrid name lay in the feeling of CIO leaders that, if the marriage of the two federations did not work, the CIO could withdraw with its identity intact, and retrieve the money it controlled through its Industrial Union Department. Later, however, affiliates of the former AFL began contributing to the fund.

This abbreviated account of the merger between the AFL and CIO is intended to show once again the significance of American developments upon the Canadian labour movement. When the merger took place in the United

States, it was expected that the affiliates of the two organizations with branches in Canada would also try to work out a merger. Both the TLC and the CCL appointed committees in December 1953 to study the possibility. These committees joined to form the Unity Committee. In February, 1954, the Committee proposed a no-raiding agreement and its provisions were subsequently approved by TLC and CCL conventions that same year. The no-raiding pact not only forbade raiding but, more importantly, set up mechanisms for dealing with alleged violations. Initially, the agreement was binding only on the directly chartered locals of each federation, but affiliated national and Canadian branches of international unions were also encouraged to become parties to the accord.

On March 9, 1955, the Unity Committee reached agreement on a statement of principles which was to govern the merger of the two federations. Two months later, a complete merger agreement was announced. This agreement was unanimously approved on June 1, 1955 by the TLC and on October 12, 1955 by the CCL. A joint TLC-CCL convention, which became the founding convention of the new Canadian Labour Congress (CLC), met in Toronto on April 23, 1956. There, the constitution drafted by the Unity Committee was ratified with some minor variations and the new Congress was formally launched.[27]

The founding convention made it clear that the CLC was to be independent of the AFL-CIO. In fact, since that convention the CLC has often taken positions on international matters that are diametrically opposed to those of the American federation.

In discussing the differences between the mergers in the United States and Canada, Forsey indicated his belief that ours more closely approached the perfect union than did that of the United States. He attributed this quality largely to the fact that the CCL was closer to equality with the TLC in power than was the CIO with the AFL. At the time of the merger in the United States, the AFL had 9.5 million

members and the CIO had about 6 million, out of a total union membership of some 18 million — a huge discrepancy compared with the distribution of Canadian membership.[28] The two Canadian organizations, Forsey added, merged more quickly, both provincially and locally, than did the American organizations at the state and local levels.[29] There was no indication that either of the Canadian organizations was contemplating pulling out of the agreement if the marriage between the two did not work. This confidence was reflected in the decision not to adopt a hyphenated name for the merged body. Furthermore, because the TLC and the CCL contained both craft and industrial unions, the traditional dichotomy between these orientations did not pose a problem at the time of the merger.

Canadian Labour and Politics

The TLC played an active part in politics from its beginning, an attribute that distinguished it from the AFL. Many of the early union members in Canada were British and they brought the traditions of the British working class with them. When the British Labour Party was formed in 1906, the TLC gave its support to provincial labour parties in Canada. Although these provincial parties were unsuccessful, the TLC also gave its support to the development of a national labour party in 1918. Such a party was formed, but it was taken over by the Communists in 1923 at which time union support was withdrawn.[30]

Forsey has suggested that as early as 1900 there were signs that the Liberal Party wanted to capture the TLC.[31] (In fact, many of the progressive policies of the Liberal Party over the years have come largely from the labour movement, both before and after the formation in Regina of the socialist Co-operative Commonwealth Federation in 1933.) However, when the CCL confronted the issue of political affiliation at its 1943 convention it resolved that it would support the

CCF Party, and encouraged its affiliates to lend it their support also. From 1943 onward, the CCL continued to endorse the CCF although there was opposition from some of its affiliated unions.[32]

When the Canadian Labour Congress was formed in 1956 it did not immediately support a political party. However, members of the labour movement were active in the development of the New Democratic Party which was founded in 1961 to replace the old CCF. Many CLC-affiliated unions allied themselves with the new party, and the CLC usually played at least a nominal role in federal elections, providing workers for getting the labour vote out and encouraging volunteers.

In the 1979 election, the CLC came out strongly in support of the NDP for the first time, providing not only its workers but its financial aid. While it is difficult to tell what impact the CLC's participation had on the results of the election, its president at the time claimed a great deal of credit for the support gained in British Columbia and in one of the Atlantic provinces. The reason for the NDP's loss in major metropolitan Ontario cities where members of the CLC and its affiliated unions were active politically is not clear. The result brings to mind Forsey's prediction, at the 1958 Canadian Political Science Association Meeting, of the potential role of the CLC in politics:

> Even if the Congress does ultimately decide on a definite line of political action . . . and even if all, or most, of the unions follow that line (which experience suggests they will not), it does not follow that the union members will pay any attention whatever.[33]

He suggested, instead, that individuals would cast their ballots as Maritimers, French- or English-Canadians, etc., rather than as union members. An American example would tend to confirm this conjecture: in the 1944 election, John L. Lewis, who was then the most powerful union figure in the United States, withdrew his support from President Roosevelt and recommended that trade union members vote for the Republican candidate, Dewey. Subsequent analysis showed that even voters in Lewis's own constituency continued to vote Democratic rather than Republican! This would seem to confirm that trade unions in North America do not have a great deal of influence on how their members vote during elections.

In the 1988 federal elections in Canada, both the NDP and the Liberals fought against the Free Trade Agreement with the United States, as did the CLC and a number of its affiliates, including the Canadian Auto Workers Union and the United Steelworkers of America. Although the NDP came out of the election with more seats than it had prior to the election, most of its gains were in western Canada and particularly in British Columbia. It received a strong endorsement from the president of the Quebec Federation of Labour, a provincial arm of the CLC, but was unable to elect a member to Parliament from that province. (However, its percentage of popular support in Quebec was higher than in any previous election.)

The president of the Canadian Auto Workers Union and the two top leaders of the Canadian division of the United Steelworkers wrote letters attacking the NDP's election strategy, claiming that it had not criticized the proposed trade agreement strongly enough.[34] However, Shirley Carr, the president of the Canadian Labour Congress, argued after a meeting between the CLC's Executive Committee members and the NDP Caucus that the criticism was "healthy." She is reported to have said that "[we] all had some criticism, but that's part of the game and [it's] very healthy for us to say that to a party that we support."[35]

The Philosophy of the Canadian Labour Movement

The philosophy of the Canadian labour movement has been a fairly pragmatic one, particularly within the craft-oriented unions. This approach is derived from the pragmatic philosophy of the AFL, and from the methods of Samuel Gompers. When asked what labour's objective was, Gompers said it was to obtain "more, more and more now." This pragmatism is balanced by the experience of the unionists who came from the United Kingdom and brought with them the idea of a working-class movement. R.J. Adams, a prolific Canadian writer, has commented that

> since its emergence, the [Canadian] labour movement has been pulled between the moderate, democratic socialism of Great Britain and the non-political approach of U.S. labour. Perhaps because of the British link, moderate socialism is more acceptable in Canada than in the U.S. Nevertheless, many Canadian unionists subscribe fully to the U.S. approach.[36]

Kumar argues that Canadian unions are "business" unions and that they are primarily interested in improving wages and working conditions through the collective bargaining process "rather than bringing about social change through direct political action."[37] He further argues that a number of unions and federations engage in political education activities "with a view to encouraging their members to participate actively in political and social affairs and to seek desired legislation."[38] He observes that the CLC supports the NDP, although "the strong financial and other support of the NDP by the CLC and its affiliated unions . . . has seldom materialized in a big labour vote."[39]

Canadian writer C.B. Williams contends that the philosophy of the Canadian labour movement reflects two primary schools of thought: namely, class collaboration and class consciousness.[40] The philosophy of class collaboration, characteristic of international unions, accepts the existing order and the government that goes along with it, and views the role of the trade union movement as that of gaining improvements in wages, hours, and working conditions from reluctant employers. The major methods of class collaboration include collective bargaining and work stoppages. The cornerstone of this philosophy, Williams claims, is self-centred self-help. Most activity in this type of trade union structure and philosophy takes place at the local level rather than at the broader societal level.

The philosophy of class-conscious trade unionism, on the other hand, rejects the existing economic and political order along with its form of government.

> As replacements, it advocate[s] various degrees of reform, ranging from direct worker control of the means of production to direct worker representation in the existing economic and political system. . . . It de-emphasize[s] collective bargaining and the strike as the method of protest against an employer, in favour of political action and the demonstration of labour solidarity through the general or industrial strike.[41]

Williams believes that if national and international unions are to succeed in contemporary Canadian society, they must redefine their role of "self-centred self-help" and become more socially aware. National and international unions, according to Williams, must become involved in issues that have so far remained the exclusive domain of the Canadian Labour Congress. He concludes by stating that "Unless the Canadian trade union movement is prepared to reshape its structure and philosophy drastically, it will continue to have great difficulty in carving for itself an accommodative role in Canadian economic and social affairs."[42]

At its eleventh constitutional convention held in Quebec City in May 1976, the CLC came out with what it called *Labour's Manifesto for Canada*.[43] After discussing economic problems in Canada, tripartitism and national planning, and the centralization of government, the document suggested that changes were required in the way important economic and social decisions were made. Specifically, it demanded that business and government share their power with labour. The *Manifesto* recognized that if labour is to play an effective role in shaping the country's economic and social policies it must do so from a position of strength. Labour's strength, it claimed, is fragmented among its affiliates and exists mainly at the plant level.

In the future the CLC must have the power which can only come from the collective strength of its affiliates. There must be agreement between all the affiliates that a full cooperative and coordinated effort will be forthcoming to guarantee that the CLC is operating from a position of strength to protect the rights, freedoms and legitimate interests of all workers. The Executive Council as a responsible decision-making body between Conventions must be assured that the policies and decisions it makes will be followed closely by all affiliates.[44]

The *Manifesto* acknowledged, as have many observers, that the CLC has very little power.

Power in Canada's decentralized collective bargaining system resides largely with national unions and Canadian branches of international unions, and particularly with the locals of these unions. Although most unions at the 1976 CLC Convention endorsed the augmentation of CLC power, no transfer of power from the affiliated national and international unions to the CLC was forthcoming. Hence, even if the CLC were to adopt a more socially conscious and a more dynamic economic program, it is unlikely that the CLC executive could gain the power necessary to influence the development and implementation of such a program.

CLC seeks reconciliation with Mulroney government

By Dave Blaikie
The Canadian Press

Shirley Carr, head of the two-million-member Canadian Labor Congress wants to bury the hatchet with Prime Minister Brian Mulroney.

And this time not in his head.

The woman who has called Mulroney a skunk, dead meat and Dracula — once even questioning his manhood — says it's time for the labor movement to come in from the cold.

But it can only happen if government treats labor as an equal partner in society, Carr said in an interview.

"We have to be a credible voice," she emphasized.

Relations between the Tories and the country's largest labor group faltered soon after Mulroney came

to power in 1984 and broke down entirely when he began negotiating free trade with the United States in 1985.

The congress refused to sit on any government committees studying free trade and has spent millions fighting free trade in general and the Tories in particular.

But now that free trade has become a fact of life, the labor movement must do what it can to make the transition for workers as painless as possible, Carr said.

The congress would be willing to take part in the government's committee on free-trade adjustment if it is restructured to give labor a more meaningful voice, she added.

"We have a situation where there are going to be very dramatic changes in this country over the next two or three years . . . What we would like to do, and what I certainly would like to do, is talk to him

about how we can play a major role."

Mulroney has accepted an invitation to a meeting. A date is expected to be set soon.

Carr said a resumption of consultation between labor and government would be healthy for both sides.

But if it occurs it must involve more than "the token" consultation that has occurred between the Tories and the congress's rival, the Canadian Federation of Labor, she argued.

If the congress does begin participating in talks at senior government levels again, it will insist on having as many representatives as business in any study groups or committees it takes part in, she added.

The *Ottawa Citizen*, Jan 25, 1989, p. A10.

Although the CLC *Manifesto* called for a form of tripartitism to oversee the development of sound economic and social programs, this objective was never reached. In 1976, the CLC withdrew from a number of government agencies, including the Economic Council of Canada, in protest against the imposition of wage and price controls. More recently, the CLC attacked the Mulroney government in very harsh terms over the free trade deal between Canada and the United States. However, early in 1989 Shirley Carr stated that she was interested in "opening the doors and keeping them open despite our differences. . . . It's important that I have access to brief [the Prime Minister] on national and international issues that are very important to us."[45]

The philosophy of the Canadian Labour Congress will likely remain much the same in the foreseeable future. The CLC will continue to express labour's point of view on economic and social policies. The impact of its views, however, will probably be minimal. The CLC's focus will almost certainly remain on bread-and-butter issues at the local level.

Nationalism and Multinationalism

Within the ranks of Canadian labour, there are those who argue for a stronger, more independent, more nationalistic trade union movement in Canada, in which Canadian workers and union leaders exercise greater control over their own affairs. Of great concern to some of these members is the growth of multinational conglomerates. A large body of literature now exists which indicates that, unless trade unions in a number of countries take concerted action to deal with multinational conglomerates, these conglomerates could start to play one country off against another in their battles with trade unions. For example, if a union goes on strike against a multinational corporation in one country, that corporation could counteract the strike by shipping material from another country in which it operates, where workers are not on strike.

Part of the trade-union response to this kind of action has been to form secretariats along broad industrial lines. These secretariats put pressure on certain parts of multinational corporations if other parts are in difficulty.

So far, Canadian unionists have not been in the forefront of the trade union response to the multinational corporation. It remains to be seen whether unions will make the connection between national independence and the need for international cooperation against the threat of multinationals.

One potential obstacle to international cooperation is conflict between international unions and national federations. In the following section, we shall deal with one such conflict which arose between the CLC and the construction unions affiliated with the AFL-CIO.

A New Canadian Federation of Labour 1982–

As we have seen, the CLC is structured in such a way that power is concentrated in the locals, rather than in the national or international unions. While the CLC does have some intermediary links, it has no building trades department, as does the AFL-CIO. Therefore, most construction unions in Canada were affiliated with international unions affiliated with both the American *and* Canadian federations.

In the 1970s and early eighties, this structure gave rise to conflict between the international building trades and the CLC. The former felt that the system of appointing delegates — one delegate for each block of members up to and including 1,000 — favoured the smaller but more numerous public sector unions, at their expense. Indeed,

> there is statistical evidence to support this argument. The Canadian Union of Public Employees [had] 267,000 members and 1,629 locals [in 1981]. The building trade unions, with a combined membership of approximately 355 [had] chartered 689 locals [in 1981]. [Thus] CUPE had almost twice as many delegates at the 1978 convention as the building trades.[46]

The construction workers wanted greater representation and decision-making power within the CLC. They also objected strenuously to the formation of an umbrella body for Quebec construction workers that had been formed by the Quebec Federation of Labour (QFL). The Quebec workers' decision to join the new group weakened the AFL-CIO-affiliated Quebec Provincial Building Trades Council.

Related to these disputes was the difference between the political orientation of the CLC executive and the building trades executive. Leaders of craft unions have a much more conservative political outlook, generally speaking, than leaders of industrial unions. The building trades had been less than enthusiastic about the CLC's political involvement with the NDP.

In 1981, fourteen international construction unions withheld their affiliation fees, and were suspended from the CLC. Immediately after the suspension, the CLC announced the formation of building trades councils, which locals of the suspended unions could join without giving up their membership in the international unions. However, the councils were largely unsuccessful in attracting members.

Sensing that the rift between the CLC and the international building trade unions could not be resolved, a number of Canadian directors of these unions issued a call for a new central federation. The founding convention of the Canadian Federation of Labour (CFL) was held in Ottawa on March 31 and April 1, 1982. Delegates representing about 200,000 workers and ten of the thirteen international building trade unions participated in the establishment of the new federation. Three of the larger unions, the United Brotherhood of Carpenters and Joiners (66,000 members), the Labourers International Union (46,715 members), plus the smaller 19,940 member International Association of Bridge, Structural and Ornamental Iron Workers did not join the new federation. All three unions are now affiliated with the AFL-CIO only.[47]

The Convention elected James McCambly, executive secretary of the Canadian Executive Board of the AFL-CIO Building Trades Department, as its president. Ken Rose, the Conference chair and an international vice-president of the International Brotherhood of Electrical Workers (IBEW), criticized the political affiliation of the CLC with the NDP and also the confrontational tactics of former CLC president Dennis McDermott in dealing with the federal government. He vowed that the CFL would seek to meet with the government regarding policies of importance to workers everywhere.

The convention adopted a resolution that the CFL would not affiliate with a political party, but that it would support any party to the extent that it espoused policies consistent with those of the CFL. Although a few delegates argued the merits of political affiliation, the resolution was enthusiastically endorsed.

Senator Edward Lawson, then Canadian head of the Teamsters' Union, addressed the convention, and among other things, stated that unions must be prepared to make sacrifices to protect their members' jobs where employers are in financial trouble. This position contrasted sharply with that of the president of the CLC, who stated that workers should not accept wage freezes or wage cuts. Prime Minister Trudeau also spoke to the convention, marking the first time in 20 years that a Canadian prime minister had addressed such a labour gathering. In his speech, Trudeau invited consultation between the federal government and the CFL, a consultative process which continued with the Mulroney government.

When the CFL was formed, many observers anticipated a fair amount of inter-union raiding. To date, however, there has been little, if any, raiding between unions affiliated with the two central federations.

Thus far, we have dealt mainly with the national and international unions in English-speaking Canada, and have only touched on Quebec very briefly. That province, however, has a unique history of trade union development. It is to the Quebec situation that we now turn our attention.

The Labour Movement in Quebec

In any history of the labour movement in Canada the Confédération des Travailleurs Catholiques du Canada (CTCC) merits special consideration. The English equivalent of the French title is the Confederation of Catholic Workers of Canada. After 1929, it was identified in English as the Canadian and Catholic Confederation of Labour (CCCL). We shall use the initials CCCL, except where CTCC appears in a quotation.

S. Jamieson states:

> The CTCC began as a movement consciously organized and controlled by Roman Catholic clergy in Quebec for the express purpose of keeping French-Canadian workers French in language and Catholic in religion in order to prevent them from becoming absorbed into "alien" and "secular" trade unions controlled by English-speaking Canadian or American elements.[48]

The movement had its origins in a lockout in the boot and shoe industry in Quebec City in 1900 over the questions of union recognition by employers and wage increases. The dispute was arbitrated by the Archbishop of Quebec. In his recommendations he called upon the unions in Quebec to change their constitutions and rules in order to bring them into line with Roman Catholic principles, as laid down in Pope Leo XIII's 1891 encyclical *Rerum Novarum*. This encyclical emphasized the right of workers to organize into trade unions, called for collective bargaining between unions and employers, and encouraged every means of settlement without a strike if at all possible.

The movement toward federation of the various local Catholic unions began in 1918 with the formation of central councils in major districts in Quebec. The CCCL was established as a permanent organization at its founding convention in Hull, Quebec three years later. As F. Isbester has pointed out, "like its affiliated unions, the Confederation was church dominated [sic] and remained so until 1946."[49] At that time, the CCCL represented one-third of the organized

workers in Quebec.

During and after World War II, the Catholic unions in Quebec changed quite dramatically in their orientation and behaviour. Large numbers of French Canadians were drawn into industries and trades in major urban centres, where they came into contact with other unionized workers. Also, the substantial wage increases won by unionized workers outside Quebec forced the CCCL to become militant.[50] With both the TLC and the CCL attempting to organize workers in Quebec, the CCCL had to assume an aggressive role in order to organize Catholic and non-Catholic workers, and in 1943 it lifted the exclusion of non-Catholics from its constitution.[51]

Accordingly, a new, combative breed of leaders was elected to fill the top executive positions in the Confederation. The outlook and behaviour of these leaders paralleled those of the leaders of rival unions. This change in leadership was accompanied by a number of unusual and significant strikes, the most important of which was the Asbestos strike of 1949. Some people have termed this the turning point in the social history of Quebec.[52] Prior to 1949, there had been a close relationship between the Church and the Duplessis government, with the Church using its influence in the Catholic trade union movement to prevent overt labour conflicts. The Asbestos strike exploded the Church-Duplessis coalition. During the seven-month strike, the Church openly supported the workers against a large American subsidiary. This support often took the form of special funds collected from congregations. The provincial government, however, declared the strike illegal, decertified the union as it had done in the meat-packing strike of 1947, and sent several hundred heavily-armed provincial police to the scene of the conflict. While the striking workers won very little monetarily, they won a great deal psychologically, for the strike lent a new sense of credibility and militancy to the CCCL. The Confederation gained wide moral support from prominent liberal and intellectual leaders in

Quebec, as well as from affiliates of the TLC and the CCL.

The Asbestos strike was important in developing close links between the CCCL, the Quebec affiliates of the CCL, and the TLC. Both the CCL and the TLC supported the CCCL in a number of important strikes after 1949. However, the Quebec affiliates of the TLC later broke ranks and supported the Duplessis government, leaving the CCCL and the CCL alone to protect what they considered to be the repressive nature of new labour legislation.[53]

When the CCL and the TLC formed the Canadian Labour Congress (CLC) in 1956, their provincial counterparts in Quebec merged to become the Quebec Federation of Labour (QFL). From the time of the merger onward, the QFL and the CCCL cooperated when it was to their mutual advantage to do so. Conflicts remained, however.

At the founding convention of the Canadian Labour Congress, a number of proposals were approved which sought the affiliation of the CCCL. In turn, the CCCL convention in September 1956 passed resolutions in favour of affiliation with the CLC. Joint committees of the CCCL and the CLC were set up and a number of meetings took place over the years with a view to reaching a merger agreement. These merger talks failed to make any significant progress, but by 1959, many observers still expected the merger to come about.

> The 1959 convention was widely expected to be the "unity convention." Such was not the case. "The fact is," Jean Marchand said, "that back in 1955 the principle of affiliation was adopted by the CCCL convention provided that the CCCL could keep its 'integrity' and its freedom to expand."[54]

In retrospect, it was this unwillingness to accommodate the CCCL as a separate entity within the framework of the CLC that foiled any attempt to merge the national central federation and the central federation in Quebec.

At its 1960 convention, the CCCL changed its name to the Confédération des syndicats nationaux (CSN) — or, in English, the Confederation of National Trade Unions (CNTU). In addition, it streamlined and centralized its structure to establish a strong, independent body, capable of competing effectively with the QFL.

The CNTU grew rapidly during the 1960s, particularly with the passage of liberal legislation in Quebec giving collective bargaining rights to public servants, many of whom are organized by the CNTU. In addition, the CNTU became much more radical during the 1960s and 1970s than had been the case before. In early 1971, the Confederal Bureau of the CNTU published a manifesto entitled *Il n'y a plus d'avenir pour le Quebec dans le system economique actuel* (There is No Longer a Future for Quebec in the Present Economic System). Another document was published a few months later entitled *Ne comptons que sur nos propres moyens* (Let us Rely Only on our Own Means). According to Quebec author J. Boivin, *Ne comptons* was a quasi-Marxist interpretation of the capitalist system in Quebec. Although more than 100,000 copies of it were printed and while about a dozen militant members organized discussion meetings at several levels of the CNTU in an attempt to have it adopted as the federation's political program, it was not discussed at the 1972 convention of the CNTU owing to a perceived lack of general support and fear of creating disagreement at the convention.[55]

In 1972, the QFL, the CNTU, and the Quebec Teachers' Corporation (QTC) formed the Common Front to bargain jointly with the provincial government on behalf of teachers and public servants. The three major groups used a "common-table" approach in order to negotiate provisions which were shared by government, school, and hospital workers. In addition, sector tables existed at which provisions particular to each sector were bargained for. When the parties failed to reach an agreement with the government, strikes were called. Spontaneous work stoppages also occurred.

In the beginning public opinion favoured the workers. But as time went on, preference swung toward the government. At that point, the government obtained an injunction which prohibited workers from going on strike and ordered others back to work. Many workers, encouraged by their leaders, disobeyed these injunctions. As a result, both the workers and the leaders of the QFL, the CNTU, and the QTC were jailed. In order to achieve a settlement, the leaders were released temporarily so that they could join negotiators at the bargaining table. The Common Front strikes were the most massive strikes ever experienced in the history of the Canadian labour movement.

One important result of the Common Front was that three members of the Executive Committee left the CNTU and called meetings of dissident union leaders who strongly disagreed with the leftist ideology of the CNTU. A majority of the dissident leaders, claiming to represent more than 75,000 of the 235,000 CNTU members, voted to secede from the CNTU and form a separate federation, the Centrale des syndicats democratiques — in English, the Centre for Democratic Unions (CDU).[56] Not too much has since been heard, however, of this new federation.

Although the CNTU is sometimes perceived to be the largest federation in Quebec, its membership is not nearly as large as that of the QFL. The reason for this perception is that more than half the membership of the CNTU comes from the public sector, and the workers in this sector have received a great deal of media attention in recent years. In 1988, the CNTU had close to 205,000 members while the QFL had over '450,000 members.[57]

Having to compete with a number of central federations in Quebec, the QFL has insisted that it is unlike other provincial federations of labour and, therefore, needs greater autonomy from the CLC to serve its members well. At the 1974 convention of the CLC held in Vancouver, the QFL sought and obtained three major concessions:

1 That it have full control over labour education in Quebec, something that other provincial federations do not have;
2 That the QFL be able to bargain with the CLC for funds which the Quebec members pay but from

which they receive little benefit because of linguistic, cultural or political differences (e.g., unilingual newspapers); and
3 That the CLC give the QFL jurisdiction over local labour councils, with the right to appoint staff workers and the money to pay them.[58]

No other provincial federations enjoy these rights: they give a special status to the QFL.

Like other federations before them, the CLC (as represented by the QFL) and the CNTU sometimes cooperate and sometimes disagree, depending upon what seems most advantageous at the time. For example, in the construction industry there have been spectacular conflicts between the CNTU and the unions affiliated with the QFL over which unions should represent workers in that industry. The employers in the construction industry negotiate through one employer association and the union with majority support must, by law, act as the main bargaining agent. Since the QFL has generally received majority support, it has become the negotiator for unionized construction workers.

In summary, the Quebec labour scene is more complex than the labour scene in any other province in Canada. The QFL, by far the largest central body, has become more radical over the years and has a special status in comparison to other provincial federations. The CNTU, more radical than the QFL, has lost membership as a result of the formation of the Centre for Democratic Unionism (CDU) as well as the breakaway of a large group of public sector workers.[59] The Quebec Teachers' Corporation professes an ideology somewhat similar to that of the CNTU. While QTC membership was at one time confined to primary and secondary school teachers, its charter was changed in the early 1970s to permit it to organize all categories of workers in the field of education. Now, the QTC competes for members in that field with the CNTU, CDU, and affiliates of the QFL. However, more than 90% of the QTC's membership comprises elementary and secondary school teachers.[60] None of the federations has been nearly as politically-oriented in recent years as they were during the 1970s.

Growth of the Canadian Labour Movement

Trade-union membership as a percentage of non-agricultural paid workers did not reach the 20% mark until around 1942. The major reason for the substantial growth during the 1940s was that, as we have discussed, Canadian workers saw that American workers had the right to organize and engage in collective bargaining as a result of the Wagner Act of 1935, and sought similar rights for themselves. Thus, Canadian Orders-in-Council during wartime, and particularly Order-in-Council P.C. 1003 of 1944, encouraged unionization and collective bargaining. The return to peacetime conditions in 1947, along with favourable legislation and a high level of economic growth, encouraged the growth of trade unions during the 1950s, with union membership as a percentage of the non-agricultural paid workers stabilizing around 33%. In the early 1960s, though, the figure hovered below 30% and it was only in 1966 and 1967 that the figure again exceeded 30%. Since then it has continued to increase to a high of 40% of non-agricultural paid workers in 1983, and in 1988 it comprised 36.6% of non-agricultural paid workers.

The major reason for the growth since the mid-1960s is that both the federal and provincial governments have given their workers the right to bargain collectively and, in some cases, the right to strike. Many of the unions representing workers at the federal and provincial levels have joined the mainstream of the Canadian labour movement by affiliation with the Canadian Labour Congress through an umbrella association, the National Union of Provincial Government Employees (NUPGE). The Public Service Alliance of Canada, which represents federal public servants, is also directly affiliated with the CLC. Most provincial unions which represent civil

servants have become part of NUPGE and it is now one of the largest components within the Canadian Labour Congress.

Although the majority of public-service unions have chosen to join the mainstream of the Canadian labour movement either through association with the CLC (or the CNTU in Quebec) uncertainty still surrounds the many unions of professional and white-collar workers, most of which are provincially based and have no national federation. The provincial nurses' associations have joined together in a national union, but it is still too early to predict whether other provincial associations will join. Some groups, particularly teachers, have had provincial organizations for many years, but no impetus seems present on their part to become part of a national Canadian labour union movement. In fact, many of them prefer the title association to union.

Also worthy of interest are certain isolated groups of engineers that have bargaining rights with a number of companies but do not belong to any central federation. Engineers, along with the other professionals mentioned above, deserve to be watched carefully in the future by Canadian labour analysts. Boivin points to the situation in Quebec, where independent labour unions accounted for 15.5% of unionized workers in 1975, and 27% by 1988.[61]

There have been a number of attempts to explain union membership growth through the use of econometric models. After surveying a number of econometric models and developing one of his own, Kumar attributes the long-term growth of union membership to the following factors:

> changes in consumer prices, lagged employment growth, the percentage change in real wages, the change in unemployment during recessionary and recovery phases of the business cycle, the inverse of union density lagged one year, the rate of change in union membership in the United States adjusted by the ratio of international to national union membership in Canada, the legislative changes following the passage of P.C. 1003 of 1944 and the extension of collective bargaining rights to public sector employees since 1963, and

changes in the ratio of employment in service and goods-producing industries and in the ratio of female and male employment. . . . [62]

While there has been some criticism of this model, it appears to provide a better explanation of union growth in Canada than any of the others. However, Kumar cautions against the use of quantitative behavioural models in explaining the growth of unions, since these models do not capture the importance of "such hard-to-quantify factors as trade union leadership, the structure of labour organizations, and the adequacy of union-organizing resources and techniques. . . ." [63] It is clear from Kumar's discussion that we have a long way to go yet before a satisfactory explanation will be provided for the growth and development of unions in Canada.

Figure 4.1

A Schematic Outline of Events in the History of Trade Union Movements in the United States and Canada

The United States	Canada
1869 *Knights of Labor* — uplift unionism — membership not restricted — craft and mixed locals	1875–1910 *Knights of Labor* — active in Que., Ont. and N.S. — uplift unionism — membership not restricted — craft and mixed locals — problems with R.C. Church in Que.
1886–1955 *American Federation of Labor* (AFL) — a loose federation of craft-oriented unions — excluded Knights of Labor because of dual unionism — little activity in politics — each affiliate was autonomous — preferred little government intervention	1886–1956 *Trades and Labour Congress* (TLC) — loose federation of craft-oriented unions and some Knights of Labor — Knights of Labor expelled in 1902 for dual unionism — little activity in politics — each affiliate was autonomous — influenced very much by AFL's philosophy and policies
	1908–1927 *Canadian Federation of Labour (CFL)* — included Knights of Labor, N.S. Provincial Workman's Assoc. and other Canadian unions — nationalistic in orientation — dominated by regional interests — wanted more Canadian control
	1919–1956 *One Big Union (OBU)* — mainly in western Canada — dissatisfaction with TLC — opposed to craft unions — felt TLC structure not suited to western Canada — influenced by radical IWW — played an active role in Winnipeg General Strike of 1919 — became part of CLC in 1956
	1927–1940 *All-Canadian Congress of Labour (ACCL)* — remnants of CFL of 1908, OBU, and CBRE — wanted industrial unions — critical of American control — critical of conservative philosophy of TLC
1938–1955 *Congress of Industrial Organization (CIO)* — unions expelled from AFL — wanted to unionize unskilled labourers — wanted industrial unions — more active in politics than AFL — organized mass production workers	1940–1956 *Canadian Congress of Labour (CCL)* — Canadian branches of CIO unions — remnants of ACCL — wanted to unionize unskilled labourers — wanted industrial unions — active in politics — organized mass production workers — wanted less control from US — wanted more government action than TLC

1955   *AFL-CIO*
— merger of AFL and CIO affiliated unions
— no raiding pacts between unions affiliated with each federation
— craft and industrial unions
— conservative philosophy
— supports Democratic Party
— code of ethical practices
— little control over affiliates

1956   *Canadian Labour Congress (CLC)*
— merger of TLC and CCL affiliated unions
— no raiding pacts between unions affiliated with each federation
— craft and industrial unions
— less conservative than AFL-CIO
— supports NDP
— code of ethics
— little control over affiliates
— standards of self-government to apply mostly to Canadian districts of international unions

1982   *Canadian Federation of Labour (CFL)*
— formed by construction unions
— has some non-construction unions
— wanted more voting power in CLC
— non-partisan political stance
— closer ties with government than CLC
— no raids between CFL and CLC

Union Developments in Quebec

1900   *Major strike in Quebec City, arbitrated by Archbishop of Quebec*
— confessional unions formed across the province
— meetings dominated largely by clergy
— influenced by Papal encyclicals

1921–1960   *Canadian and Catholic Confederation of Labour (CCCL)*
— founding convention in Hull, Quebec in 1921
— brought workers together into a confederation
— wanted to keep workers Catholic and French-speaking
— dominated largely by clergy until 1940s
— adhered largely to teachings of Papal encyclicals
— adhered largely to teachings of Papal encyclicals

1947   *Asbestos strike*
— a turning point in Quebec's economic and social history
— broke ties between government and Church
— lay leaders began to play major role in unions after mid-1940s

1960   *Confederation of National Trade Unions (Change of name to CNTU)*
— dropped Catholic from name, but adhered to Christian principles
— has about ten sectors
— became radical during the 1970s
— smaller than Quebec Federation of Labour (provincial arm of CLC)
— part of "Common Front" in 1972 and 1982
— QFL and CNTU cooperate and raid

1972   *Centre for Democratic Unionism (CDU)*
— breakaway unions from the CNTU
— very conservative philosophy
— not a very active player on the Quebec scene (Major union bodies in Quebec now are the QFL, CNTU, Quebec Teachers' Congress, and CDU)
— Part of "Common Front" in 1972 and 1982
— conflict in construction industry

Questions

1 Discuss the criminal conspiracy doctrine that hampered union development in Canada prior to 1872. How did the legal enactments of 1872 affect unions?

2 Discuss the major central labour organizations that have existed in Canada up to the present time.

3 Why has there been such a close relationship between developments in the Canadian and American trade-union movements? Do you think that this is desirable or undesirable for Canadian workers, employers, and the country as a whole? Justify your response.

4 How do you account for the demise of indigenous Canadian labour federations such as the Canadian Federation of Labour (1908), the One Big Union (1919), and the All-Canadian Congress of Labour (1927)?

5 For what reasons have labour developments in Quebec differed from developments in the rest of Canada? What do you predict for the future of the labour movement in Quebec? Make whatever assumptions you feel are needed.

6 Why has the growth pattern of the Canadian labour movement been uneven?

7 To what extent do the theories discussed in Chapter 3 explain the emergence and growth of white-collar unionism in Canada since the mid-1960s?

8 Do you consider the unions in your province to be active enough in the political arena? Elaborate by indicating those activities in which they are, should be, or should not be involved.

9 Do you think that unions in your province are influenced more by what happens in the United States than in the rest of Canada? Elaborate and give some examples.

10 Do you see any major differences between the philosophies of unions in the public and private sectors? Elaborate and give examples to support your contention.

Notes

1 A.E. Kovacs, "The Philosophy of the Canadian Labour Movement," *Canadian Labour in Transition*, eds. R.U. Miller and F. Isbester (Scarborough: Prentice-Hall Canada Inc., 1971), p. 120.

2 Bureau of Labour Information, Labour Canada, *Directory of Labour Organization in Canada 1988* (Ottawa: Supplies and Services Canada, 1988), pp. 57-60.

3 E. Forsey, *Trade Unions in Canada 1812-1902* (Toronto: University of Toronto Press, 1982), pp. X, 1. This book is a narration — analysis is left to the author's "youngers and betters." Nevertheless, Forsey is to be commended for providing us with a rich account of the development of our early unions. He constructs a picture that is partly at odds with conventional wisdom. Important dates which have been erroneously used in the past are corrected by Forsey.

4 Ibid., pp. 12-13.

5 Ibid., pp. 14-15.

6 S. Jamieson, *Industrial Relations in Canada*, 2nd ed. (Toronto: Macmillan of Canada, 1973), p. 12.

7 Forsey, *Trade Unions in Canada*, p. 31.

8 J. Crispo, *International Unionism: A Study in Canadian-American Relations* (Toronto: McGraw-Hill, 1967), p. 2.

9 Jamieson, *Industrial Relations in Canada*, p. 13.

10 Forsey, *Trade Unions in Canada*, pp. 32, 37.

11 Ibid., p. 5.

12 H.A. Logan, *Trade Unions in Canada* (Toronto: Macmillan of Canada, 1948), pp. 43-45.

13 Ibid., p. 50; Forsey, *Trade Unions in Canada*, p. 138.

14 Logan, *Trade Unions in Canada*, Table IV, p. 78.

15 Jamieson, *Industrial Relations in Canada*, p.18.

16 Ibid., p. 23.

17 Forsey, *Trade Unions in Canada*, pp. 501-2.

18 Jamieson, *Industrial Relations in Canada*, p. 17.

19 Logan, *Trade Unions in Canada*, p.301.

20 Ibid., p.324.

21 For a brief account of the rise of the CIO, see F.R. Dulles, Ch. XVI, *Labor in America*, 2nd rev. ed. (New York: Thomas Y. Crowell Co., 1960). For a more detailed account, see W. Galenson, *The CIO Challenge to the AFL: A History of the American Labor Movement 1935-1941* (Cambridge: Harvard University Press, 1960).

22 E. Forsey, "The Movement Towards Labour Unity in Canada: History and Implications," *Readings in Canadian Labour Economics*, ed. A.E. Kovacs (Toronto: McGraw-Hill, 1961), pp. 75-76.

23 I.M. Abella, *Nationalism, Communism, and Canadian Labour* (Toronto: University of Toronto Press, 1973), p. 167.

24 For an interesting account of the developments within the CCL and those between the CIO and CCL, see Ch. 9, Abella, "The CIO versus the CCL 1940-50."

25 Ibid., p. 213.

26 Dulles, Ch. XX, "The A.F. of L.-C.I.O. Merger," *Labor in America*, pp. 377-93.

27 Forsey, "Labour Unity in Canada," p. 81.

28 Dulles, *Labor in America*, p. 389.

29 Forsey, "Labour Unity in Canada," p. 86.

30 R.J. Adams, "Industrial Relations in Europe and North America," *Union-Management Relations in Canada*, eds. J. Anderson, M. Gunderson (Don Mills: Addison-Wesley, 1982), p. 461.

31 Forsey, *Trade Unions in Canada*, pp. 496-97.

32 R. Miller, "Organized Labour and Politics in Canada," *Canadian Labour in Transition* eds. Miller and Isbester, p. 209.

33 Forsey, "Labour Unity in Canada," p. 89.

34 L. Slotnick and L. McQuaig, "NDP's Election Strategy Assailed by CAW Chief," *Globe and Mail* (December 7, 1988), pp. A1 and A4. See also L. Slotnick, "Steelworker Leaders Join Critics of NDP's Campaign Strategy," *Globe and Mail* (December 13, 1988), p. A5.

35 S. Slotnick, "Criticism of NDP Healthy, Carr Says," *Globe and Mail* (December 8, 1988), p. A3.

36 R.J. Adams, "Industrial Relations Systems," p. 461.

37 P. Kumar, "Union Growth in Canada: Retrospect and Prospect," in W.C. Riddell, ed. *Canadian Labour Relations* (Toronto: University of Toronto Press, 1986), p. 103.

38 Ibid.

39 Ibid., pp. 103-104.

40 C.B. Williams, "Trade Union Structure and Philosophy: Need for a Reappraisal," *Canadian Labour in Transition*, eds. Miller and Isbester, p. 162.

41 Ibid., p. 163.

42 Ibid., pp. 171-72.

43 *Labour's Manifesto for Canada*, approved by the CLC Convention (Quebec City: May 17-21, 1976).

44 Ibid., p. 11.

45 D. Dowling, "CLC, PM Try to Bury Hatchet," *Ottawa Citizen* (March 18, 1989), p. A3.

46 J.B. Rose, "Some Notes on the Building Trades-Canadian Labour Congress Dispute," Vol. 22, No. 1, *Industrial Relations* (Winter 1983), pp. 89-90.

47 Labour Canada, *Directory of Labour Organizations in Canada, 1988*, pp. 148, 98 and 83 respectively.

48 Jamieson, *Industrial Relations in Canada*, p. 35.

49 Isbester, "Quebec Labour in Perspective, 1949-1969," Miller and Isbester, p. 242.

50 Jamieson, *Industrial Relations in Canada*, p. 37.

51 J. Boivin, "Union-Management Relations in Quebec," *Union-Management Relations in Canada*, 2nd ed., eds. J. Anderson, M. Gunderson and A. Ponak, p. 412.

52 Jamieson, *Industrial Relations in Canada*, p. 37.

53 Isbester, p. 246.

54 Ibid., pp. 250-51.

55 J. Boivin, "Union-Management Relations in Quebec," p. 415.

56 Jamieson, *Industrial Relations in Canada*, p. 43.

57 Labour Canada, *Directory of Labour Organizations in Canada 1988*, pp. 14 and 190.

58 Boivin, "Union-Management Relations in Quebec," p. 419.

59 Ibid., pp. 421–422.

60 Ibid., p. 422.

61 Ibid., pp. 422-423.

62 P. Kumar, "Union Growth in Canada," p. 110.

63 Ibid., p. 139.

The Financial Post

5

The Structure and Functions of the Canadian Labour Movement

Introduction

Studying the labour movement is somewhat akin to studying the major parts of the human body. Just as the mind and the other organs of the body must function in harmony if the body is to function properly, so do the various parts of the labour movement need to work together to accomplish their objectives.

We shall begin by discussing the structure of central federations, and of the CLC in particular. Then we will examine each of the components of the CLC shown in Figure 5.1. In the second part of the chapter we will turn to an examination of some possible future structural trends in the Canadian labour movement: towards Canadianization and consolidation. Finally, we will examine the way in which unions govern themselves.

Central Federations: The Structure and Functions of the CLC

Central labour federations perform a number of functions for their member unions and the

Figure 5.1

The Structure of the CLC-Affiliated Segment of the Canadian Labour Movement

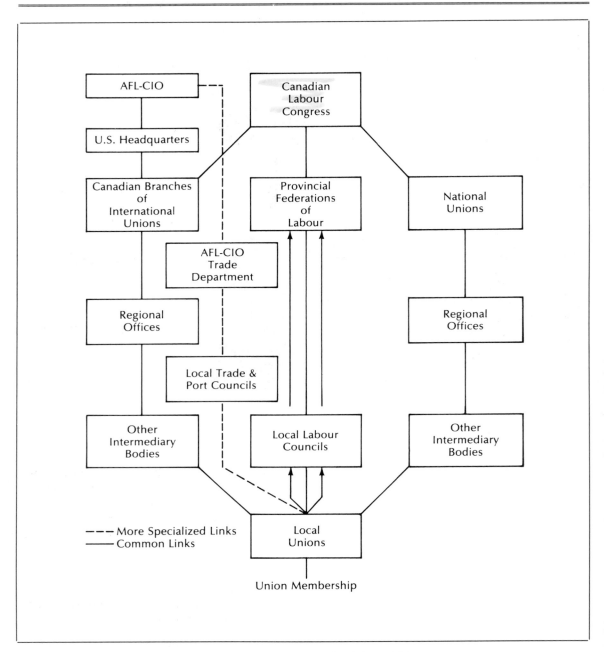

Source: John Crispo, *International Unionism* (Toronto: McGraw-Hill, 1967), p. 167.

workers they represent. They coordinate and direct a variety of activities at different organizational levels. Central federations such as the Canadian Labour Congress exist in every country in which trade unions are found. In a number of countries, such as Sweden and Australia, there are at least two central federations, one representing blue-collar workers and one or more representing white-collar workers. In other European countries, such as France and Italy, there are a number of central federations which are organized along religious and political lines. Table 5.1 summarizes the membership of the various federations in Canada.

Table 5.1	Union Membership by Congress Affiliation, 1988	
Congress Affiliation	Membership	%
CLC	2,231,697	58.1
(AFL-CIO/CLC)	812,709	21.2
CLC only	1,418,988	36.9
CNTU *CSN*	204,637	5.3
CFL	207,736	5.4
(AFL-CIO/CFL)	205,486	5.3
CFL only	2,250	0.1
AFL-CIO only	224,305	5.8
CEQ	99,114	2.6
CSD	50,379	1.3
CCU	31,407	0.8
CNFIU	3,476	0.1
Unaffiliated International Unions	15,386	0.4
Unaffiliated National Unions	662,876	17.3
Independent Local Organizations	110,478	2.9
TOTAL	3,841,491	100.0

Source: Bureau of Labour Information, Labour Canada, *Directory of Labour Organizations in Canada 1988* (Ottawa: Supply and Services Canada, 1988), Table 2, p. 14. Reproduced by permission of the Minister of Supply and Services Canada.

CEQ = Congrés d'enseignement du Québec
CSD = Congrés des syndicats démocratiques
CCU = Confederation of Canadian Unions
CNFIU = Canadian National Federation of Independent Unions

The central federations in Canada are formed of Canadian branches of international unions, national unions, and directly chartered locals. Table 5.2 presents a breakdown of union membership by type of union, and lists the affiliations of each. It shows that the CLC is by far the largest federation in the country.

As Figure 5.1 shows, the CLC structure parallels the federal-provincial-local structure of the Canadian government. In a world of big government and increasingly bigger business organizations, organized labour needs a strong and unified voice. Without federations at the national and provincial levels, organized labour would have no input into national and provincial public policy decisions. In Canada, labour relations policy falls primarily under the provincial jurisdictions, which cover 90% of workers in Canada. The CLC, therefore, has organized provincial federations in order to affect the formulation of provincial policies. Similarly, local labour councils exist to influence the policies of local governments. These organizational structures are represented by the line drawn straight down through the middle of Figure 5.1.

Functions of the CLC

Labour Canada's definition of a central labour congress provides a good description of the functions of the CLC:

> An organization having in affiliation various unions, directly chartered locals, provincial federations of labour, and local labour councils, for the purpose of broadly co-ordinating their activities at the national level including the relations between unions and governments and establishing relations with organized workers internationally. Congresses hold annual or biennial conventions attended by delegates from affiliated organizations at which policies are established and officers elected. The congress also organizes local unions known as directly chartered locals. Funds are obtained through a per capita tax on all affiliates.[1]

The supreme governing body of the CLC is the biennial convention, which establishes the

Table 5.2			Union Membership by Type of Union and Affiliation 1988	

			Membership	
Type and Affiliation	Unions	Locals	Number	%
International Unions	65	3,471	1,265,797	33.0
(AFL-CIO/CLC)	42	2,667	812,709	21.2
(AFL-CIO/CFL)	10	417	205,486	5.3
CLC only	3	29	7,911	0.2
AFL-CIO only	5	253	224,305	5.8
Unaffiliated Unions	5	105	15,386	0.4
National Unions	222	13,321	2,425,411	63.1
CLC	49	6,583	1,404,977	36.6
CNTU	8	1,864	204,562	5.3
CEQ	12	463	99,114	2.6
CCU	14	100	31,407	0.8
CSD	3	167	16,749	0.4
CFL	2	49	2,250	0.1
CNFIU	10	12	3,476	0.1
Unaffiliated Unions	124	4,083	662,876	17.3
Directly Chartered Unions	309		39,805	1.0
CSD	262		33,630	0.9
CLC	45		6,100	0.2
CNTU	2		75	*0.0
Independent Local Organizations	244		110,478	2.9
TOTAL	840	16,792	3,841,491	100.0

*Less than 0.1 percent

Source: Bureau of Labour Information, Labour Canada, *Directory of Labour Organizations in Canada 1988* (Ottawa: Supply and Services Canada, 1988), Table 6, p. 20. Reproduced by permission of the Minister of Supply and Services Canada.

policies of the Congress. While the constitution of the CLC lists thirteen sections under the article "Purposes," all 13 are derived from four main functions: (1) influencing the formulation and administration of public policy at the national level; (2) keeping peace within the Congress by resolving jurisdictional issues between its affiliated unions; (3) policing its ethical practices code; and (4) representing Canadian labour on the international trade union scene.

National Policies   The CLC attempts to achieve its objectives at the national level in a number of ways. For example, when Statistics Canada releases its monthly figures on the cost of living and unemployment rates, the CLC frequently prepares press releases setting out what policies it thinks the government should pursue. This data is also analyzed and published in *Canadian Labour*, the CLC magazine.

On occasion, the Congress makes its position known when the government prepares important legislation or appoints commissions to enquire into critical social and economic issues. In February 1981, for example, it presented a brief to the Parliamentary Task Force on Employment Opportunities in the 1980s, expressing its concern with the present serious unemployment situation and proposed remedies. In conjunction with the International Typographical Union, the CLC also co-authored a submission to the Kent Commission, which studied the concentration of newspaper ownership in Canada. In 1988, the CLC took an active part in the free trade debate, issuing numerous public pronouncements, and campaigning against the deal during the federal election campaign.

In spite of these efforts on the part of labour to participate in the decision-making processes of government, labour leaders often claim they are ignored by politicians, and the relations between labour and government are frequently shaky. For example, the former leader of the CLC, Dennis McDermott, declared publicly that "labour advice to the federal government always falls on deaf ears."[2] However, Shirley Carr, who replaced McDermott as president in 1988, has taken a more conciliatory approach. Carr met with Prime Minister Mulroney in 1989, at her request, in an effort to establish an ongoing relationship with the government. At the same time, the Congress continued to express some extremely harsh criticism of the free trade deal. Only time will tell whether this policy of conciliation will give the CLC a say in the implementation of labour policy under free trade.

Jurisdictional Conflicts Another important function of the CLC is to iron out problems of conflicting jurisdictions among its affiliated members. When the merger of the TLC and CCL took place in 1956, the constitution of the CLC stated that the jurisdictions of affiliated unions would be as they were on the founding day of the CLC (May 1, 1956), or as subsequently granted or amended by authority of the executive council and the constitution. However, some unions have attempted to maintain their jurisdictions, with the result that in some companies there are several unions, particularly where craft unions were certified before the merger took place. A multiplicity of unions can increase the number of work stoppages that

may occur over contract negotiation disputes, particularly if the unions bargain separately and at different times of the year. Also, having more than one union in a single company may cause very difficult problems if two companies merge. Which union or unions will represent the workers in the merged company, and how will the different seniority rosters among employees of the two previous organizations be resolved?

Jurisdictional disputes do not lend themselves to easy solutions, since each competing union has its own status, position, and growth concerns. Third-party assistance, in the form of mediation or binding arbitration, is sometimes necessary in such cases. However, if the disputing parties refuse to agree with a mediator, then the executive committee of the CLC will attempt to resolve the dispute.

The CLC also has a mandate to promote the unionization of workers in sectors that are not yet unionized, such as the banking industry. In 1977, the CLRB determined that a bank branch constitutes an appropriate bargaining unit. After this important decision the CLC, in cooperation with several other unions, set up a committee to organize bank workers. Generally, progress has been slow, but in 1985 members of the fledgling Union of Bank Employees at the Canadian Imperial Bank of Commerce Visa Centre in Toronto undertook a protracted strike. A subsequent decision by the CLRB in 1985 in which it found that a geographical unit of the National Bank of Canada in the Rimouski area was an appropriate unit in that situation has the potential for a turnaround in unionization in Canada's banks, since organization is easier on a geographical basis than on a branch-by-branch basis.[3]

Code of Ethics The CLC is also responsible for enforcing the code of ethical practices set out in its constitution. The code prohibits union leaders from preying on the union movement for corrupt practices. It also states that union members have the right to honest elections, to run for union office, and to fair treatment in the application of union rules, among other things.

Affiliated organizations must adhere to the CLC code. When a union violates any part of the code, it is the duty of the CLC executive or its elected officers to try to persuade the affiliated organization to correct its behaviour. The same officials have the power to suspend any organization which continues to breach these standards. Finally, if the threat of dismissal or suspension is not enough to bring the offending union into line, the matter may be brought before a regular CLC convention, at which time a vote may be taken as to whether or not to expel the malefactor.

International Relations The CLC is also active in international labour affairs, particu-

larly in the International Confederation of Free Trade Unions (ICFTU). CLC president Shirley Carr is currently vice-president of the ICFTU, and also chairs the Commonwealth Trade Union, which was founded in 1980.

The Components of the CLC

In the following sections, we will examine each of the components of the CLC shown in Figure 5.1.

Provincial and Territorial Federations of Labour Currently there are ten provincial and two territorial federations within the CLC. A

Shirley Carr (left) and Lech Walesa, 1989

provincial or territorial federation is defined as:

an organization formed by a labour congress at the provincial [or territorial] level which consists of the congress affiliates in the province [or territory]. It functions similarly to the congress in the appropriate provincial [or territorial] area except that it does not charter local unions. Funds are obtained through a per capita tax on all affiliates.[4]

According to Article XV, section 2 of the CLC constitution, all national and international unions and regional and provincial organizations affiliated with the CLC must require their local unions, branches, or lodges to join chartered federations at the provincial and territorial levels. Also, all local unions chartered directly by the CLC and all local labour councils must affiliate with the provincial and territorial federations of labour.

The Role of Provincial Federations Provincial federations react when provincial governments issue policy statements or propose legislation which affect the labour movement. For example, they played an important, albeit unsuccessful, part in attempting to convince provincial premiers not to endorse the free trade deal in the late eighties. The Ontario Federation of Labour (OFL) was particularly outspoken on this matter. The OFL presented a brief to Premier Peterson and his Cabinet calling for a training tax on employers as part of a comprehensive scheme to cushion the effects of free trade on workers in the province. The OFL said that the province would be hit hard by free trade since American plants could close branch plants and other companies could accelerate technological change to compete in the broader North American market. The federation suggested that unions should play a key role in the design of retraining policy.

The brief also "renewed the OFL's long-time call for tougher legislation on plant closings and layoffs, including increased notice, a plant closure review board with power to compel a company to provide evidence of its financial state, and a legislated severance pay formula."[5]

The efforts of the Nova Scotia Federation of Labour (NSFL) in December 1979 to block the passage of the clearly anti-labour Michelin Bill in Nova Scotia is another example of what provincial federations do. This legislation prohibits the Nova Scotia Labour Relations Board from certifying workers in one plant of a manufacturing company if the operation of that plant is integrated with the operation of another plant. The bill was enacted in response to an alleged threat by Michelin Tire not to expand its operation in Nova Scotia if any of its existing plants were forced to accept unionization. Because the NSFL did not succeed in blocking the passage of this bill, relations between the Nova Scotia government and the NSFL have remained strained.[6]

In the fall of 1983, the BC government threatened to fire 1,600 workers as part of its public-sector restraint program. The BC Federation of Labour (BCFL) insisted that the government back down and agree to hire and fire workers on a strict seniority basis.[7] Following a great deal of bitterness and name-calling on both sides, the province signed "a lucrative new contract with its employees that prevented the arbitrary dismissals that had angered unionists."[8] The president of the BCFL was also a co-leader of the Solidarity Coalition of labour and community groups, which had organized mass demonstrations against the government's restraint program.[9]

Occasionally, provincial federations must deal with internal dissensions. An incident in Manitoba in the summer of 1987 saw the Manitoba federation divided over a piece of legislation passed by the provincial government. Under the proposed legislation (to be discussed more fully in the next chapter) either a company or a union involved in contract negotiations could seek final offer selection and employees would then vote on whether to use the method. The method, if selected, would allow an impartial neutral party to accept either the union's demands or the employer's offer as the final outcome of the dispute. This is the only piece of legislation in the world that would give workers the responsibility for determining whether final offer selection would be used or not.

While CUPE and a few other unions fought the bill, the Manitoba Federation of Labour supported it. However, according to one writer, the federation "was shaken by internal feuding over its endorsement of the bill."[10] In fact, a number of CUPE representatives and other union leaders resigned from the MFL over the issue.

Local Labour Councils The CLC also includes local labour councils, which operate in a similar fashion to the CLC and the provincial federations, but at a local level. A local labour council is defined as:

> an organization formed by a labour congress at the city level. It is organized and functions in the same manner as a provincial federation, but within the scope of a city. Funds are obtained through a per capita tax on affiliates.[11]

The activities of the Ottawa and District Labour Council (ODLC) during the CLC's 1976 day of protest against wage and prices controls is a good example of what local labour councils do. The ODLC issued a very strong press release, distributed pamphlets, and used the media to urge the government to abolish its controls.

On other occasions, local labour councils have carried out research into labour-related issues, and there have also been instances of labour organizations coming together to support an attack on any one of them at the local level. This type of action is usually coordinated and directed by the local labour council.

National Unions and Canadian Branches of International Unions Labour Canada defines a national or international union as follows:

> The unit of labour organization that organizes and charters locals in the industries or trades as defined in its constitution, sets general policy for its locals, assists them in the conduct of their affairs, and is the medium for co-ordinating their activities. Funds are obtained from the locals through per capita dues. Unions usually hold regular conventions of delegates from the locals at which general policy is set and at which officers are elected.[12]

The CLC consists of 45 Canadian branches of international unions and 49 national unions. Figure 5.2 illustrates the percentage of national and international union membership in the CLC.

Figure 5.2	CLC Membership by Affiliation 1988

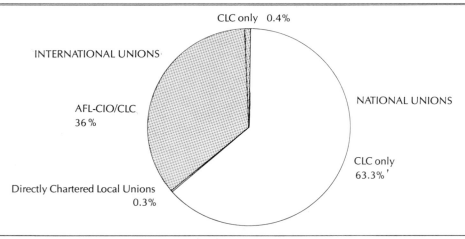

CLC only 0.4%

INTERNATIONAL UNIONS

AFL-CIO/CLC 36%

NATIONAL UNIONS

CLC only 63.3%

Directly Chartered Local Unions 0.3%

Source: Bureau of Labour Information, Labour Canada, *Directory of Labour Organizations in Canada 1988* (Ottawa: Supply and Services Canada, 1988), Table 7b, p. 21. Reproduced by permission of the Minister of Supply and Services Canada.

International unions charter locals in both Canada and the United States, while national unions restrict their activities to Canada. National unions usually have a mandate to organize within a particular jurisdiction (i.e., a trade or industry). The national union or Canadian branch of an international union serves the existing local unions within it, and organizes non-unionized workers within its particular jurisdiction.

In the early days of union development, it was easy for national unions or Canadian branches of international unions to organize in industries where large plants existed with many workers. This was particularly true in the primary, manufacturing, and transportation and communication industries. Today, however, organization is more difficult — most of the unorganized plants are small or are located in isolated areas. This situation is perceived by many as a major challenge for existing unions.

Usually a union will have its own elected executive, appointed staff, and field officers (known as national or international representatives) who are assigned particular geographic areas. In craft unions, particularly in the construction industry, field officers who organize workers and help locals are called business agents.

The Role of National and International Unions

National and international unions help their locals in a variety of ways. First, they help to organize groups of workers, and to represent them as their collective bargaining agent. Second, during contract negotiations, these unions assist the local negotiating committee in formulating demands and at the negotiating table. Third, representatives often assist locals in handling grievances, particularly when they are taken to arbitration. This assistance is extremely helpful to local union officials who may have little experience in negotiating or in presenting grievance cases before arbitrators. Many employers also prefer to deal with experienced national representatives rather than with inexperienced local officials.

The constitutions of most national and international unions give them some veto power over matters that are carried on at the local level, including the authorization of strikes and sometimes the approval of the terms of a collective agreement. For most unions, though, the power to approve terms is largely a formality. There are only a few cases on record where a national or international union has refused to accept an agreement worked out between union and management representatives at the local level, or to accept the strike decision of the majority of local union members.[13]

National unions assist their local unions, particularly if the latter negotiate separately, by building up reserve funds which are disbursed as benefits to striking workers should work stoppages occur. It is also common for one union to give donations to the striking members of another union.

The Local Union

For the ordinary worker, the most important unit within the framework of a labour movement is the local union. Labour Canada describes the local union as:

> the basic unit of labour organization formed in a particular plant or locality. The members participate directly in the affairs of their local including the election of officers, financial and other business matters, and relations between their organization and employers, and they pay dues to the local. There are locals of international, national or regional unions, locals directly chartered by a central congress, and independent local organizations. Sometimes unions have units, similar to locals, such as lodges, branches or divisions.[14]

A worker's first contact with unionism is usually with a local. Whatever occurs during that initial contact can colour the individual's whole attitude toward unions.

Each local has its own elected officers, some of whom contribute their time freely while others are paid on a full-time or part-time basis, depending on the size of the local. Every member has a right to take part in local meetings, to elect officers of the local, to have input into the formulation of contract demands, and to vote on the ratification of contract proposals for the bargaining unit to which he or she belongs.

When union representatives organize a new plant or other establishment, they first assemble a core of union members. These union members sign union cards and then try to convince other workers to join the union. It is usually this nucleus of active members that shapes the policy and direction of the local union. It has been estimated that only between 5% and 10% of the local members show up for regular union meetings. While this low turnout is often criticized by writers on the topic, it should be pointed out that meetings of voluntary associations normally have small turnouts. In this sense, local unions are no exception to the general rule. Only when matters arise of real importance to members (for example, the ratification of the terms of a collective agreement) will large turnouts occur at union meetings.

Within a local union, which may organize the workers of one company or of a number of small companies, members are normally elected to serve as shop stewards. Their function is to discuss grievances with workers and to represent workers in the grievance process, usually at the first level between supervisor and individual. Each department or area may have one or more shop stewards. In addition, there is usually a shop stewards' committee, with an individual chosen from the committee as the general shop steward. The general shop steward coordinates the efforts of all committee members.

Most union constitutions provide for initiation fees. In some unions, initiation fees are quite high. Monthly dues are normally required of members and are deducted directly from members' pay where a dues check-off clause exists in a contract. The local union distributes this money according to the constitution of the national union and the by-laws of the local. Local unions are financed entirely from the dues of union members. In the case of costly strikes, however, the general strike fund of the national or international union usually supplements local union funds.

As Bakke has pointed out, belonging to a local union gives the worker a chance to assume responsibility for his or her work environment and to feel important in relation to fellow workers. Election to an official position within the local union brings with it a certain prestige. In like manner, election as a shop steward often provides an active trade union member with a strong sense of purpose. Union officials and shop stewards often get time off to attend national or international conventions, and to participate at important regional or local policy committee meetings at which decisions are taken on items relating to future rounds of collective bargaining, or the organization of the union itself.[15]

Other Components of the CLC

National unions and Canadian branches of international unions have regional offices located in various cities and large communities across the country. The *Directory of Labour Organizations in Canada*, which is published annually, gives an indication of how many regional offices are currently in operation.

The CLC also comprises some Local trades and port councils, which are set up to handle problems among unions or among unions and employers at the local level. A good example is the Vancouver Port's Council, a CLC affiliate which consists of the locals of the major unions representing workers engaged in the transportation of goods by ship. Most cities also have councils consisting of construction industry unions. An example of such a council is the Ottawa-Hull Building and Construction Trades Council, an AFL-CIO affiliate. Other intermediary bodies include the Canadian Railway Labour Association (CRLA), a voluntary organization of eleven national and international unions which represent a large number of Canadian railway workers. The CRLA seeks to initiate and maintain cooperative action and to coordinate policy on all matters of interest and importance to its membership. Thus, although many of the individual unions involved in the CRLA bargain with more than just the railways, the Railway Association provides them with a specific context wherein they can influence government policy.

Structural Issues and Trends

The Canadianization of the Labour Movement

As we saw in Chapter 4, the number of unionized workers in Canada has been growing steadily in recent years. However, the *proportion* of non-agricultural paid workers that are unionized had declined steadily since 1983, when it reached a high of 40%. The figure now stands at around 37%. In the midst of this general trend toward organization, another major shift has been occurring: the proportion of workers who belong to strictly Canadian unions has been increasing, and there has been a corresponding decrease in the number and proportion of workers who belong to Canadian branches of international unions. Membership in Canadian unions (including unions affiliated with the CLC, other central Canadian federations, national unions, and independent local organizations) is about 67%, whereas Canadian branches of international unions now claim only 33% of the unionized labour force. These figures stand in stark contrast to those of thirty-odd years ago, when about 70% of workers belonged to Canadian branches and only 30% belonged to strictly Canadian unions.[16]

The advent of unionism in the public and parapublic sectors has greatly contributed to the growth of Canadian unions. Table 5.3 shows that the three largest unions in Canada are made up of government employees. The United Steelworkers of America, which occupied first place for many years, is now fifth, and seven of the twelve unions listed are strictly Canadian.

There are no international unions in the Canadian public sector, for at least three reasons. First, Canadian public servants have a different form of government and more collective bargaining rights than do their American counterparts, and hence they do not need the support of American unions. Second, Canadian public servants pose no threat to the jobs of American workers. Third, even before collective bargaining rights were formally granted to both federal and provincial public servants in 1967, most already had "associations" acting as their representatives in an informal manner. It was relatively easy to turn these associations into genuine bargaining agents (unions).

The increase of Canadian membership in national unions is especially significant for the CLC. Many of its policies reflect a nationalistic orientation, and the increased participation of Canadian unions in the CLC is bound to strengthen this nationalistic sentiment. In addition, many of the new national unions are more militant in their bargaining stances than most international unions.

The Canadianization of International Unions

As we have seen, around 37% of the membership of the CLC belongs to Canadian branches of international unions, and the question of Canadianization among these branches has been the subject of much soul-searching on the part of the CLC. The argument for Canadianization rests on a number of grounds:

1 Nationalists object to the inordinate degree to which the United States controls investment in Canada and influences the Canadian labour movement. They have argued vociferously for more Canadian control in these areas, and opposed the more open policies toward foreign investment adopted by the Mulroney government, which culminated in the signing of the free trade deal with the United States.

2 Many people both inside and outside the labour movement argue that by reducing the number of unions, through mergers or through the formation of strictly national bodies, the labour movement could serve its members more effectively

Table 5.3		Unions with Largest Membership 1988

		Membership (000's)	
		1988	1987
1.	Canadian Union of Public Employees (CLC)	342.0	330.0
2.	National Union of Provincial Government Employees (CLC)	292.3	278.5
3.	Public Service Alliance of Canada (CLC)	175.7	179.9
4.	United Food and Commercial Workers International Union (AFL-CIO/CLC)	170.0	160.0
5.	United Steelworkers of America (AFL-CIO/CLC)	160.0	160.0
6.	National Automobile, Aerospace and Agricultural Implement Workers Union of Canada (CLC)	143.0	143.0
7.	Social Affairs Federation Inc. (CNTU)	96.5	93.0
8.	International Brotherhood of Teamsters, Chauffeurs, Warehousemen and Helpers of America (AFL-CIO)	91.5	91.5
9.	School Boards Teachers' Commission (CEQ)	75.0	75.0
10.	Service Employees International Union (AFL-CIO/CLC)	70.0	70.0
11.	Canadian Paperworkers Union (CLC)	69.0	57.0
12.	United Brotherhood of Carpenters and Joiners of America (AFL-CIO)	66.0	66.0
13.	International Brotherhood of Electrical Workers (AFL-CIO/CFL)	64.6	68.6
14.	International Association of Machinists and Aerospace Workers (AFL-CIO/CLC)	58.5	58.6
15.	Labourers' International Union of North America (AFL-CIO)	46.7	46.7
16.	Ontario Nurses' Association (Ind.)	46.6	42.5
17.	IWA-Canada (CLC)	45.0	48.0
18.	Quebec Government Employees' Union Inc. (Ind.)	40.0	44.0
19.	United Association of Journeymen and Apprentices of the Plumbing and Pipe Fitting Industry of the United States and Canada (AFL-CIO/CFL)	40.0	40.0
20.	Communications and Electrical Workers of Canada (CLC)	40.0	40.0
21.	Canadian Brotherhood of Railway, Transport and General Workers (CLC)	39.9	39.9
22.	Alberta Teachers' Association (Ind.)	39.3	38.7
23.	Quebec Federation of Nurses (Ind.)	37.0	
24.	International Union of Operating Engineers (AFL-CIO/CFL)	36.0	36.0
25.	Ontario Secondary School Teachers' Federation (Ind.)	35.7	35.7
26.	Energy and Chemical Workers Union (CLC)	35.0	35.0
27.	Federation of Women Teachers' Associations of Ontario (Ind.)	31.1	31.5
28.	British Columbia Teachers' Federation (Ind.)	30.2	30.2
29.	Hotel Employees and Restaurant Employees International Union (AFL-CIO/CLC)	30.0	30.0
30.	Amalgamated Clothing and Textile Workers Union (AFL-CIO/CLC)	30.0	30.0

Source: Bureau of Labour Information, Labour Canada, *Directory of Labour Organizations in Canada 1988* (Ottawa: Supply and Services Canada, 1988), pp. 16–18.

than is currently possible. Policies developed by international unions, they claim, are sometimes concerned with problems more peculiar to the United States than to Canada.

3 Some writers also believe that Canadian members of international unions pay more into international trade union funds than they receive in benefits. To date, analysis of this question has been insufficient. It is still unclear whether or not Canadian workers pay more money into international unions than they receive in benefits. There are those who contend that, by being part of a continental trade union movement,

Canadian workers gain much by the combined financial contributions of workers in both countries. Certainly more research needs to be done to supplement the data contained in the annual reports of the *Corporations and Labour Unions Returns Act* (CALURA). CALURA reports do not take into account many of the indirect costs assumed by international unions in serving the needs of Canadian memberships — including the cost of research activities, the production and distribution of newspapers and circulars, salaries for non-union officers, and strike funds.[17]

The Response of International Unions To meet some of these criticisms, a number of international unions have established separate Canadian units that take into account the economic, social, and political realities of Canadian life. Large unions representing steelworkers and, until recently, autoworkers have long had branches in this country and possess the staff necessary to provide research and policy orientations which serve the needs of Canadian members.

Other international unions have also shown greater sensitivity to the Canadian situation in varying ways. As a result, a number of important developments in the international segment of the Canadian labour movement have occurred, particularly since 1968.[18] In that year, the United Packinghouse, Food, and Allied Workers merged with the Amalgamated Meat Cutters and Butcher Workmen of North America. The newly formed Canadian section adopted a Canadian name: the Canadian Food and Allied Workers Union (District Council 15). More recently, this union merged once again in both Canada and the United States with the Retail Clerks' International Union. There are now two distinct Canadian regions within the larger body of the United Food and Commercial Workers International Union. This merger resulted in a Canadian membership of 170,000 in 1988.[19]

Secessions from International Unions

Despite increased sensitivity by international unions to Canadian concerns, a number of Canadian sections of international unions broke away from their international counterparts during the 1970s and formed independent Canadian unions. Some of these are listed in Figure 5.3. (We will discuss the most recent and perhaps the most significant of these secessions, the formation of the CAW, in more detail.)

Around this time (1970), the CLC passed a resolution establishing Canadian standards of self-government for affiliated Canadian divisions of international unions. These standards were reaffirmed and expanded at the 1974 convention and now include the following five requirements:

1 Election of Canadian officers by Canadians.
2 Policies dealing with national affairs must be determined by the elected Canadian officers and/or members.
3 Canadian elected representatives must have authority to speak for the union in Canada.
4 Where an international union if affiliated to an international trade secretariat, the Canadian section of that union should be affiliated separately to ensure a Canadian presence and voice at the international industry level.
5 International unions must take whatever action is necessary to ensure that the Canadian membership will not be prevented by constitutional requirements or policy decisions from participating in the social, cultural, economic, and political life of the Canadian community.[20]

Since many nationalists within the CLC would like to see even stronger controls placed over the Canadian divisions of international unions, it is likely that there will be further developments in this regard in the future. We will now examine one example of a Canadian secession in closer detail.

United Automobile Workers The secession of the Canadian section of the United Automobile Workers in late 1984 was significant because of the good relations that existed between the Canadian section and the parent union before the split, and also because the Canadian section had enjoyed a substantial amount of autonomy over a long period of time.

The major issue leading up to the split was the alleged interference by the international union in contract negotiations in Canada. In 1984, the international office tried to influence the Canadian section of the union to agree to a contract which was practically a carbon copy of the agreement reached between the parent union in the United States and General Motors. Apparently, the president of the international union threatened to cut off benefits for Canadian workers if they pursued goals which were at variance with the agreement negotiated in the United States.[21] However, the Canadian section has its own bargaining agenda. It refused to

Figure 5.3		Major Union Secessions 1971–1989
Year	International Union	Details
1971	Communication Workers of America (CWA)	A new, fully independent union was formed — The Communication Workers of Canada (CWC). (The union is now called the Communication, Electronic and Electrical Technical and Salaried Workers of Canada.)
1974	National Association of Broadcast Employees and Technicians (NABET)	Maintains a loose multinational structure, but has its own Canadian organizations, constitutions, and elected officers.
1974	United Paperworkers International Union	Formed a fully independent Canadian union (The Canadian Paperworkers Union), but maintained good relations with the international union.
1976	Brotherhood of Railway, Airline, and Steamship Clerks (BRAC)	The new union has a separate constitution, and the three highest Canadian officers are automatically made officers of the international union.
1975	The Teamsters Union	A new Canadian conference was formed within the union, headed by an international vice president and a policy committee that is elected by Canadian members.
1985	United Auto Workers (UAW)	Formed the Canadian Auto Workers Union, a fully independent Canadian union, but maintained good relations with the American union.

bow to the pressure, and finally reached a settlement which differed from the American one in important ways.

The Canadian section had been arguing for some years for parity with its American counterparts. In fact, there was a common agreement between the union and Chrysler for many years which covered plants on both sides of the border. Because the American workers had benefited from cost-of-living allowances based on the American Consumer Price Index (which is calculated somewhat differently from the Canadian Consumer Price Index), greater and more frequent wage increases were won by the American workers. To rectify this disparity, the Canadian workers were given lump-sum payments in ensuing negotiations.

Apart from the demand of the Canadian section that the international union not interfere in Canadian contract negotiations, the only other issue between the two bodies was that all union staff in Canada be responsible solely to the Canadian director.[22] When the 25-member executive board of the international union met to discuss the demands of the Canadian section, only the Canadian director voted pro-Canadian. The executive board of the International Union is reported to have said that compliance with the demands of the Canadian division would destroy the union. It stated that, "by definition, in an international union, the international president's involvement in any set of negotiations cannot be construed as 'interference.'"[23] Since the board could not resolve the issues, a committee was set up to facilitate the orderly and cordial separation of the Canadian section from the international union.

In the end, an amicable settlement was reached whereby the Canadian section obtained $36 million of the $600 million American strike fund. This figure represented about 5% of the strike fund, while the 125,000 Canadian members comprised about 10% of total union membership. However, it was felt that the Canadian and American unions should maintain good relations with one another since there would likely be some informal arrangement between them in future negotiations, and Canadian settlements would still be governed to a large extent by what happened across the border.

In September 1985, the founding convention of the new Canadian union took place in Toronto. The name Canadian Automobile, Aerospace and Agricultural Implement Workers (CAW) was selected for the union, and Bob White was elected union leader. He was to be assisted by a Canadian council of some 300 delegates from local unions across the country. The President of the international union was invited to attend the founding convention but was unable to come. His telegrammed response read: "Although we disagree with your decision to separate, we, of course, respect it. As with workers everywhere, the international union will remain a firm friend and ally of Canadian workers."[24] The new Canadian union negotiated its first settlement that same year with the Chrysler Corporation of Canada. This settlement set a pattern for the international union, which reached its own agreement shortly after the Canadian negotiations.[25]

The CAW break is particularly significant in light of the 1965 Auto Pact between the American and Canadian governments. The Pact rationalized the North American market and the facilities for manufacturing cars in both countries. Some Canadian facilities, for example, make particular models for the entire North American market. It will be interesting to observe how the CAW break affects the future investment patterns of the American headquarters of the "Big Three" automobile companies. Will they continue to produce cars in Canada? There is some concern that American investment in Canadian operations will, in fact, decline.

Advantages and Disadvantages of Autonomy
A study of 29 international unions by two scholars in 1983 revealed some interesting results. For analytical purposes, the authors developed four models to classify the relations between the unions and their Canadian branches: (1) the assimilationist model; (2) the special-status model; (3) the self-governing model; and (4) the sovereignty-association model. Under the assimilationist model, few provisions were made for specifically Canadian issues. The Canadian divisions were treated almost exactly the same way as American divisions. In the special-status model, Canada was designated as a special region, with rights and functions not found in American regions. For example, a vice-president could be elected by Canadians, a Canadian office could be operated by Canadians, policy conferences were organized in this country by Canadians, and union dues were controlled and collected by Canadians. The self-governing model had the same features as the special-status model, but also provided for a separate Canadian constitution and Canadian control over strike funds.[26]

In the sovereignty-association model, formal international ties are maintained but the U.S. headquarters exercises no authority over the Canadian section. Canadians do not pay international dues, but may contribute to an international strike fund, contract for research and other services, and coordinate bargaining strategy with Americans.[27]

The study found that the most common reason for changing the structural links of Canadian branches of international unions was to conform to guidelines established by the CLC conventions of 1970 and 1974. Although most craft unions made some changes, they generally resisted complying fully with the guidelines. However, the Carpenters' Union, a craft union, now has a Canadian organizer and research officer.

What have been the results of greater Canadianization of Canadian sections of international unions?

> Overall, the evidence points to positive results from the shift to special or self-government . . . U.S. interviewees . . . noted that their unions have grown rapidly since the change, negotiate good collective agreements, require less assistance from headquarters, but still participate actively in affairs of the international . . . Canadian officials were also pleased with their new roles.[28]

Constitutional changes are also often accompanied by an increase in resources for Canadian operations. In addition, Canadian autonomy gives the more politically oriented Canadian unions the opportunity to debate social issues such as health insurance plans, topics which most international unions in the United States do not discuss (although there is speculation in many quarters that the free-trade deal between Canada and the United States may bring this issue to the fore).

However, there are some disadvantages to be considered. Greater Canadian autonomy may lessen the ability of Canadians to influence union policies in the United States. This is a particular disadvantage in matters such as restriction of trade. Another major limitation is cost. The 18,000-member Canadian division of BRAC levied a monthly fee of 50 cents per member to pay for a Canadian convention; the Teamsters' International office contributes 20 cents per Canadian member to support their Canadian conference. Some unions, particularly craft unions, see no benefits from greater autonomy. They operate mainly in local labour markets and negotiate their agreements at that level, so international officers play an insignificant

role. Also, the traditions of craft unions, as we pointed out in the previous chapter, tend to be much more conservative than those of industrial unions. Autonomy may become even less feasible under free trade. It remains to be seen if the changing industrial structures in the United States and Canada will draw unions in the two countries closer together in an effort to better protect their members. Autonomy, then, is a mixed blessing to Canadian workers. Full and informed debate should take place before Canadian branches of international unions rush into greater autonomy for the workers they represent.

Union Consolidation

A study by G.N. Chaison in the late seventies showed that there had been an overall increase of 38 unions in Canada between 1956 and 1977. Despite mergers, the number of national unions increased while the number of international unions decreased substantially.[29] Many of the "new" unions existed previously as consultative bodies in the public sector, but could not be included in union statistics until the introduction of collective bargaining in the federal and provincial sectors in 1967 and subsequently. Part of the growth in the number of unions can be attributed to the inclusion of these unions in the official statistics.

Given this tendency toward diversity in Canadian unions many commentators have suggested that efforts be made to consolidate unions in Canada. J. Crispo has made a case for consolidation on two grounds: (1) because union fragmentation is reducing the effectiveness of collective bargaining; and (2) because a better structure would be needed in the event that government begins seriously to consider organized labour's advocacy of national planning.[30] Another reason to reduce the number of unions in Canada is that small unions have neither the finances nor the personnel to serve their local unions adequately in contract negotiations, grievance handling, research, and education. While unions in the public and parapublic sector have bargained quite success-

Parrot's union is the winner in postal vote

BY LORNE SLOTNICK
The Globe and Mail

OTTAWA

Jean-Claude Parrot's tough-as-nails Canadian Union of Postal Workers triumphed last night by a narrow margin in a winner-take-all vote for the right to represent 46,000 employees of Canada Post.

The result means that CUPW will represent three-quarters of the federal agency's unionized work force, including mail sorters, wicket clerks, letter carriers, drivers and technicians. The result also means the death of the 21,000-strong Letter Carriers Union of Canada.

Final results showed CUPW with 20,281 or 51.1 per cent of the vote to LCUC's 19,380 or 48.8 per cent. There were 120 spoiled ballots. The vote and the count were conducted by the Canada Labor Relations Board.

A joyous Mr. Parrot, flanked by his wife and a throng of cheering supporters, emerged after hearing the result to declare that "for Canada Post there is a clear message now that they're going to have to deal properly with CUPW, not the way they have dealt with us in the past year."

He denied that the union he now heads is deeply divided, saying the big task is to draw everyone into the preparations for the next round of bargaining later this year. "It will be easy for the union if we do our job properly to unite all the workers," he said.

A shaken president of the LCUC, Robert McGarry, 55, said that there was no room for two leaders of postal workers, and that he would be heading back to his job as a letter carrier. As union president, he earned $61,500 a year.

"The democratic process has been completed," Mr. McGarry said, adding that workers who supported his union will now become involved in CUPW, attending meetings and changing things they do not like.

The vote means an immediate doubling in size for CUPW. It also ensures that the strike weapon, weakened recently by Canada Post's willingness to use replacement workers, is again a powerful tool.

But Harold Dunstan, general manager of labor relations for Canada Post, said last night that he is not thinking about strikes but about how the consolidation of unions can help improve service by ensuring that the postal service is not constantly on the brink of a strike.

"We're only going to have one round of negotiations; the issues are going to be serious and we're going to have to be zeroing in on those issues with a lot more attention than we've ever done before," said Mr. Dunstan, who congratulated Mr. Parrot on his victory.

The result is a sweet, if narrow, victory for Mr. Parrot's style of confrontational unionism, which has taken CUPW members into national strikes four times in the past 14 years.

It also will increase CUPW's clout in the labor movement, where the union has acted as a focal point for labor's left wing.

The mail ballot was conducted in November in the wake of a decision by the labor board consolidating bargaining units at Canada Post.

The new "operational unit" will include the 23,000 CUPW members, 21,000 LCUC members and smaller groups from the Public Service Alliance of Canada and the International Brotherhood of Electrical Workers.

The other three bargaining units carved out by the board comprise rural postmasters, low-level supervisory staff, and administrative employees. No votes have yet been held for those groups.

The board ruling had initially been requested by Canada Post, which was worried that frequent strikes and threats of strikes resulting from a fragmented bargaining structure was hurting business. CUPW, which has long supported the goal of one union for postal workers, supported the decision, but LCUC denounced it.

The two unions have long been adversaries, but tried to reach a merger agreement after the board decision. A tentative deal fell apart in November, amid accusations from both sides.

It was clear though that the deal was scuttled by the LCUC, which evidently felt it could win a vote easily. Top leaders of the union were predicting a 60 per cent margin, but last night they admitted they had lost their gamble.

After the merger deal collapsed, a bitter campaign ensued, with CUPW suggesting LCUC was a weak-kneed and unsophisticated group led by leaders with fat salaries, and LCUC portraying CUPW as a strike-happy union led by a fanatic.

The *Globe and Mail*, Jan 18, 1989, pp. A1,A2.

fully on their own, Chaison points out that "fewer and larger unions could still provide some advantages, notably 'enhanced lobbying activity on the national level, increased organizing and strike funds, and the ability to maintain large, full-time professional staffs for research, bargaining, and organizing.'"[31]

More recently, the process of union consolidation has been stepped up. In February 1988 the Canada Labour Relations Board (CLRB) ordered a major restructuring of the bargaining units in the Canadian post office. As a result, the eight unions operating in Canada Post were merged into four bargaining units.

The CLRB ruling may turn out to be a precedent for other sectors of Canadian industry. For example, unions in Canada's railways may also be required to merge. The workers at CN, CP, and Via Rail are represented by 14 unions, each of which guards its jurisdiction jealously. Railway union leaders have agreed that there should be some consolidation of these unions. Via Rail has already applied to the CLRB to have its bargaining units consolidated, and observers expect that CN and CP may follow suit.[32] If they do, the next logical step would be to consolidate the airline industry.

Women in Unions

Of increasing importance in coming years will be the growing proportion of women in the unionized workforce. As Table 5.4 indicates, women made up 36.4% of all union members in Canada in 1986 as compared with 17% in 1966. This substantial increase is due to the unionization of the public and parapublic sectors in recent years.

Unions must now redefine some of their policies and programs to accommodate the needs of working women. For example, more and more women are becoming aware of the appropriateness of the four-day work week to their lifestyles. Forty hours spread over four days, instead of the traditional five, allows women who have become the primary wage earners for their families three uninterrupted days per week to manage households, relation-

Table 5.4	Women Union Members as a Percentage of Total Union Membership 1966–1986

	Number of women members	% of all members
1966	322,980	17.0
1967	407,181	19.8
1968	438,543	20.4
1969	469,235	21.2
1970	513,203	22.6
1971	558,138	23.5
1972	575,584	24.2
1973	635,861	24.6
1974	676,939	25.2
1975	711,102	26.0
1976	750,637	27.0
1977	782,282	27.7
1978	835,263	28.7
1979	890,365	29.3
1980	932,883	30.2
1981	979,862	31.0
1982	985,376	32.3
1983	1,179,000	34.8
1984	1,219,100	35.4
1985	1,264,000	36.2
1986	1,310,000	36.4

Source: Statistics Canada, *Annual Report of the Minister of Supply and Services Canada under the Corporations and Labour Unions Returns Act — Part 11 — Labour Unions,* Catalogue No. 71–202 (Ottawa: Supply and Services Canada), August 1984, p. 41 for the years 1962–1982; January 1987, p. 48 for the years 1983–1984; and December 1988, p. 31 for the years 1985–1986. Reproduced by permission of the Minister of Supply and Services Canada.

ships with their children, and the stress of conducting two careers — one inside and one outside the home. Since over 44% of the labour force in Canada are women, these considerations have gained considerable weight. In some hospitals, nurses are already on four-day work schedules. Paid maternity benefits have also become a major collective bargaining issue, especially since the 1981 agreement between the federal government and the Canadian Union of Postal Workers, which included 17 weeks of paid maternity leave.

Women are also beginning to take on leading roles in the union movement. A study done for the Canadian Advisory Council on the Status of Women concluded that in 1976, 42.6% of women trade unionists were in unions where women constituted over half the total membership in contrast to 32% in 1962. Between 1970 and 1975 women represented less than 10% of people serving on trade union executive boards. By 1977, women constituted 28.6% of union membership and accounted for 16.7% of union executives.[33] However this level of representation is still out of proportion with the 36.4% of the total trade union membership that is female.

Recently, many sectors of the Canadian trade union movement have actively encouraged women to take part in executive positions. The Ontario Federation of Labour, at its annual convention in 1983, created five vice-presidential posts for women, increasing the number of vice presidents from 16 to 21. Prior to this increase, there had been only one woman among the 16 vice-presidents.[34] At its 15th constitutional convention in Montreal in the spring of 1984, the CLC extended the number of vice-presidents at large from 10 to 14, six of whom must be women.[35] Two years later, in May 1986, former CLC Secretary-Treasurer Shirley Carr replaced Dennis McDermott as president of the CLC, thus becoming the first woman to occupy that position.[36]

Shirley Carr has had a long career in unions. She started in the public sector as a member of CUPE and was active in a tripartite committee of government, management, and union officials to establish the Labour Market and Productivity Centre in 1983. Generally considered more congenial than McDermott, Carr has worked hard to improve relations between the CLC and the federal government in recent years. In 1988, she was a member of a management-union joint committee that studied the effect that free trade might have on employment.

A women's bureau exists now in the CLC, as well as a special publishing apparatus to encourage women to participate in the decision-making process. The participation of women in unions will continue to dominate much of the thinking in all ranks of the Canadian labour movement in the immediate future.

The Governance of Unions

The internal governing of trade unions is complex, and the most that we can do here is to give a very brief discussion of the subject. The topics we will discuss are: (1) the union convention; (2) the union constitution and the day-to-day running of a union; (3) the tenure and turnover of union officers; (4) democracy in unions; (5) membership control within unions; and (6) due process and remedial procedures.

Union Conventions

Union conventions, which are usually held at regular intervals ranging from one to five years, are the supreme governing bodies of unions. Their major functions include the election of union officials and the determination of the policies that the union will follow. Officers are usually elected by majority vote at conventions, although some unions elect officers by a referendum vote. However, policies which are adopted at one convention may be modified at subsequent conventions, and new policies may be added. Hence, policy formulation and changes are dynamic features of union conventions.

Conventions are attended by the senior officers of the union, delegates from intermediate bodies, and representatives of local unions. However, the senior officers have a great deal of control over the convention, and over most matters which come before it. Senior officers also control the appointment of members to the various committees which deal with these matters. One study conducted in the United States found that "in 60 of the 70 unions surveyed the major committees at conventions [were] dominated by the union's officialdom. They [were] selected by the president in 49 unions, by the executive board in 11 other unions."[37]

Most union conventions are characterized by voting on resolutions that come from local unions or union executives prior to the convention. Delegates from local unions sometimes receive instructions from members on how they should vote, or they may go to the conventions with no such mandate. In the latter case, the delegates are often subject to a great deal of pressure from national officers on how to vote during the convention itself. It has been observed that: "delegates from large locals [are] likely to submit resolutions; have delegates in attendance; and view the convention as important in the determination of policy."[38]

A study of the convention of one large Canadian union showed that there was little debate over resolutions presented to the delegates. This was partly due to events which occurred before the convention and partly due to the running of the convention itself. Pre-convention factors which were found to limit the vitality of the convention included: (1) not knowing the location to which resolutions should be sent; (2) the role of the union executive in screening and compiling the resolutions; and (3) the composition of convention committees. Factors that hampered debate within the convention itself included: (1) lack of information on resolutions; (2) instructions or pressure on how to vote; and (3) delegates' perception that they were not free agents. These factors all acted as impediments to democratic decision making.[39] Clearly, unions must make a greater effort to ensure that delegates to conventions are able to play a more meaningful role.

Constitutions and Day-to-Day Running of Unions

Usually, national or international union constitutions make provisions for the election of a president, one or more vice-presidents, and a secretary-treasurer. These officials form the union executive, which is responsible for looking after the day-to-day running of the union. There may also be provision for the election of vice-presidents to intermediate bodies, such as the various districts of international unions, including Canadian districts.

In addition to these officers, a board is usually elected at the convention to advise the exec-

utive officers on policy matters between conventions. Meetings of these bodies are held three or four times a year. Boards usually have the constitutional authority to place under trusteeship local unions whose management is suspect. In such cases local democracy is at least temporarily suspended until an investigation clears matters up. A trustee is appointed by the national office, and may include someone from that office or a local person whom the administration deems trustworthy. The constitutions of some international and national unions include suggestions for local union constitutions and by-laws.[40]

The elected officials of national and international unions have the authority to hire a staff of professionals to deal with matters such as research, education, legislation, and publicity. These appointed staff members assist not only the officers at the national level, but regional representatives and local unions. National and international unions have full-time elected officers and full-time staff members. These staff members owe their appointments to their national or international presidents, and frequently become part of the political machinery of these elected officials.

Local unions also have constitutions and by-laws to guide local officers in their day-to-day activities. Officers are elected by the local membership. Dues are collected at the local level, and per capita contributions are made to the headquarters of the national or international union and to other bodies with which the local may be affiliated, such as provincial federations of labour and local labour councils. The most important qualification for election to the leadership of a national or international union is having worked one's way up through the ranks. Having worked on the shop-floor level and having had the experience of being a shop steward are good credentials with which to enter the running for union leadership.

Union Leaders

Union leaders are unlike the managers of businesses. While the latter move across companies and industries, union leaders normally do not. In addition, little training is available to union leaders. The Labour College of Canada is one of the few sources of union management training. Each summer, a number of union members are selected by local unions to attend the Labour College. Some unions also have in-house training programs for their members. These in-house programs, however, do not involve training in management techniques.

A good deal of a union leaders' time is spent putting out brush fires. According to D.C. Bok and J.T. Dunlop, "the key problem in union government is how to encourage innovation, a longer view of the union's role and interests, and greater effectiveness in carrying out the policies and programs of the organization."[41] Union leaders also spend a good deal of their time resolving disputes and trying to maintain cohesion among different factions within their unions, assisting with the negotiation of collective agreements, handling grievances, and taking part in arbitration proceedings. They may also be active in community affairs and in community agencies.

Election and Tenure of Union Officers

The election of union officers takes place much more frequently at the local level than at the national or international levels. There is more interaction among members at the local level, and if an incumbent official is perceived to be doing a poor job, it is easy for an ambitious individual to run against him or her in local elections. Often, however, challengers make extravagant promises and cannot deliver them — sometimes a disadvantage to such individuals when they seek higher union office.

Much of the literature on union elections at the national or international levels has noted a tendency for union leaders to perpetuate their stay in office because of their ability to control the channels of communication. Thus, union leaders can develop and maintain prestigious national images which give them an advantage over their opponents. "Perhaps more important, the leader can maintain a monopoly over

the political skills within the organization and is thus able to build an effective political machine. This combination of power, prestige, and skill is said to enable the union president to perpetuate his term of office."[42]

There have been several empirical studies of the turnover among presidents of strictly Canadian unions. A study by G.N. Chaison and J.B. Rose covering the period from 1945 to 1972 concluded that turnover was attributable to union politics in only 14.1% of the cases. The greatest proportion of these turnovers were attributed to the failure of governing bodies to nominate the incumbent for further office. Slightly over 30% of the turnovers were not political in nature. They resulted from age, health, the onerous nature of the position, death in office, and union bars against successive years in office. A serious limitation of this study was that, in over half of the cases, the reasons for retiring were uncertain. Close to a third of the incumbents either retired or refused to run for office without giving reasons. About 20% changed jobs.[43]

Another study by Chaison and Rose indicated that union growth increased the likelihood of incumbents remaining in office, presumably because of their increased status, compensation, and opportunities to sharpen political skills. Also, presidents of older and larger unions tended to stay in office longer than presidents of younger and smaller unions. These findings led the authors to suggest that:

> there may be a relationship between presidential turnover and stages of union growth. The early formative years for unions would be marked by relatively unstable leadership, but as unions mature ... there is a more centralized organizational structure and reduced membership control of the governing process. Turnover rates decline, and there is an increase in the tenure of presidents.[44]

Despite these figures, union leadership changes frequently, particularly in national unions. During the period from 1963 to 1972, nearly 80% of Canadian national unions experienced at least one presidential change. Similarly, high turnover rates were found in international unions that had their headquarters in the United States. In both countries, reasons for leaving office rarely included election defeat.[45]

Democracy in Unions

S. Muthuchidambaram claims that so much has been written on the concept of union democracy, that it "is fair to say that anybody writing on 'Union Democracy' may have almost nothing 'original' to contribute."[46] My objective in this section is not to develop "something original" but rather to summarize briefly some of the major aspects of democracy or its opposite — according to Will Herberg — bureaucracy. Herberg stated in a classic piece of institutional analysis that trade unions in the United States (and probably also in Canada) constitute a paradox, inasmuch as they have dual natures:

> A modern labour union is, at one and the same time: (1) a businesslike service organization, operating a variety of agencies under a complicated system of industrial relations; (2) an expression and vehicle of the historical movement of the submerged laboring masses for social recognition and democratic self-expression.[47]

According to Herberg's analysis, unions require efficient, bureaucratic administrations, very much like those of banks or insurance companies, to fulfill their business and service functions. But unions also embody a crusading spirit of reform, and the democratic self-expression of their members is the very essence of this crusade. Unions, thus, are inherently in conflict with themselves.

Analysts and practitioners have been grappling with the whole problem of effective unionism for purposes of collective bargaining while trying, at the same time, to maximize the control of members over the organizations which the members themselves create. The CLC and the AFL-CIO both have codes which set out a whole array of ethical practices aimed at optimizing the control workers have over their organizations. These codes of ethical practices also ensure that the organizations are run honestly and democratically, and that union leaders remain responsible to rank-and-file members.

Membership Control

Many observers have noted that attendance at union meetings generally runs between 10% and 15%. Even such critical issues as contract ratification and voting for union officers may bring out only a bare majority.[48] If union leaders are adept enough to get elected, they are probably adept enough, at least most of the time, to know whether a proposed settlement can be sold to the membership. If we compare the behaviour of workers as union members and as citizens, we may find that there are few differences as far as active involvement in governmental processes is concerned.

When the rights of union officers or members are perceived to be seriously jeopardized, however, all-out member participation can be expected. Those who remember the upheaval in Quebec during the winter of 1982, when the provincial government rolled back the wages of workers in the public and parapublic sectors, realize that when workers' rights are threatened by external forces, workers will vote with their feet on the picket line. As well, the Solidarity Coalition in British Columbia during the summer of 1983 saw provincial restraints bring the province close to the brink of a general strike.

In summary, it seems that as long as things are going well, union members are content to delegate decision making to the active unionists. However, if serious and contentious matters are perceived to arise internally, rank-and-file members will probably take appropriate action to protect their interests and those of their fellow members. During the summer of 1989, the negotiating team for the B.C. nurses reached an agreement with hospital management which would have ended the nurses' strike action. However, members of the union refused to ratify the agreement, which many saw as inadequate. Some nurses even called for the resignation of their negotiating team. *The more a union member perceives his or her interests to be affected by the action of a union leader, the more that union member will participate in union business*. The converse is also true.

Due Process and Remedies

Most unions have disciplinary clauses in their constitutions. Penalties include cancellation of union membership and, depending on the type of union security clause, loss of employment. Some clauses are very specific, while others are very vague and lend themselves to various interpretations. For example, clauses such as "Engaging in any activity or course of conduct contrary or detrimental to the welfare or best interests of the Association" and "Wilfully circulating false or defamatory statements or reports concerning members of the Association" are examples of vague clauses on which disciplinary action is often taken. Although there is great variation in the ways in which such behaviour is tried, action is often initially taken at the local level, with the committee investigating the case acting as both judge and jury.

When there are allegations that union leaders or members have violated the trust of their position, there is often great concern that justice be done and that members have their say. For example, during the winter of 1989 the president and financial secretary of a local of the United Steelworkers Union were found guilty of gross financial malpractice by a three-member committee in connection with expenses charged to the local for attending a union convention in Las Vegas. The three-member committee voted that the two officials be barred from office for the remainder of their three-year term. The local's vice president recommended to the membership that a secret ballot be held. While the president of the local suggested that the president of the international union and the Canadian director of the union were against him because of his pro free-trade stance, he accepted the legitimacy of a secret membership vote. He is quoted as saying, "the members voted me into office by secret ballot,

and if they want to remove me, it should be done the same way."[49]

A person found guilty of an offence at the local level may appeal the case to the executive board of the union. If satisfaction is not obtained at that level, the case may go before a convention. At least two facts bring into question the effectiveness of this procedure. First, because of its size and number of activities, a convention is hardly an appropriate forum in which to pass important judgements. Second, a convention may be several years down the road — a long time to wait for a hearing. Even worse, the courts usually will not hear such cases until internal union processes have been exhausted.

In order to hasten the appeals procedures and to provide for a fair hearing, the UAW has a Public Review Board composed entirely of independent outside persons. A member who has been disciplined by a trial committee of his or her own local can appeal to the local union. If still dissatisfied, the member can first appeal within 30 days to the international executive board, and then to either the convention or the Public Review Board. Only cases involving the processing of grievances may, under some circumstances, come before both bodies. To ensure promptness, appeals must again be filed within 30 days. All parties have the right to counsel, and the Board must make a public report every year.[50]

When the UAW created the Public Review Board, it was assumed that many other unions would do the same. However, the Upholsterers Union is still the only other union with an independent review board.[51] One reason other unions did not follow suit was the enactment in 1959 of the *Landrum-Griffin Act,* which imposed very substantial controls on the internal operations of American unions. The Act imposed a fiduciary responsibility on persons handling union funds, set conditions for establishing and maintaining trusteeships over local unions, gave members a greater degree of control over their own activities, and allowed candidates seeking to replace incumbent officials greater publicity in union newspapers and an appeal to the Secretary of Labour for a judicial recount if there is suspicion that union elections have been rigged. A number of recounts have in fact occurred, and incumbents first declared winners have finished as losers. A 1981 assessment by an American writer of the effects of the Landrum-Griffin Act on internal union affairs concluded that:

> By and large, the provisions of the Landrum-Griffin Act respecting internal union affairs have significantly advanced the cause of union democracy while doing little, if any, damage to the structure of organized labour.[52]

No comprehensive charter of rights exists for Canadian union members, although both corporations and unions are required to submit reports annually to the Minister of Supply and Services under the Corporations and Labour Unions Returns Act. Some parts of the information are treated as confidential while other parts are published separately and on an aggregate basis for both unions and corporations annually. Some of the matters on which unions are required to report include: the name of the union, its address, the provisions of its constitution, the names and addresses of each officer, the nationality or citizenship of each officer and employee of the union resident in Canada, the name and address of each local union, the name of each local union under a trusteeship imposed by the union, the date on which the trusteeship was imposed and the reasons therefore, the name of each employer with whom the union has a collective agreement, the number of male and female members, and financial statements.[53] The annual reports contain highly aggregate data, and a special supplement gives the names of all unions filing returns. However, workers are not given any protection regarding the operation of a union under the authority of the Act.

Conclusion

Given the fluid state of the Canadian labour movement at the present time, any attempts to predict what will happen in the future may have little value. Certain issues, however, such as the decline of our economy and the nationalistic orientations of certain Canadian unions, will doubtless have a profound effect on the labour movement. In particular, these may create demands on the CLC to interface effectively with government, especially at the federal level, in order to respond to the anxieties and aspirations of Canadian labour. How strong these demands will be and how effectively the CLC will respond to them is a subject for speculation, particularly as events under the free-trade deal between Canada and the United States unfold.

Questions

1 Discuss in detail the composition of the Canadian labour movement today.

2 Discuss the structure and functions of the various components of the CLC.

3 Do you think that unions among professionals, such as teachers, nurses, and engineers, will join the mainstream of the Canadian labour movement? Elaborate.

4 A union may be defined either as a voluntary association created by workers to improve their working conditions or as a power-accumulating and power-using entity concerned mainly with ensuring its own continued institutional existence. Do you see any major contradictions between these two definitions? Explain.

5 How do you assess the alignment of the CLC with the New Democratic Party? Has the NDP done better in federal elections since it has received the full backing of the CLC? What conclusions can be drawn regarding the voting pattern of trade-unionists?

6 If you were an advisor to the President of the CLC, what strategy would you advise her to use in dealing with the federal government?

7 What is your prediction regarding future rela-tions between the CLC and the federal govern-ment? Elaborate.

8 From a philosophical point of view, are there any differences in the unions operating in the public sector and those operating in the private sector? How do you explain the differences, if they exist?

9 Are union coalitions effective in your province when compared to the power of big business and big government? Elaborate.

Notes

1 Bureau of Labour Information, Labour Canada, *Directory of Labour Organizations in Canada 1988* (Ottawa: Supply and Services Canada, 1988), p. 232.

2 V. Galt, "Unions Cool to Caccia's Request for Input in Planning by Labour," *Globe and Mail* (January 9, 1982), p. B3.

3 Canada Labour Relations Board, *58 di* (Ottawa: Supply and Services Canada, 1986), pp. 94-238.

4 Bureau of Labour Information, Labour Canada, *Directory of Labour Organizations in Canada 1988* (Ottawa: Supply and Services Canada, 1988), p. 232.

5 L. Slotnick, "OFL Recommends Training Tax to Aid Employees Hurt by Pact," *Globe and Mail* (January 26, 1989), p. A11.

6 "That's Not Democracy, Mr. Buchanan," *Canadian Labour* (January 18, 1980), p. 11.

7 J. O'Hara, "British Columbia on the Edge," *Macleans* (November 7, 1983), p. 22.

8 I. Mulgrew, "Bennett Rules: Labour Licks Wounds," *Globe and Mail* (November 1, 1984).

9 Ibid.

10 C. Mitchell, "Bill's Proclaiming Delayed," *Winnipeg Free Press* (July 3, 1987), p. 12.

11 Labour Canada, *Directory of Labour Organizations 1988*, p. 233.

12 Labour Canada, *Directory of Labour Organizations 1988*, p. 231.

13 One such case did occur in the mid-1960s, when the International Typographical Union (ITU) refused to ratify a collective agreement negot-iated by the three major newspapers in Toronto and the locals of the ITU. The ITU executive felt that certain provisions concerning the introduc-tion of new technology might establish a dan-gerous precedent for negotiations elsewhere in North America. The members eventually with-drew their acceptance of the agreement.

14 Labour Canada, *Directory of Labour Organizations 1988*, p. 231.

15 Canadian Labour Congress, "How Unions Work," No. 2, Notes on Unions (Ottawa: n.d.). The Canadian Labour Congress has published a series of Notes on Unions. No. 2 of the series, "How Unions Work," gives a very good descrip-tion of how a union organizes, acquires its bar-gaining rights, and petitions the employer to negotiate with it. This article also includes a brief description of the negotiation process and the role that third parties may play in helping the two sides reach a collective agreement. A free copy of the Notes is available from the CLC, 2841 Riverside Drive, Ottawa K1V 8X7.

16 Economics and Research Branch, Canada Department of Labour, *International Unions and the Canadian Trade Union Movement* (Ottawa: March 1956).

17 Statistics Canada, *Annual Report of the Minister of Supply and Services Canada Under the Corporations and Labour Returns Act* (Ottawa: Supply and Services Canada, July 1980), pp. 16, 69; "CALURA, Inaccurate, Incomplete, Imprecise," *Canadian Labour* (November/December, 1972), pp. 6-9.

18 R.J. Adams, "Canada-U.S. Labour Link Under Stress," Vol. 15, No. 3, *Industrial Relations* (Octo-ber 1976), pp. 295-312; and John Crispo, *International Unionism* (Toronto: McGraw-Hill, 1967), p. 327.

19 Labour Canada, *Directory of Labour Organizations 1988*, p. 150.

20 Canadian Labour Congress, "Canadian Standards of Self-Government," Addendum, *CLC Constitution*, pp. 48-49.

21 L. Slotnick, "Canadian UAW Splits from Parent Union," *Globe and Mail* (December 11, 1984), p. 2.

22 Ibid., p. 1.

23 Ibid.

24 L. Slotnick, "All-Canadian UAW Opens New Chapter in History of Labour," *Globe and Mail* (September 5, 1985), p. 18.

25 W. List, "UAW-Canada, Chrysler Pact Shows Canadians Can Cut It," *Globe and Mail* (October 28, 1985), p. B4.

26 M. Thompson and A.A. Blum, "International Unionism in Canada: The Move to Local Control," Vol. 22, No. 1, *Industrial Relations* (Winter 1983), pp. 73–74.

27 Ibid., p. 74.

28 Ibid., p. 83.

29 G.N. Chaison, "Union Mergers and International Unions in Canada," Vol. 34, No. 4, *Relations Industrielles/Industrial Relations* (1979), p. 773.

30 Crispo, *International Unionism*, p. 171.

31 G.N. Chaison, "Unions: Growth, Structure, and Internal Dynamics," *Union-Management Relations in Canada*, eds. J. Anderson and M. Gunderson (Don Mills: Addison-Wesley, 1982), p. 162.

32 L. Slotnick, "Canada's Merger-Shy Rail Unions May Get Shove from Labour Board," *Globe and Mail* (January 23, 1989), pp. A1 and A5.

33 J. White, *Women and Unions* (Ottawa: Supply and Services Canada, April 1980), pp. 22-23.

34 W. List, "Fight for Women's Equality Gains Momentum in Unions," *Globe and Mail* (December 5, 1983), p. B4.

35 Ibid.

36 L. Slotnick, "Carr Picked for Top Job on CLC Executive Slate," *Globe and Mail* (December 12, 1985), p. A24.

37 W.L. Ginsberg, "Review of Literature on Union Growth, Government and Structure — 1955-1969," Vol. 1, Industrial Relations Research Association Series, *A Review of Industrial Relations Research*, eds. W.L. Ginsberg et al. (Madison, Wis.: IRRA, 1970), p. 241.

38 J.C. Anderson, "The Union Convention: An Examination of Limitations on Democratic Decision Making," Vol. 32, No. 3, *Relations Industrielles/Industrial Relations* (1977), p. 382.

39 Ibid., pp. 395-96.

40 American Federation of Labour-Congress of Industrial Organization, *International Constitution of the United Packinghouse, Food and Allied Workers* (May 1962).

41 D.C. Bok and J.T. Dunlop, *Labour and the American Community* (New York: Simon and Schuster, 1970), p. 90.

42 G.N. Chaison and J.B. Rose, "Turnover Among Presidents of Canadian National Unions," Vol. 16, No. 2, *Industrial Relations* (May 1977), pp. 199-200.

43 Ibid., p. 202.

44 Quoted in Chaison, "Unions: Growth," p. 165.

45 Ibid.

46 S. Muthuchidambaram, "Democracy as a Goal of Union Organization: An Interpretation of the United States Experience," Vol. 24, No. 3, *Relations Industrielles/Industrial Relations* (1969), p. 579.

47 W. Herberg, "Bureaucracy and Democracy in Labour Unions," *Readings in Labour Economics and Labour Relations*, Rev. ed., ed. R.L. Rowan (Homewood Ill.: Richard D. Irwin, 1972), p. 233.

48 M. Estey, *The Unions: Structure, Development and Management* (New York: Harcourt, Brace & World, 1967), p. 49.

49 K. Sepkowski, "Steelworkers Set Vote on Officials' Expulsion Urged by Union Panel," *Globe and Mail* (March 24, 1989), p. A17.

50 United Auto Workers, *A More Perfect Union: The UAW Public Review Board* (Detroit: Solidarity House, UAW Publications, n.d.). This booklet includes the AFL-CIO Code of Ethical Practices as well as the UAW's resolution on ethical practices adopted by the 16th Constitutional Convention on April 8, 1957.

51 Ginsburg, "Review of Literature on Union Growth," p. 239.

52 T.J. St. Antoine, "The Role of Law," *U.S. Industrial Relations 1950-1980: A Critical Assessment*, eds. J. Stieber, R.B. McKersie, and D.Q. Mills (Madison, Wis.: Industrial Relations Research Association Series, 1981), p. 191.

53 *Corporations and Labour Unions Returns Act*, R.S., C.31 with amendments to March 22, 1988.

Peter Redman, *The Financial Post*

6

Legislation Governing Industrial Relations in the Private Sector

Introduction

Canada is a federal state with the central government exercising jurisdiction over only about 10% of the labour force and the ten provinces claiming the remaining 90%. From a legal perspective, Canada's industrial relations system is thus the most decentralized in the world. (For a discussion of the historical development of provincial powers, and a summary of the federal and provincial jurisdictions set forth in the Constitution, see pages 35 to 36.) As a result, parties

in the Canadian system, and especially those in the private sector who operate in more than one province, find themselves confronted with a maze of legislative provisions and with administrative machinery that varies greatly from one jurisdiction to another.

In this chapter, we will examine some of the more important developments in federal legislation governing labour-management relations. We will then turn to a more detailed analysis of current legislative provisions, both federal and provincial.

The Development of Private-Sector Legislation

The following is an overview of important federal legislation dealing with labour relations. A brief chronology of the statutes discussed here is presented in Figure 6.1, for quick reference.

Early Legislation

Before getting into a detailed analysis of the *current* legislative provisions governing labour-management relations, we should briefly examine some of the more important legislation which has had a significant impact on trade unions and labour-management relations generally. (This section will deal only with the federal legislation. Readers may refer to other sources for information on developments in the provinces.)[1]

The first major Canadian statutes in the area of industrial relations were the Trade Unions Act and the Criminal Law Amendment Act, both of which were passed by Parliament in 1872 following a strike of printers in Toronto. These laws were modelled after similar laws which had been passed in Great Britain a year earlier. The Trade Unions Act established "that the purposes of a trade union were not unlawful merely because they were in restraint of trade" and the Criminal Law Amendment Act permitted peaceful picketing.[2] Although these early statutes permitted workers to unionize, they did not require employers to recognize unions as exclusive bargaining agents for groups of workers, and they were legally free to punish workers for belonging to trade unions. It took a 1939 amendment to the Criminal Code to establish the principle that employers should not be

Figure 6.1	A Chronology of Important Federal Statutes
1872	The Trade Unions Act and the Criminal Law Amendment Act freed unions from charges of criminal conspiracy.
1900	The Conciliation Act provided for the appointment of conciliation boards, but compliance was voluntary.
1903	The Railway Labour Disputes Act applied only to railways.
1907	The Industrial Disputes Investigation Act (IDI Act) required disputing parties to appear before a conciliation board, and prohibited strikes or lockouts until the board handed down its report.
1925	The Snider case limited federal jurisdiction to a few national industries and services.
1944	The Wartime Labour Relations Regulations (P.C. 1003) contained many features of the American Wagner Act and the compulsory conciliation features of the IDI Act.
1948	The Industrial Relations and Disputes Investigation Act (IRDI Act) applied to only about 10% of the labour force. Its provisions were similar to those of P.C. 1003. The ten provinces acquired jurisdiction over the remaining 90% of the labour force.
1972	Part V of the Canada Labour Code — Industrial Relations — replaced the IRDI Act at the federal level.*

*In 1988, Bill C-94 (Revised Statutes of Canada, 1985 Act) redesignated Part V — Industrial Relations — as Part I — Industrial Relations. The most notable difference is that the provisions of the Code have been renumbered.

permitted to take away workers' rights to unionize.[3]

Another important development was the Conciliation Act of 1900 which authorized the Minister of Labour to appoint conciliation boards to aid in the settlement of disputes when requested to do so by employers or unions or both. The use of conciliation remained voluntary, however. The first compulsory conciliation legislation was the Railway Labour Disputes Act of 1903, which was passed by the federal government after a strike on the Canadian Pacific Railway. As the title suggests, it covered only railway transportation. It provided for a three-person board of conciliation, and was constituted in the now familiar Canadian pattern whereby the employer appoints one nominee jointly select a third person as chair. Strikes and lockouts were prohibited until the board's report was handed down. This law was used infrequently, and in 1906 the Conciliation Act of 1900 and the Railway Labour Disputes Act of 1903 were combined to form the Conciliation and Labour Act. (While this law still remains on the books, it is no longer used.) It provided for a three-person board of conciliation, and was constituted in the now familiar Canadian pattern whereby the employer appoints one nominee, the union a second, and the two nominees jointly select a third person as chair. Strikes and lockouts were prohibited until the board's report was handed down.

The compulsory element in labour-management relations was established more firmly by the Industrial Disputes Investigation (IDI) Act of 1907, which was passed following a major coal strike in Lethbridge, Alberta in 1906.[4] While the term *public utility* was not explained in the statute, the term *employer* was defined in such a way as to make it apply to local works and undertakings:

Any person, company or corporation employing ten or more persons and owning or operating any mining property, agency of transportation or communication, or public service utility, including . . . railways, whether operated by steam, electricity or other motive power, steamships, telegraph and telephone lines, gas, electric light, water and power works.

By a 1920 amendment, the following was added to section 2(c):

Or any number of such persons, companies or corporations acting together, or who in the opinion of the Minister have interests in common.

The major objective of the IDI Act was that parties subject to its provisions had to submit outstanding disputes to a tripartite conciliation board for investigation and recommendations *before* a strike or lockout could become legal. The Act was also important in that it gave the federal government broad jurisdiction over labour relations in mining and public utilities, whether national or local. It was equally significant that a 1920 amendment extended its application to multi-employer bargaining, either on a provincial or national basis. If the Act had not eventually been challenged and overturned by judicial decision, this provision, along with others making the Act available to any trade or industry by joint agreement of both sides, would have enabled the parties involved in any national set of negotiations to establish one conciliation board to deal with their disputes.

Following the outbreak of World War I, Parliament was called into a special session. One of the resulting laws was the War Measures Act of 1914 which authorized the federal government to take whatever steps were necessary for the security, defence, peace, order, and welfare of Canada. Under the authority of this law, the IDI Act was amended in 1918 to bring "industries essential to the war effort" under its provisions. A large number of Orders-in-Council were also enacted under the authority of the War Measures Act during World War II. The Orders-in-Council broadened the jurisdiction of the federal government.

In the 1920s, two cases arose which challenged the constitutionality of the IDI Act; both involved the application of the Act to local public utilities.[5] While in the first case, which was initiated by the Montreal Street Railway Company, the statute was upheld, the second case ultimately led to the Act being declared unconstitutional. The case at issue was the now famous *Toronto Electric Power Commissioners* v. *Snider et al* (hereafter referred to as the Snider case). The Snider case arose out of the refusal of the Toronto Electric Power Commission to recognize the authority of a conciliation board appointed to deal with a dispute between the Commission and its workers. The Commission based its argument before the Supreme Court of Ontario on the fact that the federal government did not have jurisdiction to apply the Act to municipal employers or to enact laws affecting civil rights.

Of the twelve Canadian judges who reviewed the IDI Act, ten upheld its constitutionality on the ground that labour disputes were of sufficient importance to the national life of Canada as to require their regulation by the federal government. However when the case finally came before the Judicial Committee of the British Privy Council, the court of last resort at that time (and a body far removed from the social and economic realities of Canadian life), the judgement rendered differed greatly from that of the Canadian judges. The Judicial Committee held that the Act *was* unconstitutional since it interfered with property and civil rights, and municipal institutions:

> It is clear that this enactment was one which was competent to the Legislature of a Province under s. 92. In this present case the substance of it was possibly competent, not merely under the head of property and civil rights in the Province, but also under that of municipal institutions in the Province.[6]

A number of leading Canadian authorities deplore the decision taken by the Judicial Committee.[7] Problems caused by provincial jurisdiction in the meat-packing industry — where negotiations took place on a national basis — support the contention that the Committee made a mistake in the Snider case. As recently as 1968, four distinguished Canadian academics recommended in the *Task Force Report on Labour Relations* that

> there be a relaxation in the present practice of finality in determining bargaining units in order that the structure of collective bargaining may have a better chance of finding its own level. Another set of significant recommendations bears upon conciliation and other methods of dispute settlement, especially in potential emergency disputes. Federal policy in these areas can be applicable only to industries within its jurisdiction. In industries such as meat packing, which has proved to have many national characteristics while remaining within provincial jurisdiction, a continuing scheme of co-ordination will be required in order to maintain a *de facto* national bargaining unit.[8]

What the members of the Task Force had in mind is that union and management in any industry should be able to form large bargaining units without constitutional or legislative encumbrances.

Following the Snider case, the federal government passed an act in June 1925 which attempted to salvage at least part of the IDI Act. As amended, the Act applied to all works or undertakings which were within the legislative competence of the federal government, including navigation and shipping, lines of steam or other ships, railways, canals, telephones, and other works connecting one province with another. It also contained a clause enabling the Governor-in-Council to apply its provisions to any dispute considered to be a real or anticipated national emergency. More importantly, the Act could be applied to any dispute which was within the legislative competence of the provinces, but which was made subject by provincial enactment to the amended federal statute. In this way, the federal government invited the provinces to negate the effect of the Snider case.

By June, 1926, five provinces — British Columbia, Saskatchewan, Manitoba, New Brunswick, and Nova Scotia — had passed enabling legislation which made the federal law applicable to provincial disputes of the nature contemplated in the original federal statute. The

British Columbia legislation, which was typical of the laws enacted, stated:

> The provisions of the Industrial Disputes Investigation Act, chapter 20 of the Acts of the Parliament of Canada, 1907, and amendments thereto, shall apply to every industrial dispute of the nature therein defined which is within or subject to the exclusive legislative jurisdiction of the province.[9]

By 1932, all the provinces except Prince Edward Island had taken similar legislative action. This situation remained basically unchanged until 1937 when the provinces began to pass more elaborate labour legislation of their own. This movement on the part of the provinces would undoubtedly have continued if World War II had not temporarily transferred jurisdiction over labour relations to the federal government.

Although most of the provinces did enact legislation during World War II, the federal government used its authority under the War Measures Act to play a dominant role in the field of labour-management relations.

Wartime Legislation Prior to P.C. 1003

Shortly after the outbreak of World War II, the federal government issued Order-in-Council P.C. 3495 which extended the provisions of the federal IDI Act to disputes between employers and workers engaged in defence projects and in industries producing munitions and war supplies. The extensive definition of defence projects and war supplies included many kinds of materials and equipment: it has been estimated that P.C. 3495 raised the coverage of the IDI Act from

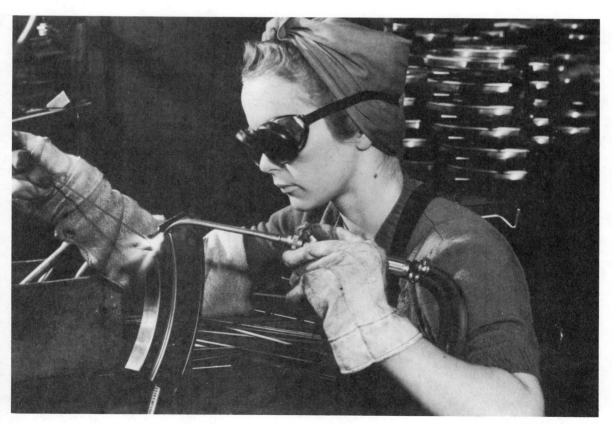

15% to 85% of the non-agricultural industries.[10] The Order also gave the Minister of Labour considerable discretion in determining which specific industries to bring under federal jurisdiction, a power which was employed extensively during the early years of World War II.

In June, 1940 the government issued a Declaration of Principles (Order-in-Council P.C. 2685) in an attempt to avoid wartime labour unrest. These principles were based largely on those of American labour legislation, specifically, the Wagner Act of 1935. P.C. 2685 advocated, among other things: (1) the recognition of fair and reasonable standards of wages and working conditions; (2) safeguards and regulations to protect the health and safety of workers; (3) no interruption in industrial operations by strikes or lockouts; (4) the freedom of workers to organize into trade unions without interference from employers; and (5) freedom of workers through their representatives to negotiate with employers or employers' associations concerning wages, hours, and other working conditions.[11] The Order, however, differed from the Wagner Act inasmuch as it did not set up an administrative body like the National Labour Relations Board (NLRB). H.A. Logan suggests that labour dissatisfaction with the 1940 Declaration of Principles, as expressed in suggestions put forward by the Canadian Congress of Labour, was largely responsible for the compulsory legislation that later came into being.[12]

Orders-in-Council P.C. 4020 and P.C. 4844 (June-July, 1941) established an Industrial Disputes Inquiry Commission to assist in settling disputes falling under the IDI Act and to investigate charges of discrimination or intimidation by employers. The Commission, composed of one or more members, could act more promptly than conciliation boards in settling disputes. In effect, the Commission also introduced the use of conciliation officers, who are still used in present-day legislation.

The right to strike in Canadian war industries was restricted by Order-in-Council P.C. 7303 of September 1941.[13] This Order made any strike in a war industry illegal until: (1) the findings of a board of conciliation had been delivered to the parties; (2) the workers had notified the federal Minister of Labour that they were contemplating a strike; (3) a vote of the workers had been taken under the supervision of the Department of Labour, subject to whatever provisions and restrictions the Minister of Labour might impose; and (4) a majority of the workers involved voted in favour of a strike.[14]

Order-in-Council P.C. 1003

By far the most important piece of federal labour relations legislation in Canada during World War II was Order-in-Council P.C. 1003 of 1944, better known as the Wartime Labour Relations Regulations.[15] The regulations combined principles taken from the Wagner Act with a compulsory two-stage conciliation procedure for the settlement of contract negotiation disputes. (Features of the Regulations are listed on page 66.)

P.C. 1003 established for all intents and purposes a national labour policy from 1944 to the last year of the war. It not only gave workers the right to join unions for the purpose of collective bargaining, it also provided for the administration of the regulations by forming the Wartime Labour Relations Board (WLRB). The Board could determine whether or not unions had sufficient support to be certified as bargaining agents on behalf of groups of workers. This was an important provision of the Regulations since, prior to that time, many strikes were conducted over the problem of union recognition. Like the NLRB in the United States, the WLRB in Canada could, upon application by a trade union, define a bargaining unit and if necessary conduct a vote to see if a majority of the workers supported the union named as their bargaining agent.

The Regulations made it illegal for unions to strike over the issue of recognition, and provided for a two-stage compulsory conciliation procedure if the parties failed to agree through negotiations of their own. Assistance would be provided first by a single conciliation officer and then, if the impasse continued, by a conciliation board. Strikes over contract negotiation disputes, however, were allowed, except in some public sector legislation. If no agreement was reached either through negotiations or with the help of third parties, unions were free to strike and employers were free to impose a lockout. These provisions remain in operation to this day.

Another major principle contained in the Regulations was that no strike or lockout was to occur during the life of a collective agreement. However, every collective agreement was assumed to contain a clause whereby any conflict over the interpretation or application of a provision of a collective agreement would be handled through a grievance procedure, the last step of which was binding arbitration.

In preparing for the return to peacetime control over labour relations, a Dominion-Provincial Conference of Labour Ministers was held in Ottawa from October 15 to 17, 1946.[16] While the federal minister made a good case for a national labour code, most of the provinces were unwilling to concede part of their jurisdiction to the federal government. Thus, the provinces maintained their pre-war control over most labour legislation; when the government enacted a new law, entitled The Industrial Relations and Disputes Investigation Act (IRDI Act) two years later, it only applied to the 10% of the Canadian labour force under federal jurisdiction.[17]

The IRDI Act contained provisions that were much the same as those of the Wartime Labour Relations Regulations: it made provision for voluntary recognition of unions by employers, the determination of appropriate bargaining units, the certification of bargaining agents (unions) by the Canada Labour Relations Board (CLRB) in industries within its jurisdiction, the duty to bargain in good faith, unfair labour practices by unions and employers, third-party assistance in the form of a two-stage compulsory conciliation process (officer to be followed by a board), no-strike and no-lockout restric-

tions, and compulsory arbitration of contract interpretation disputes.

Post-War Responses by the Provinces

When jurisdiction over labour relations returned to the provinces in the early part of 1948, the federal Wartime Regulations served as a general model for most of the provinces. Legislation in Ontario, Nova Scotia and Manitoba was also substantially the same as the federal legislation. Alberta and British Columbia consolidated previous legislation and included some provisions from P.C. 1003. Quebec and Saskatchewan continued to use their own legislation, which differed somewhat from that of the other provinces. (Saskatchewan, for example, did not require the use of compulsory conciliation in contract negotiation disputes until recently. It should also be noted that the Saskatchewan Trade Union Act covered workers in both the private and public sectors.) Prince Edward Island enacted its Trade Union Act in 1945. It required collective bargaining, but did not provide machinery for determining questions of representation or settling disputes.

During the 1950s Wartime Regulations remained the general model for labour relations legislation across the country, with minor variations from one jurisdiction to another. From the 1960s on, however, deviations from the standard model began to emerge. In the following sections, we will discuss some of the general policy concerns of current labour laws.

Public Policy Issues in Industrial Relations 1960–1989

Legislative policy regulating industrial relations has historically been directed to five major issues in Canada. These include:

1 The legal right of workers to organize into legal entities called unions or associations;
2 The process by which unions gain recognition as bargaining agents for groups of workers;

3 The duty to bargain in good faith as it applies to employers and unions in contract negotiations and the various forms of third party assistance required or provided;

4 The application of the clauses contained in collective agreements to specific and concrete work situations; and

5 The handling of jurisdictional disputes between or among unions as to which union has the right to represent workers doing a particular type of work, especially in the construction industry.

In recent years, other policy issues have been added to the traditional list:

6 The replacement of workers during a legal strike;

7 The imposition of a council of trade unions;

8 The handling of emergency disputes;

9 The imposition of first collective agreements;

10 The arbitration of unjust dismissal cases where no collective agreement exists;

11 The accreditation of employers' associations;

12 Compulsory dues check-off;

13 The duty of fair representation of members by unions;

14 Exemption from payment of union dues for religious reasons; and

15 Provisions for dealing with the impact of technological change on workers.

Many of these items have already emerged in the course of our discussion. Item 1 was discussed in some detail in Chapter 2, and will not be dealt with here. Items 2 to 5 are the classic issues with which labour relations legislation has been, and still is, concerned. They form the basis for comparison and analysis in this section. (See Figure 6.2 for an illustration of these four types of disputes and the ways in which they are resolved.) Items 6 to 15 are dealt with more briefly in the final section of the chapter. To begin, we must set the boundaries of jurisdiction of the statutes we will be discussing.

Coverage of the Statutes

The statutes of most jurisdictions in Canada governing the private sector interpret the range of workers covered under them quite broadly. However, Alberta, Nova Scotia, and Prince Edward Island exclude members of the medical, dental, legal, architectural, and engineering professions. Ontario excludes the same professions, except engineers, and adds to that list land surveyors and people employed in agriculture, hunting, trapping, horticulture, and domestic care.[18] The Prince Edward Island, New Brunswick, and Nova Scotia statutes do, however, cover police officers and accord them the right to strike.

All labour relations jurisdictions in Canada exclude workers acting in a confidential capacity in matters relating to industrial relations or who exercise managerial functions. A provision in the Manitoba statute and an amendment to Part I of the Canada Labour Code gives supervisors the right to collective bargaining. These provisions represent a new phenomenon in the private sector, and were prompted in part by recent legislation of a similar nature governing public and parapublic workers. In addition, following the publication of the *Report of the Task Force on Labour Relations*, a number of jurisdictions now grant collective bargaining rights to independent contractors such as taxi drivers, delivery workers for milk companies and retail stores, and others. In the not too distant future supervisory workers and independent contractors may be covered by the statutes of all private-sector legislation in Canada. Indeed, many critics find it difficult to understand why some jurisdictions exclude certain categories of workers while others include these same categories. They claim that there is no logical reason why *all* workers should not have the right to unionize and engage in collective bargaining.

Recognition Disputes

Prior to 1944, the only ways unions could become bargaining agents for a group of workers were through voluntary recognition by employers or the use of strike action. As we have seen, P.C. 1003 changed all of this by prohibiting strikes for recognition and establishing the Wartime Labour Relations Board through which unions could seek certification.

Figure 6.2

The Four Classical Types of Labour Relations Disputes

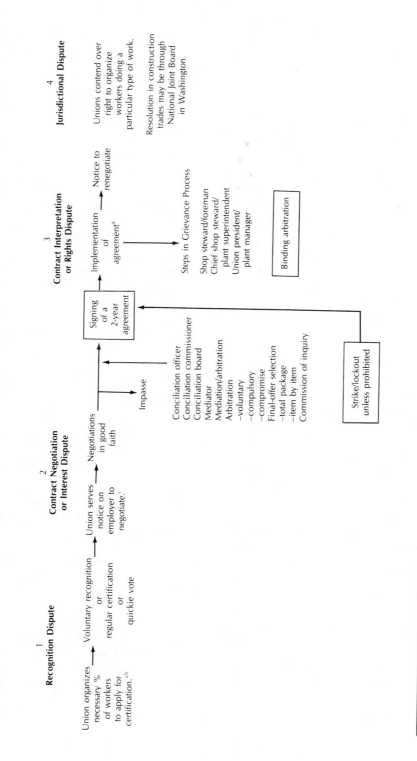

Recognition Dispute

Union organizes necessary % of workers to apply for certification.[a,b] → Voluntary recognition or regular certification or quickie vote →

2 Contract Negotiation or Interest Dispute

Union serves notice on employer to negotiate.[c] → Negotiations in good faith →

Impasse →

Conciliation officer
Conciliation commissioner
Conciliation board
Mediator
Mediation/arbitration
Arbitration
  –voluntary
  –compulsory
  –compromise
Final-offer selection
  –total package
  –item by item
Commission of inquiry

Signing of a 2-year agreement

3 Contract Interpretation or Rights Dispute

Implementation of agreement[d] → Notice to renegotiate

Steps in Grievance Process

Shop steward/foreman
Chief shop steward/
plant superintendent
Union president/
plant manager

Binding arbitration

Strike/lockout unless prohibited

4 Jurisdictional Dispute

Unions contend over right to organize workers doing a particular type of work.

Resolution in construction trades may be through National Joint Board in Washington.

Unfair Labour Practices
a Employer fires workers for trying to unionize.
b Union uses coercive tactics in trying to organize employees.
c One or both parties fail to negotiate in good faith.
d Union fails to provide fair representation.

Generally, recognition disputes involve one of three issues: (1) the determination of an appropriate bargaining unit; (2) certification of the bargaining agent; or (3) decertification.

Establishing a Bargaining Unit

A bargaining unit is normally a unit of workers considered to be appropriate for collective bargaining. Unions seek to represent workers in a bargaining unit and propose the form that the bargaining unit should take, based on the community of interests of the workers in terms of hours, wages, etc., the percentage of workers needed for certification, and the chances that the unit chosen will be accepted for certification, among other considerations.

Once the union has made its application to become the agent for a proposed bargaining unit to the appropriate labour relations board, the board sends a copy of the application to the employer. The employer must then post the application where it can be seen by all workers concerned. Should the employer or members of the proposed bargaining unit wish to take exception to the suggested make-up of the unit, they may ask the labour relations board to include or delete certain categories of workers. The board then sends a field officer to investigate the request, or holds a hearing at which all parties make their representations and petitions. The board must then decide which categories of workers form a bargaining unit appropriate for collective bargaining purposes in that particular situation. (If the employer agrees to the certification process voluntarily, the board is often bypassed completely.)

The Nova Scotia Trade Union Act includes specific guidelines to regulate the board's decisions:

> The Board in determining the appropriate unit shall have regard to the community of interest among the employees in the proposed unit in such matters as work allocation, hours of work, working conditions and methods of remuneration.[19]

While no other province sets specific criteria, labour relations boards have a long history of fleshing out the skeleton provisions contained in labour relations statutes on a case-by-case basis. According to a study conducted by E.E. Herman in the 1960s, ten criteria were used in defining appropriate bargaining units:

1. The purposes, intent, and provisions of the legislation governing the certification and determination of appropriateness of bargaining units within the particular jurisdiction;
2. The community or mutuality of interests with respect to wages, hours, and working conditions among the workers concerned;
3. The prior history and pattern of collective bargaining of the bargaining unit in question;
4. The history and nature of the proposed bargaining agent and any dealings it has had with other workers of the same employer or with other employers in the same industry or area;
5. The desires of the workers concerning which bargaining agent they wish to have represent them;
6. The eligibility of workers for membership in a particular labour organization;
7. The employer's administrative set-up and the way the unit fits into the employer's organization;
8. The collective bargaining record of an existing bargaining agent with regard to the workers in a unit previously certified as appropriate;
9. Prior decisions from which principles emerged concerning the establishment, or other establishments of the same employer or of identical, similar, or analogous industries; and
10. The agreement of the parties on a proposed bargaining unit.[20]

Not all of these criteria are used in each case; according to Herman, boards most frequently refer to the community of interest of workers. Other considerations in defining appropriate bargaining units include the status of seasonal and part-time workers, and the choice between single-plant, multi-plant, single-employer, or multi-employer units.[21]

Political considerations sometimes influence the process as well. One notable example is the Michelin Bill, passed in Nova Scotia in 1979, and referred to in the previous chapter. Under this legislation, unions in manufacturing sectors where work is organized interdependently among plants of the same employer may only be

Union challenging Ontario law that limits signing up of guards

By LORNE SLOTNICK
The Globe and Mail

A union working to sign up security guards across Ontario has launched a constitutional challenge of a law that bans the guards from joining most labor organizations.

The drive to organize the estimated 30,000 security guards in the province is part of a move by one of Canada's largest unions, the United Steelworkers of America, to expand its membership. The steel union has developed a close relationship with the 32-year-old Canadian Guards Association, which has had success recently in signing up guards in the Ottawa area.

However, a long-standing section of the Ontario Labor Relations Act prohibits a union from bargaining on behalf of guards if the union includes — or is affiliated with a group that includes — employees who are not guards.

A recent ruling of the Ontario Labor Relations Board concluded that the guards' association was affiliated with the Steelworkers, and the board refused to certify the association. The decision, which involved guards at Pinkerton's of Canada Ltd. in Ottawa, has sparked a challenge under the Charter of Rights and Freedoms that the board will probably hear this spring. The issue is expected to wind up in the courts.

"There's no reason why security guards should be prohibited from being in a union," said Brian Shell, the lawyer for the guards' association. "There's a fundamental right to join an association of your choice."

Mr. Shell said the law's ostensible purpose is to protect against possible conflicts of interest, as when security staff must guard company property during a strike.

But he said the "true purpose is to make sure that security guards are not in effective trade unions."

Without the resources of a large union such as the Steelworkers, he said, security guards have suffered from low wages and a lack of bargaining clout.

Stuart Deans, president of the guards' association, said in an interview from Ottawa that security is "one of the more highly exploited industries."

He added that when the group began signing up guards in Ottawa last year, wages were between $5.50 and $6 an hour and there were few, if any, fringe benefits.

Mr. Deans said the organizing drive is being financed by the Steelworkers and that his group — which already represents guards employed at Inco Ltd. and a handful of other companies — hopes to become part of the steel union eventually.

The Steelworkers, once a bastion of heavy industry, now represent about 12,000 security guards in Quebec, which does not have the legal restrictions that the union is challenging in Ontario. The security guards' local in Quebec is now the largest Steelworkers' local in Canada and the union says guards there are being paid about $11 an hour.

Mr. Deans said his group has had little difficulty organizing guards in Ottawa — it has applied for bargaining rights for more than 1,000 guards employed by six security companies — and he added that he expects similar success around the province if the restrictive law is struck down.

He said he has no objection to guards bargaining separately from the other employees on the site where they work, but he said no one should worry about what would happen if guards have to guard a plant against, for example, a rowdy picket line.

"I reject that argument. Guards are loyal to their jobs and we honor our collective agreements," Mr. Deans said, adding that if a guard refuses to perform his job, he can be disciplined.

Mr Shell said three provinces and the federal jurisdiction do not have Ontario's legal restriction on the unionization of security guards.

The labor board found that Mr. Deans' group was affiliated with the Steelworkers after examining a contract between the two unions under which, it said, more than two-thirds of the dues collected by the guards' union was then handed over to the steel union.

The *Globe and Mail*, Jan 4, 1989, p. A5.

certified on a multi-plant basis — that is, all such plants belonging to a company in question constitute the appropriate bargaining unit.[22] Unionization of multi-plant companies in manufacturing industries is thus very difficult in Nova Scotia.

Certification of Bargaining Agents

In almost all jurisdictions, the determination of appropriate bargaining units and the certification of bargaining agents are done by labour relations boards, most of which have a chair and a number of vice-chairs. It should be noted, however, that Quebec and British Columbia depart from the norm. In Quebec, questions regarding the appropriateness of bargaining units and the support received by bargaining agents are handled in the first instance by a certification officer. If challenged, a certification commissioner becomes involved.

The 1987 B.C. Industrial Relations Act renames the Labour Relations Board the Industrial Relations Council (IRC). The IRC is headed by a commissioner, and comprises at least two divisions, the Disputes Resolution Division, and the Industrial Relations Adjudication Division, which handles questions of certification. The commissioner may also establish panels and refer specific issues to them.[23] While the B.C. Act appears to place a great deal of authority in the hands of the commissioner, there is very little documentation to date on how the divisions and panels are functioning.

There are three basic ways in which a union can obtain recognition as a bargaining agent for a group of workers: (1) voluntary recognition; (2) the regular certification process; and (3) the prehearing vote.

Voluntary Recognition A union may organize a majority of the workers in a bargaining unit that it proposes, and then approach the employer to obtain approval as the bargaining agent for that unit. An employer who is satisfied that the union obtained a majority of the members of the bargaining unit without the exercise of undue pressure, and who considers the bar-

gaining unit appropriate may, according to most statutes, voluntarily accept the proposed bargaining unit and the union's right to act as the exclusive bargaining agent. The employer thereby becomes subject to the provisions of the statutes which provide for voluntary recognition and which specify forms of third-party assistance in the case of contract negotiation disputes.

Regular Certification The regular certification process is initiated when a union feels that it has signed up enough workers to ensure a majority of members in the bargaining unit. In virtually all jurisdictions, the process is as described under "Establishing a Bargaining Unit." If the Board finds the unit to be appropriate and if it is satisfied that the union has support from a majority of the workers, based on a count of membership cards, the bargaining agent may be certified without a vote. If the board is not certain that the union is supported by a majority of the workers, a secret ballot is held.

In 1984, British Columbia departed from the use of membership cards. Its new Industrial Relations Act requires a vote in every certification case, if the union has the 45% support needed to make an application.[24] Alberta's 1988 amendments also require a vote in every case, with 40% support. While this is the customary practice in the United States, British Columbia and Alberta are the only provinces in Canada where a vote is compulsory. Figure 6.3 outlines the steps involved in the regular certification process.

There are arguments for and against using membership cards as evidence of membership support for a union. P. Weiler, a former chair of the B.C. Labour Relations Board, points out that there are two schools of thought which underlie the route by which a union may acquire recognition under the regular certification process. One school of thought suggests that a vote should be taken in every case, drawing a parallel between secret balloting in elections for political and union offices. The secret ballot allows the person who has signed a union card and paid the union an initial fee a chance to change

Figure 6.3	Regular Certification

Union organizes required percentage of workers in proposed bargaining unit.

↓

Union makes application to board.

↓

Board defines appropriate bargaining unit.

↓

Secret vote is conducted by board.
(Or board counts membership cards issued by union.)

↓

Union is certified or not, depending on support received.

his or her mind. The assumption is that the union member may have been pressured into joining the new union. This model is followed by the National Labour Relations Board in the United States.

The other school of thought claims that it is possible — even desirable — to certify a union on the basis of majority support demonstrated by a count of membership cards. This argument rests on several grounds. First, if a union is certified on the basis of membership cards immediately, the employer has no opportunity to dissuade workers from joining the union. Second, signing up members is only the first of a number of tests which a union must undergo. A particularly difficult test is the negotiation of a first collective agreement that spells out the terms and conditions of employment. Frequently, strike action is necessary, at which point genuine membership support is important. Without it, a strike cannot be called, and without a strike or a strike threat, the employer will feel little compunction to settle.

Weiler concludes that

trade unions should be granted certification — that legal license to bargain — on the basis of signed membership cards. The real test of

whether employee support will remain steadfast will come when the trade union looks for a mandate to support its efforts at the bargaining table.[25]

He commented on the procedure he followed in the 1974 *Annual Report* of the B.C. Labour Relations Board as follows:

Upon receipt of the application [for certification], the Board immediately investigates the proportion of union membership among the employees. In the vast majority of cases, this investigation discloses that the union has more than a majority of the employees as members and the Board grants certification . . . on that basis.[26]

Figures in that report show that only about 5% of regular certification cases resulted in secret votes. It is rather ironic that the legislation governing the board that Weiler chaired for five years has become the first legislation to require a vote by secret ballot in every certification case.

Recent data from the Canada Labour Relations Board show that about 80% of certification cases are disposed of without a vote. In addition, figures from the Ontario Board indicate that votes were conducted in about 54% of the cases from 1982 to 1983 and in about 30% of the cases from 1983 to 1984.[27] It appears, then, that a vast majority of regular certification cases in Canada are processed without secret votes. Weiler's views are perhaps given more weight by recent data from the Canada Labour Relations Board, which show that fully 80% of certification cases are disposed of without a vote.

Prehearing Votes Figure 6.4 illustrates the procedure used to conduct a prehearing vote. This procedure is relatively new in Canadian labour legislation and is intended to be used in what one board chair described as "messy situations." For example, if there is some indication that the employer is committing unfair labour practices, a "quickie" or prehearing vote may be ordered to measure support before the employer has an opportunity to infringe futher upon the rights of the workers.

The membership support needed by unions to apply for regular certification and for pre-

Figure 6.4	Prehearing Vote

Union organizes required percentage of workers in proposed bargaining unit.

↓

Union applies for quickie vote.

↓

Board conducts vote and seals ballots.

↓

Board hears evidence and defines bargaining unit.

↓

Vote is counted.

↓

Union is certified if it has won sufficient support.

hearing votes varies among jurisdictions across the country. A summary of these requirements is presented in Table 6.1.

Where a prehearing vote is provided for, the usual procedure is for the board to conduct it. The voters frequently include workers whose eligibility for inclusion in the proposed bargaining unit is challenged by one or another of the parties. Therefore, the ballots are not counted until the board has ruled on who should be included in or excluded from the bargaining unit. (Contested ballots are set aside in sealed envelopes, and are only included in the ballot count if the board decides they are a part of the bargaining unit.)

The percentage support needed for a union to win a prehearing vote is the same as that required in the case of a regular certification vote. (See the third column in Table 6.1.) In the period immediately after World War II, support from 50% of the members in a bargaining unit was required to apply for certification. Once the board had determined whether or not the bargaining unit was appropriate and the majority of members in the bargaining unit supported the union, it would certify the union. The onus

was on the union to solicit membership support for its applications and for certification votes, since people who did not vote were considered not to be in favour of the union. This practice was perceived by some to be unfair to unions. It was argued that if this rule were to hold in our political system, very few members would be elected. In school board elections, where overall support for one candidate is often as low as 15% or 20% in many municipalities, it would be impossible to elect a full complement of school trustees.

Although some jurisdictions still require 50% support for the bargaining agents in a certification election, recent practice has been to accept the support of 50% of those *actually voting*. (See the differences in Table 6.1.) Workers who do not wish to have the union certified must get out and vote against it, since their absence no longer counts as a negative vote.

The complexity of Canadian industrial relations legislation raises the question of the desirability of establishing a standard percentage of membership support necessary for certification. A company operating under any one provincial jurisdiction will find it difficult enough to keep up to date with changing requirements. However, a company which operates under more than one jurisdiction, but does not fall under the federal statute, has an extremely difficult task. This is particularly true for companies in the meat-packing, pulp and paper, steel, and retail food industries, since many of them negotiate on a multi-provincial basis. As we shall see later, varying requirements for conciliation make negotiations even more complex for these companies.

At the time of certification, a trade union is certified for the occupational groups that exist at the time the application for certification is made. As new occupational categories come into existence, however, the trade union may negotiate on behalf of the workers in these new groups without applying to the respective boards for modifications to their certificates. Of the 11 statutes that deal with industrial relations in the private sector, only the Nova Scotia Trade

Table 6.1 — **A Comparison of Provisions Dealing with Certification**

Jurisdiction	% support needed to apply for certification	% support where boards are mandated to certify without a vote	% support needed to apply for a prehearing vote[a][b]	% support necessary to certify a union when a vote is taken	
				50% of those in the bargaining unit	50% of those voting
Federal	35	50 or more	35		X
Newfoundland[c]	50		40	X	
Prince Edward Island	50		N/S		X
Nova Scotia	40	50 or more	N/S[d]		X
New Brunswick	40–60	50 or more	40	X	
Quebec	35	50 or more	35	X	
Ontario	45–55	55 or more	35		X
Manitoba	45–55	55 or more	45	X	
Saskatchewan	25		N/S		X
Alberta	40	must conduct a vote	N/S		X
British Columbia	45	must conduct a vote	45		X

[a]In most jurisdictions, the boards usually have the power to certify the union or bargaining agent without a vote if there is concrete evidence that over 50% of the members want the union.

[b]Includes those statutes that make specific reference to a prehearing vote.

[c]In Newfoundland, the Board may direct its chief executive officer to conduct an investigation where an application has been made and if not less than 40% and not more than 50% of members are in good standing in the union, the chief executive officer shall cause a representation vote to be taken.

[d]Nova Scotia subjects every application to a prehearing vote.

N/S – Not specified.

Union Act refers explicitly to this particular issue. Section 26(1) of the Act specifies that where a trade union is certified an application may be made to the Nova Scotia Labour Relations Board to amend the certificate in the following respects: (1) to change the name of the union or employer; (2) to include specific additional classifications of employees in the unit; (3) to exclude specific classifications of workers from the unit; or (4) to combine previous certification orders into one order.[28] In a few other jurisdictions, these changes are dealt with by board regulations. Changes in the classifications in industries in which technology is rapidly developing is illustrated in the *B.C. Telephone Company Case* in the cases dealing with certification towards the end of this book.

As a concluding note on the certification process, it should be pointed out that an increasing number of jurisdictions are including in their statutes provisions which prevent union constitutions from barring a particular group of workers. These provisions have resulted in part from a number of court cases in which restrictive membership clauses became an issue. Section 29(3) of Part I of the Canada Labour Code is typical of these provisions:

Where the Board is satisfied that a trade union has an established practice of admitting persons to membership without regard to the eligibility requirements of its charter, constitution or by-laws, the Board may disregard those requirements in determining whether a person is a member of a trade union.[29]

Decertification of Bargaining Units

Although workers may choose a particular trade union as their bargaining agent, they can always change their minds. All statutes provide for both certification and decertification. If a certified bargaining agent is not performing well in the eyes of members of the bargaining unit, the members may, if they have majority support, apply to the appropriate labour relations board to have their union decertified.

As with certification, the board must first determine the scope of the bargaining unit. Then a vote is usually held: if a majority of the workers vote against the union, the union is decertified. In many cases, workers will have already chosen what they perceive to be a better union to represent them. Although no statistics are available on this particular question, it appears that where one union is decertified, another is usually certified.

Decertification provisions in the statutes are an important element of public policy. These provisions permit workers to dissociate themselves from weak, ineffective, or indifferent unions. This is as it should be, for trade unions have a moral and legal duty to represent fairly the workers for whom they are bargaining agents. If they fail in this respect, workers ought to be able to seek the services of other unions, or have the option of having no union.

Interest Disputes

Notice of Intent to Negotiate

Once a bargaining agent is certified, both the employer and the union are obliged to bargain in good faith over the terms and conditions of a collective agreement. The first agreement may last for one, two, or three years. Before it expires, either party may serve notice that it intends to bargain for a revised collective agree-ment. This process is referred to as a contract negotiation or "interest" dispute, to differentiate it from a contract interpretation or "rights" dispute. In a rights dispute, the arbitrator is guided in his or her decision by the clauses contained in the collective agreement. In an interest dispute, there are no agreed criteria to which the negotiators or a third party may refer.

Once a trade union is certified, it has a prescribed period of time within which to give notice of intent to negotiate for a first agreement. Similarly, before an existing collective agreement expires, the statutes prescribe a certain period of time within which the bargaining agent or the employer can serve notice of an intent to negotiate a new or revised agreement. (Generally the period of time allowed runs anywhere from 30 to 90 days.)

Provisions for Third-Party Assistance

All jurisdictions in Canada except Saskatchewan require third-party assistance before a legal strike or lockout can take place.

Until the late 1950s, most jurisdictions used a two-step conciliation process. First, a conciliation officer was appointed. If the conciliation officer failed to obtain an agreement, a conciliation board was automatically appointed. It consisted of one member chosen by each side in the dispute, plus a chair agreed upon by the first two appointees. Since the 1950s, however, most jurisdictions have been making far less use of conciliation boards.

In recent years, the use of mediation as a form of third-party assistance has increased. Mediation was first tried in Ontario during the 1960s. Since that time, many other jurisdictions have adopted this approach, using the mediator to replace either the conciliation officer or the conciliation board.

Initial Third-Party Assistance

While some jurisdictions now use mediators as the first step in third-party assistance, most still refer to a conciliation officer. In either case, the function of the first-appointed individual is to confer with the parties to help bring about an agreement between them. Most jurisdictions specify a period of time within which a conciliation officer or similar agent must report his or her findings to the minister. This time period may be extended by the consent of the parties or at the discretion of the minister. If no agreement is reached, the conciliation officer usually reports to the minister those items which have been agreed upon and those which are still outstanding. In most jurisdictions, the conciliation officer must advise the minister whether or not to appoint a conciliation board. A summary of provisions regarding the appointment of conciliation officers and mediators in the eleven jurisdictions in Canada is presented in Table 6.2. It shows that in many provinces, as well as in the federal jurisdiction, mediators are used if the conciliation officer is unable to get the two sides to agree. This provision is a relatively recent development in the area of interest disputes, and undoubtedly accounts, in part, for the decline in the appointment of conciliation boards in recent years.

Composition and Function of Conciliation Boards

Practically all Canadian jurisdictions, with the exception of British Columbia, Quebec, and Alberta, provide for the appointment of a conciliation board should the efforts of the conciliator or mediator fail. (While the Saskatchewan statute does not require the appointment of conciliation boards, it does provide for the establishment of such boards on the initiative of the Minister of Labour.) The fact that a jurisdiction provides for this type of third-party assistance does not necessarily mean, however, that

Table 6.2
Types of Initial Third-Party
Assistance

Jurisdiction	Conciliation officer or similar officer	Mediator after appointment of conciliation officer	Report of mediator replaces that of conciliation officer	Report of mediator or similar officer replaces report of conciliation board	No. of days after first stage if no board is appointed before strike or lockout is permitted
Federal	X	X		X[a]	7
British Columbia[b]	mediator				
Alberta	mediator				
Saskatchewan	not compulsory				14 when contract expires
Manitoba	X				
Ontario	X	X		X	
Quebec	X				14 no board provided for in legislation
New Brunswick[c]	X	X	X		7
Nova Scotia	X	X		X	14
Prince Edward Island	X		X		7
Newfoundland[c]	X	X		X	7

[a]Under the federal statute, the report of a conciliation commissioner replaces that of a conciliation board. Also, under the statute, the Minister may appoint a mediator.

[b]The British Columbia Industrial Relations Act provides only for mediation and a strike may take place only within the three month period after its authorization by a membership vote.

[c]Provides for the appointment of one or more conciliation officers.

the boards are used in every case. As we have seen, administrators now exercise a great deal of discretion concerning the use of tripartite conciliation boards. Generally, boards are appointed only when disputes have an important public interest component.

Where a statute provides for the appointment of conciliation boards, it will usually contain a provision which states that, within a prescribed period after the report of the conciliation officer is submitted, the minister will either appoint a conciliation board or notify the parties that one will not be appointed. In the latter case, the parties are free to initiate a strike or lockout. Conciliation boards are appointed according to a standard procedure: management and union are given a certain amount of time to name their nominees to the board, and the two nominees agree upon a third person to act as chair. In cases where the two nominees are unable to agree, the Minister of Labour appoints the third person to serve as a neutral party on the conciliation board.

If a board cannot effect an agreement between the parties, it must recommend ways in which the outstanding issues may be reconciled. Again, most statutes require that such recommendations be submitted within prescribed time periods which may be extended either by consent of the parties or at the discretion of the minister. Evidence suggests that, in practically all cases, boards far exceed the specified time period.

At one time, the report of a conciliation board was supposed to represent the views of the majority of its members. This often put the chair of a board in a position of having to write recommendations agreeable to either the union or management nominee. Legislation in some jurisdictions now permits, in the absence of a majority report, that the chair's report be taken as that of the conciliation board. This seems to be a welcome innovation, since the chair can now take advantage of input from both sides and make recommendations acceptable to both sides, or which serve as a useful basis for further negotiation.

There has been less interest in conciliation boards of late. Their decline in popularity may be due in part to criticism of the long periods between their appointments and their reports. As we have seen, the use of mediators has also obviated the need for boards to a significant extent.

One of the virtues of the tripartite boards, however, is that the two nominees appointed by management and union are normally well informed about a given industry and are therefore of great assistance to the chair in furnishing detailed knowledge about that industry. If mediators are to be effective, they should have similar expertise. Moreover, it would seem desirable to use teams of mediators or conciliation officers in attempting to improve relations in those industries which have long histories of poor labour-management relations. Ontario has developed a service within the Ministry of Labour which provides mediation teams to help repair tattered relations between unions and management.[30]

It is interesting to note that when the federal government revised the old Industrial Relations and Disputes Investigation Act of 1948 and made it Part V of the Canada Labour Code in 1972–73, provision was made for the appointment of a conciliation commissioner who would have a mandate similar to that of a conciliation board, including the power to issue a report. Similarly, the emergence of the regular use of mediation in some jurisdictions indicates clearly that governments are relying less on conciliation boards than on conciliation officers and mediators. All statutes requiring conciliation or mediation also stipulate that no strike or lockout may occur until after a certain period of time (usually seven days) has elapsed. Under Part I of the Canada Labour Code, for example, a strike or lockout may begin seven days after the minister has notified the parties that he will not appoint a conciliation officer, commissioner, or board.[31] Table 6.3 summarizes regulations concerning conciliation boards or their equivalent in each of the jurisdictions in Canada. While a discussion of all eleven jurisdictions is beyond

Table 6.3

Provisions Regarding Conciliation Boards,
Compulsory Votes, etc.

Jurisdiction	Provision made for the appointment of conciliation board or equivalent	No. of days after report before strike or lockout is legal	Supervised strike vote	Prescribed period of notice before strike or lockout may take place
Federal	X	7		
Newfoundland	X	7		
Prince Edward Island	X	7		
Nova Scotia	X	7		
New Brunswick	X	7		2 days
Quebec[a]				2 days
Ontario	X	7		48 hours
Manitoba	X	not specified in statute		
Saskatchewan	X			
Alberta	X[b]	14	X	72 hours
British Columbia			X[c]	72 hours

[a]In Quebec, the right to strike or lockout is acquired 90 days after receipt by the minister of a request for the appointment of a conciliation officer.

[b]The Alberta Labour Relations Code provides for the appointment of a Disputes Inquiry Board on the initiative of the Minister of Labour. In addition, the parties may request the Minister to appoint a voluntary collective bargaining arbitration board, the recommendations of which are binding on the parties.

[c]In British Columbia, a vote must be conducted before a strike becomes legal.

the scope of this book, it is worth mentioning again Manitoba's unique legislation concerning final offer selection.

Section 94.1 of the Manitoba Labour Relations Act empowers either the union or the employer to seek a vote of the employees, between 30 and 60 days before the expiration of a collective agreement *or* between the 59th and 71st day of a strike or lockout, to determine if they wish to resolve an impasse in negotiations by final offer selection. As we indicated in Chapter 5, this issue greatly divided the member unions of the Manitoba Federation of Labour.

Under the provision in the Manitoba statute, each party submits its final offer to the selector. The selector then holds a hearing to provide the parties an opportunity to justify their offers. The hearing may be waived or held "in camera." Section 94.3(4) states that the selector shall

(a) select the whole of the final offer of either the

union or the employer with respect to the terms and conditions of the proposed collective agreement which are still in dispute; and (b) notify the parties in writing of the decision.

This is what is referred to as the *total package* type of final offer selection. (The rationale behind final offer selection will be discussed in Chapter 8.) What is really unique in the Manitoba legislation is that final offer selection is not available at the option of the employer or the union, as is the case in every other jurisdiction in which it is made available (mostly in "essential industries" in a few American states); it is used only if a majority of the employees involved vote to have it used. To date, there have been no cases in which it has been invoked, but it will be interesting to see how employees react when and if they are confronted with making the choice of final offer selection.

Processes Required before Strikes and Lockouts

The Alberta Labour Relations Code requires that there be a supervised vote before a strike or lockout. The results of the strike vote are determined on the basis of a majority of those persons who *actually vote*. Also, a strike or lockout cannot take place until 72 hours notice has been given to the employer or union respectively.[32] The B.C. Industrial Relations Act specifies that a strike may not take place until secret ballots show that a majority of those workers voting favour a strike. A similar provision applies to a lockout by an employers' association. Also, no strike or lockout may take place until 72 hours notice has been given to the chair of the Disputes Resolution Division.[33]

In the cases cited above where a strike vote is required, a majority of those voting decides whether or not a strike will be called. The statutes of Nova Scotia and Prince Edward Island specify that, where a secret vote is to be taken, the majority of those *in the bargaining unit* must approve strike action for the strike to be legal.[34] The relevant provision of the Nova Scotia Trade Union Act reads as follows:

> No person shall declare or authorize a strike and no employee shall strike until after a secret vote by ballot of employees in the unit affected as to whether to strike or not to strike has been taken and the majority of such employees have voted in favour of a strike.[35]

The requirements of other jurisdictions concerning due process for strikes and lockouts are not precisely defined. It is likely that, in many cases, a simple voting majority would suffice. Most jurisdictions now allow a majority of those voting in a secret ballot to determine whether or not a union is certified; the same logic could be applied in determining whether or not a strike is legal.

A section of the Saskatchewan Trade Union Act (section 45(1)) provides that, where a strike has continued for 30 days, the employer, the trade union, *or 25% of the workers in the bargain-ing unit, or 100 workers (whichever is less)*, may ask the board to conduct a vote on the employer's last offer with a view to returning to work. If a majority of those voting accept the employer's last offer, then the strike is over and the workers must return to work. Section 45(3) makes it clear that only workers who are involved in the strike and who have not secured permanent employment elsewhere are entitled to vote. The danger of this means of ending a strike is that if 1,000 workers are on strike, 100 of them may request a vote on whether or not to accept the employer's last offer, and if 51 vote to accept the employer's last offer, then the strike is legally ended and all 1,000 workers must return to work.

Sections 45(1) also allows the employer to deal directly with the workers. In other jurisdictions, the union is involved in or itself conducts the vote. Section 45(1) is the only legislation in Canada which gives workers such a direct say in whether or not to continue a strike. The next closest thing to the provision in the Saskatchewan legislation is section 40 of the Ontario Labour Relations Act which permits the *employer*, before or after the commencement of a strike, to apply to the Minister of Labour for a vote on the employer's last offer. However, the Ontario provision does not give a similar right to workers. Ontario and Saskatchewan are the only provinces in Canada with such provisions in their legislation. In addition, section 11(1)(a) of the Saskatchewan Trade Union Act expressly permits an employer to communicate with his or her workers.

The above discussion has concerned the policies and procedures designed to resolve contract negotiation or interest disputes, the second of the four classical types referred to earlier in this chapter. If these procedures do not enable the parties to resolve their differences, then strikes and lockouts may legally take place. An exception is found in negotiations in the public and parapublic sectors in some jurisdictions where strikes are forbidden and compulsory arbitration is prescribed.

Rights Disputes

The statutes in every jurisdiction in Canada require that collective agreements contain clauses which forbid strikes or lockouts in rights disputes, and specify grievance procedures for their resolution, with arbitration as the final step. This provision in Part I of the Canada Labour Code is fairly typical:

> Every collective agreement shall contain a provision for final settlement without stoppage of work, by arbitration or otherwise, of all differences between the parties to or employees bound by the collective agreement, concerning its interpretation, application, administration or alleged violation.[36]

While Saskatchewan did not require arbitration of rights disputes for many years, section 44 of the recently revised Saskatchewan Trade Union Act expressly prohibits strike and lockout action during the life of a collective agreement. While there is no express provision in the new statute which requires the use of arbitration in such disputes, it is presumed to exist as the usual *quid pro quo* for the no-strike and no-lockout provision. In addition, sections 24, 25 and 26 imply the existence of such a provision.

A common difficulty with most collective agreements is that the language is general and hard to relate to specific situations. Often, provisions are ambiguous or contradictory. This ambiguity may have been deliberately incorporated by the negotiating parties, who may have compromised on a loosely worded provision in order to expedite a settlement and avoid a strike or lockout. The parties assume that the wording would be referred to a third party should the need for interpretation arise at a later date.

Note that even if the collective agreement does not contain an arbitration clause, some statutes will assume it to be present. In Ontario and a number of other jurisdictions, the clause prescribed by the statute gives an arbitrator the authority to decide whether an issue is arbitrable or not. This clause anticipates objections by either party that the arbitrator lacks jurisdiction to hear the case.

In order to cope with rights disputes, most contracts specify a grievance procedure geared to the size of the company. In small companies, the procedure may contain one to three steps, with arbitration as the final step, while larger organizations may require a more involved process before arbitration. As well, some collective agreements provide for tripartite boards of arbitration, whereas others specify a sole arbitrator. In all cases, the arbitration decision is binding upon both parties. With tripartite boards of arbitration there is usually a time period within which management and union must nominate their representatives. These two nominees must then select a chair who is mutually acceptable to both nominees. If either party fails to nominate a representative, or if the two nominees fail to agree upon a chair, most statutes in Canada contain a provision whereby the Minister of Labour or chair of the labour relations board makes the appointments.

Certain statutes also contain detailed provisions regarding the arbitration process itself, including the presentation of evidence, the calling and cross-examination of witnesses, the granting of permission to arbitrators to enter premises where infractions of collective agreements are alleged to have taken place, and so on. All jurisdictions now provide that where there is no majority decision of an arbitration board, the decision of the chair prevails.

A recent development in practically all statutes relates to cases dealing with discharge and discipline. Until recently, if a worker was suspended or discharged for just cause, the arbitrator had no legal mandate to change the decision of management. Now, however, most statutes permit the arbitrator to substitute his or her judgement for that of management, unless the collective agreement prescribes a specific penalty for the infraction. (More will be said about this subject in Chapter 9.)

Another matter of concern is the enforceability of awards. In most jurisdictions, the statutes provide that if an arbitration decision is not complied with by a certain date, it may be filed with a court and then becomes enforceable as a court order. Failure to implement an arbitration award so filed becomes a failure to comply with a court decision, with all the penalities that implies.

There has been a great deal of criticism of the arbitration process, of the lengthy delays it involves, and the costs it occasions. In response, the phenomenon of expedited arbitration has emerged, in which an arbitrator hears the case, usually right at the place where the alleged infraction occurred, and hands down a binding award almost immediately. No lengthy reasons for the decision are provided, as in conventional arbitration. Expedited arbitration was first used by the United Steelworkers Union and the ten major steel companies in the United States in 1971.[37] Its basic purposes are to reduce costs, shorten the time period from the filing of a grievance to the rendering of an arbitration award, and involve more arbitrators in the process, particularly individuals in the localities in which the disputes first arise. Parties who have used expedited arbitration find that it works well for routine grievances. The process must, nonetheless, be tailor-made to each union-management relationship.

Although expedited arbitration is beginning to find its way into a number of industries and companies, there is no wide-scale legislation dealing with it thus far. Individual jurisdictions, however, have made some effort to promote its use. During the summer of 1979, for example, Ontario passed Bill 25, which allows either labour or management to request the Minister of Labour to refer to a single arbitrator appointed by the minister any dispute arising from the interpretation, application, administration, or alleged violation or a collective agreement. (More will be said about expedited arbitration in Chapter 9.)

Jurisdictional Disputes

Jurisdictional disputes are disagreements between unions over the right to represent workers by virtue of the work to be performed. Such disputes have traditionally occurred in the construction industry. A good example is a situation where kitchens are being installed in newly constructed homes. The work involves the duties of both a carpenter and a plumber/pipefitter who connects the hot- and cold-water pipes. Both the carpenters and the plumbers unions may claim the right to organize workers performing such work.

Although the legislative provisions dealing with certification are often able to handle this kind of situation, in many cases the unions continue to compete with one another and the disputes are only settled by strike action. In some jurisdictions in Canada, construction industry panels of labour relations boards are effective in resolving these kinds of disputes. If these panels are unsuccessful, and the unions involved continue to compete, the court of last resort is the National Joint Board (NJB) in Washington, D.C. The NJB comprises an impartial chair, four representatives of the Building and Construction Trades Department of the AFL-CIO, and four contractors' associations. There is an understanding among the international construction trade unions involved that they will abide by whatever decision the NJB issues. A case may be brought before the NJB either by the employer or by the president of the international union involved. There have been a number of cases where a dispute was settled at this stage.

As far back as 1967, Abbé G. Dion of Laval University suggested that provincial entities along the lines of the National Joint Board be established in Canada, along with a national board to ensure consistency among the decisions at the provincial level.[38] To date, however, no provincial boards have been set up and a few Canadian cases still end up in Washington for final disposition.

Other Policy Issues

In recent years, a number of new policy issues have emerged which started in one of the eleven jurisdictions and then spread to other jurisdictions. We will discuss some of the more important ones briefly.

Replacement of Workers During a Legal Strike

In all jurisdictions in Canada, with the exception of Quebec, employers are permitted to replace striking workers. Workers may regain their status as workers but not their previous jobs after the strike has ended. For a large employer with a very diversified labour force, it is practically impossible to find enough skilled replacements to continue operations. For example, a company such as Stelco in Hamilton would find it extremely difficult to hire replacement workers in many steelworking occupations. A small employer, however, may be able to hire enough replacements to continue normal operations during a strike.

While it seems reasonable to assume that striking workers should be entitled to return to their jobs after a strike is over, it has also been suggested that replacements hired during strikes are entitled to some form of job security. As well, exception has been taken by some to the position that the striking worker has a right only to employee status and not to his or her job. The rights of strikers and replacement workers are a particularly difficult public policy issue.

The Ontario government has responded to this issue by including the following provision in its Labour Relations Act:

> Where an employee engaging in a lawful strike makes an unconditional application in writing to his employer within six months from the commencement of the lawful strike to return to work, the employer shall ... reinstate the employee in his former employment, on such terms as the employer and employee may agree upon, and the employer in offering terms of employment shall not discriminate against the employee by reason of his exercising or having exercised any rights under this Act.[39]

It seems clear from this provision that in order for a worker to regain his or her previous job, he or she has to seek it while a strike is still on. If this interpretation is correct, the provision might place a worker under a great deal of pressure from fellow strikers.

Manitoba has a provision whereby workers may be recalled to their previous jobs according to seniority and as such work becomes available.[40] Section 11 of the Manitoba Labour Relations Act prohibits employers from hiring permanent workers during a strike. Following a lengthy strike at the Gainers meat packing plant in Alberta in the late 1980s, the Alberta government introduced a new section to its Labour Relations Code that reads as follows:

> When a strike or lockout ends ... as a result of a settlement ... any employee affected by the dispute whose employment relationship with the employer has not been otherwise lawfully terminated is entitled, on request, to resume his employment with the employer in preference to any employee hired by the employer as a replacement employee for the employee making the request during the strike or lockout.

The employee must make his or her request in writing within 14 or 30 days following the end of the strike.

Quebec alone extends a no-replacement right to workers. In Bill 45 of 1977, the Quebec government included a section which has come to be known as the "anti-scab" provision. Under this provision, every employer is prohibited from resorting to four objectionable or unfair practices: (1) the direct replacement of workers legally on strike; (2) the hiring of additional workers prior to the commencement of a strike or lockout on the understanding that they will work during the strike or lockout period; (3) the use of workers who are in the bargaining unit on strike but who are prepared to work in another of the employer's establishments; and (4) the importation of workers from other establishments operated by the employer for the purposes of keeping a strike-bound establishment functioning. The anti-scab provision of 1977 has since been extended to include subcontractors and supervisory personnel. However, should any strike or lockout be judged to affect the health or safety of the province, the government may obtain a court order (or injunction) ordering that essential services be provided.[41]

The use of professional strikebreakers has been a controversial issue in Canada for some years. Three jurisdictions — British Columbia, Manitoba, and Ontario — now consider it an unfair labour practice for employers to employ professional strikebreakers during a strike. Manitoba and Ontario also consider it an unfair labour practice for individuals to act in such a capacity.

Imposition of a Council of Trade Unions

The British Columbia Industrial Relations Act contains a unique provision by which the Minister of Labour may direct the B.C. Industrial Relations Council to consider whether a council of trade unions would be an appropriate bargaining agent for a unit of workers. If the IRC considers such a council appropriate, it may certify the council of unions as the bargaining agent.[42]

The notion of a council of trade unions was introduced under a previous B.C. Labour Code, and was used in several cases, including the B.C. railway case in 1976. The railway had been plagued with labour problems for years. Its seven or eight unions negotiated separately, and each union based its new demands on settlements reached by the others, a practice called leap-frogging. Leap-frogging escalated the number of strikes in the railway so much that the time lost cost the provincial economy more than $100,000,000 in five years.[43]

The B.C. Board eventually forced the unions to form a council and to develop a constitution governing its operations. Under the new system, negotiations were held periodically, with all the unions participating. Before any strike action could take place, all workers took part in a secret strike vote. Each union retained its identity, however, and during the life of the agreement, each one processed the grievances of its

members. If one of the unions were to decide, for example, that its wage structure differed in important respects from those of other railway unions, it would have to persuade the other unions of the merits of its case before the matter could be considered during contract negotiations. The first two sets of negotiations resulted in peaceful settlements, but the third round of negotiations resulted in a six-week strike from December, 1979 to January, 1980. There were over 100 issues involved in the strike. However, the negotiators reached a compromise settlement which was ratified by a majority of the workers.[44] The previous B.C. Board formed councils of unions in other industries including the B.C. shipyards, and part of the construction industry.

How does one assess the advantages and disadvantages of bargaining through a highly centralized structure? As the former chair of the B.C. Board, Paul Weiler, stated, "The most obvious flaw in the growth of large bargaining units its the reduction of the capacity for self-determination by individuals or small groups within that structure."[45] Drawing on the experience of the B.C. railway, he suggested that each union leader should cast one vote on the executive board of the council, regardless of the size of the union, and that key membership decisions such as contract ratification and strike votes should take place on a one-person, one-vote basis.

On March 9, 1978, the federal Minister of Labour appointed an Industrial Inquiry Commission with a mandate to look into the advantages and disadvantages of broader-based bargaining units in federal industries, particularly in aviation, airport services, and grain-handling. In the late seventies, a federal Industrial Inquiry Commission recommended that the voluntary formation of broader-based units be encouraged in the aviation, airport services, and grain-handling industries on a voluntary basis. The Commission noted that, if voluntary efforts were not successful, the government might have recourse to legislation to effect the same end. The latter course seems more likely, since the statements made by labour and management in these sectors suggest that too many vested interests exist for the parties to adopt voluntarily broader-based bargaining units.[46] The Commission might have been more effective if it had recommended a provision comparable to that contained in the B.C. Industrial Relations Act. The mere enactment of a clause providing for the future imposition of a council of trade unions might have been sufficient to encourage voluntary creation of the broader-based bargaining units desired by the Commission.

Handling Emergency Disputes

British Columbia and Alberta are the only jurisdictions that have provisions for handling emergency disputes in industries in the private sector. The Alberta Labour Relations Code provides that, where an emergency is judged to exist or may occur that poses a threat to health or property, or where unreasonable hardship is being caused or is likely to be caused to persons who are not parties to an industrial dispute, the government may declare that all further action and procedures in the dispute be governed by the emergency provisions in the statute. Following the invoking of emergency powers, the minister responsible may establish a public emergency tribunal to mediate the dispute. The tribunal has the power to make a binding award dealing with each item in dispute.[47] The Code applies specifically to workers in community services such as water, heat, sewage disposal, and electrical and gas utilities. Health care workers are also included.

Although this provision in the Alberta statute gives a great deal of power to Cabinet, the caution exercised by government officials and by the judiciary so far indicates that it will likely be used in a responsible manner. During the spring of 1980, for example, when more than 6,000 Alberta nurses went on strike in defiance of a government back-to-work order, the government sought an interim court injunction to enforce the original order. The justice who heard the application for an injunction post-poned his ruling on the government's request and a two-year settlement was reached before any further judicial action was required. (This provision no longer applies to most nurses in the province, since sections 94-102 of the Alberta Labour Relations Code requires compulsory arbitration of interest disputes for employers who operate approved hospitals as defined in the Hospitals Act, and all the workers of those employers.)

The British Columbia Industrial Relations Act of 1988 has special sections dealing with essential services (sections 137.8 to 137.95). Under these provisions, the government may preempt a union's strike or employer's lockout option and substitute a strategy which includes fact-finding, mediation, designation and the appointment of a public interest inquiry board. Designation means that an administrative body (such as a labour relations board) declares that a specified number of persons who would normally have the right to strike are required for the continued operation of an essential industry or service, and must continue to report for duty during a work stoppage. Section 137.8 of the Act also specifies that where a dispute between the parties is not resolved and where the Minister of Labour considers that a dispute poses a threat to the economy of the province or to the health, safety or welfare of its residents or to the provision of educational services, the minister may do either or both of the following:

> (1) order a cooling off period not exceeding 40 days; (2) direct the [industrial relations] council to designate those facilities, productions and services that the council considers necessary or essential to prevent immediate and serious danger to the economy of the Province or to the health, safety or welfare of its residents or to the provision of educational services in the Province.

Where such a cooling off period is ordered no strike or lockout may take place, or if either exists, it must be suspended. There is provision for the appointment of a fact finder, but his or her report is not binding. There is also provision for the appointment of a public interest inquiry board, and where such a board conducts any hearing or inquiry, a person may be appointed as "a public interest advocate to represent the public interest at the hearing or inquiry."[48] If the parties to the dispute accept the recommendation of the public interest inquiry board, the recommendations become part of the collective agreement between the parties. If either party refuses to accept the recommendations of the public interest inquiry board and if they are in the public sector, they may be required to solve their dispute by compulsory arbitration. The Act is silent on what happens if the parties reject the recommendations of a public interest inquiry board.

The B.C. statute is broader in scope than that of Alberta since it applies to those industries in the private sector, in which work stoppages may be perceived to cause a serious threat to the economy and welfare of the province.[49] (Similar legislation in Quebec will be discussed in Chapter 10.)

In all other jurisdictions, with the exception of statutes covering essential services in the public and parapublic sectors, special ad hoc legislation is normally used to deal with so-called emergency disputes. Given the various conditions under which such disputes may arise, the strategy of ad hoc legislation may be the most appropriate one. The legislation is debated in the responsible legislative assembly, where the merits and timing of the government's proposal is subject to public scrutiny. Such is not the case when special authority is vested in one or more individuals to initiate emergency procedures.

Imposition of First Agreements

If the parties to a first agreement fail to reach a settlement through negotiation, some jurisdictions provide for its imposition by an external agency. These policies were introduced to help establish a workable union-management relationship in cases where either a newly certified union makes unrealistic demands that small employers cannot afford or, more commonly, an employer stalls negotiations in the hope that workers will tire of the idea of unionizing.

The first jurisdiction to initiate this policy was British Columbia in 1973. The relevant provision of the B.C. Industrial Relations Act states that the commissioner of the Industrial Relations Council (B.C.'s equivalent to the labour boards in most other jurisdictions) may, at the request of either party and after such investigation as he or she deems necessary, direct a panel of the IRC to enquire into a dispute of a first contract. If the commissioner considers it advisable, the panel can settle the terms and conditions for the first collective agreement, but it must give the parties an opportunity to present evidence and to make representations. It must also take into account: (1) the extent to which the parties have or have not bargained in good faith; and (2) the terms and conditions of employment for workers covered under other agreements who perform similar functions in the same or related circumstances.[50]

Most of the statutes in other jurisdictions follow this same pattern, although with some variations (see Table 6.4). In Quebec, for example, which has no labour board or IRC equivalent, the dispute is handled by a council of arbitration, which may consist of a single arbitrator. And in Ontario, the matter may be handled by a board of arbitration or, if both parties agree, by the OLRB itself.

Ontario also sets out four criteria for the board to consider:

(a) the refusal of the employer to recognize the bargaining authority of the trade union;
(b) the uncompromising nature of any bargaining position adopted by the respondent without reasonable justification;
(c) the failure of the respondent to make reasonable or expeditious efforts to conclude a collective agreement; or
(d) any other reason the Board considers relevant.

The first three criteria reflect difficulties that the Ontario Labour Relations Board confronted in a number of unfair labour practice cases, particularly the Radio Shack case, which will be discussed later in the chapter.

To varying degrees, all of the statutes encourage the parties to reach their own agreement,

Table 6.4

**Provisions for Settlement of a
First Collective Agreement**

Jurisdiction	Requested by	Availability	Arbitrator	Duration
Federal (1978)	either party	upon request	CLRB	1 year
Newfoundland (1985)	either party	upon request	NLRB	1 year
Quebec (1977)	either party	upon request	council of arbitration	not less than 1 year, not more than 2 years
Ontario (1986)	either party	after conciliation officer report, or after Minister announces no conciliation board will be appointed	1) board of arbitration 2) OLRB	2 years
Manitoba (1982)	either party	90 days after certification	MLRB	1 year
British Columbia (1973)	either party	upon request	IRC	1 year

and use arbitration as a last resort. In Manitoba, for instance, the parties may apply to the board 90 days after the union is certified. However, the board will not impose an agreement for 60 days after that, at which time it may either suggest that the parties continue to try to reach an agreement, alone or with the assistance of a conciliation officer, or go ahead and impose an agreement. If the first option is chosen the parties are given another 30 days in which to sign an agreement.

A 1980 study dealing with statutory provisions in different jurisdictions concluded that the mechanisms for imposing a collective agreement seemed to be working fairly well. It went on to suggest, however, that policy-makers should consider other measures as well.[51] One such measure was a clause enabling small unions to combine together in the certification process to withstand stonewalling by employers who sought to destroy newly certified unions by refusing to negotiate with them.

J. Sexton's more recent assessment of the first agreement policies is a favourable one, particularly as it applies to the Quebec situation where 205 cases were referred to arbitration over a six-year period, and where 88 arbitration awards were imposed. There were 36 renewals, 4

strikes, and no lockouts. He notes that the experience in Quebec has been especially successful in small bargaining units, a finding different from an assessment of the British Columbia experience. Also, a commentator on Sexton's paper suggests that Quebec's industry mix may have had an important influence on its success rate.[52]

The British Columbia experience, however, raises some doubts about the utility of imposing first agreements. In almost all the units on which the B.C. Board imposed first agreements, the unions were subsequently decertified. The "bargaining units were small, employee turnover was high, the union was not able to retain or to rebuild its support, and the employer remained hostile throughout the entire experience."[53] On the basis of this experience, Weiler has recommended that the bargaining unit be quite sizeable, that the union keep an active core of supporters who are able to act effectively, and that there be

a two-year agreement in which to engage in visible administration of the contract (that is grieving discharges, seniority cases, and the like) in order to demonstrate the value of collective bargaining in action. Only in this way will the union have the footing it needs… when it must negotiate a renewal on its own.[54]

Arbitration of Unjust Dismissal Cases Where No Collective Agreement Exists

An important policy initiative was taken by the federal government in its 1977–78 amendment of the Canada Labour Code. Part III of the Code was amended to include a provision dealing with the arbitration or adjudication of unjust dismissal cases for workers not covered by collective agreements. According to section 61.5(1) of the consolidated version of Part III of the Canada Labour Code,

> any person (a) who has completed twelve consecutive months of continuous employment by an employer, and (b) who is not a member of a group of employees subject to a collective agreement may make a complaint in writing to an inspector if he has been dismissed and if he considers his dismissal to be unjust.[55]

A person wishing to act under this provision must first file a complaint with an inspector of Labour Canada who then endeavours to assist the parties in resolving the dispute. Either the person who was dismissed or the inspector may ask the employer for a written statement giving the reasons for dismissal. If the inspector is unable to obtain a settlement, the complainant may request that the case be referred to an adjudicator.

The adjudicator must consider whether or not the dismissal of the complainant was unjust, and send a copy of his or her decision on the case, with reasons, to each party and to the minister. Where an adjudicator decides that a person has been unjustly dismissed, he or she may require the employer to:

1. Pay the person compensation not exceeding the amount of money that is equivalent to the remuneration that would, but for the dismissal, have been paid by the employer to the person;
2. Reinstate the person in his employ; and
3. Do any other thing . . . to remedy or counteract any consequence of the dismissal.[56]

Compensation is usually paid for the entire period in which the worker was out of work. Sometimes, an adjudicator will order that a reprimand be removed from the worker's file in order to mitigate the consequences of wrongful dismissal.

This federal policy initiative was indeed an important one. Workers not covered by collective agreements need this provision to protect them from being fired at the whims of their employers. Since the federal government passed this legislation, the governments of Quebec and Nova Scotia have introduced similar statutes, with minor variations. No doubt other provinces will also consider implementing similar legislation in the future to protect non-unionized workers from unjust dismissal.

Accreditation of Employers' Associations

Most jurisdictions in Canada have extensive special provisions for the construction industry. One innovative provision has been the accreditation of employers' associations. Depending on the jurisdiction, accreditation may cover a large or a limited geographic area. Alternatively, special provision can be made for specific sectors of the construction industry.

Prior to the accreditation of employers' associations, a union or group of unions would often strike against only one company so as to obtain a good agreement and then use that settlement as a standard when dealing with other employers in the industry. This tactic is known as "whipsawing." The idea behind the accreditation of employers' associations is to create a better balance of power between labour and management and to prevent any one company from signing its own agreement with the unions. Instead, the association negotiates on behalf of all member employers. As a result, whipsawing has been greatly reduced in the construction industry.[57]

Compulsory Dues Check-offs

In the early days of unionism in North America, dues check-off clauses did not exist, and local union leaders spent a great deal of time canvassing their members for payment of union dues. Dues check-off clauses relieve the union of this duty by requiring the employer to deduct union dues from the workers' wages and forward the money to the union. Deducting dues on behalf of the union and deducting income tax on behalf of the Department of National Revenue represent the same type of bookkeeping procedure. Many employers, however, see a significant philosophical difference between these two kinds of deductions.

There are several different types of dues check-off clauses. The strongest is the compulsory check-off clause under which the employer must deduct union dues from every member of the bargaining unit, and the worker cannot prevent the employer from doing so. As Table 6.5 shows, the six jurisdictions of Newfoundland, Quebec, Ontario, Manitoba, Saskatchewan, and the federal government contain statutory provisions which require that collective agreements contain compulsory check-off clauses. In most cases, the employer must withhold from the wages of every worker, whether he or she is a member of the certified association or not, the amount stated as an assessment by the union.[58] In Manitoba and Newfoundland, though, the amount deducted from workers who are not union members does not include any portion of the dues which is payable for pension, superannuation, sickness, insurance, or other benefits provided by a union.[59]

A second type of clause is the irrevocable dues check-off clause, under which the worker authorizes the employer to deduct regular union dues, but cannot rescind this authorization. A third provision is the revocable dues check-off clause under which the worker authorizes the employer to deduct regular union dues, but may rescind this authorization in writing. All other jurisdictions in Canada contain a provision requiring an employer to honour a written request by a worker for the deduction of union dues from his or her wages. In some jurisdictions, the worker must allow three months to pass before revoking authorization. Most statutes require that dues be forwarded to the union at least once a month, accompanied by a statement containing the names of all workers in the bargaining unit.

Duty of Fair Representation

A somewhat troublesome problem of great concern to the courts, and more recently to legislators, is that of reconciling the rights of an individual as a willing participant in the collective bargaining relationship with the rights of the union as an effective collective bargaining agent. Sometimes, collective agreements suit one group to the detriment of another. A good

Table 6.5	Provisions Regarding Dues Check-Offs	
Jurisdiction	Compulsory dues check-off	Negotiable dues check-off
Federal	X	
Newfoundland	X	
Prince Edward Island		X
Nova Scotia		X
New Brunswick		X
Quebec	X	
Ontario	X	
Manitoba	X	
Saskatchewan	X	
Alberta		X
British Columbia		X

example of this imbalance is the gaining of benefits for full-time workers through the erosion of rights for part-time workers. Most of the concern, however, has been with the administration of collective agreements.

The Task Force on Labour Relations addressed the issue of administering collective agreements in the following terms:

> [A] troublesome issue concerns the relative rights of the collectivity and of individuals in the negotiation and administration of a collective agreement. The problem can best be illustrated in relation to the individual member's right of access to the grievance procedure and to arbitration. Normally such access is controlled by the union, and this is as it must be if collective bargaining is not to be undermined. Yet the union should be expected to exercise this discretionary power in a fair and impartial manner if it is not to have arbitrary control over its members. This suggests that a union should be able to show that it acts in good faith whenever it chooses not to pursue a member's grievance or to pursue another one contrary to his interests. This must be the limit to any concept of fair representation if responsible collective decision making within and between union and management is not to be jeopardized.[60]

Since the publication of the *Report of the Task Force on Labour Relations* in 1968, six jurisdictions — the federal, Ontario, British Columbia, Manitoba, Saskatchewan and Quebec — have enacted special provisions on the duty of fair representation (see Table 6.6). Two jurisdictions — Newfoundland and Alberta — deal with this issue under prohibited or unfair labour practices.[61] The wording in some of the statutes makes it clear that the provisions apply to the administration of the collective agreement only. For example, a 1983 revision of the Saskatchewan Trade Union Act is very specific in this respect, as is indicated in section 25.1:

> Every employee has the right to be fairly represented in grievance or rights arbitration proceedings under a collective bargaining agreement by the trade union certified to represent his bargaining unit in a manner that is not arbitrary, discriminatory, or in bad faith.

(The Newfoundland provision also clearly refers to grievances, while the Manitoba and federal acts refer to the rights of workers under a collective agreement, which presumably means the same thing.)

Far from being a monolithic organization, a union consists of a number of sub-groups: older workers and younger workers, full-time and part-time, male and female, etc. Of particular importance are older workers who have accumulated benefits such as the right to promotions, recall from layoff (both based in part on seniority), medical plans, and pensions. Balancing collective agreement clauses to meet the needs of all union members is no easy task.

Table 6.6	Jurisdictions Which Contain a Duty of Fair Representation by Unions	
Jurisdiction	Yes	No
Federal	X	
Newfoundland	X	
Prince Edward Island		X
Nova Scotia		X
New Brunswick		X
Quebec	X	
Ontario	X	
Manitoba	X	
Saskatchewan	X	
Alberta	X	
British Columbia	X	

As a result, in B.C. the statute regulating fair representation includes not only the administration but also the negotiation of collective agreements. However, it is questionable whether this inclusion is beneficial. The negotiation of collective agreements involves the internal politics of unions, and administrative tribunals might not be able to reflect the internal dynamics of union membership participation in contract negotiations. Part V of the Canada Labour Code at one time involved the CLRB in these internal politics, but the legislation was soon changed so that the Board would not have to make the kinds of decisions that union members and leaders are in the best position to make.

The Ontario Labour Relations Board has adopted a number of standards to be applied in determining the merits of a claim. One such standard is the immediate and long-term impact of a grievance decision on the whole bargaining unit when the union declines to take such a decision to arbitration. In general, the Ontario Board has accepted the principle that the individual worker does not have an absolute right to have a claim arbitrated. Furthermore, the Ontario Board places the burden of proof on the complainant in cases involving the duty of fair representation. The complainant is further expected to exhaust all other available internal remedies within the union before initiating action before the Ontario Board.

Union leaders, for their part, are obliged to consider seriously the desires of subgroups within their unions. This responsibility puts union leaders in a very delicate position, for there is often a very fine line between what does and what does not fall within the ambit of fair representation. While union leaders must be given some discretion, they must exercise it with caution: if they err, they should err on the side of aggrieved workers.

J. Rose, a long-time observer and writer on construction labour relations in Canada, has suggested that fair representation be applied to employers' associations as well as unions.[62] This suggestion is particularly relevant since all provinces except Manitoba have legislation enabling multi-employer associations to be accredited as the exclusive bargaining agents for all employers they represent. He points out that

> in many respects, the accreditation process is similar to trade union certification. The acquisition of exclusive bargaining rights is normally based on majority support, the appropriateness of the bargaining unit and the employers' association being a properly constituted organization.[63]

It would follow that the duty of fair representation should apply as much to employers' associations as to unions, given that both have similar powers of representation. To date, however, only B.C. and Ontario have such provisions.

In the absence of any statute explicitly requiring fair representation, courts in Canada have generally used the common law concept of natural justice to resolve unfair representation complaints. The two major principles of natural justice are the rule against bias, and the right to a fair hearing.

Religious Grounds for Exemption from Joining or Financing a Trade Union

In five jurisdictions — the federal, British Columbia, Manitoba, Saskatchewan and Ontario — workers who have religious objections to joining or financially supporting a trade union or both may apply to the appropriate labour relations boards for exemption (see Table 6.7). Except in Manitoba, the respective boards may not exclude such a worker from an appropriate bargaining unit as long as the worker pays an amount equivalent to union dues to a specified charity as determined jointly by the worker and the trade union or, in cases where they cannot agree, by the respective boards. (In Manitoba, the union simply ceases to be obliged in any way to represent or act on the worker's behalf.[64]

Much debate still exists regarding the pros and cons of compulsory unionism and compulsory payment of union dues. One school of thought contends that individuals should have the right to decide whether or not they will join a trade union, and make payments to the union

Table 6.7	Jurisdictions Which Exempt Union Members from Payment of Union Dues for Religious Reasons	
Jurisdiction	Yes	No
Federal	X	
Newfoundland		X
Prince Edward Island		X
Nova Scotia		X
New Brunswick		X
Quebec		X
Ontario	X	
Manitoba	X	
Saskatchewan	X	
Alberta		X
British Columbia	X[a]	

[a]B.C. exempts workers from union membership, but not from payment of union dues.

if they do not join. Other experts contend that, since all workers in the bargaining unit benefit from any provisions that the union negotiates on their behalf, all workers should belong to the union, or at least make financial contributions equal to those of union members.

This debate is not a new one. As early as 1946, a six-month strike occurred in the Ford Motor Company of Canada over the issue of union security. The UAW demanded that the collective agreement between the parties contain a clause requiring all workers to become union members, whereas the company took the position that it did not wish to compel workers to belong to the union. Eventually, an arbitrator, Justice Ivan C. Rand, concluded that since all workers benefit from the provisions of a collective agreement, it was incumbent upon them all to support financially the trade union which had won those benefits for them.[65]

Protection from the Adverse Effects of Technological Change

The problem of technological change and its impact on workers has been a major policy issue for legislators for a number of years now. Part I of the Canada Labour Code and the statutes of British Columbia, Manitoba and Saskatchewan currently provide for the reopening of negotiations when a significant or major technological change takes place.

Part I of the Canada Labour Code defines technological change as

the introduction by an employer into his work, undertaking or business of equipment or material of a different nature or kind than that previously utilized by him in the operation of the work, undertaking or business; and a change in the manner in which the employer carries on the work, undertaking or business that is directly related to the introduction of that equipment or material.[66]

Other statutes define technological change in much the same way. For example, Saskatchewan includes in its definition of technological change: "the removal by an employer of any part of his work, undertaking or business."[67]

Provisions for the settlement of disputes arising out of the introduction of technological change by the employer may be negotiated and included in a collective agreement between the parties. British Columbia requires a mandatory clause which makes provision for a settlement without stoppage of work, by arbitration or another method agreed to by the parties, of all disputes relating to adjustment of technological change.[68] All statutes referred to above specify that a significant number of workers must be affected in order for their provisions to apply, although the method of determining what constitutes a "significant number" varies.

In all of the jurisdictions with technology clauses, the employer must notify the union at least 90 days (federally, 120 days) before the change is introduced. Once notified, the union can in turn serve notice that it wishes to commence negotiations to revise the terms of the collective agreement. In cases where the employer fails to give proper notice, the union can appeal to an arbitration board in B.C. and Manitoba, or to a labour relations board in Saskatchewan and the federal jurisdiction. The powers of these tribunals vary from jurisdiction to jurisdiction, but if the ruling recognizes that a change has occurred or is being planned, the union may request that negotiations begin. Under the federal and B.C. legislation the employer must name the persons whose job are affected, and if they have been laid off, the employer must compensate them or reinstate them.

When policy makers introduced these provisions in the statutes, the intent in some jurisdictions was to encourage the parties voluntarily to include provisions in their collective agreements to cushion the impact of the effects of technological change on workers. As was noted earlier, the B.C. Industrial Relations Act *requires* that such clauses be included in every collective agreement. Whether other jurisdictions will see the problem as sufficiently serious to require amendments to their labour relations statutes remains to be seen. Given the accelerated rate of change in technology in many industries in Canada, policy makers may find such legislation increasingly important.

Unfair Labour Practices and the Roles of Labour Relations Boards

In addition to their responsibilities in the certification process and the duty to bargain in good faith, labour relations boards in Canada are charged with the responsibility of handling many other subjects in the labour relations field. One important subject is unfair labour practices.

All statutes contain provisions which prohibit employers from interfering with workers' rights to unionize and to avail themselves of the benefits of collective bargaining. According to the deputy ministers, chairs of labour relations boards, and senior union and management officials interviewed in the conduct of this study, the most common form of unfair labour practice is the dismissal of workers for exercising the rights granted to them under the statutes. A perusal of the annual reports of a number of labour departments supports this assertion.

Unions are also prohibited from using coercion in trying to influence prospective members. Like employers, unions are required to bargain in good faith in attempting to reach or revise a collective agreement, and must meet certain conditions before they may legally strike. As noted earlier, in some jurisdictions, unions are also charged with the duty of fair representation on behalf of their members. Charges of lack of fair representation are handled by labour relations boards, except in Quebec and Ontario, unless the parties request that the dispute be handled by the OLRB.

In all jurisdictions in Canada except Quebec, labour relations boards investigate allegations of many unfair labour practices. Hence, the boards play a fundamental and constructive role in the Canadian industrial relations system. In some jurisdictions, labour relations boards are quite large: they include a chair, associate or vice-chairs, and a number of union and employer representatives. Many boards with very heavy case loads prefer to sit in panels consisting of a chair or vice-chair, one union

Figure 6.5   **The Radio Shack Notice**

NOTICE TO EMPLOYEES

Posted by Order of the Ontario Labour Relations Board

We have issued this notice in compliance with an Order of the Ontario Labour Relations Board issued after a hearing in which both the Company and the Union had the opportunity to present evidence. The Ontario Labour Relations Board found that we violated the Ontario Labour Relations Act and has ordered us to inform our employees of their rights.

The Act gives all employees these rights:

To organize themselves;

To form, join or help unions to bargain as a group, through a representative of their own choosing;

To act together for collective bargaining;

To refuse to do any and all of these things.

We assure all of our employees that:

WE WILL NOT do anything that interferes with these rights.

WE WILL NOT threaten our employees with plant closure or discharge or with any other type of reprisals because they have selected the United Steel Workers of America as their exclusive bargaining representative.

WE WILL NOT attempt to get employees to inform on union activities and the desires of their fellow employees.

WE WILL NOT engage in surveillance of employee activities with respect to union organization.

WE WILL NOT intimidate or coerce employees in any way into withdrawing from the United Steel Workers of America or from supporting the United Steel Workers of America.

WE WILL NOT refuse to bargain collectively with the United Steel Workers of America as the certified bargaining agent representative of all employees as directed by the Board in the following units:

(1) All employees of the respondent in Barrie save and except foremen and persons above the rank of foreman, office and sales staff, persons regularly employed for not more than 24 hours per week and students employed during the school vacation period.

(2) All employees of the respondent who are regularly employed for not more than 24 hours per week and students employed during the school vacation period, save and except foremen, and persons above the rank of foreman, office and sales staff.

WE WILL NOT in any other manner interfere with or restrain or coerce our employees in the exercise of their rights under the Act.

WE WILL make whole the United Steel Workers of America for all losses suffered by reason of our refusal to bargain in good faith as directed by the Board.

WE WILL make whole all bargaining unit employees who suffered losses by reason of our failure to bargain in good faith as directed by the Board.

WE WILL comply with all other directions of the Ontario Labour Relations Board including:

(1) Providing the United Steel Workers of America with reasonable access to employee notice boards in our warehouse facility for a period of one year;

(2) providing the United Steel Workers of America with a list of names and addresses of all bargaining unit employees and to keep this list up to date for a period of one year;

(3) providing the United Steel Workers of America with a reasonable opportunity to be present and to reply to any speech made by management representatives to assembled employees;

(4) providing the United Steel Workers of America with an opportunity to address bargaining unit employees on company time and company premises for a period of time not exceeding thirty minutes following the reading of this notice.

WE WILL bargain collectively with the United Steel Workers of America as the duly certified collective bargaining representative of our employees in the above units as directed by the Board and if an understanding is reached, we will sign a contract with the Union.

                                                  RADIO SHACK

                                         Per: (Authorized Representative)

This is an official notice of the Board and must not be removed or defaced

This notice must remain posted for 60 consecutive working days

representative, and one management representative. In the smaller provinces, the chairs of labour relations boards are usually appointed on a part-time basis since the case load is not large enough to justify a full-time appointment.

The powers of Canadian labour relations boards differ from one jurisdiction to another. The boards derive their powers from the provisions of the labour relations acts under which they were created. Where an employer has wrongly dismissed a worker for union activities, most boards have the power to reinstate the worker with compensation to cover the loss of wages. Recently, the Ontario Labour Relations Board has ordered transgressing employers to compensate workers and, in some cases, has also required them to pay interest on any monetary loss a worker may have suffered, such as lost wages, damages, and legal expenses. The extensive remedial powers of some boards are spelled out in the statutes, usually pursuant to precedents set by other boards.

The OLRB and most others may also certify a trade union without a vote in those situations where it appears that the wishes of the workers would not be served if a vote were ordered. It was under this authority that the Ontario Labour Relations Board certified the United Steelworkers Union at the Radio Shack operation in Barrie, Ontario, on November 24, 1978. The broad range of powers possessed by labour relations boards in Canada was demonstrated through a notice which the Ontario Labour Relations Board, in December, 1979, required Radio Shack to post on its bulletin boards for 60 consecutive working days. It also required the company to send copies of the notice to the homes of workers in the bargaining units involved.[69] (A copy of the notice is included as Figure 6.5.)

This case represents one of the more blatant violations of the law by an employer in recent memory. Among other things, Radio Shack threatened its workers with plant closures, undertook surveillance of staff for union activities, used other forms of intimidation and threats, tried to deal with employees directly rather than through the union, and was charged with refusing to bargain in good faith. (This is reminiscent of similar actions taken by some employers during the 1930s, and does not typify employer reaction to unionization today.)

As indicated above, some boards in Canada may also have to impose first collective agreements on employers, deal with worker complaints against their bargaining agents, and fashion remedies appropriate to the unfair practices of the unions in question. In most jurisdictions, if one party wishes to prosecute the other party in court, permission must first be granted from the appropriate labour relations board. The boards, in determining whether there are grounds for prosecution, must investigate to some extent the merits of the case before consenting to prosecute.

Conclusion

In this chapter, we have discussed major policy issues in Canadian industrial relations and have also attempted to describe the administrative machinery established by the various jurisdictions to accomplish the policy objectives set out in their statutes. In addition to drawing comparisons among various jurisdictions, some basic philosophical questions have been raised regarding different policy approaches they take in handling the same or similar problems: should the certification of a bargaining agent be determined by 50% of those voting or by 50% of the membership? Why do British Columbia and Alberta now require a vote in every certification case? Should the payment of union dues be compulsory? It is hoped that both students and practitioners of labour relations will give some thought to these and other questions.

Questions

1 Trace the evolution of labour relations legislation in Canada.

2 Do you think Canadian governments have legislated excessively in the collective bargaining field? Elaborate.

3 Identify and discuss the four classical types of labour-management disputes. Indicate how the legislation and the machinery established by it have dealt with each of these kinds of disputes.

4 Do you consider recent policy initiatives to have favoured unionization and collective bargaining? Elaborate.

5 The Landrum-Griffin Bill, passed in the United States in 1959, concerns itself with the internal affairs of unions with a view to ensuring the democratic elections of union officers and the financial accountability of unions. The Bill also gives the Secretary of Labour the power to conduct inquiries in cases of suspected wrongdoing. Do you see the need for similar legislation in Canada? Elaborate and give some details to support your position.

6 Using the Radio Shack notice, discuss some of the unfair labour practices committed by the company. What do you think of the OLRB's decision?

8 Does labour legislation in your province favour unions or management? Why?

9 Do you think that legislation should be available to unions to have a first agreement imposed on the parties? Elaborate.

10 If you were the Minister of Labour in your province, what major changes, if any, would you make in the present legislation? Elaborate.

11 Discuss the effects of legislating labour relations provisions (such as those concerning wrongful dismissal) for non-unionized workers. Compare the advantages and disadvantages of such legislative protection with those of union protection. Do you think all jurisdictions in Canada should legislate protection for non-unionized workers? If so, what parameters do you think should exist for such legislation?

Notes

The consolidated versions of labour relations statutes have been used in the notes to this chapter. The long title of the consolidated versions will be given here, and shorter forms may be used through the remainder of the chapter. For example, rather than using repeated references to Part I of the Canada Labour Code, we will refer simply to R.S. 1985, c. L-2 and the appropriate section, e.g., s.51. This shorter form means Revised Statutes (Canada in this case), year, Chapter L-2. In some cases the R. does not appear, as is the case in Alberta and a number of provinces. Hence, S.A. refers to the Statutes of Alberta. With this brief introduction, the long titles of the consolidated versions of the 11 statutes will be indicated here. Part I of the Canada Labour Code, R.S., 1985, c. L-2; The B.C. Industrial Relations Act, 1979, R.S. Chap. 212; (This includes all of the revisions up to 1987); Alberta Labour Relations Code, 1988, Chapter L-1.2; Saskatchewan Trade Union Act, Chapter T-17 as amended in 1980-81 by c.43, 1986, c.66 and c.81, and in 1983-84, c.54; Manitoba Labour Relations Act, L.R.M. 1987, c.L10; the Ontario Labour Relations Act, R.S.O., 1980, c.228 as amended by 1983, c.42, 1984, c.34, 1986, c.17 and

1986, c.64, s.23; Quebec Labour Code, R.S.Q., Chapter C-27, updated to November 1986; New Brunswick Industrial Relations Act, Chap. 1-4, consolidated to March 31, 1987; The Nova Scotia Trade Union Act, Chapter T-17, with amendments to August 1986; P.E.I. Labour Act and Regulations, (R.S.P.E.I. 1974, Chap. L-1 as amended to September 7, 1987); and the Newfoundland Labour Relations Act, 1977, Chapter 64, with amendments to June 1986.

1 D.H. Woods, *Labour Policy in Canada*, 2nd. ed. (Toronto: Macmillan, 1973); S. Jamieson, *Industrial Relations in Canada*, 2nd ed. (Toronto: Macmillan, 1973). For an excellent and detailed analysis of Canadian labour law, see G.W. Adams, Q.C., *Canadian Labour Law: A Comprehensive Text* (Aurora, Ontario: Canadian Law Book Inc., 1985). See also H.W. Arthurs, D.D. Carter and H.J. Glasbeek, *Labour Law and Industrial Relations in Canada* (Toronto: Butterworths, 1981) and J.E. Dorsey, *Canada Labour Relations Board: Federal Law and Practice* (Toronto: Carswell, 1983).

2 For a brief overview of Canadian labour law, see J. Sack and T. Lee, "The Role of the State in Canadian Labour Relations," Vol. 44, No. 1, *Relations Industrielles/Industrial Relations* (1989), pp. 195-223; P. Verge, "Law and Industrial Relations in Quebec: Object and Context," *The State of the Art in Industrial Relations*, eds. G. Hebert, H.C. Jain, and N.M. Meltz (Kingston: Industrial Relations Centre, Queen's University and Toronto: University of Toronto Centre for Industrial Relations, 1988), Chapter 4; See also B. Adell, "Law and Industrial Relations: The State of the Art in Common Law Canada," *The State of the Art in Industrial Relations*, Chapter 5.

3 Woods, *Labour Policy in Canada*, pp. 41-42.

4 Alton Craig, *The Consequences of Provincial Jurisdiction for the Process of Company-Wide Collective Bargaining in Canada: A Study of the Packinghouse Industry* (unpublished Ph.D. Dissertation, Cornell University, 1964). Much of the material regarding the IDI Act and legislation up to the early 1950s is taken from this doctoral dissertation which is copyrighted in the author's name. A copy may be found in the Labour Canada library.

5 Canada Department of Labour, *Judicial Proceedings Respecting Constitutionality of the Industrial Disputes Investigation Act, 1907 and Amendments of 1910, 1918, and 1920* (Ottawa: Queen's Printer, 1925).

6 1925 A.C., pp. 404-05.

7 R.M. Dawson, *The Government of Canada*, 3rd rev. ed. (Toronto: University of Toronto Press, 1957), particularly the chapters dealing with the powers of the federal and provincial governments; F.R. Scott, "Federal Jurisdiction over Labour Relations — A New Look," *Proceedings*, 11th Annual Conference (Montreal: McGill University Industrial Relations Centre, 1959), pp. 35-51.

8 *Canadian Labour Relations: Report of the Task Force on Canadian Labour Relations* (Ottawa: Privy Council Office, December, 1968), pp. 210-11. The four members who formed the Task Force on Labour Relations were: Professor H.D. Woods, then of McGill University; Abbé Gérard Dion, of Laval University; John H.G. Crispo, of the University of Toronto; F.W.R. Carrothers, then president of the University of Calgary.

9 Quoted in B.M. Selekman, *Postponing Strikes: A Study of the Industrial Disputes Investigation Act of Canada* (New York: Russell Sage Foundation, 1927), p. 287.

10 H.D. Woods and S. Ostry, *Labour Policy and Labour Economics in Canada* (Toronto: Macmillan of Canada, 1962), p. 24, footnote 21.

11 Vol. XL, No. 7, *Labour Gazette* (July 1940), pp. 678-79.

12 H.A. Logan, *State Invervention and Assistance in Collective Bargaining: The Canadian Experience, 1943-1954* (Toronto: University of Toronto Press, 1956), p. 11.

13 Vol. XLI, No. 10, *Labour Gazette* (October 1941), p. 1209.

14 Ibid., p. 1209.

15 Logan, *State Intervention*; Vol. XLIV, No. 11, *Labour Gazette* (February 1944), pp. 135-43.

16 Vol. XLIV, No. 11, *Labour Gazette* (November 1946), pp. 1523-25.

17 *Industrial Relations and Disputes Investigation Act* (1948), c. 54.

18 Alberta Labour Relations Code (1988), c. L-1.2, s.1(1)(ii); Ontario Labour Relations Act, R.S.O. (1980), c. 228 as amended to 1986, c. 34, ss. 1(3)(a) and 2 (a)(b)(c); The Nova Scotia Trade Union Act, S.N.S. 1972, c. 19, s.2; Prince Edward Island Labour Act, R.S.P.E.I. (1974), Chap. L-1 with amendments to 1987, s. 7(2)(a).

19 Nova Scotia Trade Union Act, S.N.S. 1972, c. 19 as revised and amended to August 1986, s.24(14).

20 E.E. Herman, *Determination of the Appropriate Bargaining Unit by Labour Relations Boards in Canada* (Ottawa: Canada Department of Labour, November 1966), pp. 12-13.

21 Those interested in pursuing the subject of appropriate bargaining units should read Herman's work, *Determination of the Appropriate Bargaining Unit by Labour Relations Boards in Canada*.

22 Nova Scotia Trade Union Act, Chapter T-17 with amendments to August 1986, s. 24A (1)(2)(3).

23 B.C. Industrial Relations Act, 1979, R.S. Chap. 212, ss. 12, 12.1 and 13.

24 B.C. Industrial Relations Act, 1979, R.S. Chap. 212, s. 43.(1).

25 P. Weiler, *Reconcilable Differences* (Toronto: Carswell, 1980), pp. 15-49, 48-49.

26 B.C. Labour Relations Board, *Annual Report* (1974), pp. 12-13.

27 Data for the Canada Labour Relations Board were received from the Research Branch of the Board. Data for Ontario were taken from the Ontario Ministry of Labour, *Annual Report* (1982-

83), pp. 86-87; and Ontario Ministry of Labour, *Annual Report* (1983-84), pp. 81-82.

28 S.N.S., 1972, C.19, s. 26.

29 R.S., 1985, c. L-2, s. 29(3).

30 W. List, "Mediators Heal TTC's Old Wounds," *Globe and Mail* (July 3, 1979), p. 4.

31 R.S., 1985, c. L-2, s. 89.

32 S.A., 1988, c. L-1.2, ss. 73-76.

33 S.B.C. 1979, RS Chap. 212, ss. 81-82.

34 S.N.S., 1972, c. 19, s. 45(3)(a); R.S.P.E.I., 1974, c. L-1, s. 40(4).

35 Ibid.

36 R.S., 1985, c. L-2, s. 57(1).

37 "Expedited Arbitration Breaks Grievance Log-Jam," *Steel Labour* (April 1973); and Ben Fischer, "The Steel Industry's Expedited Arbitration: A Judgement after Two Years," *Arbitration Journal* (September 1973), pp. 185-90.

38 G. Dion, "Jurisdictional Disputes," Ch. 8, *Construction Labour Relations*, eds. H.C. Goldenburg and J.H.G. Crispo (Ottawa: The Canadian Construction Association, 1968), pp. 333-75.

39 R.S.O., 1980, c. 228, s. 73.(1).

40 L.R.M. 1987, c. L10, s. 12(1)(2).

41 R.S.Q., Chapter C-27, ss. 109.1-2.

42 S.B.C., 1979, RS Chap. 212, s. 57.

43 Weiler, *Reconcilable Differences*, p. 168.

44 Ibid., p. 170.

45 Ibid., p. 173.

46 Labour Canada, *Report of the Inquiry Commission on Wider-Based Collective Bargaining* (Ottawa: December, 1978).

47 Alberta *Labour Relations Code*, 1988, Chap. L-1.2, ss. 148-50.

48 S.B.C. 1979, RS Chap. 212, s. 137.93.

49 Ibid., s. 137.8.

50 S.B.C., 1979, c. 212, s. 137.6.

51 S. Muthuchidambaram, "Settlement of First Collective Agreements: An Examination of the Canada Labour Code Amendment," Vol. 35, No. 3, *Relations Industrielles/Industrial Relations* (1980), pp. 387-409.

52 J. Sexton, "First Contract Administration in Canada," and P.B. Beaumont, "Comments on First Contract Administration in Canada" (J. Sexton), *Proceedings* of the 1987 Spring Meeting of the Industrial Relations Research Association, Boston, Mass., April 29-May 1, 1987. Reprinted from *Labour Law Journal* (August 1987), pp. 508-518.

53 Weiler, *Reconcilable Differences*, p. 54.

54 Ibid.

55 Part III, Canadian Labour Code, R.S., c. L-1, with amendments to July, 1982, s. 61.5(1).

56 Ibid., s. 61(9).

57 J. B. Rose, *Public Policy, Bargaining Structure and the Construction Industry* (Toronto: Butterworths, 1980).

58 R.S.Q., 1983, c. C-27, s. 47.

59 L.R.M. 1987, c. L10, s. 76 and S.N., 1977, c.64 as amended by s.83.1 in 1985.

60 *Canadian Labour Relations: Report of the Task Force on Labour Relations*, p. 104.

61 R.S., 1985, c. L-2, s. 37; RS B.C., Chap. 212, s. 7.(1); S.A., 1988, s. 151(1)-(3); L.R.M. 1987, c. L10, s. 20; S.S., 1983, c. 81, s. 8; R.S.O., 1980, c. 228, ss. 68-69; R.S.Q., 1983, c. C-27, ss. 47.2-.5; S.N.S., 1972, c. 60, s. 53.

62 J.B. Rose, *Employer Accreditation: A Retrospective*, Research and Working Paper Series No. 206 (Hamilton: School of Business, McMaster University, June, 1983). See in particular the section on the duty of fair representation, pp. 13-17.

63 Ibid., p. 2.

64 RS B.C., 1979 Chap. 212, s. 7.(2).

65 Justice Ivan C. Rand's decision, in *Labour Gazette* (1946).

66 R.S., 1984, c. L-2, s. 51(1).

67 S.S. 1983, c. 81, s. 43.(1)(c).

68 RS B.C., 1979, c. 212, ss. 74-76.

69 Ontario Labour Relations Board, "United Steelworkers of America, *complainant* and Radio Shack, *respondent*," decision (December 5, 1979), para. 125, pp. 71-75 (Mimeographed).

Peter Redman, *The Financial Post*

7

The Negotiation Process

Introduction

The collective bargaining process constitutes a complex of activities and relationships occurring daily or continuously in the workplace, concerning both the rewards workers receive for their services and the conditions under which these services are rendered. The negotiation process, by contrast, occurs periodically and seeks to define or redefine the rewards and conditions of employment.[1] Chapter 7 treats the negotiation process as the means by which inputs (the demands of the two actors, labour and management) are converted into outputs

(the rewards to workers for services performed and the conditions under which work is performed).

Hence, the collective bargaining process consists of numerous subsets of activities, including the negotiation and implementation of the terms of collective agreements. The rewards for, or guides to, daily activities in the workplace are important to both workers and employers. If the terms of collective agreements meet the needs and expectations of the workers, are spelled out clearly, and the parties share a common understanding of them, then these terms may be implemented with few difficulties. However, if differences do occur, provisions exist for reviewing alleged breaches. The differences are often discussed on the spot by the supervisor and worker, with or without the aid of a shop steward. If such discussion does not succeed in resolving the differences, then the parties normally use the grievance process, which we will discuss in Chapter 9. This chapter, however, concentrates solely on the periodic negotiations that define the major terms and conditions under which workers provide their services.

The Negotiation Process

Within the organized segments of the private, public, and parapublic sectors, the negotiation process is the main means for converting inputs (demands) into worker-oriented and organization-oriented outputs. Should the parties fail to reach agreement through their own periodic negotiations, a variety of third-party processes exist to help break the impasse. The use of these processes may be prescribed by legislation or agreed upon between the parties, and there may be different provisions governing the private and public sectors. (The forms and functions of these supplementary processes comprise the subject matter of the following chapter.)

Among the many topics included under the rubric of industrial relations, probably none is more difficult to analyze than the negotiation process — despite the growing body of literature on the subject.[2] Rather than summarizing the several formal approaches, this chapter will explain how the negotiation process works, using the following topics: (1) negotiation units; (2) the preparation of demands; (3) the composition of negotiation committees; (4) negotiation strategy; (5) multidimensional demands; (6) bargaining power; (7) a non-deterministic approach; (8) ratification of new agreement clauses; (9) compulsory provisions; (10) the duty to bargain in good faith; and (11) concession bargaining.

Negotiation Units

The broad concept of bargaining structure and particularly the concept of the negotiation unit are critical to our discussion of the negotiation process. It is crucial to understand the term "negotiation unit" precisely in order to avoid the confusion that is often caused by the numerous meanings inherent in the term "bargaining structure." Hence, we shall begin this chapter by discussing four components of the negotiation unit, and their importance for the parties involved in negotiations.

The Components of the Negotiation Unit

Some years ago, an excellent article pointed out a number of components in the term "bargaining structure" were not always differentiated clearly, which makes the task of defining the phrases more difficult.[3] However, since we have just looked at legislation in the preceding chapter, let us begin this discussion by defining the bargaining structure from a legislative point of view.

Certified Bargaining Unit   The discussion of the regular certification process and the quickie vote in the previous chapter pointed out that labour relations boards first determine whether or not a unit proposed by a bargaining agent is an appropriate bargaining unit, except in cases of voluntary recognition. This determines the extent of the election district or certified bargaining unit. In a company that consists of only one establishment, this unit may become the "negotiation unit" which the parties use for negotiating a collective agreement. On the other hand, a certified bargaining unit may be one of a number of building blocks in a negotiation unit which will eventually emerge by mutual agreement of the parties — a situation which typically occurs in a company consisting of more than one establishment.

Decision-Making Unit   A second component, and for our purposes the most important, is a kind of negotiation unit defined as the "decision-making unit" through which the parties engage in formal discussions leading to a settlement of the outstanding issues. The settlement reached between the parties may result in one collective agreement covering all the workers in all the certified units, or it may result in as many separate collective agreements as there are certified units. Hence, the number of negotiation units may be fewer than the number of certified bargaining units. The number of certified bargaining units, however, will never be greater than the number of negotiating units.

The negotiating unit may include members from some or all of the separately certified bargaining units. For example, all of the packinghouse plants of Canada Packers across the country hold separate certificates issued by the appropriate provincial labour relations boards. The parties, however, formed a national negotiation unit which, until recently, brought together not only senior representatives from the head office of the company and the union, but also company and union representatives from plants all across the country. All these people represented one large negotiation unit. The collective agreement reached by this particular unit covered over 5,000 production workers in Prince Edward Island, Quebec, Ontario, Manitoba, Saskatchewan and Alberta, although some of the terms of the agreement varied from one province to another.[4] For example, the statutory civic holiday falls on different days in each of the provinces. Hence, single collective agreements may contain global provisions with applications which vary from plant to plant. The most common way such provisions are embodied is through master agreements with supplementary local agreements, as is the case in the auto industry.

Unit of Direct Impact   A third component of the bargaining structure is the unit of direct impact[5] — that negotiating unit which affects directly the agreements of other units. When a settlement is reached between Canada Packers and the union representing its workers, for example, the terms of that settlement are incorporated directly into the collective agreement between the union and Swifts, another large meat-packing company. This pattern began during World War II and continued up until the early eighties, when local labour market conditions combined with the different ages of the plants to create a more decentralized structure of bargaining.

Appropriate Bargaining Unit   One board chair has pointed out that labour relations boards are confronted with two competing concepts of an appropriate bargaining unit. To begin with, the unit may be deemed the one in which the union has sufficient worker support to give it the greatest chance of acquiring bargaining rights with the employer. This was a major consideration of the Canada Labour Relations Board in a 1977 decision in which it decided that the appropriate unit for a bank union was the branch, rather than all of the bank's workers across Canada.[6] However, the most appropriate unit for certification purposes may *not* be the most appropriate for negotiation purposes later on. This conflict has been pointed out by P. Weiler:

> It is a common experience of labour boards to find that these two uses of the "unit" point in opposite directions when the board must decide on the precise boundaries of an appropriate unit. What looks like an optimal structure for long-range negotiations may also be worlds removed from any grouping of employees within which the trade union could hope to obtain majority support in the short run.[7]

The appropriate bargaining unit, the negotiation unit, and the unit of direct impact represent three overviews of the concept of bargaining structure. For the purpose of this chapter, we shall be concerned mainly with the negotiating unit as our unit of analysis. There will be some discussion, however, of the unit of direct impact as it relates to pattern bargaining.

Determinants of Negotiation Units

Legislative Framework One of the major determinants of the negotiation unit is the legislative framework. This framework serves as the foundation on which the union-management relationship is built. In Canada, there are two aspects to the legislative foundation. First, Canada's decentralized system means that most of our certified bargaining units are confined to the provincial level. However, there is nothing preventing the parties from informally or extra-legally forming multi-provincial negotiating units which include a number of separately certified bargaining units. These broader types of negotiating units are found in industries such as meat-packing, automobile and steel manufacturing, canning, and pulp and paper production.

Decentralization Second, most labour relations boards in Canada define the appropriate bargaining unit as including both production and craft workers in an establishment. Some even include professional engineers if the majority of these workers wish to be included. The major exception to this means of certification occurs in British Columbia where unions are often certified as bargaining agents for all the establishments of a company, and where councils of trade unions may be certified as bargaining agents for all of the workers affected directly by employers' associations in any industry whatsoever (rather than simply in the construction industry, as in most other Canadian jurisdictions).[8] The major point to keep in mind here is the strong emphasis placed on single-establishment certification by most provincial labour relations boards. This emphasis contributes greatly to Canada's decentralized negotiation structure.

Some governments play a centralizing role in the public sector where, as in British Columbia and Ontario, the negotiation units are two-tier: one for working conditions only and others for wages only. As we shall indicate in Chapter 10, bargaining agents for public-sector workers are named by some provincial statutes.

Market Forces Another major determinant of negotiation structure is the role played by market forces. As A.R. Weber has pointed out, unions have generally sought negotiation units which are "coextensive with the specific market(s) encompassed by their jurisdictions."[9] As a general rule, industrial unions press for negotiation units which are as broad as the scope of the product market, while craft union are more concerned with conditions in local labour markets. A good example of an industrial union is the Canadian Auto Workers. Until the recent separation, the Canadian and United States sections tried to reach similar agreements with the Big Three auto companies for workers in both Canada and the United States. A good example of a craft union is one which operates in the construction industry. In both situations, unions are trying to take labour "out of competition" in order to require companies to compete on a basis other than wages.

Centralization An employer's operations can also have a significant effect on the nature of the negotiation unit. Unions will press for company-wide negotiations, for example, when the employer operates autonomous establishments. This is particularly true in industries like meat-packing, where each plant of a company operates as an autonomous unit. If one plant is struck, the company can usually supply the market from another plant which is located nearby. The United Packinghouse Workers Union (Now the United Food and Commercial Workers International Union) won the right to national negotiations with the Big Three meat-packing companies (Canada Packers, Swifts, and Burns) during World War II — a right which the union and its successors have, until recently, clung to despite the fact the companies operate under different provincial jurisdictions.

The United Steelworkers Union has also carried on joint negotiations with the southern Ontario and Quebec plants of the Steel Company of Canada despite the fact that this industry, too, operates under provincial jurisdiction. No agreement is acceptable to the union unless it meets the minimal demands of the big local unions at both Stelco in Hamilton and the Notre Dame works in Montreal. Clearly, some unions are strong enough to obtain and maintain multi-provincial negotiation units despite the fact that the employers with whom they deal fall under provincial jurisdiction.

In some cases, however, it is employers who initiate more centralized forms of negotiation in order to increase their bargaining power with one or more large unions. This practice occurs in much of the clothing and printing industries in Ontario and Quebec as well as the trucking industry in a number of provinces where negotiations take place through multi-employer bargaining councils. By joining together and forming a consolidated structure these small companies minimize the economic harm which might be inflicted on them by large unions. For example, the Council of Printing Industries in Ontario and Quebec negotiates with the Graphic Arts International Union on behalf of 55 companies.[10] Most of these small companies would not be able to withstand a lengthy strike.

In some cases, both unions and employers prefer larger negotiation units in order to obtain uniformity in fringe benefits and to facilitate administration.[11] From the workers' point of view, however, centralized bargaining may not seem desirable, since workers may have little input into the negotiation process.[12] In addition, internal trade-offs between union and management may be much more difficult in such large structures. Managers at the local level may also object to highly centralized negotiation structures if they erode decision-making powers that managers presume to be part of their own function. Administrators in hospitals and schools in Quebec are isolated from the negotiation process because of the very highly-centralized negotiations which take place in the parapublic sectors in that province. (Chapter 10 will deal with the legislative structure of negotiations in Quebec.)

An enormous diversity of negotiation structures exist in Canada. Negotiations for collective agreements take place almost every day.

There is no such thing as a major national case around which all others revolve, as there is in Australia: once an agreement is settled in Australia's metal industries, it spreads to others very quickly.

Some calendar years, however, see much more negotiation activity than others, particularly when many of the groups in the federal and provincial public sectors come up for negotiations during the same year.

The highly unionized public sectors in Canada at the federal, provincial, and municipal levels have made for somewhat more centralized negotiation structures than would otherwise exist. The increased incidence of unionization in these sectors since 1964 has seen a pronounced shift in the direction of multi-establishment negotiation units, as we will see later. In the federal and provincial sectors, negotiations for each major group of workers takes place for all workers in the group no matter how scattered they may be across the province or country.

Pattern Bargaining What the system of negotiations in Canada lacks in centralized negotiation structures may be made up for in part through the adoption of pattern bargaining. As indicated earlier, the outcome of a particular set of negotiations may have a significant impact on other negotiations. Pattern bargaining revolves around the notion of the unit of direct impact. Pattern bargaining tends to occur where negotiations in one industry, company, or local level serve as a fulcrum for negotiations in other industries, companies, or localities. One major study concluded that "wage spillovers can only be found for bargaining units in similar industries within a region."[13] The auto industry has traditionally been characterized by informal pattern bargaining; the UAW focuses its efforts on one company while dragging on negotiations with the other two companies. Once a settlement is reached with the target company, the union then uses this settlement as a standard in negotiations with the other two large companies. A similar situation exists in the steel industry. The United Steelworkers Union will use either Stelco or Algoma Steel as a target, and then use the settlement reached with the target as a standard in concluding an agreement with the rival company.

J.C. Anderson gives an example of a formal, intercity pattern-bargaining situation which is unique: In British Columbia, where fire fighters' negotiations in Vancouver dominate the outcome of negotiations in the rest of the province,

> over 80 percent of the municipalities in the province with collective agreements have included a provision agreeing to either settle for the same salary as the Vancouver fire fighters or to give some fixed proportion (for example, 90 percent) of the Vancouver salary to their fire fighters.[14]

This kind of iron-clad pattern bargaining is unusual, but it demonstrates again how pattern bargaining can actually act as an almost perfect substitute for a broader negotiating unit.

Types of Negotiation Units

Table 7.1 shows the different types of negotiation units that concluded negotiations for each year cited, while Table 7.2 gives the percentage of workers covered by each type. An eight-type topology is used to differentiate among negotiation units in the two tables. Note that the single-union type accounts for more than 90% of the negotiation units and workers in most years. Most of the multi-union types occur in the railway and pulp and paper industries, as well as in the federal government drydocks.

On the employer side, a different pattern exists. Single-employer negotiation units generally comprise over 85% of negotiation units (Table 7.1, columns 1 to 4), covering from 54% of workers in 1967 to 87% in 1977 (Table 7.2, columns 1 to 4). At the single-employer level, an interesting contrast appears between single-establishment and multi-establishment units. Although single-establishment negotiation units comprise around 40% to 50% of all negotiation units (Table 7.1, columns 1 and 2), they

generally cover only about 20% of workers (Table 7.2, columns 1 and 2). The proportion of negotiation units that fall into the single-establishment category is relatively high in comparison with the others, partly because 500 workers is the cut-off point for inclusion. Many negotiation units just barely attain this level. School boards and teacher negotiation units in some provinces, especially Ontario, are very decentralized and small. Negotiations in this sector take place at the local rather than the provincial level.

Multi-establishment negotiation units, on the other hand, cover only about one third of all negotiation units that bargain each year. Nevertheless, multi-establishment negotiation units have accounted for from 36% (1967) to 72% (1973) of workers because of the inclusion of federal and provincial public-sector workers in this category. A number of larger companies in the private sector, such as Stelco and Canada Packers, and members of the auto industry, negotiate on a multi-establishment basis. Allowing for differences in calculations, it is still evident that the multi-establishment, single-employer category covers a higher proportion of workers now than it did prior to 1967.[15]

Multi-employer negotiation units comprise about 4% to 8% of the negotiation units that bargain each year. The percentage of workers covered varies considerably from year to year depending upon the size of the negotiation units. For example, railway agreements in 1967, 1971, and 1979 account for a fairly large proportion of the workers whose agreements were concluded in those years, while the 6% in 1976 includes province-wide negotiations among Quebec hospitals and their unions.

Employer-association bargaining (Tables 7.1 and 7.2, columns 7 and 8) ranges from a low of 6% of negotiation units in 1969 to highs of 13% and 16% in 1967 and 1984 respectively. More dramatic, however, is the variation in the percentage of workers covered by this type of negotiation unit which ranges from a low of 8% in 1971 to highs of 27% in 1974, 10% in 1976 and

Table 7.1   Percentage Distribution of Negotiating Units Covering 500 or More Employees by Type for Negotiations Concluded Each Year, Excluding Construction, 1966-1984

Type of Negotiating Unit	1966	1967	1968	1969	1970	1971	1972	1973	1974	1975	1976	1977	1978	1979	1980	1981	1982	1983	1984
Single Employer																			
Single Establishment, Single Union	55	51	49	47	45	45	43	44	40	48	51	43	48	51	49	48	43	49	45
Single Establishment, Multi-Union	1	3	5	a	4	2	1	2	1	a	2	5	2	1	4	2	1	3	1
Multi-Establishment, Single Union	30	25	30	40	34	39	38	39	43	39	30	38	35	36	30	40	46	39	35
Multi-Establishment, Multi-Union	a	1	2	1	2	1	a	3	a	1	2	1	1	a	2	1	1	a	1
Multi-Employer																			
Single Union	4	6	3	4	4	4	4	6	4	4	4	4	3	3	4	3	1	3	2
Multi-Union	a	2	1	1	1	1	a	1	a	1	1	a	a	a	1	a	a	a	a
Employer Association																			
Single Union	8	13	8	6	9	7	11	8	7	7	9	9	8	9	6	5	4	4	14
Multi-Union	a	a	a	1	a	a	1	1	1	1	1	a	a	1	1	2	1	1	2
n	181	175	283	328	295	322	325	327	403	391	525	544	578	484	485	410	412	487	455

[a]Less than .5%.

Source: Labour Data Branch, Labour Canada, *Collective Bargaining Review,* 1966-1984. The Labour Canada data deal with major collective agreements, and not negotiating units. Hence, in coding the information according to the concept of the negotiating unit, many judgment calls had to be made and my role in supervising the data compiled for the study published in 1968 was extremely useful. See Alton W. J. Craig and Harry J. Waisglass, "Collective Bargaining Perspectives," Vol. 23, No. 4, *Industrial Relations/Relations Industrielles* (1968), pp. 570-90, Tables 1 and 2. The term *n* refers to the number of negotiating units each year. Our figures are lower than those reported in the *Collective Bargaining Review* since we deal with negotiating units and not collective agreements. The construction industry is included for the first time in 1984.

Table 7.2 Percentage Distribution of Employees in Types of Negotiating Units Covering 500 or More Employees During Negotiations Concluded Each Year, Excluding Construction, 1966-1984

Type of Negotiating Unit	1966	1967	1968	1969	1970	1971	1972	1973	1974	1975	1976	1977	1978	1979	1980	1981	1982	1983	1984
Single Employer																			
Single Establishment, Single Union	23	23	19	15	18	17	15	16	13	21	18	20	22	19	18	19	12	15	15
Single Establishment, Multi-Union	a	1	2	a	2	1	a	1	1	a	1	4	2	1	2	1	a	2	1
Multi-Establishment, Single Union	45	30	47	64	54	57	56	65	55	62	49	62	52	57	51	62	63	61	45
Multi-Establishment, Multi-Union	a	a	6	a	7	1	a	7	a	2	a	1	1	a	2	1	a	a	a
Multi-Employer																			
Single Union	11	12	2	3	2	5	5	2	4	4	4	4	4	6	10	6	1	8	4
Multi-Union	1	20	11	4	1	12	a	1	1	a	6	a	a	5	1	a	a	a	2
Employer Association																			
Single Union	19	13	13	13	14	8	24	8	12	13	13	11	13	11	13	10	9	7	16
Multi-Union	2	a	1	a	2	a	a	1	15	2	7	1	a	a	3	2	14	6	17

aLess than .5%

Source: Labour Data Branch, Labour Canada, *Collective Bargaining Review*, 1966-1984. The Labour Canada data deal with major collective agreements, and not negotiating units (see source to Table 7.1). The total employee figures in our study are very close to those reported in *Collective Bargaining Review* except for the year 1977.

1978 and 33% in 1984. In 1974, a railway association negotiated on behalf of more than 70,000 railway workers that year.

The year 1978 witnessed negotiations by the Railway Association of Canada, the Newfoundland Hospital Association, the Alberta Hospital Association, the Saskatchewan Health Care Association, the Health Labour Relations Association of British Columbia, the Quebec Motor Transport Industrial Relations Bureau, and the Fisheries Association of British Columbia. Also included were employer associations in the pulp and paper and food industries in British Columbia, and in the printing and clothing industries in British Columbia, Ontario, and Quebec. The construction industry was represented for the first time in 1984. Most of the negotiations in this industry are conducted with employers' associations.

Although insufficient data exist to show an increase in association bargaining, the figures for the 1966 to 1984 period give the general sense that such a development is underway, although likely at the provincial level since few industries fall under federal jurisdiction. The extent of association bargaining was much higher in 1984, since the data collected and analyzed by Labour Canada that year included the construction industry for the first time. An increase in association bargaining has occurred in this industry with the advent of accreditation of employer associations in the late 1960s.[16]

Employer association bargaining has possible implications for bargaining outcomes. Since one of the objectives of employer association bargaining is to unite employers and to offset whipsawing tactics by unions, one could hypothesize that bargaining outcomes in association bargaining would be lower than if employers bargained individually. Also, employer association bargaining, which usually occurs on an industry-wide basis, is likely to result in more uniform settlements than would be true if the individual companies of the association negotiated their own collective agreements. From the employees' point of view, there may be more external equity in the wage structures among the companies that bargain on an association basis. These hypotheses, however, are subject to empirical testing for verification.

The Preparation of Demands

Virtually all North American collective agreements have a specified term of duration. This term may range from less than a year to five years. The significance of a fixed-duration agreement is that the parties prepare for, and engage in, negotiations some time before it expires in the hope of replacing it with a new agreement. This is what Stevens calls the "deadline rule." The deadline rule refers to the threat or actual use of a strike or lockout at the end of an agreement. The deadline rule has a significant impact on how negotiations proceed, particularly during the latter stages when the parties may hastily agree to trade-offs so as to avoid a work stoppage.[17]

Long before the two parties begin actual talks they start preparing demands and counterdemands, which form the agenda items for the negotiations. The preparation of demands has at least two dimensions: (1) the structural process of formulating demands; and (2) the actual sources from which demands emerge. The structural aspects will be discussed first.

Structures for the Determination of Demands

There has been no systematic study of the ways in which bargaining demands are prepared in the industrial relations systems of Canada or the United States. This is probably due to the large number of unions and the highly decentralized nature of negotiations in each country, which make for a variety of negotiation structures. However, it is still possible, by using examples, to indicate some of the ways in which demands are prepared.

Since unions are not homogeneous organizations, divergent demands sometimes emerge even within a small negotiation unit. For example, workers nearing retirement may be interested in improving the pension plan whereas young workers may be more concerned with immediate take-home pay. The negotiating committee's job of reconciling these competing claims is what Walton and McKersie call "intra-organizational bargaining."[18] Similarly, within the management group, the marketing manager may wish to avoid a strike in order to meet commitments to customers while the finance officer may wish to keep labour costs to a minimum.

If bargaining is conducted largely between a local union and a single plant, the demands of the union are likely to be prepared by local members. In these cases, a negotiating committee is usually formed. This committee normally canvasses members of the local to see what items they would like to have negotiated. After receiving suggestions, the negotiating committee will sometimes try to reconcile competing demands from various subgroups before proposing a negotiation package to the entire membership for approval. If representatives of a national union or Canadian branch of an international union are members of the negotiation committee, they may wish to include items that the union has included in collective agreements with other employers.

In a multi-establishment structure, the preparation of demands may be somewhat more complex. The members of the various locals may hold meetings or policy conferences to formulate a package of demands. This package may be sent to representatives of the head office who will then sift through the demands and sort out, where possible, the conflicting ones. Prior to the commencement of negotiations, a meeting of all members of the negotiation committee may take place to finalize the package.

The Meat-Packing Industry The history of preparing demands in the meat-packing industry has been characterized by a number of methods. In the 1940s, the Canadian division of the United Packinghouse Workers Union some-times sent letters to the locals seeking their demands. This approach usually met with indifference and it was left to the National Office of the Canadian District to form demands which were then discussed by delegates from the various locals on the negotiation committee prior to talks with management. The officers of the Canadian District had a fair amount of say in preparing the demands, particularly since they usually tried to get uniform benefits for union members in the Big Three — Canada Packers, Swifts and Burns. Since the plants of the three companies were often in close proximity, the workers could meet to compare notes on their respective wage-benefit packages. As the union evolved and international conventions were held more frequently, the members of the Canadian District started to meet separately from their American counterparts to formulate a package of demands to be served on the Big Three in Canada and also on the smaller companies.[19]

The Steel Industry In the steel industry in Ontario and Quebec, the main negotiations usually take place between the United Steelworkers Union and the Steel Company of Canada (Stelco) in Hamilton, or sometimes the Algoma Steel Company. Representatives from other local unions in Stelco plants usually play an active part in preparing the demands to be served on Stelco, because the agreement at the Hamilton plant serves as a pattern for other Stelco basic steel and fabricating plants in Ontario and Quebec. While the Canadian director has a substantial input into the formulation of demands, so do workers from the Notre Dame Works in Montreal, since the final settlement at Stelco in Hamilton also serves as a pattern for the Montreal plants and to some degree for the fabricating plants.

The Railways Negotiations in the two major Canadian railways, CN and CP, have a very complex structure for determining demands, particularly since the unions sometimes negotiate as two major groups — one for the operating personnel (those who run the trains) and another for the non-operating personnel (repair and maintenance workers, etc.). On some occasions, as many as 17 unions have been involved in the process.

Let us take one union as an example: the Canadian Brotherhood of Railway, Transport and General Workers (CBRT&GW) which is one of the major non-operating unions. In the preparation for the 1977 negotiations with the railways, the national office of the union asked the locals to send in their demands by January 21, 1977. Some 500 to 600 demands were received from the locals, many of which were similar in content. A five-member resolutions committee was set up to study, correlate, amalgamate, and reword the demands. In addition, proposals were submitted by the National Executive Board of the union. Then a three-day meeting of the Brotherhood's Railway Local Chairman's Conference was held. This conference adopted more than 100 major and addendum demands, the latter covering local work practices. The addendum proposals were to be submitted to the railways at the end of March 1977. The major demands were to be processed by the National Executive Board of the union and were to be presented to the railways in October 1977. To further complicate the picture, the Brotherhood's demands became part of the overall demands adopted by all of the non-operating unions involved in the negotiations.[20]

The Automobile Industry Until recently, bargaining in the Canadian automobile industry has been closely tied in with that in the United States, in part because the same union and companies operate on both sides of the border. The 1965 Auto Pact agreement between the Canadian and American governments was designed to rationalize production facilities and narrow the gap between automobile prices in Canada and the United States. J. Crispo has pointed out that the Canadian negotiators for the Big Three automakers always attended the pre-negotiation sessions held in the United States:

> The bargaining tie-in between the two countries is so close in some industries that Canadian negotiations are not seriously begun until the appropriate settlements have been wrapped up in the United States. This is usually a reflection of corporate as well as trade-union practices.[21]

Now that Canadian auto workers have their own union, a new pattern may well emerge in the coming years, but it is too early at this stage for any structure to have become firmly established.

In most of these industries, local union members' desires are taken into account in local supplements to the master agreements which allow for variation in contract terms among different plants of the same company (as long as these are consistent with the terms of the master agreement between the company and the union). The Canadian union will likely formulate demands and establish priorities on its own terms. However, as the wounds from the UAW-CAW split heal, informal links between the two unions are likely to develop.

The Public and Parapublic Sectors The unions and associations in the public and parapublic sectors formulate demands in a variety of ways because of the relatively recent advent of unionism in these sectors and the particular legislative provisions that govern collective bargaining for public-service workers. In the federal public service, a large number of negotiation units are grouped into specific occupational categories. Each of these groups formulates its own demands, although the bargaining agent (whether it be the Public Service Alliance of Canada (PSAC), the Professional Institute of Public Service (PIPS), or some other union) will have specific proposals that it would like to see incorporated into all agreements which it negotiates. In 1985, PSAC negotiations became sector-wide on many issues, with each subgroup negotiating for its own demands.

Public-sector bargaining is more centralized in Quebec than in Ottawa: in 1972, the Common Front (the CNTU, QFL, and the Teachers' Corporation) representing provincial public servants and parapublic workers negotiated with the Quebec government at a common table over such issues as wages and salaries, job security, and social insurance. Issues peculiar to specific groups such as hospital workers, teachers, and professional and non-professional public servants were negotiated at sector tables.[22] (More will be said about this in Chapter 10.)

Some Comparisons The few examples cited above do not cover all the ways in which union demands are prepared, but they do indicate some of the typical procedures. They also serve to demonstrate the varying degrees of influence exerted by the leading officials of national unions, Canadian directors of international unions, and trade union and corporate links between Canada and the United States.

Employers, like unions, use a variety of methods to develop their proposals and counter-proposals. In a single-plant company, bargaining proposals are likely to be developed by the company's management, possibly with the aid of industrial relations specialists. In a multi-plant company, proposals and counter-proposals may be developed by the chief personnel officer or designated negotiator, who receives inputs from responsible officials of the various plants that form part of the negotiation unit.

In a number of cases, employer associations may be responsible for developing proposals and counter-proposals. Many suggestions come from the companies themselves, and are submitted to the association membership for acceptance. CN and CP, for example, establish an informal negotiation unit, sometimes with other smaller railways, for the purpose of bargaining jointly with unions representing operating and non-operating personnel. Although no formal structure exists for preparing joint proposals and counter-proposals, there is a good deal of discussion between the two companies in developing their agenda items.

In the public sector, bureaucrats are often faced with a different problem: that of reconciling the need for autonomy in bargaining with the explicit requirement of public accountability. Often conflict manifests itself in a wrangle with the union over who the real employer is. This situation is true not only for the public service but also for such institutions as hospitals and school boards. Simply put, the important question is this: Is the designated employer the real employer, or is the government the real employer? Under the federal Public Service Staff Relations Act, the Treasury Board is the official employer for government departments and a number of agencies. But on a number of occasions, the federal Cabinet has seemed to be the real power behind management.[23]

The government, being both legislator and employer, is sometimes placed in an awkward position in negotiations. While private employers are profit-oriented, a government is a collector of revenue, mainly taxes, which it is presumed to spend for the common good. Ultimate responsibility to the taxpayer, therefore, creates a political problem when it comes to satisfying union demands. In times of recession, Cabinet may be faced with the need to cut back on spending because of a large deficit, and thus cut back employment and deny requests for salary increases — all of which creates resentment, confrontation, and low morale. The restraint programs in effect from 1982 to 1984 had devastating effects in some jurisdictions, particularly in British Columbia where the possibility of a province-wide strike loomed large. In 1985, the federal government cut back spending in agencies such as the CBC, Canada Council, and National Research Council, and encouraged early retirement among employees of government departments to reduce employment costs. In 1989, the federal government, in its efforts to reduce the deficit, once again cut back the CBC budget, abandoned its commitment to nuclear submarines, and trimmed social programs such as the unemployment insurance program, day-care centres, and others. These actions provoked bitter attacks by a number of unions.

Parapublic entities such as hospitals and schools boards derive their revenue from provincial funds. By the time fixed expenditures are allocated and other facilities provided for, there may not be much room for manoeuvering in the negotiation of wage increases, particularly where the government pays the full cost of hospital and other services.

Sources for the Determination of Demands

If the parties are bargaining for the first time, the union may take an existing agreement with which it is satisfied and present the provisions contained therein as its set of demands, or proposals (management responses are sometimes referred to as "counter-proposals"). This method of beginning negotiations has been used in the construction industry and in a number of parapublic organizations (hospitals and nursing homes). In most cases, however, union leaders and members will also include in their proposals some kind of a union security clause and a dues check-off provision, to ensure the strength and continuity of the union, and provide its leaders with the security to concentrate more on the workers' needs and less on political concerns.

Even after it concludes its first agreement, a union may look to the bargaining positions of unions in the same industry as the basis for its own demands in subsequent rounds. We discussed this "pattern bargaining" tactic in the section on the structure of negotiation units. In a union-management relationship that has existed for some time, however, one of the prime sources for determining demands on both sides is experience with the present collective agreement. If certain clauses cause many grievances, it is in the interest of the two parties to try to have those clauses changed, even though disagreement may exist over what needs changing. Supervisors and shop stew-

ards are good sources of information and advice to management and union negotiators in this respect.

The economic climate and business prospects for the future may spur some union leaders to make demands for which there are no precedents. For example, the fear of unemployment due to technological change prompted the later Walter Reuther, former president of the UAW, to seek a form of guaranteed annual wage in the mid-1950s. More recently, unions have been seeking other provisions to protect workers who lose their jobs due to technological change. Such attempts have been difficult, since union demands for some measure of control over the introduction of technological change challenge what management perceives to be its traditional prerogative.

A company may use its poor financial performance as a reason for offering a smaller wage increase than that given by companies in the same industry. For example, in February 1977, negotiators for the American Motors Corporation and the UAW agreed to terms that were lower than those negotiated with Ford, Chrysler, and General Motors. Union representatives were reported to have said that the settlement would permit the company to stay afloat financially.[24]

Early in 1982, American workers at both Ford and General Motors also agreed to give up previously won concessions to help their companies out of serious financial difficulties. However, the 1984 settlement with GM and Ford restored many of the 1982 concessions: benefits such as paid holidays, lump-sum payments, and profit-sharing plans. Moreover, the agreements contained provisions to help avoid situations such as those which occurred prior to the 1982 negotiations.

The rate of inflation is a key factor in the preparation of wage demands. The high rate of inflation in Canada during the 1970s led many unions to seek high wage settlements. Changes in productivity, ability to pay, and other factors are also relevant in the formulation of proposals and counter-proposals by unions and employers. An employer's competitive position with respect to domestic or international markets may determine to some degree the benefit package that it will be prepared to offer as a counterproposal.

Unions also use factors such as increased inflation and higher productivity to justify the demands that they put forward. However, non-monetary issues, such as a union's demands that all new workers become members of the union, may be supported by highly developed philosophical arguments. Likewise, an employer's opposition to such a proposal may also have strong ideological underpinnings. These issues are some of the more difficult ones to resolve in negotiations since they represent well-entrenched philosophical extremes.

The Composition of Negotiation Committees

The composition of negotiating committees may be as diverse as the various ways in which demands are prepared. To negotiate on a plant-by-plant basis, a negotiating committee for the union will probably be elected by the local membership. Such a committee usually represents the many interest groups in the local. Generally, there is also a field officer from the larger union of which the local is a part. The field officer often acts as the union's main spokesperson, and is constantly kept informed of the members' wishes by the elected local representatives on the negotiating committee.

In complex bargaining structures involving a number of plants and locations, a senior officer of the national union or a Canadian director of an international union will probably be involved. In the meat-packing industry, for example, the Canadian director of the international union leads the negotiation committee, but there are usually representatives of the various locals involved, as well as plant superintendents on the management side. This arrangement allows local individuals to speak to the issues that apply to the particular plants they represent. These individuals also act as information sources to the union members and plant management when it comes to explaining the provisions of the agreements and are useful in processing grievances since they know the original intent of certain clauses. Sometimes, however, negotiating committees become unwieldy. In these cases, a small number of delegates may be elected to form a negotiating committee, while the other members act as observers or take part in sub-committees set up to study particularly difficult issues.

Top union officials are sometimes accused of making too many decisions without ascertaining the wishes of members of their locals. For this reason, the appointment of representatives from the various special interest groups helps to bring a greater sense of democratic decision-making to the bargaining table. However, if the representatives of the various locals have divergent views on similar problems it may become difficult for negotiations to proceed effectively, since the union may not be speaking with one voice. Large negotiating committees run into the problem of maintaining democracy at the local level while preserving enough centralized control to keep negotiations on track. Forming a small negotiating committee with side members on subcommittees helps to alleviate this problem to some extent.

The employer is usually represented by one or more senior management members, who in turn may be aided by an expert from personnel or industrial relations staff, if the company is large enough to have a well-developed personnel department. The company president, however, is usually the chief management spokesperson and must assume responsibility for the final management offer. The president may also be co-chair of the negotiating committee, along with the chief union negotiator.

Negotiation Strategy

In the ordinary course of events, the union initially presents its set of demands to the employer, either before or at the initial meeting between the two negotiating teams. Management is then given some time to study the union's demands or proposals, and to develop its counter-proposals. The employer may initiate demands of its own, of course, on items that may or may not be among the union's demands. After this first exchange, the bargaining agenda begins to become clear to each side and serious negotiations begin. Usually the parties will have more demands than they expect to obtain. This is what C. Stevens calls the "large-demand rule" of the negotiation game.

Although the negotiation process involves a relationship between two interdependent organizations, this relationship is mediated by the principal representatives or negotiators for each side, whose job it is to try to find the true settlement position of the other party. To start, each side puts forward a large number of demands, some of which are considered essential and others tradeable or indicative of what will become serious issues in the future. The large agenda gives both sides room to manoeuvre.

The Contract Zone

Through the negotiation process, the number of demands will gradually be narrowed down as each party gains a better understanding of the other's true position. Eventually, this will lead to the discovery of a contract zone — that is, some intermediary area between the two sets of demands wherein both parties would rather settle than undertake a strike or lockout. Stevens describes the first step in negotiations in the following terms:

> The initial bargaining proposal is an information-seeking device. During the early stages of negotiations, each party, in addition to giving information about (and concealing) his own preferences, is attempting to discover the true preferences of his opponents. In part, the negotiator will infer these preferences from his opponent's bargaining position. He will also infer them from his opponent's reaction to his own bargaining position. The parties at this stage are attempting to demarcate the limits of the contract zone. The movement from initial bargaining positions to some fairly clear perception of the range within which (if any) an outcome by agreement can lie is devious. There is reliance upon ceremonial and semi-ritual modes and upon sign language as each side attempts to estimate the meaning of what is said by the other side.[25]

Essentially what Stevens is saying here is that initial bargaining proposals act as information-seeking devices whereby each party is trying to infer the bottom line of the other party. Each party seeks to gauge the position of the other by observing their reactions to the various proposals put forward. This exchange sets the upper and lower limits of the contract zone, but any miscalculation of what these limits are can be dangerous. There are certain ceremonial and semi-ritual modes of behaviour that each negotiator is expected to use to try to influence the other party — and also to impress his or her constituents. Voice intonation, gestures, etc. are as important, if not more important, than the actual language used.

Figure 7.1 depicts two situations that are characteristic of negotiations when the parties are trying to map out a contract zone. In Situation A, there is no overlap between the management's upper limit and the union's lower limit. Therefore, no contract zone exists since the union is not prepared to agree to management's highest offer. The only way a contract zone could come into being is if the parties were prepared to shift their positions so an overlap could occur. In Situation B, the employer's upper limit is above the union's lower limit and, hence, a contract zone exists.

As a general rule, it is useful to separate monetary demands from non-monetary items and to settle the easy issues first. This helps to create a climate conducive to settling the difficult issues.

Figure 7.1	Determination of the Contract Zone

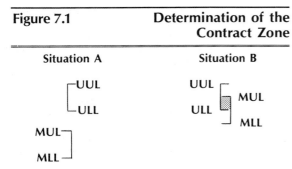

Situation A	Situation B

UUL = Union's upper limit (the initial demand of the union).

ULL = Union's lower limit (the lowest increase the union will accept).

MUL = Management's upper limit (the highest offer management is prepared to make).

MLL = Management's lower limit (the initial offer by management).

▨ = Contract zone.

As each issue is dealt with, an agreement is drafted and initialled by each side. Such specific agreements are tentative until a final, comprehensive settlement has been reached. It is not at all unusual to trade off some of the earlier items upon which agreement has been reached in order to arrive at a final settlement.

Negotiation Tactics

Stevens points out that the tactics used in the negotiation process are those of competition and conflict in the early stages and those of cooperation and coordination in the later stages.[26] The first set of tactics are designed to help map out a contract zone, while the latter are instrumental in helping to find a settlement point within the contract zone.

Competition and Conflict Among the tactics of competition and conflict available to the parties are those of bluff, not-bluff, commitment, persuasion, and rationalization. A party using the *bluff* tactic claims that they will do something that they will not do. This tactic is a delicate one and can inadvertently lead to a work stoppage. *Not-bluff*, on the other hand, is a frank

statement by a one side in the negotiations that they will do what they threaten to do. *Commitment* involves taking a position and sticking to it. This can be done by tying an issue to a principle, or by going public. However, this can cause problems if one party takes a firm stand early in the negotiations and finds it difficult to retreat at a later date.[27] Generally, negotiators find it preferable to take a flexible, step-by-step approach rather than commit themselves too early on and thus risk an unwanted and unnecessary work stoppage. *Persuasion* is an attempt by one party to convince the other of the reasonableness of a position. *Rationalization*, however, is used primarily to give the other negotiators the material with which to develop: (1) a reason which allows them to retreat from their current negotiating position; and (2) a justification of the retreat which will satisfy their constituents.

Coordination and Cooperation Once a contract zone is estimated by the parties, tactics of coordination and cooperation are used to reach agreement within the contract zone. Although the chief negotiators may perceive a contract zone, other participants in negotiations may not. In a mature bargaining relationship the chief negotiators may hold off-the-record discussions, wherein they reveal their true positions without prejudice. It is understood that they may withdraw any statement which is publicly imputed to them. Often, caucuses are used by negotiators at this stage to persuade constituents that the best possible deal has been negotiated for them. Sometimes, too, a negotiator may have to grandstand (revert to an adversarial role) for the benefit of his or her constituents, knowing that the other negotiator will correctly perceive this as putting on a show with the full knowledge that a better settlement is unlikely.

In fact, the ability to prevent the opposing negotiator from losing face with his or her constituents is often extremely important when the two chief negotiators realize that a mutually acceptable agreement is in sight, especially if a strike or lockout deadline is approaching. If the

Canada Post accused of stall tactics during talks

BY JANE COUTTS
The Globe and Mail

Postal workers marched in front of the Gateway postal station in Mississauga, Ont., yesterday to demonstrate anger over what they call Canada Post's stalling tactics at the bargaining table.

Bargaining between Canada Post and the 45,000-member Canadian Union of Postal Workers began in July but little progress has been made, the union's national president Jean Claude Parrot said at the demonstration.

"Progress can only occur when the two parties agree to deal with their problems," he said. "They are just stalling, trying to force us into conciliation without ever really having negotiated at all."

Job security tops the list of union concerns, Mr. Parrot said.

"And I mean job security in the form of job creation programs to get back work they're taking away by contracting out, and creating new services so workers who lose their jobs in new technology can do other work," he said.

Fears over job security are linked directly to Canada Post's new emphasis on profit, he said.

The Crown corporation earned a profit of $96-million this year, the first time in 30 years its revenues have exceeded expenditures.

Now, Mr. Parrot said, the company is using its current position as a starting point toward an annual goal of 15 per cent profit, which he believes has been set as the target figure necessary to attract a private-sector buyout of the Crown corporation.

That was not the intention when Parliament made the post office a Crown corporation, he said.

"The law doesn't say Canada Post has to make a profit, it says it should 'try to be self-sufficient.' But Canada Post is interpreting that as meaning they have to have a 15 per cent profit, I think because the government is trying to get Canada Post to the point where it can sell shares, like Air Canada."

No wage proposals have been tabled yet, Mr. Parrot said, but the union is looking for a "real increase," that will keep pace with inflation and put more money in workers' pockets.

The union also wants to use the bargaining table to address health and safety problems and what they say is a climate of harassment being created in an effort to pressure workers to quit, he said.

Ida Irwin, a spokesman for Canada Post, denied that the company is trying to force workers to quit.

We've heard this before. It's a response to our attendance management program, which we began in 1984 to try to get a handle on runaway absenteeism."

Postal employees were averaging 19 sick days each per year, well above the industry average of eight or nine days, she said.

"We have it down to 13 days and we're proud of that, and we know the people who did not abuse sick leave are proud of it too."

She also denied that the post office is stalling negotiations. Instead, she blamed the union for creating delays by demanding that all the company's questions on contract demands be put in writing.

"It is not our practice to waste time while bargaining," she said. "There is nothing obstructive about attempting to clarify the union's demands."

This is the first round of bargaining between Canada Post and the new amalgamated Canadian Union of Postal Workers, which absorbed the Letter Carriers Union of Canada in January.

Ms Irwin said it's too early to say how the combined union will affect bargaining.

"Certainly, bargaining with a group that represents 45,000 people, the responsibility is greater and we expect to see that level of responsibility on the union's part as well," she said. "We are in a very, very competitive business."

Mr. Parrot said local union leaders from across Canada will meet in Toronto Sept. 10 to discuss strategy for negotiations. He said there is pressure from within the union to take job action, possibly including a nation-wide strike.

The *Globe and Mail*, Sept. 1, 1989, p. A4.

two chief negotiators agree, for example, that a demand by the union should be dropped, the union's chief negotiator may let a delegate from the local argue the case and have the management spokesperson effectively refute it. This is quite often done when one delegate feels very strongly about a demand which is not important to the others.

One party may also aid the other by providing a way for the other to back down on a commitment in an earlier demand. When the chief negotiators see, for example, that a settlement is in sight, they may resort to sign language to communicate their flexibility about certain outstanding items. This may pave the way for both sides to retreat from earlier demands without losing face. The retreat, however, must be made in such a way that it does not convey weakness to one's own constituents. Making too great a concession may be interpreted as weakness by the other side.

As Stevens states,

> By the use of sign language a party signals the direction in which it wants to go, and then waits for some answering signal. Either the parties go arm-in-arm, as it were, or do not go at all. . . . To communicate successfully by means of sign language and symbols, the negotiator must be willing to take some chances.[28]

The tactics of cooperation and coordination, including sign language, should bring the parties to an agreement if a contract zone has been established and if the negotiators have done a good job. However, if no contract zone exists or can be found, a strike or lockout is likely to occur unless some form of third-party assistance is successfully employed. Such assistance may involve the kind of eleventh-hour marathon bargaining sessions that constitute the most dramatic form of contract negotiations.

Multidimensional Demands

It is useful to view bargaining demands as falling into the two categories proposed by Stevens. First, there are those that seek to alter the terms of trade (rewards or conditions of employment) within a given collective bargaining game. A change in the wage rate is a good example of this type. Second, there are those which seek to alter the basic ground rules of collective bargaining or the definition of the role relationships of the parties. According to Stevens, "demands which are perceived as a union's challenge to management's control are of this variety."[29]

Non-monetary demands such as job security and management's right to contract out work pose a problem owing to their multidimensional character; that is, it is difficult to achieve a trade-off on them because their objective value cannot be fixed precisely in monetary terms. This is one reason that some of the bargaining models, such as Stevens', which portray a point of determinacy (single point of settlement) are of little use in the development of a theory of negotiations involving a mixed package of monetary and non-monetary items. How, for example, can a monetary value be placed on the demand for a union shop security provision which requires all members of the bargaining unit to be union members?

Stevens argues that there are both necessary and sufficient conditions for a settlement. The necessary condition is that the equilibrium position of the two parties be consonant: the two parties must be willing to settle for exactly the same thing. The sufficient condition requires mutual awareness of this consonance.[30] Thus, Stevens assumes that each negotiator knows precisely what the other negotiator's settlement position is. This is a rather unrealistic assumption to impose on a bargaining model, because although each party has its perceptions of the other's settlement position, their perceptions may not in fact correspond to reality. Moreover, even after an agreement has been reached, a negotiator may feel that he or she could have obtained a better settlement by holding out a little longer. Rather than assume a predetermined settlement point, it is preferable to think of negotiations as a process whereby each negotiator first tries to find the contract zone, and then uses whatever leverage is available to arrive at a determinate resolution within that zone. (This is in line with the discussion of the negotiation process in Chapter 1, in which it was stated that the ultimate source for determining a specific point of settlement in contract negotiations is through the use of bargaining power.)

Bargaining Power

In Chapter 1, bargaining power was defined as the ability to obtain objectives despite the resistance of others. It consists of two components: (1) a strong attachment to something that is desired or to the possession of something that is threatened; and (2) the ability to impose sanctions. We will now expand upon this definition.

Chamberlain's Conception

The most widely used definition of bargaining power is that of N. Chamberlain who defines it as:

> The ability to secure another's agreement on one's own terms. A union's bargaining power at any point in time *is* for example, management's willingness to agree on the union's terms. Management's willingness in turn depends upon the cost of disagreeing with the union's terms, relative to the cost of agreeing to them.[31]

Management's bargaining power may be defined in a similar way. The bargaining power of the parties may thus be summarized in the following equations:

Union's bargaining power =

$$\frac{\text{Cost to management of not agreeing to union terms}}{\text{Cost to management of agreeing to union terms}}$$

Management's bargaining power =

$$\frac{\text{Cost to union of not agreeing to management terms}}{\text{Cost to union of agreeing to management terms}}$$

Chamberlain uses the term "cost" in the broad sense of "disadvantage" and includes in it both monetary and non-monetary items. While other models deal only with the issue of wages,

Chamberlain is concerned that issues of a non-monetary nature be incorporated in the concept of bargaining power. He states that:

> The sort of balancing of costs which is contemplated in the definition of bargaining power just given does not require measurement of costs in an arithmetical sense. . . . What these costs of agreement and disagreement may be to the bargainers cannot be known precisely enough to permit balancing, except through the exploratory process of negotiations.[32]

Chamberlain further states that it is through negotiations that feasible or infeasible combinations are revealed which form the basis of a settlement. He does not, however, explain the mechanics of the process. Rather, he discusses overt tactics such as strikes, picketing, and lockouts which influence the cost to management and to the union of disagreement.

Bargaining power depends on the skills of the negotiators and on various external factors surrounding negotiations. Bargaining power cannot be precisely measured. The most that one can do is indicate the factors that affect the bargaining power of the union and the employer, and show how their perceptions of bargaining power derive from their assessments of these factors. Such perceptions may be faulty: it is all too easy for a negotiator — especially an inexperienced one — to overestimate or underestimate the influence of different factors in a negotiation situation. During the 1981 Stelco strike, for example, the union believed it had a strong bargaining position. After the strike began, however, the bottom fell out of the steel market, thereby reducing the union's leverage considerably.

Hicks's Conception

J.R. Hicks's diagram of a determinate wage outcome is helpful in explaining how various factors affect bargaining power.[33] In Hicks's model, shown in Figure 7.2, an employer originally offers a wage rate at level E and the union initially demands a wage rate at level U. According to Hicks, the parties are likely to settle at level P where the curves EE' and UU' intersect.

Figure 7.2   Hicks's Bargaining Schedules

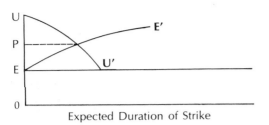

Expected Duration of Strike

Source: J. R. Hicks, Ch. 7, *Theory of Wages* (London and Basingstoke: Macmillan, 1932).
EE' = Employer's concession curve
UU' = Union's resistance curve
P = Wage

Note: After a certain period, time is on the side of the employer, because unions can maintain a strike only as long as their strike fund lasts. Thus, both curved configurations may change daily.

Hicks made a number of assumptions in this model, the first of which was that the parties had perfect knowledge of the two curves. This assumption, like that of Stevens, is ambitious. Hicks also assumes that anything below the union's resistance curve (UU') would be more costly to it than a strike. The same would hold true, in the case of management, for anything above the employer's concession curve. Hence rational behaviour, according to Hicks's model, would dictate a settlement at point P. While this model makes for a neat, determinate solution, the assumptions are too great to even approximate the real world. The reason for including Figure 7.2 in this chapter is to indicate that the employer's bargaining power — the concession curve — and the union's bargaining power — its resistance curve — are not static and may be influenced by many factors. These will be discussed in the following section.[34]

Factors That Affect Management's Bargaining Power

The following are some of the more important factors affecting an employer's concession curve or bargaining power.

Size of Inventory A large inventory gives management more bargaining power than a low inventory, since in the former case, customers can be supplied from accumulated stocks. A rough estimate of how long any employer could endure a strike without serious damage to sales can be calculated by dividing the accumulated inventory by an average week's shipment.

Structure of Business If the company is an integrated operation in which production units depend on inputs from feeder plants it is more susceptible to strikes and slowdowns. If it is composed of autonomous units which can meet market demands should a part of the operation be closed down, it will be better able to withstand a strike. A good example of an autonomous-unit company is a meat-packing company which has a number of plants operating autonomously in different locations. If a strike is conducted against one plant, it is possible to supply the market area affected with meat processed at other plants, assuming that these other plants are operating at less than full capacity. By contrast, in the automobile industry some plants specialize in making parts which feed into the assembly operations. A strike at one feeder plant could affect all the other plants after the inventory was used up.

Competitiveness of Company In a tight product market, especially where the product is a fairly common one, there is always the possibility that customers may switch permanently to competitors, as they discover substitute products or alternative sources of supply. The fear of losing business to competitors may weaken an employer's bargaining power.

Seasonal Nature of Business Generally, employers find that their bargaining power is lowest at the peak period of the season. Canners of fresh vegetables are more vulnerable at canning time than any other time of the year, and shipping companies are weaker at the beginning and end of the shipping season. In these and other seasonal industries, unions try to bring negotiations to a head near the beginning or end of the seasonal period, knowing that time constraints on management will expedite a settlement and increase union gains.

The Willingness and Ability of Supervisory Personnel to Replace Striking Employees As indicated in Chapter 6, when a large organization's labour force goes on strike, it is virtually impossible for the company to find replacement workers. However, Bell Canada has made it a policy to use supervisory and managerial personnel to do the work of striking workers. During the summer of 1988, Bell used about 9,000 managers to replace striking employees. While the company claimed that the work was going smoothly, by the end of the 14-week strike many managers were very displeased at having to put in such long hours, often at distances far from their homes. It is questionable how long the company could have kept the system working under these adverse circumstances.

Strike Insurance An employer's bargaining power can be enhanced by strike insurance. A number of airlines in the United States devised a "Mutual Aid Pact" before deregulation, whereby if one company was struck, any extra profits made by the other airlines were given to the airline whose workers were on strike. Two strikes by workers at Western Airlines resulted in substantial payments received by that company. A 160-day strike in 1970 turned a potential loss into a large profit: 5.4% return on investment, the third highest return in the industry that year. Under the Airline Deregulation Act of 1978 the Mutual Aid Pact was made illegal.[35] A similar provision is found among major railroads in the United States, however.

Factors That Affect Union Bargaining Power

The factors which weaken a company's bargaining power usually increase a union's bargaining power. There are, however, a number of other factors that have an important bearing on the union's power.

Strength of Commitment to Issues If the union is fighting for some cause with which the workers have little immediate concern, then it may not be in a strong bargaining position. A classic example of this was the 1959 strike in the United States steel industry. A number of surveys that preceded the 116-day strike showed that the workers were not strongly committed initially to striking over pay and fringe benefits. It was only when management introduced proposed changes in local work rules that the workers got strongly behind the union. Since changes in local work rules would affect them directly and immediately, the workers became very militant.

Access to Liquid Assets The size of a union's strike fund often determines how long it can maintain a work stoppage. Walter Reuther, former head of the UAW, always made it a point to build up a large strike fund when he wanted to obtain a major concession from the automobile companies. Another component of a union's financial strength is its ability to obtain grants or loans from other unions if its strike fund runs out. Interest-free loans or outright grants are often made to striking unions from those not on strike.

Strike Timing There would be little point in workers who operate ships on the Great Lakes going on strike during the winter when the shipping season is closed. Generally, unions will time negotiations to coincide with the period when worker's services are most needed, the employer's inventory is low, or both. The construction unions in Ontario brought their negotiations to a head in May and June 1988 when work stoppages took place on a number of major projects in a number of Ontario cities, including the Skydome in Toronto.

Strike Effectiveness If the workers of a large company with many skilled workers go on strike, it is difficult for the employer to recruit strike-breakers with sufficient skills to keep the

Canapress Photo Service

company operating. By contrast, a small local employer with a few workers might be able to recruit enough extra workers to keep operations going. It was a strike of this nature — with associated violence — that prompted the Quebec government to pass its anti-scab legislation in 1977. Under the Quebec Labour Code, a struck employer is now prohibited from hiring replacement workers during a strike. Employers are also prohibited from producing at non-striking plants goods that would normally be produced at the struck plant. They are further prohibited from contracting out work done by the striking workers. The Quebec law is the only legislation of its kind in North America.

Picketing Primary picketing is aimed at the employer against whom the strike is called. Unions have every right in law to picket peace-fully during a strike and the more the picket lines are respected, the more the union's power will increase. Sometimes, however, it may be a violation of a contract for members of another union working in the same establishment to refuse to cross a picket line. In these cases, the workers cannot legally respect the picket line of the other union.

Another form of picketing is the secondary boycott whereby a union, either through its own organization or in conjunction with another union, tries to put pressure on a third party to influence the struck company. The third party may be a supplier of materials to, or a purchaser of goods from, the struck employer.

Unemployment Insurance While striking workers in Canada do not qualify for unemployment insurance until production reaches

80%, worker in New York do qualify for such benefits after a certain waiting period. During the 1960s, workers on strike against some of the New York newspapers were receiving a high proportion of their regular pay, when both their strike benefits and unemployment insurance were combined.

Relative Power   If the components affecting the union's bargaining power are favourable to it, it may, through skillful negotiations, obtain something at or near the employer's upper limit (point c in Figure 7.3). On the other hand, if the employer's bargaining power is greater, the settlement will probably be nearer the union's lower limit (point b).

If bargaining power is relatively equal, the settlement will fall about halfway between b and c. However, given the present state of knowledge about the variables involved in strikes, it is futile to suggest a determinate solution at a specific point. Bargaining power helps determine the specific settlement point, but this cannot be determined *a priori*, unless some very great assumptions are introduced into a model of contract negotiations. A realistic model with a determinate solution must, in my view, await a better formulation of the variables in the negotiation process and a more accurate measurement of the concepts.

T. Kochan, a well known American writer, indicates a troubling contradiction between conceptual discussion of the determinants of bargaining outcomes and empirical analysis. The conceptual argument is cast in terms of a whole range of bargaining outcomes, whereas the empirical testing is limited to wage determination only. Kochan further observes:

> This contradiction mirrors the general state of empirical research on private-sector bargaining outcomes. The study of nonwage outcomes is still in a very primitive stage of development. The central difficulty in studying nonwage outcomes lies in constructing measures of nonwage outcomes that are amenable to quantitative analysis.[36]

A Non-Deterministic Approach to Negotiations

Walton and McKersie break the negotiation process down into four subprocesses: (1) *distributive bargaining*, which represents a set of activities the results of which are viewed as gains for one and losses for the other; (2) *integrative bargaining*, which represents a set of activities whereby a gain for one party is a gain for the other as well; (3) *attitudinal structuring*, which represents those activities that promote the attainment of the desired patterns of relationships between the two parties; and (4) *intraorganizational bargaining*, which are those activities that bring the expectations of constituents into alignment with those of the chief negotiator.[37] After describing each of the subprocesses, the two writers analyze the tactics appropriate to each. Under distributive bargaining, for example, they emphasize the notion of utility functions (what an actor considers an item or service to be worth) and indicate that for the negotiator the utility function increases up to a certain point and then begins to drop off. Thus, if the going rate for a service in a community is $10.00 an hour, a negotiator's utility is highest when he or she obtains this wage, since anything beyond that might seriously increase costs to the employer and result in layoffs. Walton and McKersie also indicate the types of commitment strategy appropriate to various situations and

---

Figure 7.3   Power and Settlement Level

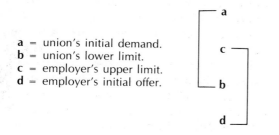

a = union's initial demand.
b = union's lower limit.
c = employer's upper limit.
d = employer's initial offer.

identify, under various conditions, the point in the sequence of bargaining moves when the maximum commitment should be made. They have developed nine hypotheses regarding commitment strategy, the first of which reads as follows: *"The more knowledge Party has about the resistance point of Opponent, the fewer the bargaining moves before Party commits himself to a final position."*[38]

This principle applies well in the case of distributive bargaining. However, an early commitment pattern under distributive bargaining can seriously hamper the benefits to be a-chieved in the integrative bargaining subprocess. Similarly, attitudinal structuring suggests that there is a fairly high degree of trust between the parties. A high degree of trust, however, conflicts to some extent with a take-it-or-leave-it approach.

The tactic appropriate to intraorganizational bargaining raises the question of what degree of control a chief negotiator should try to exercise over his or her constituents. The question is whether to try actively or passively for an internal consensus. Adopting an active role will likely make it easier to persuade constituents to adopt the negotiator's views. Whether the chief negotiator takes an active or passive role, his or her actions will affect the tactics appropriate to the other three subprocesses of bargaining.[39]

The framework presented by Walton and McKersie is a very useful one for analyzing the negotiation process. It does not, however, lead to a determinate solution nor does it suggest how a solution may be obtained.

Ratification of New Collective Agreement Clauses

Once an agreement is reached on the items in dispute, these must be written in the form of a collective agreement. In the case of a new bargaining relationship, this will mean the preparation of a new agreement containing all the clauses agreed upon in the negotiation process.

For a renewal of an existing collective agreement, the issues finally agreed upon in negotiations take the form of a "memorandum of understanding," which is usually signed by all the union and management negotiators. The new clauses agreed upon must then be incorporated into the existing collective agreement, which may mean modifying existing provisions or adding new ones.

Although neither the law nor the constitutions of most unions in North America require negotiators to present newly negotiated contracts to union members for ratification, the tradition of most unions is to do so. In recent years many negotiators who have presented their proposed agreements for membership approval have found that a majority of the members refuse to ratify the collective agreements. For example, both the B.C. and Quebec nurses' unions rejected contracts negotiated on their behalf in 1989.

C.W. Summers and other labour writers have done some excellent work on this topic.[40] Summers found that in some instances agreements were not accepted by the members because the terms of settlement were not clearly presented, particularly where job security was concerned. He speculated that rejection may also have occurred because initially inflated union demands raised the expectations of the membership beyond the level any negotiator could be reasonably expected to deliver. Management may also have contributed to the rejection of agreements at times, by dragging its heels during negotiations and only slowly and grudgingly consenting to some of the union's important demands. If negotiators on both sides were more realistic than they have been and were to try to conclude their negotiations without long delays, there might be a greater rate of acceptance of settlement terms by union members.

Summer points out, however, that the ratification problem is a result of the separation of the responsibility to negotiate an agreement and the authority to make it binding. This partly explains why two schools of thought exist on this subject. Some eminent labour relations specialists feel strongly that negotiators should have the authority to make agreements binding. While some negotiators do have this power, a recent survey of union leaders and members in the United States indicates that about 90% of union leaders and members agree that union members should have the right to ratify the proposed collective agreement, since it is the members who must live with its terms. There is some agreement, however, that delegates one step removed from the negotiators could be granted the authority by the general membership to make the agreement binding.

The major function of the ratification process, as Summers suggests, is to test the acceptability of the terms of settlement by those who have to work under its provisions. If workers say "yes" to the agreement, it becomes *their* agreement and not merely that of the union's negotiating committee or the union executive. Also, dissenters will feel bound by the majority's vote. As Summers states, "The democratic character of the union and its statutory role as representative make acceptability the primary test of the legitimacy of a collective agreement."[41] And an agreement, to be accepted, must contain provisions which satisfy, at least to a minimum degree, the competing interests of the diverse groups within a union.

As stated earlier, one of the functions of the union negotiator is to try to establish the priorities of the various groups which make up the union membership. Effective two-way communications between the negotiator and the members are essential to this purpose. As a first step, intraorganizational negotiations within the union and management must precede the negotiations between the two parties. If these internal negotiations are carried out effectively, it is more likely that the settlement finally reached at the negotiation table will be acceptable to the constituents of both negotiation teams. In the final analysis, it is the constituents of both the union and management negotiators who decide the content of a negotiated settlement.

Compulsory Provisions in Collective Agreements

All jurisdictions in Canada require that collective agreements contain clauses which prohibit strike and lockout action during the life of a collective agreement. The intent of this provision is to guarantee some degree of stability in the employment relationship during the life of the agreement.[42] As a *quid pro quo*, all jurisdictions also require that collective agreements contain a provision for final and binding arbitration of disputes arising over the interpretation and application of the clauses in the collective agreement. In some jurisdictions, the legislation spells out the applicable clause where collective agreements fail to include one.

Another legal requirement is that collective agreements operate for a minimum period of one year. Most jurisdictions also require collective agreements to contain a provision which recognizes the union as the exclusive bargaining agent for the group of workers it represents; that is, only the duly certified union can negotiate on behalf of the members in the bargaining unit. In addition, six jurisdictions now require that the agreement contain a compulsory dues check-off clause if the bargaining agent so requests. B.C. legislation requires collective agreements to contain provisions for assisting workers affected by technological change. H.W. Arthurs *et al* claim that "These mandatory provisions have the effect of reducing the scope of bargaining to the extent that they establish a minimum below which the parties cannot bargain."[43]

The Duty to Bargain in Good Faith

While there is a tremendous amount of jurisprudence on the duty to bargain in good faith in the United States, there is surprisingly little on this subject in Canada. There are two reasons for this dearth. First, labour relations boards in Canada have only recently been given the authority to issue remedial orders in cases where good faith bargaining was found to be lacking.[44] Prior to this, a party who felt that the other had failed to bargain in good faith was obliged to obtain consent from Canadian labour relations boards to prosecute the other party in court. In order to obtain such consent, the aggrieved party had to demonstrate a *prima facie* case (one which seemed justifiable from the evidence presented) before the labour boards showing that their cases might receive a favourable decision before a court of law.

The second reason for the lack of a large body of jurisprudence on this topic in Canada is that if the parties fail to meet and negotiate, conciliation officers or mediators are appointed to assist the parties. A strike or lockout becomes legal only after this procedure is complied with. According to H.D. Woods, the obligation of conciliation officers to get the parties together in the same room to begin negotiations is the major reason for the lack of bad faith bargaining charges in Canada. No such obligation exists in American law, and Professor Woods thought that this difference partly explained the large number of unfair practice cases in the United States.

Actions Deemed to Indicate Bad Faith

Now that most labour relations boards in Canada have the authority to issue remedies in these situations, a body of jurisprudence is emerging. A brief summary follows of some of the actions which constitute a failure to bargain in good faith.

Failure to Meet and Threats Since collective bargaining is viewed as an exercise not only in economic strength but also in human relations, Canadian labour relations boards have placed far greater emphasis on the manner in which negotiations are conducted than on the content of negotiations.[45] The right of bargaining agents to bargain for a collective agreement imposes a duty on the employer to bargain with a view to concluding a collective agreement: the serving of notice to bargain by one party requires that

the other meet with it. A refusal to meet at the commencement of negotiations constitutes a refusal to bargain in good faith. Unlawful strike threats by a union before negotiations begin also constitute bad-faith bargaining. However, where the parties have discussed the issues at numerous meetings, a refusal to meet further until some condition is altered is deemed acceptable. Labour relations boards have even held that since workers are entitled to negotiate through their chosen representatives, "an employer's objection to the composition of the union bargaining committee (even where it contains an employee of a business competitor) cannot justify a refusal to meet with the union."[46]

Circumvention of Bargaining Agent An employer may not circumvent a union by negotiating with the workers directly or through another union. Employers who have attempted unilaterally to change the conditions of employment after the negotiation and conciliation period has expired have been found, in some instances, to have violated the duty to bargain in good faith.

Suppression of Information Full and informed discussion during negotiations is required for good faith bargaining. An explanation of the rationale underlying an offer or demand must be included in such discussions. The opposing side is not obliged to accept the rationale, but the union or management representative must give one. Furthermore, the offer or demand does not necessarily have to be "reasonable," but it must be an honest one. If the parties, having negotiated in good faith, feel that further discussions are useless, then a take-it-or-leave-it position does not constitute bad faith. Another aspect of a full and informed discussion concerns the extent to which the employer must supply data to the bargaining agent:

> While it has been recognized that there is some duty upon the employer to supply information,

the full extent of that duty has never been denied. In one case a refusal by an employer to supply existing wage and classification data was taken into account in determining that a failure to bargain in good faith had occurred.[47]

Failure to Use A Prescribed Form of Third-Party Assistance As we discussed in the previous chapter, the parties in all jurisdictions in Canada must go through certain forms of third-party assistance before the right to strike or lockout accrues. Untimely strikes and lockouts are clearly illegal, and remedial legislation may be invoked to stop them. A failure to bargain in good faith exists also in the refusal of one of the parties to comply with a method previously agreed upon by both parties to resolve the dispute. In one case, the parties signed a collective agreement requiring arbitration to be used in the next round of negotiations should they be unable to resolve the dispute themselves. When the employer refused to proceed to arbitration, he was found guilty of bargaining in bad faith, and was ordered to submit to arbitration.

Reneging and Introduction of New Demands Attempts to renege on commitments previously made constitutes a failure to bargain in good faith. Conversely, the introduction of additional demands by a party after the agenda has already been clearly established is also considered to be a failure to bargain in good faith. The parameters of the negotiations are set early in the exchange of proposals and counterproposals, and the introduction of new matters near the end of the negotiations has been held to "effectively destroy the decision-making framework."[48] In the past labour boards have ordered employers to execute a formal agreement where a mutual understanding has been reached on all issues.

Demands that Are Illegal Under Other Statutes While Canadian labour law does not distinguish between mandatory demands (those which the parties must negotiate) and voluntary demands (those which a party may refuse

to negotiate) as is the case in the United States, Canadian boards have considered demands that are tainted with illegality to be a breach of good faith.[49] For example, a party which attempts to bargain for a national agreement in an industry which falls under provincial jurisdiction may be found liable. Attempts by employers to restrict the scope of the bargaining unit, to rearrange the assignment of work between competing unions, or to interfere with the internal operation of a union are all illegal. A demand that a union not discipline workers who have crossed picket lines during a strike is one example of illegal interference with the internal operation of unions.[50] Demands which are illegal under other statutes, such as human rights statutes, also constitute bad faith bargaining. However hard bargaining, even if accompanied by harsh words and insults, does not constitute a failure to bargain in good faith. This is one reason why many employers and unions probably take a very tough stance during the conduct of negotiations.

Elapse of Time Some negotiations seem to drag on for a long period of time. The duty to bargain in good faith does not diminish with the passage of time, but may take different forms where extensive negotiations have already taken place.

Surface Bargaining A smooth operator may respect all legal procedures associated with the duty to bargain in good faith, but have no intention whatsoever of entering into a collective agreement. This practice is called surface bargaining. An example of surface bargaining is the tabling of unreasonable and predictably unacceptable proposals while refraining from any conduct which is noticeably inconsistent with a desire to enter into a collective agreement.

What remedy, if any, does a party have against surface bargaining? Labour relations boards refuse to deal with this kind of situation since it revolves around the concept of motives, and motives are extremely difficult to prove.

Bendel suggests that labour relations boards "should be prepared to hold that an employer whose contract proposals it considers unreasonable by reference to a particular objective standard is *prima facie* guilty of failing to bargain in good faith."[51]

Remedies for Failure to Bargain in Good Faith

The measure usually put forward as a remedy for the failure to bargain in good faith is, quite simply, a directive that further negotiations be conducted in good faith. Such a directive is usually accompanied by the appointment of a mediator. However, the directive is not in itself a remedy, especially since boards do not supervise their directives. It has been suggested that one effective remedy would be to impose the terms that might have been reached had good faith bargaining occurred and postpone any pending decertification vote. However, these proposals have been expressly rejected by most labour relations boards on "the basis that they would interfere unduly with the existing balance of bargaining power."[52] However, the Ontario Labour Relations Board (OLRB) has ordered an employer to reimburse union negotiators for extra costs resulting from the failure of management negotiators to bargain in good faith. The Board also ordered the company (Radio Shack) to reimburse the workers for the earnings they lost as a result of the bad faith bargaining.

The ORLB went as far as a board should go, in the absence of a legal mandate to impose the terms of a collective agreement. It is extremely difficult, if not impossible, to determine how much the union and the workers lost as a result of the failure of the employer to bargain in good faith. The Ontario government has since given an arbitration board or the ORLB the power to impose a settlement in the case of first collective agreements. The Board will henceforth use settlements by other employers in the same industry where the employees are engaged in similar work as the norm for the settlement of first agreements.

Concession Bargaining

During the recession of the early 1980s, a new term was added to the lexicon of industrial relations literature: concession bargaining. It represented a break from the long-established practice of pattern bargaining in the US and Canada, and arose as a result of drastic changes in the previously fairly stable economic background. Faced with the recession, deregulation, and increasing foreign competition, management in many companies pleaded with workers to accept reductions in wages, benefits, or work rules, or to forego future benefits.

Concession bargaining was particularly devastating in the United States, where the union movement is much weaker; the pressure for concessions, and the threat posed by the existence of a non-union belt, has decimated the pattern bargaining system there. While the results in Canada were less dramatic, P. Kumar reported that wage freezes and nominal wage cuts occurred in 10% of collective agreements in 1983 affecting 14% of workers covered; in 25% of agreements in 1984 affecting about 25% of workers in 1984 and 16% of agreements in 1985 covering 168,000 workers. Wage freezes or cuts were much more prevalent in Western Canada than elsewhere, with one of every two settlements including a wage freeze or cut. In addition, concessions were most predominant in the construction industry.[53] These results stand in stark contrast to Canadian trade union rhetoric.

While unions made many concessions in the early eighties, E.M. Kassalow believes that the process has not been a one-way street, particularly in large companies. Unions have often been able to obtain bargaining rights in new areas in return for granting economic concessions. Kassalow points out that

> in auto and meatpacking new rights have been gained on the matter of plant closing or outsourcing to non-union companies. These new rights are by no means comprehensive, but they represent an important breakthrough in an area where companies in those industries have not yielded ground in the past.[54]

The kinds of improvements achieved by unions through concessions can be summarized as follows:[55]

1 *Symbolic improvements*: These require that management take a cut in benefits along with production workers.

2 *Job security*: Xerox agreed to employment security and no-layoff clauses at one of its plants in return for concessions over work rules. United Airlines made a similar deal with its pilots. The most common example of job security, however, is embodied in agreements by employers not to proceed with planned layoffs.

3 *Implicit job security*: This includes guarantees of plant investments, and similar concessions.

4 *Contingent compensation*: Promises may be made for improvements in future compensation. These improvements include stock ownership plans, profit-sharing, and arrangements which tie future benefits to improvements in the company's performance. However, when companies enter into stock ownership or profit-sharing plans, they may have to open their books to workers later on. These plans represent a latent benefit to workers, since companies would not normally have to reveal this type of information.

5 *Formal arrangements to include the union in business decisions*: These arrangements have been the most publicized, but probably the least common form of *quid pro quo*, or concession received in exchange for benefits foregone. Sometimes union leaders are allowed to sit on company boards; there are also shop-floor participation plans dealing with specific issues. Decisions about equipment purchases and crews fall in this category.

6 *Union bargaining gains*: These include access to continuous information about the company's performance and future plans. It is suggested that these arrangements meet current union needs and may also improve their bargaining power in negotiations. Furthermore, they are weighted heavily in favour of gain-sharing and job security.

Some management spokespersons have argued that companies may have actually given away too much: the gains have been short-term, the cost has been long-term intrusion of unions into the prerogatives of management. On the other hand, concessions may be asked for and extracted from unions even though such concessions are not necessary to the continued operation of companies.

It is not yet clear whether concessions bargaining is here to stay, or is a passing phase in industrial relations. Given the strength of unionization in Canada, it could represent a new trend in industrial relations, whereby unions and management cooperate at every organizational level to make North American companies competitive with companies anywhere in the world.

Conclusion

This chapter examined the structure of negotiation units, and the factors that have influenced it. It then focused on two major phases of the negotiation process: the mapping out of a contract zone, and the process of reaching a settlement within the contract zone. The pivotal role that bargaining power plays in determining bargaining outcomes was discussed, as were the factors that influence the bargaining power of both unions and employers. The ratification of negotiated settlements is a crucial matter for both negotiators and workers, with the latter usually having the final say. The duty to bargain in good faith, which has recently become a matter of great concern to labour relations boards as well as to unions and employers, was discussed insofar as jurisprudence on this subject has developed in Canada. The chapter concluded with a look at concession bargaining as a possible future trend in the negotiation process.

Questions

1 Differentiate between the negotiation process and collective bargaining. Why is it important to make this distinction?

2 By comparing periodic events with day-to-day relationships, describe the components of the bargaining structure. Use conventional terminology.

3 Why is the concept of the negotiation unit important?

4 Name the major determinants of the negotiation unit. Explain the importance of each component to each party.

5 Discuss how unions and employers prepare for contract negotiations. At what point should the parties start preparing for the next round of negotiations?

6 What is the major function of the chief negotiator on each side of the bargaining table?

7 According to C. Stevens, what are the major phases of the negotiation cycle? Which strategies and tactics are appropriate to each phase?

8 What is the role of bargaining power in the negotiation process and what are the major factors that affect the bargaining power of each party?

9 Do you think it is possible to develop a model that will give a determinate solution to a particular set of negotiations? Justify your opinion.

10 Discuss fully the factors which constitute good faith bargaining. Do they play a significant role in the negotiation process? Elaborate.

11 Do you think that workers should have the right to ratify the terms of negotiated collective agreements, or should this matter be left in the hands of the negotiators? Elaborate.

12 Discuss the concept of concession bargaining and some of the factors that have brought it about. Who are the winners and losers in the process and what determines this? Elaborate.

Notes

1 N.W. Chamberlain and J.W. Kuhn, *Collective Bargaining*, 2nd ed. (New York: McGraw-Hill, 1965), p. 141.

2 J.R. Hicks, *The Theory of Wages* (London: Mac-Millan Co., 1932); J. Pen, "A General Theory of Bargaining," *American Economic Review* (March 1952, pp. 24-42); C.M. Stevens, *Strategy and Collective Bargaining Negotiations* (New York: McGraw-Hill, 1963); R.E. Walton and R.B. McKersie, *A Behavioral Theory of Labour Negotiations* (New York: McGraw-Hill, 1965); B.M. Mabry, Chs. 8-10, *Labor Relations and Collective Bargaining* (New York: The Ronald Press, 1966); Pao Lun Cheng, "Wage Negotiations and Bargaining Power," Vol. 21, No. 2 *Industrial and Labor Relations Review* (January 1968), pp. 163-82, and comments and replies in subsequent issues of the same journal; *Essays in Industrial Relations Theory*, ed., G.G. Sommers (Ames: the Iowa State University Press, 1969); S.M. Bacharach and E.J. Lawler, *Bargaining: Power, Tactics and Outcomes* (San Francisco: Jossey-Bass Publishers, 1981); J. Barbash, "Collective Bargaining and the Theory of Conflict," Vol. XVIII, No. 1, *British Journal of Industrial Relations* (March 1980), pp.

82-90; and S.M.A. Hameed, "A Critique of Industrial Relations Theory," Vol. 37, No. 1, *Relations Industrielles/Industrial Relations* (1982), pp. 15-31; G. Hébert, H.C. Jain, and N.M. Meltz, eds., *The State of the Art in Industrial Relations in Canada* (Kingston: Industrial Relations Centre, Queen's University and Toronto: University of Toronto, Industrial Relations Centre, 1988); and J. Sen and S. Hameed, *Theories of Industrial Relations* (Littleton, Mass.: Copley Publishing Group, 1988).

3 A.R. Weber, "Stability and Change in the Structure of Collective Bargaining," *Challenges to Collective Bargaining*, ed. L. Ulman (Englewood Cliffs, N.J.: Prentice Hall Inc. 1967), p. 23.

4 Labour Canada, No. 6, *Collective Bargaining Review* (Ottawa: Supply and Services Canada, June 1982), p. 61.

5 Weber, "Stability and Change," p.14.

6 1977, *di* 319; 1977 Can LRBR 99; and 77 CLLC 16,089.

7 P. Weiler, *Reconcilable Differences* (Toronto: Carswell, 1980), pp. 154-55.

8 Ibid., p. 162.

9 Weber, "Stability and Change," p. 15.

10 Labour Canada, No. 2, *Collective Bargaining Review* (February 1982), p. 35.

11 Weber, "Stability and Change," p.23.

12 W.E. Hendricks and L.M. Kahn, "The Determinants of Bargaining Structure in U.S. Manufacturing Industries," Vol. 35, No. 2, *Industrial and Labor Relations Review* (January 1982), pp. 181-95.

13 D.A.L. Auld *et al*, *The Determinants of Negotiated Wage Settlements in Canada (1966–1975)* (Hull: Supply and Services Canada, 1979), p. 157.

14 J.C. Anderson, "The Structure of Collective Bargaining," eds. J. Anderson and M. Gunderson, *Union-Management Relations in Canada* (Don Mills: Addison Wesley Publishers, 1982), p. 176.

15 A.W.J. Craig and H.J. Waisglass, "Collective Bargaining Perspectives," Vol. 23, No. 4, *Relations Industrielles/Industrial Relations*, Table 2, p. 583.

16 J.B. Rose, Ch. 3, *Public Policy, Bargaining Structures and the Construction Industry* (Toronto: Butterworths & Co. Ltd., 1980), pp. 35-51.

17 Stevens, *Strategy and Collective Bargaining Negotiations*, pp. 46-47.

18 Walton and McKersie, *A Behavioral Theory*.

19 For a history of bargaining in the Big Three of the packinghouse industry, see Alton W. Craig, "The Consequences of Provincial Jurisdiction for the Process of Company-Wide Collective Bargaining in Canada: A Study of the Packinghouse Industry" (unpublished Ph.D. dissertation, Cornell University, 1964).

20 Vol. 36, Nos. 2-3, *Canadian Transport* (February and March 1977).

21 J. Crispo, *International Unions* (Toronto: McGraw-Hill Canada, 1967), p. 182.

22 For a very good analysis of the first three rounds of negotiations in the Quebec public service, see Jean Boivin, *The Evolution of Bargaining Power in the Province of Quebec Public Sector (1964-1972)* (Quebec: Department des relations industrielles, Université Laval, January 1975). This study has since been published as a book by the Laval University Press.

23 Ibid.

24 "AMC, Union Reach Pact on Contract," *Globe and Mail* (February 17, 1977), p. 5.

25 Stevens, *Strategy and Collective Bargaining Negotiations*, p. 63.

26 Ibid., p. 10.

27 For a good discussion of commitment tactics, see Walton and McKersie, *A Behavioral Theory of Labor Negotiations*, pp. 82-125.

28 Stevens, *Strategy and Collective Bargaining Negotiations*, p. 106.

29 Ibid., p. 120.

30 Ibid., p. 12.

31 Chamberlain and Kuhn, *Collective Bargaining*, p. 170.

32 Ibid., pp. 171-72.

33 J.R. Hicks, *The Theory of Wages*, Chapter 7.

34 Hicks and Chamberlain continue to be influential. Bacharach and Lawler, for example, rely heavily on them in developing their theory of contract negotiations. See Bacharach and Lawler, *Bargaining: Power, Tactics and Outcomes*, pp. 43-44.

35 M.L. Kahn, "Airlines," *Collective Bargaining: Contemporary American Experience*, ed. G.G. Sommers (Industrial Relations Research Association Series, 1980), pp. 354-358.

36 T.A. Kochan, *Collective Bargaining and Industrial Relations: From Theory to Policy and Practice* (Homewood, Ill.: Richard D. Irwin, Inc., 1980), p. 324.

37 Walton and McKersie, *A Behavioral Theory*, pp. 4-5.

38 Ibid., p. 123.

39 For a more extensive discussion of the problems associated with adopting various tactics, see Walton and McKersie, *A Behavioral Theory*, Ch. X.

40 For an excellent treatment of this subject, see C.W. Summers, "Ratification of Agreements," *Frontiers of Collective Bargaining*, eds., J.T. Dunlop and N.W. Chamberlain (New York: Harper and Row Publishers, 1967), pp. 75-102. Some of the ideas in the following section are taken from this article.

41 Ibid., p. 83.

42 Sources for the material in this and the next section are H.W. Arthurs, D.D. Carter and H.J. Glasbeek, *Labour Law and Industrial Relations in Canada* (Toronto: Butterworths and Co. Ltd., 1981), pp. 200-207 (originally published as a monograph in *The International Encyclopedia for Labour Law and Industrial Relations* (Deventer, The Netherlands: Kluwer, 1981); M. Bendel, "A Rational Process of Persuasion: Good Faith Bargaining in Canada," *University of Toronto Law Journal*, 30 (1980), pp. 1-45.

43 Arthurs *et al*, *Labour Law and Industrial Relations in Canada*, p. 206.

44 Bendel, "A Rational Process of Persuasion," p. 2.

45 Arthurs *et al*, *Labour Law and Industrial Relations in Canada*, p. 201.

46 Ibid., p. 202.

47 Ibid., p. 204.

48 Bendel, "A Rational Process of Persuasion," p. 19.

49 Arthurs *et al*, *Labour Law and Industrial Relations in Canada*, p. 205.

50 Ibid.

51 Bendel, "A Rational Process of Persuasion," p. 32.

52 Arthurs, *et al*, *Labour Law and Industrial Relations in Canada*, p. 207.

53 P. Kumar, "Recent Wage Deceleration in Canada: Short-term Response or Structural Change," Vol. 42, No. 4, *Relations Industrielles/Industrial Relations*, pp. 690-691.

54 E.M. Kassolow, "Concession Bargaining — Something Old, But Also Something Quite New," *Proceedings*, Thirty-Fifth Annual Meeting of the IRRA (Madison, Wis.: IRRA, 1982), p. 376.

55 P. Capelli, "Union Gains Under Concession Bargaining," *Proceedings*, Thirty-Sixth Annual Meeting of the IRRA (Madison, Wis.: IRRA, 1983), pp. 300–304.

J. Chris Christiansen, *The Financial Post*

8

Forms of Third-Party Assistance in the Negotiation Process

Introduction

As we have seen, if the two parties in the negotiation process are unable to reach an agreement by themselves, various types of third-party assistance are available to them. Conciliation is compulsory in a majority of jurisdictions in Canada before a strike or lockout can be deemed legal, and in most cases some form of mediation is also available, either to supplement or replace the services of a conciliation officer or board or both. In addition to conciliation and mediation, arbitration is sometimes used, primarily in the public and parapublic sectors.

Labour Canada provides very little reliable information regarding the overall use of third-party assistance in negotiation disputes.[1] It is therefore difficult to assess the degree to which the various methods are used, and with what success. However, some trends can be clearly discerned from the statistics in Table 8.1.

The table shows that, while conciliation is being used less and less often in negotiations, there has been a definite increase in the use of mediation in recent years, both in the private sector, and in public and parapublic sector disputes. The use of arbitration has also been increasing over the last few decades, largely

Table 8.1 — Stages at Which Settlements Were Reached per Calendar Year from 1968 to 1988 for Collective Agreements Covering 500 or More Employees, by Percentage of Total Agreements for Canada as a Whole

Stages of Settlement	1968	1969	1970	1971	1972	1973	1974	1975	1976	1977	1978	1979	1980	1981	1982	1983	1984	1985	1986	1987	1988
Direct Bargaining	34.7	44.6	36.0	35.0	41.3	39.1	41.7	39.9	42.2	50.1	42.2	43.9	45.8	41.6	40.8	22.4	41.0	50.0	49.0	46.0	55.0
Conciliation Officer	38.4	26.1	29.7	20.7	26.8	18.3	19.0	19.5	18.4	19.8	15.7	16.9	14.4	18.2	12.1	9.0	12.0	15.0	16.0	14.0	15.0
Conciliation Board	8.2	4.7	2.0	5.1	2.3	3.4	1.7	4.0	1.2	1.4	2.4	2.1	1.5	1.0	2.0	—	0.1	a	1.0	a	a
Post-Conciliation Bargaining	2.4	6.7	9.3	9.3	5.1	9.4	6.1	7.5	8.0	8.6	9.6	7.1	4.9	6.7	5.7	2.4	4.7	6.0	4.0	4.0	4.0
Mediation	—	1.2	5.3	5.7	4.8	4.9	9.3	8.0	10.4	8.8	15.6	7.8	11.9	7.3	11.9	6.1	8.3	12.0	13.0	14.0	10.0
Post-Mediation Bargaining	—	.6	.7	.6	.6	—	—	—	—	—	.2	.9	1.3	1.5	1.2	.6	4.2	2.0	1.0	9.0	1.0
Mediation after Work Stoppage	—	—	—	—	—	1.1	—	—	—	—	.2	.2	.6	—	—	—	—	—	—	—	—
Arbitration	2.4	3.8	5.0	9.0	5.4	6.1	6.6	8.2	5.8	5.6	7.6	9.3	7.7	9.0	7.4	2.7	5.4	6.0	6.0	3.0	7.0
Post-Arbitration Bargaining	—	.6	.7	—	—	—	—	—	—	—	.2	—	—	—	—	—	—	—	—	—	—
Work Stoppages	14.0	11.7	10.7	13.2	9.0	16.9	15.4	11.7	11.2	5.3	5.3	10.5	8.6	14.6	3.7	6.4	6.5	8.0	6.0	9.0	7.0
Bargaining after Work Stoppages	—	—	.3	.6	4.0	1.4	.2	1.0	2.3	.2	.7	.5	3.1	.2	2.9	—	—	—	4.0	—	1.0
Other	—	—	.3	.6	.9	.3	—	.3	.5	.2	.3	.7	.2	—	12.1*	50.3*	17.7	a	a	—	—
Total Percentage	100.1	100	100	100.1	100.2	99.9	100	100.1	100	100	100	99.9	100	100	99.9	99.9	99.9	99.0	100	99.0	100.0
Number of Agreements	294	341	300	334	354	350	410	401	599	567	656	561	547	479	488	595	552	515	552	468	530

*The high percentage under *Other* in 1982 and 1983 represent a pass-through of the public-sector wage (income) restraint program at the federal and provincial levels.

Source: Data for 1968–1969 and 1981 were obtained from *Collective Bargaining Review*, Labour Canada, Ottawa. Data for the period 1970–1980 were obtained from *Wage Developments Resulting from Major Collective Bargaining Settlements*, Labour Canada, Ottawa. Data for 1985–1988 were obtained from Bureau of Labour Information, Labour Canada. The original data are in absolute terms. The total is given in last row. Agreements in the construction industry covering 500 or more workers are included from 1984 to 1988.

a Less than 1%

because of the increase in unionization and collective bargaining in the public sector. Finally, although the press gives wide coverage to work stoppages, thereby exaggerating their overall importance, only about 10% to 15% of negotiations actually result in strikes or lockouts.

It should be noted, however, that the data presented in Table 8.1 understates the extent of third-party assistance, since Labour Canada's figures do not show how many stages disputes have gone through prior to reaching an agreement. For example, the extent to which conciliation officers have been used before resorting to conciliation boards is not stated, since the appointment of a conciliator normally precedes the appointment of a conciliation board. Also ignored are the times conciliation officers or mediators may have unsuccessfully intervened following work stoppages.

This is not the only example of under-reporting of third-party activity. Implicit in Labour Canada records of settlements reached at the work stoppage stage is the idea that mediators have assisted in the resolution of disputes. However, in coding its information Labour Canada does not identify this or any other type of third-party assistance unless special legislation is passed or an inquiry commission is convened to end a work stoppage. Hence, the figures ignore much mediation (and post-mediation) bargaining. Clearly, Table 8.1 must be read with a great deal of caution.

In this chapter, we will describe the various forms of conciliation, mediation, and arbitration being used in North America today, and attempt, on the basis of the evidence available, to evaluate the effectiveness of each. Some attention will also be given to the utility of fact-finding, and of mediation cum arbitration, or med-arb.

The Compulsory Conciliation Process

Compulsory conciliation began with the IDI Act which was drafted by MacKenzie King, then the Deputy Minister of Labour. Public opinion, according to King, would support the recommendations of conciliation boards, and thus create strong pressure on the parties to settle on the terms the boards recommended.

King felt that the Conciliation Act of 1900 was too weak. His drafting of the IDI Act reflected both his intention to give the new legislation more bite and his very definite ideas about conciliation, investigation (which was a precursor of fact-finding), and the role of public opinion in implementing recommendations issuing from conciliation boards. With respect to investigations, King made the following observations:

> The benefits of Compulsory Investigation do not lie in its coercive features, but in the opportunities it guarantees for conciliation at the outset, and for continuous efforts at conciliation throughout the entire course of an investigation.[2]

King recognized investigation as secondary in importance to conciliation, but essential when the latter did not function well. Although he may have been right in his original assessment of public opinion as a factor in the resolution of labour-management disputes, it became apparent with the increasing use of conciliation boards after World War II that public pressure did not play the important role that he assigned it, particularly when conciliation boards were appointed with little regard for the nature of the dispute.

Although conciliation officers and boards under most statutes are required to attempt to mediate a settlement between the parties when an impasse has been reached (the accommodative approach), more often than not they also play a fact-finding role, and are required to make recommendations (the normative approach).

The late H.D. Woods contended that these two approaches reflect most Canadian legislation dealing with state assistance in union-management conflicts. According to Woods, the accommodative approach is intended

> to provide a catalytic influence and make it easier for the parties to concede, compromise and agree

... [The normative approach is used where] one or both of the parties are believed to be unreasonable or ill-informed, and this condition may be corrected by third-party appraisal and evaluation, which will lead to recommendations.[3]

We will deal first with conciliation and mediation and then with fact-finding with recommendation.

Conciliation Officers

Usually, a conciliation officer is the person first appointed when the parties, having reached an impasse in negotiations, request government assistance. In most jurisdictions, the conciliation officer attempts to keep the parties together in a joint conference and may act as a catalyst in resolving outstanding issues. If within a short period of time, the conciliation officer is unable to help the parties resolve their differences, he or she will file a report with the Minister of Labour, or another appropriate authority such as the PSSRB, on the items agreed upon and those still in dispute. When filing the report, the conciliation officer may recommend the appointment of a board.

Conciliation officers are used in the private sector, and in many parts of the public sector, including the federal, provincial, and municipal public services. Most statutes that give collective bargaining rights to provincial public-sector workers contain a provision which requires conciliation or mediation before the appointment of an arbitration board and before a strike or lockout. The same is true for many parapublic-sector workers (hospital workers, teachers, etc.).

Conciliation officers rarely settle disputes. This is partly because, as we have seen, the parties often perceive the conciliation officer's appointment as the first of a potential two-part process and they may not be willing to compromise at that stage. Also, the work of a conciliation officer is not as long and intensive as that of a mediator and is carried out in accordance with a requirement for strict neutrality. A mediator is free, however, to point out unreasonable demands, particularly when these are proposed by or presented to inexperienced negotiators.

The Mediation Process

Negotiations do not stop once a mediator enters a dispute, but are, or should be, facilitated. The major objective of the mediation process is to assist the parties to arrive at an agreement that is acceptable to both of them. This, of course, is the most visible form of successful mediation. However, if a mediator is able to reduce the number of unresolved issues in a dispute, get the parties to narrow the differences on outstanding issues, or prevent the parties from delaying concessions until later in the dispute-resolution process, then the mediation process has been partially successful.[4]

Common sense suggests that it is easier for a mediator to bring the parties to a settlement if they have already mapped out a contract zone. If the parties are unable to establish a contract zone because of inexperience or inflexibility, a mediator may be able to bring one into existence, but this is a more difficult task than getting a settlement within an established contract zone.

Ohio introduced a system of collective bargaining for public sector employees in 1983. The law allows the parties to agree upon a procedure for resolving disputes, but if they cannot settle there is provision for mediation and fact-finding. The statutory provision regarding the appointment of a mediator is very unusual: if the parties do not reach an agreement, a mediator may be appointed 45 days *prior to* the expiration of an existing collective agreement. In addition, the mediator is given only 14 days in which to obtain a settlement. These are unusual time frames to impose upon the mediation process and apparently the legislation has been severely criticized by almost everyone who works under it plus many neutral observers. It is interesting to note that during the first 17 months' experience under the Act, 55% of all disputes resulted in the parties developing their own procedures to escape the strictures it imposes.[5]

If both sides come to the bargaining table with a large number of demands but no priorities attached to them, then part of the function of the mediator is to assist the parties in establishing priorities. The mediator thus performs an important educational function. Once the parties have a clear sense of the relative importance of their demands, they can begin to trade off low-priority items and reactivate the negotiation process.

Another major function of the mediator is to discover the final position of each party. Without this information, he or she will find it very difficult to establish the parameters of his or her role. This knowledge is particularly important in the later stages of the process, since at that point the mediator may be offering suggestions of his or her own for the parties to consider. In most cases, however, the parties are reluctant to reveal their final positions to the mediator. The mediator must, therefore, be adept at reading between the lines and willing to exert a great deal of effort.

Another important duty of the mediator is to maintain control over the mediation process, and act as the only source of public information on the progress of the negotiations, since the parties cannot negotiate freely in a public forum. Mediators should also avoid being manipulated by either party; once compromised, their influence is reduced to nil.

Mediator Profile

Unions and management prefer to deal with mediators who have had previous experience.[6] This poses a paradox: it is very hard to break into mediation unless one has experience, yet one needs experience to get involved in mediation. Probably the best way for a person to enter this field is to take on fairly simple situations, then more involved ones in order to gain a high profile among management and union negotiators. Prior experience as a negotiator may be very helpful. Many of Canada's top mediators, however, have never negotiated an agreement themselves.

Major characteristics of the mediator are impartiality and acceptability to both parties in the dispute. Mediators with a reputation for fa-

vouritism generally have brief careers. Another characteristic of a good mediator is the ability to gain the trust and confidence of the parties. A mediator who is not well known normally encounters exceptional difficulties early in the process, prior to any discussion of the issues.

The mediator's ability and willingness to give a sympathetic hearing to the positions of both sides, and to deal with the technical issues at hand, win him or her the confidence of the parties. However, it is important that the mediator seek clarification of technical issues where necessary. In fact, this is one area in which the mediator has to be perfectly honest with the parties. Asking to be fully informed on at least a few issues will not destroy his or her credibility.

A mediator must also be able to treat matters in confidence. One of the first things that a party may do is entrust the mediator with confidential information on a minor issue in order to assess his or her ability to act with discretion. D. Kuechle cites an example of this tactic:

> One union negotiator described his recent experience with such a [test of the confidentiality of the mediator]. He told the mediator that he could not proceed unless he gained one point: an additional $50 a month on full-benefit pensions, knowing that the company was willing to give that amount. But he said 'I would like to explore $75 first to see how the company is thinking on this line.' The mediator said 'O.K.' and went to the company.
>
> Soon after that he called the parties together and announced that he had been successful in getting a $50 pension increase: now he saw no reason why the parties could not proceed to other points. When that happened, the union's chief negotiator met privately with the company's negotiator and told him what had happened. The two then agreed that they should dismiss the mediator and proceed alone, that he could not be trusted.[7]

The mediator mentioned in Kuechle's example revealed confidential information without permission to do so and, therefore, lost the confidence of both union and management negotiators.

In addition to discretion, a mediator must also possess a sense of timing. Union members know generally how long contract negotiations and the mediation process take from past experience. If the mediator tries to settle prematurely, before either the negotiators or their constituencies are ready, the attempt is unlikely to be successful.

Certain times of the day are more favourable for announcing an agreement than others. For example, if the parties have been negotiating for a lengthy period of time and have been involved in prolonged and intensive mediation, it would be inappropriate to announce an agreement at four o'clock in the afternoon. Four o'clock in the morning would be a better time, since an early-morning announcement creates the impression that the mediation process was a difficult one and that the settlement came only after some very hard bargaining on all sides. Such an impression is likely to leave members with the feeling that their interests have been well represented, fought for, and incorporated as much as humanly possible into the new agreement. Feeling this way about an agreement, members will likely accept it, and such easy acceptance will likely facilitate labour peace.

The mediator must also know whether or not the parties are relating their settlement to another benchmark agreement. If such is the case, it would obviously be unwise to try to force an agreement before the decision in the benchmark case is announced, since the chief negotiators will probably want to study the decision in the benchmark case.

A good mediator is able to pace the negotiations and help to maintain momentum once the parties have started compromising and agreeing on certain items. And it is crucial to sense the precise moment when an agreement is possible. This moment could be when the union has announced a strike or just hours prior to the commencement of a work stoppage. The mediator must be able to sense which of a series of key moments is the most critical for getting the parties to come to an agreement. Should this moment be missed, the future chances of success are diminished.

Sometimes the mediator may have to *create* a critical moment. If the time for agreement is near, the mediator may inform the parties of other cases pending and of the difficulties and delays likely to be encountered in booking further mediation time. Should the parties at this point be relying fairly heavily on the mediator to reach a settlement, the imposition of a time limit may be sufficient to achieve it. An astute mediator employs such a stratagem, however, only if convinced that it will work.

Another important aspect of the mediator's job is what Kressel refers to as the "bulking of items." Through this process, problems are identified and handled as a unit. For example, all the major monetary issues may be grouped together and a subcommittee created to handle these items. Using bulking, it may be easier to get the parties to compromise on bread-and-butter issues. Multidimensional issues, however, are more difficult to bulk since there may not be enough of them in the union's or management's demands to permit the necessary concessions and compromises.

An effective mediator is able to determine the real power figures among the negotiators. Quite often, these power figures may be discerned in caucuses — that is, in sessions when the negotiators for each side meet separately to determine what their next step(s) should be. During caucus meetings, the mediator should be looking for the individual who has veto power and whose ideas seem to serve as a basis for group consensus.

It is also during these caucuses that the important constituents may be revealed. Within unions there are usually important subgroups who feel strongly about the inclusion of certain items in the collective agreement. The same is true for management. For example, a negotiator representing a school board may be accountable to the school trustees who have given the negotiator his or her mandate and parameters. The more the mediator knows about the constituents, the more effective the mediator's efforts are in helping the parties frame an agreement acceptable to them. Sometimes, in fact, the mediator will help negotiators sell an agreement to their constituents.

In the early stages of the mediation process, the mediator is concerned with establishing his or her credibility and gaining the trust and confidence of the parties. Upon meeting the two parties for the first time, the mediator will hear a lot of arguments and counter-arguments. Each party starts out striving for the better negotiating position, and tries to get sympathetic treatment by the mediator. As the talks proceed and the mediator comes to understand the parties, wins their confidence, and gains some appreciation of the issues, he or she assumes a more active role. At this point, an attempt might be made either to establish a framework or to arrange the bargaining agenda so as to encourage the parties to negotiate and make compromises on their own. The mediator may also make suggestions concerning tentative compromise positions.

The final stages of the mediation process are usually characterized by a frantic exchange of proposals in an attempt to reach a settlement before a strike deadline or some other critical time. This is normally the time when the parties ask for suggestions to resolve outstanding issues. A mediator will make proposals only if confident of the "bottom-line" positions of the parties and of his or her ability to satisfy these minimum requirements.

It is usually easier to assess the positions of experienced negotiators than those of novices. For one thing, experienced negotiators know that at some point the mediator may have to come up with his or her own proposals for settlement and, with that expectation, they may in confidence offer suggestions or hints to help the mediator to formulate an acceptable compromise. The mediator may then have off-the-record sessions with the two chief negotiators, who are often very anxious to reach a settlement. The greatest difficulty for a mediator during this crucial stage of mediation is working with inexperienced negotiators who do not realize that they themselves are expected to be of some help in forming final proposals.

At the point where a mediator feels that a mutually acceptable agreement is imminent, the negotiating teams may be called together and asked to give their views on the proposed settlement terms. Sometimes these views take the form of general statements, which are then spelled out in detail so that the parties have a clear understanding of the meaning of the final agreement clauses.

The Effectiveness of Mediation

A few fairly recent empirical studies of the effectiveness of the mediation process exist. One study found that the larger the number of issues at the impasse stage and the greater their severity, the less effective the mediation.[8] Three sources of impasse were found to be particularly difficult to mediate: (1) low motivation by the parties to settle; (2) the inability of the employer to pay; and (3) unrealistic expectations by both parties. None of these sources is surprising, particularly since the data used were from negotiations involving police and firefighters. In recent years, local governments have been having difficulties in raising funds. Inability to pay, therefore, has been a common complaint at the local level. Low motivation may reflect the fact that there were further stages in the dispute resolution process. The sources of impasse most conducive to mediation were: "(1) lack of experience on the part of the negotiators (especially the union negotiators), and (2) disputes involving what the parties viewed as issues of 'principle,'"[9] This success with inexperienced parties reflects the educational aspect of the mediator's role, as he or she teaches the parties that compromise is an essential part of the negotiation process. More surprising, however, is the finding that issues of "principle" were amenable to mediation, since these issues normally culminate in bitter disputes. One is left wondering how the participants in the research project interpreted "principle at stake." It could be that issues of principle such as union security and dues check-off are specified in the statutes governing collective bargaining in the public sector.

The perceived quality of the mediator was helpful in facilitating progress and concessions

B.C. nurses, hospitals both cool to 20.9% raise in deal set by mediator

Canadian Press
VANCOUVER

Both sides in the B.C. nurses' dispute reacted coldly yesterday to a mediator's decision imposing a two-year contract with a total wage increase of almost 21 per cent.

"Job action may be over but our dispute continues," said Pat Savage, president of the B.C. Nurses Union.

"We will begin now to prepare for the next round of negotiations and develop mechanisms to make sure the public understands that patient-care problems are sure to result from this shortsighted setttlement. The mediator's report is binding and we accept it under duress."

Gordon Austin, president of the Health Labor Relations Association, which bargains for 144 hospitals and health care centres, said: "Over all, HLRA is extremely disappointed with the term of this collective agreement."

Mediator Vince Ready's decision means the nurses' starting hourly wage of $15.07 is immediately increased to $17.02 and will move to $19.68 by the end of the contract.

Starting wages for nurses in Canada currently range from a low of $12.57 an hour in New Brunswick to a high of $15.85 in Ontario, the association said.

Mr. Ready imposed salary increases of 6.25 per cent retroactive to Aug. 1; 3 per cent on April 1, 1990; and 4 per cent Dec. 1, 1990. That translates into a compounded increase of 20.9 per cent.

The 17,500 nurses, who have been without a contract since March 31, had refused to work overtime or perform non-nursing duties since staging a 13-day strike in June.

Terms of the contract are virtually the same as those in the first two years of a three-year offer rejected by nurses last month. The only difference is that Mr. Ready ruled the second 6.25 per cent increase this year should be effective Aug. 1 rather than Oct. 1.

That will cost the association an extra $5-million, Mr. Austin said, adding that he had no assurances the provincial government would provide that extra money.

The union had asked for a two-year contract while the hospitals wanted a three-year contract.

Mr. Ready said he chose the shorter contract because issues such as the union's frustration at staffing shortages had to be addressed "on a continuing basis. A shorter-term collective agreement will allow the parties to return to the bargaining table within 16 months to address these very legitimate concerns raised during this prolonged round of negotiations."

The union says there are almost 600 nursing vacancies in the province and that the number is growing. Ms Savage said the wages of other Canadian nurses will vault past those of the B.C. nurses as contracts expire in other provinces.

"It's not much better than what we turned down before," Barb Berryman, a general duty nurse at Royal Inland Hospital in Kamloops, said of Mr. Ready's ruling. "The only thing that it has going for it is that it's a two-year deal."

Premier William Vander Zalm, who is on vacation, had threatened government intervention in the event talks broke down in the summer-long labor dispute.

The nurses, ignoring their union executive's recommendation, rejected an offer last month that called for a 29.5 per cent increase over three years.

The union's original demand called for a 33 per cent increase over one year.

Elective surgery waiting lists grew by an average of 30 per cent during the dispute, a spokesman for the hospitals said.

Health Minister Peter Dueck said the arbitration solution was preferable to government intervention.

The *Globe and Mail*, Aug. 19, 1989, pp. A1, A2.

in bargaining. Somewhat surprisingly, however, no significant relationship existed between the parties' perceptions of the quality of the mediator and the probability of actually reaching a settlement in mediation.[10] (The inability of the employer to pay might have contributed to this finding.)

A number of personal and occupational characteristics of mediators were also examined. The experience of a mediator correlated strongly with the effectiveness of mediation, including the probability of settlement. It was also found that no consistent relationship existed between the educational background of the mediators and whether or not they were full- or part-time members of the appointing agency.[11]

The same study found that aggressive mediation strategies correlated strongly with progress in bargaining and making concessions, but not with the probability of settlement. Also, it was found that mediators were more successful in resolving non-salary disputes than salary ones, with the exception of complex fringe benefits such as pension plans. An aggressive strategy was more effective in winning concessions from unions than from management, probably because union demands, many of which are inflated for the purpose of being subsequently traded off, are easier to concede than those of management.[12]

Another study, based on data drawn from recent negotiations in 24 municipal blue-collar bargaining units in six states found that the intensity of mediation (which was measured somewhat differently from the aggressiveness of strategies) was positively related to the effectiveness of mediation. Intensity of mediation was "characterized by complete immersion in a dispute and full concentration on resolution of the issues. An intense mediator will try new substantive and procedural approaches to identify issues or individuals who will help to resolve the dispute."[13] The major conclusion of this study was that "where disputes are difficult or subject to extended impasse procedures beyond mediation, intense mediator behaviour is

critical for mediation to be effective."[14] Effective in this study was defined as getting a settlement. The study also found that intensive mediation was often able to control or eliminate the "chilling effect," or the failure of a weak party to make concessions while negotiating, in the expectation that an arbitrator will order a desirable settlement. However, the *lack* of intensive mediation was likely to *result* in a chilling effect. The authors conclude that mediation *per se* is not the answer in public-sector disputes, but that "intense mediator behaviour does appear to be effective in difficult negotiations or ones subject to impasse procedure beyond mediation."[15]

Yet another study of the effectiveness of mediation was conducted with 1980 data from teacher negotiations in Iowa. The results of mediation in these negotiations were classified as settlement or non-settlement. A. Karam and R. Pegnetter, the authors of the study, attempted to determine if there were differences between the reactions of unions and management to various types of mediation strategies and qualities. They concluded that, for unions, the most important factors in mediation were devising a framework for negotiations, changing expectations during the mediation process, and maintaining the neutrality and confidentiality of the mediators. Management negotiators found mediation to be most effective where the mediators engaged in face-saving activities, where there was discussion of the cost of disagreement and where they respected the mediator's expertise, trust, and impartiality. The authors found no evidence that testing proposals or emphasizing other settlement patterns bore any relation to settlement in public-sector mediation.[16]

The Conciliation Board Procedure (Fact-Finding with Recommendations)

Specific reference in Canadian legislation to fact-finding with or without recommendations is very rare, although this type of third-party assistance is well-established in the United States. Nonetheless, since conciliation boards function in an analogous way to fact-finding and recommendations, we will consider the use of conciliation boards as equivalent to fact-finding with recommendations.

Under Canadian legislation, the mandate of a conciliation board is to try to mediate settlements between unions and management. If the board is not successful in its mediation efforts, it must make its recommendations public. Only after a certain number of days following the release of the conciliation board's report may workers go on strike or an employer initiate a lockout. In preparing its report, the members of a conciliation board must adopt what the late H.D. Woods referred to as a normative approach to third-party intervention; that is, the board members must investigate the matters in dispute and make pertinent recommendations.

As indicated in Chapter 6, conciliation boards were used as one of the major forms of third-party assistance in contract negotiation disputes until well into the 1960s. However, boards have been voluntary in Saskatchewan and are now partly voluntary in Manitoba, and they have been eliminated completely in Quebec and British Columbia. Other jurisdictions still retain provisions for their establishment in private-sector disputes. However as indicated earlier, very few of these jurisdictions now establish conciliation boards and when they do, it is mainly in cases that have a serious public-interest component.

Disadvantages of Conciliation Boards

One of the major criticisms of conciliation boards is the long delay inherent in the process. Private-sector legislation in Canada provides no guidelines for board members; consequently, they must develop their own criteria for determining the kinds of recommendations they will make. This freedom sometimes slows down the negotiation process. Ill-conceived recommendations may also "heat up" rather than "cool off" a dispute. Thus, the overall success rate for conciliation boards is low.

Another major objection to compulsory conciliation is that it hampers direct negotiations between the parties. For example, if the two sides feel in their private negotiations that their dispute may go to a conciliation officer, they are inclined to withhold concessions until later in the process. If the dispute proceeds to the conciliation board stage, there is an inclination to withhold the last offer until the conciliation board has reported. Only after the report do both parties really begin serious negotiations.

While the elimination of work stoppages, which is one of the major objectives of the compulsory conciliation process, is a laudable objective, one may question whether delaying the work stoppage until after the issuance of the conciliation board report is conducive to genuine negotiations, since the more time there is to settle at the negotiation table, the less pressure there is to settle. Furthermore, a conciliation board report may make a recommendation which strongly favours one party over the other. In that event, the favoured party may use the board's recommendation as an argument to support its position and thus prolong subsequent negotiations.

In addition, as H.D. Woods says:

> the fallacy in the Canadian compulsory conciliation procedure is that it ignores the role of the work stoppage as a catalytic agent in bringing about agreement. When the parties are confronted with the possibility of a strike or lockout, each is brought face to face with a choice between (a) the losses to be incurred by the strike and (b) the price that may have to be paid to avoid these losses. But the delay on resort to work stoppages suspends the need to face these alternatives.[17]

In fact, a conciliation report favourable to one side may actually prolong a subsequent work stoppage, should the favoured side persist in seeking to obtain what the report recommended.

Declining Use of Conciliation Boards

The decline in conciliation board appointments is apparent at the federal level, which until recently relied more on conciliation boards than any other form of third-party assistance, especially in disputes with a fairly heavy public interest component. When Part V of the Canada Labour Code was amended in 1972, provision was made for the use of conciliation commissioners as well as conciliation officers and boards. In addition, section 195 of Part V (now section 105 of Part 1) of the Labour Code empowers the Minister of Labour to appoint a mediator, either upon request or on his own initiative. This gives the federal minister a great deal of discretion in the choice of conciliation strategies; namely, the appointment of a conciliation officer, and/or a conciliation commissioner, and/or a conciliation board, and/or a mediator. Over the years, there has been a decline in two-stage conciliation: there are now fewer appointments of conciliation boards and more appointments of conciliation commissioners in private-sector disputes.

While we are seeing fewer and fewer boards appointed in the private sector, the Public Service Staff Relations Act (PSSRA), which covers workers in the federal government, still contains a mandatory provision whereby a bargaining agent choosing to exercise its strike option must first go through a two-stage conciliation process. The process is not always very successful. For example, up to 1981, lengthy conciliation board reports were used in negotiations between the Canadian Union of Postal Workers (CUPW) and the Treasury Board. In fact, in the 1978 and 1981 negotiations, three separate (and lengthy) board reports were written, one by each of the nominees and one by the chair. Just once, though, in the spring of 1980, was a settlement reached on the basis of a conciliation board report. And in that case, the conciliation board recommended favourably on almost every item that the union wanted. In fact, in the post-conciliation negotiations, CUPW made it very clear that is would settle without a strike only if the government gave substantially what was contained in the conciliation board report. An added factor in these post-conciliation negotiations was the presence of the President of the Canadian Labour Congress — the first time that such a high-ranking official in the labour move-

ment had ever taken part in negotiations between a union and an employer. In light of the move away from conciliation boards in the private sector, it will be interesting to see what, if anything, will be done about their use in the federal and provincial public sectors.

Effects of the Decline If all the criticisms directed at conciliation boards in the past are true, their decline should mean that the negotiation process takes less time. Since provisions for conciliation boards vary from province to province, the decrease should also facilitate negotiations in multiprovincial bargaining situations. Furthermore, as the activities of conciliation boards are curtailed or eliminated, the role of the conciliation officer should become more effective in achieving contract settlements. However, no studies have been conducted to determine if any of these outcomes have transpired.

One thing that the reduction of conciliation boards *has* achieved is the extension of the role and function of mediation. Not too many years ago, the appointment of mediators in contract negotiation disputes was something of a rarity in Canadian industrial relations. In recent years, however, increasing references have been made to the appointment of mediators in such disputes in the public, parapublic, and private sectors. It is expected that mediators will gradually replace conciliation boards and possibly conciliation officers.

Effectiveness of Conciliation

Only a small proportion of settlements are reached at the conciliation board stage. Whether this is due to their declining use or their ineffectiveness is difficult to say. Conciliation boards have often been viewed as an interim step to be endured before hard bargaining can take place. In this sense, they are considered to have a chilling effect on negotiations.

W. List suggests that conciliation boards may be more useful if their members are perceived as mediators, with the union and management nominees playing a mediation role with the parties they represent. This arrangement would enhance the possibility of obtaining informal agreements, which could then be set down officially in the conciliation report issued by the board. This tactic was used by one conciliation board chair in disputes in the meat-packing industry.

This form of conciliation-mediation would certainly be preferable to the traditional fact-finding with recommendations, which sometimes widens rather than narrows the differences between the parties' positions, and which may also undermine third-party credibility. For example, during the 1982 doctors' dispute in Ontario, a fact-finder charged with recommending a new fee schedule for medical services came up with a figure which the Ontario Medical Association claimed was less than the original government offer. The OMA further alleged that the fact-finder's report seemed to be based entirely on his personal concern with inflation and did not seriously examine the legitimacy of the doctors' demands.[18] The result was a temporary disruption of medical services in the province.

While the compulsory conciliation process has been seriously criticized in the private sector for many years, it found some support in a study which deals with impasse disputes in the federal public sector of Canada.[19] The PSSRA governs collective bargaining between federal public servants and the federal government. While the most salient features of the Act will be discussed in Chapter 9, it is sufficient to indicate here that where two parties are unable to reach an agreement through the negotiation process,

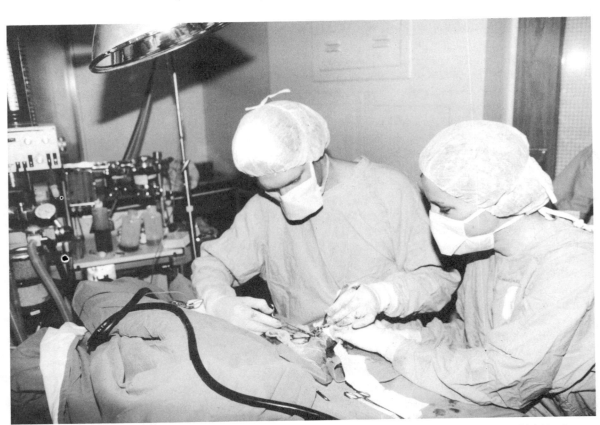

Dick Hemingway

the Act provides for two dispute settlement routes: (1) conciliation with the right to strike; and (2) binding arbitration. The bargaining agent for each group of workers chooses a route before each round of negotiations begins. An agent may change routes at the beginning of each round of negotiations but not during their course. The results of the study showed that a higher proportion of disputes were settled in the intermediate stages (conciliation and mediation) of the conciliation and strike route than by the arbitration route. The authors stated that the "data suggest that the costs of disagreement associated with a strike provide much higher pressure or motivation for the parties to settle in mediation or conciliation than the associated costs of going to arbitration."[20] In the public sector, therefore, the incentive to use the conciliation route with a strike as its final step appears to be much greater than that for the route with arbitration as its final step.

The Arbitration Process

Conciliators, mediators, fact-finders, and conciliation boards may recommend the terms of a settlement, but their recommendations are not *binding* on the parties to the dispute. The results of arbitration, on the other hand, are not negotiable; both parties are bound to accept them.

Arbitration of Contract Negotiation or Interest Disputes

While arbitration has been practiced in the private sector to a very limited extent in the past, it is only the recent, widespread adoption of collective bargaining in the public sector that has made this method a major form of third-party assistance in Canada. Public servants in Ontario, Alberta, and several other provinces have the right to bargain collectively, but not to strike, so arbitration is a useful tool for settling disputes. In addition, the federal PSSRA and the New Brunswick legislation both provide for either arbitration or the conciliation and strike routes, and allow the bargaining agent to select

which route will be used. (More will be said about these approaches in Chapter 10.)

In some parapublic sectors, too, arbitration is the final form of settlement. For example, under the Ontario Hospital Disputes Arbitration Act, workers in hospitals and other health-care facilities do not have the right to strike. Instead, the parties must submit any unresolved issues in negotiations to binding arbitration.

A conceptual distinction exists among the types of arbitration currently employed in Canada. Compulsory arbitration is mandated, or required by law, as the final stage in contract negotiation disputes. The example cited in the previous paragraph is a form of compulsory arbitration since health care workers and hospitals cannot legally conduct strikes or lockouts. Voluntary arbitration, on the other hand, involves a mutual agreement between the two parties to be bound by third-party recommendations. The parties may, for example, decide before or during the proceedings of a conciliation board that they will be bound by the recommendations of that board.

Although many private employers recommend compulsory arbitration as a means of resolving contract negotiation disputes in the public and parapublic sectors, they have made it quite clear that they themselves do not wish to be bound by such measures. Unions are also generally opposed to compulsory arbitration in both the private and public sectors, although weaker unions sometimes prefer to have their disputes settled by arbitration rather than deal directly with powerful employers. Weak employers may also prefer arbitration to a strike or lockout.

Voluntary Arbitration

Management and unions in the private sector generally do not like using compulsory arbitration to settle unresolved contract negotiation issues. However, a bold experiment in voluntary arbitration was initiated in 1972 by the United Steelworkers Union and the ten major steel companies in the United States. This bargaining procedure is officially known as the

Experimental Negotiating Agreement (ENA). Under the ENA, one bargaining procedure exists to resolve national issues and another to resolve local issues. (Since no provision exists for binding arbitration to settle local issues, the strike option remains.) If a national agreement cannot be reached by a specified date, either party may submit the unresolved issues to an impartial arbitration panel with the authority to render a final and binding decision on the outstanding issues. The arbitration panel is made up of one union representative, one management representative, and three impartial arbitrators selected by both parties. At least two of the three arbitrators are thoroughly familiar with collective bargaining agreements in the steel industry.[21] This procedure has been used in negotiations since 1974. During these negotiations, the parties were able to reach agreement without having recourse to the arbitration panel stage.

The major impetus behind the ENA was the boom and bust phenomenon which provided the background for negotiations between 1959 and 1974. During each round of negotiations prior to 1974, the steel companies stockpiled extensively in anticipation of a strike. While the workers made a good deal of money in overtime building up this large inventory, they were often without necessary funds during the layoffs which occurred while the inventory was being liquidated. However, in each case following 1959, a settlement was reached without a strike. Consequently, union members were laid off and company production was more or less halted until the stockpiled steel had been sold. The desire to prevent this situation led the union and the companies to try out the ENA.

There were some incentives for each party to enter into the ENA. For example, each member of the union having employee status as of August 1, 1974 received a bonus of $150, in recognition of the savings in production costs anticipated from not stockpiling. Also, there were certain fundamental safeguards in the existing collective agreements that each side wanted to protect and preserve. These per-

tained to local working conditions, past practices, union-shop and check-off guarantees, no-strike/no-lockout provisions, and a management rights clause. The 1974 agreement also assured the union that the cost-of-living clause won in 1971 would continue to operate to 1977. The ENA was intended, as well, to force the parties to reach settlement terms of their own, rather than having terms imposed by outside third parties. Mr. Abel, president of the union at that time, claimed that

> a third party dictating the terms of a settlement might not be aware of technical problems that may, unwittingly, stem from an imposed settlement.
>
> The need to formulate contract conditions that are workable and acceptable to both sides will serve as an additional pressure to resolve issues independent of the arbitration machinery that has been established.[22]

Mr. Abel predicted accurately that the parties would make every attempt to reach an agreement on their own. It should also be pointed out, however, that part of the agreement allowed strikes over local issues. Strikes over these issues had always been a very thorny problem in steel industry negotiations. Since the companies bargain on a multi-company basis, it is extremely difficult to deal with local issues at the national level.

Surprisingly, only a few other industries and services have attempted an ENA. Voluntary final offer selection arbitration is used in American major league baseball, as well as in a number of Canadian universities, including the University of Ottawa.[23]

Compulsory Arbitration

Most writers who analyze compulsory arbitration enter immediately into discussions of its labour relations aspects, without specifying the criteria by which its effectiveness may be assessed and without providing a framework for their discussions. What I wish to do here is to provide a framework for discussing the fundamental aspects of compulsory arbitration and to indicate the difficulty of assessing its effectiveness.

Strike Prevention One of the presumed benefits of compulsory arbitration (which is used primarily in the public and parapublic sectors) is that it protects the public interest, however that may be defined, from the adverse consequences of strikes. From this perspective, then, compulsory arbitration has a strike-prevention function. The prevention of strikes assures the delivery of goods and services to the public and the maintenance of labour peace. However, to date not one study has surveyed the public to ascertain if it wishes its interests to be protected by the use of compulsory arbitration.[24] It is quite possible that the public has not suffered sufficient hardship or inconvenience to favour compulsory arbitration as the preferred way of resolving public-sector disputes. Furthermore, rather than thinking in terms of a unitary public interest, perhaps we should be thinking in terms of multiple public interests. For example, an individual who always walks to and from work may not find a transit strike inconvenient.

Protection of Public-Sector Workers Compulsory arbitration is a dispute settlement procedure which protects the interests of public-sector workers. Collective bargaining without the right to strike or without an arbitrated settlement may not be sufficient to bring a public-sector employer to the negotiation table. In the absence of the threat of a strike or of compulsory arbitration, the employer would have little or no incentive to negotiate in good faith. In fact, it is quite possible that the employer would unilaterally impose the terms and conditions of employment. The evidence supports the proposition that arbitration has worked effectively in promoting good faith bargaining, although much depends on the types of arbitration procedures used. Also, the fact that arbitrators use the same labour market data in making their awards suggests that arbitration may provide roughly even results, particularly concerning wages, for groups of workers across bargaining units in the same labour market areas.[25] Hence, arbitration appears to protect the interests of public-sector workers quite well.

Regulation of Conflict It has been suggested that collective bargaining with arbitration has become a regulator of interest-group conflict.[26] That is, collective bargaining has brought into the open the fact that a set of group interests exists among public-sector workers which is potentially costly and which has made overt the potential conflicts between public-sector workers and the public sector as an employer.

Public-sector workers have as much interest in protecting their wages and working conditions as private-sector workers do. One response to collective bargaining in the public sector has been the provision of procedures for third parties to resolve impasses. These procedures include arbitration. Arbitration not only resolves impasses between the public-sector employer and union, but may also resolve disputes among members of either or both groups. It is argued that arbitration "performs this regulatory function primarily through the finality, impartiality, compromising and face-saving features of the process."[27] Arbitration can help both union leaders and management spokespersons in dealing with their constituents since both parties can save face by blaming the arbitrator for unfavourable outcomes.

Inhibition of Representative Government The critics of compulsory arbitration argue that it inhibits representative government. The political system, they claim, should reflect the will of the governed by holding publicly elected officials accountable for allocative decisions and by allowing interest groups to be heard during public decision-making processes.[28] Arbitration, however, lacks accountability, and the determination of wages and working conditions by arbitrators has led to a high degree of bureaucratization in decision-making, as labour relations professionals concern themselves only with how their decisions will affect the union and management representatives they deal with, and ignore other groups, such as taxpayers, who are affected by the decisions. It has been suggested that this criticism of compulsory arbitration could be largely overcome through a reformulation of the arbitration process. It has been stated, for example, that

> legislative bodies may restrict the scope of arbitrable subjects, limit the coverage of the arbitration legislation, specify exceedingly tight decision criteria, require that the decisions be made by tripartite panels instead of single arbitrators, and mandate final-offer selection rather than conventional decision making.[29]

It is questionable whether or not these measures would be sufficient to control arbitrators' decisions. A number of Canadian jurisdictions which give collective bargaining rights to their workers specify criteria which arbitrators must follow, but they are not precise enough to ensure specific arbitration outcomes.

The Government of Quebec has always refused to have wages and working conditions in the public and parapublic sectors arbitrated. It claims that to do so is to lose control over its budget, about one-half of which comprises the cost of wages and other benefits. The problem is even more acute in Quebec since negotiations for all public and parapublic workers take place about the same time every three years. Hence, settlement terms have an immediate and substantial impact over the distribution of government revenues.

Inhibition of Genuine Bargaining It is alleged that compulsory arbitration (and particularly compromise arbitration, in which the arbitrator more or less splits the differences between the parties) acts to inhibit genuine bargaining. Of all the research done on arbitration in recent years, this aspect has received the lion's share of attention. Research findings suggest that compromise arbitration has a chilling effect on negotiations, since one or both of the parties may withhold concessions during bipartite negotiations in the hope of gaining a better settlement if the dispute goes to arbitration. This practice prevails among weak unions or weak employers. Research findings also suggest that compromise arbitration has a narcotic effect on bipartite negotiations, since the parties may build up a dependence on it during consecutive rounds of negotiations.[30]

Reliance on Impasse Procedures While empirical research literature is abundant on the subject of the chilling and narcotic effects, there is no consensus on the extent to which the parties rely on going beyond the bilateral negotiation process. Three recent articles debate the appropriateness of statistical techniques used to determine if a narcotic effect exists.[31] One article claims that the definition generally fitting the popular usage of the concept is "repeated or heavy reliance on an impasse procedure."[32] Precisely what repeated or heavy reliance means is still open to conjecture. The most recent study concludes that after an initial period of adjustment

> there were no positive narcotic effects, and only scattered negative effects, under any of the bargaining laws or for any of the employee groups analyzed. The concern frequently expressed over the positive narcotic effect therefore appears to be exaggerated, if not groundless. To the extent it exists at all, a positive narcotic effect is apparently a phenomenon only of early experience under a public sector bargaining law.[33]

A study of collective bargaining among British Columbia school teachers under a system of compulsory arbitration between 1938 and 1973 concluded that "compulsory arbitration can avert strikes without causing collective bargaining to disappear and without leading to wage awards far above or below negotiated settlements."[34] Another writer subsequently analyzed the same data, manipulated it in different ways, and concluded that "arbitration has significantly reduced the incentive to bargain among British Columbia teachers' unions and school districts during the period studied, and the authors therefore overstate their case when they refer to the 'success' of the B.C. teachers' arbitration system."[35]

Choice of Settlement Routes In the section on mediation, we stated that the PSSRA provides for two types of impasse settlement procedures: (1) conciliation and strike; and (2) arbitration. The bargaining agent must choose a route before negotiations begin. One study compared the results of the two dispute settlement routes for the first four rounds of negotiations between 1968 and 1975 and found an increasing trend for disputes to be settled at the arbitration stage over the four rounds. The percent of cases going all the way to arbitration in each of the four rounds was as follows: 5%, 32%, 33%, and 54%.[36] The authors of this study concluded that

> the overall pattern of results supports the existence of a chilling effect. Over time the proportion of units settling on their own, with no third-party assistance, steadily decreased. Furthermore, the chilling effect appeared to be greater under the arbitration route than under the conciliation-board strike route.[37]

This study also found that there was preliminary evidence of a narcotic effect: "a history of experience with the impasse procedure increases the probability of relying on third parties in the subsequent rounds of bargaining."[38] While this study concluded that both a chilling and a narcotic effect existed under the compulsory arbitration route, it did not specify the criteria used to determine the existence of these effects.

Experience with compulsory arbitration between the Ontario government and its workers shows that, since 1963, about 30% of settlements were reached at the arbitration stage. An examination of some of the awards revealed that, by the time they went to arbitration, the parties were often very far apart.[39]

In addition to the Canadian studies cited above, numerous American studies exist, particularly of police officers, firefighters, and teachers. Most of these studies confirm that the chilling effect and narcotic effect result from the use of compromise settlements handed down under compulsory arbitration. Two prominent American writers recently concluded that, ultimately, the line between an acceptable and an unacceptable rate of impasse under any system is subjective. Judgement must be balanced against other policy objectives as well as the effectiveness of the impasse resolution procedure.[40]

Criticisms of Arbitration

Compromise arbitration has been criticized on the grounds that it is not an innovative process. If one looks at the major innovations in collective agreements over the years, one will find that very few of them have come about through arbitration. One exception to this rule, at least in Canada, was the union security clause which was established following a strike by the United Automobile Workers against the Ford Motor Company in 1946. In that particular dispute, the union wanted a union-shop provision whereby all members of the bargaining unit would be required to become union members. The Ford Motor Company of Canada refused to accept this proposition and, after about a six-month work stoppage, the issue was submitted to arbitration. The arbitrator in that case was the late Ivan C. Rand, the Chief Justice of the Supreme Court of Canada. His decision, later called the "Rand Formula," did not require workers within a bargaining unit to become union members, but did require that they pay union dues. This was, however, one of the few major innovations under the compromise or conventional form of arbitration in Canada.

Another major criticism of the conventional form of arbitration is that arbitrators act in a normative context. Usually the arbitrator or arbitration board in an interest or contract negotiation dispute will hear evidence by both parties in which each tries to justify its own position. It is only by selecting criteria presented by the parties, or in some cases adopting criteria of their own, that the arbitrators or arbitration tribunals are able to provide a rationale behind the award which they hand down.

Thus far in Canada, only the PSSRA and a few provincial public sector statutes which specify arbitration as the final stage of dispute resolution provide guidelines for arbitrators in those situations in which the bargaining agent selects the arbitration process. However these acts still permit the introduction of any other factors that the arbitrators deem relevant.

In an effort to eliminate the detrimental effects of the compromise form of arbitration on the negotiation process, a number of variants of compulsory arbitration have been introduced in a number of American states and in at least one important Canadian parapublic sector. The most prominent of these is final-offer selection (FOS) — sometimes referred to as final-offer arbitration (FOA).

Final-Offer Selection

One of the alternatives which arose as a result of the criticism of conventional or compromise arbitration is final-offer selection, or FOS. C.M. Stevens was one of the first to propose what he called "either-or" arbitration, in an article entitled "Is Compulsory Arbitration Compatible with Bargaining?"[41] Stevens suggested that if the parties could not reach an agreement through negotiations, either one should be allowed to appeal at any time to an arbitrator or arbitration tribunal which would select the total bargaining package of one party or the other. This system would create a high degree of uncertainty regarding the arbitration award, and encourage the parties to negotiate a settlement. A major hypothesis of Stevens' article, then, was that the greater the degree of uncertainty, the more likely the parties were to negotiate to finality. The threat of an either-or type of arbitration award was almost equivalent to the threat of a strike.

> Compulsory arbitration of this type provides an instrument through which each party may impose a cost of disagreement upon his opposite number. Generally speaking, it seems quite possible that a threat to arbitrate, like a threat to strike, might invoke the negotiatory process of concession and compromise which are characteristic of normal collective bargaining.[42]

Three types of final-offer selection now exist: (1) total package; (2) final offer by item; and (3) tri-offer selection.

Total-Package In total-package selection, the arbitrator or arbitration panel chooses either the final package of the union or the final package of the employer. The selector or arbitrator under this system has to select the final offer of either side *in toto*, and cannot take items from both packages. Figure 8.1 illustrates how the system works.

Let us suppose that at time X a union is demanding a 30% wage increase and a company is offering 5%. Settlements in the industry are averaging 10% to 12%. Final-offer selection is available to both sides and may be invoked at any time. Neither party, at this point, would want an arbitrator to choose between the two packages, since an adverse decision would represent a significant loss. Hence, there is an incentive to negotiate further. By time X1 the union's demand has declined to 20% and management's offer has risen to 7%. Since the two sides are still far apart — neither is in the 10% to 12% range — there is continued reason to negotiate for further concessions. At time X2, the union demand is 12.5% and the management offer is 9.5%. Neither side stands to lose too much if the final offer arbitrator accepts the other side's offer, so arbitration could be invoked to bring the negotiations to a close.

This scenario demonstrates how the use of final-offer selection can encourage parties to remain at the bargaining table. Total-package FOS thus seems an effective third-party procedure in cases where well-defined monetary issues are being negotiated. It is less well suited,

Figure 8.1   **Total-Package, Final-Offer Selection**

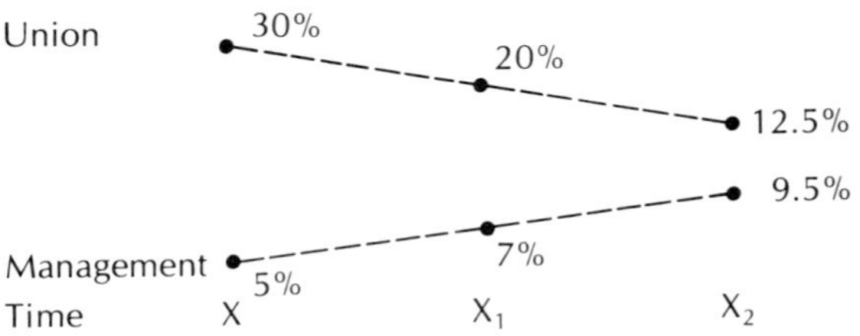

however, to negotiations involving non-monetary matters or questions of principle. Nonetheless, this form of arbitration is vastly superior to traditional methods, which rarely give the parties any incentive to continue bargaining.

Final-Offer by Item This form of FOS enables the arbitrator or arbitration tribunal to select specific positions from either the union's or management's final offers, and comes somewhat closer to compromise arbitration; that is, the award is based on both sides' offers and what the arbitrator perceives as a fair settlement, given the final positions of the two parties. The selector may choose items from either party's package, but cannot change the quantum of the item selected.

Tri-Offer Selection Under tri-offer selection, the arbitrator may choose the last offer of the union or management, or the recommendations of a fact-finder. These recommendations are made known to the parties before the arbitrator arrives on the scene. Tri-offer arbitration has not yet been used in Canada, but has been utilized in Massachusetts for public-safety workers, and was recently introduced into Iowa as well for all categories of public-sector workers. (In Iowa, the arbitrator selects on an issue-by-issue basis.)[43]

Effectiveness of FOS To what extent, if any, does FOS alter the conclusions reached earlier on the compromise form of compulsory arbitration? First, FOS is better able to protect the public interest, by acting to prevent strikes. While there is very little literature on this subject, one can be sure that if FOS *was* correlated with the incidence of strikes, there would be some evidence of it in the research. We can take the lack of concern as a positive sign that FOS helps to prevent strikes. However, there is no evidence that the public prefers FOS to strikes. Hence, FOS is more or less taken as an article of faith on the part of the politicians who have introduced it.

Insofar as there is no negative correlation between public-sector wages and FOS, FOS probably protects the interests of public-sector workers, since it appears to have a levelling effect in labour markets. As well, it appears to act as a regulator of interest-group conflict by protecting public-sector workers vis-à-vis the government as employer. It acknowledges that public-sector workers have a right to protect themselves against arbitrary or capricious action by the government, since the last step in the procedure is impartial third-party arbitration.

Final-offer selection tends to promote genuine bargaining, since the parties are pressured to make concessions at certain points in the process when more might be lost by forcing an award through inflexibility than by ceding on an issue. The tri-offer method used in Iowa not only has these critical pressure points built into it, but an additional decision to be considered by the arbitrator — namely, the recommendations of the fact-finder as well as the packages of the two parties.

Despite these benefits, it should be noted that FOS is perhaps as much an inhibitor of representative government as compromise arbitration is. Decisions about government allocation of scarce financial resources are not made by elected politicians, but by industrial relations specialists whose main preoccupation is the prevention of strikes and the promotion of harmonious relations between the government as employer and the unions. Professional arbitrators seldom show much concern for the citizenry at large.

In summary, FOS appears to contribute greater benefits than costs as contrasted with compromise arbitration. The one function that it does not appear to perform well is representation, except in cases where public policy establishes tight criteria to guide arbitrators in the selection of their awards. The available evidence suggests that FOS performs much better than conventional or compromise arbitration. Theoretically, tri-offer FOS is the most desirable method and, according to the empirical evidence to date, it appears to be working well.

Fact-Finding, Mediation, and Voluntary Arbitration

There is only one piece of legislation in Canada which provides for all of the various types of third-party assistance (fact-finding, mediation, and arbitration, whether voluntary or in the form of total-package, final-offer selection). This statute, the Ontario School Boards and Teachers Collective Negotiations Act (1975), provides for the appointment of a fact-finder at the request of the parties or on the initiative of the Ontario Education Relations Commission, the body that administers the statute.[44] The fact-finder is given 30 days to prepare a report, which *may or may not* contain recommendations for settlement. Upon receipt of the report, the parties are given 15 days to settle, after which time the report is made available to the local news media, in order to bring public pressure to bear on the negotiators.

Section 14 of the statute gives the Commission the right to assign a person to assist the parties to make or renew an agreement. This is usually interpreted as the right to appoint mediators following fact-finding efforts. The union may legally strike only after mediation has been attempted. There is also a provision in the statute allowing the parties to submit their outstanding issues to binding arbitration of the compromise form, or to refer their unresolved issues to a third party for total-package final offer selection. To date the FOS method has been used in a very small percentage of cases.

The Ontario Education Relations Commission has a very extensive data bank upon which the parties to the negotiations or a fact-finder, mediator, or selector may draw. Moreover, the Commission has a program for training fact-finders and mediators involved in school negotiations, and has recently embarked upon a program to improve long-term union-management relationships in those cases where the two sides have been unable to develop some measure of mutual trust.

One study, by B. Downie which assessed the first two years under the Act, criticized the way in which various aspects of it functioned, particularly the fact-finding process.[45] In the first round of negotiations, fact-finders were appointed in nearly 50% of the cases in the first year, and over 40% in the second.[46] The response to a questionnaire sent to the parties indicated that in only 36.4% of the cases did the parties claim that an impasse had been reached, and that only slightly over 50% of the parties felt the appointment of a fact-finder to be necessary.[47] Teacher negotiators felt more strongly about the need to appoint fact-finders than school board negotiators did. This disparity indicates that very few meaningful negotiations had taken place prior to the appointment of fact-finders, a conclusion supported by the fact that "the forty-eight fact finders' reports written in the first round of negotiations listed 590 items in dispute, or more than 12 items per fact finder."[48]

Despite this gloomy picture, the study concludes that fact-finding does have the potential to encourage bargaining. Part of the problem with the fact-finding process in the first two rounds was that fact-finders made recommendations on only about 45% of the issues. In addition, fact-finders often failed to give a rationale for their recommendations. In about 45% of the cases, moreover, the recommendations made were of a compromise or non-directional nature. The researcher sums up the fact-finding process by suggesting that

> a possible conclusion, then, is that fact finders are not making, or not able to make, the hard choices that would give a report some strategic or therapeutic importance. It may be in the future that we will see stronger language, more recommendations, and more presentation of rationale by fact finders.[49]

Little mention of mediation was made in the study, since mediation had been used in only about 18% of the first round cases. On some occasions, mediators were appointed for training or strategic purposes. Mediators were appointed in only 35 cases during the second round as well.[50]

A later study indicated that the duration of teacher-school board negotiations had increased dramatically. In each round of negotiations from 1976 to 1982, the average length of negotiations exceeded eight months.[51] In an effort to decrease the time spent in negotiations and to increase the effectiveness of the procedures under the legislation, particularly the fact-finding process, the Commission adopted a number of changes in the use of fact-finding and mediation. For one thing, the parties were encouraged to use fact-finding only if absolutely necessary and to continue their negotiations after the agreement expired. And, in 1980 and 1981, the Commission recruited highly qualified individuals who were very familiar with both industrial relations and school board negotiations. As a result of these changes, the fact-finders produced reports with recommendations, rationales, and data which were more acceptable to the parties.[52]

The Commission also adopted a new policy of releasing fact-finders' reports to the local media in *every* case. Fact-finders were required to provide a summary of their reports so that more accurate reporting could be made by the media. Starting in 1980, the Commission also started recruiting and training individuals as intensive mediators. And, from 1980 to 1982, there was much greater use of mediation *before* fact-finding. Concurrent with this change, a dramatic drop occurred in the use of fact-finders: from 61% to 37% of all negotiations. Fact-finding was used in only 25% of the cases in the 1980 to 1982 rounds.[53] B. Downie, who is a former chair of the Commission, made the following comment about the fact-finding process:

> Fact-finding and the procedures of Bill 100 have been a conspicuous success and a model to which industrial relations specialists should pay heed. Certainly, one of the key factors of this success is reports that include specific recommendations on substantive terms.[54]

Downie concluded that if a public-disputes tribunal such as the Ontario Education Relations Commission were to be successful, it needed a variety of tools at its disposal and the discretion to implement new and different proposals.[55] Since both compromise and final-offer arbitration were included in the strike category, we can safely assume from the figures that arbitration was used very sparingly.

Mediation-Arbitration (Med-Arb)

Mediation-arbitration is another form of third-party assistance sometimes used to help resolve contract negotiation disputes. Med-arb, like FOS, has both its advocates and its detractors. Some critics argue that it is very difficult for any one person to play the roles of both mediator and arbitrator. It is suggested that if a person plays both roles, the negotiating parties are not likely to reveal their final positions to that individual.

On the other hand, a number of people contend that a good mediator is able to detect the final settlement positions of the two parties, and the mere fact that he of she may become an arbitrator should not prevent him or her from detecting what these final positions are. Overall, there does not seem to be any clear-cut consensus among industrial relations specialists concerning the effectiveness of med-arb. This does not mean, however, that the topic is being ignored.

Judge J.C. Anderson has proposed a type of med-arb with a number of unique characteristics.[56] The process would substitute for the right to strike or lockout in the public sector an agreement between the parties to continue direct negotiations, using mediation, if required, until a specified date. The mediator/arbitrator would be completely independent and fully experienced in the labour field, and would only function as an arbitrator if mediation failed. The report of the arbitrator would become final and binding on the parties. However, a procedure would be added to the med-arb process whereby either party could appeal to a special tribunal against the arbitration decision.

Judge Anderson sees the following advantages to his proposal: (1) it allows the parties to obtain an agreement between themselves; (2) if agreement does not occur, it gives the parties the opportunity to negotiate with the assistance of a mediator; and (3) if mediation is not successful, the arbitrator, while acting as a mediator, is able to establish the priorities which each party places upon outstanding issues.[57] Judge Anderson also suggests that the arbitrator's report would not differ much from the kind of agreement that the parties might fashion for themselves.

There are, however, admitted drawbacks to this form of med-arb: (1) the hesitation on the part of the parties to submit their dispute to a third party; (2) the lack of skilled mediators/arbitrators; and (3) the fact that acting as mediator may prejudice a person's decision as arbitrator. Since the publication of Judge Anderson's article in 1975, however, there has been no great rush in Ontario or any of the other provinces for the parties to adopt this med-arb procedure.

Industrial Inquiry Commissions

Legislation in most jurisdictions provides for the appointment of industrial inquiry commissions. These commissions are usually composed of one or more experts in particular fields of industrial relations. The federal government and the provinces often set up special inquiry commissions to look into particularly difficult labour-management situations.

One notable inquiry examined the "run-throughs" on the Canadian National railways. Before the diesel engine came into being, railway cars were pulled by coal engines, which were unable to make very long runs. As a result, many small towns grew up around railway terminal stations, where the trains would stop to pick up enough fuel to take them to their next destination. When the diesel motor came along, trains were able to travel longer distances without refueling. Former terminal stations were bypassed or "run through" and in effect became ghost towns.

In 1964, the federal government appointed a one-person commission to look into the effects of run-throughs on the towns and railway workers involved.[58] The commissioner found that run-throughs were indeed creating major adjustment problems for the railway workers and unions, as well as for the communities affected. He made some very strong recommendations to the federal government on this problem, which are reflected in Part 1 of the Canada Labour Code: employers are required to give 120 days advance notice to the unions of technological change which may have a serious impact on a substantial number of workers.

Arsenal of Weapons

We have now discussed practically all types of third-party assistance that have been proposed or utilized in North America. It has often been suggested that all of these mechanisms be included in statutes governing labour-management relations. This "arsenal of weapons," as it is sometimes called, would be available to a government or government agency at any time during a labour-management dispute. The idea behind including a variety of techniques is to enable the administrators of legislation to select the procedures which seem most appropriate at the time and for a particular dispute. An arsenal of weapons has considerable appeal since it avoids building in a pre-determined sequence of forms of third-party assistance. With a pre-determined scheme, serious negotiations often do not begin until a very late stage.

By contrast, if the parties do not know in advance which form of third-party assistance they will receive, they will have a strong incentive to reach an agreement themselves. Since unions and management generally dislike arbitration, they are likely to engage in any negotiations which minimize the chances of compulsory arbitration.

Conclusion

In this chapter, we have discussed a variety of forms of third-party assistance in the negotiation process. The major conclusion that has emerged from this discussion is that there is no one best form. In fact, it is still unclear which instruments measure most appropriately the effectiveness of different forms of third-party assistance. Totally different conclusions may be drawn from the same body of evidence, depending on the statistical tools used.[59] In addition, personal preferences often dictate the method chosen.

From a policy point of view, it seems clear that provision should be made for a number of types of third-party assistance, and that the administrative agencies charged with implementing the policies should use procedures appropriate to each type of dispute. It would be useful for future studies to include not only procedures as independent variables, but also environmental, organizational, and interpersonal characteristics. Inclusion of these additional variables will make rigorous research more difficult, but will aid in attempts to develop more effective forms of third-party assistance under given conditions.

Questions

1 What does Table 8.1 tell you about the use of various forms of third-party assistance in contract negotiations in the Canadian industrial relations system?

2 Distinguish among the types of third-party assistance with binding recommendations and those with non-binding recommendations.

3 Discuss the major types of third-party assistance prescribed by law in the various Canadian jurisdictions. What is your assessment of the prescribed procedures? Elaborate.

4 Tomorrow you are to begin as a mediator in a major high-profile dispute. How will you proceed and what are some of the things you will do and not do to get a settlement in this dispute? Elaborate.

5 Given the criticisms of conventional arbitration in interest disputes and the strong case for FOS, how do you account for the continued reliance in most instances on conventional arbitration?

6 What is your assessment of the arsenal-of-weapons approach as a form of third-party assistance?

7 Differentiate among the three forms of final-offer selection. Theoretically which one should be most effective? Why?

8 What is meant by the "chilling" and "narcotic" effects of compromise arbitration, and what do you perceive as a means of avoiding them?

9 Which third-party dispute settlement procedure would you prefer in the private sector? Would you suggest the use of the same procedure for public-sector disputes? Elaborate.

Notes

1 Up to 1984, the No. 12 December issue of Labour Canada's *Collective Bargaining Review* (Ottawa: Supply and Services Canada) contained a table each year giving the number of collective agreements and the workers covered for the various stages at which negotiations were completed each year. They are no longer published. The figures for 1985-1988 are taken from a computer printout by the Bureau of Labour Information, Labour Canada, June 12, 1989.

2   Hon. W.L. MacKenzie King, *Industry and Humanity* (New York: Houghton Mifflin, 1918), p. 219.

3   H.D. Woods, *Labour Policy in Canada*, 2nd ed. (Toronto: Macmillan of Canada, 1973), p. 158.

4   T.A. Kochan and J. Jick, "The Public Sector Mediation Process," Vol. 22, No. 2, *Journal of Conflict Resolution* (June 1978), pp. 211-12.

5   E.E. Herman and H.M. Leftwich, "Mediation and Fact-Finding Under the Ohio Public Employee Collective Bargaining Act," *Proceedings* of the Thirty-Eighth Annual Meeting, IRRA (Madison, Wis.: IRRA, 1986), pp. 316-323.

6   For an excellent discussion of the strategies to be used by a mediator see K.K. Kressel, *Mediation: An Exploratory Survey* (Albany: Association of Labour Mediation Agencies, 1972). See also C.M. Stevens, "Mediation and The Role of The Neutral," *Frontiers of Collective Bargaining*, eds. J.T. Dunlop and N.W. Chamberlain (New York: Harper & Row, 1967), pp. 252-90; A. Karim and R. Pegnetter, "Mediation Strategies and Qualities and Mediation Effectiveness," Vol. 22, No. 1, *Industrial Relations* (1983), pp. 105-14; B. Keller, "Mediation as a Conflict-Solving Device in Collective Industrial Disputes," Vol. 43, No. 2, *Relations Industrielles/Industrial Relations* (1988), pp. 431-446; R. Singh, "Dispute Settlement and Mediation," and J.M. Hiltop, "Reply to Professor Singh," Vol. 26, No. 3, *Industrial Relations* (Fall 1987), pp. 314-317.

7   David Kuechle, "How To Prepare For Mediation," *Labour Gazette* (February 1974), p. 128.

8   Kochan and Jick, "The Public Sector Mediation Process," pp. 213, 221.

9   Ibid., p. 221.

10 Ibid.

11 Ibid., pp. 223-24.

12 Ibid., p. 225.

13 P.F. Gerhard and J.E. Drotning, "Dispute Settlement and the Intensity of Mediation," Vol. 19, No. 3 *Industrial Relations* (Fall 1980), p. 354.

14 Ibid., p. 352.

15 Ibid., p. 358.

16 Karam and Pegnetter, "Mediator Strategies and Qualities and Mediator Effectiveness," p. 112.

17 H.D. Woods, *Labour Policy in Canada*, p. 201.

18 G. York, "MDs Livid Over Weiler Report Calling for 14% Fee Increase," *Globe and Mail* (April 2, 1982). For a good discussion of the possibility of the OMA becoming a formalized union, see G. York, "OMA May Seek Union Powers if MDs

Lose Fee Fight," *Globe and Mail* (April 12, 1982), p. 8.

19 J.C. Anderson and T.A. Kochan, "Impasse Procedures in the Canadian Federal Service: Effects on the Bargaining Process," Vol. 30, No. 3, *Industrial and Labor Relations Review* (April 1977), pp. 283-301.

20 Ibid., p. 291.

21 I.W. Abel, "Basic Steel's Experimental Negotiating Agreement," *Monthly Labor Review* (September 1973), pp. 39-42.

22 Ibid., p. 42.

23 J.D. Dworkin, "The Impact of Final-Offer Interest Arbitration On Bargaining: The Case of Major League Baseball," *Proceedings*, Twenty-Ninth Annual Winter Meeting of the IRRA, (Madison, Wis.: IRRA, 1977), pp. 161-69; J.R. Chelius and J.B. Dworkin, "Arbitration and Salary Determination in Baseball," *Proceedings*, Thirty-Third Annual Meeting of the IRRA, (Madison, Wis.: IRRA, 1981), pp. 105-12.

24 P. Feuille, "Selected Benefits and Costs of Compulsory Arbitration," Vol. 33, No. 1, *Industrial and Labor Relations Review* (October 1979), pp. 66-67.

25 Ibid., p. 69; J. Delaney, P. Feuille, and W. Hendricks, "Police Salaries, Interest Arbitration, & the Leveling Effect," Vol. 23, No. 3, *Industrial Relations* (Fall 1984), p. 423.

26 Feuille, "Selected Benefits and Costs of Compulsory Arbitration," p. 70.

27 Ibid.

28 Ibid., p. 71; R.D. Horton, "Arbitration, Arbitrators, and the Public Interest," Vol. 28, No. 4, *Industrial and Labor Relations Review* (July 1975), p. 499.

29 Feuille, "Selected Benefits and Costs of Compulsory Arbitration," p. 72.

30 Ibid, p. 73.

31 R.J. Butler and R.G. Ehrenberg, "Estimating the Narcotic Effect of Public Sector Impasse Procedures," Vol. 35, No. 1, *Industrial and Labor Relations Review* (October 1981), pp. 3-20; T.A. Kochan and J. Baderschneider, "Estimating the Narcotic Effect," Vol. 35, No. 1, *Industrial and Labor Relations Review* (October 1981), pp. 21-28; and J.R. Chelius and M.M. Extejt, "The Narcotic Effect of Impasse-Resolution Procedures," Vol. 34, No. 4, *Industrial and Labor Relations Review* (July 1985), pp. 629-637.

32 Kochan and Baderschneider, "Estimating the Narcotic Effect," p. 27.

33 J.R. Chelius and M.M. Extejt, "The Narcotic Effects of Impasse-Resolution Procedures," p. 637.

34 M. Thompson and J. Cairnie, "Compulsory Arbitration: The Case of British Columbia Teachers," Vol. 27, No. 1, *Industrial and Labor Relations Review* (October 1973), p. 14.

35 P. Feuille, "Analyzing Compulsory Arbitration Experiences: The Role of Personal Preferences," Vol. 28, No. 3, *Industrial and Labor Relations Review* (April 1975), pp. 432-35; M. Thompson and J. Cairnie, "Reply," Vol. 28, No. 3, *Industrial and Labor Relations Review* (April 1975), pp. 435-38.

36 Anderson and Kochan, "Impasse Procedures in the Canadian Federal Service," p. 291.

37 Ibid.

38 Ibid.

39 G.W. Adams, "The Ontario Experience with Interest Arbitration," Vol. 36, No. 1, *Relations Industrielles/Industrial Relations* (1981), p. 245.

40 T.A. Kochan and J. Baderschneider, "Dependence on Impasse Procedures: Police and Firefighters in New York State," Vol. 31, No. 4, *Industrial and Labor Relations Review* (July 1978), p. 432. For an excellent treatment of compulsory arbitration in the public sector, see B.M. Downie, *The Behavioural, Economic and Institutional Effects of Compulsory Interest Arbitration* (Ottawa: Economic Council of Canada, December 1979).

41 A 1986 article by J.G. Treble entitled, "How New is Final-Offer Arbitration?" (Vol. 25, No. 1, *Industrial Relations*, Winter, 1986, pp. 92-94) suggests that FOS was used in a number of British industries as early as 1860. However, since Stevens is usually credited with introducing the modern-age forms of final-offer selection, our discussion will centre on his ideas. See C.M. Stevens, "Is Compulsory Arbitration Compatible with Collective Bargaining?" Vol. 5, No. 2, *Industrial Relations* (Feb. 1966). Other sources of useful information include D.G. Gallagher and R. Pegnetter, "Impasse Procedure Under the Iowa Multistep Procedure," Vol. 32, No. 3, *Industrial and Labor Relations Review* (April 1979), pp. 328-29; D.G. Gallagher, "The Use of Interest Arbitration in the Public Sector," *Pro-*

ceedings, 1982 Spring Meeting of the IRRA, rpt. *Labor Law Journal* (August 1982), pp. 502-3.

42 C.M. Stevens, "Is Compulsory Arbitration Compatible With Collective Bargaining?" Vol. 5, No. 2, *Industrial Relations* (Feb. 1966), pp. 38-52 and J.G. Treble, "How New Is Final-Offer Arbitration?" Vol. 25, No. 1, *Industrial Relations* (Winter 1986), pp. 92-94.

43 D.G. Gallagher and R. Pegnetter, "Impasse Resolution under the Iowa Multistep Procedure," Vol. 32, No. 3, *Industrial and Labor Relations Review* (April, 1979), pp. 328-29.

44 *Statutes of Ontario*, 1975, c. 72.

45 B.M. Downie, *Collective Bargaining and Conflict Resolution in Education: The Evolution of Public Policy in Ontario* (Kingston: Industrial Relations Centre, Queen's University, 1978).

46 Ibid., p. 11.

47 Ibid.

48 Ibid., p. 112.

49 Ibid., p. 115.

50 Ibid., p. 101.

51 B.M. Downie, "Collective Bargaining Under an Essential Services Commission," *Conflict or Compromise: The Future of Public Sector Industrial Relations*, eds. M. Thompson and G. Swimmer (Montreal: The Institute for Research on Public Policy, 1984), p. 283.

52 Ibid., pp. 393-96.

53 Ibid., pp. 395-96.

54 Ibid., p. 396.

55 Ibid., p. 397.

56 Judge J.C. Anderson, "Labour Relations — Changing Concepts — New Techniques." *Viewpoints* (Society of Professionals in Dispute Resolution, summer 1975), pp. 13-15.

57 Ibid., p. 14.

58 The Honourable Mr. Justice Samuel Freedman, *Report of Industrial Inquiry Commission on Canadian National "Run-Throughs"* (Ottawa: Queen's Printer, 1965).

59 Butler and Ehrenberg, "Estimating the Narcotic Effect of Public Sector Impasse Procedures," pp. 3-20; Kochan and Baderschneider, "Estimating the Narcotic Effect," pp. 21-28.

9

Administration of the Collective Agreement

The Financial Post

Introduction

The purpose of this chapter is to define and discuss the objectives and procedures of the grievance process, particularly arbitration. We will discuss the steps involved and some substantive issues emerging in jurisprudence as a result of arbitration decisions. Judicial review and enforcement of arbitration awards, criticisms of conventional arbitration, the emergence of expedited arbitration in a number of industries, and some recent innovations to improve the ongoing relationship between unions and management will also be discussed.

The Grievance Process

At the beginning of Chapter 7 I referred to the collective bargaining process as a daily complex of interactions among workers, their superiors, and union leaders, particularly shop stewards. The grievance process is at the heart of the collective bargaining process since it ensures that all workers are treated fairly on a daily basis. In Canada, grievances and contract interpretation disputes are common occurrences. If collective agreements do not contain clauses that deal with grievances, then clauses are set out by the labour relations boards or statutes.

Grievance procedures are necessary for three reasons: First, in all Canadian jurisdictions the parties are mandated by law to settle any differences of opinion which arise concerning the meaning, application, and interpretation of the various clauses of the collective agreement without a work stoppage. Second, the parties must agree on how to apply the general terms contained in a collective agreement to specific actions on the shop floor, the hospital ward, or whatever the daily workplace may be. Third, the duration of agreements has been increasing, and unions and managers must deal realistically with worker and management demands for local adjustments during the life of the agreement.[1]

The potential for grievances arises from ambiguous collective agreement clauses. Negotiators simply cannot spell out the clauses in enough detail to cover every concrete situation which may arise during the life of the agreement. Sometimes, ambiguities are even condoned, to expedite settlement. Grievances may also arise where two or more provisions of a collective agreement appear contradictory, and a complaint is lodged by a worker under the provision most favourable to him or her. If both parties know that some ambiguity or contentious point exists in a provision, then they should anticipate the need for arbitration at some point during the life of the collective agreement. Nevertheless, only when a provision is allegedly violated may a grievance be lodged.

Formal Aspects of Grievance Handling

All statutes in the private, public, and parapublic sectors prohibit strikes and lockouts while an agreement is in force. This is intended to provide stability during the life of the agreement. To compensate for this restriction on strikes and lockouts, the statutes further stipulate that collective agreements provide for the resolution of disputes concerning the interpretation, application, or alleged violation of the agreement's provisions. In most jurisdictions, the grievance procedure specifies binding arbitration by outside neutrals as the last step in the process. It is generally agreed that using such a procedure is preferable to seeking judicial action through the regular court system.

The grievance procedure varies widely from one organization to another and may have as few as two or as many as five steps in the union-management hierarchy. Most grievance procedures impose time limits on each step in the process. For example, a worker may have a certain number of days within which to present a grievance from the time that the alleged infraction occurred. Management, upon receiving the grievance, has a certain number of days within which to reply, at each stage of the grievance process. The union is also allotted specified periods of time within which to appeal management's decision, if it so wishes, to higher levels. Failure to file an appeal or submit a response on time or in the correct order may invalidate the whole grievance procedure, particularly if the matter is later referred to arbitration.

In the first step of the grievance procedure, the shop steward plays an important role. Shop stewards act on behalf of the employees they represent. There may be as many as 15 or 20 shop stewards in a large organization. Their main functions are to hear the grievance as it is presented by the worker and to take part in processing it through the lower levels of the grievance procedure. Most collective agreements contain provisions which permit shop stewards to leave their place of work, usually with the permission of their supervisor, to handle the grievances of other workers within the same working unit. The shop steward has "superseniority" — the highest seniority in the unit. They are usually the last ones to be laid off, even though their ordinary seniority may be much less than that of other workers whose employment is temporarily or permanently terminated. The superseniority clause ensures availability of a steward for the immediate handling of grievances.

Generally, a worker with a grievance first takes it up with the supervisor of the work group, either with or without the assistance of the shop steward. The supervisor is required to respond positively or negatively to the worker's complaint within a given time frame. If the supervisor disagrees with the worker, the worker and shop steward must decide whether or not to pursue the matter to the next level in the grievance procedure.

In one sense, shop stewards perform an important managerial function by pre-screening potential grievances. This is usually done by informal discussion with the aggrieved worker, during the course of which the shop steward may advise the worker whether or not a legitimate grievance exists. Undoubtedly, many complaints do not go to grievance because the shop steward advises the worker that the case is not well founded. A low incidence of grievances, however, is not necessarily a good indication of the quality of union-management relationship. It may indicate, for example, that the supervisor is "giving the shop away." In such a case, management may instruct the supervisor to get tougher with the union or, failing that, may arrange for the supervisor's transfer.

When the worker files a grievance it must relate to a specific provision in a collective agreement. An argument can be made, however, that anything which bothers a worker at the place of work automatically interferes with his or her performance, and should therefore be given a thorough hearing by management. The collective agreement of the National Capital Commission workers in Ottawa provides for complaints to be heard at all stages of the grievance process except the adjudication stage.

The grievance procedure gives a worker who feels unjustly treated by management an opportunity to present his or her case before those in managerial and supervisory positions, and ultimately before an outside third party, if necessary. One problematic aspect of the process, however, is the fact that workers may grieve only after management has given an improper order. Some critics have argued that workers should be given a chance to make their formal objection before management required them to obey an offensive instruction, since

> workers are, perhaps, as interested in assurance of justice before the act as in justice through the grievance procedure after the act. They want a manager to hear and explicitly to consider their interest before he acts, as well as afterward.[2]

It is interesting to note that some of the recent legislation concerning health and safety permits workers to refuse to do a job if they feel that the job poses a significant threat to their health. Previously, they had no recourse but to perform the work and subsequently file a grievance.

Informal Aspects of Grievance Handling

J.W. Kuhn, a long-time student of the grievance process, has discussed the various ways in which workers may use bargaining power daily in the workplace.[3] He discusses, for example, the informal shop-floor tradeoffs that take place between supervisors and shop stewards. Generally, if shop stewards and the particular work group they represent are fairly strategic to any operation within an organization, they will have a high degree of bargaining power which may be used to win concessions from the supervisor. In the same way, adept supervisors may win concessions from shop stewards and the informal work group by offering certain benefits in exchange for a faster rate of production to meet a particular daily or weekly standard. These informal tradeoffs work very well as long as both sides live up to mutual expectations. The tradeoffs also forestall grievances resulting from unilateral changes to the conditions of employment.

However, should one party make a commitment to give concessions and subsequently renege on that promise, the informal understandings or expectations between the parties may be destroyed. This is one reason why those higher up in their respective organizations should not tamper with the way that people at the local level work out their own accommodative arrangements. Kuhn claims that

Charles Bryant/De Havilland Aircraft

a major problem of industrial relations arises if either union or management tries to resolve issues arising out of negotiations at the place of work between foremen and stewards with no regard for the complexity of the activities that brought them about.[4]

The grievance procedure is also a way for both unions and management to obtain information on the adequacy of the collective agreement. For example, if one particular clause is the source of many grievances, then the wording of that clause should be changed during the next round of negotiations. Since management is usually the one to initiate communications in the workplace, it bears the major responsibility for advising managers and shop stewards of decisions significantly affecting working condi-

tions. These decisions may not only trigger individual grievances but generalized union demands.

Not all items can be resolved informally. For example, discipline and discharge cases should always be adjudicated by higher authorities who are far removed from the scene of the initial action. Also, special committees may have to be set up to deal with complex issues such as job evaluation, job classification, and apprenticeship. Some agreements also provide for special procedures and personnel to deal with highly technical matters, such as supplemental unemployment benefits, pension plans, and health and welfare plans. Grievances arising out of the administration of these fringe benefits require expert handling.

The Requirement for Arbitration

Where informal bargaining has proved ineffective and the steps in the grievance process involving different levels in the union and management hierarchies have been systematically followed without satisfying the grievor, all Canadian jurisdictions prescribe arbitration as the final step in the grievance process. The award of the arbitrator or arbitration tribunal is binding on the union, management, and the worker or workers affected.

Arbitration Tribunals

Several types of arbitration tribunals are available to the parties in the grievance process, including a single *ad hoc* arbitrator, a tripartite arbitration board, and what is often referred to as a permanent umpire. (A permanent umpire is an arbitrator named by the parties either in the collective agreement or by mutual agreement to serve for a specific period of time.) The usual practice, however, is to employ *ad hoc* arbitrators or arbitration boards which are appointed every time a new arbitration case arises. Sometimes, the parties name a number of arbitrators to serve on a rotating basis as grievance disputes arise.

Every form of arbitration tribunal has its advantages and disadvantages. A permanent umpire, for example, usually gets to know the parties and the industry very well and quite often makes decisions that become part of the jurisprudence of the parties involved in that particular collective bargaining relationship. In other words, these decisions or awards may set precedents which may be invoked in similar disputes, thus obviating the need for the umpire's services. In addition, the permanent umpire has the advantage of being readily accessible to the parties, and this helps cut down on time delays which are often characteristic of the arbitration process. However, a possible disadvantage is that the parties may rely too heavily on the permanent umpire to help resolve their problems for them. It is generally conceded that

it is much better for the parties to reconcile their differences over the interpretation and application of the terms of a collective agreement themselves, rather than having a neutral party do so, particularly where a deliberately vague clause has been included in a collective agreement.

If the parties choose to employ a tripartite board rather than a permanent umpire, they benefit from the experience of the union and management nominees. These nominees generally have a fairly sophisticated understanding of the industry in question and are thus able to advise the chair on relevant technical problems. This advice is particularly important in the case of *ad hoc* arbitration boards, where the chair may not be familiar with the technical aspects of the question being arbitrated. Tripartite arbitration boards also have their shortcomings, however. It can be time-consuming to hear an arbitration case, since meetings must be scheduled to accommodate the three members of the board as well as the management and union personnel who appear before it. As well, until recently the decisions of arbitration boards had to be majority decisions. This requirement meant that the chair of the board had to ensure that either or both union and management nominees concurred.

These shortcomings caused the late Bora Laskin, who was Chief Justice of the Supreme Court of Canada and a professor at the University of Toronto, to observe: "The conclusion is inescapable, and is amply fortified by experience, that a three-man board of arbitration is a waste of manpower and time."[5] He further maintained that the use of a single arbitrator would avoid post-hearing pressure being exerted on the chair by the union and management members of a tripartite board. As we have seen, present legislation covering contract interpretation disputes in the private sector in all jurisdictions in Canada states that, where there is no majority decision of an arbitration board, the decision of the chair rules.

The advantage of using a single arbitrator is that the parties have to rely on the availability of only one person, which can substantially reduce both the time and costs involved in the arbitration. In addition, if the same arbitrator is selected by the parties each time, he or she will become familiar with the technical details of the industry. The decisions of these arbitrators are thus more likely to be appropriate to the given circumstances. Appointing a different arbitrator each time around, however, may encourage the parties to settle their disputes among themselves and avoid overdependence on the decisions of third parties.[6]

At one time, most cases in Canada were handled by tripartite arbitration boards. (In Ontario, the use of arbitration boards is still almost double that of single arbitrators.) However, adjudication (arbitration) of disputes in the public sector is now handled much more frequently by single arbitrators than by arbitration boards. For example, the federal PSSRA does not provide for a tripartite arbitration board at all. Rather, either full-time or part-time members of the Public Service Staff Relations Board are used as adjudicators. (The term adjudication rather than arbitration is used in the Public Service Staff Relations Act.) Many provincial governments that have given their workers the right to collective bargaining have followed this same pattern.

Selection of Arbitration Tribunals The method for selecting a type of arbitration tribunal is usually contained in the collective agreement. However, if the parties are unable or unwilling to select the members or the chair of an arbitration board, then ministers of labour in practically all jurisdictions have the right to nominate members to the board. In those provinces which make a list of arbitrators available to the parties, an arbitrator or chair of an arbitration board is appointed when both parties have selected the same name.

Often the parties make use of what is known as the "box score" in the selection of arbitrators. If a union or management finds that an individual has fairly consistently ruled in favour of the other side, it will probably not want him or her

as an arbitrator. This method is not always the best way to judge an arbitrator's impartiality, since it fails to take into account the rationales for previous decisions.

Once it is decided who is to be the arbitrator, either the union or management will contact the person chosen. At this point, the prospective arbitrator does not seek any further information about the case but merely accepts or declines the appointment. Once the arbitrator is seized of a case, however, it is up to him or her to arrange for the time and place of the arbitration hearings, to see that they are conducted properly, that all interested parties are given a chance to present evidence, and that appropriate awards are determined.

Arbitrator's Fees and Expenses When a case is heard by a single arbitrator, the two parties share the cost of the arbitration proceedings, including the arbitrator's fees and any fees for hotel rooms where the arbitration proceedings take place. In addition, the parties jointly share the cost of any verbatim transcript. C.H. Curtis, after having done a study of arbitration in Ontario some years ago, indicated that, in some Ontario cases, arbitrators have experienced difficulty in collecting their fees and expenses: "From the arbitrator's point of view, it is probably sound practice to have an understanding with the parties about fees before the arbitration is undertaken."[7] As a rule of thumb, arbitrators are generally permitted two days' fees for each day of hearing to cover the time of going through the submissions of the parties, the collective agreement, the material obtained during the hearing, analyzing the information, and writing the award. In addition to the fees mentioned above, if either or both parties engage legal or other counsel in assisting with their presentation, each party bears its own costs for such counsel.

The Arbitration Process: Two Interpretations

Most writers on the arbitration of contract interpretation disputes refer to it as an adjudication process. D.J.M. Brown and D.M. Beatty define this kind of arbitration as

> the primary, if not the exclusive, process for the final and authoritative settlement of disputes arising out of the application of collective agreements ... The arbitrator ... adjudicates upon specific, concrete disputes which he resolves by applying the legal regime established by the collective agreement to the facts which he finds on the basis of the evidence and arguments presented to him.[8]

In earlier days, however, some analysts, including Selekman and Shulman, believed that arbitration was more of a clinical than an adjudicative process. Those who adopted the clinical approach emphasized the importance of getting at the problem behind the stated grievance, since it was their contention that very often the stated grievance did not reflect the real complaint of the worker. J.W. Kuhn takes a somewhat similar position and indicates that it takes a sophisticated ear to read between the lines of a grievance: "Written grievances and answers may be purely formal, describing problems in conventional terms that hide or distort more than they reveal."[9] Notwithstanding the clinical approach to grievances, it appears that the adjudicative interpretation prevails in Canada and the United States.

There is another aspect of arbitration about which there are two schools of thought. One school sees arbitration decisions as a means of prescribing appropriate forms of behaviour, through primarily *punitive* measures. The second school sees arbitration awards as *corrective* in nature, and designed to encourage workers and management to adopt a more positive form of behaviour. Arbitrators belonging to the second school of thought are more inclined than those of the first school to give the actors "a second chance."

Arbitration Hearings   One of the principle responsibilities of an arbitrator is to ensure that hearings are conducted properly. To accomplish this task requires that certain rules be followed: (1) all interested parties must receive notice of the time and place of the arbitration hearings

and be given an opportunity to attend; (2) the parties must be permitted without unreasonable restrictions to introduce evidence; (3) the parties must be permitted to present witnesses and there must be ample opportunity for cross-examination of witnesses; (4) the parties must be allowed to make concluding oral arguments which, in effect, summarize the major thrust of their evidence during the arbitration proceedings; (5) if the parties so desire, they must be allowed to file written, post-hearing briefs; and (6) witnesses should not be permitted in the hearing room until called upon. The assumption behind the latter practice is that if the presence of more than one witness is permitted in the hearing room, individual testimonies may be tainted.

These ground rules are important since

> a refusal to permit cross-examination, a refusal to compel the attendance of a witness at the instance of a party, or the exclusion of admissible and relevant evidence will provide grounds for review and may result in an order quashing the award if a substantial injustice has resulted therefrom.[10]

Defining Issues and Making Awards   It is extremely important for an arbitrator or an arbitration board to have a very clear statement of the issue under consideration. Such a statement sometimes takes the form of what is called a "submission to arbitrate" in which the parties make a joint submission to the arbitrator indicating the precise basis of the grievance. On other occasions, however, the parties come to an arbitration hearing without a clear statement or submission of the issue, and it is up to the arbitrator or arbitration board to obtain a concise expression of the grievance. If such a statement is not available, the arbitrator, after hearing from both parties, may try to formulate a statement of the issue by using words the two parties agree upon. A statement of the issue is important to the arbitrator because an award may be overturned by a court if it finds that the arbitrator has gone beyond his or her jurisdiction. The submission to arbitrate should not only state the nature of the dispute but also the remedy

Brotherhood members retain rights when business sold

After the sale of CN Hotels to Canadian Pacific Hotels, some members of Local 270 working at the Chateau Laurier Hotel in Ottawa — one of the hotels sold — were told to turn in their rail passes.

The Brotherhood objected on behalf of 53 members, saying the old employer had included the right to rail passes in the collective agreement and the new employer, when it bought the hotel, was obligated to honour the collective agreement and provide rail passes.

It all began when the General Manager, Peter M. Howard, in a memo dated April 5, 1988 wrote:

TO: ALL CN RAIL
PASS HOLDERS
Please be advised that all CN Hotel employees currently holding rail passes will lose their privileges with the effective date of the sale to CP Hotels Corp., therefore rail passes will not be honoured after March 31, 1988. Would you kindly return your rail passes to the Human Resources Department.

Earlier, on January 12, 1988, the Brotherhood had signed a collective agreement with CN Hotels which ended on December 31, 1990. Annexed to the collective agreement was a letter to Brotherhood Representative Andy Wepruk from General Manager Howard dated October 30, 1987 which said:

Further to our discussions during contract negotiations, this letter of understanding will serve to confirm that as long as the Canadian National continues to provide rail pass privileges on

VIA Rail to CN employees, those Chateau Laurier employees, who according to the policy, are entitled to pass privileges, shall continue to enjoy the same pass privileges during the life of the present Collective Agreement.

At arbitration

At arbitration, the company said the 53 members could no longer qualify under "the policy" because after the sale of the hotel, they no longer were employees of Canadian National Railway Company.

The Brotherhood said the letter of understanding was clear and unequivocal. The new owner had assumed the responsibility of providing rail passes when it bought the Chateau Laurier as if it too had signed the collective agreement.

It said that Section 63(2) of the Ontario Labour Relations Act says:

Where an employer who is bound by or is a party to a collective agreement with a trade union or council of trade unions sells his business, the person to whom the business has been sold, is until the Board otherwise declares, bound by the collective agreement as if he had been a party thereto.

The arbitrator decides

The arbitrator, Harvey Frumkin, agreed with the Brotherhood. He wrote, "it is true that the policy referred to in the letter of understanding annexed to the collective agreement envisaged only employees of Canadian National Railway Company.

While "the company's assertions that these employees, following the sale of the Chateau Laurier by Canadian National Company were no longer eligible for the rail pass privileges they claim, by reason of the loss of their status as Canadian National Railways employees, must be taken as valid, the matter of eligibility for rail pass privileges is not the issue.

"In the final analysis the rights of the employees on whose behalf the grievance has been filed could not, by operation of Section 63 of the Labour Relations Act be affected by the sale and transfer of the Chateau Laurier in which they played no role. "The company in acquiring the business conducted at the Chateau Laurier by Canadian National Railway Company assumed all of the obligations of that company towards the employees under its agreement as if Canadian National Railway Company has remained (the) employer under its collective agreement for its duration.

"It could not expect that the employees covered by the collective agreement could have their rights in any way diminished by reason of a sale and transfer over which they had no control and in which they played no role.

"Accordingly the company must bear responsibility to provide the affected employees with rail pass privileges or their equivalent in substance or compensation."

Representative Andy Wepruk presented the case at arbitration.

Canadian Transport, Jan. 1989, p. 8.

sought. Otherwise the arbitrator would not be able to order a remedy even if he or she finds that there has been a breach of the collective agreement.

The statement of the issue or the submission to arbitrate, plus the provisions of the collective agreement, may greatly inhibit the arbitrator's manoeuvrability. In addition, an arbitrator must be very careful that any submission is not phrased in such a way that the provisions of the collective agreement will not allow him or her to deal with it. For this reason, it is in the interest of both parties to state the submission to arbitrate in fairly general terms.[11] In making an award, the arbitrator must take into account the record of the arbitration hearing and any other data both generated by the arbitrator and known to the parties. To summarize then, the collective agreement, the submission to arbitrate, and the record or evidence produced at the hearing or deposited with the arbitrator form the sole basis for the arbitration decision.

Objections to the Arbitrator's Jurisdiction
At the beginning of the hearings, an arbitrator will usually try to get the parties to agree that: (1) if he or she is the sole arbitrator, the appointment has been duly made and accepted by the parties; or (2) if he or she is a chair of an arbitration board, that the board is appropriately constituted. At this point, either of the parties may object that the arbitrator or board does not have jurisdiction over the case and provide evidence to support this contention.

There are a number of grounds on which the parties may challenge jurisdiction. They may, for example, claim that the time allowed between the day on which the last reply was given and a request for arbitration was made has expired. This is usually referred to as a "procedural irregularity." Alternatively, one of the parties may challenge the arbitrator's appointment when, for instance, it is suspected that the appointee has discussed the case with one of the parties before the hearing, or allege that the arbitration board is not properly constituted

because one of the board members appears to have a financial interest in the arbitration award. In addition, since arbitration deals with the interpretation, application, or alleged violation of a collective agreement, one of the parties may argue that the subject matter before the arbitrator does not fall under the terms of the collective agreement. Whatever the objection to the arbitrator's jurisdiction, it is usually a matter to be disposed of before beginning the hearing. However, an arbitrator may take the objection under advisement and proceed with the hearing, since in many instances arbitrability is inextricably bound up with the merits of the case itself.[12]

Burden of Proof When an arbitration hearing begins, the side bearing the burden of proof must give a general opening statement setting forth the issue in dispute, an outline of the pertinent facts, and the conclusion that the party expects the arbitrator to reach. When the moving party has finished speaking, the opposing party makes its opening statement along similar lines. In most arbitration proceedings, the burden of proof is on the party bringing the grievance. The main exception to this general rule is in cases involving discipline and discharge. In such cases, the grieving party is obliged only to establish that there is a collective agreement, that the person was employed by the organization, and that the person has either been disciplined or discharged.[13] Beyond that point, the burden of proof shifts to the employer, who must prove why the discipline or discharge should be upheld. However, once the employer has shown a *prima facie* case or just cause for the action, the burden of proof shifts again to the worker, who must present a defence or indicate mitigating circumstances that would warrant a lesser or no penalty.

The reason why the burden of proof in discharge cases falls upon the employer is that discharge in the industrial relations system is the equivalent of "capital punishment" in the legal system: just as the Crown Attorney prosecuting a homicide case must prove that the person charged with the crime is guilty, so must the employer justify to an arbitrator the dismissal of a worker. The assumption in both situations is that the individual is innocent until proven guilty. The same reasoning applies to discipline, since an accumulation of upheld discipline grievances on a worker's record may be used at some point in the future as a basis for discharge under the doctrine of culminating incident. One school of thought argues that, if a worker has spent some time on a job, a kind of tenure right accrues. Also, as workers age (older workers have sometimes been defined as those over 40 years of age), it becomes more and more difficult for them to find other jobs. The burden of proof in discharge and discipline cases, therefore, is also a way of discouraging employers from acting in an arbitrary or capricious manner against older workers and other minority-groups.

Examination of Witnesses   In an arbitration case, the party with the right to lead off the hearing also has the right to call witnesses first. After the moving party has adduced evidence from a witness, the opposing party may cross-examine. Following cross-examination, the initiating party may re-examine the witness but only to fortify or clarify the original evidence. No new evidence may be introduced during the re-examination of a witness.

Before legal counsel or the person presenting the case calls a person to testify, that individual usually ensures that the witness is very knowledgeable on the subject matter on which he or she is to be examined and cross-examined. When giving evidence, there should be no hesitation in responding to a question in either the original presentation of evidence or on cross-examination. A weak witness or one who appears to lack credibility can do more damage than good to the party presenting evidence, particularly when subjected to cross-examination by the opposing side. As is the case in courtroom procedure, the person question-ing the witness should ask direct questions, should avoid leading questions or putting words in the mouth of the witness, and should let the witness relate the facts in his or her own words with little or no interruption.

The purposes of cross-examination are to weaken or destroy an opponent's case, to adduce evidence to support one's own position, and to discredit a witness.[14] The examiner in cross-examination should be careful to avoid asking leading questions or badgering a witness. Too many questions of the latter type may be objected to by the moving party and those objections, if upheld by the arbitrator, may harm the cross-examiner's case. Since arbitrators have a fair amount of discretion in controlling cross-examinations, they may on occasion forbid questions that do not appear to be relevant to the case or that are meant to catch the witness off guard. Arbitrators may also ask questions of the witnesses, but only with the intent of clarifying matters for their own benefit, and without appearing to support one party or the other.

At the end of the arbitration proceedings, the arbitrator should give the parties time to present closing arguments, in which they summarize succinctly the issue in dispute and the points they made in support of their case. A further objective of the final summation is to give the parties a last chance to impress upon the arbitrator or the members of the arbitration board the importance of the matter in question and the merits of the case.

Standard of Proof   In legal proceedings before the courts, two standards of proof are required. One is the balance of probabilities which relates to civil law proceedings: if, on the basis of the evidence presented, the balance of probabilities appears to lie against one side, then that side is found guilty. In criminal cases, courts usually require proof beyond a reasonable doubt (the second standard of proof). Two recent outstanding Canadian books suggest that arbitrators generally follow the civil law standard of proof. At one time, some arbitrators argued that something approaching the criminal law burden of proof should apply in discharge cases. However, this view is no longer generally accepted.[15]

Making the Award   Once the arbitrator has heard the issue in dispute, looked at all the relevant provisions in the collective agreement, and examined all the evidence on record, he or she must render an award. Sometimes the submission to the arbitrator is in two parts. For example, a discharged worker may ask to be both reinstated and compensated. In such cases, the arbitrator will usually retain jurisdiction over the case until the parties have resolved the financial problem; and, should they be unable to agree upon the amount of compensation, the arbitrator will make that determination.

Ambiguity in Contract Language

As pointed out earlier in this chapter, one problem often faced in arbitration is that of applying ambiguous language to a specific and concrete situation. Brown and Beatty observe that there are differences of opinion among arbitrators as to what constitutes ambiguity:

> One view holds that more than the arguability of different constructions of the collective agreement [is] necessary to constitute an ambiguity. Another view is that an ambiguity exists if there is no clear preponderance of meaning stemming from the words and structure of the agreement.[16]

One way of dealing with the problem of ambiguity is to invoke past practice, as it "has occurred during the life of the collective agreement and . . . has come to be relied on by one of the parties,"[17] since this implies a tacit understanding between the parties regarding their mutual obligations. Another method is to look at the negotiating history of the parties, so as to determine what meaning they attributed to the ambiguity in the original collective agreement. A transcript of the record of the negotiations or the notes kept by the parties can greatly assist such an investigation. Where research discloses

that the parties have always attributed different meanings to a particular phrase, past practice may be the only method invoked to resolve the ambiguity.

Just Cause for Discipline and Discharge

There are very few topics involving arbitration which have received as much attention as discipline and discharge. In particular, the concept of "just cause" has become the subject of a great deal of arbitral jurisprudence. Prior to the introduction of just cause clauses into collective agreements, common law permitted employers to sever the employment relationship for cause, or, in the absence of cause, upon proper and reasonable notice.[18] Today, even in those collective agreements that do not contain a just cause provision, both arbitrators and courts appear to take the view that an employer's right to discharge depends upon his or her ability to prove "cause" or "just cause."[19]

Dealing with the concept of just cause for discharge has posed problems for some arbitrators. Some feel that, since workers in these situations have very much more at stake than employers do, there must be certainty that the evidence adduced constitutes just cause for discharge. American arbitrator S.J. Rosen claims that arbitrators "ultimately must feel comfortable with the decision. Perhaps, just cause eventually becomes a matter of being able to retire at night with an untroubled feeling."[20]

In preparing the worker's case, it is wise for the union advocate to grill the worker and his or her witnesses thoroughly with the kinds of difficult questions likely to be posed by the management advocate in cross examination during the arbitration hearing. This preparation is extremely important for, should the management advocate find the grievor or the grievor's witnesses hesitant in responding to a question or should either volunteer information which may potentially damage the grievor's case, then the management advocate will be presented with an opportunity to discredit the grievor. Good preparation will help the grievor and the grievor's witnesses to give quick, crisp, and credible replies, and also greatly help the arbitrator, for the arbitrator cannot take on the task of representing the grievor in the absence of adequate preparation on the part of the grievor and/or the grievor's representative.

Cases involving discipline or discharge pose two questions: (1) are there sufficient grounds for discipline or discharge; and (2) if so, is the penalty imposed appropriate in the given situation? While there are many factors which justify an employer's using suspension and discharge to punish certain types of behaviour, there are other factors which could mitigate the severity of the penalty:

1 The previous good (and unblemished) record of the grievor.
2 The long service of the grievor.
3 Whether or not the offence was an isolated incident in the employment history of the grievor.
4 Provocation (which may have been initiated by an agent of the employer).
5 Whether the offence was committed on the spur of the moment as a momentary aberration, due to strong emotional impulses, or whether the offence was premeditated.
6 Whether the penalty imposed has created a special economic hardship for the grievor in the light of his particular circumstances.
7 Evidence that the company's rules of conduct, either written or posted, have not been uniformly enforced, thus constituting a form of discrimination. (This, in effect, means that if breaking a rule results in discipline, it is up to the employer to ensure that the rule is well known and consistently enforced.)
8 Circumstances negating intent (e.g., the likelihood that the grievor misunderstood the nature or intent of an order, and as a result disobeyed it).
9 The seriousness of the offence in terms of company policy and company obligations.
10 Any other circumstances which the board should properly take into consideration (e.g., failure of the grievor to apologize and settle the matter after being given an opportunity to do so).[21]

Only one of the conditions noted above need be established in order for an arbitrator to mitigate the severity of the penalty imposed by the employer.

Arbitral Authority Versus Managerial Authority

The original view of arbitration generally did not allow an arbitrator to modify a judgement imposed by management on a worker. For example, if an employer discharged a worker, an arbitrator did not have the authority to substitute a lesser penalty. By 1965, however, arbitrators were taking the view that they could indeed change the penalty imposed by management even if just cause were established by the employer. In other words, employers were obligated not only to prove the worker's wrongdoing, but also to justify the severity of their own response.

The Port Arthur Shipbuilding case, however, deprived arbitrators of this discretionary power. In that instance, the arbitrator substituted suspension for discharge in the case of three workers, all of whom had many years of seniority with the company. This decision was eventually quashed by the Supreme Court of Canada. Mr. Justice Judson, who delivered the Supreme Court decision, observed that

> the sole issue in this case was whether the three employees left their jobs to work for someone and whether this fact was a proper cause for discipline. Once the board had found that there were facts justifying discipline, the particular form chosen was not subject to review on arbitration.[22]

Following this decision, a group of Ontario arbitrators successfully appealed to the provincial Minister of Labour to pass legislation confirming their authority in arbitration cases and making court intervention more difficult. The Ontario Labour Relations Act was amended in 1966 to include section 44(9):

> Where an arbitrator or arbitration board determines that an employee has been discharged or otherwise disciplined by an employer for cause and the collective agreement does not contain a specific penalty for the infraction that is the subject-matter of the arbitration, the arbitrator or arbitration board may substitute such other penalty for the discharge or discipline as to the arbitrator or arbitration board seems just and reasonable in all the circumstances.[23]

Practically all other provinces in Canada have

since enacted similar legislation to confirm an arbitrator's power to amend an excessive penalty imposed by an employer, if there is no explicit provision made for such a penalty in the collective agreement.

Enforcement of Arbitration Awards

Section 44(11) of the Ontario Labour Relations Act states that:

> where a party, employer, trade union or employee has failed to comply with any of the terms of the decision of an arbitrator or an arbitration board, any party, employer, trade union or employee affected by the decision may file in the office of the Registrar of the Supreme Court a copy of the decision, . . . whereupon the decision shall be entered in the same way as a judgement or order of that court and is enforceable as such.[24]

Other jurisdictions in Canada have legislation somewhat similar to that of the Ontario provision. Once a decision is filed with the court it then becomes a court order. Parties who fail to comply with the award leave themselves open to contempt of court proceedings.

Judicial Review of Arbitration Awards

All jurisdictions require the use of arbitration as the last step in the grievance procedure. Hence, the courts tend to look upon arbitration as a quasi-judicial process, and therefore subject to judicial review. There are a number of grounds upon which the judiciary may review arbitration decisions. While this area is a fairly complicated one, a simplified analysis yields four grounds for court intervention: (1) belief that an arbitrator has exceeded his or her jurisdiction; (2) an alleged lack of impartiality on the part of the arbitrator; (3) procedural defects in the arbitration hearing and in rendering the award; and (4) an alleged error of law on the face of the award.

An arbitrator can exceed his or her jurisdiction by answering a question not under consideration, by failing to respond to the question to be considered, or by amending, altering, or varying the collective agreement. It is impor-

tant, therefore, to ensure that the question submitted is dealt with according to the terms of the collective agreement.

Generally, it is conceded that bias, or interest on the part of the arbitrator in the outcome of the case, or reasonable fear thereof, justifies a court either in prohibiting an arbitrator from proceeding or in setting aside an award which has been rendered. Fraud and corruption would also be grounds for questioning impartiality.

Procedural defects encompass a number of irregularities. For example, an arbitrator who does not permit all interested parties to participate in the arbitration process may be found guilty of denying the parties natural justice. In addition, rulings such as the refusal to permit cross-examination or the exclusion of admissible and relevant evidence may result in the decision being reviewed and quashed if a substantial injustice has resulted therefrom. *Ex parte* fact-finding by an arbitrator (i.e., the taking of evidence in the absence of one of the parties of interest) may also result in the quashing of an award.

An error of law on the face of the award is somewhat difficult to explain. The legal definition of an error of law is an error in the application or interpretation of some legal standard, statutory or otherwise. Since questions of interpretation of collective agreements have always been viewed as questions of law in most jurisdictions in Canada, a court will review an arbitrator's interpretation of provisions in a collective agreement with a view to assuring itself that it is a plausible construction (understanding) of the document. The court itself may not agree with the arbitrator's interpretation but, if it finds that the construction is a "reasonable one" (i.e., one that would be made by a reasonable person), it will not necessarily quash the award.

An arbitrator may also commit an error of law if he or she misconceives that law. For example, if a labour relations act indicates the applicability of a directive to both union and workers, the arbitrator who applies such a directive to only one of the parties will be committing an error of law.[25] The term "on the face of the award" (or record) is a time-honoured formulation which conveys no precise legal meaning in grievance proceedings, but is merely a way of referring to the documentation upon which an arbitrator bases his or her decision. For example, if an arbitrator bases a decision on an argument that was not presented by either party, and if that argument is so far out that it could not be accepted by a "reasonable" person, a court could find that the arbitrator committed an error "on the face of the record." A court, upon finding that an award is defective, may quash it, set it aside, or send it back to the arbitrator for reconsideration. Wherever possible, the latter course is followed.

Criticisms of the Traditional Form of Arbitration

The conventional form of grievance arbitration has been severely criticized by unions, management, academics, and many practitioners as a time-consuming process that can make the parties wait years for a final arbitration award. In addition, the traditional arbitration process tends to be a very expensive proposition, particularly for small companies and unions with limited financial resources. The process has also been criticized on the grounds that many arbitrators write lengthy dissertations in formulating their awards and rationales. This not only increases costs, but also deprives the grievor of a swift determination of the case.

One of the major reasons for the long delay an expense occasioned by arbitration is that about 10% of the arbitrators do about 90% of the work. This often means that cases must be booked for arbitration hearings many months in advance because the arbitrator whom the parties want is not available until that time. Parties generally prefer an experienced arbitrator, well-versed in the arbitration process and familiar with the jurisprudence. Novices to the arbitration field may have neither the technical qualifications and expertise to rule on many of the issues that come up during an arbitration hearing, nor the background necessary to understand the kind of award that would be appropriate to the collective agreement and industry.

Despite these criticisms, conventional arbitration is certainly preferable to using the courts as a vehicle for resolving problems between unions and management. Although the courts should review arbitration awards to safeguard the system, they are no substitute for the grievance procedure and arbitration as it is practiced in North America.

Expedited Arbitration

In 1971, the ten major American steel companies in the United States and the United Steelworkers Union adopted an expedited arbitration procedure on an experimental basis. This procedure is designed to deal with routine grievances and ordinary discipline cases. Grievance cases are presented by local union representatives and companies are usually represented by industrial relations personnel. High-echelon personnel who normally present arbitration cases do not participate in the expedited arbitration process. Furthermore, it is well understood by the parties to expedited arbitration that any decisions resulting therefrom do not form precedents for the normal arbitration process.

Workers and management in the American steel industry were so impressed with the expedited arbitration procedure that they have included it in all agreements since 1971. Now, some 200 panel members (arbitrators) are assigned to various local centres. Each panel has an administrator who assigns panel members to cases in alphabetical rotation depending on their availability for the time and place designated by the local union and management representatives. Hearings are kept informal; no briefs are presented and no transcripts are made. Arbitrators present awards within 48 hours after completion of the hearing.

This new procedure has not only resulted in prompter decisions, but has allowed arbitrators to examine the particular conditions under which the grievance was submitted. Costs have been reduced substantially. Most importantly, more grievances can be settled at the lower levels, thereby decreasing the number of cases reaching the regular arbitration stage.[26]

L. Stessin, writing in 1977, stated that more than 500 American companies and unions use expedited arbitration. He observed that it is rare for a case channelled through the expedited route to stay on the books for more than 60 days. In addition, in most expedited procedures, the arbitrators are formally charged with the duty of rendering their opinions by the next day.[27]

***Examples of Expedited Arbitration in Canada*[28]**
The United Steelworkers of America and the International Nickel Company of Canada Limited have a form of expedited arbitration called the grievance commissioner procedure which is in use at both the Sudbury and Port Colborne operations. Two grievances commissioners act as sole arbitrators and alternate serving on a monthly basis. Hearings are held on the third Thursday of each month, but are only convened if there are at least four cases outstanding. Once a grievance has been processed through the regular procedure without being resolved, the union's general grievance committee and the company's industrial relations supervisors meet to determine if it should be heard by a regular tripartite arbitration board or if expedited arbitration will be used. Expedited arbitration may be chosen only by mutual consent of the parties. Failing such consent the grievance must undergo regular arbitration.

The grievance commissioner procedure is a very informal one. Not less than ten days prior to the hearing, the Commissioner is provided with a copy of the grievance, a written summary of the stage-two grievance meeting which outlines the facts agreed to, the facts in dispute, the union's position, the company's position, and a copy of the written decision of the management representative at stages two and three of the grievance procedure. In addition, the parties supply brief written arguments supporting their positions. The purpose of the hearing is solely to clarify issues or facts in dispute. Usually, no witnesses

are called; the written material generally serves as the basis of a decision, although the parties may make further representations or present such evidence as the Commissioner may permit or require. There is, however, no obligation to conform to strict rules of evidence. A written decision must be rendered within seven days of the hearing. Brief reasons for the award accompany but do not form a part of the award. The parties understand that decisions in the grievance commissioner procedure establish no legal precedents.[29]

Another example of expedited arbitration in Canada is the procedure used by the British Columbia Maritime Employers' Association and the International Longshoremen's and Warehousemen's Union for handling urgent grievances. These involve safety on the job, handling damaged cargo, or situations where a work slowdown or stoppage is in effect. These cases are referred to a job arbitrator for a summary disposition. The job arbitrator serves on a full-time basis and possesses practical waterfront experience, and is empowered to render oral awards on the spot. The oral award takes effect immediately and is binding on the parties, but it must be confirmed in writing as soon as possible thereafter, usually within 48 hours.

The summary disposition is generally a short award that takes into account the background of the case, the positions of both parties and the appropriate clauses of the collective agreement. The job arbitrator is paid a retainer of a certain amount per month, the cost of which is shared equally by the parties. The arbitrator must be available 24 hours a day and may be called at any time by either of the parties. An alternate may be called in when the full-time job arbitrator is on vacation or not available.

Should either of the parties request a rehearing of a matter on which the job arbitrator has rendered a decision, the question is referred to the Joint Industry Labour Relations Committee, but such rehearings are rare. The Committee, moreover, has set aside only a small number of decisions rendered by the job arbitrator.[30] Expedited arbitration can be tailored to each industry in which it is used and is eminently well suited for handling relatively routine types of grievances. It may also be used for handling discipline and discharge cases in which quick decisions are usually desirable. In complex discharge cases, which involve the testimony of witnesses, the regular arbitration process may be more appropriate than the expedited form. Even where expedited arbitration has been introduced, the regular arbitration process will continue to play an important role in resolving major disputes between the parties over the interpretation, application, or alleged violations of collective agreements. Policy issues, such as contracting out, should not be dealt with in expedited arbitration proceedings.

One benefit of the expedited arbitration process is that it encourages people interested in arbitration to become active in the field and thereby gain the experience required to handle more complex cases. The resulting increase in the availability of arbitrators may reduce the cost and delays currently associated with regular arbitration.

Expedited Arbitration in Ontario and Manitoba During the summer of 1979, the Ontario government passed legislation which provides for a form of expedited arbitration. Bill 25 amended the Ontario Labour Relations Act by adding section 45. Under this section, a party to a collective agreement may request the minister to appoint a single arbitrator. If the minister agrees to the appointment, the arbitrator must attempt to resolve a dispute regarding the interpretation, application, administration, or alleged violation of an agreement. A request may be made for the appointment of a single arbitrator after the grievance procedure under the collective agreement has been exhausted or after 30 days have elapsed from the time the grievance was first brought to the attention of the other party, whichever occurs first. (Grievances concerning discharge require only a 14-day period to elapse, rather than 30 days.)

The minister can also appoint a settlement

officer to confer with the parties and endeavour to bring about an agreement *prior* to the arbitration hearing. However, the arbitrator must start to hear a case within 21 days after the request for an arbitrator is received, and must deliver an oral decision as soon as practicable.

In 1984 Manitoba also adopted a form of expedited arbitration, based largely on the Ontario Act. Manitoba, however, also makes provision for the appointment of a grievance mediator on the joint application of the parties. The function of the grievance mediator is similar to that of the settlement officer in Ontario. The Manitoba statute also provides for a grievance mediator to be named in the collective agreement.

Ontario's expedited form of arbitration has been used often since it was passed into law. The same is expected to occur in Manitoba. And, while no big rush is evident among the other jurisdictions to enact a form of expedited arbitration, one may speculate that they may follow the examples of Ontario and Manitoba.

A further incentive for the use of quicker forms of arbitration was revealed in a major study of arbitration in Ontario discharge cases. This study found that, the sooner the case was heard after a discharge, the more likely the discharged worker was to be reinstated:

> Where the hearing was held within three months, 42 percent of the grievors were reinstated with a lesser penalty; 29 percent were completely exonerated; and 29 percent were not reinstated. However, where the hearing was held more than nine months after the discharge, 74 percent of the grievors were not reinstated; 21 percent received a lesser penalty; and 5 percent were completely exonerated.[31]

Grievance Arbitration and the Charter of Rights and Freedoms

The Charter of Rights and Freedoms has given rise to a number of problems in the arbitration of grievances. D.D. Carter has recently highlighted some issues that have arisen in arbitration awards and court proceedings involving arbitration.[32] He argues that our grievance arbitration process consists of the "internal values" of the collective agreements and the "external values" of general legislation. The external values were implanted when legislation during the 1940s mandated that collective agreements contain clauses for resolving conflicts over their interpretation and application. The internal values have emerged from the particular processes that have been incorporated into collective agreements. Carter sums up the possible conflict between these two systems in the following terms:

> Here one is faced with the central question of whether grievance arbitration should function as a purely private process, or whether there is some public dimension to the process that requires a consideration of standards found outside the confines of the collective agreement.[33]

While there has been a balancing between the private and public ordering so far, the Charter has the potential of disrupting this balancing. The reason for the potential disruption is the Charter's emphasis on broad political values, such as freedom of speech and expression, freedom of conscience and religion, equality under the law, and due process. Carter argues that

> Charter arguments could be used to challenge virtually every aspect of the present arbitral jurisprudence defining just cause for discipline and discharge, and even the hallowed principle of seniority could run afoul of the Charter's guarantee of equality if the courts were to hold that the Charter does apply to collective agreements.[34]

Already the courts have added an overlay to the internal value system by insisting that an arbitrator give notice to parties other than the employer and union where the other parties may have a stake in the outcome of the arbitration award. They have also made it clear that arbitration boards not be composed of members who have a close relationship with one of the parties.

Carter raises a number of Charter issues which need to be resolved before the air is clear.

They include the following:

1 Does the Charter apply to the basic legislative framework established for grievance arbitration?
2 Does the Charter apply directly to collective agreements negotiated between the parties?
3 Does the Charter have indirect application to collective agreements because general legislation must now be read subject to the Charter?
4 Do arbitrators have the authority to apply the Charter, or is this task the exclusive responsibility of the courts?[35]

Carter also cites a number of cases that show that arbitrators and the courts have not yet reached a consensus on the extent to which the Charter applies to these questions. For example, with respect to the application of the Charter directly to collective agreements, one arbitrator concluded that it does apply by stating that "We believe that the Charter is intended to stand four-square as the guarantor of the fundamental rights and freedoms in all corridors of our Canadian society."[36] In another case, an arbitration board held that the Charter did *not* apply, even though one of the parties was a Crown agent:

> Private contracts are not of general application to the population of the province as a whole, even though they may affect individuals in various parts of the province. If the rights of the grievors guaranteed by s. 6(2) of the Charter are being violated they are . . . being violated by a collective agreement between their union and a Crown agent which is not of general application throughout the province.[37]

Carter contends that the present uncertainty regarding the application of the Charter to grievance arbitration ". . . reflects the lack of a clear perception by the courts of the institutional role of the collective agreement and grievance arbitration."[38] He concludes that what the courts must do is to decide "whether the collective agreement and grievance arbitration are essentially instruments of private ordering or whether they play some wider public role."[39] Given the diverse decisions being handed down at various levels in the courts, it may be some time yet before we know whether and to what extent the Charter will become part of the grievance arbitration process.

Grievances and Arbitration of Rights Disputes in the Public Sector

Although various types of appeal procedures for public servants exist under the auspices of public service commissions, it was only with the advent of public-sector collective bargaining that arbitration of rights disputes, often referred to as adjudication, became available to public-sector workers in Canada. (Adjudication has not done away entirely with various types of appeals still subject to public service commissions, such as the protection of the merit principle in appointments, promotions, transfers, and termination of employment for lack of competence.)

Since the phenomenon of a collective bargaining regime for public-sector workers is relatively new, there is a paucity of information on the subject.[40] What we shall attempt to do, therefore, is to outline the types of adjudication tribunals that exist in a few jurisdictions, some aspects of public-sector adjudication unique to that sector, an example of one of the challenges with which adjudicators have had to contend, and the development of grievance mediation which had its origin in the public sector.

The various jurisdictions in Canada have taken different approaches to grievances in the public sector. The private-sector model of appointing *ad hoc* arbitrators has been adopted in the public sector of Nova Scotia. In British Columbia, the Industrial Relations Council makes appointments from a panel whose members are selected by the parties. In Alberta, the parties have made provision in their collective agreements for a Public Service Grievance Board with a chair and a number of vice-chairs. The federal, Ontario and New Brunswick statutes provide for panels of adjudicators. Under the federal Public Service Staff Relations Act,

adjudication is usually carried out by a single adjudicator who is either a full- or part-time member of the Public Service Staff Relations Board. One of its three deputy chairs administers the adjudication system. The parties may use a tripartite board of adjudication under the federal Act, but so far they have not elected to do so. The Ontario Crown Employees Collective Bargaining Act provides for a grievance settlement board made up of a panel of neutral adjudicators, plus panels of employer and union nominees.[41]

K. Swinton points out several advantages to the use of a panel of adjudicators, including the speedier handling of cases, since no time is lost in searching for someone to act as chair, and a greater consistency in decisions. (This consistency may be jeopardized, however, if the panels become too large.) Also, during the early phase of a collective bargaining regime, the adjudicators may play an educational role for inexperienced parties.[42] Part-time federal and Ontario adjudicators operate in both the private and public sectors.

In some ways, adjudication in the public sector is different from arbitration in the private sector. One major difference is that in the public sector a statute may confer a right on an individual to have a grievance taken all the way to adjudication. No such legislative right exists in the private sector. Private-sector grievances relate solely to the interpretation, application, or alleged violation of the terms of a collective agreement.

One example of a situation where a statute confers a right to the grievance process and adjudication in the public sector is contained in sections 90 and 91 of the PSSRA (which will be discussed in detail in Chapter 10). In effect, these provisions say that if a worker feels aggrieved by the application of a statute, regulation, provision of a collective agreement, or an arbitral award, the grievance may be addressed to all levels of the grievance procedure, including adjudication if there is no other administrative procedure for redress. If the case involves the interpretation of a collective agreement or arbitral award, the worker must have the support of the bargaining agent. All workers who have been subject to disciplinary action resulting in discharge, suspension, or financial penalty may take their cases all the way to adjudication, and may be represented by a bargaining agent, irrespective of whether or not the worker is a member of a bargaining unit.

When a person accepts a position in a public service, that person is on probation for a specified period of time, which may range from six months to two years in the federal public service. The same applies if a person is promoted to a higher level in the same classification. Workers are seldom aware of this fact, however. Let us assume that, before the end of the probationary period, the person is discharged on the grounds of incompetence. The worker may feel that he or she is being disciplined rather than dismissed. In this situation, the individual may take the case to arbitration, with or without the assistance of a bargaining agent. There are similar provisions for what are referred to as "critical job interests," in some provincial statutes.[43]

The employer will often argue that an adjudicator has no jurisdiction to hear such cases. Writers J. Finkelman and S. Goldenberg, however, disagree:

> From the outset adjudicators [under the PSSRA] have taken the position that they are entitled to entertain a grievance by an employee who has been rejected by a deputy head during the probationary period in order to ascertain whether the termination of employment really constituted disciplinary action resulting in discharge.[44]

Where adjudicators have found that the person was discharged, they have ordered reinstatement, sometimes with an extension of the probationary period. In other cases, financial compensation has been awarded.[45] The courts have generally upheld such action by public-sector adjudicators.

Another important difference between arbitration in the private and public sectors is that the concept of public interest may arise in public-sector cases. For example, if a worker in a home for retarded persons should spontaneously hit a patient, should that worker be dismissed or given a lesser penalty? Such cases are likely to attract media attention. In addition, not only the public interest but also employer interests may be involved. A competing concern exists in such cases, particularly when workers have records of long and competent service. While arbitrators are acutely aware of the delicate nature of such cases, "they have adopted the jurisprudence of progressive discipline from the private sector, even where that has been controversial."[46]

As indicated earlier, mediation is sometimes used in public-sector grievance cases. Between 1980 and 1981, there was quite a backlog of cases in Canada Post. Two special tripartite committees, each chaired by a mediator/adjudicator, were appointed on a one-time basis to resolve the outstanding cases. In Ontario, there has been continuous grievance mediation since 1979, when one vice-chair was appointed specifically for that purpose. While the vice-chair hears no cases, he or she meets regularly with the parties in an attempt to settle and consolidate cases of the same nature. Although the success of this system is difficult to measure, a substantial number of cases have been withdrawn in recent years.[47] Grievance mediation is not used in the Canadian private sector. The reason for its more widespread use in the public sector is because of the large number of grievances to be processed, and also because it is a speedier and less costly way of dealing with large numbers of grievances. An informal poll conducted in Michigan in 1978 showed that mediators from the Federal Conciliation and Mediation Service and from the state agency had success rates of well over 80%.[48] In the United States, widespread use of grievance mediation occurs on an *ad hoc* basis, and some parties are including it as a part of their regular grievance procedures. Grievance mediation is not a substitute for arbitration, but it can be an important step in the grievance procedure. It is quite possible, moreover, that grievance mediation will help remove some of the high degree of legalism from the grievance and arbitration process, and perhaps result in a more clinical approach to grievance handling.

Conclusion

In this chapter, we discussed the pros and cons of the grievance arbitration process. We also outlined the steps in an expedited form of arbitration which seems to be gaining acceptance in the labour-management field. Finally, a discussion of arbitration (adjudication) in the public sector was included, and we looked briefly at grievance mediation in the public sector, which could foreshadow things to come in both the public and private sectors.

Questions

1 What is the major objective of the grievance process?

2 What is the nature of clauses in collective agreements that lead to the filing of grievances, some of which go all the way to arbitration?

3 What are the pros and cons of the legalistic vs. the clinical approach to resolving grievances?

4 Arbitration as the final step in the grievance procedure is the *quid pro quo* for no-strike and no-lockout provisions during the life of collective agreements as required by the statutes in all Canadian jurisdictions. What is your assessment of this arrangement?

5 Explain what is meant by the "submission to arbitrate" and the nature of the "burden of proof" in arbitration decisions?

6 Assume that you will be conducting your first arbitration hearing tomorrow. What factors will you take into account in conducting the hearing and the rendering of your award to assure that it will not be overturned by a court?

7 What is your assessment of expedited arbitration as an alternative to the traditional grievance arbitration process? What kinds of grievances lend themselves best to this procedure?

8 Do you think that the differences between arbitration in the private sector and adjudication in the public sector are significant? Do those things which are unique to the public sector pose problems for adjudicators in that sector? Elaborate on both questions.

9 Do you think that there should be a total ban on strikes and lockouts during the life of collective agreements, or are there some issues on which the parties should have the right to strike or lockout? Elaborate.

10 There were a number of references in the chapter to "judicial review" of arbitration cases. Do you think that courts, which often lack members with expertise in industrial relations, should have the right to review decisions made by experts? Elaborate.

Notes

1 N.W. Chamberlain and James W. Kuhn, *Collective Bargaining*, 2nd ed. (New York: McGraw-Hill, 1965), p. 141.

2 J.W. Kuhn, "The Grievance Process," *Frontiers of Collective Bargaining*, eds. J.T. Dunlop and N.W. Chamberlain (New York: Harper & Row, 1967), p. 257.

3 Ibid., pp. 252-70.

4 Ibid., p. 256.

5 Bora Laskin, "Legal Issues in Labour Relations: Some Problems of Arbitration," *Labour Relations Trends: Retrospect and Prospect*, ed. H.D. Woods, Proceedings of the Tenth Annual Conference of the McGill Industrial Relations Centre (Sept. 11-12, 1958), p. 27.

6 For those wishing a more complete statement on the advantages and disadvantages of different types of arbitration tribunals, see F. Elkouri, and E.A. Elkouri, *How Arbitration Works*, 3rd ed.

(Washington: Bureau of National Affairs, 1973), Chapter 4.

7   C.H. Curtis, *Labour Arbitration Procedures* (Kingston: Industrial Relations Centre, Queen's University, 1957), p. 45.

8   D.J.M. Brown and D.M. Beatty, *Canadian Labour Arbitration*, 2nd ed. (Aurora: Canada Law Book Limited, 1984), pp. 9-10. For the second of the two excellent books referred to in the text, see E.E. Palmer, *Collective Agreement Arbitration in Canada*, 2nd ed. (Toronto: Butterworths, 1983).

9   J.W. Kuhn, "The Grievance Procedure," p. 259.

10 Brown and Beatty, *Canadian Labour Arbitration*, pp. 29-30. For an excellent discussion on the procedures of arbitration, see A.W.R. Carrothers, *Labour Arbitration in Canada* (Toronto: Butterworths, 1961), Chapter 4. This book was the first major book on arbitration in Canada.

11 For a more detailed analysis, see Brown and Beatty, *Canadian Labour Arbitration*, pp. 58-59; Palmer, *Collective Agreement Arbitration in Canada*, pp. 28-34; P. Praslow and E. Peters, *Arbitration and Collective Bargaining: Conflict Resolution and Labour Relations* (New York: McGraw-Hill, 1970), pp. 17-28.

12 Palmer, *Collective Agreement Arbitration in Canada*, pp. 22-28; and J.P. Sanderson, Q.C., *Labour Arbitration and All That* (Toronto: Richard De Boo, 1976), pp. 45-50.

13 Brown and Beatty, *Canadian Labour Arbitration*, pp. 129-30.

14 Ibid., p. 142.

15 Palmer, *Collective Agreement Arbitration in Canada*, pp. 268-71; Brown and Beatty, *Canadian Labour Arbitration*, p. 133.

16 Brown and Beatty, *Canadian Labour Arbitration*, p. 154. Brown and Beatty also differentiate between latent or patent ambiguity. Basically, a patent ambiguity is one that appears on the face of the agreement, whereas a latent ambiguity exists where it is not apparent on the face of the agreement.

17 Palmer, *Collective Agreement Arbitration in Canada*, p. 83.

18 Brown and Beatty, *Canadian Labour Arbitration*, pp. 330-31.

19 Palmer, *Collective Agreement Arbitration in Canada*, pp. 234-35.

20 S.J. Rosen, "How Arbitrators View Just Cause," *Proceedings*, Twenty-Fifth Annual Meeting of the IRRA (Madison, Wis.: IRRA 1983), p. 133.

21 *Re: United Steelworkers of America, Local 3257 and the Steel Equipment Company Ltd. (1964) 14 L.A.C.*

356, quoted in Labour Relations Law Casebook Group, *Labour Relations Law: Cases, Material and Commentary* (Kingston: Industrial Relations Centre, Queen's University, 1970), pp. 262-63. For a much more complete discussion of the above mentioned topics, see Palmer, pp. 215-34, and Brown and Beatty, pp. 361-84.

22 *Port Arthur Shipbuilding Co. v. Arthurs* (1968), D.L.R. (2d) 693, quoted in Labour Relations Law Casebook Group, *Labour Relations Law*, p. 293.

23 *Ontario Labour Relations Act, R.S.O.*, 1980, c. 228, s. 44(9).

24 *Ontario Labour Relations Act, R.S.O.*, 1980, c. 228, s. 44(11).

25 Brown and Beatty, *Canadian Labour Arbitration*, pp. 31-42.

26 For more details on this procedure, see "Expedited Arbitration Breaks Grievance Log Jam," *Steel Labor* (April 1973); B. Fischer, "The Steel Industry's Expedited Arbitration: A Judgement After Two Years," *Arbitration Journal* (September 1973), pp. 185-90.

27 L. Stessin, "Expedited Arbitration: Less Grief Over Grievances," *Harvard Business Review* (January-February 1977), pp. 128-34.

28 Those who wish to study the Canadian industries which have some form of expedited arbitration should refer to the following two documents: Federal Mediation and Conciliation Service, Labour Canada, *Industry and Expedited Arbitration: Alternatives to Traditional Methods* (Ottawa: Supply and Services Canada, 1978); *Expedited Arbitration—An Alternative* (Montreal: McGill University, Industrial Relations Centre, 1977).

29 *Industry and Expedited Arbitration*, pp. 18-21; *Expedited Arbitration—An Alternative*, pp. 101-05.

30 Ibid., pp. 14-18, 96-100.

31 G.W. Adams, *Grievance Arbitration of Discharge Cases: A Study of the Concepts of Industrial Discipline and Their Results* (Kingston: Industrial Relations Centre, Queen's University, Research and Current Issues Series, No. 38, 1978), p. 50.

32 D.D. Carter, "Grievance Arbitration and the Charter: The Emerging Issues," *Relations Industrielles/Industrial Relations* Vol. 44, No. 2 (1989), pp. 337-353. This section is based on Carter's excellent article.

33 Ibid., p. 338.

34 Ibid., p. 339.

35 Ibid., p. 340.

36 Quoted in ibid., p. 344.

37 Ibid., pp. 344-45.

38 Ibid., p. 351.

39 Ibid.

40 For two good Canadian articles, see K. Swinton, "Grievance Arbitration in the Public Sector," *Conflict or Compromise: The Future of Public Sector Industrial Relations,* eds. M. Thompson and G. Swimmer (Montreal: The Institute for Research on Public Policy, 1984), pp. 343-71; and J. Finkelman and S. Goldenberg, *Collective Bargaining in the Public Sector: The Federal Experience in Canada* (Montreal: The Institute for Research on Public Policy, 1983), Chapters 11, 12.

41 Swinton, "Grievance Arbitration in the Public Sector," pp. 344-45.

42 Ibid., pp. 345-48.

43 Ibid., p. 350.

44 Finkelman and Goldenberg, *Collective Bargaining in the Public Sector,* p. 589.

45 Ibid., p. 590.

46 Swinton, "Grievance Arbitration in the Public Sector," p. 359.

47 Ibid., p. 348.

48 G.A. Gregory and R.E. Rooney, Jr., "Grievance Mediation: A Trend in the Cost-Conscious Eighties," *Proceedings,* Spring Meeting of the IRRA, (Madison, Wis.: IRRA 1980), p. 507.

10

Collective Bargaining in the Public and Parapublic Sectors

Peter Redman, *The Financial Post*

Introduction

In recent years, collective bargaining for workers in the public and parapublic sectors has become a major topic in the field of industrial relations. It is of great concern to policy-makers, public servants, administrators, academics, journalists, and, perhaps most importantly, to the public at large. The term "public sector" refers to workers who are employed by the federal, provincial, and municipal governments. The "parapublic sector" includes such groups as teachers, health-care workers, firefighters,

and police officers, who are not directly employed by governments, but by organizations which are extensively supported by government funding.

Our discussion of collective bargaining in the public sector will begin with a brief history of federal and provincial public-sector collective bargaining, and with an analysis of the provisions governing these workers today. This analysis will be followed by a consideration of collective bargaining among municipal workers. The chapter will conclude with a comparison of collective bargaining among teachers and health-care workers in several provinces.

The Historical Development of Collective Bargaining Among Federal and Provincial Workers

One of the most controversial topics regarding collective bargaining for public servants is whether they should have the right to strike, or whether their services are so essential that strikes should be prohibited and that their contract negotiations should be settled by arbitration. As well shall see later in this chapter, there is no consensus in Canada regarding this question since some jurisdictions allow their public servants to strike while others impose compulsory arbitration in contract negotiation disputes. A strong argument could be made that some private-sector workers provide essential services, and should not have the strike option. For example, most of us depend on the services of gas and oil delivery drivers to run our furnaces and to keep our houses warm. So far, however, no serious comparison has been made between the services rendered by public- and private-sector workers, except in Quebec where the legislation covers some workers included in the private sector. With the exception of Saskatchewan, which granted collective bargaining rights to both public- and private-sector workers in 1944, no Canadian government gave such rights to their workers until the mid-1960s, when Quebec amended its Labour Code to include professional and other government workers. However, what has been termed the "bold experiment" occurred in 1967, when the federal government passed the Public Service Staff Relations Act. In the election preceding the passage of the PSSRA, Lester Pearson, then leader of the official opposition, stated in a speech given in Ottawa that if the Liberals were elected to form the next government, he would implement a collective bargaining regime for federal public servants. When the Liberals were elected, Mr. Pearson set up the Heeney Committee to propose a collective bargaining regime which would have arbitration as its final dispute resolution mechanism. As we shall see later, however, the federal PSSRA provides for the settlement of contract negotiation disputes by arbitration or the use of the conciliation/strike route (see Figure 10.1). The Act gives collective bargaining rights to workers in federal departments, a number of federal agencies for which Treasury Board is designated as the employer, and a number of government agencies referred to as "separate employers" who do their own negotiations.

Following the passage of this legislation, all provincial governments have given public servants the right to collective bargaining, including the right-to-strike in some jurisdictions and arbitration in others. With the exceptions of Quebec, Manitoba, and Prince Edward Island, all provinces have special public-sector labour relations statutes. (Manitoba and PEI give their workers the right to collective bargaining through their respective civil service statutes. In Quebec, workers in the public and parapublic sectors come under the Quebec Labour Code.) The British Columbia Industrial Relations Act of 1988 repeals the Essential Services Act and brings practically all workers in the province under its jurisdiction, including those in the public- and parapublic-sectors. However, at the time of writing the part of the Act which deals with the public sector has not yet been proclaimed. The Province's Public Service Labour Relations Act has *not* been repealed, and presumably it still governs collective bargaining for public servants. The situation in British Columbia makes for a very untidy legislative scheme for public servants at the time of writing this chapter, and it is hoped that the situation in that province will soon be clarified.

The Sovereignty Issue

The historical resistance to collective bargaining in the federal public service was based largely on the principle of the sovereignty of the state. Collective bargaining and the right to strike were considered incompatible with this principle and with the essential nature of many government services.[1] W.B. Cunningham, writing in 1966, contended that the conventional wisdom in the United States and Canada viewed

Figure 10.1   **Collective Bargaining in the Public Sector**

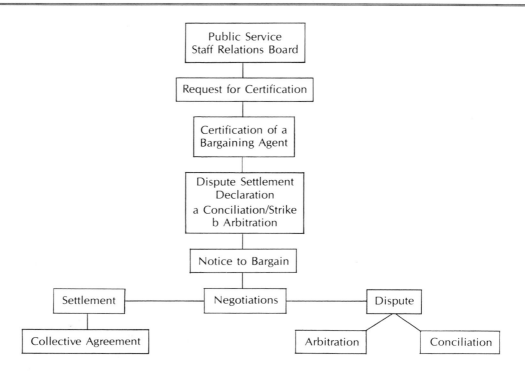

the advent of collective bargaining in the public service as unnecessary, impractical, illegal, and supportive of the notion that the sovereign state "cannot be compelled by lesser bodies to do anything that it chooses not to do, and it cannot enter into contract arrangements that bind its freedom to exercise its sovereign power in the future."[2] American writer R.W. Fleming later asserted that the original debate over whether public-sector workers should be permitted to organize and bargain was over. He went on to say that "Remnants of it [the sovereignty issue] persist, and there are jurisdictions where there is no such right, but in the overall the battle is now on a different front."[3]

One aspect of the whole question of public-sector collective bargaining that is still the focus of controversy is the delegation to arbitration boards of the power to make binding decisions.

Canadian scholar K.P. Swan, aware of both American and Canadian jurisprudence, claims that:

> a clear majority of judicial pronouncements in the United States have rejected constitutional objections to the validity of compulsory binding interest arbitration statutes, but the opposition is not entirely routed, and ammunition for further assaults is readily available.[4]

Overall, however, it appears that the sovereignty argument carries little weight, and that public-sector collective bargaining, is likely to continue, at least in Canada.

The Actors in Public Sector Bargaining

In every industrial relations system in which workers are unionized, there are three major actors: (1) the union or unions; (2) those bodies designated to represent the government as employer; and (3) the administrative tribunals which help to regulate the relations between the first two.

Unionism at the Federal Level

Worker organizations at the federal level existed long before the emergence of collective bargaining. Many of these organizations acted as consultative bodies through the National Joint Council (created in 1944), in which employer and worker organizations were represented equally. The Council dealt with several matters, one of which was salary. In the late 1950s and early 1960s, worker organizations and the Public Service Commission often consulted and agreed on salary increases. Their recommendations, however, were frequently ignored by the Treasury Board.[5]

Union membership at the federal level increased by 200% between 1966 and 1970, and doubled in 1967. However, the rate of growth from 1970 to 1981 increased less than 4% each year on average, levelling off in 1977.[6] What's more, most of the increases resulted from the certification of existing units. Recruitment of new members from some previously non-unionized groups proved difficult. Clerical and stenographic groups were particularly hard to organize, because the workers were largely young married women whose involvement in the labour force tended to be limited to the years preceding periods of full-time childbearing. Unions appeared low on the scale of needs experienced by members of these groups.

Many of the new unions arose out of earlier worker associations — for example, the Civil Service Federation of Canada (CSFC), which had its origin in 1909. The original CSFC membership of 5,223 grew to 80,000 in 1958. The Civil Service Association of Canada (CSAC), a breakaway from the CSFC, had a membership of 33,000 in 1966.[7] These two associations are singled out because it was their merger in 1967 which resulted in the formation of the Public

Service Alliance of Canada (PSAC) with a membership of over 175,750 in 1988.[8]

The PSAC, now the third largest union in the country, represents a very large majority of all federal public servants. Its structure is complex: it contains 17 components, each with its own elected officers. While the components are organized along departmental lines, the bargaining units in the federal public service are organized along occupational lines.[9] Hence, a number of departmental components may have a keen interest in negotiations for the same occupational units. The components help their members to handle grievances. Some PSAC components are strong, others are weak, and the fair management of these unequal components is difficult.

Seventeen unions represent federal public servants. The Professional Institute of the Public Service of Canada (PIPS) was established to represent professional workers. Its membership has shrunk in recent years, due to the establishment of The Economists', Sociologists', and Statisticians' Association (ESSA) and several other groups which formerly belonged to PIPS. One of the more militant federal unions is the Canadian Union of Postal Workers (CUPW). The Canadian Air Traffic Control Association, with a membership of about 1,900, will likely have a lot of clout unless all air traffic controllers continue to be designated as essential workers in future disputes as they have been since a recent Supreme Court decision. (More will be said about this topic later in the chapter.)

Unionism at the Provincial Level

The organization of provincial workers is similar to that at the federal level. Prior to the mid sixties, most provincial government workers had associations that were concerned mainly with social and recreational activities, and which sometimes acted as pressure groups to improve general welfare and working conditions. By 1966, membership in these associations was over 90,000, and membership increased steadily during the 1970s.[10] By 1978, there were more workers in unions at the provincial level than at the federal level.[11]

In the early stages of the CLC, some provincial associations, such as the British Columbia Employees' Association (BCEA), were affiliated directly with the CLC. This caused strained relations between the PSAC and CUPE, each of which wanted to incorporate these provincial associations. To circumvent this problem, the National Union of Provincial Government Employees (NUPGE) was formed in 1976, thus removing these workers from the realm of competition between the PSAC and CUPE. All provincial associations, including those which had been directly affiliated with the CLC but excluding those of New Brunswick and Quebec, are now affiliated through this umbrella union.[12] In 1988, NUPGE was the second largest union in Canada with a membership of over 292,000 — considerably more than even PSAC with its more than 175,700 members.[13]

Bargaining rights were acquired by statutory recognition in six provinces.[14] When bargaining rights were granted to public servants in Quebec in 1964, the Quebec Government Employees' Union was designated by statute as the bargaining agent for clerical and blue-collar employees.[15] The apparent unevenness in the growth of unions at the provincial level has been due in part to the practice whereby union members are included in the statistics only when collective bargaining rights have been accorded these members.

In concluding this section, it seems fair to say that favourable government legislation was the major catalyst in the phenomenal growth of unionization in the federal and provincial public sectors. In fact, it is quite possible that the saturation point in union growth may now have been reached in these sectors.

Public Sector Employers

When a government gives collective bargaining rights to its public servants, one major problem is that of determining which government agency is the employer. A number of options exist, the most notable of which are the Treasury Board or its equivalent and the public service commissions. In the cases of the federal government and New Brunswick, authority is vested in the treasury boards of the two governments. The Ontario statute designates "the management board of cabinet" as the employer. Newfoundland defines the government negotiator as the President of the Treasury Board, or a person authorized by the President to bargain collectively under his supervision, on behalf of the employer. The Prince Edward Island regulations specify that Her Majesty the Queen in right of the province shall be represented by a person designated by the Treasury Board. Nova Scotia designates its Public Service Commission as the employer.

All public-sector negotiations at the provincial level in Quebec are conducted with the government on one side of the bargaining table and often a common front of public-service unions on the other side.[16] The Alberta, Saskatchewan, and Manitoba statutes make no specific reference to the body responsible for negotiations on behalf of public servants. However, as pointed out by a number of authors, the Public Service Commission is the negotiation authority in the province of Saskatchewan.[17]

A major problem with negotiations in the public sector is to make it very clear to the union and other interested parties that the appointed negotiating body has full authority to conclude a collective agreement. If the negotiating committee is not given full authority to do so, the parties of interest are likely to appeal to politicians to influence the outcome of negotiations — a practice that is referred to as "making an end run." Saskatchewan has been very successful in avoiding end runs. Its Public Service Commission, which is fully in charge of negotiations, keeps in close touch with Cabinet. The bargaining parameters within which the Public Service Commission (PSC) negotiators must operate are approved by the Cabinet Committee on Collective Bargaining, with final authority residing in Cabinet. Wetzel and Gallagher have pointed out that:

> The government has found little need to become directly involved in negotiations since it can safely assume that the PSC comprehends its interests and will see that they are protected. The level of trust and comfort which the government feels with this relationship is manifested by the fact that it does not feel the need to have a non-PSC government representative to report on the pulse and direction of talks as it does where the immediate employer is outside of government, e.g. hospitals and nursing homes. Aside from an occasional direct communication between the Minister-In-Charge and the unions, the unions expect to deal with the PSC, as the government's spokesperson.[18]

Other governments might do well to follow the example set by the Saskatchewan government by delegating sufficient authority to experienced negotiators both to make deals and to inspire confidence in union negotiators that they have the authority to do so. If such is not the case, cabinet ministers may very well have to come to the bargaining table.[19]

Tribunals Which Administer Public-Sector Statutes

Politicians are very interested in the processes and outcomes of collective bargaining in the public sector. This interest sometimes results in political interference in collective bargaining.

One example of political meddling occurred in the spring of 1981, when the president of the federal Treasury Board requested that the PSSRB designate all air traffic controllers as essential workers in case of a strike in the aviation industry. The Board refused to comply. However, an appeal to the Federal Court of Appeal overturned the Board's decision and the Supreme Court upheld the Appeal Court ruling. Many critics argue that it was arbitrary in the extreme for the government to act as it did, without consulting the unions concerned or proceeding duly through Parliament.

In order to lessen such interference, it is generally accepted that independent machinery be established to administer the provisions of public-sector statutes. For this reason, the federal government set up the entirely independent Public Service Staff Relations Board (PSSRB). Practically all other jurisdictions have established similar separate administrative tribunals to administer the provisions of their public-sector legislation. In some cases, the functions of these tribunals are related to those of private-sector labour relations boards. In fact, three provinces — British Columbia, Newfoundland, and Saskatchewan — use their labour relations boards or equivalents to administer their public-sector statutes. Quebec no longer has a labour relations board but uses certification officers, certification commissioners, certification commissioners general, a labour court and an essential services council. These functionaries administer the Quebec statute for the public and parapublic sectors and are sometimes aided in their task by advisory bodies to the provincial government. Under the Prince Edward Island regulations, the tribunal or authorizing body for the public sector is a group of three persons: the minister responsible for the Civil Service Act acts as chair, and two additional members are appointed by the Lieutenant-Governor-in-Council.[20]

These tribunals have a number of important functions. First, they act as agencies which define bargaining units and certify bargaining agents — functions performed in the private sector by labour relations boards. Second, since most statutes list a whole series of unfair labour practices, these tribunals must hear charges or complaints about such activities and make decisions with respect to them. Third, if a government department such as the Treasury Board wishes to designate (deny the right to strike to) all workers in a specific category, the tribunals must hear and interpret these requests.

While appointments of conciliation officers, mediators, and conciliation boards are usually made through ministers of labour in the private sector, the same appointments in the public sector are made by the separate tribunals. The tribunals use either full-time or part-time members as adjudicators in contract interpretation disputes. Hence, the administrative tribunals perform the combined functions of labour relations boards and ministers of labour and are thus extremely important to the collective bargaining process in the public sector.

Statutes Covering Collective Bargaining for Public-Sector Workers

Having discussed the three actors, we now turn to a discussion of the nature and coverage of statutes in the public sector. As indicated in Chapter 6, eleven statutes govern bargaining in the Canadian private sector. While the Quebec Labour Code, the Saskatchewan Trade Union Act and perhaps the British Columbia Industrial Relations Act apply equally to the public and private sectors, all other jurisdictions have separate statutes to govern public-sector workers. Some of these statutes, such as that in New

Brunswick, also cover hospitals, schools, and public utilities. Hence, in Canada we have a variety of statutes governing workers in the public and parapublic sectors, ranging from one statute covering all groups in Quebec, Saskatchewan and perhaps British Columbia to seven in Ontario, including those for police and fire fighters. What has developed is a "crazy quilt" of legislative provisions.

In every jurisdiction, with the exception of Saskatchewan, Quebec and possibly British Columbia, there are at least two relevant statutes — one for employers and workers in the private sector and at least one other for workers in the public (and in some cases parapublic) sectors. For example, the federal government uses Part 1 of the Canada Labour Code to govern workers in transportation, communications, banking, and radio and television broadcasting (the private sector), and the Public Service Staff Relations Act to cover workers in all federal departments and a number of federal agencies (the public sector).

Federal government heads off strike by public-service union

BY SUSAN DELACOURT and LORNE SLOTNICK
The Globe and Mail

The federal government has headed off a massive strike by its largest public-service union — at least temporarily — with a tentative agreement that also represents a staff relations breakthrough for new Treasury Board president Robert de Cotret.

But opposition to the settlement, reached on Sunday night, was already surfacing yesterday within the Public Service Alliance of Canada, and union sources predicted that at least some of the 27 bargaining classifications would reject the contract and launch strikes.

The deal, which covers more than 160,000 public-service employees — including clerks, meat inspectors, customs officers, jail guards and tradesmen — provides for wage increases totalling 14.4 per cent over a 42-month period retroactive, in

most cases, to the end of 1987.

Union sources said bargaining teams were severely split on the merits of the offer, with the result that the deal is being put to a mail vote with no recommendation to either accept or reject. Ratification, in 27 separate votes, is expected to take eight to 10 weeks.

PSAC president Daryl Bean, saying it was up to the members to decide, nevertheless praised the settlement. "It is a substantial package. There are major improvements in it; there are some new breakthroughs," he said.

But at least one senior official of the union was urging a rejection yesterday, saying the settlement falls short of projected inflation and makes no headway on job security or pay equity.

"In real terms, it's a pay cut, but if the members are transfixed by the money, they could be taking a serious risk," said John Baglow, the union's national director for the Ottawa area. "If they vote for this they could be voting for their own unemployment."

Mr. de Cotret told reporters that "I'm certainly quite pleased with the outcome and I think the unions are also."

Mr. de Cotret placed great emphasis on improving the government's relations with the public service when he was put back in the Treasury Board role in January.

Yesterday, both he and Mr. Bean acknowledged that this agreement represented the first step in that process.

According to Mr. Bean, the agreement was at least in part a result of Mr. de Cotret's willingness to settle the longstanding dispute. He signalled very quickly that he was prepared to move and present a substantive package" when he came to office, Mr. Bean said, "and it is a substantive package."

Mr. de Cotret, for his part, said: "It was obviously a mandate I had

to resolve the issue. A government depends enormously on its employees and we want our employees to be well treated and equitably treated."

But he denied that this agreement was an attempt by the government to clear the decks for a budget that is expected to stress fiscal restraint and cost cutting in every part of federal operations.

"It was never mentioned in that perspective," he said.

The package provides for wage increases of 5 per cent in the first 14 months of the 42-month agreement, 4.8 per cent in the second 14 months and 4.6 per cent in the third 14 months. Factored on an annual basis, the increases represent an average yearly increase of 4.2 per cent.

In addition, it provides improved vacation time, larger employer contributions to a medical plan, training and separation benefits for laid-off workers and a promise of child-care facilities.

But on the issue of job security, which the union has made a priority since the government began chopping the public service four years ago, there is little change. An existing clause that committed the government to make "every reasonable effort" to effect cuts through attrition is unchanged despite the union's stated goal of a no-layoff guarantee.

Mr. Bean said he was not concerned by this, citing improvements

in retraining and severance pay. He added the Tories have cut 11,000 public service jobs since 1985 and only 800 of those have been by layoff. None of the 800 has grieved under the job-security article, he said.

Mr. Bean said he expected the deal would be approved by the members, but Mr. Baglow said a campaign to reject the contract would likely develop quickly.

Mr. Bean said that while the agreement does not accomplish all the union's goals, members would have to go on strike to extract any substantial improvements.

Even if the agreement is ratified, a new dispute could arise when the two sides sit down to overhaul the Public Service Staff Relations Act, which governs the way negotiations are carried out.

Mr. Bean used the occasion of yesterday's news conference to once again call for the act to be scrapped, in favor of the Canada Labor Code, which governs other bargaining in federal labor jurisdiction.

Mr. de Cotret said yesterday that he agreed the act needed to be overhauled, but that nothing would be done until this agreement is ratified. He also ruled out any notion of totally scrapping the act.

The Globe and Mail, March 7, 1989, p. A3.

Coverage of the Statutes

The federal Public Service Staff Relations Act applies to all government departments and a lengthy list of commissions and agencies for which the Treasury Board acts as the employer. The statute also mentions separate employers or agencies which negotiate for themselves, such as the Atomic Energy Control Board, the Economic Council of Canada, the Medical Research Council, and the National Film Board.[21] Public-sector statutes in most provinces also refer to a number of other agencies and Crown corporations.

While the Quebec Labour Code at one time included a host of organizations and services in its definition of the public sector, it has now restricted this list to the following:

In this division, "public service" means
(1) a municipal corporation or intermunicipal agency;
(2) an establishment or regional council within the meaning of paragraphs a and f of section of the Act respecting health services and social services . . . that is not contemplated in paragraph 2 of section 111.2;
(3) a telephone service
(4) a fixed schedule land transport service such as a railway or a subway, or a transport service carried on by bus or by boat;
(5) an undertaking engaged in the production, transmission, distribution or sale of gas, water or electricity;
(6) a home garbage removal service;
(7) an ambulance service or the Canadian Red Cross Association or
(8) an agency that is a mandatory of the Government, except the Société des alcools du Que-

bec and an agency or body whose personnel is appointed and remunerated in accordance with the Public Service Act.[22]

The Ontario *Crown Employees Collective Bargaining Act* of 1972 covers not only all public servants *per se* but also workers in the Liquor Control Board, Workers' Compensation Board, Niagara Parks Commission, and the Ontario Housing Corporation within the Municipality of Metropolitan Toronto.[23] The public sector in the B.C. Industrial Relations Act includes the provincial government, a municipality, a board of school trustees, a university or college, a community care facility, a hospital, a library board and a schedule of assorted organizations listed in the schedule at the end of the statute. (While this section of the B.C. Act has been assented to — that is, given approval in third reading of the provincial assembly — it has not at the time of writing been proclaimed by the Lieutenant Governor-in-Council.)[24]

Ontario Provincial Police

The Public Service Staff Relations Act does not cover members of the Royal Canadian Mounted Police or the Canadian Armed Forces. There have been some rumblings, however, that one or both of these groups should be included. Provincial police officers have collective bargaining with arbitration as the formal mechanism for resolving contract negotiation disputes, and a number of European countries grant collective bargaining rights to members of the military, but without the right to strike. Most jurisdictions exclude police and firefighters, since they are covered by separate statutes.

As with private sector statutes, most of the statutes governing workers in the public sector exclude persons who act in a confidential capacity in matters relating to industrial relations and who take an active part in policy development and implementation. In general, the cut-off mark for management workers is higher in the public sector than it is in the private sector. But in the federal jurisdiction, more managerial exclusions exist than in most of the provinces.

At this point, it will be helpful to recall the three major types of classical labour relations disputes used in discussing the legislation covering collective bargaining in the private sector. First, a discussion of recognition disputes will deal with the determination of bargaining units and the certification of bargaining agents. Second, a discussion of contract negotiation or interest disputes will deal with negotiable issues and impasse resolution. Third, a discussion of contract interpretation or rights disputes will deal with grievance handling, arbitration procedures, and matters subject to arbitration. Figure 10.2 (overleaf) presents a summary of all three types of dispute settlement procedures.

Recognition Disputes

Determination of Bargaining Units

In some jurisdictions, the composition of bargaining units its determined by the statutes which give collective bargaining rights to public-sector workers. In other jurisdictions, labour relations boards, or special tribunals for the public sector, review union submissions in order to determine the appropriateness of proposed bargaining units. In making such decisions, the boards may refer to existing regulations, if any, respecting the original composition of the units.

In the federal public service, literally hundreds of occupational groups existed within the service before the PSSRA was passed. As part of the new regime under collective bargaining, the Public Service Commission was charged with the responsibility of defining occupational groups within five broad occupational categories. Table 10.1 lists these categories and the number of groups that each comprises.

This revamping made for a total of 72 occupational groups, each generally equivalent to a bargaining unit. (Bargaining units may consist of workers plus supervisors, workers only, or supervisors only.) Two years after the Act came into effect, 98% of the workers belonged to bargaining units for which bargaining agents had been certified. As of December 1987, however, 19 unions had been certified as bargaining agents in the federal public service. Fourteen of these have agreements with the Treasury Board, and 8 have agreements with separate employers, although 3 of the 19 are common to the central administration and separate employers. These bargaining agents represented 167 bargaining units, 81 of which were in the central administration. Of the 19 separate employers, 11 were unionized, and these accounted for the remaining 86 bargaining units. (Separate employers do their own negotiating. In other cases, the Treasury Board is the employer and does the negotiating.)[25]

The New Brunswick statute contains the same occupational categories as the federal statute, but exactly what percentage of workers now comprise bargaining units is unknown. In addition, the New Brunswick statute recognizes the distinction between supervisory and non-supervisory bargaining units.[26]

Figure 10.2

Actors
—Employer: TB, PSC
—Unions
—Administrative Tribunals

Recognition Dispute

* **Bargaining units determined in statutes**

Federal (72 groups)
—workers
—supervisors   } 122 negotiating units
—both   81 in central administration
                            41 separate employers

Quebec (3 negotiating units)
—professionals
—white collar
—blue collar

Some other jurisdictions
—master agreements
—negotiation units for 8-10 groups

* **Certification of bargaining agents**
—no voluntary recognition
—no quickie vote

Federal
—if 52%, then certify
—if less than 52%, then vote

Provinces which determine bargaining agents
P.E.I. Public Service Association
Nova Scotia Government Employees Association
Ontario: OPSEU
Manitoba Government Employees Association
Quebec Government Employees Union
British Columbia Employees Association[1]

Interest Dispute

* **Negotiations**
—all jurisdictions
—Federal chooses route
and designates at this
stage

Issues (Federal and New Brunswick)
—rates of pay
—hours of work
—leave entitlement
—standards of
discipline
—other

* **Impasse**
—further negotiations
—appointment of
conciliation officer
—mediation in some
jurisdictions
—conciliation in some
jurisdictions
—strike or lockout
—New Brunswick
chooses route and
designates at this
stage
—Federal: conciliation
and strike route or
arbitration route

[1]The British Columbia statute does not name a bargaining agent,
but the statutes of the other provinces do.

Dispute Settlement Provisions Under Federal and Provincial Public-Sector Statutes

Rights Dispute

•**Essential Service Methods**
—designation
—compulsory arbitration
—court injunction if above two are not conformed with
—special *ad hoc* back-to-work legislation

Designation
—Federal
—New Brunswick
—Quebec
—British Columbia
—Newfoundland

Compulsory Arbitration
—Alberta
—Ontario
—Manitoba
—Nova Scotia
—P.E.I.

•**Collective agreement**
•**Grievance procedure**
—last step is adjudication

—Federal: The grievance is in the name of the worker, but the bargaining agent must approve and usually supports the worker. Disciplinary action consists of discharge, suspension, or financial penalty. Membership in bargaining unit unnecessary to have discipline cases adjudicated. Only single adjudicators.

Ontario: adjudication is broader in scope than federal one. Grievance Settlement Board interprets, classifies, appraises performance and decides on cases of discipline or dismissal without just cause.

Table 10.1	Occupational Categories and Groups Under the Federal Public Service Staff Relations Act
Occupational categories	Number of groups
Scientific and Professional	28
Technical	13
Administrative and Foreign Service	13
Administrative Support	6
Operational	12

Source: Alton W.J. Craig, "Collective Bargaining in the Federal Public Service of Canada," Vol. 5, No. 2, *Optimum (1974), p. 28.*

According to the Alberta statute, workers for the Crown in right of Alberta constitute a single bargaining unit.[27] However, the statute mentions that a number of professions, including doctors, dentists, architects, engineers, and lawyers should not be included in the bargaining unit unless the board is satisfied that a majority of such workers wish to be included.[28]

Although the Ontario statute does not name the bargaining units in the statute, it does indicate that those designated in the regulations under the Crown Employees Collective Bargaining Act are appropriate for collective bargaining purposes.[29] The following groups comprise the bargaining units in Ontario: social services, operational services, scientific and technical services, administrative services, general services, law enforcement, and correctional officers. While the Registrar of the Ontario tribunal refers to these as salary units, others contend they they are more appropriately entitled negotiation units.[30] Only the Liquor Control Board of Ontario, the Workers' Compensation Board, the Niagara Parks Commission, and the Ontario Housing Corporation are listed in the regulations, but it would appear that the theory underlying the selection of these organizations resembles the separate employer concept under the PSSRA.

An interesting case arose in Ontario in the early eighties, when the correctional officers, who were then part of a larger group, went on strike to carve out for themselves a separate bargaining unit. The correctional officers claimed that they did not properly belong to the occupational group containing social workers. The President of the Ontario Public Service Employees Union was jailed because he advised these workers to strike, in contravention of the Ontario statute. The issue was resolved by arbitration — an unusual way for determining a bargaining unit, since the tribunal responsible for administering an act usually makes this decision.

During the summer of 1989, 350 Crown attorneys in Ontario were also given collective bargaining rights, and now negotiate through the Ontario Crown Attorneys Association. The members of this group had been seeking bargaining rights for years, claiming that their salaries had fallen far behind those for lawyers in the private sector. Unresolved disputes go to binding arbitration.[31]

The Quebec Labour Code provides for three types of bargaining units for public-sector workers: professional bargaining units, white-collar units, and blue-collar units.[32] The Nova Scotia statute identifies eight different bargaining units, some of which apply to the health services and education areas.[33] The statutes of Manitoba, Saskatchewan, Prince Edward Island, and Newfoundland do not define bargaining units.

Determination of Bargaining Agents

In some provinces, the provincial associations or unions are listed in the public sector statutes. Even those statutes which name the bargaining agent in the statute provide for the replacement of the bargaining agent should a majority of workers become dissatisfied. In addition, practically every statute provides for bargaining agents to represent new groups of workers not previously certified. Most of the statutes also provide for special tribunals, rather than the existing labour relations boards, to certify unions.

Bargaining Agents As can be seen from Table 10.2, the British Columbia, Alberta, Saskatchewan, Ontario, Quebec, and Newfoundland statutes specify the proportion of workers in bargaining units necessary to make application for certification and the proportion of support that is needed in order for a bargaining agent to be certified. Manitoba, New Brunswick, Nova Scotia, and Prince Edward Island do not specify any precise figures relating to the certification process. However, their statutes do name the bargaining agents.[34] Some statutes require *50% of those voting* to support bargaining agents for them to be certified. Another four, including the federal statute, require that the bargaining agent obtain the approval of *50% or more of those in the bargaining*

unit. The Former Chair of the federal Public Service Staff Relations Board, J. Finkelman, did an exhaustive analysis of the federal statute and recommended that the PSSRA be amended to allow a bargaining agent to apply for certification where it claimed to have the support of 35% of those in the proposed bargaining unit, and that it be certified if it was supported by a majority of workers voting, provided that not less than 35% of eligible voters cast ballots.[35] If the study's proposals were implemented, they would bring the federal law more into line with most of the statutes governing workers in the private sector. The growing tendency in Canadian statutes to adopt the principle of a simple voting majority would require those who oppose certification to cast a vote rather than allow them to stay home and expect their abstention to count as a "no" vote. Following the will of the active voting membership corresponds with established democratic practice in the political sphere.

This completes our discussion of the ways in which recognition disputes are handled in the different jurisdictions. The following sections deal with contract negotiation (interest) disputes.

Table 10.2

A Comparison of Provisions Dealing with Certification

Jurisdiction	% support needed to apply for certification	% support necessary for a union to be certified when a vote is taken	
		50% + of those in the bargaining unit	50% + of those voting
Federal	Not specified	X	
British Columbia	35–51%		X
Alberta	50% +	X	
Saskatchewan	25%		X
Manitoba	Not specified	Not specified	
Ontario	35%		X
Quebec	35%	X	
New Brunswick	Not specified	Not specified	
Nova Scotia	Not specified	Not specified	
Prince Edward Island	Not specified	Not specified	
Newfoundland	50% +	X	

Source: Alton W.J. Craig, "Collective Bargaining in the Federal Public Service of Canada," Vol. 5, No. 2, *Optimum* (1974), p. 28.

Interest Disputes

The Scope of Bargainable Issues

From looking at the definition of a collective agreement in the statutes of the various jurisdictions, it would appear that almost anything is negotiable, except those items which require the enactment or amendment of a statute or the amendment of pension legislation. However, under the PSSRA, the following matters are *not* subject to arbitration:

> the standards, procedures or processes governing the appointment, appraisal, promotion, demotion, transfer, lay-off or release of employees, or with any term or condition of employment of employees that was not a subject of negotiation between the parties during the period before arbitration was requested in respect thereof.[36]

This provision is designed to protect the merit principle in the appointment, promotion, etc. of public-sector workers. Such staffing regulations are to be found in a separate law: the Public Service Employment Act.

While the federal statute contains what is probably the most exhaustive statement of subjects which are not subject to arbitration, the statutes of Alberta and Ontario contain clauses almost as comprehensive as those of the federal statute.[37] The B.C. Public Service Labour Relations Act prohibits collective agreements from containing clauses relating to the merit principle and its application in the appointment and promotion of workers. This statute also prohibits negotiation over all matters included under such acts as the Public Service Act and the Pension Act.[38]

The number of items negotiable under most statutes governing collective bargaining in the public sector is relatively small in relation to the number of items negotiable in the private sector. In some jurisdictions, the fact that so few issues are subject to arbitration is cause for considerable concern and frustration among unions and workers alike. While the parties may jointly negotiate over a substantial number of issues, it sometimes happens that if government negotiators do not wish to deal with a particular item, they may threaten to go to arbitration where the issue is not arbitrable. This kind of tactic is hardly conducive to genuine collective bargaining.

In some jurisdictions, two-tier bargaining exists. The British Columbia Public Service Labour Relations Act contains the following provision:

> Two collective agreements shall apply to each bargaining unit, as follows: (a) a master agreement including all the terms and conditions of employment common to all employees in the bargaining unit, or to 2 or more occupational groups in the bargaining unit, and (b) a subsidiary agreement for each occupational group, including the terms and conditions of employment that apply only to employees in a specific occupational group in the bargaining unit.[39]

The specific occupational groups mentioned in (b) above are determined by negotiation between the parties.

This form of bargaining is close to ideal, for those items which are common to all workers in the public sector may be covered by one major or master collective agreement. In addition, subsidiary agreements containing provisions that are unique to each occupational group may be negotiated by the groups concerned.

The Ontario government has three types of collective agreements. The first relates to each of the eight or ten specific occupational groups or negotiation units discussed earlier in this chapter. Under this type of negotiation, each group may negotiate salary scales peculiar to its own occupational group. In addition to these multiple salary agreements, there is another general agreement for the entire civil service relating solely to working conditions and terms of employment such as overtime, hours of work, and grievance procedures. Finally, there is a service-wide collective agreement negotiated at two- or three-year intervals on fringe benefits for the entire Ontario public service. As with the two-tier structure in British Columbia, the Ontario system makes a good deal of sense by providing for one set of negotiations on items that are common to all public-sector workers and at the same time enabling particular groups of workers to negotiate salaries for their specific occupations. A number of bargaining units in the federal government now negotiate two-tier agreements, an extra-legal practice that was started several years ago.

To summarize, thus far we have dealt with those workers covered by the public-sector statutes, the administrative agencies which are independent of the government, who the employer is in the various jurisdictions, the determination of bargaining units and bargaining agents, and the scope of bargainable issues. In the following section we will describe the means by which negotiations are initiated and the various methods for resolving interest disputes.

Dispute Settlement Procedures Under the Federal and New Brunswick Statutes

The Federal and New Brunswick Statutes

When a public-sector bargaining agent is certified, it is entitled — as are bargaining agents in the private sector — to serve notice to negotiate for a new collective agreement, or for the renewal of an existing one. The negotiation process in the public sector is very much the same as it is in the private sector, and the processes explained in the chapter on "The Negotiating Process" apply to the private, public, and parapublic sectors. If the parties are successful in reaching an agreement, the provisions agreed upon will be written into the collective agreement just as they are in the private sector.

If an impasse occurs in negotiations and the parties are unable to reach an agreement, various forms of third-party assistance are available to them. (The effectiveness of these different forms was discussed in Chapter 8.) In the pri-

vate sector, a strike or lockout usually follows if conciliation or mediation (or both) are unsuccessful. Public-sector disputes generally contain more of a public interest component than do those in the private sector. There are also many more ways in which public-sector disputes may be handled. It is to a discussion of these procedures that we now turn our attention. We will focus on the federal and New Brunswick statutes and, where appropriate, compare their provisions with those prescribed in different provinces.

One of the unique features of the federal PSSRA is that it provides for two methods of dispute resolution, namely, conciliation with the right to strike *or* arbitration. After the initial set of negotiations, the bargaining agent must make its choice before a specific round of negotiations begins and may not change the route once the negotiations have begun. The New Brunswick statute is similar in this respect to the federal statute, except that the bargaining agent must decide between the conciliation-and-strike route or the arbitration route only when an impasse is reached in the negotiations. These are the only two jurisdictions in Canada where such a choice is available.

An interesting question is why one should require the bargaining agent to determine its route prior to the commencement of negotiations and the other at the impasse stage. A partial answer to this question is found in a report prepared by a Royal Commission for the New Brunswick government:

> The choice [under the PSSRA], however, must be indicated *after* a group has been certified as a bargaining agent and *before* negotiations begin. Both sides are thus committed in advance to the method that could be used ultimately to resolve a deadlock. Yet, it may be argued that this very element of certainty about the final method of settling differences has serious disadvantages. Students of collective bargaining have noted on the basis of many empirical studies that a degree of uncertainty about how far either of the parties is prepared to go in pressing its case encourages the

give-and-take and flexibility that are necessary for successful negotiations. Bargaining tends to be inhibited or ritualized when the parties know they must go through predetermined procedures at given stages of their negotiations. The procedural steps proposed by this Commission are designed to avoid some of this difficulty. They seek to maintain the atmosphere of uncertainty that is considered conducive to effective negotiations by delaying the choice between the strike or arbitration to the end of the bargaining exercise.[40]

Students of industrial relations would agree that a degree of uncertainty about the procedural steps involved may encourage the parties to reach an agreement on their own.

Both statutes specify that an arbitrable award may deal only with "rates of pay, hours of work, leave entitlements, standards of discipline and other terms and conditions of employment directly related thereto."[41] Hiring and firing practices are not bargainable.

Arbitration   The federal Act provides for the appointment by the Public Service Staff Relations Board of two panels, one consisting of at least three persons representing the interest of the employer and the other consisting of at least three persons representing the interest of the workers. If a dispute reaches the arbitration stage, the PSSRB appoints one of its own members to chair the arbitration board and selects one person from each panel, thus forming a three-member arbitration board. It should be noted that a number of boards may sit at the same time to handle different disputes as long as there are enough members on the panels representing the employers and workers and enough members of the board to chair them. Under the federal statute, the arbitration board, in conducting its proceedings and in formulating its award, is required to take into consideration the following criteria:

a the needs of the Public Service for qualified employees;
b the conditions of employment in similar occupations outside the Public Service, including such geographic, industrial, or other variations as the Board may consider relevant;
c the need to maintain appropriate relationships in the conditions of employment as between different grade levels within an occupation and as between occupations within the Public Service;
d the need to establish terms and conditions of employment that are fair and reasonable in relation to the qualifications required, the work performed, the responsibility assumed and the nature of the services rendered; and
e any other factor that to it appears to be relevant to the matter in dispute.[42]

The New Brunswick statute is almost identical.

While Mr. Finkelman, the first Chair of the Board, was not responsible for the two-route system, it is quite obvious from his report that he prefers the arbitration route to that of conciliation with the right to strike. He states in his report that, "if an impasse is reached, every possible step should be taken to encourage resort to arbitration, a technique whose time appears to have come."[43] This preference no doubt reflects Mr. Finkelman's experience as an arbitrator for over thirty years in the men's clothing industry in Toronto with a union whose philosophy has been traditionally to submit interest disputes to binding arbitration.[44] With obvious reservations, he suggests that the parties should have the right, by mutual consent, to use final-offer selection in whatever form they may deem appropriate to the situation.

There has been some criticism of the arbitration route, especially when it can be instituted only at the request of the bargaining agent, as is presently the situation under the federal Act. One argument for the use of arbitration is that only through arbitration can weak groups achieve equity. This assumption is open to question since little consideration has been given to other alternatives. For example, leaders of weak unions could use pattern-setting as a vehicle for strengthening their bargaining position. Similarly, coalition bargaining could be instituted to permit weak groups to join with the stronger ones to increase their bargaining power. While Finkelman downplays the desirability of using the strike route as a norm in negotiations, he does not develop all the drawbacks of the arbitration procedure. According to Crispo, some of these drawbacks include: (1) the difficulty in appointing an arbitrator acceptable to both sides and determining a suitable tenure for the person chosen; (2) the potentially detrimental effects of compulsory arbitration on the process of collective bargaining itself; (3) the fact that union leaders may use the arbitrator or arbitration tribunal as a scapegoat in the event they they do not make a proper internal trade-off among the conflicting interests of their own members; and (4) the potential for the haphazard determination of criteria by arbitrators in interest disputes. Furthermore, strikes sometimes provide a release for worker frustration and are therefore helpful in restoring morale and self-respect.[45] While the federal Act provides the criteria mentioned above to be followed by arbitrators, the final section — "any other factor that to it [the arbitration board] appears to be relevant in the dispute" — gives just about as much flexibility as would exist were no criteria specified.

It would seem, therefore, that discussions leading to any future legislative amendments to the Act might well take the strike norm into serious consideration. It is generally accepted that arbitration of interest disputes is not an instrument for innovation; this has been demonstrated in the federal public sector. In addition, if it were not for the use of strikes or strike threats in the private sector, there would be less creative provisions in private-sector agreements than there are today.

The New Brunswick arbitration procedure differs from that of the federal government. Under the New Brunswick statute, the maximum period for collective bargaining is 45 days unless otherwise agreed to by the parties. Where the parties have bargained in good faith with a view to concluding a collective agreement but have failed to reach one, they may, by mutual written agreement, submit their differences to binding arbitration. The New Brunswick statute also makes provision for a Public

Service Arbitration Tribunal, consisting of a chair responsible for the administration of the system of arbitration, and two panels of three persons each, representing the respective interests of employer and worker. The Lieutenant Governor-in-Council may authorize the board to designate one or more persons to be alternative chairs of the Arbitration Tribunal. This provision is obviously meant to allow for the simultaneous sitting of two or more arbitration boards. If the two parties agree jointly to submit their dispute to arbitration, the arbitration board is guided by the same criteria as the federal government, except that in New Brunswick "the interest of the public" would be an additional factor.

Conciliation and Strikes The other option open to parties under both the federal and New Brunswick statutes is the conciliation/strike option. Both statutes empower the chairs of the respective boards to appoint a conciliation officer at the request of either party or on the chair's initiative. A conciliation officer may also be appointed as part of the arbitration route. If, however, a conciliation officer is unable to bring the parties to an agreement, a conciliation board *must* be established, again at the request of either party, or on the initiative of the chair of the board.[46]

A provision introduced as part of the federal Act and now adopted by a number of provincial jurisdictions specifies that no conciliation board may be established until the parties have agreed or the board has determined the workers or class of workers, the performance of whose duties are considered *essential to the safety or security* of the public. These "designated workers" may not legally take part in a strike.

Under the federal statute there are two occasions on which a list of designated workers must be furnished by the employer. The first occurs before a bargaining agent specifies the dispute resolution process. This list cannot be challenged by the bargaining agent, but the proportion designated helps in determining which route to choose. The second occasion arises if the bargaining agent has chosen the conciliation route as the dispute resolution procedure. In this case, the employer is required to provide a list to the bargaining agent and to the board within 20 days after the notice of bargaining has been given. The bargaining agent is then given 20 days to file an objection to the employer's list. If the two parties cannot resolve their differences, the board holds hearings and makes a final determination. The New Brunswick statute, which also has a method of designation, differs from the federal statute inasmuch as the designation of essential workers takes place only when an impasse in negotiations is encountered.

When a federal conciliation board is established, the chair of the PSSRB presents the board with a statement setting forth the matters on which the conciliation board shall report its findings and recommendations. The original statement of issues may be amended at any time in the interest of assisting the parties to reach an agreement.

Conciliation boards are established in the same way as they are in the private sector. It is interesting to note, however, that a federal conciliation board may not make recommendations concerning "the standards, procedures or processes governing the appointment, appraisal, promotion, demotion, transfer, lay-off or release of employees."[47]

Under both the federal and New Brunswick statutes a majority of the members of a conciliation board speak for the board in deciding upon any matter referred to it. In addition, the New Brunswick statute provides that, where there is no majority decision by the conciliation board, the chair must report his or her own findings and recommendations, but in no case can the findings and recommendations of the minority be reported.[48] Under the PSSRA each member of a conciliation board may publish his or her report. Both statutes contain a clause providing for voluntary arbitration, in the sense that before a conciliation board has made its report

the parties may agree in writing to accept its recommendations as binding.

Under the federal statute, if the workers reject the recommendations of a conciliation board and the bargaining agent is authorized to call a strike, it may do so seven days after the receipt of the conciliation board's report by the chair of the PSSRB. The New Brunswick statute is more complex. In principle, a strike vote may take place after seven days have elapsed from the publication of any conciliation board report. One of the parties, however, must first ask the chair of the Public Service Labour Relations Board (PSLRB) to declare that a deadlock exists, and the chair must subsequently make an offer to the union and management of voluntary binding arbitration. Only when the latter offer is refused by at least one of the parties is the union finally free to ask for a strike mandate which must be sanctioned by a majority vote of the bargaining unit's membership. If the union does not obtain a strike mandate, the chair can order both sides back to the bargaining table for 21 days, at the end of which time the union may take another strike vote, if no settlement has been reached. This procedure offers the possibility of a prolonged stalemate, which can be ended only by a successful strike vote or by the conclusion of a negotiated agreement. In the event that a strike is authorized, it may take place only after seven days have elapsed from the date on which the bargaining agent has notified the chair and the employer that the workers in the relevant bargaining unit have authorized strike action.[49]

Dispute Settlement Procedures in Other Jurisdictions

Compulsory Arbitration Five provinces — Alberta, Ontario, Manitoba, Nova Scotia, and Prince Edward Island — do not allow public servants to go on strike but require that arbitration be the final step in the dispute resolution procedure. Most of the pertinent statutes also provide for the use of conciliation services prior to the imposition of arbitration, and for voluntary arbitration if the parties agree in advance to be bound by the terms of a conciliation board report. Each of the statutes also contains criteria to guide arbitrators in formulating their awards, including an item with respect to the interest of the public. The Nova Scotia statute includes an interesting provision to the effect that the Governor-in-Council and the Civil Service Commission are not bound to implement an arbitration award which would result in any department exceeding its appropriateness unless the Minister of Finance includes in the estimates for the next ending fiscal year an amount sufficient to implement the arbitration award retroactive to the date on which the arbitration award was to be effective.[50] Also, no arbitration award may require the government to amend a statute for its implementation.

Conciliation and Strikes The use of strikes in the public sector is a controversial issue. Six jurisdictions — federal, British Columbia, Saskatchewan, Quebec, New Brunswick, and Newfoundland — allow work stoppages after conciliation or mediation has failed; other jurisdictions insist upon compulsory arbitration. Why the rules differ on this issue is not at all clear, although in the case of New Brunswick and the federal jurisdiction, the collective bargaining regime was the subject of a special study in which the two options were recommended.

Among the six jurisdictions that allow strikes, all except Saskatchewan also designate some employees as essential. (While Saskatchewan has allowed strikes among all its public servants since 1944, very few strikes have taken place in that province.) The federal jurisdiction permits the bargaining agent the choice of conciliation with the right to strike, while the B.C. statute makes provision for the parties to seek the assistance of a mediator should they fail to reach a collective agreement on their own. If mediation fails, the parties are asked to agree to have any issues in dispute submitted to arbitration for a final and binding decision. Should

either side refuse, the union is free to exercise its strike option. A majority of the members of the union must vote in favour of a work stoppage and the strike must begin within the three-month period following the taking of the vote. In addition, the bargaining agent must notify the government negotiators at least three days before any strike begins.

British Columbia strike votes reflect the two-tier bargaining system in that province. If the issues in dispute are those in a master agreement covering various occupational groups, then a strike vote must be taken among all members covered by the agreement. However, if the matters in dispute refer to a subsidiary agreement covering the members of an occupational group, then the strike vote must be taken among these members only. In either case, a majority of the members must vote in order for a strike to be deemed legal.[51] In 1977, the B.C. government passed the Essential Services Disputes Act, which applied to a number of agencies, including certain provincial public servants. Part 3 of the Act provided for the Lieutenant-Governor-in-Council to designate those facilities, productions, and services which he considered necessary or essential to prevent immediate and serious damage to life, health, safety, or an immediate and substantial threat to the economy and welfare of the province and its citizens. This statute is repealed by the B.C. Industrial Relations Act, but the provisions in the new Act dealing with essential services has not been proclaimed as of the time of writing this chapter.

The Newfoundland statute makes provision for the appointment of conciliation officers and conciliation boards if the parties are unable to reach agreements on their own. The findings of the conciliation board, however, are not binding on the parties, and workers in the Province of Newfoundland have the right to strike. In 1983, Newfoundland amended its legislation to make it possible for the Minister of Manpower and Industrial Relations to appoint a mediator from within the public service or outside, either on his or her own initiative or by the request of the parties. A mediator may also be appointed when a request is made for the appointment of a conciliation board. Furthermore, a conciliation board may be appointed if the efforts of a mediator prove unsuccessful.[52]

The Newfoundland statute has always provided for the designation of essential workers in the event of a strike. In 1983, however, the designation process was changed. Under the amendment, the bargaining agent or the board may seek, any time after the certification of the bargaining agent, a statement from the employer regarding the number and names of essential workers in each classification. Where a majority of employees are considered essential, the legislation makes all members of the bargaining unit essential.[53]

A strike may be undertaken when a majority of the workers in the unit actually vote by secret ballot in favour of such action. There is, however, a waiting period of seven days between the time the bargaining agent gives notice in writing to the Minister of Labour of the workers' intentions and the beginning of the work stoppage. The Newfoundland Act also provides that, where less than a majority of the workers in the unit vote in favour of a strike, either party may by notice in writing request the resumption of collective bargaining. Also, when the provincial assembly resolves that a strike is or would be injurious to the health or safety of persons or any group or class of persons or the security of the province, it may declare that a state of emergency exists and forbid the strike of all workers in the unit or units specified in the resolution. The assembly may, in addition, order the workers of such unit or units to return to duty if they have already gone on strike. In the event that a state of emergency has been declared, any dispute concerning outstanding issues is referred to adjudication, which is equivalent to compulsory arbitration. The adjudication board is guided by criteria similar to those contained in those statutes which make arbitration the norm for settlement.

When the Quebec Government revised its Labour Code in 1964, it gave the right to strike to all public- and private-sector workers, with the exception of police and firefighters. In addition, both Liberal and Péquiste governments have come out against arbitration, since they prefer to retain control over how their budget is allocated and spent rather than delegate any part of that responsibility to an arbitrator.

In 1978, the Quebec National Assembly passed Bill 59, a complicated piece of legislation which outlined provisions for negotiations and dispute settlement in the public and parapublic sectors, including education and social affairs. The Bill created a Committee of Information on Negotiations which is responsible for informing the public on the state of negotiations. The intended effect undoubtedly is to bring public opinion to bear on public- and parapublic-sector disputes. The Bill also provides that the negotiation stage begin 180 days before the date of expiration of a collective agreement, and that every certified association in the public and parapublic sectors must, through its bargaining agent, present in writing to the other party its proposals on all the matters that are to be negotiated at the national and regional levels no later than 150 days before the date of expiration of a collective agreement. In turn, the management negotiating committee in these sectors must, within 60 days following receipt of these proposals, present in writing to the other party and to the Committee of Information on Negotiations their proposals on all the matters that are to be negotiated.

The Bill also sets out procedures for designating essential workers to whom the right to strike is denied. This designation process is a matter of negotiation between both sides, with the Essential Services Council having the final say in the case of any disagreement about the designation of specific workers.

In June, 1982, the Quebec government passed Bill 72 to ensure the continuance of essential services *at all times* in the health and social service sectors. The Bill applies also to telephone services, subways, buses, ferries, agencies responsible for the production, transmission, distribution or sale of gas, water and electricity, garbage removal services, ambulance services, the Canadian Red Cross Association, and unspecified government agencies. In addition, the government, on the recommendation of the Minister of Labour, may require the employer and union to maintain essential services in the event of a strike if the government believes that a strike in the public service might endanger public health and safety. Such an order must be made not later than 15 days before the union acquires the right to strike.

Similar action may be undertaken after a strike has already begun if the government believes the essential services are insufficiently covered and that there is therefore a danger to public health and safety. The suspension of strike activity is effective until it is proved to the government that adequate essential services will be rendered. In order to ensure the maintenance of essential services, the parties are required to reach agreement on the essential services to be maintained. If they are unable to reach agreement, the union must establish a list of the services which, in its view, must be maintained in the event of a strike.

An important part of the Bill is the establishment of an Essential Services Council composed of eight members — a chair, two persons chosen after consultation with management and two after consultation with labour, and three other members. The Council has the responsibility of assessing whether an agreement by the parties on essential services, or the list supplied by the union, is adequate to maintain the necessary level of essential services. If the Council finds the proposed services inadequate, it may propose amendments to the joint agreement of the parties or the list supplied by the union — the Council is not empowered, however, to impose amendments. The Council must report every case to the Minister of Labour where essential services provided for in a joint agreement or a union list are inadequate, or

where they are not rendered during a strike. It must also indicate the extent to which this constitutes a danger to the pubic. The Council must inform the public of the contents of any such report made to the Minister. The Bill prohibits lockouts by employers in establishments deemed to be providing essential services. It also imposes heavy fines for workers, union leaders and managers, and unions and employers who declare or instigate a strike or lockout contrary to the provision of the Labour Code.

By establishing a mechanism for determining and requiring the provision of essential services during a strike, and by giving the Cabinet the power to prohibit or suspend a strike for an indefinite period, the Quebec government is moving away from the frequent use of special back-to-work legislation which has characterized labour relations in the public sector in that province for years. The Bill also contains provisions which facilitate class-action suits.

The Essential Services Council (Conseil des services essentiels) was established on December 1, 1982 and now has a full complement of members, a support staff, and a Professional Services Branch which includes several mediators. From the time the Council was established until December 31, 1984, it handled well over 500 essential services cases. These cases included the maintenance of essential transportation services in the City of Montreal during the morning and evening rush hours. Transportation services were maintained in other communities as well. The Council has also dealt with such services as snow removal (in order for ambulances and police vehicles to operate), garbage removal, radio communications in police departments, telephones, and sanitation. Ninety-five percent of the cases were resolved without recommendations by the Council. Most of the other 5% were settled on the basis of recommendations made by the Council after consultation with the parties involved.

One of the strengths of the Council is that it tries to mediate with the parties when it believes that insufficient services are being supplied.

Council mediators work with the parties to try to obtain negotiated settlements, and sometimes engage in bench mediation where the parties appear before the full membership of the Council. In difficult cases, the Council conducts public hearings to which the press and public are invited. The resultant publicity brings pressure to bear on the parties to make concessions and thus to agree on the number of people needed to provide essential services. Thus far, only one of the Council's recommendations has been refused. In that case, the workers went back to work, however, one day after the recommendation was made.[54]

In 1987 Quebec passed Bill 30 to establish a Commission on Industrial Relations (Commission des relations du travail), which was to have functions similar to those of labour relations boards. It would ensure the rights of employees to unionize and administer the certification process. It would also have the power to enforce most provisions of the Labour Code by mediation, and if necessary, by ordering the persons concerned to comply with its directive. The commission was also designed to replace the Essential Services Council in seeing that essential services were provided in the event of a strike, as well as taking charge of the certification process. The duties of the Labour Court and the Essential Services Council would also have been part of its mandate. However, there has been such hostility to the proposed commission by the parties that the legislation establishing it, while passed by the Quebec Assembly, has not been proclaimed. However, it is possible that the Quebec government wishes to maintain the Bill as a threat to motivate the parties to try to resolve their disputes without its implementation.

Ever since collective bargaining was granted to public and parapublic workers in Quebec, many serious confrontations have occurred between unions and the Quebec government. The use of special back-to-work legislation had become almost commonplace in practically every round of negotiations. It is to be hoped that the Essential Services Council will continue to play an effective role. Since no government has lasted more than two sets of negotiations, some correlation may exist between the incidence of public-sector negotiations and changes in government.[55]

Summary of Dispute Resolution

In studying the literature on public-sector bargaining, it becomes clear that Canada has been bolder than the United States in experimenting with different forms of dispute resolution. "One of the more apparent differences between the two countries is the relative toleration displayed by Canadians toward public-sector strikes and strike rights compared to the *de jure* strike paranoia which exists in many parts of the United States."[56] In order to complete an already complex picture, we should indicate that, if a group of workers in any jurisdiction should go on strike and the government has used any or all of the means mentioned above, special back-to-work legislation may always be used as a last resort. There have been many cases, in both the federal and provincial sectors, where governments have enacted special back-to-work legislation in order to terminate a strike when it was felt that the public would no longer tolerate it. This might happen in a province where arbitration is the final form of dispute resolution, or in the federal jurisdiction should an arbitration decision be considered so meager that the workers affected would rather strike than accept the award. In some critical public-sector disputes, the final judgement concerning the prevention or ending of a strike must be exercised by elected politicians.

Since we have discussed in some detail the contract negotiation dispute at the federal and provincial levels, we shall now briefly discuss contract interpretation disputes at these levels. Wages and strikes in the public and parapublic sectors will be discussed in the following chapter, which deals with the outputs of the Canadian industrial relations system.

Rights Disputes

The Grievance Process and Adjudication of Rights Disputes at the Federal Level

All collective agreements covering federal public servants contain a provision requiring adjudication of contract interpretation or rights disputes. Some statutes contain the words "by arbitration or otherwise," but do not specify what "otherwise" means. Since the PSSRA contains a fairly elaborate statement on the grievance procedure, we shall discuss this legislation in some detail and then look briefly at a few provisions in some of the other jurisdictions. ("Adjudication" is used to refer to grievance arbitration, since the PSSRA uses the term "arbitration" with reference to contract negotiation or interest disputes.)

Section 90(1) of the Act states that a worker who feels aggrieved by the interpretation or application of "a provision of a statute, or of a regulation, bylaw, direction or other instrument made or issued by the employer, dealing with terms and conditions of employment, or a provision of a collective agreement or arbitral award" or as a result of any occurrence or matter affecting the terms or conditions of employment, may carry a complaint through the various steps of the grievance procedure from the level of the direct supervisor up to that of the department's deputy minister. However, a worker is not entitled to present a grievance relating to the interpretation or application of a provision of a collective agreement or an arbitrable award without the approval and participation of the responsible bargaining agent. The only kinds of grievances that may go to adjudication are those relating to the interpretation or application of a provision of a collective agreement or an arbitral award, or those relating to disciplinary action resulting in discharge, suspension, or financial penalty. Otherwise, the final appeal is to the deputy minister.

In the case of discharge, suspension, or disciplinary action, any worker, whether a member of a bargaining unit or not, may seek the help of a bargaining agent in presenting the case to adjudication. In the federal public sector, the worker initiates and pursues the grievance, not only through the grievance procedure, but also to adjudication, although the case may be prepared with the support and active assistance of the bargaining agent. This differs somewhat from arbitration in the private sector, where the arbitration of rights disputes is in the name of the union and not in the name of the worker.

In his report, Mr. Finkelman recommended that the federal Act be amended to allow a bargaining agent and the employer to include in a collective agreement a provision that the bargaining agent be entitled to present grievances on behalf of a worker with certain safeguards built into the process to protect the worker if he or she does not wish to pursue a grievance.[57] This recommendation seems valid since the bargaining agent, for example, may want to have a clause in a collective agreement brought to arbitration in order to obtain a clear and definitive interpretation of its meanings.

Mr. Finkelman makes a number of other suggestions for changes in matters subject to adjudication. Among these are that classification grievances be made adjudicable and that a provision be included in any revision of the Act which would give an adjudicator the right to substitute his or her judgement for that of management in cases involving suspension or discharge which, in most cases, results in lesser penalties. It would seem reasonable that any revision of the Act should incorporate the latter provision since it is provided in all private-sector statutes and is also part of the Ontario Crown Employees Collective Bargaining Act.[58]

Grievance Procedures in Provincial Jurisdictions

Only the Manitoba Civil Service Act makes no reference to a grievance procedure. The B.C. statute contains provisions relating to arbitration of grievances under the Public Service Act and also refers to grievances regarding dismissal, discipline, or suspension in addition to the traditional interpretation, application or alleged violation of a collective agreement. The Ontario statute provides for the establishment of a Grievance Settlement Board, to deal with the interpretation, application, or alleged violation of a collective agreement. The Ontario statute also states that, in addition to these kinds of grievances under a collective agreement, a worker claiming:

(a) that his position has been improperly classified, (b) that he has been appraised contrary to the governing principles and standards, or (c) that he has been disciplined or dismissed or suspended from his employment without just cause, may process such matters in accordance with the grievance procedure in the collective agreement, and failing final determination under such procedure, the matter may be processed [by the Grievance Settlement Board].[59]

The Ontario provision has a broader application than any other statute in Canada governing public-sector workers.

Collective Bargaining at the Municipal Level[60]

Collective bargaining for municipal government workers was introduced at the same time that the provinces passed legislation giving collective bargaining rights to workers in the private sector. The main reason for this is that municipal governments and members of municipal services were defined as "employers" and "employees" respectively under the labour relations legislation enacted in each province. However, in the case of firefighters and police, separate legislation has modified the application of collective bargaining. In most jurisdictions, firefighters and police come under separate statutes, and collective bargaining for the latter group usually ends in binding arbitration. Nowhere in Canada do firefighters have the strike option and in only one or two jurisdictions do police officers have the right to strike.

Most municipal governments with a population of 10,000 or more are now involved in a collective bargaining relationship. At least two or three hundred municipal corporations exist in this category.[61] Apart from police and firefighters, municipal workers are usually divided into two groups, outside and inside workers. Outside workers are defined in the following terms:

employees engaged in maintenance and operational activities relative to municipal services and facilities, e.g. water and sewage services, road and street maintenance, refuse collection and disposal, maintenance of parks, recreational facilities, and public buildings.[62]

Inside workers are defined as:

employees engaged in clerical, accounting and stenographic duties.... Also, ... many ... employees engaged in technical duties relative to engineering, building inspection, property valuation, etc.[63]

In addition, some municipal corporations have to negotiate with other bargaining units. For example, in some provinces municipal governments must deal with unions of public health nurses and technicians.

The largest union in the municipal field in Canada is the Canadian Union of Public Employees (CUPE). In 1988, CUPE had 2,086 local unions across the country with a total membership of 342,000.[64] The major groups represented by CUPE in the municipal field are the inside and outside workers and in most of the medium to large cities there are usually two locals of this union. Quebec is the only province which has developed a sizeable union for municipal workers other than CUPE. This is the Federation canadienne des employés de services publics (Canadian Federation of Public-Service Employees) which is affiliated with the CNTU.[65]

In municipal bargaining, one of the most serious problems is who will represent the municipal corporation as an employer in bargaining with its unions. In this respect, practice varies widely among municipalities of various sizes within and among provinces. In some municipalities, paticularly the smaller ones, negotiations are frequently conducted by a committee of the municipal council assisted by a senior officer who provides staff support. In such cases, the governing body may be reluctant to delegate this responsibility or there may not be a person with sufficient skills to negotiate. Furthermore, where collective bargaining is conducted in this manner, it generally suffers from a lack of continuity since municipal officials are subject to periodic elections.

In many medium to large municipal corporations, the management structure is uncoordinated (i.e., there is no chief executive officer) and comprises a number of departments which report to a committee or council. Such municipalities usually have personnel departments. Responsibility for negotiations may be delegated to the personnel manager. Problems arise, however, when the personnel manager's mandate is not clearly defined: the result may be that union negotiators will undertake direct contact with the council members where negotiations are normally concluded.

In a municipal jurisdiction which has a chief executive officer or agency such as a city manager or city administrator, the responsibility for conducting negotiations is generally assigned to such a person. Under this kind of situation, negotiations may be delegated further to a personnel director or labour relations officer operating under a clear mandate concerning the limits within which he may negotiate. Under this kind of an arrangement, the municipal council as such is not usually directly involved in the negotiations.

A 1977 study of 26 large Canadian cities showed that 21 had a labour relations director or city manager responsible for negotiations, three had elected negotiation officials, and two hired labour lawyers as needed. The study also indicated "that professional and formally trained labour relations specialists had more discretion and authority, less trouble obtaining a mandate from the political officials, and less interference in bargaining than their nonspecialist peers."[66]

In major metropolitan areas, municipal collective bargaining may present special difficulties. For example, a union involved in negotiations in one municipality may be very reluctant to settle until it has a good idea of what the terms of settlement will be in an adjacent municipality. This is a pattern-leader, pattern-follower situation. While the municipalities in these situations may try to coordinate their negotiations, the unions may whipsaw, using an increase obtained from one municipality as a precedent to obtain the same or a larger increase from another municipality.

Other considerations are associated with collective bargaining at the municipal level. The revenues received by municipalities vary. This variation implies much in collective bargaining. Since approximately 60% to 70% of the annual operating budget of a municipality is devoted to salaries, wages, and fringe benefits for its workers, the negotiated salary and wage increases clearly may have a direct effect on the real property tax rate.[67] Although growing municipalities with an increasing tax base may be able to cushion the impact of wage and salary increases, static municipalities or those in decline may find themselves in very serious financial difficulties if they have to raise the tax base substantially in order to meet new wage and salary commitments. A problem is also inherent in the determination of wages and salaries for non-unionized workers. Most municipalities pay their non-union employees, including their managerial and supervisory personnel, increases which are relatively in line with those increases paid to other groups.

While this description of collective bargaining among municipal workers is somewhat abbreviated, it at least provides a basis for understanding what goes on at that level. In times of high inflation and property tax increases, managers and negotiators at the municipal level have difficulty in offering fair wage increases on the one hand, without raising taxes beyond what is economically or politically acceptable to local citizens.

Collective Bargaining in Education and Health Care

Rather than discussing the legislation governing collective bargaining in education and health services in each of the ten provinces, we shall deal here only with the provinces of Quebec, Ontario, and Saskatchewan. A study of these jurisdictions offers an insight into contrasting parapublic systems.

Quebec Education and Health Care

In June, 1978, the Quebec National Assembly passed Bill 55 dealing with the organization of management and union parties for collective bargaining in the sectors of education, social affairs, and government agencies. Under this Bill, the government contemplated a highly centralized form of bargaining in education and social affairs. The result has been the statutory expression of what has been taking place informally for a number of years (i.e., a two-tiered system of negotiations).

Both worker groups (such as local teachers' associations and hospital workers' unions) and management teams are organized into national negotiating committees which wrestle with most of the substantive wage and policy issues in collective bargaining. A separate national negotiating committee is established for education, health care, and the public sector. Usually, these committees will negotiate separately but, in some years (such as in 1972 and 1982), they form a common front.

The national committees may allow certain subjects to be negotiated at a lower (local or regional) level, thus permitting the insertion of clauses in the national contract which reflect specific regional concerns. In general, however, the contract negotiated by the national committees is binding on all affiliated worker and management groups. Management negotiators are directly responsible to the ministers of social affairs and education. In fact, these ministers must personally sign any contract approved for the educational sector. The Quebec Treasury Board is responsible for ensuring the orderly progress of talks and for authorizing the management committee's negotiation positions where these represent a particular concern to the provincial government.

Politicians play a very prominent role in education and social affairs in Quebec. This role is important because both Liberal and Péquiste governments in Quebec have totally opposed the use of compulsory arbitration in the public and parapublic sectors. The government allocates a certain amount of money to the educational sector and a certain amount to the social affairs sector which includes health care. It is then up to the minister concerned to engineer an agreement which respects as closely as possible these budget estimates.

It is not known what effect highly centralized negotiations have on parties at the local level. However, it is reasonable to assume that local parties may feel greatly frustrated in being obligated to live with agreements negotiated with little of their own input. Nonetheless, J. Boivin contends that centralized bargaining in the public health and educational sectors reflects and is generally supported by the cultural situation of French Canadians:

> Each successive government since 1960 has clearly affirmed the necessity to build a strong and centralized administration in order to preserve and maintain the peculiar cultural distinction of Quebec in North America. Such need for a centralized form of government in Quebec contrasts singularly with the home rule or local community syndrome which is typical of the rest of North America.[68]

During the summer of 1989, nurses in Quebec adopted a work-to-rule campaign and also cut down sharply on the use of part-time work. The President of the Quebec Federation of Nurses, which represents 90% of the province's 40,000 nurses, commented that "when a lot of nurses [cut down on overtime and part-time work] at the same time, it highlights the problems of the health-care system and gives a real insight into its shortcomings."[69] The Essential Services Council was trying to determine if the refusal of full-time nurses to do overtime and the refusal of part-time nurses to work more than two days a week at 51 hospitals constituted a breach of the Quebec Labour Code.[70]

Education and Health Care in Ontario

Prior to the passage of the School Boards and Teachers Collective Negotiations Act of 1975, the province of Ontario permitted school boards and teacher associations to bargain independently of government. However, with the passage of the Act, a more elaborate scheme was put into place. The Act, administered by a special body designated as the Education Relations Commission, provides for negotiations between local school boards and teachers' association branches, although representatives from national teacher associations attend local negotiations. Bargaining takes place separately for elementary and secondary school teachers, but nothing in the Act prohibits the parties from negotiating jointly for both levels.

With respect to third-party assistance, the Act provides for the appointment of a fact-finder who, in the event of stalled negotiations, may make recommendations on any items in dispute. The report of a fact-finder is meant to serve as a basis for further negotiations toward the attainment of a settlement, but it may be made public if an agreement is not reached within 15 days. The underlying assumption is that making the report public in the local community will put pressure on both school board and teacher negotiators to come to a settlement. Should negotiations drag on, the statute provides for the appointment of a mediator who may become more actively involved than a fact-finder in the actual negotiations. The statute also provides for arbitration which allows for final-offer selection of the total-package type. This provision, however, has seldom been used.

Unlike the situation in Quebec where school board and teacher negotiations are highly centralized, Ontario negotiations tend to be very decentralized. So far, it does not appear as if there is any trend toward greater centralization of school board and teacher negotiations.[71]

Hospitals and nursing homes in Ontario operate under the Ontario Hospital Labour Disputes Arbitration Act of 1965, which provides for binding arbitration of contract negotiation disputes in hospitals and nursing homes. Until relatively recently, the hospitals bargained on a decentralized basis, each hospital negotiating its own agreement with nurses and other groups. In recent years, however, and particularly since 1981, a dramatic move has occurred toward centralized negotiations.

During the winter of 1981, a large number of hospitals attempted to negotiate a settlement with CUPE, which bargains for many hospital workers. A negotiating team was drawn from a representative number of hospitals. When negotiations broke down, CUPE negotiators refused to go along with the provision of the Ontario statute requiring the appointment of a member to an arbitration board. In fact, CUPE leaders recommended a strike in protest against the arbitration proceedings, since the union felt that it would not catch up or get a settlement large enough to bring its workers into line with other groups. CUPE, furthermore, advised workers to disobey a court injunction ordering striking workers to return to work.

It is generally conceded by observers that the strike was badly organized. Not surprisingly, therefore, it failed after a couple of weeks. A number of CUPE leaders were sentenced to prison or were fined for encouraging workers to defy the court injunction.[72] Even when an arbitration board was set up under the chairmanship of the highly respected P. Weiler, a former chair of the B.C. Labour Relations Board, CUPE refused to name its representative to the arbitration board, and the government was obliged to name a person to represent the union. When the arbitration decision was handed down, many workers and union leaders felt the decision was slanted in favour of management.

The trend toward centralization of collective bargaining among hospitals in Ontario is, as we mentioned before, a fairly recent phenomenon. However, it is significant that over 100 hospitals joined together to bargain on a provincial basis during the round of negotiations in the winter of 1981. While there is no province-wide bargaining among Ontario hospitals, developments in recent years point to increasing centralization.

With respect to nursing homes, the picture in Ontario is a very different one. Practically all the nursing homes in the province negotiate on an individual basis. Few, if any, signs exist that coordinated or province-wide bargaining among nursing homes is likely to begin. This indication may be because some of the nursing homes are government-owned and operated while others are private concerns. In addition, nursing homes do not rely solely on provincial funds as hospitals do: they receive money from both residents and government.

In summary, then, one may identify a developing trend toward more centralized bargaining among hospital workers in Ontario which has yet to make itself felt among nursing home staff. Also, there is a growing disenchantment with the arbitration process in the health care field.

Education and Health Care in Saskatchewan

Negotiations for teachers in Saskatchewan are conducted under the Teacher Collective Bargaining Act (1973) which is administered by the Education Relations Board. The Act provides for two-tier bargaining with one set of clauses negotiated at the provincial level and another at the local level. The Saskatchewan Teachers' Federation is the bargaining agent in provincial negotiations. The employers' association is the Saskatchewan School Trustees Association.

The statute provides that the Federation shall, prior to the commencement of negotiations and in any case no later than 101 days prior to the date on which an agreement negotiated

pursuant to the Act expires, prepare written notice specifying the process for resolution, whether mediation, conciliation, or arbitration. The Saskatchewan statute does not allow teachers to strike. Stewardship of the employers' interests is shared by the Saskatchewan School Trustees Association (SSTA) and by government representatives.[73] The management negotiating team consists of nine members, four appointed by the SSTA and five by the government. Of the five government representatives, four are from the Department of Education and one from the Department of Finance.

Under this hybrid structure, the government contingent has a controlling vote in policy and position formulation. The government's main concern is with the high cost of settlements. Currently it pays in the range of 30% to 85% of the local operating costs of school districts. Hence any significant concessions would likely require a substantial increase in public spending. Although the SSTA wants to become the major negotiator for management, the government is reluctant to give up the control it now exercises. A recent study by Wetzel and Gallagher concludes that

> to varying degrees, the Saskatchewan government has managed to divest itself of direct bargaining roles, assured that its legitimate interests will be adequately protected. Having been reasonably satisfied with the system during the recent bargaining round, there are no signs that the government wants any drastic change.[74]

Negotiations have become centralized not only in the Saskatchewan educational sector but also in the Saskatchewan health care sector. The government has encouraged hospitals and nursing homes to sign their bargaining rights over to two non-governmental provincial industry associations. The Saskatchewan Health-Care Association (SHA) represents the province's 107 unionized hospitals in bargaining, a responsibility it has carried since 1973. The Saskatchewan Association of Special Care Homes (SASCH) negotiates for 38 of its 110 member nursing homes, a function it took over in 1975. A government observer is present at negotiations for both hospitals and nursing homes.

The government seems anxious to avoid direct participation in these bargaining relationships. Wetzel and Gallagher point out that, "by placing distance between itself and the negotiations, the government endeavours to reduce its vulnerability to direct pressure from unions for bargaining concessions."[75] The SHA and SASCH both believe that maximum freedom from government interference can be attained by demonstrating trustworthiness in evolving reasonably stable relationships with the unions and in producing prudent settlements. Hence, in Saskatchewan, the highly centralized structure of bargaining in the educational and health care fields parallels the centralized structure of negotiations in the province of Quebec, except that Quebec politicians play a more active role.[76]

Conclusion

In this chapter, we analyzed the collective bargaining process in the public sector, at the federal, provincial and municipal levels, as well as in the parapublic sectors of education and health care in three provinces.

We began by discussing the historical evolution of unions and collective bargaining in the public and parapublic sectors along with the "sovereignty issue." By using three of the four classical types of disputes discussed in Chapter 6 for the private sector, we discussed the recognition process, the contract negotiation process and forms of third party assistance if negotiation between the parties fail, and the contract interpretation dispute. Finally, we discussed the collective bargaining process at the municipal level, and then focused on the education and health care sectors in Ontario, Quebec and Saskatchewan.

Questions

1　What kinds of workers are usually referred to as public and parapublic workers?

2　Do most jurisdictions in Canada have one statute governing both private and public-sector workers, or do most have at least two statutes?

3　Do you think that public-sector workers should have the right to collective bargaining? Should they have the right to strike?

4　How does the collective bargaining regime for public-sector workers, especially those covered by the federal Public Service Staff Relations Act, differ from the regime for workers in the private sector?

5　How have the various jurisdictions in Canada attempted to cope with strikes in essential services in the public and parapublic sectors? What is your assessment of these attempts?

6　How does collective bargaining apply to the educational and health care sectors in the provinces of Ontario, Quebec, and Saskatchewan?

7　If you were an advisor to a government contemplating the establishment of collective bargaining for its public servants, what would be the essential components of the scheme that you would suggest? Elaborate.

8　Prepare a list of services which are so essential that workers who perform them should not have the right to strike. Elaborate on the rationale for the inclusion of each service.

9　Are there goods or services in the private sector which are so essential that workers involved in them should not have the right to strike? Elaborate.

10　Do you feel that you have suffered personally as a result of an essential-service strike? Elaborate.

Notes

1 S.B. Goldenberg, "Collective Bargaining in the Provincial Public Services," *Collective Bargaining in the Public Sector* (Toronto: Institute of Public Administration of Canada, 1973), p. 11; "Public Sector Labour Relations in Canada," *Public-Sector Bargaining*, eds. B. Aaron, R. Grodin, and J. L. Stern, Industrial Relations Research Association Series (Washington: The Bureau of National Affairs Inc., 1979), p. 256.

2 W. B. Cunningham, "Public Employment, Collective Bargaining and the Conventional Wisdom: U.S.A. and Canada," Vol. 21, No. 3, *Relations Industrielles/Indusrial Relations* (July, 1966), pp. 408-09. Cunningham provides an excellent critique of the conventional wisdom regarding the sovereignty of a state.

3 R. W. Flemming, "Public-Employee Bargaining: Problems and Prospects," *Proceedings*, Thirty-First Annual Meeting of the IRRA, (Madison, Wis.: IRRA, 1979), p. 6.

4 K. P. Swan, "Public Bargaining in Canada and the U.S.: A Legal View," Vol. 19, No. 3, *Industrial Relations* (Fall 1980), p. 278.

5 C. A. Edwards, "The Public Service Alliance of Canada," Vol. 23, No. 4, *Relations Industrielles/Industrial Relations* (1968), p. 636.

6 J. B. Rose, "Growth Patterns of Public Sector Unions," *Conflict or Compromise: The Future of Public Sector Industrial Relations*, eds. M. Thompson and G. Swimmer (Montreal: The Institute for Research on Public Policy, 1984), p. 97.

7 Edwards, "The Public Service Alliance of Canada," p. 635.

8 Bureau of Labour Information, Labour Canada, *Directory of Labour Organization in Canada 1988* (Ottawa: Supply and Services Canada, 1988), p. 123.

9 Ibid., pp. 124-129.

10 Rose, "Growth Patterns of Public Sector Unions," p. 100.

11 Ibid.

12 J. Finkelman and S. Goldenberg, *Collective Bargaining in the Public Sector: The Federal Experience in Canada* (Montreal: The Institute for Research on Public Policy, 1983), p. 4. This comprehensive study of collective bargaining under the federal PSSRA will go down as a classic piece of analysis in the annals of industrial relations research in Canada.

13 Bureau of Labour Information, Labour Canada, *Directory of Labour Organizations in Canada 1988* (Ottawa: Minister of Supply and Services, 1988), p. 16.

14 Rose, "Growth Patterns of Public Sector Unions," p. 100.

15 Ibid.

16 S. Goldenberg, "Collective Bargaining in the Provincial Public Sector," p. 29.

17 Ibid., p. 37; K. Wetzel and D. G. Gallagher, "The Saskatchewan Government's Internal Arrangements to Accommodate Collective Bargaining," Vol. 34, No. 3, *Relations Industrielles/Industrial Relations* (1979), pp. 452-70.

18 Wetzel and Gallagher, "The Saskatchewan Government's Internal Arrangements to Accommodate Collective Bargaining," pp. 455-56.

19 Goldenberg, "Collective Bargaining in the Provincial Public Sector," p. 37.

20 P.E.I. Civil Service Act, *Regulations*, Part XV, 66(d).

21 Public Service Staff Relations Act, R.S.C., c. P-35 with amendments up to 1978-79, Schedule 1, Parts 1 and 2.

22 Quebec Labour Code, R.S.Q., C-27 with amendments up to November, 1988, s. 111.0.16

23 Ontario Regulations 577/72 under the Crown Employees Collective Bargaining Act, 1972, ss. 1-10.

24 British Columbia Industrial Relations Act, R.S. Chap. 212, 1979, ss. 137.1 and 154.

25 Statistics provided by the Public Service Staff Relations Branch, Treasury Board of Canada.

26 S.N.B., 1968, c. 88, s. 24(5) (a).

27 R.S.A., 1980, c. P-33, s. 18.

28 R.S.A., 1980, c. P-33, s. 22(3).

29 R.S.O., 1980, c. 108, s. 56(c)(i).

30 The information contained herein was derived, at least in part, from a telephone conversation with the Registrar of the Ontario Public Service Labour Relations Tribunal, June 19, 1981.

31 "Ontario Crown Attorneys Granted Bargaining Rights," *Globe and Mail*, June 20, 1989, p. A8.

32 Goldenberg, "Collective Bargaining in the Provincial Public Services," p. 26.

33 S.N.S., 1978, c. 3, Schedule "A."

34 R.S.C., c. P-35 with amendments up to 1978-79,

s. 34(c); R.S.B.C., 1979, Ch. 346, s. 5(b); R.S.A., 1980, c. P-33, as amended up to January 18, 1984, ss. 25 and 29; S.S. as of October 1983, c. T-17, ss. 6(2) (b) and 8; R.S.O., 1980, c. 108, s. 4; R.S.Q., c. C-27 with amendments up to April 1, 1984, ss. 21 and 28; S.N. 1973, No. 123, ss. 6 and 7. The Ontario statute also makes provision for prehearing votes which are conducted in the same way as they are conducted in the private sector.

35 J. Finkelman, Q.C., Pt. 1, *Employer-Employee Relations in the Public Service of Canada: Proposals for Legislative Change* (Ottawa: Information Canada, 1974), p. 232.

36 R.S.C., c. P-35 with amendments up to 1978-79, s. 70(3).

37 R.S.A., 1980, c. P-35, s. 48(2); R.S.O., 1980, C. 108, s. 18.

38 R.S.B.C., 1979, Ch. 346, s. 13.

39 R.S.B.C., 1979, Ch. 346, s. 11(1) (a) (b).

40 *Report of the Royal Commission on Employer-Employee Relations in the Public Service of New Brunswick* (1967), p. 34.

41 R.S.C., c. P-35 with amendments up to 1978-79, s. 70(1); S.N.B., 1968, c. P-25, s. 84(1).

42 R.S.C., c. P-35 with amendments up to 1978-79, s. 68.

43 Finkelman, Pt. 1, *Employer-Employee Relations in the Public Service*, p. 125.

44 Finkelman, "Voluntary Arbitration," an address prepared for delivery to the Electrical Contractors Association of Ottawa, May 5, 1972; mimeographed and unpublished.

45 J. Crispo, "Collective Bargaining in the Public Sector: Seminar Report," *Collective Bargaining in the Public Sector*, pp. 95-105, particularly pp. 101-05.

46 R.S.C., c. P-35 with amendments up to 1978-79, s. 78; and S.N.B., 1968, c. 88, s. 49.

47 R.S.C., c. P-35 with amendments up to 1978-79, s. 86(3).

48 S.N.B., 1968, c. 88, s. 57(1).

49 Much of the material on the federal statute is taken from the author's own study which is cited as the source for Table 10.1.

50 S.N.S., 1978, c. 3, s. 33(2).

51 R.S.B.C., 1979, Ch. 346, s. 17(7)-(10).

52 S.N., 1983, c. 24, s. 3. This became section 17.1 of the Public Service (Collective Bargaining) Act, 1973.

53 S.N., 1983, c. 24, s. 2. This section replaces section 10 of the Act, ibid.

54 The author is deeply indebted to Mr. B. Bastien, former chair and Mr. A. Gagnon, member, of the Quebec Essential Services Council for the information which they so freely supplied on the operations of the Council. The present chair is Madeleine Lemieux.

55 G. Hebert, "Public Sector Bargaining in Quebec: A Case of Hypercentralization," *Conflict or Compromise: The Future of Public Sector Industrial Relations*, eds. Thompson and Swimmer, pp. 229-81.

56 P. Feuille and J. C. Anderson, "Public Sector Bargaining: Policy and Practice," Vol. 19, No. 3, *Industrial Relations* (Fall, 1980), p. 316.

57 Finkelman, Pt. 1, *Employer-Employee Relations in the Public Service of Canada*, pp. 179-80.

58 R.S.O., 1980, c. 108, s. 19(3).

59 R.S.O., 1980, c. 108, s. 18(2).

60 Much of the information in this section is drawn from T. J. Plunkett, "Municipal Collective Bargaining," *Collective Bargaining in the Public Service*, pp. 1-10.

61 Ibid., p. 4.

62 Ibid.

63 Ibid.

64 Bureau of Labour Information, Labour Canada, *Directory of Labour Organizations in Canada*, 1988, p. 57.

65 Plunkett, "Municipal Collective Bargaining," p. 6.

66 Feuille and Anderson, "Public Sector Bargaining: Policy and Practice," p. 313.

67 Plunkett, "Municipal Collective Bargaining," p. 9.

68 J. Boivin, *The Evolution of Bargaining Power in the Province of Quebec's Public Sector (1964-1972)* (Quebec City: Department des relations industrielles, Université Laval, January 1975), p. 313.

69 "Quebec Queries Legality of Boycott by Nurses," *Globe and Mail*, June 20, 1989.

70 Ibid.

71 For a recent discussion of negotiations in the Ontario grade school system, see B. M. Downie, "Collective Bargaining Under an Essential Services Disputes Commission," *Conflict or Compromise: The Future of Public Sector Industrial Relations*, eds. Thompson and Swimmer, pp. 373-401.

72   W. List, "Hartman Sentenced to Forty-Five Days in Prison," *Globe and Mail* (June 12, 1981), p. 1.

73   Wetzel and Gallagher, "The Saskatchewan Government's Internal Arrangements to Accommodate Collective Bargaining," p. 464.

74   Ibid., p. 468.

75   Ibid., p. 459.

76   For an interesting comparison of the approaches of Canada's three western provinces in hospital negotiations, see K. Wetzel and D. B. Gallagher, "Management Structures to Accommodate Multi-Employer Hospital Bargaining in Western Canada," *Conflict or Compromise: The Future of Public Sector Industrial Relations*, eds. Thompson and Swimmer, pp. 282-313.

Dick Hemingway

11

The Outputs of the Canadian Industrial Relations System

Introduction

In Chapter 1 we defined the emerging discipline of industrial relations as a complex of private and public activities, operating in a specified environment and concerned with the allocation of rewards to workers for their services and the conditions under which the services are rendered. So far, our discussion has centred primarily on the actors, the environment, and the complex of private and public activities — under which we include the labour movement, the legislative provisions, the negotiation process, the forms of third-party assistance, the grievance procedure and the arbitration of contract interpretation disputes — that make up the industrial relations system. It is now time to turn our attention to a discussion of the outputs of industrial relations systems.

The outputs or rewards to workers for their services are at the very core of the dependent variables of our framework. They are the raison d'être of industrial relations systems. While most of a collective agreement's clauses benefit

Figure 11.1 **Sample Table of Contents of a Collective Agreement: Index**

Article	Page	Section
1. Scope	1	1.01-1.04
2. Recognition	1	2.01-2.03
Contracting Out	2	2.04
3. No Discrimination	3	3.01-3.03
4. Management	4	4.01
5. Union Security	4	5.01-5.03
6. No Cessation of Work	5	6.01
7. Adjustment of Grievances		
Differences Between the Company and Workers	5	7.01-7.07
Differences Between Company and Union	9	7.08
Time Limit Extensions	10	7.09
General Grievance Committee—Grievance Stewards and Plant Committeemen	10	7.10-7.22
8. Third Party Determination	14	8.01
Grievance Commissioner	14	8.02-8.05
Arbitration Board	15	8.06-8.13
9. Discharge and Discipline	18	9.01-9.04
10. Workers in Armed Forces	19	10.01
11. Seniority		
Definitions	20	11.01
Applications of Seniority on Layoff	21	11.02-11.07
Application of Seniority in a Department	24	11.08-11.09
Application of Seniority—Curtailment in Operations	25	11.10
Temporary Promotions, Demotions, and Transfers	26	11.11
Job Posting	26	11.12-11.20
Transfers General	31	11.21-11.23
Leaves of Absence	32	11.24-11.31
General (Designated Individuals, Summer Workers, Seniority List)	36	11.32-11.36
12. Establishment of New Department, Transfers, and Special Seniority Provisions	37	12.01-12.05

Article	Page	Section
Stationary Engineers, Refrigeration Operators, and Compressor Operators	69	20.12-20.15
Incentive for Study Courses	70	20.16
21. General Training	71	21.01-21.06
22. Incentives	73	22.01-22.07
23. Pensions	75	23.01-23.02
24. Insurances, Health, and Hospital Services	76	24.01-24.05
25. Cost of Living Allowance	77	25.01
26. Authority	79	26.01
27. Further Conferences	79	27.01-27.02
28. Termination	80	28.01
Signatures	81	
Schedules		
"A" Classifications of Workers Excluded from the Bargaining Unit	82	
"B" Rules Governing Proceedings of Grievance Commissioner	89	
"C" Rules of Arbitration	90	
"D" Departments	91	
"E" Classifications Entitled to Preferential Recall	92	
"F" Wages Rates	93	
"G" Apprentice Wage Rates	94	
"H" Plant Committeeman Areas	96	
"J" S.H.E. Committee Areas	98	
Worker Benefit Plans		
Group Term Life Insurance Plan	100	
Group Non-Occupational Accidental Death and Dismemberment Insurance Plan	103	
Prescription Drug Plan	105	
Non-Occupational Sickness and Accident Insurance Plan	106	
Dental Plan	107	
Letters of Agreement		

workers, they may benefit *or* detract from management's objectives.

Most of the benefits that unions obtain for their members result from the power they wield in the negotiation process. Management is often confronted with the threat of strikes or actual strikes, and it must determine how far it is willing to go in opposing union demands. If it perceives its bargaining power as relatively weak compared to that of the union, it is more likely to settle closer to the union's position than would otherwise be the case. This is in keeping with our discussion of the role of bargaining power in Chapter 7.

We will discuss two kinds of outputs — organizational and worker-oriented — and will follow the breakdown given by Beal, Wickersham, and Kienast in *The Practice of Collective Bargaining*.[1] Among the organizational outputs, we will examine management rights, union recognition, union security, and dues check-off. Three types of worker-oriented outputs will be considered: (1) the wage and effort bargain including wage rates, hours, and pay for time not worked, such as holidays and paid vacations; (2) job rights and due process, which will involve items such as seniority, just cause in cases of discipline and discharge, some aspects of the grievance process, and the establishment of reasonable rules and fair treatment; and (3) contingency benefits, including compensation for layoffs, permanent separation from a job, illness, accidents, or untimely death, provisions to protect workers' health and safety, and superannuation, pensions, and insurance plans for workers. In addition to organizational and worker-related outputs, this chapter will also deal with a third output of the industrial relations system: industrial conflict, be it in the form of strikes or lockouts.

When collective bargaining first started in North America, collective agreements were basically one page in length. Workers would post a new wage schedule on the employer's door and await the employer's approval. Over the years many items other than wages have become the subject of negotiations, and present-day collective agreements are, as a result, very complex. A quick glance at Figure 11.1, which sets out the table of contents from a Canadian collective agreement, shows the tremendous amount of detail now involved.

Organizational Outputs

Management Rights Clauses

It is important to consider this clause since anything not contained in the collective agreement usually gives management the right to do whatever it perceives to be best for the organization. Management rights clauses usually refer to the prerogatives of management to operate the enterprise subject to the terms of a collective agreement. The following is an example of these clauses:

> Nothing in this agreement shall be deemed to restrict the management in any way in the performance of all functions of management except those specifically abridged or modified by this agreement.[2]

Table 11.1 shows that the vast majority of agreements covering about three-quarters of workers contain management rights provisions.[3] A major controversy exists over the so-called "residual rights theory" of management. Management claims to have unilateral control over all decision-making unless otherwise stated in the collective agreement. Management further contends that if there is no clause in a collective agreement with respect to a particular issue, it has the right to make unilateral decisions on that issue. Most union leaders argue, on the other hand, that no such thing as residual management rights exist since the mere ownership and operation of capital does not give management the authority to rule on all matters concerning workers. Some labour leaders also argue that unions have the right to bargain not only over personnel matters, but also investment policy, pricing policy, and a variety of

Table 11.1	The Incidence of Management Rights Clauses in Collective Agreements Covering 500 or More Workers	
	Agreements	Workers
	%	%
General statement of management rights	30.0	36.0
Enumerated list of management rights, residual with management	24.5	18.3
Enumerated list of management rights, residual rights silent	22.7	19.2
No provision	22.7	26.3
Total	100.0	100.0

Source: A special computer printout from Labour Canada as of February 1985. The universe for this analysis is 963 collective agreements in force covering 2,044,660 workers.

other areas in which management has traditionally had sole discretion.

An example of where management takes unilateral action is in ordering workers to do certain things that they feel they are not obligated to do by the collective agreement. In such cases management insists that workers do the work that they are instructed to do and then take the matter up through the grievance procedure if they feel that the collective agreement has been breached.

We noted in Chapter 9 that J.W. Kuhn believes that workers prefer a hearing and a decision *before* an act rather than justice *after* the act. It is also instructive to note that in a number of Canadian jurisdictions workers may refuse to do work which they *believe* to be harmful to their health or safety.

Irrespective of the merits of the two schools of thought on this issue, there is no question that unions have, through collective bargaining, acquired a much broader role in decision-making than was the case some years ago. For example, management at one time claimed that pension plans were not negotiable and that the administration of such plans was a management prerogative. Following a lengthy strike in the United States in 1947, however, pension plans became negotiable in the steel industry. This decision set a precedent which soon affected practically all other industries on the North American continent. Hence, as unions have gained the right to bargain over more and more issues, the area of management discretion or residual rights has narrowed considerably. This trend has not, however, eliminated the major philosophical differences between union and management spokespersons over the whole issue.

Union Recognition Clauses

Provisions to recognize a union as the sole bargaining agent for a group of workers resemble management rights clauses, since both serve to define the relationship between two organizational entities. Usually, specific reference is made to the group of workers represented; for example, all the production and maintenance workers at Plant X located in City Y. The practice of including such clauses in collective agreements is, in some cases, a holdover from the days of voluntary recognition, where there were no laws requiring employers to negotiate in good faith with a certified bargaining agent. Today, most certificates issued by labour relations boards name the bargaining agent and also the group of workers for which it is the exclusive representative. This sometimes creates difficulties at a later stage when occupations in the original certificate begin to disappear and new ones evolve. Unless unions and management can agree to define the term "employee" in the certificate to include individuals in jobs not explicitly mentioned, those individuals who logically should be part of the bargaining unit may be technically excluded. (The B.C. Telephone Case in Appendix 1 deals with this problem.) Generally, union recognition clauses are helpful in dealing with this sort of difficulty, which may account, in part, for their survival. In addition, such clauses may also be invoked in filing grievances over matters not explicitly covered in collective agreements.

Union Security Clauses[4]

Union security clauses define the relationship between the union organization and its members. The different types of union security clauses include the closed shop, the maintenance of membership, the union shop, the modified union shop and the Rand formula.

Closed Shop   The term "closed shop" refers to compulsory union membership and to recruitment by and through the union. Labour Canada defines a closed shop as follows:

> The employer is required to hire union members, through the union or from lists supplied by the union. Only if there are none available is the employer permitted to hire others, who must then become and remain union members as a condition of employment.

Closed shops are frequently found in the construction and long-shore industries and are often associated with hiring halls, which represent an arrangement between the union and employer whereby the union agrees to supply the number of workers required.

Maintenance of Membership   Under maintenance of membership clauses, workers are under no obligation to join the union; however, those who do must, as a condition of employment, maintain their union membership throughout the life of the contract.

Union Shop   In a union shop agreement, the employer is entirely free to employ non-union workers, but they must joint the union within a specified period after being hired, and the employer must discharge any who fail to do so.

Modified Union Shop   Under a modified union shop clause,

> employees who are already members are required

to maintain their membership as a condition of employment as with the union shop, but certain groups (usually employees who were not members at the time the workplace was first organized) are exempted. All new employees must, however, join the union.

Rand Formula   The principle behind the Rand Formula is that since the union provides service to all members of the bargaining unit, not just union members, all employees should share in the cost of providing this service. So, while union membership is not compulsory, all employees must pay dues, or their equivalent, to the union. In the United States this type of union security clause is called the "agency shop." In practice, the Rand Formula includes those collective agreements which refer to a union dues check-off procedure for all employees in the absence of any additional information.

Table 11.2 shows that over 90% of agreements, covering over 93% of workers, have union security clauses. The most prevalent of which are the union shop, the modified union shop, and the Rand Formula.

Table 11.2	Union Security Clauses	
	Agreements	Workers
	%	%
Closed Shop	2.8	2.0
Union Shop	22.8	15.7
Modified union shop	19.2	27.7
Maintenance of membership for present and/or future workers	4.4	3.5
Other	0.1	0.0
No provision	50.7	51.0
Total	100.0	100.0

Source: Labour Data Branch, Labour Canada, *Provisions in Collective Agreements in Canada Covering 500 and More Employees: All Industries (Excluding Construction)* (Ottawa: Supply and Services Canada, July 1985), pp. 4-5. Reproduced by permission of the Minister of Supply and Services Canada.

Use of Union Security Clauses The whole issue of union security clauses, and particularly those which require compulsory union membership, is a very controversial one. Some employers take the view that they should not have to require workers to join unions as a condition of employment. They argue that it is the union's job to convince the workers of the merits of union membership and that only those who favour joining unions should be made to do so. Unions respond that membership is a means of increasing solidarity in the bargaining unit and also enables a larger number of workers in the bargaining unit to take part in union affairs, to run for union office, etc.

Employers also argue that the closed shop is a means of enabling unions to restrict the supply of workers by having control over the number of people admitted to a trade. Unions, however, contend that the closed shop, in conjunction with a hiring hall, is a real advantage to employers since the union acts more or less as the employers' recruiting agency. Many heated debates have taken place over compulsory unionism in the past, and they continue today. Among the general public, there is also much disagreement over the appropriateness of union security clauses, a fact which doubtless reflects the divergent opinions of people coming from union and non-union backgrounds.

The use of the closed shop in the Ontario construction industry was challenged under the Charter in the Arlington Crane case in Ontario in 1988. In that case, the owners of a company in Hamilton who operated a crane rental company protested that their grandson could not work for them because of the closed shop provision in the collective agreement governing their segment of the construction industry. Not only did the union have a closed shop, but it required members to take its apprenticeship course in order to belong to it. The Supreme Court of Ontario ruled that the Charter did not apply, since the legislation permitting the closed shop "neither requires nor encourages the parties as a matter of policy to agree to such a union security clause. It only "authorizes" such a provision.[5] The judge who wrote the decision added that the grandson was not being forced to associate with the union. He also stated that "The evidence is that there are non-union crane rental operators carrying on business in Ontario although few in number." The grandson's recourse, "if he so chooses, is to obtain employment with one of them," the judge added.[6]

Check-off Clauses

A check-off clause refers to the practice whereby the employer, by agreement with the union, regularly withholds union dues from workers' wages and transfers these funds to the union. The check-off is a common practice in organized establishments and is not dependent upon the existence of a formal union security clause. The arrangement may also provide for deductions of related initiation fees, assessments, and fines. There are various types of check-off clauses: (1) compulsory check-off, whereby the worker has no option but to have the dues deducted; (2) voluntary revocable check-off, whereby the worker may sign dues over to the union but may subsequently revoke such assignment; and (3) voluntary irrevocable check-off, whereby the worker, having once authorized the deduction of union dues, may not revoke such authorization. An additional form of check-off clause is one that is compulsory for union members only. Below are sample clauses relating to dues check-off:

Compulsory for all Workers
In the case of an employee covered by this agreement who is not a member of the union and who is not required to become a member of the union, the employer agrees to deduct and forward to the union, monthly, the regular weekly union dues in accordance with the Rand formula.

Compulsory for Union Members Only
The employer agrees to deduct at such intervals, as may be agreed upon by the parties, from the wages of each of its employees, who are members of the union and who have authorized the same, the prescribed dues and to remit the same once

each month to the union. Each authorization shall be in writing, signed by the employee, and shall be delivered by the union to the employer.

Voluntary Revocable

The company shall remit to the union not less often than once each calendar month, amounts deducted from employees' wages in respect of initiation fees, regular monthly dues and duly authorized union assessments, pursuant to an assignment by individual employees in the following form:

To: (Company)

Until this assignment is revoked by me in writing, I, _____, hereby authorize you to deduct from wages earned by me the sum of $_____ for the month of _____ and thereafter the regular monthly dues and such assessments as may be generally levied by the local union in accordance with the constitution and by-laws thereof, and to forward these amounts to said union.

(Employee's Signature)

The local union hereby agrees that the company shall be saved harmless with respect to all deductions made and paid to the said Union in respect of provisions herein.

Use of Check-off Clauses Table 11.3 shows that compulsory dues check-off clauses are by far the most predominant type in Canada. Unions have been very successful in negotiating these clauses into their collective agreements. This success has enabled union officers and shop stewards to devote their time to more important matters, such as handling grievances. During the early days of unions, union officers would collect dues from members as they entered their places of employment — a time-consuming method.

Dues check-off clauses, like union security clauses, have serious philosophical implications for both unions and management. During the winters of 1979 and 1980, a number of major strikes occurred over compulsory dues check-offs. The problem became so serious in Ontario during the spring of 1980 that the government of that province passed legislation requiring that, if a union made a request for a dues check-off clause, the employer was compelled to include such a clause in the collective agreement. This measure effectively took the com-

Table 11.3	Check-Off Clauses	
	Agreements	Workers
	%	%
Voluntary (whether revocable or irrevocable)	5.4	3.6
Compulsory check-off for all workers	59.3	70.6
Voluntary for old workers, compulsory for new	1.5	2.6
Compulsory only for union members	24.7	17.3
Other	0.3	0.1
No provision	8.9	5.8
Total	100.0	100.0

Source: Labour Data Branch, Labour Canada, *Provisions in Collective Agreements in Canada Covering 500 and More Employees: All Industries (Excluding Construction),* (Ottawa: Supply and Services Canada, July 1985), pp. 6-7. Reproduced by permission of the Minister of Supply and Services Canada.

pulsory dues check-off out of the strike arena in Ontario. In 1977, the Quebec government revised its legislation to makes dues check-off compulsory. Other provinces have taken similar action. The legislative initiatives could explain in good part why dues check-off provisions are so prevalent in collective agreements today. (As indicated in Chapter 6, certain jurisdictions also provide for the payment of an amount of money comparable to the amount of the union dues to be paid to a charitable organization if a worker, because of religious beliefs, objects to the payment of union dues to the union.)

The Charter of Rights and Freedoms has recently been used to challenge the question of dues check-off provisions. One such case is the Lavigne case in which the payment of union dues is the central theme.[7] Francis Lavigne, a community college teacher in Ontario for which the Ontario Public Service Employees Union (OPSEU) is the bargaining agent, sought a ruling that he should not have to pay any part of his union dues that did not go directly to cover the cost of collective bargaining. The union to which he belongs contributes to the Ontario Federation and the Canadian Labour Congress, which support a variety of causes. Lavigne argued that contributions to the Ontario Federation of Labour and the Canadian Labour Congress to support causes that he did not accept infringed on his individual freedom, as guaranteed under the Charter. An Ontario trial judge ruled in favour of Mr. Lavigne, but the Ontario Court of Appeals overruled the lower court's ruling. The judges of the Appeals Court stated that by playing an active role beyond collective bargaining,

> the union is merely doing what trade unions have traditionally done in Canada and in political democracies everywhere . . . The court should not be called upon to monitor and examine every jot and tittle of union expenditure objected to by a non-member, as the judgment in appeal would indicate.[8]

The judges in this case also stated that the payment of union dues did not identify Lavigne personally with any of the political, social, or ideological objectives of the union, nor did it impose any obligation on him to conform to the views advocated by the union.[9] The Appeals Court decision is being challenged in the Supreme Court of Canada, and we will not have a definitive statement of the role of the courts in such issues until the Supreme Court hands down its decision.

Worker-Oriented Outputs

In the preceding section, we discussed the organizationally oriented outputs or clauses in collective agreements. We will now turn our attention to worker-oriented outputs, beginning with the wage and effort bargain.

Wage and Effort Bargain

As we noted in Chapter 3, most theorists believe that workers join unions to improve their

wages, working conditions, job security, protection from arbitrary management action, and in general their lot in life. It should come as no surprise, then, that the vast majority of provisions in collective agreements are worker-oriented clauses which define workers' incomes and conditions of work. We must be quite selective in discussing worker-oriented outputs, since many modern-day collective agreements are over 100 pages in length, comprise some 100 or more sections, and include clauses on wages, COLA, hours, and various types of time paid for but not worked, all of which come under the heading of the "wage and effort bargain."

In discussing the wage and effort bargain, we are looking at two sides of a coin. Workers are compensated for the services they perform, but this compensation is a cost for the employer — a cost which must be justified by the productivity of the workers. During periods of inflation, workers are likely to demand large wage increases so as to maintain real income. If this occurs, the balancing of wage costs and productivity becomes both critical and difficult.

It should also be noted that the wage and effort bargain is not always dealt with in collective agreements. There are often daily bargains that are made on the shop floor. For example, a job description may be drawn up with a wage scale attached. However, the actual number of units produced is often determined by the interaction between the worker and the supervisor.

Wage Increases Very few provisions in collective agreements are more important to workers than those covering the wages they receive in the performance of their duties. Table 11.4 gives an indication of percentage wage increases for the commercial and non-commercial sectors and an all-industry average for the years 1972 to 1988.[10] The percentage changes in the tables are increases in base rates for new settlements during the year in question. These percentage increases for Canadian workers, which are based on the lowest or "sweeper" rate, are inflated in comparison with the figures published by the Bureau of Labour Statistics in the United States which uses average rather than base rates. Also, American settlements are based on major agreements covering 1,000 or more workers, while the Canadian data are restricted to major agreements covering 500 or more workers — the only negotiated wage data now available. This distinction should be kept in mind when readers see Canada-US comparisons in the press, since the press does not differentiate the bases on which the data are computed in the two countries.

Table 11.4 shows that the average annual percentage increases in the commercial sector are slightly higher for the years from 1972 to 1974

than they are for the non-commercial sector, which includes the public sector. However, the average annual percentage increases in the non-commercial sector for the years from 1975 to 1977 are somewhat higher than the increases in the commercial sector; this is particularly significant for the year 1975. As we shall see later, this is explained in part by the spread of unions and the great demand for labour in the public sector during this period. The increases for the years 1978 and 1979 again show that increases in the commercial sector are slightly higher than increases in the non-commercial sector, whereas 1980 and 1981 reverse this two-year

Table 11.4	Average Effective Annual Percentage Changes in Base Rates for New Settlements Covering All Collective Bargaining Units of 500 or More Workers by Year[a]		
Year	Commercial	Non-Commercial[b]	All Industry
1972	9.2	7.7	8.0
1973	10.9	10.0	10.4
1974	14.9	14.8	14.8
1975	15.1	19.6	17.4
1976	9.6	11.0	10.4
1977	7.4	7.8	7.6
1978	8.2	7.0	7.6
1979	10.8	8.5	9.8
1980	11.6	10.8	11.1
1981	12.9	13.0	13.0
1982	10.1	10.5	10.2
1983	5.5	4.5	4.9
1984	3.5	3.7	3.6
1985	3.5	3.7	3.6
1986	3.1	3.8	3.5
1987	3.8	4.2	4.1
1988	4.5	4.0	4.3

[a] Construction industry included from 1985 onwards.
Source: Collective Bargaining Division, Labour Data Branch, Central Analytical Services, Labour Canada for the year 1972 to 1977. Effective increases were calculated starting in 1978. The figures for the years 1978 to 1983 are taken from Collective Bargaining Division, Labour Data Branch, Central Analytical Services, Labour Canada, *Major Wage Settlements — Fourth Quarter and Annual Summary 1983,* Table F-1, p. 16. The figures for 1984 are taken from Labour Canada, *Major Wage Settlements: Second Quarter,* 1985 p. 1. The figures for 1986 to 1988 are taken from the Bureau of Labour Information, Labour Canada, *Major Wage Settlements: Annual and Fourth-Quarter,* 1988, Table A-1, p. 17. The effective rates are based on an assumed CPI figure as a proxy for the inflation rate. The figures are adjusted if the actual CPI is different from the assumed level.

pattern and show the negotiated average annual increases to be slightly higher in the non-commercial sector.[11] The figures for 1983 to 1988 are dramatically lower than those for any year since the 1950s. The figures are slightly lower in the non-commercial sector, resulting at least in part from the various public-sector restraint programs for two of these years and from the serious recession of the past few years. The figures for 1985 to 1988 are still relatively low and vary between the commercial and non-commercial sectors.

The figures in recent years are comparable to the average annual percentage increases during the early 1950s when they were in the neighbourhood of 3.5%. While the negotiated increases in Table 11.4 are somewhat high — especially for the years 1974, 1975, 1976, and 1980 to 1982 — the figures alone tell us little, if anything, about workers' real income. Labour Canada in recent years has attempted to adjust negotiated settlements in accordance with increases in the Consumer Price Index (CPI).

In recent years, there have been a substantial number of studies on the wage determination process, both under collective bargaining and in the non-union sector. These studies adopt different methodologies and produce, to varying degrees, varying results.[12] While we will not examine their findings in detail, we will show what some of these studies have concluded with respect to the wage determination process in both the unionized and non-unionized sectors.

Effects of Inflation One study presents a model of wage determination which includes an analysis of the impact of price increases, labour market developments, and wage spillovers or pattern bargaining. The authors also compare the effects of direct bargaining, mediation, and work stoppages on wage determination. Inflation is seen to affect wage outcomes in two respects: (1) as an anticipated factor which is built into a negotiated wage increase and (2) as a past reality that has not been compensated for.

The researchers summarize their findings on these points in the following terms:

> The empirical results indicate that in the private sector approximately 40 percent of expected future inflation is built into the wage rate at the time the contract is signed and approximately 60 percent of past uncompensated inflation is corrected for at the next contract negotiation. Under a steady, fully-anticipated inflation, the combined price effects suggest that approximately 75 percent of the movement in consumer prices will be incorporated into wage rates.[13]

Thus, inflation, which we discussed in Chapter 2, has a significant impact on wage outcomes.

Labour Market Effects As far as the labour market is concerned, this study used various measures of unemployment and job vacancy rates in order to determine whether or not a relationship exists between unemployment and wage increases. The authors conclude that "negotiated wage changes are remarkably insensitive to changing labour market conditions."[14] In fact, negotiated wages seldom decline at all but move up, level off, and then move up again — a phenomenon called the "ratchet effect."

Pattern Bargaining Effects The impact of pattern bargaining is of great importance. The three types of spillover or pattern bargaining mentioned in the study include regional, industry, and combinations of the two. The strongest type was industry-related for a particular region. National patterns seem to be very weak and have very little if any impact on wage settlements, whereas patterns for a given industry within the same region do have pronounced effects on the outcome of negotiated wage settlements.[15]

In assessing the negotiating process on wage outcomes, the researchers used three stages at which settlements are reached: direct bargaining, mediation-conciliation, and work stoppages. While the three processes show significant differences, the differences may be

Wages increase 5% in quarter, Ottawa reports

BY ELIZABETH MOORE
The Globe and Mail

Canadian workers negotiated sharply higher wage settlements during the spring.

The federal Labor Department said new union contracts signed in the second quarter provided for average yearly wage increases of 5 per cent, up from 4.3 per cent in the first quarter.

The strongest gains were recorded in Ontario and British Columbia, where companies and unions struck deals that gave increases of 6.6 per cent. The figure for Quebec was 5.5 per cent. Consumer prices were rising at a 5 per cent annual rate during the same period.

Although the increase in wage settlements may stall any decline in interest rates, economists say it is unlikely to put upward pressure on rates. Nor, they say, will it necessarily fuel further inflation.

Edward Carmichael, senior economist at Burns Fry Ltd., said the Bank of Canada is unlikely to tighten its monetary policy in response to these numbers, noting that higher wage settlements alone do not fuel inflation.

The central bank, which has kept interest rates high to fight rising inflation, carefully watches the outcome of wage negotiations.

Mr. Carmichael said the bank will take the wage numbers into consideration in determining monetary policy and interest rates. But it will also pay attention to yesterday's news of a weakening Canadian

trade surplus and today's report on the consumer price index for July.

He attributed the higher wage settlement to rising inflation, tax increases, low unemployment and the strong demand for labor in Ontario.

Tim Whitehead, economist at the Canadian Imperial Bank of Commerce, said the increase does not support an early and dramatic drop in interest rates., However, economists had already been forecasting the rates would not drop until sometime this fall.

"If people are concerned about a wage-price spiral, those numbers add a little bit of substance to those concerns," he said.

Mr. Carmichael said higher wage settlements are consistent with what has already happened on the inflation front, and is more of a lagging than a leading indicator of inflation, reflecting workers' concern to keep pace with inflation.

"It's not at all surprising that union people would try to maintain their real purchasing power," he said.

Mr. Whitehead said regional differences reflect the relative strength of the regional economies. Workers in the Prairies settled for an average wage gain of only 3.7 per cent, the lowest in the country, during the April-June period.

The Ontario economy has been booming for several years, while British Columbia may have the highest economic growth rate this year among Canadian provinces, he said.

B.C. settlements were at 6.2 per

cent in the first quarter, after a 5.2 per cent increase in 1988, 3.1 per cent in 1987 and 1.5 per cent in 1986, suggesting that workers there are catching up on previous losses in the face of inflation.

Demand in the Quebec labor market is weakening, meaning that the province, which saw an increase to 5.5 per cent from 4.1 per cent in the first quarter, will probably see moderating wage settlements in the next quarter, Mr. Whitehead said.

The Atlantic provinces were the only region to post a decline in the second quarter to 5.1 per cent from 5.6 per cent in the first quarter.

Workers in Toronto especially are trying to protect their real income from inflation, Mr. Whitehead noted.

In June, Toronto had the highest inflation among Canadian cities at an annual rate of 6.4 per cent compared with the national average of 5.4 per cent.

The second-quarter numbers don't show a lot of easing in the demand for workers in Ontario or Toronto, he said.

Mr. Carmichael said the numbers also show a break in the trend towards more moderate wage settlements in the private sector.

In the second quarter of 1988, private sector wage settlement increases averaged 5.3 per cent, declining to 5.1 per cent in the third quarter, 4.8 per cent in the fourth quarter, and 4.5 per cent in the first quarter of 1989, before rising to 5.5 per cent in the second quarter.

There was concern that some high-profile public sector wage

negotiations would be leading the way in wage increases, but the annual average rise in the public sector in the second quarter was 4.8 per cent, Mr. Carmichael said.

During the second quarter, wages also increased in all industry sectors except manufacturing, the department said.

The trade sector, which includes those employed in retail trade and wholesale retailers, jumped from an annual increase of 2.6 per cent in the first quarter to 7 per cent in the second quarter. The four agree-

ments in this sector included workers of the Ontario Liquor Control Board, the Saskatchewan Liquor Board and a division of the Ontario Produce Co.

The average annual wage increase in construction was 5.9 per cent, up from 5.0 per cent; 5.1 per cent in community, business and personal services, up from 4.6 per cent; 4.4 per cent in transportation, communication and utilities, up from 3.3 per cent; and 4.6 per cent in public administration, up from 3.9 per cent.

High wage settlements in manufacturing, which declined to 5.3 per cent in the second quarter from 5.7 per cent in the first quarter, will increase Canadian labor costs, and combined with a higher Canadian dollar, may make it harder for Canadian companies to compete against their U.S. counterparts under the free-trade deal, Mr. Carmichael said.

The *Globe and Mail*, Aug. 18, 1989, pp. B1, B4.

attributed principally to price considerations and spillover effects. By themselves, these three processes have very moderate influences.[16] The researchers also found no evidence that settlements in the public sector spill over into the private sector.

Another study was concerned with a comparison of wage changes in major collective agreements in the private and public sectors, with more emphasis on the public sector than on the private sector. Like the previous study, it was based on the average annual percentage wage increases in base rates for major collective bargaining agreements covering 500 or more workers in Canada, excluding those in constructions and deals with approximately the same period (1967 to 1975). While the major dependent variable in this study is changes in wage rates, the major independent or explanatory variables are excess demand for labour and anticipated inflation. The authors assert that the economic environment creates an upper limit and a lower limit within which a wage settlement will take place. In addition, they indicate that the power of unions and management will indicate where the minimum and maximum wage levels fall within the range determined by the market.[17] This supports our own assertion in Chapter 7 that bargaining

power is very significant in determining a specific settlement point.

Public Sector Effects In a chapter on wages in the public sector, Cousineau and Lacroix suggest that government production of goods and services responds relatively little to typical variations in economic activity. In the early phases of public-sector unionization, wages increased markedly — a circumstance also noted for initial unionization in the private sector. This substantial wage increase could be absorbed, in part, because government derives its revenues from taxes and borrowing, rather than from the marketplace. The main beneficiaries of these initial wage increases were workers at the bottom end of the pay scale. Over the survey period, rates of increases in wages were found to be consistently higher for workers at the bottom of the wage scale than for those with moderate or high wages. This phenomenon was not found, however, in the private sector. Another difference between the private and public sectors was that labour market conditions (e.g., high unemployment) affect public servants' wage rates less than those of workers in the private sector. On the other hand, wage rates were more responsive to inflation in the public sector than in the private sector.[18]

The authors of this study forecast that, in periods of recession and high inflation, wages in the public sector would act as a factor in causing an economic slowdown:

> Indeed, wages in the public sector will increase even though they would decrease during a recession in the private sector. Business will then be faced with excessive wage demands even when it finds itself in serious financial difficulty.[19]

Furthermore, they claim that in an open economy such as Canada's, the pressure of public-sector wage increases on private-sector settlements results in a weakness in the competitive ability of Canada's economy, especially those sectors which are exposed to international competition.[20]

To the extent that these findings are accurate, they support the contention in Chapter 2 concerning the impact of unions and collective bargaining on the export sector of our economy. The picture painted in this study was dismal, and as a consequence the study received considerable attention when it was first released. However, the first study found no evidence to support the hypothesis that settlements in the public sector significantly spilled over into settlements in the private sector.[21]

Catch-up Effects One study which analyzed the bargaining outcomes (both wage and non-wage) of 49 of the 72 occupational groups in the federal public service for the first four rounds of negotiations found that the first three rounds were characterized by a high degree of pattern bargaining, in which the clerical and manual occupations gained in relation to the professional occupations, thus narrowing the wage differentials. This is explained at least in part by the fact that the first three rounds of negotiations were characterized as a catch-up phase, in comparison to private-sector occupations and internal comparisons. A large proportion of the non-wage outcomes appear to have occurred during the first round. During the fourth round of negotiations, many bargaining units switched from arbitration to the conciliation board and strike route.

The resulting strikes affected wage and non-wage outcomes significantly. This round ended the catch-up phase and resulted in greater wage dispersion.[22]

Human Capital Effects Gunderson, one of the most prolific writers on comparisons between wage increases in the private and public sectors, has come to several conclusions. One conclusion — based on 1971 census data and human capital variables (human resource endowments) such as education, experience and training, along with other independent variables of wage determination — was that public-sector workers have greater human capital endowments than do their private-sector counterparts. Another conclusion he reached was that male and female public-sector workers with human capital endowments equivalent to their private-sector counterparts earned 6.2% and 8.6% more, respectively, than their private-sector equivalents.[23]

A subsequent study by the same author, in which the data used were all-industry averages for various occupations in various cities during 1977, showed that the public-sector advantage was about 1% for male blue-collar occupations and about 3% for predominantly female white-collar jobs. The author concluded that, since the private-public wage differentials are very volatile, the public-sector advantage which appeared in his earlier study had probably dissipated by 1977.[24] Using more recent data, the same author's most recent finding is that,

> although there was a rising trend from a public sector wage disadvantage to a wage advantage over the period from 1952 to 1980, that advantage peaked sometime in the latter part of the period. In addition, the advantage, even at its greatest, was not very large.[25]

Gunderson concludes that, with the maturation of unions in the public sector, the new taxpayer militancy, and the fiscal crises of many governments, the public sector may not be the place to be in the future.[26]

Effects of Unionization A study undertaken by G.F. Starr dealt with the general effect of unionization on wages, and concluded that the "union-nonunion wage differential for production workers in manufacturing lies in the range of 10 to 17 percent."[27] This study concluded that, while spillover effects between unionized and non-unionized sectors may be important, it would be difficult to indicate with any degree of accuracy the difference between wage increases in the unionized sector and wage increases in the non-unionized sector.[28]

Johnson's study of non-union wage changes in Canada listed the factors which are taken into account when decisions are made regarding wage adjustments.[29] Johnson differentiated between primary and secondary factors, primary factors being those which had the greatest impact on a given wage change and secondary factors being those which contributed in a less significant way to a wage change. The primary and secondary factors were then summed for each item to show its overall impact on wage settlements. Outside wages, inside wages and turnover (number of workers who quit relative to number of workers hired) headed the list as having the most influence on wages, followed by profits, cost-of-living, minimum wages, market conditions, employment changes, and arbitrary (miscellaneous) items.[30]

Overall, outside wages (the going rate for this type of work in the same industry or area or both) far outstripped other items in determining wage adjustments, including inside wages (a rate of pay for other jobs within the same company or institution). Many of the factors noted in these studies were discussed in Chapter 2. These factors demonstrate how important the environment of an industrial relations system can be on the outcomes of the system, even in the non-union sector.

In recent years, other writers have attempted to develop and test general models of industrial relations systems to explain bargaining outcomes and, in particular, wage settlements. Many of these studies show very low correlations between the variables in the models and the outputs of the industrial relations system.[31]

It may be some time yet before we will be able to quantify the variables in industrial relations in order to adequately explain and predict the increases and the levels of the outputs of the system, because there are far too many variables in our frameworks to quantify and too many outputs to explain. What is needed is the development of proxy variables for a number of the more detailed variables in the frameworks in order to develop an explanatory and — more importantly — a predictive model.

Cost-of-Living Allowances Cost-of-living allowances are regular cents-per-hour or percentage increases made to workers through the operation of escalator clauses or other types of cost-of-living adjustments. In Canada, the rate is determined in accordance with changes measured by Statistics Canada's Consumer Price Index for the whole country. A sample clause of a cost-of-living allowance is the following:

> In addition to the wage rates set out in this Schedule, any increase or decrease in the cost of living, during the period of this agreement, shall be based on changes in the Consumer Price Index as published by Statistics Canada and pegged on the figure of 126.8. Adjustment either upward or downward will be made on the basis of 1¢ per hour for each 0.6 change in the CPI, but in no event will a decline in the CPI below 126.8 provide a basis for reduction in the negotiated wage schedule.[32]

Table 11.5 summarizes the major collective agreements on file from 1975 to 1988 (covering 500 or more workers in all industries, except construction prior to 1984) which have COLA clauses and the percentage of workers covered by such clauses. The figures indicate that COLA clauses become more important during periods of high inflation because they are a means of trying to maintain real income. COLA clauses reached a peak of 49% in 1976 when the CPI was still above 10%, declined somewhat when inflation fell below 10%, but reached an all-time peak of about 50% of workers covered in 1981 when the CPI hit 12.5%. Hence, the incidence of COLA clauses appears to follow the inflation

Table 11.5	Cost of Living Allowance Provisions in Force at the End of Each Year Covering 500 or More Workers, 1975–1988[a]	
Year	% Agreements	% Workers
1975	38.1	43.7
1976	45.5	49.0
1977	33.2	45.3
1978	36.9	43.0
1979	34.2	42.3
1980	37.8	46.6
1981	39.4	49.7
1982	36.1	43.5
1983	26.6	33.5
1984	24.3	32.4
1985	26.7	35.8
1986	28.4	39.2
1987	28.1	41.2
1988	27.8	39.9

[a] Construction industry is included from 1983 onwards.
Source: The data for the years 1975 to 1978 are taken from Collective Bargaining Division, Labour Data Branch, Labour Canada, "Cost-of-Living Allowance Provisions in Major Collective Agreements, 1977, 1978 and the first half of 1979," December, 1979. The data for the years 1979–1988 were provided by the Bureau of Labour Information, Labour Canada, in a special computer printout, June 12, 1989. The figures for these years are based on all agreements in force.

Table 11.6	Types of Cost of Living Allowance Clauses, 1989	
	Agreements	Workers
	%	%
Provision is effective immediately	16.5	19.6
Provision exists but to be implemented at a later date	9.4	16.7
Provision inoperative	1.7	1.0
Other	—	—
No provision	72.4	62.7
Total	100.0	100.0

Source: Bureau of Labour Information, Labour Canada, Special Computer Printout, June 12, 1989. The data in this table include all collective agreements covering 500 or more employees, including the construction industry.

rate fairly consistently. Note that only about 33% of workers were covered by COLA clauses during 1984, a year of low inflation and also the first year for which construction collective agreements were included in Labour Canada's data base. There are very few, if any, agreements in the construction industry that contain COLA clauses. The latter point is probably responsible to a large degree for the lower incidence of COLA clauses since 1984.

Table 11.6 shows the types of COLA clauses in force for the year 1989. They included about one-quarter of agreements covering about 33% of workers: with inflation running relatively low for a number of years, the incidence of COLA clauses could be expected to decline also. The table also shows that only about one-fifth of workers were covered by COLA clauses that were effective immediately. In the public sector of Quebec, COLA clauses were more prevalent than in any other jurisdiction in Canada.

From a worker's point of view, COLA clauses are particularly important in multi-year collective agreements when the rate of inflation is very difficult, if not impossible, to predict. There is a serious disagreement as to whether or not COLA clauses are inflationary in nature, and the evidence is so mixed that it is impossible to reach a definite conclusion on this issue. What studies on this matter do indicate, however, is that the "money illusion," or the tendency to judge wage raises in absolute rather than relative terms, does not exist in these economic times. Workers are very much aware that their actual negotiated increases could be substantially eroded if they were not protected by some kind of COLA provision in the case of increasing or sustained inflation.

The evidence shows that quarterly and annual adjustments are the most frequent provisions in COLA clauses. One of the more interesting aspects of the COLA phenomenon is the variety of methods used in making adjustments for increases in the cost-of-living.

As can be seen from Table 11.7, the two most important methods used for calculating COLA

Table 11.7	Method of Calculating COLA Rate of Payment for Agreements with COLA	
	Agreements	Workers
	%	%
Cents per point increase in CPI	49.4	50.4
Percent increase in wages per percent increase in CPI	36.2	42.3
Cents per percent increase in CPI	3.9	1.4
Other	10.5	5.8

Source: Bureau of Labour Information, Labour Canada, Special Computer Printout, June 20, 1989.

adjustments are the cents-per-point increase in the Consumer Price Index and the percent increase in wages per percent increase in the CPI. The first method accounts for close to 50% of agreements covering over 50% of workers. The second accounts for 36% of agreements covering over 43% of workers. As indicated in Table 11.8 the percentage increase in the CPI is the

Table 11.8	Triggering Formulae Used to Determine Amount of COLA in Collective Agreements	
	Agreements	Workers
	%	%
Percent increase in CPI (COLA is generated only after the CPI has increased by a certain percentage)	39.7	48.9
Cents per point increase in CPI (COLA generated once the amount calculated according to the formula exceeds a specified number of cents per hour)	10.5	15.3
No trigger mechanism specified	49.8	35.8
Total	100.0	100.0

Source: Bureau of Labour Information, Labour Canada, Special Computer Printout, June 20, 1989.

prevalent method of triggering COLA clause adjustments, accounting for over 39% of agreements, covering close to 50% of workers with COLA clauses. About 50% of agreements specify no triggering mechanism. Past practice or common understanding, however, probably governs the implementation of these COLA clauses.

Hours of Work According to the most recent statistics on hours of work per week, about 45% of agreements covering about 36% of workers specify 40 hours or less per week. Thirty-seven hours or more, the next most prevalent length of workday, is required of slightly more than 12% of workers. Slightly less than 15% of workers work about 35 hours per week. Unions have been making slow but steady gains in reducing the length of the workday. Now, only about 2% of workers are required to work more than 40 hours per week.[33]

Overtime Compensation Usually, workers who put in time beyond normal hours are compensated for overtime by a rate of pay much greater than normal hourly wages. The available evidence indicates that about 45% of the collective agreements covering over 49% of the workers make provision for time-and-a-half. Another 29% of the agreements covering more than 30% of workers provide for time-and-a-half to be followed by double time. Over 17% of agreements covering about 15% of workers make no provision for overtime.[34] An interesting aspect of these figures is the provision for double time — a fairly recent development. Recently, 7% of agreements covering over 4% of workers makes provision for double time only, and it is likely that demands for double time will increase in the future.

Paid Holidays A substantial proportion of collective agreements stipulate that workers must be paid for statutory holidays. In order to be eligible for this payment, however, workers must meet certain conditions with respect to days worked before and after the statutory holiday. The following is a sample clause setting out the most common requirement:

> In order to be eligible for pay for a statutory holiday, an employee should work his scheduled hours the day immediately preceding and immediately succeeding the holiday unless he has received permission in writing to be absent.

Table 11.9 indicates that the most prevalent provision (34.9%) requires workers to work both the day before and the day after the holiday. A significant proportion (16.8%) of workers are paid for statutory holidays if they work *either* the day before or the day after the statutory holiday.

Table 11.9 Eligibility Requirements for Paid Statutory Holidays

	Agreements	Workers
	%	%
Must have worked the last scheduled working day before	0.4	0.3
Must have worked the next scheduled working day after	0.0	0.0
Must have worked both working days immediately before and after	41.4	34.9
Must have worked either working day immediately before or after	10.4	16.8
Must have worked a specified length of time prior to the holiday	9.6	10.2
Other	0.2	0.1
No provision	38.0	37.8
Total	100.0	100.0

Source: Agreement Analysis Section, Labour Data Branch, Labour Canada, *Provisions in Collective Agreements in Canada Covering 500 and More Employees: All Industries (Excluding Construction)*, (Ottawa: Supply and Services Canada, July 1985), pp. 88-89. Reproduced by permission of the Minister of Supply and Services Canada.

Paid Vacations In addition to the provisions shown in Table 11.10, previous data from Labour Canada for 1985 showed there is often some arrangement for unused vacation time to be carried over from year to year. About 30% of workers are covered by such a provision in their collective agreement. Only 16% of collective agreements covering 12% of workers prohibit such a carry-over. For the remaining 51% of workers, there is no specific provision in their contracts in this regard. In some instances, however, an informal arrangement with management might hold.[35] Five- and six-week vacations, a fairly recent phenomenon, may become more prevalent in the future as a means of sharing available work.

Job Rights and Due Process

This category of benefits relates to job rights such as the use of seniority in promotion, layoff and recall, and the procedures set out for handling workers' grievances.

Seniority Seniority may be defined broadly as a workers' total length of continuous service with the employer. Seniority is based on the principle that greater priority or preference is accorded to the worker with longer service. The term is used to fix a worker's status relative to other workers as a criterion to be used in determining promotions, layoffs, vacations, etc. Seniority may be on a departmental basis, plant-wide basis, or some combination of these.

Superseniority (or special seniority) is a position higher than the worker would acquire solely on the basis of length of service or other general seniority factors. Usually such treatment is reserved for union stewards who are entitled to special consideration in connection with layoff and recall to work, since they help workers in the handling of their grievances, and have the most experience in the shop and in the grievance procedure. The following is a sample clause relating to the use of seniority in promotions:

> The company agrees to recognize the principle of departmental and plant seniority in job progres-

Table 11.10   **Selected Data for Paid Vacation Clauses in Collective Agreements Covering 500 or More Workers**

	Minimum years of service	% Agreements	% Workers
3 weeks: most common provision	1 year	28.2	32.3
2nd most common provision	5 years	13.7	12.1
no provision		29.8	39.1
4 weeks: most common provision	10 years	18.1	14.9
2nd most common provision	9 years	15.0	15.9[a]
no provision		26.1	22.9
5 weeks: most common provision	20 years	19.6	20.2
2nd most common provision	16–19 years	23.5	19.7
no provision		30.3	29.7
6 weeks: most common provision	25 years	15.0	11.3
2nd most common provision	29 years	6.9	7.9
no provision		56.7	59.6

[a]These workers are concentrated in the Community, Business and Personal Services sector which includes such fields as education, health and retail trade.
Source: Bureau of Labour Information, Labour Canada, Special Computer Printout, June 3, 1989, pp. 22–29.

sion and in the layoff and rehiring of employees in a fair and equitable manner having regard not only to the length of service, but as well to the knowledge, training, skill, efficiency and physical fitness of the employee or employees concerned to do the work assigned.

It will be observed in the sample clause that although seniority is one of the major factors taken into account in promotion, skill, efficiency, and physical fitness are also considered. Table 11.11 gives some statistics regarding the role of seniority in promotions.

Seniority is one criterion for determining layoff priority (see Table 11.12). A layoff is an involuntary separation from employment for a temporary or indefinite period that results from no fault of the workers. Although layoff usually implies eventual recall, or at least an intent to recall workers to their former jobs, the term is occasionally used for separations plainly signifying permanent loss of jobs, as, for example, in plant shutdowns. A sample clause relating to the use of seniority in layoffs is as follows:

In cases of transfer to avoid layoff, other than those of a temporary nature, and layoff due to lack of work, the company agrees that seniority in the classifications and in the classes within the classifications shall be the prime consideration, but the union recognizes the company's right to have regard for ability and to retain a limited number of employees of lesser seniority who, because of special training or ability, are essential to the efficient operation of the plant, provided such employees are placed in jobs making use of such special training or ability.

Interesting contrasts appear when one analyzes the use of seniority in promotion and in layoff. While provision is made in 17.8% of agreements covering 17.9% of workers for layoff on the basis of straight seniority, only 0.6% of agreements covering 0.3% of workers make provision for promotion on this basis. Also, while straight seniority is the most common provision respecting promotion, such is not the case with layoffs (all other things being equal), where seniority is given more weight than factors such as ability, skill, knowledge, and physical fitness. This possibly reflects employers' desires to bring back workers with skill levels above the minimum required, in case promotional opportunities occur before the end of the layoff.

Table 11.11	The Use of Seniority on Promotion	
	Agreements	Workers
	%	%
Straight seniority	0.6	0.3
Seniority with other factors such as ability, skill, knowledge, and physical fitness	34.3	30.7
Straight seniority if other factors are equal or sufficient	39.3	33.4
No provision	25.8	35.6
Total	100.0	100.0

Source: Agreement Analysis Section, Labour Data Branch, Labour Canada, *Provisions in Collective Agreements in Canada Covering 500 and More Employees: All Industries (Excluding Construction)* (Ottawa: Supply and Services Canada, July 1985), p. 11. Reproduced by permission of the Minister of Supply and Services Canada.

Seniority is also a criterion for determining recall (see Table 11.13). Recall is the process of bringing laid-off workers back to work, usually based on the same principles that governed the order of layoff, but in reverse (e.g., the last worker laid off is the first to be recalled). A sample clause dealing with the use of seniority in recall is the following:

> When the working force is increased after a layoff . . . employees will be recalled according to seniority, providing the greater seniority employees are able to perform the available work.

While numerous strikes were conducted in the past over the role of seniority in promotions, layoffs and recalls, there have been very few within recent memory. Unions argued that the longer workers remained with an employer, the more rights they acquired to available jobs. Employers, on the other hand, wanted as much flexibility as possible in dealing with their workers. Over the years, the parties seem to have

Table 11.12	The Use of Seniority on Lay-Off	
	Agreements	Workers
	%	%
Straight seniority	17.8	17.9
Seniority with other factors such as ability, skills, knowledge and physical fitness	40.6	40.9
Straight seniority if other factors are equal or sufficient	21.4	15.5
No provision	20.2	25.8
Total	100.0	100.0

Source: Labour Data Branch, Labour Canada, *Provisions in Collective Agreements in Canada Covering 500 and More Employees: All Industries (Excluding Construction)* (Ottawa: Supply and Services Canada, July 1985), p. 12. Reproduced by permission of the Minister of Supply and Services Canada.

Table 11.13	The Use of Seniority in Cases of Recall	
	Agreements	Workers
	%	%
Straight seniority	13.5	12.9
Seniority with other factors such as ability, skills, knowledge, and physical fitness	43.1	38.2
Straight seniority if other factors are equal or sufficient	17.3	13.3
No provision	26.0	35.6
Total	100.0	100.0

Source: Agreement Analysis Section, Labour Data Branch, Labour Canada, *Provisions in Collective Agreements in Canada Covering 500 and More Employees: All Industries (Excluding Construction)* (Ottawa: Supply and Services Canada, July 1985), p. 14. Reproduced by permission of the Minister of Supply and Services Canada.

resolved the dilemma by recognizing the validity of both the seniority criterion and criteria of ability, suitability, etc. in determining promotions, layoffs, and recall.

Worker Grievances — Initial Presentation

As we saw in Chapter 9, a worker may take a grievance to the supervisor alone or in the company of a shop steward. The following sample clause is one which makes provision for both cases:

> An employee may make a complaint to his foreman or other immediate supervisor either individually or accompanied by a shop steward. Such complaint shall be submitted within 30 calendar days of the occurrence or cause thereof.

The latest available evidence indicates that in about 73% of agreements covering 70% of workers, grievances may be submitted to supervisors with or without union representatives. The next most frequent provision requires that workers alone submit grievances to supervisors. The submission of grievances by union representatives alone is less frequent still.[36]

Special Grievance Procedures in Discipline and Discharge Cases

Discipline and discharge cases are initiated at higher levels of the grievance procedure than other cases. A sample clause providing for a special procedure in the case of dismissal is as follows:

> A claim by an employee that he has been unjustly discharged shall be treated as a grievance if a written statement of such grievance is lodged at Step No. 3 of the Grievance Procedure within three working days after the discharge, or within three working days after the union has been notified of the discharge, whichever is the later.

Table 11.14 indicates that 46% of the agreements covering about the same percentage or workers provide for a reduction in the number of steps in the grievance procedure in disciplinary or dismissal cases. The relatively high incidence of such provisions indicates how seriously disciplinary and dismissal cases are taken.

Table 11.14   Special Grievance Procedure in Disciplinary or Dismissal Cases

	Agreements	Workers
	%	%
Number of steps in the grievance is reduced	46.4	45.1
Duration of delays between steps is reduced	4.0	5.3
Reduced number of steps in grievance & reduced duration of delays between steps	7.5	6.4
Other	—	—
No provision	42.2	43.2
Total	100.0	100.0

Source: Agreement Analysis Section, Labour Data Branch, Labour Canada, *Provisions in Collective Agreements in Canada Covering 500 and More Employees: All Industries (Excluding Construction)* (Ottawa: Supply and Services Canada, July 1985), p. 28. Reproduced by permission of the Minister of Supply and Services Canada.

Contingency Benefits

Contingency benefits are intended to cover situations that cannot be anticipated precisely for any individual worker. Such benefits may be activated in response to a number of unforeseen events including layoff, bereavement, or illness. It is to some of these items that we now turn our attention.

Severance Pay and Supplemental Unemployment Benefits (SUB)

Severance pay is defined in general terms as monetary payments made by employers to displaced workers, generally upon permanent termination of employment with no chance of recall. Sometimes, however, severance pay is given upon indefinite layoff with recall rights intact. The plans usually provide for lump-sum payments but may allow several payments over a period of time. Plans normally calculate such payments in accordance with length of service. Severance pay is also sometimes called termination pay, dismissal allowance, separation benefit, or layoff allowance (where layoff implies permanent layoff). The following is a sample clause of the use of severance pay on retirement:

> An employee who has ten or more years continuous service in the employ of the employer is entitled to be paid on resignation or retirement severance pay equal to the amount obtained by multiplying the number of completed years of continuous employment by his weekly salary to a maximum of twenty weeks pay.

Supplemental unemployment benefit plans (SUB) provide regular weekly payments to laid-off workers. Usually SUB plans are funded by an employer contribution to the fund in terms of so many cents per hour worked and are used primarily in cases where workers are laid off due to cyclical downturns in the industry or, sometimes, in cases of major seasonal variations. A sample supplemental unemployment benefit plan is as follows:

> The regular benefit payable to an eligible employee for any week beginning on or after December 31, 1989 shall be an amount which, when added to his unemployment insurance benefit and other compensation, will equal 95% of his weekly after-tax pay.

The use of averages mask a great deal of disaggregated information. For example, while close to 43% of the total agreements covering 30% of workers have no provision for severance pay and supplemental unemployment plans, wide variation exists among industry classifications. There is no such provision in fishing because of the extremely seasonal nature of the industry. In mining, which is a year-round operation, 34% of agreements covering 27% of workers have no provisions. Hence, the environment of the industry is an important factor influencing the outputs of industrial relations systems. Within the manufacturing sector, the presence of such provisions range from a high of about 100% in agreements covering 100% of workers in tobacco products to no agreements in knitting mills.[37] The latter industry in Canada

must compete with cheaper foreign-made imported goods. The fact that many employers in this industry are barely able to exist could be the major reason for the low incidence of severance pay and supplemental unemployment insurance.

Paid Leaves of Absence

Death in the Immediate Family The vast majority of collective agreements make provision for paid leave of absence in cases of death in the immediate family. What one has to watch for in examining these kinds of clauses is how the collective agreement defines immediate family. The following sample clause indicates the provisions contained in one particular agreement:

> In the event of death in the family of an employee with three months or more service, the employee will be granted a leave of absence for a reasonable period of time to attend the funeral and will be reimbursed for wages lost by reason of time lost, provided, however, that the amount reimbursed will not exceed three days' wages at average earnings or hourly rate. The term member of an

Table 11.15	Paid Leave of Absence — Death in Immediate Family	
	Agreements	Workers
	%	%
1 day	0.4	0.5
2 days	0.2	0.1
3 days	51.9	45.0
4 days	10.5	15.7
5 days	26.0	28.4
More than 5 days	1.4	2.2
Other	2.9	3.1
No provision	6.7	5.0
Total	100.0	100.0

Source: Agreement Analysis Section, Labour Data Branch, Labour Canada, *Provisions in Collective Agreements in Canada Covering 500 and More Employees: All Industries (Excluding Construction)* (Ottawa: Supply and Services Canada, July 1985), p. 108-09. Reproduced by permission of the Minister of Supply and Services Canada.

employee's family means a husband or wife, son or daughter, brother or sister, mother or father and mother-in-law or father-in-law.

Table 11.15 indicates the provisions in collective agreements which require paid leave of absence in case of death in the immediate family. Most collective agreements contain a provision allowing at least three days of paid leave of absence in the case of a death in the immediate family. Four and five days are the two next most prevalent provisions, with five days being more prevalent than four days.

Paid Maternity Leave An increasing number of collective agreements provide for leave of absence with or without pay in maternity cases (see Table 11.16). A sample clause reads as follows:

> Maternity leave of not more than six months shall be granted, with pay for four weeks.

Maternity leave with pay, a relatively new phenomenon, is provided for in agreements covering about 0.2% of workers. About 15% of agreements covering 30.9% of workers provide for maternity leave without pay. In some cases, sick leave may be used as maternity leave.

These figures, taken by themselves, would appear to indicate that unions still have much to do in order to provide paid leave for maternity cases. The maternity leave provisions negotiated in the Canada Post agreement during the summer of 1981 and by Bell Canada in 1982 will no doubt be a target which many unions will seek to achieve in the future. Nonetheless, the figures used here grossly underestimate the coverage given to women since the percentages apply to all workers under collective agreements covering 500 or more workers, and such agreements, in many cases, cover bargaining units which are predominantly or exclusively composed of male workers, such as the construction industry. (Thus far, paternity and adoption leave are somewhat of a rarity and usually do not extend beyond a few days.)

Labour standards legislation, which covers such things as minimum wages, hours, paid holidays, vacations, and maternity leave, usually follows well behind provisions found in collective agreements. An examination of all 11 labour standards acts revealed that none of them requires an employer to grant paid maternity leave. While every act requires employers to grant maternity leave, some specify that such leave will be without pay. As more workers gain paid maternity leave under collective agreements, eventually most jurisdictions will probably require a minimum period of paid maternity leave.

Medical, Dental, and Disability Coverage Among the other important contingency benefits that are contained in collective agreements, basic medicare, dental, and long-term disability coverage are among the most important. Employer-paid medicare premiums have been of concern to unions ever since medicare was first introduced in Canada. Contributions by employers vary between 100% (in about 30% of agreements) and 75% (in 10.5% of agreements). Nevertheless, close to 53% of workers still must pay 100% of their medicare premiums — a situation which may soon change in the workers' favour.[38]

Close to one-third of workers are covered by dental plans for which premiums are fully paid by the employer. A number of other arrangements exist for the payment of dental care premiums by employers, but close to 40% of workers are still not covered by dental plans.

Table 11.16	Maternity Leave With Pay	
	Agreements	Workers
	%	%
With pay	0.3	0.2
Without pay	13.8	30.9
With and without pay	1.5	0.8
No provision	84.5	68.1
Total	100.0	100.0

Source: Bureau of Labour Information, Labour Canada, "Provisions in Collective Agreements" (Covering 500 or more Employees, Including Construction), June 6, 1989, p. 34.

This situation, too, may soon change in the worker's favour.[39] Long-term disability coverage is a recent development. Sixty percent of workers are not yet covered by such plans. A small percentage (16%) have their premiums paid in full by their employers. A smaller proportion still (5.5%) have their premiums partially (75% to 99%) paid by their employers.[40] With respect to sick leave, the most common provision is for fifteen days a year.[41] It is interesting that about 25% of workers are covered by a provision dealing with alcohol and drug addiction.[42] This is a recent development and probably has its basis in arbitral jurisprudence which is quite understanding of alcohol and drug abuse.

Contracting-Out

Contracting-out refers to a practice of allowing certain steps in a manufacturing process, plant maintenance, or other functions to be performed by outside contractors using their own workforces. The following clause is a sample of a contracting-out clause in a collective agreement:

> It shall be the policy and intention of the company to use its workers as much as practicable for work at the plant. The company has the right to contract out work as required when such action does not result in a regular qualified employee of the bargaining unit being replaced.

Quite a controversy exists over the right of management to contract out work. A majority of collective agreements do not contain a provision regarding contracting-out, since employers are averse to concessions that challenge the management residual rights theory. Unions, for their part, wish to safeguard the jobs of their members from encroachment by contract workers.

But, despite the general aversion of actors in the industrial relations system to contracting-out, agreements covering 21% of workers specifically permit it. It is interesting to compare this figure to the 25% of workers covered by agreements which prohibit contracting-out leading to layoffs or failure to recall. It is surprising that employers have made such concessions

concerning layoffs and recall, particularly since the jurisprudence on this issue has been clear for some time:

> it is now universally accepted that bargaining unit work may be subcontracted to non-employees, provided that the subcontracting is genuine and not done in bad faith. Whatever the view may have been in earlier awards, it is now settled that to prohibit subcontracting, the agreement must expressly so provide.[43]

Such subcontracting must be *legitimate* in the sense that it must be performed by independent contractors or the workers of independent contractors.[44] Table 11.17 summarizes the inclusion

Table 11.17	Provisions in Collective Agreements Regarding the Contracting-Out of Work	
	Agreements	Workers
	%	%
Permitted	16.9	21.0
Prohibited	1.5	0.6
No contracting-out if it leads to layoffs or failure to recall members of bargaining unit	26.1	25.8
No contracting-out to non-union employer	1.3	1.4
No contracting-out if it leads to layoffs or failure to recall members of bargaining unit & if it is to a non-union employer	1.1	0.6
Other	0.1	0.2
No provision	53.0	50.3
Total	100.0	100.0

Source: Agreement Analysis Section, Labour Data Branch, Labour Canada, *Provisions in Collective Agreements in Canada Covering 500 and More Employees: All Industries (Excluding Construction)* (Ottawa: Supply and Services Canada, July 1985), pp. 152-53. Reproduced by permission of the Minister of Supply and Services Canada.

of contracting-out clauses in Canadian agreements.

Some Concluding Comments on Worker-Oriented Outputs

This section has covered some of the major provisions in collective agreements dealing with remuneration for work and the conditions under which work is performed. Outputs are determined by general management philosophy, personnel policies, and by workers' attempts, through their unions, to have an impact on the terms and conditions that govern their employment. The latter is one of the most important aspects of an industrial relations system, for without the desire of workers to have some control over the conditions under which they work and over the compensation and other benefits they receive, neither unions nor collective bargaining would be necessary.

Industrial Conflict as an Output of the Industrial Relations System

A collective agreement reached between union and management without a strike may have a positive feedback to the participants in the industrial relations system. For example, if a settlement satisfies the vast majority of workers, then they are likely to be happy with their work, working conditions, and benefits. Consequently, there may be a decline in absenteeism or turnover and, possibly, higher output or productivity. While there is certainly no hard evidence to support the statements we have made here, there are some indications that these kinds of results will likely take place if a collective agreement is reached peacefully and if the provisions of that agreement are acceptable to the vast majority of workers. Should union and management not be able to reach an agreement on their own, or with third-party assistance, then they may resort to strikes or lockouts. Thus, work stoppages can be considered another type of output from the industrial relations system.

Strikes *can* have a beneficial effect, insofar as they enable workers to relieve frustrations. They can also act as catalysts — as lockouts do — in the negotiation process. Nonetheless, strikes and lockouts can also have potentially detrimental consequences for various aspects of the economy and society. We shall deal more fully with this topic when we deal with the concept of the feedback loop.

Strikes may be defined as a cessation of work or a refusal to work by workers in combination, in concert, or in accordance with a common understanding which is directed at getting the employer to agree to terms and conditions of employment. Strikes are also defined in a number of statutes as a slow-down or other concerted activity on the part of workers to restrict or limit output. They are legal during the negotiation or renegotiation of collective agreements only after certain conditions have been met. They are illegal, however, if conducted during the life of a collective agreement. A wildcat strike is one which is conducted during the term of the collective agreement and without the approval of union officers. A lockout may be defined as the closing of the place of employment or the suspension or refusal of work by an employer to compel workers, or to aid another employer to compel workers, to agree to proposed terms or conditions of employment.

The Charter of Rights and Freedoms may eventually have a significant impact on the right to strike. Section 52(1) of the Charter provides that

> the Constitution, of which the Charter is a part, "is the supreme law of Canada," and that "any law" inconsistent with it, "is, to the extent of the inconsistency, of no force or effect." Section 32(1) provides that the Charter applies "to the Parliament and government of Canada" and "to the legislature and government of each province. . . ."[45]

Adell argues that the Charter purports to protect traditional individual rights beyond interference by government. The Charter also gives the courts "the power to strike down any law or other act of government which they find violates those rights."[46]

The central question here is whether the Charter should emphasize individual worker's rights, as Beatty argues in his book *Putting the Charter to Work*, or whether it will reach so far as to emasculate the system of collective bargaining that has evolved in Canada over a number of years.[47] Thus far the Supreme Court of Canada has dealt with one case which concerns the right to strike and to picket. In the Dolphin Delivery case, the Court held that legal restrictions on picketing constituted a violation of the guarantee of freedom of expression in s. 2(b) of the Charter. However, the Court held that legal restrictions of secondary picketing could be justified under s.1 of the Charter by "keeping a labour dispute from having an undue effect on parties not directly involved in it."[48]

In a subsequent trilogy of cases, the Supreme Court of Canada held that freedom of association, which is guaranteed in s. 2(d) of the Charter, does not include the right to collective bargaining and the right to strike.[49] We can be certain that a number of cases will have to come before the Supreme Court comes down with a definitive ruling on the Charter and the right to strike (including how far the right to strike extends).

There are a number of ways of measuring the incidence of strikes; a major problem, however, is finding an *appropriate* way. This is true particularly in comparing strikes among jurisdictions or countries. The number of strikes occurring during a specified period of time is one measure, but this tells us little, since some countries may have a large number of very short strikes while others may have a small number of very long ones. The number of person-days lost is another measure sometimes used, but this too tells us little unless we know something about the size of the labour forces, particularly for purposes of comparison. The number of workers involved in strikes during a specified period is another measure, but this too tells us little unless we know something about the size of the labour forces being compared.

Time lost due to strikes and lockouts as a *percent* of estimated working time is the most widely used method of measuring the incidence of strikes. By giving a percentage or relative measure, this method makes meaningful comparisons possible. However, one must be careful in comparing strikes among countries since the reporting of strikes may vary from one country to another. For example, one-day walkouts in protest against government policies may be counted as strikes in some countries, but not in others.

Strikes and Lockouts in Canada from 1901 to 1988

The most important element in Table 11.18 is the last column, which shows the percentage of estimated time lost due to strikes and lockouts. This table reveals a high number of person-days lost following both world wars (.6% in 1919 and .54% in 1946). More recently, the percentage of estimated working time lost began to increase in 1966 when it jumped to 0.34% from 0.17% in 1965. The figures continued to be high during the late 1960s, throughout the 1970s (with the exception of 1971 and 1977) and the early 1980s, and then fell again after 1982. An examination of this data will reveal the cyclical nature of increases and decreases in the frequency of work stoppages.

Before proceeding to attempt an explanation for the high incidence of strikes in Canada, we should first put strikes in their proper perspective. If we look at the number of person-days lost in 1980 due to unemployment (217 million) or due to accidents or illness for which money was claimed through workers' compensation (13.4 million), the figures for strikes and lockouts (approximately 9 million) fade into pale insignificance.[50] In recent years, absenteeism has become an increasingly important phenomenon among workers and, if allowed to grow, will become a much more important cause of person-hours lost. Furthermore, as pointed out previously, about 90% of collective agreements in Canada are settled without strikes.

Table 11.18   **Strikes and Lockouts in Canada, 1901-1988**

Year	Number beginning during year	Number	Workers involved	Man-days	% of estimated working time
1901	97	99	24,089	737,808	—
1902	124	125	12,709	203,301	—
1903	171	175	38,408	858,959	—
1904	103	103	11,420	192,890	—
1905	95	96	12,513	246,138	—
1906	149	150	23,382	378,276	—
1907	183	188	34,060	520,142	—
1908	72	76	26,071	703,571	—
1909	88	90	18,114	880,663	—
1910	94	101	22,203	731,324	—
1911	99	100	29,285	1,821,084	—
1912	179	181	42,860	1,135,786	—
1913	143	152	40,519	1,036,254	—
1914	58	63	9,717	490,850	—
1915	62	63	11,395	95,042	—
1916	118	120	26,538	236,814	—
1917	158	160	50,255	1,123,515	—
1918	228	230	79,743	647,942	—
1919	332	336	148,915	3,400,942	0.60
1920	310	322	60,327	799,524	0.14
1921	159	168	28,257	1,048,914	0.22
1922	89	104	43,775	1,528,661	0.32
1923	77	86	34,261	671,750	0.13
1924	64	70	34,310	1,295,054	0.26
1925	86	87	28,949	1,193,281	0.23
1926	75	77	23,834	266,601	0.05
1927	72	74	22,299	152,570	0.03
1928	96	98	17,581	224,212	0.04
1929	88	90	12,946	152,080	0.02
1930	67	67	13,766	91,797	0.01
1931	86	88	10,736	204,238	0.04
1932	111	116	23,390	255,000	0.05
1933	122	125	26,558	317,547	0.07
1934	189	191	45,800	574,519	0.11
1935	120	120	33,269	288,703	0.05
1936	155	156	34,812	276,997	0.05
1937	274	278	71,905	886,393	0.15
1938	142	147	20,395	148,678	0.02
1939	120	122	41,038	224,588	0.04
1940	166	168	60,619	266,318	0.04
1941	229	231	87,091	433,914	0.06
1942	352	354	113,916	450,202	0.05
1943	401	402	218,404	1,041,198	0.12
1944	195	199	75,290	490,139	0.06
1945	196	197	96,068	1,457,420	0.19
1946	223	226	138,914	4,515,030	0.54
1947	231	234	103,370	2,366,340	0.27

| Table 11.18 continued | | | Strikes and Lockouts in Canada, 1901-1988 | | |

Year	Number beginning during year	Number	Workers involved	Man-days	% of estimated working time
1948	147	154	42,820	885,790	0.10
1949	130	135	46,867	1,036,820	0.11
1950	158	160	192,083	1,387,500	0.15
1951	256	258	102,793	901,620	0.09
1952	213	219	112,273	2,765,510	0.29
1953	166	173	54,488	1,312,720	0.14
1954	155	173	56,630	1,430,300	0.15
1955	149	159	60,090	1,875,400	0.19
1956	221	229	88,680	1,246,000	0.11
1957	238	245	80,695	1,477,100	0.13
1958	251	259	111,475	2,816,850	0.25
1959	201	216	95,120	2,226,890	0.19
1960	268	274	49,408	738,700	0.06
1961	272	287	97,959	1,335,080	0.11
1962	290	311	74,332	1,417,900	0.11
1963	318	332	83,428	917,140	0.07
1964	327	343	100,535	1,580,550	0.11
1965	478	501	171,870	2,349,870	0.17
1966	582	617	411,459	5,178,170	0.34
1967	498	522	252,418	3,974,760	0.25
1968	559	582	223,562	5,082,732	0.32
1969	566	595	306,799	7,751,880	0.46
1970	503	542	261,706	6,539,560	0.39
1971	547	569	239,631	2,866,590	0.16
1972	556	598	706,474	7,753,530	0.43
1973	677	724	348,470	5,776,080	0.30
1974	1,173	1,218	580,912	9,221,890	0.46
1975	1,103	1,171	506,443	10,908,810	0.53
1976	921	1,039	1,570,940	11,609,890	0.55
1977	739	803	217,557	3,307,880	0.15
1978	1,004	1,058	401,688	7,392,820	0.34
1979	987	1,050	462,504	7,834,230	0.34
1980	952	1,028	441,025	8,975,390	0.38
1981	943	1,048	338,548	8,878,490	0.37
1982	608	677	444,302	5,795,420	0.25
1983	576	645	329,309	4,443,960	0.19
1984	652	716	186,993	3,883,400	0.19
1985	760	829	162,231	3,125,460	0.13
1986	643	735	483,615	7,108,730	0.28
1987	569	656	582,659	3,978,760	0.15
1988	471	549	208,167	5,045,700	0.18

Source: For the figures 1901 to 1973, *Strikes and Lockouts in Canada*, Information Canada, 1975, pp. 7–8; and the figures for the years 1974 to 1980 are taken from Labour Data, Labour Canada, *Strikes and Lockouts in Canada* (Ottawa: Supply and Services Canada), p. 9. Reproduced by permission of the Minister of Supply and Services Canada. The figures for 1981–1983 are taken from Labour Data, Labour Canada, *Strikes and Lockouts in Canada* (Ottawa: Supply and Services Canada, 1983), Table 1, p. 13. Reproduced by permission of the Minister of Supply and Services Canada. The figures for 1984–1988 were obtained from the Bureau of Labour Information, Labour Canada, Special Computer Printout, June 20, 1989.

Major Cause of Strikes

The continued high incidence of strikes in Canada relative to that of other countries in recent years has led to an increased interest in the topic. One of the better studies which attempts to analyze industrial conflict in Canada is that of S.M. Jamieson, a long-time commentator on this subject.[51] Jamieson indicates that, for the period from 1966 to 1975, Canada experienced the highest incidence of strikes (as measured by person-days lost per 1,000 workers) of any nation except Italy. He contends that this high level of conflict seems to have been caused by two particular features of Canada's political economy and industrial relations system:

(1) the unique pattern of economic instability in Canada, arising from the high degree of specialization of her export trade and highly unstable and capital-intensive resource industries. These have exerted a strong and destabilizing "multiplier effect" on other sectors of the economy, particularly the construction and "heavy" capital goods industries; and (2) the highly decentralized trade union movement, and its political weakness and inability to exert any significant influence over the economic policies of business and governments.[52]

He goes on to point out that economic instability generates high levels of industrial conflict for a variety of reasons. These include:

the rapid increase in profits as compared to wages during boom periods; the widespread feelings of insecurity created by periodic labour shortages and over-expansion, by mass layoffs and unemployment; and, most important perhaps, the widely unequal gains in wages and fringe benefits for workers in different industries.[53]

In addition, Jamieson claims that six industries which employ less than 15% of all workers accounted for more than 50% of all person-days lost due to strikes during the period from 1966 to 1975. These six industries are construction, mining and smelting, transportation, primary metals, pulp and paper, and wood products. Between 1966 and 1970, these industries accounted for 53.5% of person-days lost. The addition of transportation, communication, and public utilities raised the total to 73%.[54]

Construction is the leader in person-days lost due to strikes. Jamieson has claimed for some time that economic instability is one of the major factors in the high incidence of strikes in Canada. In his more recent study, he contends that this factor has accounted for a disproportionate share of all strike activity in Canada during the 1960s and 1970s. With respect to the period from 1966 to 1975, he observes that:

the half-dozen or so goods-producing industries which accounted for more than one half of all man-days lost in strikes during 1966-75 were also among the most cyclically sensitive, and enjoyed among the largest wage increases during the 1960's. These, in turn, appeared to have a pattern-setting role, stimulating workers in other major sectors such as transportation, public utility and public sectors generally to demand and strike for larger gains in the 1970's.[55]

In keeping with his earlier analysis, Jamieson also claims that more than three-quarters of all person-days lost due to strikes during the period from 1966 to 1975 were concentrated in the three main industrial provinces of Ontario, Quebec, and British Columbia. He suggests that if the person-days lost due to strikes under federal jurisdiction were estimated for each province in proportion to its share of workers in the industries or occupations involved, these three provinces would account for more than 90% of all person-days lost. However, he indicates that the timing of strikes, the different percentages of person-days lost, and the uneven strike record for these three provinces in the sixties and seventies may be attributed to different provincial responses to the same broad economic force.[56]

One may also attribute the high percentage of person-days lost in Canada to the long duration of strikes. From 1960 to 1976, the percentage of strikes which lasted over 25 days increased from 19% to 40%. In 1977, Canada experienced 100 strikes, 10% of which lasted between 50 and 99 days and accounted for 30% of all time lost that year. In addition, about 4% of the strikes lasted from 100 to 199 days and accounted for 17% of the time lost. Thus 14% of the strikes in 1977 accounted for approximately 47% of the time lost, a fact which confirms the view that Canada's problem is not the number of strikes, but their duration, since so few account for the time lost due to strikes.[57]

Strikes reached a peak in 1976 when there was a one-day national protest against the wage-and-price controls then in effect, and declined to comparatively low levels in the 1980s. Part of the reason for the low incidence of strikes in the early part of the decade may be the public-sector wage constraint programs for federal and most provincial public-sector workers. The low inflation rate, and the negotiation of close to "real wages" may explain the low incidence of strikes in the late eighties.

Public- and Private-Sector Strikes

We will now discuss strikes in the public sector and compare them with strikes in the private sector. The analysis here is based in part on a study of strikes in the Canadian public sector by D. A. Smith.[58] The basic issue explored in this study is which sector — the public or private — is more strike-prone. Smith compared the frequency, size, and duration of strikes between the two sectors. Using the frequency of strikes as a measure of strike activity, he concluded that there was a slight upward trend in the proportion of public-sector strikes. However, when allowances were made for the degree of employment and unionism in the public sector, Smith concluded that

> since public employees constitute approximately 25 per cent of the Canadian labour force and approximately 45 per cent of union members, it is clear that in terms of frequency the public sector is less strike prone than is the private sector.[59]

Using time lost due to strikes for the period from 1972 to 1981 as a measure of strike activity, Smith found that in only two of the ten years studied did time lost exceed the employment rate in the public sector. However, for the entire period from 1972 to 1981, "the average share of the public sector in the total number of work-days lost is just over 20 per cent, a figure which is below the employment share of the public sector."[60]

On a sectoral basis, strikes were found to be more frequent in the education and health care sectors. Over 61% of public-sector strikes occurred in these two sectors in 1980, compared with just over 30% in 1972.[61] In attempting to discover explanatory variables for the frequency of public-sector strikes, Smith found that when inflation, unemployment, and other variables were accounted for, the number of strikes continued to increase in the public sector.[62] In addition, strikes in the public sector were found to be less responsive to labour market conditions than were strikes in the private sector.

The MacDonald Royal Commission of Canada's economic union and development prospects commissioned a study of "Strike Activity in Canada" by R. Lacroix.[63] In this study, Lacroix discusses the explanations that have been offered for strikes generally, and then focuses his attention more on the Canadian scene. He explains that according to one school of thought strikes are at least in part a result of the differences in bargaining power between the parties, and are associated with the swings in the business cycle. However, as Lacroix points out, one of the major problems with this argument is the difficulty of linking an increase in bargaining power with a higher incidence of strikes.[64]

Lacroix refers to a popular model developed in 1969 by Ashenfelter and Johnson, who contended that there are three parties involved in contract negotiations: management, union leaders, and union members. In order for union leaders to expand the union and secure their own position, they had to satisfy the expectations of their constituents. If union members expected wage increases greater than those which management was willing to offer, union leaders would call a strike. The strike would last until members lowered their expectations to correspond with the employer's final offer. This model assumes that employers will try to optimize profits. It also assumes that the employer is the only party who has all of the information required to make decisions about strikes, since the employer knows the employees' resistance curve (which was discussed in Chapter 7). However, it may be argued that rather than being passive, workers may decide whether to call a strike or not by maximizing a function of "new benefit" from the strike in accordance with the employer's concession function and thus derive a wage scale and strike duration. This worker role was developed by Eaton in 1972.[65]

Lacroix, in his review of the literature on strike causation, also states that a theory of strikes has been proposed and empirically verified which views strikes as *accidents* which occur during the course of contract negotiations. According to this theory, both parties have a vested interest in negotiating until they reach a settlement because both parties wish to avoid a strike, workers obtain better benefits than those initially offered by the employer, and the employer signs a less costly agreement than that originally demanded by the workers. "The bargaining process is actually an exchange of information on the firm's ability to pay and the union's ability to support a strike."[66] Since both parties incur costs during the negotiation process, they must choose an optimal bargaining duration — a duration in which marginal costs equal marginal gains. "In most cases, the choice of an optimal duration implies that, by limiting the duration of the negotiations, the parties accept a strike probability that is greater than zero."[67] Lacroix believes that, by using this model, variations of strikes can be explained among industries, by firms in the same industry, and among countries. Strikes can vary between industries since the tradeoff between strike probability and bargaining duration varies from one industry to another. For example, firms operating in a competitive, international market require extensive information on the state and prospects of foreign competition, exchange rates, transportation costs, etc. There is a higher probability of strikes in these types of industries than there is in stable industries since the parties to the negotiations will experience greater difficulty in reconciling their different perceptions of these factors.[68]

In analyzing the Canadian situation in comparison with some European countries where the incidence of strikes is less severe, Lacroix contrasts the centralized negotiations in some countries, in which the parties work closely together at the national level, with the much more decentralized level of negotiations in Canada. Also, he points out that in several instances, employee benefits are provided by law rather than negotiated in collective agreements as in Canada, with the result that there are more negotiable items in Canada. This, in turn, enhances the opportunities for strikes.[69]

The Feedback Loop and the Outputs of the Canadian Industrial Relations System

In keeping with the framework set out in the first chapter, it is appropriate, at this point, to discuss the outputs of the industrial relations system as they feed back into the system itself and into the environmental subsystems. The concept of the feedback loop is a very useful one in analyzing the outputs of the industrial relations system, as they are perceived as rewards to employees and often as costs for employers. Also, strikes and actions taken to end them can easily be analyzed by using the loop.

Among the organizationally oriented outcomes of the industrial relations system, dues check-off clauses and union security clauses have aroused the most controversy and have generated a fair amount of industrial conflict in a number of jurisdictions. The degree of conflict was so great in Ontario that the Ontario government felt it necessary to legislate compulsory dues check-off so as to avoid strikes over the issue. Union recognition clauses in collective agreements have served to legitimize unions not only in the workplace, but also at higher societal levels. Many public and parapublic white-collar workers now belong to unions because of union security clauses, and pay union dues according to dues check-off provisions. This fact has been responsible in part for the widespread acceptance of unions in Canada as the legitimate voice for the aspirations of practically all categories of Canadians.

With respect to worker-related outputs, wages and other items which have a cost component to them are sometimes seen as causes of inflationary spirals. It can be argued that at the micro or plant level a high increase in wages in any one year, if not offset by a substantial increase in productivity, could cause an increase in costs and eventually an increase in prices. Yet, while most economists agree that unions may have some "wage push" effects on inflation, no one has yet been able to specify precisely what impact negotiated wage increases and other cost items have on the inflationary process. Nevertheless, it is the real or perceived effects of wage increases on cost, prices, and hence inflation which prompt governments to introduce wage-and-price controls (sometimes called incomes policies) in an effort to reduce the rate of inflation.

Unions have a long history of lobbying governments and trying to negotiate shorter working hours. Shorter hours of work, negotiated holidays, and the increasing length of vacations are now giving workers more leisure time in a highly-paced and stressful society. In addition, the 40-hour work week in most collective agreements has also had an impact on governments setting standard hours per week and establishing regulations concerning overtime for non-unionized workers.

Negotiated group medical and dental plans give workers a sense of security should they become ill, and retirement plans, including early retirement, allow workers a good deal of flexibility in deciding how to spend their later years. The recent emergence of negotiated maternity leave should also add to this sense of security, especially among those working women who are important contributors to fam-ily incomes or who are primary wage-earners. In addition, such measures in collective agreements may eventually serve as a model for legislation governing the provision of maternity leave.

On the general question of job security, unions have been instrumental in establishing seniority as an important factor in matters of promotion, lay-off, and recall. Here, too, there is evidence that clauses in collective agreements have served as models for legislation covering both unionized and non-unionized workers.

Industrial Conflict and Back-to-Work Legislation

A strike in one industry may very well have serious detrimental effects on other industries in our economic system, as well as affecting the well-being of citizens, nationally or in a given province. If it seems clear that the public strongly objects to such work stoppages and if the politicians are convinced that hardships are occurring, government will likely pass back-to-work legislation. This is a good example of how the feedback loop helps in analyzing the outputs of the industrial relations system.

Some governments monitor the effects of a strike and pass special back-to-work legislation only when a strike begins to have serious consequences. In 1966, for example, when railway workers struck, the federal Department of Labour watched the impact of the strike on the movement of grain and other goods. It was only when the movement of goods came close to a halt that special legislation was enacted. Department officials knew from experience that railway workers do not undertake strike action lightly and that, in this case, there were many pent up frustrations that a short strike might alleviate.

Governments are not always sensitive, however, to the need for workers to relieve tensions resulting from stalled bargaining talks. In the 1978 postal strike, for example, where postal workers had been working for a year or more

The Financial Post

without a renewed agreement and where there was much hostility on both sides, the federal government passed special back-to-work legislation very soon after the strike was called — a puzzling decision since two previous postal strikes of a month or more were settled without back-to-work orders. It was later revealed that the Postmaster-General had been erroneously advised that the workers would not obey a strike call by the president of the union. It was only the day that special legislation was intro-

duced in Parliament that the Postmaster-General discovered that the workers were in fact prepared to strike.

In the above case, the government may be criticized for basing the decision to invoke back-to-work legislation on the anticipated outcome of a strike vote rather than on any clear-cut notion of a strike's detrimental effects. As such, the decision was potentially damaging to respect for the rule of law because it invited defiance of the back-to-work order.

As may be seen from these examples, the problem of strikes is particularly acute in public-sector bargaining. J. Boivin observed that, while there seems to be no superior alternative to collective bargaining in determining the working conditions of public-sector workers, there is also no universal solution to problems in public-sector labour relations.[70] "What should be recognized in the end," he claims, "is that the final solution to labour relations conflict in the public sector will always be a political one."[71]

I concur with this view, inasmuch as there seems to be no final answer as to what the most appropriate form of action should be with respect to disputes in the public sector and in essential areas of the private sector. Arbitration as a method of resolving interest disputes is often violated, as was demonstrated in the Ontario hospitals case in the winter of 1981. Back-to-work legislation tends to be habit-forming because governments, as well as the parties involved, often look to it as a face-saving device. Fines and imprisonment do not seem to be effective remedies to collective bargaining problems, particularly in the public and essential-service sectors.

One must finally conclude that the ultimate responsibility for resolving industrial disputes resides with the elected members of Parliament or the provincial legislators, who are there to act on behalf of society as a whole. This principle implies, however, a respect both for the parties involved in an industrial dispute and for the public good.

Questions

1 Describe the relationship between the outputs (particularly the wage settlements and COLA clauses) contained in this chapter and some of the environmental factors discussed in Chapter 2? Elaborate.

2 What are the major organization-oriented outputs? Elaborate.

3 Is the three-fold conceptual distinction of worker-oriented outputs a useful one? Why or why not?

4 What is the significance of each of the three types of worker-oriented outputs? In which category do you expect to see the most changes in the next five years?

5 Discuss the incidence of industrial conflict as an output of the industrial relations system. What are the major causes for its high incidence and how may it be reduced?

6 Using the concept of the feedback loop, analyze the significance of the outputs of the Canadian industrial relations system for other subsystems of Canadian society.

7 Do the sample clauses and tables in this chapter give you a better understanding of collective bargaining than you had when you began the course? Elaborate.

8 Do you now see why increases in wages, if not offset by increases in productivity, might account for increases in prices? Through what process might this occur for a small company operating in the community from which you come?

9 Does the evidence presented in this chapter on the incidence of strikes in the private and public sectors accord with what the public generally thinks? Elaborate.

10 Do you agree with the assessment of back-to-work legislation presented in this chapter? Do you see any alternatives to it? Do you consider an essential-services council, such as that in Quebec, to be a good solution to essential-service disputes? Elaborate.

Notes

1 E. F. Beal, E. D. Wickersham, and P. K. Kienast, *The Practice of Collective Bargaining*, 5th ed. (Homewood Ill: Richard D. Irwin, Inc., 1976) in particular Pt. 3, Chs. 9-13.

2 The sample clauses contained in this and other sections are taken from Labour Data Branch, Labour Canada, *Sample Clauses for the Analysis of Collective Agreements*, Annex to the Coding Manual for the Analysis of Collective Agreements (1974), and Bureau of Labour Information, Labour Canada, *Collective Agreement Coding Manual*, December 1, 1987.

3 All tables, with the exception of this one and a few others, are based on an analysis of 1,081 collective agreements covering 2,393,000 workers.

4 Definitions of union security clauses are taken from those provided by Labour Canada in the publications cited above.

5 *Arlington Crane Service Ltd. et al. v. Ont. Min. of Labour et al.*, (1989), 89 C.L.L.C., at p. 12,160.

6 Ibid., p. 12,167.

7 L. Slotnick, "Use of Union Dues for Political Causes Does Not Violate Charter, Court Rules," *Globe and Mail*, January 31, 1989, p. A2.

8 Ibid.

9 Ibid.

10 The annual figures were obtained by taking all negotiations settled in any given calendar year and calculating the average annual percentage increase over the life of the agreement. These figures were then weighted by the total number of workers covered by the agreements, summed, and the weighted mean for the calendar year was obtained. The effective wage increase is arrived at by assuming an estimated inflation rate based on the CPI and used as a proxy for the rate of inflation. The CPI is applied to those agreements which contain COLA clauses. Adjustments are made subsequently if the increase in the CPI is different from the assumed increase.

11 The non-commercial industries consist of highway and bridge maintenance, water systems and other utilities, hospitals, welfare organizations, religious organizations, private households, education and related services, public administration, and defence. Commercial industries consist of all industries except the non-commercial industries.

12 J.-M. Cousineau and R. Lacroix, *Wage Determination in Major Collective Agreements in the Private and Public Sectors* (Ottawa: Supply and Services Canada, 1977); D.A.L. Auld, L. N. Christofides, R. Swidinsky, and D. A. Wilton, *The Determination of Negotiated Wage Settlements in Canada (1966-1975)* (Hull: Supply and Services Canada, 1979); G. G. Johnson, *Non-Union Wage Changes in Canada: Theory and Survey Evidence* (Hull: Supply and Services Canada, 1979); A. A. Porter et al., *Wages in Canada and the United States: An Analytical Comparison* (Ottawa: Queen's Printer, 1969); G. F. Starr, *Union-Nonunion Wage Differentials: A Cross Sectional Analysis* (Toronto: Research Branch, Ontario Ministry of Labour, March 1973); N. M. Meltz and D. Stager, *The Occupational Structure of Earnings in Canada, 1931-1975* (Hull: Supply and Services Canada, 1979); J. C. Anderson, "Determinants of Bargaining Outcomes in the Federal Government of Canada," Vol. 32, No. 2, *Industrial and Labor Relations Review* (January 1979), pp. 224-41; M. Gunderson, "Earnings Differential Between the Public and Private Sectors," Vol. XII, No. 2, *Canadian Journal of Economics* (May 1979), pp. 228-42; M. Gunderson, "Public Sector Compensation in Canada and the U.S.," Vol. 19, No. 3, *Industrial Relations* (Fall 1980), pp. 257-71; M. Gunderson, "The Public/Private Sector Compensation Controversy," *Conflict or Compromise: The Future of Public Sector Industrial Relations*, eds. M. Thompson and G. Swimmer (Montreal: The Institute for Research on Public Policy, 1984), pp. 5-43.

13 Auld et al., *The Determination of Negotiated Wage Settlements in Canada*, p. 8.

14 Ibid., p. 118.

15 Ibid., pp. 131-52.

16 Ibid., pp. 183-84.

17 Cousineau and Lacroix, *Wage Determination in Major Collective Agreements in the Private and Public Sectors*, p. 25.

18 Ibid., p, 63.

19 Ibid., p. 66.

20 Ibid., p. 67.

21 Auld et al., *The Determinants of Negotiated Wage Settlements in Canada*, p. 157.

22 Anderson, "Determinants of Bargaining Outcomes in the Federal Government in Canada," pp. 232-33.

23 Gunderson, "Earnings Differentials Between the Private and Public Sectors," p. 238.

24 Gunderson, "Public Sector Compensation in Canada and the U.S.A.," p. 264.

25 Gunderson, "The Public/Private Sector Compensation Controversy," p. 19.

26 Ibid.

27 Starr, *Union-Nonunion Wage Differentials: A Cross Sectional Analysis*, p. 115.

28 Ibid., p. 125.

29 Johnson, *Non-Union Wage Changes in Canada: Theory and Survey Evidence*, pp. 124-25.

30 Ibid., p. 125.

31 For an example of one such study see John C. Anderson, "Bargaining Outcomes: an IR System Approach," Vol. 18, No. 2, *Industrial Relations* (Spring 1979), pp: 127-43.

32 Bureau of Labour Information, Labour Canada, *Collective Agreement Coding Manual*, December 1, 1987, p. 5.

33 Bureau of Labour Information, Labour Canada, "Provisions in Collective Agreements (Computer Printout), June 3, 1989, p. 10.

34 Labour Data Branch, Labour Canada, *Provisions in Major Collective Agreements in Canada Covering 500 and More Employees, All Industries (Excluding Construction)* (Ottawa: Supply and Services Canada, 1985), pp. 43-45.

35 Ibid., p. 104.

36 Ibid., pp. 26-27.

37 Ibid., p. 23.

38 Bureau of Labour Information, Labour Canada, "Provisions in Collective Agreements," p. 36.

39 Ibid., p. 37.

40 Ibid., pp. 36-37.

41 Ibid., p. 40.

42 Ibid., p. 5.

43 D. J. M. Brown and D. M. Beatty, *Canadian Labour Arbitration* (Aurora: Canada Law Book Limited, 1984), pp. 215-16.

44 Ibid.

45 Quoted in B. Adell, "Law in IR in Common Law Canada," *The State of the Art in Industrial Relations*, eds. G. Hébert, H.C. Jain, N.M. Meltz (Kingston: Industrial Relations Centre, Queen's University and Toronto: Industrial Relations Centre, University of Toronto, 1988), p. 112. See also D.D. Carter, "Canadian Labour Relations Under the Charter, Exploring the Implications," Vol. 43, No. 2 (1988) *Relations Industrielles/ Industrial Relations*, pp. 305–321.

46 Adell, p. 109.

47 D.M. Beatty, *Putting the Charter to Work: Designing a Constitutional Labour Code* (McGill-Queen's University Press, 1987).

48 Adell, pp. 130-31.

49 *Reference re Public Service Employee Relations Act (Alta.)*, [1987] 1 S.C.R. 313; *Psac v. Canada* [1987] 1 S.C.R. 424 and *RWDSU v. Saskatchewan* [1987] 460.

50 From preliminary figures of the Occupational Safety and Health Branch, Labour Canada, and *Historical Labour Statistics*, Catalogue #77-201 (Annual), p. 128.

51 S. M. Jamieson, *Industrial Conflict in Canada 1966-1975* (Discussion Paper No, 142, Centre for the Study of Inflation and Productivity, Economic Council of Canada, December 1979). See also the large number of studies cited in the footnotes to Jamieson's paper.

52 Ibid., Summary, p. 1.

53 Ibid.

54 Ibid., p. 13.

55 Ibid., p. 30.

56 Ibid., p. 34.

57 Alton W. J. Craig, "Canada's Industrial Relations in International Perspective," Vol. 3, No. 1, *Foreign Investment Review* (Autumn 1979), p. 9.

58 D. A. Smith, "Strikes in the Canadian Public Sector," *Conflict or Compromise: The Future of Public Sector Industrial Relations*, eds. Thompson and Swimmer, pp. 197-228.

59 Ibid., p. 204.

60 Ibid., p. 206.

61 Ibid.

62 Ibid., p. 215.

63 R. Lacroix, "Strike Activity in Canada," *Canadian Labour Relations*, W.C. Riddell, Research Coordinator (Toronto: University of Toronto Press, 1986), pp. 161-209.

64 Ibid., pp. 162-164.

65 Ibid., pp. 164-166.

66 Ibid., p. 168.

67 Ibid., p. 169.

68 Ibid., p. 170.

69 Ibid., pp. 171–202.

70 J. Boivin, "Collective Bargaining in the Public Sector: Some Propositions on the Causes of Public Employee Unrest," *Collective Bargaining in the Essential and Public Services Sectors*, ed. M. Gunderson (Toronto: University of Toronto Press, 1975), p. 13.

71 Ibid., p. 15.

Postscript
Some Concluding Observations

The Financial Post

Industrial Relations: A Limited-Purpose Instrument

The practice of industrial relations — or, more narrowly, collective bargaining — should be looked upon as a limited-purpose instrument and not as a panacea for all problems in the workplace. This book has defined industrial relations systems as complexes of private and public activities, operating in specific environments, and concerned with the allocation of rewards to workers for their services and the conditions under which work is performed. By definition, then, industrial relations systems are not designed to handle major social and economic problems such as unemployment, technological change, and inflation. They may be of partial assistance in helping workers to adjust to technological change, but they can neither assume the responsibility for the adverse consequences, nor amend the difficulties arising from such change. Similarly, while industrial relations systems may assist in alleviating inflation, they cannot solve it.

Even the best efforts of economists and politicians are insufficient when applied to resolving these major problems in highly industrialized countries. Yet some observers of the industrial relations scene, particularly socialist writers, seem to think that industrial relations should be able to succeed where politics and economics have failed. A good example of a popular writing which has been critical of industrial relations systems for their failure to cure social ills is a book by Paul Jacobs: *Old Before Its Time: Collective Bargaining at 28*. Jacobs, a long-time socialist and supporter of unionism in the 1930s, concludes that unions have become too conservative. He accuses them of failing society by failing to end inflation, unemployment, and maladaptation to technological change — all of which were subjects of great concern during the early 1960s.[1] Such a view lacks a genuine appreciation of the limited but important objectives that an industrial relations system serves; it is dangerous to ask any system to perform functions for which it was not intended since this could very well inhibit or destroy its capacity to carry out its intended functions.

Dunlop's assessment of industrial relations systems is very much more pertinent than Jacobs':

> It is a system to establish, revise and administer many of the rules of the workplace; ... it is a procedure to determine the compensation of employees and to influence the distribution of the economic pie; ... it is a method for dispute settlement during the life of agreements and on their expiration or reopening, before or after resort to the strike or lockout.[2]

According to Dunlop, three forces compete to perform these functions: unilateral management action, unilateral union action, and government fiat. Various combinations are possible among the three. Again, fundamental social issues such as poverty, civil rights, and unemployment are not amenable to solution by means of actions undertaken by industrial relations systems. Any assessment of industrial relations systems, Dunlop claims, must be made against their intents.[3]

Critical Issues for Labour, Management and Government During the 1990s

Critical Issues for Labour

Nationalism and Consolidation There has already been a number of mergers among sizable unions, and several Canadian branches of international unions have formed autonomous Canadian unions. Although one can predict that this trend will continue in the years ahead, the major question is how much consolidation will in fact take place. The answer probably lies in the degree to which existing unions adequately serve their membership. If a substantial number of workers perceive that the present structure of unions is not doing the job they expect, then the degree of consolidation may be substantial. On the other hand, if workers are satisfied with the service the present union structure gives them, then the trend to consolidation may be insignificant.

Should the high level of nationalistic sentiment continue in Canada, there are likely to be a number of breakaway movements, especially among larger Canadian branches of international unions. Conversely, if nationalism subsides, so will the desire for autonomous organizations. International unions cannot count on such a development, however, and would be wise to review past disaffections of Canadian branches of international unions in order to determine how to better serve their Canadian members. Such concern on the part of international unions would, doubtless, inhibit further breakaway movements.

The breakaway of the Canadian section of the United Auto Workers in 1984 to form a strictly Canadian union in 1985 exemplifies what can happen if the head office of an international union tries to dictate what Canadian workers should do, particularly if the Canadian section is headed by dynamic leaders. A sense of nationalism may have been involved in the CAW case, since Canadian unions in general refrained from concession bargaining to the extent that American unions did in the early 1980s, including the UAW.

A major policy decision that will confront a number of independent unions that do not now belong to the mainstream of the Canadian labour movement is whether or not to join the Canadian Labour Congress, the Canadian Federation of Labour, or some other national body. Groups such as engineers in private industry, nurses, and teachers, among others, may decide to remain independent. Most teachers' and nurses' associations, for example, have been independent for a long time at the provincial level and are unlikely to join a national federation. The recent formation of a national union among nurses may, however, serve as a model for similar groups. Engineers not employed in the public sector have only recently formed associations. These associations are isolated and local in nature and it may be some time before they form autonomous entities at the provincial and national levels.

If the teachers and engineers do join the CLC, they will add to the growing presence of public and parapublic workers within the Congress. The PSAC, representing federal workers, has long been affiliated with the CLC and is, indeed, one of the largest components within that body. The largest union in the CLC (and in Canada) is the Canadian Union of Public Employees (CUPE) which represents municipal workers, non-professional workers in hospitals and hydroelectric companies (Ontario Hydro, for example), and school board and university workers. Since 1975, an umbrella association, the National Union of Provincial Government Employees (NUPGE), representing public servants in provincial associations, has also been a member of the CLC. Although some problems in leadership had emerged in the past, NUPGE is now ready to maintain its position as another important member of the Congress.

Duty of Fair Representation   Another critical issue which unions are going to have to face in an increasing number of jurisdictions is the duty to represent workers fairly in grievance cases. Eight jurisdictions in Canada now have a legislative requirement that unions represent their members fairly. In a recent case, the Ontario Labour Relations Board stated that a union must act in a manner that is not arbitrary, discriminatory, or in bad faith. In the case before the Board, a worker alleged that she had been fired for union activities but that her union had refused to file a complaint with the OLRB. The Board found the union guilty of not representing the worker fairly, had her reinstated, and ordered the union to pay the women's legal costs since she took the case to the Board at her own expense.[4] In the future, union leaders are going to have to be very careful in dealing with members' complaints about the quality of union representation. If they fail to do so, there will be many unfair labour practice cases filed by members against their own unions.

Possible Increasing Role of Women   Women have been steadily assuming more and more leadership in Canadian unions. The Ontario Federation of Labour and the CLC have now increased the number of women on their executive councils. With Shirley Carr as the new CLC president, it is likely that women will feel encouraged to run for executive office in their unions. In 1985, for example, a 23-year-old woman was elected president of the Winnipeg Labour Council, which represents 33,000 workers.[5] Since women now constitute over 43% of the labour force and over 36% of unionized workers, many women will be seeking not only a greater role in union leadership, but improvements in benefits, such as paid maternity leave and daycare.[6]

Legislative Protection   At common law, workers had few rights attached to their jobs. Their employment could be terminated upon the employer giving reasonable notice, a concept which has caused a great deal of controversy.[7] However, as we indicated in Chapter 1, one close observer of the Canadian labour scene has argued that unorganized workers are becoming a force to be reckoned with.[8] In the non-unionized sectors, a host of laws govern workers in matters such as unemployment insurance, minimum wages, maximum hours, statutory holidays, equal pay for work of equal value, and human rights or equality under the law irrespective of colour, race, creed, national ancestry and, in some cases, age. Some human rights legislation prohibits sexual harassment in the workplace. Also, in some jurisdictions, workers can refuse to do work which they consider a serious threat to their health and safety. Most of these provisions apply to both the unionized and non-unionized sectors of the economy, and are usually found in what is referred to as labour standards legislation.

Federal legislation and legislation in Nova Scotia and Quebec gives non-unionized workers the right of appeal in cases where they feel that they have been dismissed (and in some cases disciplined) without just cause. These cases can go all the way to binding arbitration by an impartial arbitrator. Many cases have been reported where arbitrators have ordered workers reinstated with compensation from the time of their dismissal. While much labour standards legislation lags behind the unionized sector, procedural rights are at the leading edge of labour-management relations.

Group Action   In addition to extensive and growing individual protections, support is building for group action, particularly in the area of health and safety. Joint union-management and worker-management committees have functioned very effectively in Saskatchewan in the health and safety field since the 1970s. In these committees, workers and management are able to resolve issues quite successfully on their own. One major reason for their success is that both workers and management know that government administrators are committed to making the actors in the industrial relations system the prime agents for ensuring compliance.[9] The Ontario Occupational Health and Safety Act requires the establishment of committees consisting of at least two people. Worker members are selected by the workers where no unions exist, and by unions where they do exist.

The use of universal committees in non-union as well as union organizations was introduced under the federal Labour Adjustment Benefits Act of 1982, which deals with redundancies. When an employer plans to terminate the employment of 50 or more workers within a four-week period in an establishment under federal jurisdiction, a joint planning committee of not less than four members must be established. In non-unionized organizations, the workers are entitled to select members of the committee, just as a union is in unionized organizations. The joint committees are charged with the development of adjustment programs to eliminate the necessity for termination or to minimize its adverse impact on redundant workers by helping them to find other employment. Unless the members agree otherwise, joint planning committees may only deal with matters normally addressed in collective agreements with respect to termination of employment. "The members shall cooperate and make every reasonable effort to develop an adjustment program as expeditiously as possible."[10] These words are similar to those which impose an obligation on unions and management to bargain in good faith under a collective bargaining relationship.

It is possible that this type of government-sponsored procedure will encourage the formation of unions, particularly when workers experience what it is like to deal with employers on a united rather than individual basis. Adams sees the possibility of committees undertaking a multitude of tasks, including redundancy, technological change, health and safety, training, and the joint management of pension plans. Instead of having a committee to deal with each of these issues, he forsees one general-purpose committee emerging which would be responsible for coordinating all of these different programs. "Should collective employment decision making become as widespread as the current trend suggests it might," he claims, "the term [unorganized] will cease to have any real meaning. Everyone will be organized."[11] Another writer, however, sees these government initiatives as obstacles to the formation of unions since, as he argues, governments seem to be doing so much that there is little need for unions in many instances.[12]

We need hardly take sides with one or the other of these predictions. Workers in non-unionized organizations in some jurisdictions already have some input into the ways in which their rewards and the conditions under which they work are established. A central question is whether they will be satisfied with what they have now or will attempt to gain more by unionizing.

The Charter of Rights and Freedoms The Canadian Charter of Rights and Freedoms will affect unions, workers, and employers greatly in the immediate future. The provisions of the Charter apply to Parliament, the legislatures, and federal and provincial governments. Any action which is perceived to contravene guaranteed rights and freedoms may be challenged.[13] Section 1 of the Charter guarantees rights and freedoms "subject only to such reasonable limits prescribed by law as can be demonstrably justified in a free and democratic society."[14] Every time a court invokes one of the rights or freedoms, it must determine if the infringement is justified under the words quoted above. "Reasonable limits" and "demonstrably justified" can mean different things to different judges, and differing judgments are being handed down at lower court levels. It will take many years before a body of jurisprudence evolves from the Charter of Rights and Freedoms.

Freedom of association is guaranteed under section 2(d) of the Charter. An important ques-

tion is whether freedom of association carries with it the right to collective bargaining and the right to strike. In the few decisions handed down to date involving wage restraints in public-sector jurisdictions, one concluded that the right to collective bargaining and strike action *are* part of the freedom of association, and two others disagreed.[15] The courts viewed the restraint programs as temporary or exceptional. One writer, after reviewing legislation such as the restraint program and back-to-work statutes in various Canadian jurisdictions, concludes that the courts have failed to note the restructuring that is taking place in Canada and which is denying rights to trade unions — rights attained at great cost, rights which should be protected.[16]

Section 15(1) of the Charter states:

> Every individual is equal before and under the law and has the right to the equal protection and benefit of the law without discrimination and, in particular, without discrimination based on race, national or ethnic origin, colour, religion, sex, age or mental or physical disability.[17]

This section is expected to usher in a flood of cases, which may take years to resolve. One such case is that initiated by the CLC in the Supreme Court of Nova Scotia to have section 24A of the Nova Scotia Trade Union Act (the Michelin Bill) declared illegal.[18] As we have discussed, this 1979 amendment requires that for a union to be certified as the bargaining agent of a manufacturing company with interdependent plants, the bargaining unit must include workers at all interdependent locations, and the union must win over a majority of them in order to be certified. This means, in effect, that a union cannot apply for certification at one plant only. This is the only legislation of its kind in North America.

In addition to these two examples, numerous cases arising from the Charter have been brought before the courts. Some noteworthy issues have been challenged: the use of compulsory union dues for political causes, the use of

Union wins ruling on dues

Appeal court says they can be funnelled to non-union causes

TORONTO (CP) — The Ontario Court of Appeal has struck down a ruling that would have restricted the use of union dues to support political parties and social causes.

In its decision released Monday, the high court said a contract between the Ontario Public Service Employees Union and the province's community colleges doesn't breach the constitutional rights of teacher Merv Lavigne.

Lavigne, a teacher at the Haileybury School of Mines in Northern Ontario, won a landmark Ontario Supreme Court decision in 1986 that said his rights were violated because a portion of his annual union dues — about $2 — supported causes other than bargaining.

But an appeal by the union reversed that decision.

The conservative National Citizen's Coalition, which has paid about $500,000 for Lavigne's legal fees so far, said the engineering teacher will appeal the ruling to the Surepeme Court of Canada.

"Merv Lavigne doesn't quit and neither does the National Citizen's Coalition," said president, David Somerville.

Lawyers for Lavigne argued the 1984 contract between the union and the council of regents, the governing body for Ontario colleges, violated his right to freedom of association and speech.

Lavigne is not a member of the union but must pay dues. He objected to his dues being spent on political parties and causes with which he disagrees such as the New Democratic Party, abortion clinics and a strike by British coal miners.

The original decision was considered a major blow to organized labor, which has supported causes beyond the bargaining table for more than 40 years.

Union president Jim Clancy said the union's successful appeal means organized labor can continue to lobby for causes such as disarmament, a cleaner environment, measures to reduce poverty and pension reform.

"We reserve the right to speak out on those issues, and to take on government and to take on business when they are leaving workers holding the bag," Clancy told reporters, describing the court ruling as a victory for all workers against big business.

"We always thought this was an important case," Clancy explained. "We never saw this case as one person against the union.

"But rather, we saw this case as a situation where big business, through the National Citizens' Coalition, was trying to trample the traditional rights that trade unions have enjoyed in this country."

The Ontario Court of Appeal also ordered the National Citizens' Coalition to pay all legal costs. But those costs will not have to be paid until the Supreme Court of Canada makes a decision on the case.

Clancy estimated that the Ontario Public Service Employees Union alone has spent between $350,000 and $400,000 in legal fees so far.

The *Ottawa Citizen*, Jan. 31, 1989, p. A3.

---

closed shop union security provisions whereby workers must be members of a union in order to be hired, the imposition of first collective agreements designed to help weak unions, the use of union shop arrangements whereby workers must become union members within specified time periods after they are hired, and the use of accreditation in the construction industry whereby employer associations bargain on behalf of employers. In fact, the very rights to bargain collectively and to strike are being challenged.[19]

Since judges tend to interpret statute law conservatively, it is quite possible that some of these issues may be ruled invalid. Imagine what would happen if the courts were to find that compulsory union dues check-off clauses are illegal: much of a union officer's time would be spent trying to collect union dues! This would set us back to a situation typical of the period prior to 1944 when there was very little legislative support for unions and collective bargaining. The decisions of the courts on these issues could very well change the nature of unionism and collective bargaining as we have come to know them and even wreck what constructive arrangements have been worked out between employers and unions over the years — a bleak scenario, and one that will, I hope, not come about.

B. Adell, a leading Canadian legal scholar, recently stated that

> if the courts refuse to hold that the Charter prohibits legislative encroachments on collective bargaining or on other forms of public or collective regulation of employment conditions, social justice dictates that they also refuse to use the Charter to strike down provisions designed to protect collective employee rights and interests.[20]

Social Partners The above issues are a few of the many that the labour movement in Canada will have to confront in the very near future. In addition, there are the larger concerns about the joint relationship between unions and management or the three-way relationship between unions, management, and government. Such matters as humanizing the workplace (whatever that may come to mean in the North American context) and worker participation in management may also be issues that labour will wish to consider in the future. In addition, if the labour movement wants greater input into the formulation of national policy, it may have to consider, along with management and government, the possibility of some kind of forum in which consultation among the three partners can take place. At the very least, such a forum would allow both unions and management to air their views with respect to proposed government policies.[21]

The creation in 1984 of the Canadian Labour Market and Productivity Centre might be the beginning of more effective cooperation between unions, management, and government in the years to come. Such cooperation may be critical to Canada's competitiveness in international markets in the future, particularly if it improves Canada's low rate of productivity during the 1970s and 1980s.[22]

With respect to worker participation in management, trade unions in North America have long taken the view that they do not wish to take part in managerial decision-making outside the framework of collective bargaining. However, with the problems that many companies are now facing with respect to productivity, absenteeism, turnover, and increasing foreign competition, particularly as a likely consequence of the free-trade pact between Canada and the United States, unions in Canada and in North America generally may have to rethink their position. Canadian unions, in particular, may have to formulate demands more in line with those proposed by their counterparts in the United States. They may also have to consider policy options such as having representatives on the boards of directors of companies, profit-sharing schemes, and greater worker participation in management decision-making. Worker safety and product safety may be improved by greater worker participation — if Canadians are willing and able to face these challenges.[23]

Critical Issues Facing Management

Union Acceptance Many employers accept unions as an integral part of today's industrial society; some, however, merely tolerate their existence. In addition, a significant number of employers would prefer to fight unionism to the bitter end, as has been demonstrated by a number of labour relations board decisions in recent years. Management in the latter category may very well have to rethink their position with respect to unions, particularly in light of the fact that the federal and all ten provincial governments have given collective bargaining rights to their own workers.

Canadian employers as a whole, however, have been more receptive to unions, even during the recession, than their counterparts in the United States. It has become fashionable in the United States for employers to attempt to keep their companies union-free. The same has not been true of employers in Canada. The approaches of the Canadian and US governments have generally stood in very sharp contrast.

Human Rights Legislation With the recent enactment of human rights legislation which bars discrimination on the basis of colour, race, creed, and age, employers are going to have to become much more sophisticated in the development of their human resource policies so that they can justify their decisions before administrative tribunals under various types of legislation. In the past few years, there has been a substantial number of cases in which employers, found guilty of violating these laws, have embarrassed themselves before administrative tribunals, or courts, or both, by trying to justify out-moded human resource policies. What emerges from these cases is the fact that some employers have not done a very sophisticated analysis when determining the types of qualifications necessary to fill their personnel positions, and nor have they confronted other issues, such as discrimination against women and visible minorities, or the problem of sexual harassment.

Group Action Another issue relates more specifically to union-management relations. Traditionally, employers in North America have withheld important information from unions in negotiating collective agreements. As one observer pointed out, all Western European unions receive more relevant data at the enterprise level than North American unions do. He predicts that sooner or later employers in Canada and the United States will have to start sharing information in order to make the collective

bargaining system more effective.[24] The change will probably take some time, and it may occur initially only in those cases where companies are in dire enough financial conditions to plead with unions to help them remain solvent.

The experience of the Chrysler Corporation in 1980 and 1981, and of General Motors and Ford in the United States in 1981 and 1982, is typical of what some companies will do when their financial positions become precarious. The question that many employers are going to have to face is whether to share information with unions only during hard times or on an ongoing basis, so that unions understand the financial positions of companies during negotiations. Even companies that make excess profits may eventually choose to disclose this information to unions. A few companies in Canada disclosed such information several years ago while giving increases to workers during the closed period of the contract but just prior to the release of quarterly or annual financial reports which showed record-breaking profits.

Issues of the *World of Work Report*, which is published monthly by the Work in America Institute Inc., show that a substantial number of companies in the United States are developing programs to increase job satisfaction, worker participation, and quality of work life. Most of these have as their primary objective an increase in productivity. In some cases, these programs are initiated unilaterally by the employer, but often they are undertaken jointly by employers and unions. Such experiments have generally resulted in lower rates of absenteeism, higher morale, and better union-management relations — all of which have contributed to higher productivity. In some cases, these programs have also led to greater community involvement on the part of both unions and management.

Critical Issues Facing Governments

In recent years, most governments in Canada have amended their legislation to make it easier for unions to become certified bargaining agents, to require workers to pay union dues, and to require employers to engage in good faith bargaining. These have all been attempts to improve labour-management reactions generally. However, the new legislation in British Columbia may very well undermine much of the creative efforts that went into improving industrial relations in that province during the late 1970s and early 1980s.

Redundancy A problem that has received a good deal of attention on the part of governments has been that of plant closures which render redundant substantial numbers of workers. These problems are bound to become even greater under the free-trade pact between Canada and the United States. Unfortunately, governments so far have not implemented policies in anticipation of the likely adverse consequences on workers of the pact.

Before the free-trade deal, the Ontario government did initiate legislation to help cope with redundancies. In 1982, the federal government passed the Labour Adjustment Benefits Act, based on the report of an inquiry commission.[25] The provisions in the Act went further than the Commissioner's recommendations in providing benefits to workers affected by plant closures and industrial restructuring, including some aspects of technological change. It is to be hoped that other jurisdictions will enact similar legislation.

The Royal Commission on the Economic Union and Development Prospects for Canada (also known as the Macdonald Commission) has recommended that "increased consultation and cooperation between labour and management should be an objective of Canada's labour relations policy, as well as of employers and employees generally."[26] In the Commission's view, increased cooperation would improve relationships, reduce the incidence of strikes and lockouts, provide more enjoyable work environments for workers, involve workers in more planning and decision making, improve productivity, product quality, and competitiveness, and produce higher profits and wages.[27]

These themes have been familiar ones in labour-management relations in Canada for at least 20 years. I doubt that the Commission's recommendations will have any more impact on employers and unions now than such exhortations have had in the past, for the adversarial nature of the Canadian industrial relations system is still very firmly embedded in the thinking of both employers and unions.

The Macdonald Commission has also recommended arbitration as a viable alternative to strikes or lockouts in sectors where the cost of work stoppages are deemed by the public to be excessive.[28] It may be very difficult to withdraw the right to strike from those who already have had it.

Group Action Another issue which governments, and the federal government in particular, must face is whether or not to consult with labour and management before passing legislation relating to industrial relations and social and economic policies. Both the Quebec and Manitoba governments have joint labour-management committees which examine proposed changes in labour legislation. The same was true in Nova Scotia until the passage of the Michelin Bill in 1979. The federal government has no permanent consultative machinery, but it has usually, until recently, consulted major union and management groups before passing legislation in the industrial relations field. With respect to the larger problem of developing macro-economic and social policies, however, the question is whether or not the federal government is willing to set up consultative machinery and use it in a meaningful way, so as to pass the most appropriate forms of legislation.

Essential Services Another major issue or policy with which governments are going to have to deal is the increasing use of special back-to-work legislation when work stoppages develop in the so-called essential services or industries. There has been a trend in recent years in some jurisdictions to use back-to-work legislation. This legislation is adding, in effect, a predetermined step to the procedure used in handling contract negotiation or interest disputes. Too frequent recourse to back-to-work legislation not only invites defiance of the law, but also diminishes the possibility of the parties to the dispute developing a satisfactory collective bargaining relationship. For this reason, governments may be better advised, in some cases, to allow strikes to continue and let both parties suffer until they come to an agreement by themselves. Granted, a laissez-faire attitude could mean inconvenience and even hardship in some cases. The benefits would, however, outweigh the short-term considerations, since any movement toward restoring bargaining in good faith in specific situations has the effect of engendering greater trust among the participants, especially between government negotiators and union leaders.

During the winter of 1985, the Mulroney government invited labour, management, and other groups to Ottawa for a two-day session. Labour representatives took part in the exercise, but with some skepticism. Since the CLC thought that none of the recommendations it put forth during the session were taken into account when the government's budget was prepared, it convened a two-day conference in early 1986 to discuss the proposals it had put forward, along with some new ones. Although government and management were invited to take part in the conference, neither accepted the invitation. This incident appears to signal that more joint union, management, and government action will not be forthcoming under the Mulroney government, unless Shirley Carr is able to acquire greater access to the corridors of power in Ottawa, or the government changes its mind and accepts a greater role for the union movement in the formulation of national policy. It is doubtful, however, that either of these developments will occur.

Human Rights It is imperative that governments at the federal and provincial levels enact adequate legislation in the areas of human rights, employment standards, and sexual harassment. A reading of some of the cases examined by special tribunals and human rights commissions reveals some deplorable practices. Undoubtedly, the cases investigated represent a small fraction of the actual cases in which harassment takes place. Many occurrences are not investigated since no complaints are lodged. The 1984 federal government legislation requiring all employers in the federal jurisdiction to develop and inform employees of such policies should be emulated by other jurisdictions.

Conclusion

The history of union-management relations in Canada, as in most other countries, has been characterized by a certain amount of conflict. This may be inherent in union-management relations, since there will always be some disagreement as to how the profits of organizations should be shared by the owners of capital and the workers. However, a certain degree of cooperation *does* exist between unions and employers, for their relationship is a symbiotic one — each side needs the other. Many innovations mentioned in this book, in fact, tend to stress a cooperative as opposed to the adversarial approach, and are aimed at reducing labour strife, delivering fair and swift justice to aggrieved parties, and improving the overall working environment for both employers and workers.

The systems approach adopted in this book (see Figure 12.1) is valuable since it allows for a sophisticated analysis of the motivations of the parties, their tactics and rewards, that goes beyond the level usually associated with industrial relations. For example, we have raised basic philosophical questions about the different ways in which various jurisdictions treat the same policy issues. In addition, the systems approach is an appropriate analytical tool by which to gauge a maturing relationship between unions and management, a relationship in which both sides are able to recognize destruc-

Figure 12.1

A Framework for Analyzing Industrial Relations Systems (A Structural-Functional Approach)

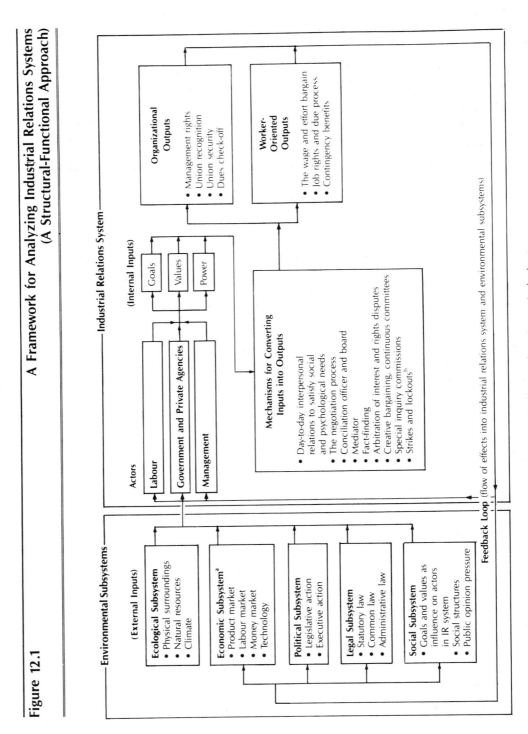

[a]This model presupposes but does not explicitly show the interrelationship between the various societal subsystems.

[b]A work stoppage may also be considered an outcome or output of the industrial relations system.

tive patterns and seek to replace them with more pragmatic and productive alternatives.

Throughout this book we have emphasized the decentralized and atomistic nature of the Canadian industrial relations system. With eleven political jurisdictions in Canada, no one voice can speak on behalf of any one of the major actors. As a result, many of our trade-union, employer, and government structures seem geared toward serving parochial interests. There is a serious void at the national level — a crying out for strong and courageous leadership from unions, management, and government to develop integrated policies and programs. In fact a greater degree of real centralized decision making by unions, management, government, and possibly other interest groups is now critical in Canada.

It is well recognized that leaders must satisfy their constituents' aspirations and, perhaps more importantly, allay their fears, especially in facing the loss of previously hard-won gains. In the long run, however, leaders can influence, as well as be influenced by, their constituents' opinions. It is in the best interest of management to involve our highly educated workforce in some of the day-to-day decision making. It is equally advantageous that trade-union members be persuaded to voluntarily forgo their strike option in given situations.

Adoption of these ideas, however, requires an awareness and courage not normally associated with the kind of political expediency seen during past years, but present in the long-term creative relationships between organizations and individuals. These qualities have characterized the leaders of union-management relationships at various times in the past. Will they continue to do so in the precarious years which we now face?

Questions

1   What scenario do you see for Canadian industrial relations in the near future? Elaborate.

2   Do you foresee more or less cooperation among unions, management, and government in the near future? Give a rationale for your answer.

3   Do you consider unions to be limited-purpose instruments? Elaborate.

4   Do you think that non-union group action will prove to be as effective as union action? Do you think that non-union group action will lead to unionization in those situations in which workers are not yet unionized? Elaborate.

5   Do you consider the Macdonald Commission's suggestion that arbitration of interest disputes is a viable alternative to strikes in those situations in which society deems the cost of strikes to be excessive? Who do you propose should decide whether or not the cost of strikes in certain sectors is too high? What reaction do you expect from sectors that will lose the right to strike? Elaborate.

6   Discuss some of the recent court decisions arising from the Charter of Rights and Freedoms and their impact on unions, management, and governments.

7   What impact do you expect the free-trade pact between Canada and the United States to have on the structure of Canadian industry, its competitiveness and its industrial relations system? Elaborate.

Notes

1 P. Jacobs, *Old Before Its Time: Collective Bargaining at 28* (Santa Barbara: Center for the Study of Democratic Institutions, 1963).

2 J.T. Dunlop, "The Social Utility of Collective Bargaining," *Challenges to Collective Bargaining*, ed. L. Ulman (Englewood Cliffs, N.J.: Prentice-Hall Inc., 1967), p. 169.

3 For a more developed statement of the views expressed above, see A.H. Raskin and J.T. Dunlop, "Two Views of Collective Bargaining," *Challenges to Collective Bargaining*, pp. 155-80.

4 W. List, "Labour Board Attacks CUPE Failure to Aid Woman Fired Over Union Role," *Globe and Mail* (June 15, 1981), p. 1.

5 B. Gory, "Woman, 23, Is New Head of Labour Body," *Globe and Mail*, (January 2, 1986), p. A10.

6 L. Hossie, "Union Women Are Revving Up and Moving Up," *Globe and Mail* (January 2, 1986).

7 H.J. Glasbeek, "The Contract of Employment at Common Law," *Union-Management Relations in Canada*, eds. J. Anderson and M. Gunderson (Don Mills: Addison-Wesley Canada Ltd., 1982), p. 69.

8 R.J. Adams, "The Unorganized: A Rising Force," a paper presented to the 31st Annual McGill Industrial Relations Conference (Montreal, April 6, 1983); also as Research and Paper Series No. 201, Faculty of Business, McMaster University (Hamilton: April 1983).

9 Ibid., p. 11.

10 *Labour Adjustment Benefits Act* (Bill C-78, 1982), s. 60. 13(3).

11 Adams, "The Unorganized: A Rising Force," p. 19.

12 C.R. Brookbank, "The Adversary System in Canadian Industrial Relations: Blight or Blessing?" Vol. 35, No. 1, *Relations Industrielles/ Industrial Relations* (1980), p. 34.

13 J. Fichaud, "Analysis of The Charter and Its Application to Labour Law," Vol. 11, 20th Annual Meeting of the Canadian Industrial Relations Association, Vancouver, B.C., pp. 599-600.

14 Ibid., p. 603.

15 A. Bartholomew, "The Guarantee of Freedom of Association in Canada's Charter of Rights and Freedoms: A Double-Edged Sword for Labour?" A paper presented to the 26th Annual International Studies Association Conference (Washington: March 5-9, 1985) p. 21.

16 Ibid., pp. 12-29.

17 Quoted in Fichaud, "Analysis of The Charter and Its Application to Labour Law," p. 599.

18 "CLC Files Suit Challenging Michelin Bill," *Globe and Mail* (May 9, 1985), p. 8.

19 L. Slotnick, "Charter Cases Major Challenge Facing Unions," *Globe and Mail* (January 13, 1986), pp. A1, A23.

20 B. Adell, "Law and IR in Common Law Canada," *The State of the Art in Industrial Relations*, eds. G. Hébert, H.C. Jain and N. Meltz, (Kingston: Industrial Relations Centre, Queen's University and Toronto, Centre for Industrial Relations, University of Toronto, 1988), p. 115.

21 J. Crispo, *Industrial Democracy in Western Europe: A North American Perspective* (Toronto: McGraw Hill Ryerson Limited, 1978); C.J. Connaghan, *The Japanese Way: Contemporary Industrial Relations* (Ottawa: Supply and Services Canada, 1982).

22 B.J.C. Smith, "Canada Falling Behind in Productivity," *Globe and Mail* (February 25, 1985), p. B8.

23 D. Drache and H. Glasbeek, "A New Trade Union Strategy," Vol. 9, No. 7, *Policy Options*, September 1988, pp. 15-18.

24 J. Crispo, *Industrial Democracy in Western Europe: A North American Perspective*, pp. 150 ff.

25 *Report of the Commission of Inquiry into Redundancies and Lay-Offs*, A.W.R. Carrothers, Chair (Ottawa: Supply and Services Canada, 1979).

26 Vol. 2, *Report of the Royal Commission on Economic Union and Development Prospects for Canada* (Ottawa: Supply and Services Canada, 1985), p. 707.

27 Ibid., pp. 698-707.

28 Ibid., p. 705.

appendix one

Certification

A Question of Jurisdiction — The Agnew Lake Mines Case*

Reasons for Judgment in Applications for certification affecting
Labourers' International Union of North America
(Applicant No. One)
United Steelworkers of America
(Applicant No. Two)
and
Agnew Lake Mines Limited (Respondent)

1 These are two counter applications for certification of the Applicant therein, each being a trade union, as bargaining agent for substantially the same unit of employees of the Respondent therein, namely a unit of employees employed by the Respondent in the development and operation of a uranium mine at the Respondent's mine site in Hyman Township in the province of Ontario, excluding office and clerical employees employed in a confidential capacity in matters relating to labour relations. Application No. One was dated March 24, 1969, and Application No. Two was dated April 3, 1969.

2 The classifications of employees of the respondent appearing on the respondent's payroll as at the dates of the applications and comprising the proposed bargaining units were those of trades leader, hoistman (with compressor papers), tradesman-group 1- "A", tradesman-group 1- "B", tradesman-group 2- "A", heavy equipment operator "A", journeyman helper-group "1", general labour, light truck driver, dryman, general miner, and skiptender, excluding the classifications of manager, secretary, engineering supervisor, layout engineer, surveyor, mine accountant, chief warehouseman, paymaster, clerk-typist, surface foreman, mechanical foreman, electrical foreman, mine captain, and shift boss.

---

* Permission to use this case was granted by the Canada Labour Relations Board. Minor deletions were made by the author for the purposes of this book.

Based upon the report of the Board's investigating Officer following upon his check of the payroll records of the Respondent and the membership and attendant records of each of Applicant No. One and Applicant No. Two, the Board finds that at the date of application No. One there were 24 employees in the proposed bargaining unit of whom 15 were claimed by Applicant No. One to be members in good standing of the said Applicant, and finds that at the date of application No. Two there were 31 employees in the proposed bargaining unit of whom 18 were claimed by Applicant No. Two to be members in good standing of the said applicant.

3 The Respondent submits that both applications are premature as its uranium mining operation is still in the process of underground development, no ore has as yet been taken out of the mine, and the mill which the Respondent has decided to build at the mining site to process the mined ore into the form of uranium concentrate for marketing purposes, is not in operation as yet. The Respondent's evidence is that the 12 classifications of employees in the proposed bargaining unit on the payroll at the time of the making of the applications constitute only 30 per cent of the number of classifications of employees who will be employed and who would be covered in the proposed bargaining unit when the mine comes into full production and the build-up of employees is completed. Based upon its presently planned production and its progress estimates, the Respondent anticipates that the build-up of employees in the proposed bargaining unit will result in an increase to 100 by the end of 1969, to 200 by the end of 1970, and to a minimum of 400 at full production by the end of 1971.

The Respondent submits that any application for determination of the wishes of the employees in the proposed unit as to their choice of a bargaining agent would be premature until the build-up has reached at least roughly 50 per cent of the ultimate build-up total. It considers this percentage would constitute a representative group of employees for such purpose. The Respondent made representations also in relation to an appropriate description of the proposed bargaining unit in the event the applications are further processed at this time. Counsel for Applicant No. One submits that in view of the uncertainties of the future build-up in the Respondent's mining development and production operation, there is no reason why at least the employees in the categories now employed should be denied bargaining rights at this time. Counsel for Applicant No. Two concurs in this view.

Counsel for Applicant No. Two and Counsel for the Respondent cited also for the Board's consideration the practice followed by the Ontario Labour Relations Board in dealing with applications for certification in the mining industry in Ontario of tying the certification granted to the currently appropriate stage of mining operation then being carried on at the mining site designated as either the construction, development, or production stage as an alternate to a deferral of certification pending further anticipated build-up (see O.L.R.B. judgment in International Union of Mine, Mill & Smelter Workers (Canada), vs. Surlaga Gold Mines Ltd. dated July 13, 1967, for an outline of this policy).

Questions

1 Does this case fall under the jurisdiction of the Canada Labour Relations Board? If not, why not? If so, under what authority?
2 Do you see any discrepancy in the figures claimed by the two applicants and the total number of workers on the job?
3 How is the proposed bargaining unit defined?
4 As a member of the Board, would you consider the unit proposed to be appropriate?
5 If you do consider the unit appropriate, for what stage of operations do you consider it appropriate?
6 What would happen when that stage of the mine was completed?
7 How would you define the next stage of operations?
8 Which union, if either, do you think will be certified in this case? Why?

Two Unions Attempt to Represent Security Guards — The Eastern Provincial Airways (1963) Case*

Canadian Air Line Employees Association, applicant,
and
Eastern Provincial Airways (1963) Limited,
Gander, Newfoundland,
employer
International Association of Machinists
and Aerospace Workers, applicant,
and
Eastern Provincial Airways (1963) Limited,
Gander, Newfoundland, employer

1 These cases involve two competing applications to represent the same group of employees, namely, a group of security guards of the respondent, Eastern Provincial Airways (1963) Limited. The first is an application for review presented pursuant to section 119 of the Canada Labour Code (Part V — Industrial Relations) by CALEA seeking to have its existing certificate for a unit of employees of the employer amended in order to include said security guards therein. The second is an application for certification made pursuant to section 124 of the Code by the IAM for the same group of security guards. The first application was filed on August 1, 1978, and CALEA claimed to

* Permission to use this case was granted by the Canada Labour Relations Board. Minor deletions were made by the author for the purposes of this book.

represent all of the security guards. The second application was filed on August 18, 1978, and the IAM claimed to represent all of the same employees.

2   The Board first wishes to state that it will decide whether or not both applications are receivable in the light of the provisions of Sections 119, 124 and 126 of the Code. The first aspect is whether or not the Board can entertain, at the same time, an application filed under section 119 and another application made under section 124. Let us first state that the Board, as a matter of policy, is not formalistic as to the procedure in which applications are made to the Board. In the present instance, both unions wish to represent a group of employees who were not formerly represented by any union. According to section 124, an application for certification can be presented for such a group at any time. Whether or not such a group would be made part of an existing certificate or would form a distinct unit is a decision that the Board will take after the filing of the applications and after having completed its investigation. It seems to us that whether an application to represent a group of employees filed at an appropriate time, be presented by way of section 119 or 124, is not essential to its admissibility. The goal pursued in each case is to be declared the certified bargaining agent for a group of employees. The Board will not, as a matter of policy, dismiss an application for revision under section 119 to include a group of employees in an existing unit on the sole basis that the application should have been made under section 124 when such application is otherwise timely and satisfies the prerequisites of other pertinent sections of the Code relating to certification and more precisely, the provisions regarding the wishes of the employees. In short, the Board finds that the application for review under section 119 in this case will be considered both as an application for review under section 119 in the event the Board decides that the security guards are to be included in the existent certificate, or as an application for certification if the Board decides that the security guards must form a distinct bargaining unit and the employees wish to be represented by the applicant, CALEA.

The next question the Board must ask itself is whether or not it will consider the application for certification presented by the IAM in the light of section 126(c) which reads as follows:

> 126. Where the Board
> (c) is satisfied that, as of the date of the filing of the application, or of such other date as the Board considers appropriate, a majority of the employees in the unit wish to have the trade union represent them as their bargaining agent, the Board shall, subject to this Part, certify the trade union making the application as the bargaining agent for the bargaining unit.

At the time of the filing of the application for revision by CALEA, the Board's investigation revealed that all of the security guards had signed membership cards with CALEA. Normally, since the coming into force on June 1, 1978, of the revised subsection (c) of section 126, the Board, as a policy, will consider the wishes of the employees at the date of the application. Before the amendment to the Code, the Board had to follow the interpretation of the original subsection (c) as given by the Federal Court of Appeal in the case CKOY Limited [1972] 2 F.C. 412, and as a result the Board had to consider the wishes of the employees at the time it was making its decision. Because of this decision, the Board had to change its policy, as stated in the case of Swan River The Pas 1 di 10 [1974] 1 Can LRBR 254, and in which decision the Board had explained why it wanted to consider the wishes of the employees as of the date of application. As stated above, the Board can now resume the policy it had developed in 1974 and consider the wishes of the employees at the date of application. In this case, however, the other applicant, IAM, filed an application for certification 17 days later and our investigation revealed that all of the security guards had expressed their wish to be represented by IAM. The Board was then confronted by the situation in which a group of employees had indicated to the Board that they wished to be represented but by different unions. In such circumstances, the Board cannot ignore this conflicting situation as to the wishes of the employees. We are in a situation similar to the one in which more than one union applies to represent the same group of employees, each union claiming to represent a majority. In such cases, Labour Relations Boards when given reasonable grounds to doubt the true wishes of the employees, have normally ordered a vote and considered as valid both applications, even though they were not presented at the same time. This is not a situation where the employees are trying to get out of union representation but a situation where the employees have clearly expressed their wishes to be represented by a union, and the question to decide is which union will represent them. Because of the above given reasons, the Board is of the opinion that we are in a situation where we must consider the wishes of the employees at another date than the dates of the filing of the applications. The Board has, on August 25, 1978, directed that a vote be held among the security guards covered by both applications, giving them the choice to express their wishes as to whether they would like to be represented by CALEA, the IAM or not to be represented by a union at all. This vote was ordered according to the provisions of section 118(i), which gives the Board power to order a vote in a precautionary way, as a matter of speaking, in order that the wishes of the employees be expressed and the ballots sealed until such time as the Board decides if the vote is to be considered or not.

The employer has contested both applications on the following grounds. First of all, it contends that the security guards are not employees as defined by the Code, as they are employed in a confidential capacity in matters relating to industrial relations. This is based on the interpretation of the employer as regards the work performed by the security guards and mainly because their duties consist of:

1 screening passengers emplaning on the employer's aircraft in accordance with section 5.1 of the Aeronautics Act;
2 protecting the employer's property and prevention of fire;

3 prevention of public intrusion upon the employer's property and theft of the employer's property by the public;

4 monitoring all the employer's employees in relation to theft in this connection, security guards have authority to check and search the person and possessions of employees while on the employer's premises;

5 inspecting all aircraft that terminate their flight plans at Gander and to check for shortage of inventory;

6 inspecting commissary supplies;

7 conducting special investigations of cases of observed theft or alleged theft committed by either employees or the public; and

8 other investigations relating to industrial relations.

The Board, in its decision Canadian Union of Bank Employees v. Bank of Nova Scotia 21 di 439; 1977 CLLC 16090, has reviewed the jurisprudence and restated the threefold test under which a person will not be considered an employee because he is performing functions in a confidential capacity related to industrial relations. The Board at page 16,625,21 di 460 said

> To this end this Board and other Boards have developed a threefold test for the confidential exclusion. The confidential matters must be in relation to industrial relations, not general industrial secrets such as products formulae (e.g. Calona Wines Ltd. [1974] 1 Can LRBR 471, headnote only, BCLRB decision 90/74). This does not include matters the union or its members know, such as salaries, performance assessments discussed with them or which they must sign or initial (e.g. Exhibit E-21). It does not include personal history or family information that is available from other sources or persons. The second test is that the disclosure of that information would adversely affect the employer. Finally, the person must be involved with this information as a regular part of his duties. It is not sufficient that he occasionally comes in contact with it or that through employer laxity he can gain access to it. (See Greyhound Lines of Canada Ltd. 1974 CLLC [16,112] 4 di 22, and Hayes Trucks Ltd. [1974] 1 Can LRBR 284).

After having reviewed the results of its investigation, the evidence and the submissions of the employer, the Board is of the opinion that none of the security guards perform work in a confidential capacity in matters relating to industrial relations.

The employer also contended that certification should not be extended so as to include the subject employees within a trade union which has an existing collective bargaining relationship with the employer. Further, the employer stated that certification should not be granted nor extended so as to include the subject employees within a unit for which a trade union already has a collective agreement with the employer.

The Board, being of opinion that the security guards are employees within the meaning of section 107 of the Code, must decide if they are appropriate for inclusion in an existing unit or should form a separate unit, and in this second alternative whether they can be represented by a union which already has ties with the employer. It is to be noted that both CALEA and IAM have ties with the employer as they hold certificates and have bargained collective agreements with the employer for its operations at Gander.

The Board is convinced that even though the security guards are working in the same premises and in close relation with members of the applicant

CALEA, this fact is also true of their relation with the members of IAM. The whole question is whether or not the security guards should form a distinct bargaining unit or be included in a general unit. In Ontario, section 11 of the Ontario Labour Relations Act reads as follows:

> The Board shall not include in a bargaining unit with other employees, a person employed as a guard to protect the property of his employer and no trade union shall be certified as bargaining agent for a bargaining unit of such guards and no employer or employer's organization shall be required to bargain with a trade union on behalf of any person who is a guard if, in either case, the trade union admits to membership or is chartered by, or is affiliated, directly or indirectly, with an organization that admits to membership persons other than guards.

As we see it, this section expressly forbids the Ontario Board from certifying a union for a unit of security guards if that union does not exclusively represent security guards. We have no such provision in our Code. In British Columbia, where there are no provisions such as in the Ontario Labour Relations Act, the Board, in the case of The Hospital Employees Union Local 180 and St. Vincents Hospital, [1974] 1 Can LRBR 363, has taken the following view at page 367:

> This Board has no firmly determined policy on security guard units. The question of whether security guards should be placed in separate units or in general employee units has received considerable attention elsewhere (e.g., Ontario Labour Relations Act, s. 11). Any policy development will focus its attention on conflicts of interests between employees who have authority over fellow employees and their fellow employees. The nature of this authority will have to be examined to determine whether the employees designated as guards are employed to monitor the actions of their fellow employees and perhaps to admonish or report employees for actions tainted with illegality. Where persons are employed principally to exercise this sort of surveillance over fellow employees, the Board may find it inappropriate to include them in the same unit as their fellow employees. Central to a policy developed on the appropriateness of the unit for guards will be concern as to whether the guards and the employer are placed in a position where the guard's duties conflict with his interests as a member of a bargaining unit.

This Board adopts the approach of the B.C. Labour Relations Board.

In order to decide, this Board must then look at the functions of the security guards and it becomes a question of facts whether or not they perform security functions or surveillance over fellow employees. In the present instance, the security guards perform a dual role. Fifty percent (50%) of their time consists of screening passengers emplaning on the employer's aircraft and the other 50% consists of surveillance of the company premises, and this includes, as stated above, the monitoring of all the employer's employees in relation to theft, conducting special investigations of cases of observed theft or alleged theft committed by either employees or the public. The Board's investigation revealed that, in numerous cases, the security guards had to report and investigate thefts by fellow employees. It is also important to mention that the security guards are on a rotating shift so that they are all performing the dual functions described above.

· · ·

As to the argument raised by the employer that the Board should not certify a group of security guards with a union which already negotiates with the employer for different groups, the Board, in United Steelworkers of America v Denison Mines Limited case, 8 di 13, 75 CLLC 16,150, has already decided that security guards, such as those in the present instance, are not private constables and as such are not covered by section 135 of the Code, which reads as follows:

> The Board shall not certify a trade union as, and a trade union shall not act as, the bargaining agent for both a bargaining unit comprised of private constables and a bargaining unit comprised of employees other than private constables if any or all of the employees in both such bargaining units are employed by the same employer.

However, it must be pointed out that the limitation expressed in Section 135 of the Code is restricted by the definition of "private constable" given in Section 107 of the Code which reads:

> "private constable" means a person appointed as a constable under the Railway Act or the National Harbours Board Act;

The Board, 8 di 14, of the Denison Mines decision, said:

> There was no evidence that the security guards under study were appointed private constables under the "dominium" of either of these two Statutes. Therefore, the provisions of section 135 do not avail to the Respondent in the circumstances and this Board is not directed to deny certification to a bargaining agent seeking to represent these security guards although it already represents other bargaining units of employees of the same employer.

· · ·

Questions

1 What is (are) the major issue(s) that the Board has to decide in this case?
2 How could both applicant unions claim support of all of the workers at the same time?
3 What is the operative date on which the Board will determine the wishes of the workers in this case?
4 On what date did the Board conduct a vote among the workers? Is this the regular certification procedure or is it a prehearing vote? Elaborate.
5 Should the security guards form a separate bargaining unit or should they be included with other workers all in one unit? Elaborate.
6 Can only one of the unions or both or neither be considered as a bargaining agent for these workers? Elaborate.
7 Assume that a vote has been conducted on ballots which show the names of both unions and a designation of "no union," and that neither union gets 50% support of the members voting. What happens then? Elaborate. Should legislation make provision for such an outcome? If so, what form should the provision take?

The Impact of Changing Technology and Public Policy — The B.C. Telephone Co. (1977) Case*

Society of Telephone Engineers and Managers, applicant,
and
British Columbia Telephone Company, Vancouver, B.C., employer,
and
Telecommunication Workers' Union
(Formerly: Federation of Telephone Workers of British Columbia),
Intervenor,
and G. Fred Pearson, et al,
Employee Intervenor.

The Society of Telephone Engineers and Managers has filed with the Board an application for certification as bargaining agent for a unit comprising all persons employed in the first four levels of management of the Marketing Department of the British Columbia Telephone Company.

Because of a number of special circumstances surrounding this application and the existence of similar or related applications filed with the Board, the Board determined that it would be appropriate to conduct a hearing and issue a decision in order to determine whether all or some of the persons employed in the proposed bargaining unit were "employees" within the meaning of the Canada Labour Code (Part V — Industrial Relations). The relevant facts are fully outlined in the interim decision by the Board on February 26, 1976.[1]

In its interim decision, the Board ruled that "all persons employed as managers in the Marketing Department of the British Columbia Telephone Company with the exception of the Vice-President — Marketing and the Marketing Operations Manager are "employees," within the meaning of section 107(1) of the Canada Labour Code (Part V — Industrial Relations)." Accordingly, the Board advised the parties that it intended to convene further hearings in order to allow the parties to lead evidence and present arguments with regard to the issues raised by the instant application for certification and particularly with regard to the appropriateness of the bargaining unit proposed by the applicant. In view of the conflicting positions of the applicant and of the intervenor, the Board raised the following question:

> Should these employees be included in a separate bargaining unit for which STEM wishes to be certified or should all or some of them be included in the bargaining unit which is already represented by the Federation of Telephone Workers of British Columbia.

---

* Permission to use this case was granted by the Canada Labour Relations Board. Minor deletions were made by the author for the purposes of this book.

The parties were subsequently convened to further hearings. All parties were also requested to file further written evidence and submissions on the issue.

The Society of Telephone Engineers and Managers is a relatively new organization which, as its name indicates, wishes to represent the engineers and managers employed by the British Columbia Telephone Company. In support of its application, it has provided the Board with the usual documentation in order to establish that it is a trade union within the meaning of the Canada Labour Code (Part V — Industrial Relations). After having reviewed that evidence, the Board is satisfied that the Society of Telephone Engineers and Managers is a trade union within the meaning of section 107(1) of the Canada Labour Code (Part V — Industrial Relations).

In 1949, the Federation of Telephone Workers of British Columbia was certified as bargaining agent by the Canada Labour Relations Board to represent all employees of the employer except the incumbents of certain classifications, specified in the Certification Order, which were to be excluded from the bargaining unit.

On March 13, 1975, the intervenor applied to the Board for a revision of its certificate of bargaining authority which would have the effect of substantially increasing the number of persons included in the bargaining unit which it represents. Many of the persons employed in the Marketing Department and included in the bargaining unit which the applicant wishes to represent are included in this application for revision.

Since then, the Federation of Telephone Workers of British Columbia has revised its constitution and changed its name to Telecommunication Workers' Union. It will be referred to hereinafter by its new name.

Because of the overlap between the application for certification filed by the applicant and the application for review filed by the Telecommunication Workers' Union with regard to persons employed in the managerial ranks in the Marketing Department, the Board allowed the intervenor to file evidence and submissions with regard to that group of employees in the course of the hearing on the application for certification filed by the Society of Telephone Engineers and Managers.

Circumstances of Instant Case

This case is unusual in a number of respects. The position of the applicant is, to say the least, somewhat unusual since it wishes to be certified as bargaining agent to represent a group of employees employed in the first four levels of management of the Marketing Department. The instant application is only one of a number of similar or related applications filed with the Board. The applicant itself, the Society of Telephone Engineers and Managers, has filed two other applications for certification to represent a unit of employees in the Finance Department and to represent a group of engineering employees. In all cases, the persons who it wishes to represent have been considered by the employer to be Level I to Level IV managers who heretofore have been excluded from the existing bargaining unit of classified employees. The

Board has also received an application for certification from the Telephone Supervisors' Association in which it seeks to be certified as bargaining agent for a unit comprising first level plant supervisors. Finally, on March 13, 1975, the Telecommunication Workers' Union filed an application for review made pursuant to section 119 of the Canada Labour Code (Part V — Industrial Relations) asking the Board to decide that some 600 additional persons, employed at different levels of the management structure of the employer, were and should be included in the bargaining unit which it represents. Although there is no overlap between the application for review filed by the Telecommunication Workers' Union and the application for certification filed by the Telephone Supervisors' Association, there is a substantial measure of conflict between the application filed by the Society of Telephone Engineers and Managers and the Telecommunication Workers' Union.

The employer has reacted to these various applications in a similar fashion. B.C. Tel. has intervened to oppose each application asking that it be dismissed because the persons proposed for inclusion in the various bargaining units were not "employees" within the meaning of section 107(1) of the Canada Labour Code (Part V — Industrial Relations) as they performed management functions or, in some cases, were employed in a confidential capacity in matters relating to labour relations. In no case has the employer disputed the appropriateness of the bargaining unit proposed by the applicant. In some cases, the employer has deliberately and continuously refrained from taking a position on the appropriateness of the bargaining units. In other cases, after being expressly invited to do so by the Board, it has contested the appropriateness of the proposed unit suggesting instead that the appropriate unit be company wide and include only persons employed at one level of management. It is worth noting that, at this stage, none of the applicants has proposed such a bargaining unit.

When a trade union files an application for certification, it must, in order to be certified by the Board, meet the requirements outlined in section 126 of the Canada Labour Code (Part V — Industrial Relations). Therefore, the application of the normal rules of procedure and evidence require the applicant to satisfy the Board that it meets the requirements prescribed in section 126 of the Code. Of course, the Board is not bound by the rules of procedure and evidence normally applied in the common law courts. Often, an application for certification can be disposed of without a hearing. Information and evidence elicited by the Board in the course of its investigation of an application will often make it unnecessary for the Board to require an applicant to establish that it meets one or the other of the requirements outlined in section 126 of the Code. In the instant case, prior to the resumption of the hearing, the Board notified the parties as follows:

> Following a review of the file for the purpose of determining an appropriate procedure, the Board finds there is at least a prima facie case to suggest that the proposed bargaining unit may be appropriate for collective bargaining. Accordingly, any party disputing the appropriateness of the proposed unit or objecting to the inclusion of certain classifications in that unit will be invited to lead evidence first.

When the hearing resumed on the instant application for certification, the employer, although expressly invited to do so by the Board, declined to take any position with regard to the appropriateness of the bargaining unit proposed by the applicant or by the intervenor in its application for review. It also declined to lead further evidence although it did provide the Board with information and submissions expressly requested by it. The employer also informed the Board that a reorganization had taken place within the Computer Communications Group of the Marketing Department which had the effect of substantially increasing the number of persons employed at levels I to IV in the managerial ranks of the Marketing Department of the British Columbia Telephone Company. It indicated that it felt that the incumbents of these various classifications were not employees under the provisions of the Canada Labour Code. However, the employer has until now provided the Board with no further information or submissions regarding the duties and responsibilities of these persons.

There can be little doubt that the procedure outlined above, which was designed to facilitate and speed up the determination of the various issues raised by the applications now before the Board, has caused a number of problems. Certainly, it was well designed to assist in the determination of the "employee" status of the various persons proposed for inclusion in the bargaining units. It was not, however, particularly well designed to allow the Board to familiarize itself with the overall organization of the British Columbia Telephone Company particularly as regards the relationship between the various departments or branches and the possible community of interest existing among the managerial employees of the company. Accordingly, in a letter dated April 15, 1976, the Board requested from the parties to the various cases further information and submissions on this point. It is worth noting, however, that these were requested and obtained following the conclusion of the hearing on the instant application for certification. It is only in the documentation thus requested by the Board that the British Columbia Telephone Company eventually let the Board know its position on the appropriateness of the bargaining units proposed by the various applicants.

It is clear that there is a marked conflict between the position of the applicant and the intervenor with regard to the right of representation of quite a number of managerial employees in the Marketing Department of the B.C. Tel. In many respects, the position of the intervenor and that of the applicant are incompatible and diametrically opposed.

The Evidence

In view of the circumstances of the case and in the light of the evidence submitted during the preliminary hearing conducted by the Board with regard to the "employee status" of the marketing managers employed by B.C. Tel., the position of the applicant with regard to the appropriateness of the bargaining unit for which it seeks to be certified is fairly clear and straightforward.

Briefly, the applicant contends that the marketing managers are a distinct group sharing a particular community of interest and, in view of the circumstances, a departmental unit is appropriate for collective bargaining. In so arguing, it does not dispute that a single all-inclusive bargaining unit comprising all the managerial employees of B.C. Tel. would also be appropriate for collective bargaining. In fact, it has stated quite bluntly that its overall objective was the creation of such an all-inclusive unit.

Since the employer had taken the position that it declined to lead further evidence, the Telecommunication Workers' Union was invited to lead evidence. In rebuttal, the applicant led further evidence in support of its contention that the Telecommunication Workers' Union's position should not be upheld and that the applicant should be certified as bargaining agent to represent the unit described in its application for certification. The position of the intervenor is fairly simple. On February 23, 1949 it was certified by order of the Canada Labour Relations Board as bargaining agent for a unit described as follows:

> A unit of employees of the British Columbia Telephone Company, comprising all employees of the Company save and except those employed in the following occupational classifications.

Therefore, the intervenor contends that it is the certified bargaining agent for a unit comprising all the employees of the British Columbia Telephone Company save for the classifications specifically excluded in the Certification Order issued by the Board.

Over the years, however, this relatively simple definition of the bargaining unit represented by the union has become a source of problems. In particular, a practice has developed of describing the bargaining unit in a manner completely opposite to the terms of the Certification Order. This has its origins in a practice or understanding which apparently developed quite early in the negotiations between the employer and the intervenor.

Therefore, over the years, the Telecommunication Workers' Union, which was the certified bargaining agent for a unit comprising all employees of the employer excluding certain named classifications, has negotiated collective agreements applicable to a unit comprising only certain listed classifications. The Board has received no evidence as to when this practice originated but it is understood to go back to the early 50's.

The intervenor contends that, over the years, the employer has engaged in various practices which have had the effect of eroding the bargaining unit which it represents. In some cases, new job titles or job descriptions have been assigned to existing classifications which have then been unilaterally declared by the employer to be excluded from the bargaining unit because the incumbents allegedly performed management functions or were employed in a confidential capacity in matters relating to industrial relations. Alternatively, new positions or classifications have been created and the employer has refused to recognize that they were properly included in the bargaining unit represented by the Union.

The evidence discloses that since 1967 the intervenor has attempted to assert its jurisdiction over a number of disputed classifications. In particular it protested decisions of the employer to create "management trainee" and other allegedly managerial positions which were then deemed to be excluded from the bargaining unit. It was, and still is, the contention of the intervenor that these positions were properly included in the bargaining unit which it is certified to represent.

In an attempt to resolve this issue, the intervenor first resorted to the grievance and arbitration provisions of its collective agreement with the employer. This occurred as a result of the creation of five new positions designated as "Communications Consultants — Data." The Telecommunication Workers' Union sought a ruling that these employees whom the employer contended were performing management functions and thus were not subject to the terms of the collective agreement were, in fact, employees subject to the collective agreement and particularly to the dues check off provisions of the agreement. The arbitration board ruled in favour of the intervenor. Shortly thereafter, these classifications were abolished and the employees affected by the arbitral award were assigned to new duties. The intervenor soon concluded that the problem could not be satisfactorily resolved in this manner since each instance would have to be the subject of a new grievance and of a new arbitral award and nothing precluded the employer from abolishing the classifications which had been the subject of an arbitral award and creating new ones.

The intervenor then filed various applications with the Canada Labour Relations Board pursuant to section 61 of the Industrial Relations and Disputes Investigation Act which reads as follows:

> 61(1) If in any proceeding before the Board a question arises under this Act as to whether a person is an employer or employee; . . . . a group of employees is a unit appropriate for collective bargaining; . . . .
>
> (2) A decision or order of the Board is final and conclusive and not open to question, or review, but the Board may, if it considers it advisable so to do, reconsider any decision or order made by it under this Act, and may vary or revoke any decision or order made by it under this Act.

The intervenor sought a determination that persons employed in 14 different classifications were employees within the meaning of the Canada Labour Code and included in the bargaining unit under the certification order issued in 1949. The classifications in question were the following: Programmer, Programmer Analyst, Programmer Assistant, Programmer Trainee, Temporary Programmer, Associate Programmer, Computer Input-Output Analyst, Computer Scheduling Assistant, Systems Design Coordinator, Technical Services Coordinator, Data Processing Training Coordinator, Computer Shift Supervisor, Accounting Machine Supervisor and Home Consultant. The Telecommunication Workers' Union was then advised by the Board that "while this is an application to have the Board vary the existing certificate, it will be processed in accordance with the Board's established practice for the investigation of applications for certification." Accordingly, the Union was advised that an investigating officer had been appointed. It was further advised that it would be required to provide to the Board's investigation officer its membership and financial records in order to determine whether the employees in the additional classifications were members in good standing of the Union. At all times, the position of the Union was that it was simply requesting the Board to make a ruling pursuant to section 61(1) of the Code to determine that the persons affected were employees within the meaning of the Code and were included in the bargaining unit for which it was already certified. The position of the Board, as expressed in correspondence under the signature of its then Chief Executive Officer, was that the matter could only be dealt with pursuant to section 61(2) of the IRDI Act and that the applicant union was required to establish to the satisfaction of the Board that it had "a mandate from the employees in the classifications listed in the request for review". The position of the Board was apparently that it was without authority to make the decisions requested by the Union. It may be useful to quote from a letter addressed by the Chief Executive Officer of the Board to the Telecommunication Workers' Union and dated June 29, 1971:

> It is quite right, as stated in your application of May 12, 1971, that the wording of the Board's certificate issued on February 23, 1949 is sufficiently broad to include additional classifications initiated by the company after the date of the said Order of certification providing both parties are in mutual agreement regarding such inclusion. Where the parties fail to agree that the incumbents of newly created classifications are employees within the meaning of the Act and hence within the meaning of the order of certification, the bargaining agent has two options opened to it, namely (a) the filing of a new application for certification under Section 7 or Section 8 of the Act, and (b) the filing of a request for review pursuant to the provisions of subsection (2) of Section 61 of the Act. Under either option, the Board's policy is to ascertain whether the applicant trade union has as members in good standing a majority of the employees comprising the group which it wishes added to the unit and in respect of whom it seeks the right to bind them by collective agreement.

Shortly afterwards, the Union withdrew its application for review.

A similar application filed on behalf of the Plant Division of the intervenor met with a similar fate.

At that time, proposals for amending Part V of the Canada Labour Code were being considered by the Parliament of Canada. Therefore, the Telecommunication Workers' Union wrote to the then Minister of Labour suggesting that suitable provisions should be incorporated in the new Code to obviate the defects of the existing legislation which had the effect of "enabling Companies under Federal jurisdiction to rape initially established certifications." They received a reply which suggested that their suggestion was ill-founded.

Eventually, the Telecommunication Workers' Union sought to resolve this problem in its negotiations with the employer over the renewal of the collective agreement. A Conciliation Board report issued on May 4, 1973 recognized that there was a serious problem arising out of "a long out-dated Certificate of Bargaining Authority and the apparent lack of appropriate machinery to update it as becomes necessary from time to time." The Conciliation Board felt that it could not adequately deal with the issue but recommended that the parties resume negotiations with a view to reaching agreement. In the event of a failure to reach agreement by November 1, 1973, the parties would receive the assistance of an officer of the Department of Labour. If the parties came to an agreement, a joint application would be made to the Canada Labour Relations Board for appropriate amendments to the certificate of bargaining authority. Failing agreement prior to January 1, 1974, the matter would be referred to an arbitrator for binding decision. The parties would be required to file a joint application with the Canada Labour Relations Board to amend the certificate of bargaining authority in accordance with the award. The arbitrator or board should deliver its award by March 1, 1974 or some later date agreed to by the parties. The employer and the Union eventually concluded a collective agreement embodying the recommendations contained in the report of the Conciliation Board. Shortly thereafter, negotiations commenced. On May 10, 1974, the Union applied to the Department of Labour for the appointment of a mediation officer to assist the parties in their negotiations. On May 16, 1974, the Department of Labour appointed one of its officers as mediator pursuant to the provisions of section 195 of the Canada Labour Code (Part V — Industrial Relations) to deal with the jurisdictional dispute between the Telecommunication Workers' Union and British Columbia Telephone Company.

It is while this process was under way that the supervisory or managerial employees of the British Columbia Telephone Company began to organize into associations of their own. Shortly thereafter, applications for certification were filed by the Society of Telephone Engineers and Managers and by the Telephone Supervisors' Association of British Columbia. By filing these applications for certification, these associations sought bargaining rights for many of the employees in the classifications which the intervenor was itself seeking to represent. These applications for certification clearly had the support of the employees affected as shown by the evidence of membership tendered to the Board in the course of its investigations, whereas the intervenor could not claim any significant support from these employees. Therefore, in March 1975, the intervenor filed with the Board an application for review made pursuant to section 119 of the Canada Labour Code (Part V — Industrial Relations) seeking a determination that a number of disputed classifications were and should remain included in the bargaining unit which the Union already represents.

Position of the Parties

1   The Applicant
The evidence demonstrates that the managerial employees of the Marketing Department are a cohesive group, generally working as a team and sharing a distinct community of interest. Although they have much in common with other managerial employees of the British Columbia Telephone Company, those in the Marketing Department constitute, by themselves, a separate unit which is appropriate for collective bargaining.

The intervenor does not now and has never in the past represented the employees in the proposed bargaining unit. Therefore, any expansion of the bargaining unit represented by the intervenor to include additional positions or classifications not now represented by it amounts to an application for certification for the additional group. Whether the application is filed pursuant to section 124 of the Code or pursuant to section 119, the Board cannot and should not ignore the wishes of the employees involved. Therefore, the fact that the intervenor has made no attempt to organize these employees, and does not even claim that a majority of the employees in the additional group wish to be represented by it, can only lead the Board to reject the contention of the intervenor.

This evidence becomes even more significant in view of the fact that a majority of the employees affected have clearly indicated their wish not to be represented by the intervenor but have opted instead to be represented by the applicant union.

2 The Intervenor

Pursuant to the Certification Order issued in February 1949, all employees of the employer who are not clearly and primarily supervisors are included in the bargaining unit which the intervenor was certified to represent. Therefore, these employees cannot and should not be included by the Board in a separate unit represented by a different bargaining agent.

Accordingly, the Telecommunication Workers' Union contends that a number of the classifications proposed for inclusion in the bargaining unit for which STEM seeks to be certified should really be included in the existing bargaining unit which it represents. It claims jurisdiction over the following classifications because the persons involved do not supervise anybody: Marketing Services Administrator, Product Analyst, Liaison Assistant, Sales Promotions Supervisor, Phone Mart Coordinator, Market Methods Analyst, Operations Research Coordinator, Methods Analyst, Pricing Practices Administrator, Market Research Supervisor, Market Training Supervisor, Market Research Analyst, Market Support Analyst, and Systems Development Analyst. They further wish to represent some employees who have only very limited supervisory duties such as: Product Manager, Product Coordinator, Communications Companies' Relations Supervisor, Marketing Methods Supervisor, Phone Power Supervisor, Product Manager, Computer Communications Group, Computer Communications Consultant, Computer Communications Group — Market Support Supervisor, Systems Development Supervisor and Communications Consultant. Finally the intervenor also contends that the classifications of Pricing Assistant, Marketing Training Assistant, Marketing Operations Analyst Supervisor and Inter-Company Services Coordinator should be included in the same unit as the classified employees because they devote only a very small proportion of their time to the supervision of other employees.

Since the application for review filed by the intervenor simply involves a clarification and an updating of the original Certification Order issued in

1949, the Board does not need to and should not consider the wishes of the employees in the additional classifications which are proposed for inclusion in the existing unit.

In any event, in view of the nature of the operations of B.C. Tel. and in view of its operational and organizational structure, the bargaining unit proposed by the applicant is not appropriate for collective bargaining. It would be absurd to fragment bargaining units along departmental lines since the evidence discloses that the activities of the Marketing Department and of its managerial employees are closely integrated with the overall operations of B.C. Tel.

3   The Employer

Because of the stance it took following the issuance of the Board's interim decision in this case, the employer has not taken a position as such. However, it has already indicated that it felt that the Board should be governed in its decision by the wishes of the employees affected.

Subsequently, the employer has indicated that the bargaining units proposed by both the applicant and the intervenor were not appropriate for collective bargaining and has suggested that the Board should find appropriate company wide units comprising all managerial employees at the same level of management.

Reasons for Decision

In its earlier decision in the instant case, the Board found that all persons employed as managers in the Marketing Department of the British Columbia Telephone Company, with the exception of the Vice-President — Marketing and the Marketing Operations Manager, were "employees" within the meaning of section 107(1) of the Canada Labour Code (Part V — Industrial Relations). This decision affected at the time approximately 100 employees. The intervenor contends that, under the terms of the Certification Order issued in its favour in February 1949, it is entitled to represent some 70 of these employees and that these employees cannot and therefore should not be included in the separate bargaining unit for which the applicant seeks to be certified. It is necessary to deal with this contention before we consider the appropriateness of the bargaining unit proposed by the applicant.

It is reasonable to first consider and discuss the merits of the application for review filed by the Telecommunication Workers' Union, insofar as it affects managerial employees in the Marketing Department, before dealing with the issues raised by the application for certification.

1   The Application for Review Filed by the Telecommunications Workers' Union

The position of the intervenor is quite understandable and, in view of the circumstances, it deserves some sympathy. For nearly ten years, the Telecommunication Workers' Union has sought a binding ruling on its contention that the employer had acted illegally in failing to recognize that a number of

classifications were properly included in the bargaining unit which the intervenor represented pursuant to the Certification Order issued in February
1949. When this proved to be of no avail, it sought to resolve its dispute with
the employer at the bargaining table. When some progress was achieved in
the negotiations on this issue, new associations or trade unions were created
which applied to the Board to be certified as bargaining agent for many of the
classifications which it felt it was entitled to represent.

Because of the importance of the issues raised by the intervenor's contention, we feel that it is appropriate to discuss the general principles
involved, before considering the merits of the application for review as it
affects employees of the Marketing Department.

a General Principles

Pursuant to the provisions of the Canada Labour Code (Part V — Industrial
Relations), a trade union which wishes to become the bargaining agent for a
unit of employees has two avenues open to it. It may apply to the Board for
certification but it may also attempt to obtain recognition from the employer.
This possibility is recognized in a number of provisions of the Code but is
particularly reflected in the definition of "bargaining agent" found in section
107(1).

> 'bargaining agent' means
> 1 a trade union that has been certified by the Board as the bargaining agent for
>   the employees in a bargaining unit and the certification of which has not been
>   revoked, or
> 2 any other trade union that has entered into a collective agreement on behalf
>   of the employees in a bargaining unit
>   a the term of which has not expired, or
>   b in respect of which the trade union has, by notice given pursuant to
>   subsection b 147(1), required the employer to commence collective bar-
>   gaining.

Therefore, a trade union that has concluded a collective agreement with an
employer which is applicable to a group of employees is the bargaining agent
for this group of employees, and as such enjoys basically the same rights and
privileges as a trade union that has been certified by the Board.

Should the employer refuse to "recognize" the trade union as bargaining agent or should the trade union prefer to avail itself of the certification
procedure provided by the Code, it may file with the Board an application for
certification. When the Board is seized with an application for certification
and when it finds that the applicant trade union meets the requirements of
the Code, section 126 provides that:

> the Board shall, subject to this Part, certify the trade union making the applica-
> tion as bargaining agent for the bargaining unit.

Section 136 of the Code further provides that:

> 1 Where a trade union is certified as the bargaining agent for a bargaining unit,
>   a the trade union so certified has exclusive authority to bargain collectively
>   on behalf of the employees in the bargaining unit. . . .

Therefore, pursuant to section 146 of the Code, the bargaining agent may, by notice, require the employer to commence collective bargaining. When notice to bargain collectively has been given, the bargaining agent and the employer are required, pursuant to section 148 of the Code, to "bargain collectively, in good faith, and make every reasonable effort to enter into a collective agreement." There is, however, a fundamental difference between the two processes. Recognition depends entirely on the agreement of the employer and becomes effective only upon the execution of a collective agreement between the employer and the trade union concerning the group of employees to which the collective agreement is applicable. A certification order is an "order or decision of the Board" which is "final" pursuant to section 122(1) of the Code. Therefore, once a certification order has been issued by the Board, the employer is no longer free to recognize or refuse to recognize the trade union as the bargaining agent for the group described in the order.

When a collective agreement is entered into, section 154 of the Code provides that it is binding not only on the bargaining agent and the employer but also on "every employee in the bargaining unit". Section 107(1) of the Code contains the following definition:

> 'bargaining unit' means
> a unit as determined by the Board to be appropriate for collective bargaining or
> b to which a collective agreement applies

This would appear to indicate that, at least when the Board has certified a trade union as bargaining agent for the employees in a bargaining unit, the parties to the collective agreement are no longer free to exclude from the application of the collective agreement any employee included in the unit "determined by the Board to be appropriate for collective bargaining."

Of course, a bargaining relationship need not for that reason remain forever static. In bargaining collectively with a certified trade union, an employer may recognize the trade union for a unit larger than the one to which the certification order originally applied and, in such a case, the execution of a collective agreement amounts to the recognition of the trade union as bargaining agent for the additional group of employees. Therefore, once a bargaining relationship has been established, the bargaining unit originally defined by the Board in the certification order may expand and may, by this process of incremental recognition, extend to cover a larger group of employees. When an application is filed with it pursuant to section 119 of the Code, the Board may sanction such arrangements and grant a corresponding amendment to the original certification order issued by the Board. Should such recognition not be achieved in this fashion, a trade union may only become the bargaining agent for such an additional group of employees by filing an application for certification or for review with the Board in order to obtain additional bargaining rights. In such a case, it will of course be required to satisfy the Board that it enjoys the necessary membership support among the new group of employees which it wishes to represent, as would any trade union wishing to be certified to represent a group of employees for which it does not already have bargaining rights.

If a bargaining unit originally defined by the Board in a certification order can thus be expanded, the possibility that it can be contracted must also be considered.

Situations where this occurs inadvertently are not particularly bothersome. However general the language used by the Board in a certification order, the parties may by their behaviour demonstrate that they understand the bargaining unit to be smaller than the one apparently originally determined. A typical example of this might be a situation where a union is certified as bargaining agent for a unit comprising "all employees" but where, over the years, the parties clearly show by their behaviour that they consider the sales staff or the office employees to be excluded from the unit. In such a case, little more can be done but to give effect to the "new" description of the bargaining unit, as evidenced by the behaviour of the parties over a long period of time. Thereafter, should the trade union wish to acquire bargaining rights for the "forgotten employees", it will be required to proceed by way of application as if, in fact and in law, it had never had any right to represent these employees.

A more serious problem arises if the employer and the certified bargaining agent deliberately enter into a collective agreement which is expressly made applicable to a bargaining unit which is smaller than that described in the certification order. In such a situation employees included in a bargaining unit for which a trade union has been certified by the Board are effectively deprived of the benefits of the collective agreement and of their right to be represented by the bargaining agent in collective bargaining with their employer. As between the employee and the bargaining agent, such an agreement appears to involve a breach of the duty of fair representation which is owed by the bargaining agent to every employee in the unit.

In such a case, the Board should at the very least be extremely cautious against endorsing or otherwise giving effect to an agreement between the employer and the bargaining agent which is in contravention of the Board's certification order and which further has the effect of infringing on the rights of the employees affected. Since an agreement has been concluded between the employer and the bargaining agent, the Board must also be wary of undermining the very collective bargaining system which the Code was designed to uphold by making it possible for a party to a bargain to renege on its part of the deal.

Certainly, and whether such agreements between the employer and the bargaining agent are valid or not, an employer may not lawfully compel or seek to compel the bargaining agent to conclude a collective agreement which is expressly made applicable to a group which is smaller than the unit that the trade union has been certified to represent as bargaining agent pursuant to a certification order issued by the Board. As the Board has already indicated a party may be in breach of its duty to bargain collectively in good faith under the provisions of section 148(a) of the Code if it seeks to compel the other party to include in a collective agreement a provision which is illegal or otherwise contrary to public policy. Therefore, an attempt to compel the inclusion in a collective agreement of a "scope clause" under which the collective agreement would not be applicable to "every employee in the bargaining unit," despite the clear language of section 154 of the Code, might very well amount to a failure to comply with section 148(a) of the Code. Furthermore, since a certified bargaining agent has, pursuant to section 136(1)(a) of the Code, the "exclusive authority to bargain collectively on behalf of the employees in the unit," an employer may not evade its obligation under the Code by refusing to recognize a trade unit [sic] duly certified as the bargaining agent for all or part of the unit described in the certification order.

In any event, and whether we like it or not, it is a well-known fact of industrial relations in this country that, over the years, employers and trade unions have bargained over the application of a collective agreement and have concluded agreements which may be incompatible with the terms of a certification order issued by the Board. We have already expressed serious reservations as regards the validity of such agreements, which appear to contravene both the language and the policies of the Canada Labour Code. While such agreements certainly cannot allow either party to the contract to evade their legal obligations vis-à-vis the employees affected, it would be equally unacceptable to allow a party to renege on its agreement, because it is no longer convenient or acceptable to it. In the name of preserving the effectiveness and continuous validity of a certification order issued by it, the Board will not use the discretion vested in it by section 119 of the Code to rescue a trade union from "poor deals" made at the bargaining table, particularly when a union later seeks to invoke bargaining rights against the very employees which it has abandoned or ignored over a long period of time. Although a certification order issued pursuant to the provisions of the Code normally continues to have full force and effect until such time as it is revoked whether expressly pursuant to section 138(1) or implicitly pursuant to section 136(1)(b) of the Code, the bargaining rights which it confers may lapse as a result of the failure of the bargaining agent to exercise them over a long period of time. Whether or not a trade union can be allowed to invoke its own dereliction as regards the employees affected by it, it should not be able to invoke it against those very employees or against the employer who is entitled to rely on the agreement reached with the union and implemented over a period of time. Therefore, a certified bargaining agent who has, over the years, voluntarily relinquished its bargaining rights with regard to some employees who were originally included in the bargaining unit for which it was certified should be in no better position than a trade union which has done so inadvertently or one which has entirely failed to exercise its bargaining rights over a long period of time. In such a situation, if the certified bargaining agent wishes to obtain anew the bargaining rights which it has relinquished, it is entirely normal and appropriate that the Board should take into account in reaching its decision the wishes of the employees affected, as if a new application for certification were involved.

We must nevertheless recognize that, over the years, problems may arise over the interpretation or application of a certification order issued by the Board. The language used in the description of the bargaining unit may become out-of-date. New positions or classifications may be created or the duties and responsibilities of certain positions may vary. Often, the parties may be able to resolve such disputes themselves by agreeing that the newly-created classifications were meant to be covered under the terms of the original certification order or that certain persons clearly do or do not per-form management functions or are or are not employed in a confidential capacity in matters relating to industrial relations. Of course such an agree-ment does not bind the Canada Labour Relations Board which, pursuant to section 118(p) of the Code, is expressly empowered to make such a determi-nation. Nevertheless, it is only reasonable that the Board should, as a general rule, give effect to such agreements unless they appear to it to directly contravene the policies or provisions of the Code.

Direct negotiations between the employer and the bargaining agent are not, however, the sole means of resolving such disputes. Pursuant to section 119 of the Canada Labour Code (Part V — Industrial Relations):

> the Board may review, rescind, amend, alter or vary any order or decision made by it, and may rehear any application before making an order in the [sic] respect of the application. . . .

In the course of determining such an application, the Board may certainly invoke the powers given to it by section 118(p) of the Code to determine whether a person is an employee or whether a person performs management functions or is employed in a confidential capacity in matters relating to industrial relations. Only after such a determination has been made, can the Board determine whether it is appropriate to review or vary an existing certification order so that the description of the bargaining unit properly reflects the existing situation.

The Board has already indicated that the powers conferred upon it by section 119 of the Code could and would be used to update or otherwise clarify an order or decision of the Board having a continuing effect.

> Whenever an order or decision of the Board has a continuing effect, and this is typically the case where a Certification Order has been issued, various circum-stances may change which may require corresponding amendments or clarifi-cations of the Board's original decision. For example, the name of the bargaining agent or that of the employer may have changed or the classification titles referred to in the Board's order may be replaced by new ones. Alternatively, new classifications may have been created and it may be unclear whether they are dealt with by the Board's original decision. In such a case, an application may be filed under section 119 asking the Board to review and alter its decision or to clarify it. Here, an eventual decision on the application for review will not change the nature and effect of the original Board's order. It will simply up-date or clarify the wording of the decision and accordingly, the Board must simply be satisfied that these changes are in order.

In this way, the parties can seek and obtain from the Board a ruling with regard to the scope of the bargaining unit described in a certification order issued by the Board. The Board can determine whether the incumbent of a new classification is an employee who was meant to be included in the bargaining unit originally defined by the Board or whether the person in question performs management functions or is employed in a confidential capacity in matters relating to labour relations, in which case it may be appropriate to vary the existing certification order so as to add the new classification to the list of exclusions.

Furthermore, for the purpose of making that determination, it should matter little whether the person or persons whose status is raised in the application wish the trade union to represent them as their bargaining agent. Obviously, in order to be certified as bargaining agent for a bargaining unit, a trade union must enjoy the support of a majority of the employees in the unit found appropriate by the Board. However, in order to make the determination required by section 126(c) of the Code, the Board does not and must not consider the wishes of individual employees or of employees in given positions or classifications but the overall wishes of all the employees included in the unit which it has found appropriate. It is a basic principle of our labour relations legislation that the wishes of the majority of the employees in an appropriate bargaining unit must prevail with regard to the question of whether a trade union will be certified as bargaining agent for the whole unit, and which trade union must be so certified. In such a context it is unavoidable that some employees or groups of employees may disagree with the majority and that their wishes may have to be subjected to those of the majority. There appears to be no valid justification to depart from this principle in the context of an application for review made pursuant to section 119 of the Code simply because an employer may have created a new position or classification and may contend that the incumbent is not an employee within the meaning of the Code or because the employer contends that the duties and responsibilities of a particular individual have changed in such a manner that that individual is no longer an "employee" under the Code.

The Board cannot and should not ignore the "facts of life." When an employee is hired or promoted into a position by an employer and is led to understand by that employer's representatives that he is now a "manager" and entitled to receive the "privileges" normally accruing to the managerial ranks, it is not very likely that this person will be inclined to obtain or retain membership in the trade union representing the "ordinary" employees of that employer. If, as a result of his alleged promotion from the bargaining unit, the employer stops deducting union dues from that employee's salary, as required under the collective agreement, only a very determined and exceptional individual will take the necessary steps to maintain his membership by directly forwarding to the trade union the requisite financial contribution. It is clear that a union attempting to recruit a member under these conditions is at least severely handicapped. Furthermore, it is equally clear to us that, normally, a trade union should not be required to do so. An employer may not, by creating a new classification and labelling the incumbent a "manager", vary or alter a bargaining unit defined by the Board in a certification order. If the nature of the duties and responsibilities of that person are such that the position is clearly included in the bargaining unit for which the Board has certified a trade union, only the Board can determine whether that person performs management functions or is employed in a confidential capacity in matters related to industrial relations so that the position should, accordingly, be expressly excluded from the bargaining unit for which the trade union is certified. In making that determination, it is clear that the Board must focus on the nature of the duties and responsibilities of the person involved and not on the subjective beliefs of that person or of the employer as to the importance of his alleged managerial function.

It is clear, however, that in order to secure a determination from the Board on the basis of these principles, a trade union must act without delay. At the very least, it must not acquiesce in the contention of the employer that persons employed in "disputed classifications" are excluded from the bargaining unit. Failing that, the Board may very well find that the parties have, by their agreement or by their behaviour, interpreted the certification order issued by the Board in a manner that is binding on both the employer and the bargaining agent. In such a case, it would not be proper for the Board to invoke the discretion conferred upon it by the provisions of section 119 of the Code to disturb a long established relationship, without regard for the wishes of the employees involved.

b The Instant Application for Review
The contention of the intervenor is that, pursuant to the Certification Order issued in its favour in February 1949, it is entitled to represent all the employees of the British Columbia Telephone Company except those who devote a major portion of their time to the supervision of other employees. Therefore, the Board should refuse to give effect to the unilateral actions of the employer which have eroded the bargaining unit over the years, and review the 1949 order so as to restore the bargaining unit which it had originally certified. Since what is at stake is a simple up-dating and clarification of the Certification Order originally issued by the Board, the wishes of the approximately 600 employees which it claims should be added to the unit are irrelevant.

The facts are not quite as simple and straightforward. The Certification Order at issue in this application for review was issued by the Board on February 23, 1949. A review of the Board's files with regard to the original application for certification is singularly uninformative. The file contains little or no information with regard to the employer's organizational structure or with regard to the reasons which warranted the exclusion of certain classifications from the unit and it is therefore difficult to ascertain the intended scope of the bargaining unit described by the Board in the Certification Order. In fact, the file makes it clear that the Certification Order which was issued by the Board in February 1949 simply reflected and endorsed an agreement reached between the employer and the Federation of Telephone Workers of British Columbia with regard to the scope of the bargaining unit. Certainly, it is not possible to conclude, as does the intervenor, that the unit originally defined by the Board included all employees except those who were involved in the supervision of other employees. The list of exclusions outlined in the Certification Order is now rather useless. Some job titles can still be related to existing ones which are supervisory in nature. The basis for a number of the exclusions can still be fairly easily ascertained when the job title is that of "manager" or indicates that the incumbent must have been a "professional" and, as such, was not an employee under the legislation as it then existed. Unfortunately, the justification for a large number of exclusions is not all that clear. The original unit description can be interpreted as the intervenor proposed but it is equally consistent with the interpretation proposed by the applicant, according to which only "ordinary" employees were originally included and all positions with important managerial, supervisory, professional or technical functions were excluded. According to this latter interpretation, the employees whom the applicant now wishes to represent comprise the very group which was originally excluded, for one reason or another, from the unit represented by the intervenor. In view of this, it is neither possible nor desirable to attempt to interpret or clarify the Certification Order issued in 1949, without considering the changes which have taken place in the organization of the employer over a period of twenty-five years. We are far from satisfied that it is possible, as the intervenor contends, to restore the bargaining unit originally determined by the Board to be appropriate in view of the fact that the evidence is far from conclusive.

Furthermore, even if it were possible to do so, it is far from clear that it would be appropriate to do so in this case. The intervenor was certified in 1949. Since then, it has negotiated several collective agreements with the employer. It now protests the fact that these collective agreements have not been applicable to the entire bargaining unit for which it had originally been certified. We recognize of course that, for a period of close to ten years, the intervenor has been trying to obtain a resolution of its dispute with the employer over this issue and to counteract what it considers to be an erosion of the bargaining unit which it represents. It is extremely regrettable that its efforts in this regard have proven to be of no avail and that various circumstances have deprived it of the opportunity to obtain a final decision on the validity of its claim. The fact remains, however, that, from 1949 to 1967, the intervenor did little or nothing to remedy the situation. In view of this, the Board can only conclude that, if the intervenor ever did have the authority to bargain on behalf of a group of employees wider than that which is now covered by its collective agreement with the employer, these bargaining rights have now lapsed.

Since 1949, the telecommunications industry has undergone major transformations. The nature of the operations of B.C. Tel. has changed as well as have the skills and qualifications required of its employees. Over the years, the number of employees employed in supervisory positions or in highly specialized staff positions has grown dramatically and these employees have, in fact, been excluded from the bargaining unit represented by the union. Although the bargaining unit represented by the union may to some extent have been eroded by this phenomenon, we are not prepared at this stage to rule that this occurred solely or mainly as a result of the employer's determination to restrict the bargaining rights of the intervenor. In fact, this seems to be due in large part to the development of the industry and of this enterprise over a period of many years.

It is now clear, from the earlier decisions of this Board in this or in related cases, that a number of persons employed in the managerial ranks of the British Columbia Telephone Company do not in fact perform management functions and are indeed "employees" within the meaning of the Code. Whatever the reasons for this, these employees are not now and have not for many years been represented by a trade union. The Telecommunication Workers' Union has not seriously attempted to recruit these employees and does not claim that they wish to be represented by it.

2   The Application for Certification

In the instant case, the Board has already ruled that the employees proposed for inclusion in the bargaining unit were "employees" as that term is defined in section 107(1) of the Canada Labour Code (Part V — Industrial Relations).

We also find on the basis of the documentary evidence filed with the Board that the applicant is a trade union within the meaning of section 107(1) of the Canada Labour Code. In this regard, we note that the employer had contested the trade union status of the applicant on the grounds that its members were not "employees" but managers. This assertion has been disposed of, at least in part, by the interim decision of the Board in the instant case. We recognize, however, that many managerial employees of B.C. Tel. are members of the Society and that, at this stage, it would be premature for the Board to rule that these persons are all "employees." Nevertheless, we find that the applicant is an "organization of employees ... the purposes of which include the regulation of relations between employers and employees." We are confident that, should some of the members or leaders of the Society be found not to be "employees," the applicant will nevertheless be able to continue to operate as a trade union and will take whatever steps are necessary to remove any possible inference of "managerial interference."

Therefore, there remains for us to determine, pursuant to section 126(b) of the Code, "the unit that constitutes a unit appropriate for collective bargaining" and pursuant to section 126(c), whether the applicant enjoys the support of a majority of the employees in that unit. In so doing, we are aware that it is up to the applicant to establish to the satisfaction of the Board that it meets the requirements outlined in section 126 of the Code.

The position taken by the other parties to the application has been of little assistance to the Board in reaching a determination on that issue. The employer has not contested the appropriateness of the bargaining unit proposed by the applicant. It has also refused to take any position with regard to this issue although it has provided the Board with the written information and submissions which it had expressly requested. The intervenor has indeed disputed the appropriateness of the bargaining unit proposed by the applicant. It is clear, however, that its position has been largely influenced by its concern to protect and promote its own claim that it is entitled to represent more than two-thirds of the employees in the proposed bargaining unit. The intervenor does not dispute the right of the applicant to represent those managerial employees of the Marketing Department who are involved, to a considerable extent, in the supervision of other employees. It has however questioned the appropriateness of a supervisory unit which would comprise only the employees of that department.

To some extent, the applicant itself may have been hampered in presenting evidence and submissions to the Board on the issue of appropriateness. It may have been led to rely unduly on the Board's statement that at least a prima facie case has been established with regard to the appropriateness of the bargaining unit which it proposes. It may also have been handicapped by its own frankness as to its goals and ideals. It is the clearly avowed goal of the Society to eventually secure bargaining rights for a single bargaining unit comprising all the employees of B.C. Tel. in the managerial ranks. It recognizes that such a bargaining unit would be appropriate, indeed would be the most appropriate and desirable from the point of view of the effective representation of the employees involved. In view of the circumstances of this case, however, it nevertheless requests that, for the time being, the Board find appropriate the bargaining unit which it proposes and which would include only employees in the managerial ranks of the Marketing Department.

Section 125(4) of the Code provides that:

> Where a trade union applies for certification as the bargaining agent for a unit comprised of or including employees whose duties include the supervision of other employees, the Board may, subject to subsection (2) determine that the unit proposed in the application is appropriate for collective bargaining.

It is obvious that the unit proposed here is not one that comprises only supervisory employees but one that includes both supervisory and non-supervisory employees. Subsection 125(4) of the Code makes it clear that the Board may find appropriate either type of unit.

In support of its position, the applicant has relied to quite an extent on modern management theory. Counsel for the applicant has quoted in argument Galbraith and Drucker. It contends that, in the modern enterprise, it is neither possible nor desirable to draw a line between managers and ordinary employees. Because of the explosion of knowledge and of the ever increasing complexity of the modern enterprise, a "technostructure" has developed in larger corporations. It is composed of "knowledge workers" who, by the nature of their work which often involves the supervision of other employees, by the nature of their skills and by their working conditions, are different from "ordinary" employees although they are "employees" themselves, as that term is defined in section 107(1) of the Canada Labour Code. According to the applicant, these persons share a distinct community of interest which warrants the creation of separate bargaining units.

On the other hand, it is clear that this application for certification applies only to those employees of the Marketing Department who are not already represented by the intervenor. In this regard, the applicant contends that, because the Marketing Department is organized as a team and because of the unique function of the Marketing Department in the employer's operation, a unit comprising only the employees of the Marketing Department would be appropriate for collective bargaining. In support of this contention, the applicant invokes the difficulty of organizing persons who have, until very recently, been considered not to be "employees" and deprived of the right to bargain collectively under the provisions of the Canada Labour Code. It further indicates that it intends and hopes to continue to organize the managerial employees of the employer and to file subsequent applications for certification. In this respect, it is prepared to concede that the granting of additional bargaining rights to this applicant should not lead to the creation of numerous additional units. Instead, all the various units for which the applicant may become certified should be merged into a single unit.

The British Columbia Telephone Company employed, as of December 31, 1975, more than 10,500 persons. Of this number, 1,902 persons were considered to be "management." In October 1976, the number of "managerial" employees had grown to 1,983. Of this number, some 100 persons were employed in the Marketing Department as of the date of the instant application for certification. Following a reorganization which has since been implemented, new services and groups were brought into the Marketing Department, particularly in the Computer Communications Group. Accordingly, in the Fall of 1976, there were more than 140 employees in the managerial ranks of the Marketing Department.

In earlier decisions, particularly in the decision of the Board in Trade of Locomotive Engineers and Canadian Pacific Limited and Brotherhood of Locomotive Engineers, the Board has already indicated that, in most circumstances, a bargaining unit comprising all the employees of a given employer is appropriate for collective bargaining. Indeed, in most cases, such a bargaining structure is best designed to ensure the effective representation of the interests of the employees, while promoting "effective industrial relations" and the "constructive settlement of disputes." The Canada Labour Code, however, has not mandated the Canada Labour Relations Board to determine in any given case the "most appropriate" bargaining unit. It is a well-known fact of industrial relations that, in most situations, more than one unit may be appropriate for collective bargaining. The Board should not, however, endorse the creation of a number of small bargaining units unless it is satisfied that there exist valid considerations for departing from the concept of a broad overall unit.

Within the British Columbia Telephone Company, there already exists one bargaining unit represented by a certified bargaining agent. This unit of "classified employees" comprises office and clerical employees, telephone operators and other traffic personnel as well as tradesmen, technicians, installers, construction or maintenance employees and other blue collar workers. In order to effectively represent these rather diverse groups of employees, the intervenor is organized as a federation comprising three relatively autonomous divisions: clerical, traffic and plant. The success of the Telecommunication Workers' Union in negotiating a single collective agreement on behalf of some 9,000 employees testifies to the fact that it is possible to accommodate diverse and varied interests within a single unified bargaining structure. There can be little doubt that the intervenor could further adapt its structures to include in its ranks and to effectively represent other employees of the employer, even if they are employed in a supervisory or managerial capacity or perform highly skilled work. It is however clear that, at this stage, these employees do not wish to be represented by the Union and many of them have expressed a wish to be represented by another trade union.

In view of the circumstances of this case, the Board is not prepared to find that the only unit appropriate for collective bargaining is one which would include all employees of the British Columbia Telephone Company, or all the employees of the British Columbia Telephone Company except those who perform supervisory functions. To so rule would amount to a finding that all those employees who are not already represented by the intervenor could only exercise the rights which are granted to them by section 110(1) of the Code by becoming members of the intervenor in such numbers that the Board would be justified to review the existing Certification Order so as to expand the existing bargaining unit to include these additional classifications. Under this reasoning, these employees could only avail themselves of the provisions of the Code with regard to certification and collective bargaining by opting to be represented by the Telecommunication Workers' Union. While we recognize that such an outcome may be unavoidable in some cases, we feel strongly that such a conclusion should be avoided if at all possible, since it severely restricts the freedom of employees to select the bargaining agent of their choice. Therefore, in this case, while reiterating our opinion that a single all-inclusive unit would be appropriate for collective bargaining, we are prepared to find appropriate for collective bargaining a separate unit comprising only those employees who are not presently represented by the Telecommunication Workers' Union. The concept of the "technostructure" proposed by the applicant is certainly novel in industrial relations terms. Yet, we feel that it is a useful concept. The modern enterprise does employ large numbers of "knowledge workers." Whether they perform a staff or a line function, these employees will often share a distinct community of interest. In many circumstances, such as in the instant case, it may be appropriate to recognize this fact by sanctioning the creation of a separate bargaining unit comprising only these employees. Accordingly, as we have indicated in our decision on the application for certification filed by the Telephone Supervisors' Association, the Board is prepared to find appropriate for collective bargaining a separate unit of "supervisory" or managerial employees of the British Columbia Telephone Company. It may even be that more than one "supervisory" unit could be found to be appropriate for collective bargaining.

The Board is fully aware of the difficulty of organizing into a trade union employees who have, at least until recently, been led to believe that they are "managers" and that belonging to a trade union is somehow incompatible with their status as "managers." As a result, it is not entirely surprising that these employees, when they choose to organize pursuant to the provisions of the Code, should be inclined to do so through organizations created specifically for that purpose and should favour the creation of separate "supervisory" bargaining units. In this context, it is clear that any decision on the appropriateness of such supervisory or quasi-supervisory units may have a tremendous impact. If the right of these employees to join a trade union and bargain collectively with their employer through the bargaining agent of their own choice is not to remain a dead letter, it may well be that the Board should, at least for the time being, adopt a fairly sympathetic approach as regards proposals for the creation of such units, where they are not otherwise inappropriate. Nevertheless, the wishes of the employees involved or the extent of a union's organizing campaign cannot by themselves establish the appropriateness of a bargaining unit for collective bargaining.

Questions

1 Why would the Society of Telephone Engineers and Managers (STEM) have filed separate applications for certification of workers in the marketing and finance departments and for a group of engineers? Elaborate.

2 What is the difference between certification by the Canada Labour Relations Board (CLRB) and voluntary recognition? Elaborate.

3 Why did the intervenor not try to get support from the workers whom it wished to have included in its bargaining unit?

4 The CLRB refers to the possibility that the intervenor and the employer may not have been bargaining for workers who may technically have been covered by the collective agreement. How could the parties have known this in an industry where occupational changes and job duties were changing so quickly?

5 How would you assess the intervenor's arguments? Would you find it appropriate to represent the group it sought to represent?

6 What does the intervenor's experience with its 1949 certificate tell you about the dynamics of bargaining units and how they might be kept up to date?

7 What order, if any, would you make for the intervenor?

8 Why did STEM make its application for workers in separate departments when it eventually wanted to represent all levels of management in the company?

9 a) Why did STEM raise the issue of knowledge workers and technostructure?

   b) Did this issue increase or decrease its chances of becoming certified as the bargaining agent for the first four levels of management in the marketing department? Elaborate.

10 If you were writing the decision for the Board, would you find the unit proposed by STEM appropriate for collective bargaining? Elaborate.

11 a) This case lends itself beautifully to role-playing. Have three members of the class act as members of the Board, with your professor as chair and another two as representatives of employer and union interests. Have other class members play the roles of the chief spokespersons for the two unions involved, the president of the company, and Fred Pearson, *et al.* Role-play the case as if it were a real-life one and assume that all of the players would like to take on cases of a similar nature in the future.

   b) What is the assessment of each actor with respect to the roles played by the others?

   c) How does the class as a whole assess each of your roles?

   d) If you have audio-visual equipment, tape this case, replay it, and critique it.

   e) Did you find the exercise worthwhile?

appendix two

Unfair Labour Practice Cases

An Alleged Union Unfair Practice — The Kenneth Cameron Case*

Kenneth Cameron,
complainant,
and
Canadian Brotherhood
of Railway, Transport and
General Workers, CBRT,
respondent,
and
Via Rail, Montreal, Quebec,
employer.

• • •

1 On April 18, 1980, Mr. Kenneth Cameron filed a complaint with the Canada Labour Relations Board, alleging that his union, CBRT, breached its duty of fair representation by its refusal to refer to arbitration his grievance against his discharge. The section of the Code alleged to have been contravened is section 136.1.

> 136.1 Where a trade union is the bargaining agent for a bargaining unit, the trade union and every representative of the trade union shall represent, fairly and without discrimination, all employees in the bargaining unit.

Efforts by the Board's officer to assist the parties to reach a settlement were unsuccessful. A hearing was held in Montreal on October 6, 1980. Although Via Rail was made a party, it chose not to appear at the hearing.

2 The complainant was, at the time of his discharge, a dining car steward. He had been assigned to that position two and a half years previously. His

---

* Permission to use this case was granted by the Canada Labour Relations Board. Minor deletions were made by the author for the purposes of this book.

length of service for CN and Via Rail, its successor, totalled five years and a half. He had an untarnished work record. The events giving rise to the dismissal concern a trip made on July 18, 1979, between Montreal and Winnipeg on a skyline car. The salient facts can be summarized as follows.

The complainant worked on two types of cars — the skyline car and the café car. Both wagons are for dining, bar and take-out services. However, their layout is different. On the café car, a closed area exists for each kind of service whereas on the skyline car, the services are provided for in an open area.

The teams assigned to these cars differ in their composition as well as in their responsibilities. For the café car, the staff comprises a take-out attendant, a bar attendant, a chef and a steward, whereas on the skyline car, there is a chef, an assistant chef, two waiters and a steward. On the café car, each employee is accountable for his/her work area, whereas on the skyline car, the steward is accountable for the quality of service as well as the money involved in the total operation. Furthermore, detailed instructions and forms exist for the café car whereas for the skyline car, few directives on how to operate had been issued at the time of the run in July 1979.

It was also established that when the skyline cars were acquired in June 1978, by Via Rail, its employees were not given the opportunity to familiarize themselves with the new equipment whereas the employees of CP used to the skyline car were provided training on the café cars.

The evidence also showed that a written complaint from a client to Via Rail on July 31, 1979 prompted the employer to investigate the matter. The quality of the food, the filthy condition of the skyline car and the poor service on the train en route from Winnipeg to Thunder Bay were concerns of the client. The complainant was the steward on duty for that trip. In the preliminary inquiry made by the employer some discrepancies in reporting funds were discovered and statements of employees were gathered. With these elements on hand, the employer charged the complainant with gross dereliction of duty, unbecoming action for a supervisor contrary to sanitary and hygiene regulations and misreporting revenue for saleable take-out items on trains 1 and 2, ex. Montreal, July 18, 1979. As required by article 24.7 of the collective agreement (No. 2) in cases of major offences, the employer held a hearing on August 30, 1979. The purpose of such a hearing is to establish and determine the facts upon which action may be taken.

Mr. Cameron was notified by telephone, on August 28, by Mr. Durand, his supervisor, that he was being held out of service and that he had to appear at a hearing and be interrogated. The complainant declared that he was never served the written notice which spells out the charges.

Following his telephone conversation with his supervisor, Mr. Cameron contacted Mr. Kiley, member of the local grievance committee in order to obtain his assistance. The union did inquire to find out the charges generally. Mr. Kiley was present at the investigation hearing. At the end of the hearing, Mr. Cameron stated:

I think the treatment I have received from Mr. de Cotret has been fair and civil. But I do feel that it is not right that I received no specifics regarding the accusation before coming to the hearing. Also I wish to reserve my right to have the Brotherhood Regional V.P. cross-examine witnesses who have testified against me. (article 24.9).

The hearing was recorded and each party revised the copy and signed it.

When Mr. Cameron was informed of his dismissal, he went to Ottawa with his Local Chairman, Mr. Rouleau, to meet Mr. Thivierge, the Regional Vice-Chairman. Mr. Rouleau, acting under the instructions of Mr. Thivierge, filed a grievance at Step 1 of the procedure against the discharge. Later on, Mr. Thivierge pursued the procedure at Step 2. Following the employer's reply not to amend its decision, Mr. Thivierge turned the matter to Mr. J.D. Hunter, National Vice-President of CBRT, and recommended a referral to arbitration as he felt the penalty was too severe. In his correspondence, he also raised the possible collusion of the employees who had filed statements against Mr. Cameron. All along, Mr. Cameron had requested verification of the employees' statements.

In view of Mr. Thivierge's concern of possible collusion between the employees who accused the complainant, Mr. Hunter proceeded to Step 3 of the grievance procedure. At the meeting with Via Rail, he raised the possibility of collusion and requested the employer to verify it. In reply, the employer rejected the suggestion of collusion and turned down the grievance.

Mr. Hunter, after reviewing the file which contained the investigation report, the statements of the employees, the letter of the client and the remittance form from Cameron for commodities sold, decided against a referral to arbitration.

3   As the duty of fair representation under the Quebec legislation was raised in argumentation as a basis for establishing the extent of the obligation of a bargaining agent under the Canada Labour Code, it is appropriate to examine extensively the Quebec system.

Section 38b of the Quebec Labour Code statutorily expresses the duty of fair representation in the following terms:

> a certified association shall not act in bad faith or in an arbitrary or discriminatory manner or show serious negligence in respect of employees comprised in a bargaining unit represented by it, whether or not they are members.

There exists a rigorous procedure for this type of complaint. It is initiated by the filing of a written complaint to the Minister within six months from the circumstances giving rise to the complaint. On receipt of a complaint, the Minister appoints an investigator who shall endeavour to settle the dispute in fifteen (15) days. Within the fifteen (15) ensuing days if no settlement is reached or if the association does not honour the agreement, the employee shall apply to the Labour Court for authorization to submit the claim to arbitration. The Court, before granting it, must determine if the association has contravened Section 38b. Following a positive ruling, the claim is heard by an arbitrator and judged on its merits.

Since the duty of fair representation has been included in the Code, the Quebec Labour Court has rendered a number of decisions. It emerges from its jurisprudence that the section has a very limited coverage. It was ruled that section 38e, which establishes the procedure, restricted the scope of section 38b. Consequently, the legislation envisages complaints relating strictly to disciplinary measures including all forms of dismissals . . .

It also flows from the jurisprudence that the onus of proof rests on the complainant, the reasoning being . . . that the legislator presumed that unions represent fairly all employees of a bargaining unit.

The complainant, therefore, has to demonstrate that a serious prejudice would result if denied a recourse to arbitration. . . . To evaluate the seriousness of the prejudice, the reasonable success of a claim in arbitration is taken into consideration. . . . The consequences of the dismissal are used in determining the extent of the prejudice. The complainant had demonstrated a violation of seniority rights as well as a loss in earnings that an extra year of employment would have granted. Furthermore, the cooperative behavior of the complaint is also taken into account. . . .

The most important factor in the evidence is the alleged violation of the duty of fair representation. The union and the complainant share the burden to establish, for the complainant, the union's violation: for the union, its compliance to the requirements of section 38b. . . .

> If the union enjoys such discretion shielding it from the tribunal's intervention, it must still demonstrate that it took steps in order to have been able to take a decision with full knowledge of the facts (page 96) (Our translation).

The extent of the obligation for a bargaining agent . . . as stated in another case is

> The duty stipulated in Section 38b of the Labour Code cannot be qualified as being the best authority to exercise nor is it the most advantageous. It is negative in the sense that in representing an employee a certified association must not act in bad faith or in an arbitrary or discriminatory manner or show gross negligence. . . . That is a far cry from a duty unconditionally imposed upon a certified association . . . not to lack proficiency or to take the part of any employee who believes he is in difficulty or declares he is dissatisfied (page 158) (Our translation).

Therefore, the conduct of an association, to be declared in contravention to the Code, has to be arbitrary, discriminatory, of bad faith or gross negligence. Of all these qualifications, only the latter seems to cause a difficulty. Two schools of thought have emerged. . . . The concept of gross negligence could include a simple error but which resulted in serious damage.

> In my view, here the legislator did not wish, in spite of the ambiguity of the text which seems in fact to require proof of gross negligence, to limit this remedy to the point where an employee would, for example, be absolutely deprived of his right to have his grievance taken to arbitration if he could establish merely simple negligence on the part of his union.

The concept of negligence which can be more or less serious, of great or minor consequence or of another type is always difficult to deal with. On the one hand, a simple negligence can result in serious damage, on the other hand, a gross one can have no consequences. The law must be appreciated by taking into account the whole of the facts and their effects, the negligence and its consequences, the cause and the resulting prejudice. That is why I do not hesitate to say that a simple negligence (for example, a simple oversight) which results in an employee being deprived of his recourse to arbitration where that recourse would prevent him from losing his position, truly constitutes gross negligence (page 335) (Our translation).

However, . . . only blatant errors would be considered gross negligence:

Sometimes the grievance can first appear to be without any merit where there is however evidence of gross negligence. Sometimes also, the association may have acted in a satisfactory manner but simply erred by wrongly refusing to defend an employee's dismissal.

Unless there is a clear and obvious situation where it appears that the discretion was not manifestly exercised in a judicious manner, the remedy provided for in Sections 38b. et seq. of the Code will not be available to the employee. The legislator certainly did not intend, through the actions of union officers, to deprive an association of employees existing within the concrete reality of a business of the choice and the appropriateness to act or not in view of rectifying a situation which an employee covered by the certificate judges to be prejudicial towards him. That is why an employee does not have an absolute right to arbitration, nor an absolute right to have his association act according to his instructions. He does, however, possess a clearly established right — and that is where the law affords him protection — that his association not abuse its discretion by acting in bad faith, or in an arbitrary or discriminatory manner or showing gross negligence, when the employee asks it to file a grievance on his behalf (pages 326 and 327) (Our translation).

. . . it is further elaborated:

Section 38b. of the code has the effect of slightly broadening the parameters of fair representation. Not only must a union take a malevolent attitude, but it must not demonstrate gross negligence. In taking a grossly negligent attitude, the union will therefore not be able to rely on its good faith and lack of intention to prejudice the employee in order to escape any judgement condemning its attitude (page 235) (Our translation).

and:

Serious negligence involving an association of employees must therefore be related to an attitude characterized by gross negligence, by a negligence of great consequence attributable to its representatives, by an unpardonable oversight of the required precautions, by an undisguised or obvious lack of ability or by a manifest lack of concern revealing the association's inability to look after the interests of the employees in its bargaining unit seriously and efficiently (page 236) (Our translation).

Failure to appoint representatives to a meeting with the employer before any decision on a grievance can be made . . . to investigate, file a grievance and call a grievance committee . . . withdrawal of a grievance based on the record and word of the employer . . . failure to request from a complainant her version of the facts . . . refusal to file a grievance based on the employer's opinion . . . were all ruled gross negligence.

To qualify a union's behaviour as being arbitrary, discriminatory, of bad faith or gross negligence, various tests are adopted. Thus borrowed from civil law, the concept of a prudent administrator (conduite du bon père de famille) is a norm applied to the actions of an association. . . . The merits of a grievance are also considered for the same reason with the proviso that they be examined strictly in relation to an association's actions to assess the nature and extent of inquiry made by a union. . . . Other criteria of evaluation are also proposed. . . .

> Our labour law affords little room to individual rights. It could certainly have been otherwise, but there was a clear desire to favour collective organization in the work place over any other type of employer-employee relationship which would have allowed individual rights more latitude.
>
> Since, on an individual basis, employees have access to grievance and arbitration procedures with respect to the application of the collective agreement only to the extent which that agreement permits, the duty of a union regarding individual grievances must be appreciated in this light. The duty of the union is that much more vital as, only it, is empowered to enforce these rights.
>
> Furthermore, the union's discretion can be appreciated in a different light according to the nature of the grievance (general, group or individual).
>
> Finally, the possible divergent interests between the union and the employee who may be concerned, must be taken into account.
>
> The more the interests diverge, even to the point of being contradictory, or the more individual interests are pronounced, then the union will have to be more cautious in exercising its discretion and in fulfilling its duty of fair representation.
>
> Otherwise, the union runs the risk of playing the twofold role of judging and being judged, or simply violating the rules of natural justice which require that all interested parties be heard (Our translation).

It should be mentioned that the Quebec Labour Court, on a petition under section 38 of the Code, sees its mandate as being:

> In exercising its jurisdiction in accordance with section 38d., the Court's role is not per se one to assess the quality of the decisions taken by a certified association and, finding it appropriate, to substitute its own assessment of a case to that of the said association; in order to intervene, the Court must have proof of violation of section 38b (Our translation). . . .

Having perused the jurisprudence on the duty of fair representation under the Quebec Labour Code, the question to turn to now is how does it relate in the federal legislation?

4 Section 136.1 states the duty of fair representation under the Canada Labour Code. The section was proclaimed in force on June 1, 1978.

As in Quebec, the procedure in the federal jurisdiction is initiated by a written complaint. It must be filed not later than ninety days (90) from the date on which the complainant knew, or in the opinion of the Board ought to have known, of the action or circumstances giving rise to the complaint.

It should be stressed that the delay of ninety days is strict. The Board has not the power to extend the time limit under any circumstances. . . .

Contrary to Quebec legislation where the person who alleges unfair representation must apply to the Labour Court when dissatisfied with the investigator's efforts, under the federal legislation, once a person has initiated the procedure, the Board remains seized of the complaint and retains total jurisdiction. It uses mediative techniques to seek early resolution of complaints. On failure of settlement the Board adjudicates the complaint and may exercise remedial authority under Sections 189 and 121.

The recourse under the federal legislation is available to all employees comprised in a bargaining unit, the bargaining agent being certified or not. Even though it would seem that the accessibility is greater under our jurisdiction (member of certified or recognized bargaining union being covered) than in Quebec where it is specifically referred to members of a certified union, in reality, it is not so, as only certified unions have legal status to enter into collective bargaining with an employer under the Quebec legislation.

Although the federal text is positive and broad, contrary to the Quebec legislation, the Board has been cautious in delineating its coverage. Until recently, the Board has made a distinction between complaints relating to collective agreement administration and those concerning collective bargaining. It has recognized that both types of complaints were envisaged by section 136.1. The Board has also expressed its intention not to fetter the wide latitude of discretion an exclusive bargaining agent must have in collective bargaining. . . . It also stated that section 136.1 did not cover the internal appeal procedure of a union relating to grievance which was accessible strictly to members of the union, precluding therefore, its recourse to non-members. . . .

The burden of proof under the federal regime, like in Quebec, rests on the complainant. The onus can be overturned by a preponderance of evidence.

The legislated standards imposed in the federal jurisdiction are for a union to act "fairly and without discrimination". In provincial legislations, the test is negative and states that a union's conduct should not be arbitrary, discriminatory or of bad faith (see B.C. and Ontario legislations) and includes gross negligence in Quebec. Although aware of these provincial standards, the Board has expressed several times its preference for a prudent attitude in the imposition of any standard. . . . It has voiced its difficulty in combining the provisions of the Code, the intentions of Parliament and the need to protect the individual. . . . However, it rejected an allegation made that the words "fairly and without discrimination" should be read conjunctively and as requiring an element of bad faith. . . .

As far as tests are used in the evaluation of a union's conduct, the furthest the Board went was to adopt the seriousness of a grievance as a factor to be considered in assessing the quality of an association's behaviour. . . .

In summary, the federal and the Quebec systems appear similar in many respects. The scope of the duty to represent fairly under section 136.1

of the federal Code encompasses the subjects covered by the Quebec legislation. However, in view of the federal text being affirmative and broad, the Board opted for a case by case approach and refrained from adopting any specific criteria.

5   With this understanding of the Quebec and federal concepts of fair representation, we now turn to the task of assessing the conduct of CBRT in the handling of the complainant's grievance.

On the one hand, it must be kept in mind that the union is the bargaining agent, and as such, has an exclusive bargaining authority pursuant to section 136(1) of the Code. On the other hand, its authority must be exercised fairly and without discrimination in the representation of employees.

Therefore, it must be recognized that in the processing of a grievance and its control, a union has the exclusive right to make a decision at any step of the procedure, be it to proceed with the grievance, to settle it or to abandon it, and the Board should not interfere in this respect. The rationale is analyzed in *Rayonnier Canada (B.C.) Ltd.* [1975] 2 Can LRBR 196 (B.C.L.R.B.) and *Frederick Carl Vincent*, [1979] 2 Can LRBR 139 (O.L.R.B.) and [1979] OLRB Feb. Rep. 144.

However, its conduct can be subject to scrutiny under the duty of fair representation. Consequently, the question to be addressed is "Did CBRT, in processing the grievance of Mr. Cameron, satisfy its obligation under section 136.1?"

The evidence has established that Mr. J.D. Hunter, Vice-President, is the union official with the responsibility of determining whether or not a grievance should be referred to arbitration. When he made his decision, he relied on the grievor's version as taken by the employer, the client's complaint, the employees' statements (chef and assistant chef) as gathered by the employer and their remittance form as prepared jointly by them and the employer as well as the remittance form of Mr. Cameron as submitted to the employer.

From Mr. Hunter's testimony, it was clear that based on those documents, he would also not have proceeded to Step 3 of the procedure if Mr. Thivierge, the Regional Chairman, had not insisted on his suspicion of collusion between the employees accusing Mr. Cameron and on the merit of the grievance.

Questions

1 On whom does the onus of proof lie in duty of fair representation cases? Why is this so?

2 Why does the Canada Labour Relations Board (CLRB) discuss the duty of fair representation as it exists under the Quebec Labour Code?

3 What is your assessment of the procedure followed in Quebec whereby the Labour Court must find that an association (union) has contravened the relevant section of the Quebec Labour Code and the case is heard by an arbitrator? How

does this procedure differ from that of the Canada Labour Relations Board? Elaborate.

4 What are the factors that have been held to constitute gross negligence under the Quebec Labour Code? Do they seem adequate to you?

5 What is the difference between stating the duty of fair representation in a positive sense and in a negative sense? Elaborate.

6 The CLRB, until recently, made a distinction between complaints relating to both the negotiation and administration of collective agreements. Do you see any difficulties with this comprehensive approach, particularly as it applies to the negotiation process?

7 If you had written the reasons for decision in this case, would you have found the union guilty of an unfair labour practice? Elaborate on the rationale for your decision.

8 Assume that you have found the union guilty of an unfair labour practice by virtue of its failure to take Mr. Cameron's case to arbitration. Sections 121 and 189 give the Board remedial powers. What remedies, if any, would you have granted to Mr. Cameron? Which party would bear responsibility for awarding them? Elaborate.

9 In 1984 Part V of the Canada Labour Code was amended to read as follows:

> A trade union or representative of a trade union that is the bargaining agent for a bargaining unit shall not act in a manner that is arbitrary, discriminatory, or in bad faith in the representation of any of the employees in the unit with respect to their rights under the collective agreement that is applicable to them.

What are the practical implications of this reworded section, and why do you think the change was made? Elaborate.

An Alleged Employer Unfair Practice — The Inland Broadcasters (1969) Ltd. and Twin Cities Radio Ltd. Case*

Inland Broadcasters (1969) Ltd. and
Twin Cities Radio Ltd.,
Kamloops, B.C.,
employer,
and
National Association of Broadcast
Employees and Technicians,
respondent.

The Board was composed of Mr. James E. Dorsey, Vice-Chairman and Messrs. Robert J. Arseneau and Hugh R. Jamieson, members.

* Permission to use this case was granted by the Canada Labour Relations Board.

Appearances:
Messrs. D.S. Clark and J.W.R. Pollard representing the employer. Mr. Ken Mowers representing the respondent.

1   This case involves a request by Inland Broadcasters (1969) Ltd. and Twin Cities Radio Ltd. for review of a certification order issued to the National Association of Broadcast Employees and Technicians for a unit of this employer's employees. The certification order was issued on April 17, 1979. The application for review was filed on September 27, 1979 under section 119, which states:

> 119. The Board may review, rescind, amend, alter or vary any order or decision made by it, and may rehear any application before making an order in respect of the application.

Because of the events leading up to this application and the various allegations made by both parties, the Board is publishing these reasons. No hearing has been held in this case.

2   The union applied for certification on February 19, 1979. The application was received in the Board's Vancouver office and processed in the usual manner with notice to the employer and employees.

At the request of the employer's counsel the time to reply was extended to March 12, 1979. The employer's reply was filed on that date. At the same time there was some debate or other activity going on among the employees.

The Board's offices received several untimely employee replies which the Board's administrative offices returned as untimely. On March 20 the Board's officer had completed his investigation and issued a letter to the parties setting out his understanding of their positions with respect to the appropriate bargaining unit.

By telex on March 21, the Board received a request by counsel for several employees for an extension of time to file a submission. This request was granted and the counsel was given until April 2 to reply. The union strongly protested this action and also alleged employer inspired action in opposition to the application. The employer denied any improper action.

On March 30, counsel for thirty-six persons filed a reply which simply expressed a wish in opposition to the application. A thirty-seventh person acting for himself followed the same procedure and filed a similar reply. On April 17, the Board considered the application and determined the appropriate bargaining unit. A unit of employees of both corporate entities was determined appropriate because the Board declared on September 25, 1974, in connection with a previous unsuccessful application for certification, that the two were a single employer under section 133 of the Code. (The union's 1974 application for certification was dismissed following a representation vote.) The unit determined appropriate in 1979 encompassed over fifty people on the date of application of which a sound majority were members of the union. In keeping with the purpose, intent and spirit of section 126(c) of the Code, the Board granted certification (see *Canadian Imperial Bank of Commerce, Sioux Lookout* 33 di 432, [1979] 1 Can LRBR 18).

So as of April 17, 1979 the situation was this. The union had majority support among the employees as of February 19. Notice of the application was posted on the employer's premises on February 22. No employee replied within the ten-day period allowed alleging any impropriety. The employer had sought and received an extension of time to March 12. On March 21 counsel for employees sought and received an extension of time to reply. The same extension was granted to another individual. The replies when received purported to show a wish late in March of persons who were later found not to be in the appropriate bargaining unit as well as some in the unit. If given weight, which the Board did not, the union's support would have been just short of a majority. At the same time the union was alleging and the employer was denying improper employer prompting and support for the group expressing views opposed to the union's application. The Board's decision granting certification prompted no further communication from any party or employee.

The next event before the Board was an unfair labour practice complaint by the union on May 9, 1979 seeking reinstatement of an employee and other Board directives. A Board officer met with the parties and the matter was settled by an agreement between the parties.

The union and employer met to bargain on June 5 and July 24. Further bargaining has been delayed pending this application.

3   This brings us to these proceedings which really commenced on September 27, but had an interesting prelude. On July 30 the employer wrote its Member of Parliament, Mr. Don Cameron, protesting the Board's decision and requesting him to intervene to have the Board reopen the case. He referred the employer's letter to the Minister of Labour by letter of August 9 expressing the view that the Board should reopen the case. The Minister recognizing the impartial and apolitical nature of the Board wrote Mr. Cameron as follows:

> Mr. Don Cameron, M.P.
> Kamloops-Shuswap
> Room 421WB
> House of Commons
> Ottawa, Ontario
> K1A 0A6
>
>
> Dear Don,
>
> Thank you for your letter of August 9, 1979 concerning correspondence you have received from Inland Broadcasters Ltd.
>
> As you are no doubt aware, the Canada Labour Relations Board is a quasi-judicial body and it would of course be inappropriate for me to intervene in its activities. I have, however, referred your letter to the Board Chairman for any action which he may deem necessary.
>
> Yours sincerely,
>
>
> Lincoln M. Alexander

The Chairman of the Board then wrote Mr. Cameron as follows:

September 14, 1979

Mr. Don Cameron, M.P.,
Kamloops-Shuswap,
Rom 421WB,
House of Commons,
Ottawa, Ontario.
K1A 0A6

Dear Mr. Cameron:

Your letter of August 9, 1979, to the Honourable Lincoln Alexander in the matter of Inland Broadcasters Ltd. has been referred to me for reply.

The Canada Labour Relations Board granted certification to the union (the National Association of Broadcast Employees and Technicians) under Section 124 of the Canada Labour Code (Part V — Industrial Relations) in April 1979. Messrs. Clark and Pollard of Inland Broadcasters (1969) Limited, in their letter to you of July 30, 1979, appear to be requesting a review of the Board's decision of April 1979. Section 119 of the Code provides for such a review procedure and if the employer wishes to make an application under this Section of the Code, the Board would be pleased to entertain it. This application may be made through the Board's Vancouver office to the attention of Mr. P. Kirkland, Regional Manager, at 1090 West Pender Street, 12th floor, Vancouver, B.C., V6E 1N7, Telephone No. (604) 666-6001.

Yours truly,

Marc Lapointe, Q.C.

This reply prompted the employer's application.

The grounds for the employer's review are not that the Board erred in its original decision or that there was some legal impediment to the grant of certification or on any other basis in the Code. Rather the employer says it pleas for "justice."

On application day, February 19, 1979, the unit as proposed by the union totalled 53 people. Since they were granted automatic certification, presumably they had more than 50% of the unit signed up as union members, by one means or another. Two months later, April 17, 1979, NABET was certified as the bargaining agent for these 53 people in the unit. As of August 30, 1979, only **five and one half months** after certification, 22 members of that original 53 member unit have left the employ of the company; one by a lay-off, and **twenty-one** by resignation. Included in the resignations were the president of the local, the secretary-treasurer of the local, and a member of the local's negotiation committee. We have very strong indications that most of the employees who resigned were also members of the union. To date, the local has still not elected a new secretary-treasurer of the local, apparently because no one will allow their name to stand.

In short, while the company agrees that every employee is free to join the trade union of his choice, and to participate in its lawful activities, we do **not** agree that a trade union should have the right to bargain for the unit unless that trade union truly represents a majority of the members of that unit. It is apparent that on February 19, 1979, NABET had collected enough signatures (by one means or another) of their proposed unit of the employees of the two companies to qualify as their agent. It is our sincere belief that that group, even on that date, did not truly represent a majority of the unit, due to the aforementioned coercion and intimidation that was reported to us by our employees. And further, it is our sincere belief that because of the fact that more than 40% of the original unit have since left the employ of the company, the percentage of the unit that the union now represents is a very small minority. Surely it is a miscarriage of justice to allow the union to direct the working lives of our employees if this is true. We submit that there is **only one way** to determine if there is justice being served in this case . . . **only one way** to determine if the majority of our employees are being treated fairly under the Labour Code, and that way is for the CLRB to conduct a representation vote, as was originally requested by us to Mr. Anderson. If a vote were held, and it shows that a majority of the people wish to be represented by the bargaining agent of NABET, then the company will accept that mandate completely.

But should a secret ballot indicate that NABET does not represent a majority of the unit, as circumstances overwhelmingly indicate, *then let justice be done*. If NABET believes that they represent a majority of the unit, surely they cannot fear a secret representation ballot that will show this. If NABET represents only a minority of the unit, then surely they should not be allowed to represent the majority, and assuming that they are an honourable organization, surely they would not wish to bargain for the majority unless they truly represent them.

. . .

Mr. Kirkland, this is the application under Section 119 of the Code. It is **not** an application for de-certification. It is an application for a secret ballot representation vote conducted by the Board, so that the **true** wishes of our employees can be determined, with **no** outside pressure or intimidation being exerted upon them, so that **justice may be completely served**.

The union does not dispute this exceedingly high employee turnover nor does it dispute that there has been active debate among employees even expressed in personal letters to the local press. It says the request is untimely and seeks to counterbalance the picture by filing letters from eight former employees. Each was a union supporter and chronicles the reason he or she felt compelled to leave even though they may have had two or three years employment service. The employer undoubtedly has some explanation for each of the allegations made or events described. We need not go into them here or assess which is an accurate account. The union's reply and letters of former employees were forwarded to the employer. The Board then received a request from the employer of an extension of time to file a reply. The next communication was from several employees in the form of letters or petitions. They were dated the same day or subsequent to the employer's request for an extension of time and all supported the employer's application. We do not know how the employees learned of these proceedings. No notice was sent to them by the Board.

What we can safely say is that the resignation of twenty-one persons in five and a half months is a truly sad event in an enterprise of this size and nature. We are dealing with a daily broadcasting operation, not a seasonal or climate affected industry. The union alleges its members are resigning because of the pressure on them because they are union members. We have not inquired into this and pass no judgment on it. We only wish to say that should they have approached their Member of Parliament and had he referred the matter ultimately to the Board, he would have received the same courtesy as Mr. Cameron did.

• • •

Questions

1 Why do you think that the employer failed an application under section 119 of Part V of the Canada Labour Code when there is a provision in the Code which permits an application for decertification? Elaborate.

2 Who may make an application for decertification under Part V (now Part 1) of the Canada Labour Code and what is the applicable time frame in such cases?

3 What are some of the possible reasons for the high rate of turnover among employees in this organization?

4 Do you think that the employer was motivated by seeing that "justice be done" or was he motivated by a desire to get rid of the union? Elaborate.

appendix three

Negotiation

A Question of Strategy — The Bridgetown Manufacturing Company Case*

Prepared by:
Mr. E. L. Roach,
Department of Management Studies,
Algonquin College, Ottawa

Bridgetown Manufacturing Company is located in a city in Eastern Ontario with a population of about 100,000. It is a medium size manufacturer of home and office furniture, with a smaller plant in a suburban city located 30 miles outside of Montreal.

Bridgetown Manufacturing employs 250 employees, many of whom have been with the company for over 15 years. The employees are represented by the Canadian Brotherhood of Cabinet and Furniture Workers, Local 555. Two hundred of the employees are hourly wage employees and the contract provides for a union shop.

Bridgetown Manufacturing has been in operation for fifty years and has always had a healthy profit. In recent years, however, the margin of profit has gradually declined in the face of competition from other furniture manufacturers, and the general slump in the economy.

The relationship between the company and the union has been cordial and most of the contracts were negotiated without any third-party assistance.

During the 1987 contract which expired in June 1989, some cracks began to appear in the cosy relationship which hitherto existed between the company and its employees. The rank and file were unhappy about the impact of inflation on their wages and their inadequate fringe benefits package. The union had fought for a COLA clause in the last agreement, but management was adamant in its refusal to discuss this demand.

---

* Permission to use this case was granted by Mr. Roach. Minor deletions were made by the author for the purposes of this book.

The 1987 settlement was ratified by only 60 percent of the membership after a bitter and acrimonious ratification meeting. A small but militant faction in the union voted for rejection and called for strike action. Management was dissatisfied with the way that union stewards were performing. They conducted most union business on company time and, while the company allowed this practice to continue, it expressed a desire to impose limits on it.

In an attempt to improve its profit position, the company recently subcontracted work to a private contractor which would normally have been done by the workers in the plant. This reduced the overtime available to the workers and caused a great deal of resentment and frustration.

Three months before the contract was to expire, the company dismissed a shop steward for drinking on company premises during his lunch period. Another employee, with 10 years' service, was suspended one week without pay for excessive tardiness and absenteeism.

In the union elections conducted in January 1987, a young, aggressive and militant executive was elected on the platform of "increased democratic control over production," a better pension plan and greater job security. Jim Trimble, a member of the Marxist-Leninist Party and leader of the militant faction, was elected president of Local 555.

Negotiations

Week 1

Negotiations in past years were based on "a cooperative bargaining" concept. Two months prior to negotiations both sides submitted to each other proposals for changes in the existing contract and their initial bargaining positions. Because relationships between the union and the company had deteriorated, this practice was not followed in 1987, and the union waited for the first formal negotiation session to submit its demands.

They included the usual demand for changes in vague and ambiguous wording in the hundred paragraphs of the old agreement. Since some recent arbitration decisions supported management's position, some amendments were requested to the relevant clauses to nullify management's advantage. The union also presented an impressive list of new demands, some of them obviously "fillers" to be traded away later in the negotiation sessions.

The company's negotiation team accepted the new demands without comment and agreed to meet within a week. This would give them time to study the demands and prepare counterproposals.

It was agreed that the next session would start with a revision of the contractual language of the existing contract, and then proceed with the new demands. There was an air of cautious optimism at the bargaining table and each party left the initial session with renewed confidence that a settlement would not be difficult. They agreed in advance that they would try to conclude negotiations within four weeks. The union set a strike deadline four weeks from the commencement of negotiations.

Representing the union were:

1 Jim Trimble — newly elected president of Local 555, Chairman;
2 Peter Tull — representative of the Canadian Cabinet and Furniture Workers Union;
3 Rick Kennedy — Secretary Treasurer, Local 555;
4 Peter Hermann, Don Lindsay, Lloyd Campbell — shop stewards;
5 Arthur Black — representing the membership at large.

Representing the management were:

1 Lance Gibbs — General Manager, Chairman;
2 Andy Jacobs — Director of Personnel and Industrial Relations;
3 Dale Andrews — Production Manager.

Week 2 (Monday)

There were very few disagreements over the revision of the contractual language in the existing contract and the management team was anxious to begin discussing the list of forty-two union demands. It was confident that the union was serious about twelve of them, and that the others were mere bargaining tools to gain concessions later in the negotiations.

Its strategy, therefore, was to determine which of these demands had "top priority" status and to focus the negotiations on them. The quicker this was done, the easier it would be to reach an early settlement.

Peter Tull, the union's national representative, was not interested, however, in discussing specific demands, but preferred to review in great detail job titles, job descriptions and classifications which had already been discussed and revised by the Joint Management-Union Evaluation Committee. A recent evaluation resulted in 8 job classes being upgraded and 4 job classes being down graded.

The next two days were spent on this exercise much to the annoyance of the management team. Management perceived the analyzing and questioning of the judgment of the Joint Committee as an obvious "go slow" tactic on the part of the union.

Week 2 (Wednesday)

Lance Gibbs, Chairman of the management's negotiation team, attempted to counter the union's delaying tactics at the start of the meeting.

Mr. Gibbs: Let's get on with the job at hand. Your strategy is clear. You are trying to stall, and force us into a strike to squeeze the last dollar out of us, but it won't work. The decisions of the Joint Evaluation Committee are not topics for negotiations.

Mr. Trimble: We have a responsibility to our membership to look after their welfare to the best of our ability. We feel that it is the duty of the negotiation team to review the deliberations of the Committee.

Mr. Gibbs: You have that right, but not at the negotiating table. When you are ready to enter into serious negotiations let us know." (Mr. Gibbs and his team stormed out of the room, muttering that the union was not bargaining in good faith.)

Later, an agreement was finally reached on this contentious issue, and the decision of the Joint Committee, by agreement, was considered as binding on both parties.

Mr. Gibbs was convinced that the union's strategy was to extend negotiations to the strike deadline, and to coerce management into accepting their demands under the threat of strike action. "Crisis bargaining" was clearly their game plan. He, therefore, reported his suspicions to John Chapman, plant manager, and advised him to make the necessary preparations for a strike. Extra overtime was scheduled and instructions were sent to their suppliers of raw materials to "hold off" on deliveries. The services of a security guard firm were also secured.

Week 3 (Monday)

No serious negotiations took place, since the management team had abruptly left the last session. Attempts to resume serious bargaining were rebuffed by the union. Mr. Gibbs was prepared to begin serious negotiations, but he was no longer willing to be taken in by the union's games.

Mr. Gibbs:	Are you ready to tell us what exact wage increases you are demanding?
Mr. Trimble:	For the past three years our workers have been receiving wages must less than the average for this region, and the high cost of living is making it difficult to feed our families and meet our mortgage payments. The company is making substantial profits, and we are expecting a substantial increase.
Mr. Gibbs:	What I want to hear from you is an exact amount. What is a substantial increase?
Mr. Trimble:	First we want to hear what the company is prepared to offer.
Mr. Gibbs:	O.K., can we have a half-hour coffee break?

The parties returned to their respective hotel suites to plan strategy. Each side wanted the other to take the initiative and put an exact wage increase on the table. The company representatives did not want to take the initiative since they wanted to start well below the union's initial demand. The union team was in no hurry to state a precise wage demand with the hope that, as the deadline approached, management would be forced to offer a higher wage increase.

After the recess, Mr. Gibbs revealed the company's offer to make the union tip its hand.

Mr. Gibbs:	I will give you the total package amount by which the company is willing to increase its overall labour costs. You can break up the amount any way your membership wishes for all your economic demands. You can allocate the total dollar package between wages and the usual fringe benefits. The company cannot afford any more and remain in business. If you press for more, we might have to consider shifting some production to our non-unionized Quebec plant.
Mr. Trimble:	How are we to determine how this total amount should be broken down? We have no way of determining the cost of each of our demands, such as the cost of O.H.I.P., shift premiums, etc., to

the company. We will, however, discuss your offer over the weekend and meet with you again next Monday.

During the weekend there was considerable activity on both sides. The company was busy preparing for a strike and managers were told to prepare for a three- or four-week work stoppage. On the union side, the word went out to the membership to refuse overtime. Union officers and stewards began to condition the membership for strike activity. "We have been shafted long enough" became somewhat of a slogan. Strike signs were hastily prepared and picket captains were being instructed as to their conduct and responsibilities on the picket lines. Letters went out to the District Labour Council enlisting moral and monetary support from the locals of the Council.

Week 4 (Monday)

This was the final week of negotiations, and Friday at midnight was the strike deadline set earlier by the union. The company persisted in negotiating a package deal while the union preferred to negotiate on an item-by-item basis.

The company offered a package totalling $200,000 to cover a three-year contract. The union promptly turned down this offer and countered with its proposal.

Mr. Trimble: We have decided to negotiate for a one-year contract.
Mr. Gibbs: Forget it.
Mr. Trimble: Then we shall not give you any proposals at all.
Mr. Gibbs: Sure you can — just adjust them to a three-year contract.

At this point in the negotiations Mr. Trimble gave the company the union's detailed demands based on a one-year contract.

The list consisted of ten major demands including a 25-cent-an-hour general wage increase — the first time that a precise wage increase was put on the table. In addition, there were some non-economic items; e.g. plant-wide, instead of departmental, seniority governing lay-offs, a sub-contracting clause, and a job security clause.

The company's negotiating team left the room to discuss the union's demands. On returning, Mr. Gibbs said that he was willing to negotiate a one-year contract, but that the cost of the union's demands was far beyond what the company was capable of paying. The 25-cent-an-hour wage increase was absolutely ridiculous. Uncertain economic conditions, declining sales and lower profit margins made the union's wage demands a joke.

Mr. Gibbs: Do you want to drive us into bankruptcy? The most we can afford — and I am being generous — is a 10-cent general increase. I am very upset over the conduct of these negotiations. In the past we had a good working relationship and negotiations were conducted with very little rancour. We compromised, made concessions, and signed contracts that were fair and realistic. I am very dissatisfied with the slow pace of negotiations, and I am not going to be "sucked in."

> Mr. Trimble: The union will adjust its demands if you allow our accountants to inspect your financial statements. Our membership helped to make your company a success over the years, and we are entitled to a fair share of its wealth.

Mr. Gibbs did not reply to the union's request to examine the company's financial statements, but reiterated that if the union persisted in making unreasonable demands, and if the company could not be assured of labour stability in the plant, management would postpone plans for further expansion. It would seriously consider moving the plant to their other location.

Week 4 (Wednesday)
The union resumed negotiations with some significant changes in its demands. It would accept a two-year agreement calling for fifteen cents an hour in each year of the agreement, 4 weeks vacation after 10 years of service instead of 8 as set out in the demands, and 12 paid holidays instead of 14.

> Mr. Gibbs: I thought as much. You come to the negotiations with a large shopping list and you expect me to raise my offer a couple of cents each time you drop a demand.

It was decided to postpone negotiations on the wage issue and discuss some of the non-economic demands. The session lasted until midnight, and agreement was reached on most of the clauses. The parties agreed to take another look at "job security" the following morning.

Week 4 (Thursday)
With the strike deadline only 24 hours away, the pressure was on. Both sides wanted to avert a strike, but each side was waiting for the other side to make concessions. The union picket leaders had met to plan the final strike strategy, but the membership was having second thoughts although by an overwhelming majority it had given the negotiation team a strike mandate earlier. Most of them could not survive a strike of more than two weeks, and the union's strike find would last for only about three weeks.

Little was achieved in the first hour of negotiations, since both sides merely traded insults. After lunch, however, the company submitted its final contract offer — 12 cents an hour general wage increase for each year of a three-year contract together with an improved life and health benefits package.

The union assessed its position. It would agree to a three-year contract as proposed by management with the addition of COLA and sub-contracting clauses. The company's representatives agreed to discuss the union's latest position with senior management and meet the following day. The union negotiators reminded Mr. Gibbs that the strike deadline was only hours away.

Week 4 (Friday — contract expires midnight)
The management team disagreed as to what should be done about the union's latest proposal.

Mr. Jacobs
(Personnel Director):
Our relations with the union have been very stable lately, and I think that a compromise now would be a great help in improving relationships. Further, I think we should consult more with the union committee before bringing about changes in the plant — anything to restore our workers' morale and confidence in the company. I do not think that they can afford to strike, but we should offer them a few more cents, or at least try to negotiate a COLA clause.

Mr. Andrews
(Production Manager):
With the new executive in charge and the present mood of the workers, a strike is a distinct possibility, if only for a couple of weeks. We have a backlog of production orders and I am afraid that we could lose some of our customers if there is a strike. Let's "sweeten the pot." We can find ways of increasing production and we can still be competitive with a moderate increase in prices.

Mr. Gibbs
(General Manager):
The union is bluffing. They are in no position to withstand a lengthy strike. If they do strike, they will be begging us to take them back when their credit has dried up. They are behind in their mortgage payments, and their wives are beginning to get on their backs. We should show the new executive who runs the plant. If we stand up to the union, its influence with the membership would be somewhat weakened. We should 'hang tough.'

The management team, unable to reach an agreement, decided to let Jack Anderson, the company president, review the situation and resolve the impasse. The president, after a thorough analysis of the situation, agreed with Mr. Gibbs, and directed the management team to reject the union's proposal.

Mr. Gibbs met with Mr. Trimble at 10:00 p.m. and informed him that the company was not prepared to accept the union's latest proposal. The company, however, would now pay 70% of O.H.I.P., and 100% of the premiums for the employees' group insurance package. It would not consider a COLA clause.

Mr. Trimble hastily convened a meeting of the union executive. They decided to submit the company's latest offer to the membership with a recommendation that it be rejected.

Questions

1 Why did the union want to bring the issue of job evaluation to the negotiation table?
2 Evaluate the negotiation strategies employed by:
   a the management team
   b the union's bargaining team
3 Why is the package approach particularly important to bargaining on economic issues?

4 Did the presence of the strike deadline force the negotiating teams to engage in "good faith" collective bargaining?

5 Is the exchange of demands and other proposals for change prior to negotiations preferable to the submission of demands at the first negotiating session? Elaborate.

6 Which party seems to have the advantage?

7 Do you think the union membership will accept the company's final offer or opt for a strike? Elaborate.

8 If you had been called in to mediate this dispute just prior to the impasse, what would you have done to head off a strike? Elaborate.

Municipal Collective Bargaining: The Northville Simulation*

By
Gene R. Swimmer,
School of Public Administration,
Carleton University, Ottawa
and
Allan M. Maslove
Updated by Nancy Douglas and Pat Steenberg
1987-88 version

Introduction and Ground Rules

The following exercise is designed to give the participants some feeling for municipal collective bargaining. To simplify the scope of this simulation, the negotiations will involve amending an existing collective agreement, which expires at the end of this month.

1. Participants will be divided into Union and Employer teams, containing four to six members in each team. In large classes, several sets of negotiations will take place simultaneously. All team members will be assigned roles for the simulation. The role profiles will help clarify the areas of special interest in the upcoming negotiations. For example, the objectives of the Chief Administrative Officer may differ from those of the Director of Personnel on the management team. As much as possible, participants are expected to stick to their roles during the entire simulation.

2. Each union or management team will hold meetings to determine their negotiating positions. As a result of their preliminary strategy sessions, each team will develop a "bargaining book" to be presented to the Instructor. This paper should include the team's original demands or offers, fallback or true positions, and an analysis of what the opponents' final positions are likely to be in the negotiations. In developing their initial position, both teams *should not rewrite the entire contract*. Remember that much of the existing contract serves both sides well. Teams should limit their changes or additions to 5 or 6 Articles. All changes in wording should be *underlined* in your initial position. All documentary and/or cost evidence which will be used to strengthen the team's position should also be included. Each team is free to obtain whatever evidence from outside sources it wishes. Finally, any specific strategy which the team plans to use should be summarized. Success in the negotiations will likely be determined by the care taken in the preparation of this bargaining book.

3. The legal environment for the simulation will be determined by the relevant Provincial Labour Relations and Labour Standards Acts.

4. Actual bargaining will commence shortly after the deadline for completion of the bargaining book. Before the first session, both sides will present their opponents with a written statement of demands and clauses they wish to have incorporated into the new contract (this list should be identical to the initial position as outlined in the team's bargaining book). After receiving the opponent's initial position, both sides should caucus individually in advance of actual negotiations.

5. Negotiating sessions that follow will have specific time limits determined by the instructor (general three 2 1/2 hour sessions). At any time during the bargaining, either team may call for a short caucus (one to five minutes) to discuss a specific proposal or counter-proposal.

6. All strategy and negotiations are in the strictest confidence. DO NOT DISCUSS THE NEGOTIATIONS WITH YOUR OPPONENTS OR ANY OTHER STUDENTS UNTIL ALL BARGAINING HAS BEEN COMPLETED.

7. All teams must continue bargaining until the end of the final negotiating session as designated by the Instructor. At this time, the teams have either settled on a new collective agreement or have reached an impasse.

If a settlement has been obtained, the Union and Management teams will jointly submit a copy of the new agreement to the Instructor. In addition, both teams should prepare an oral presentation for the whole class, comparing what they originally wanted prior to the negotiations to what actually resulted.

If an impasse has been reached, both sides will present a written submission to a mediator or arbitration board, explaining those issues resolved, those still unresolved, and why they believe the unresolved issues should be decided in their favour. Both sides should also be prepared to present their cases before the entire class.

The City of Northville

The City of Northville is a community of about 400,000 people. It is the principal city in an agricultural area mainly devoted to dairy farming and market gardening. Northville is the capital city of the province and the provincial government is the largest employer in the city; about 40,000 people are provincial government employees. The other major employers in the city are the university (about 10,000 students, 600 faculty members and 1,500 other employees), a major insurance company head office with about 3,000 employees, and the city itself, which provides approximately 4,000 jobs.* Other sources of employment are primarily located in the retail and service sectors and a number of smaller establishments employing mainly "white collar" workers (financial services, consulting and research).

The city's median income is the ninth highest in Canada. Employment levels in the city are quite stable and the local unemployment rate is slightly below the national average. The inflation rate (as measured by the C.P.I.) is about the same as the national rate.

In the late 1960s and early 1970s the city experienced a rapid growth in population but in more recent years the population growth has been very slow. In large part this levelling-off is due to the austerity in provincial government spending, a common trend in the public sector over the last few years. One consequence of the slowdown in the city's growth has been a stabilization in the value of the taxable assessed property in the municipality. In combination with continuing expenditure growth (in part caused by the rapid population growth of earlier years) this has resulted in higher than average property tax rates (mill rates) in relation to comparable cities in the province.

The elected city government is composed of a mayor and 15 councillors. The mayor is elected by city-wide balloting** and the city council is orga-

---

* This figure does not include bus drivers and other employees of the public transit system. The Northville Transit System is a separate agency that bargains directly with its own employees.

** The turnout in the last municipal election was only 30%. It is interesting to note that a recent study by a professor at the University found that over the last five Northville municipal elections, turnout of provincial and municipal union members has been double the average.

nized on a ward system. Municipal elections are held every two years and the next election is scheduled for 6 months after the current round of contract negotiations. Much of the Council's business is conducted in a series of committees, each of which oversees a major administrative department or area of concern. The Chairman of the Finance Committee is the councillor most closely in touch with the contract negotiations. The current mayor has already announced that for personal reasons he will not seek re-election and it is generally felt that the Chairman of the Finance Committee will run for mayor in the next election although as yet he/she has not announced his/her intentions.

The Budget

The following tables outline the financial position of the municipal corporation in terms of expenditures (Tables 1 and 2) and revenues (Tables 3 and 4). Over the past ten years the assessed value of taxable property has increased at between 2.0% and 4.0% per year. In the coming year the expectation is that the increase in taxable assessment will be 3%. The second major source of revenue is the provincial grants paid to the city; these can be expected to increase by about one percentage point less than the annual change in the National Consumer Price Index in the coming fiscal year. All other revenues, on average, can be expected to increase by the rate of inflation.

Early on in its budget deliberations the City Council made it clear that it would attempt to limit the mill rate increase to 2 percentage points below the expected inflation rate. Hoping to ensure that its target is achieved, the Council decided that, for the first time, one of its members would sit on the management's bargaining team during contract negotiations. The Chairman of the Finance Committee was selected for this role.

Table 1
City of Northville
Operating Expenditures
Functional Analysis
Fiscal Year — Concluding _____

		%
General Government	_____	12
Protection to Persons and Property	_____	16
Transportation Services	_____	20
Environmental Services	_____	8
Health & Social Services	_____	34
Planning & Development	_____	5
Recreation & Cultural Services	_____	5
TOTAL		100

Table 2
City of Northville
Operating Expenditures
by Major Object of Expenditure
Fiscal Year Concluding _____

		%
Personnel Services	_____	41.0
Material and Supplies	_____	7.3
Purchased Services-External	_____	11.4
Purchased Services-Internal	_____	11.3
Grants and Contributions	_____	19.0
Financial Expenses	_____	10.0
TOTAL	$	100

Table 3
City of Northville
Operating Revenues
Fiscal Year Concluding _____

		%
Property Taxes	_____	34.2
Payments-in-Lieu of Taxes	_____	12.0
Provincial Government Grants	_____	25.8
Licences, Fines, Concessions	_____	10.7
Service Charges	_____	11.0
Other Revenues	_____	6.3
TOTAL	$	100.0

Table 4
City of Northville
Tax Rates for Fiscal Year Concluding _____

	Taxable Assessment	Tax Levy	Mill Rate*
Business & Commercial	$_____	$_____	$
Residential & Farm	$_____	$_____	
TOTAL	$_____	$_____	

*Does not include the mill rate for educational purposes.

The city department in which most of the outside workers are employed is the Department of Physical Environment. The major divisions of the Department that employ the outside workers of Local 353 are Road Maintenance, Sanitation, Sewer Maintenance, and Grounds and Recreation Facilities Maintenance. Among the activities engaged in by these departments are maintaining, repairing, and removing snow from city streets and sidewalks, supervising the resurfacing of streets and sidewalks, operating a recycling program for glass, tin and newspapers, supervising garbage collection, maintaining sanitary sewers, storm sewers and combined sewers, trimming and maintaining trees along roadways and in city parks, maintaining and landscaping city parks, and maintaining city outdoor rinks and other recreation facilities.

There are currently 900 outside workers represented by Local 353 of C.U.M.W.

History of the Union and Its Relationship with The Employer

In 1947 the City of Northville passed a by-law which recognized the Northville Municipal Service Association as the sole bargaining agent for all of its employees except those in the Police and Fire Departments. This Association was the forerunner to Local 353 of the Canadian Union of Municipal Workers (C.U.M.W.). The by-law went on to say that: "When the City and the Association find it impossible to reach a satisfactory agreement on any matter affecting salaries, wages or working conditions, such matter shall, upon the demand of either party, be submitted to arbitration."

The original recognition of the Association by the City soon proved unworkable because of its broad coverage. All employees, including department heads, professionals, inside (office) and outside workers, were lumped together in a single bargaining unit. In 1955 the Association and City agreed to formalize the collective bargaining arrangement. The Provincial Labour Board, acting at the request of the parties, decided that the employees should be broken up into four categories: managers who were to be excluded from collective bargaining, and three separate bargaining units for professionals, inside workers, and outside workers. The Northville Municipal Service Association was certified as the exclusive bargaining agent for the latter two groups, inside employees and outside workers. Professional employees decided to set up a separate local association.*

From 1955 onward the negotiations between the City and the Association adhered to the general private sector model, with one major exception. Under Provincial statute, municipal operations are considered as part of the private sector for purposes of industrial relations. As such, municipal

---

* Northville's 1500 police and firemen also have separate Associations that bargain with the city. There has never been a direct wage pattern set between settlements for these groups and Local 353.

employees and employers have all the rights and privileges of their private sector counterparts, including the union's right to strike and the employer's right to lockout. In part due to previous good relations and also a lack of employee militancy, the Northville Association and the City retained arbitration as a dispute resolution process. In other words, the parties agreed to give up voluntarily their respective rights to strike and lockout. The two units bargain separately; sometimes the outside workers bargain first, other times their negotiations follow a settlement by the inside workers. Both the Association and the City have been aware that the first unit to settle in any specific round tends to set the pattern in wages and major benefit increases for the other group.

In 1965, members of the Northville Municipal Service Association decided to join the Canadian Union of Municipal Workers (C.U.M.W.), a national union which was rapidly organizing non-professional municipal, school board, and hospital employees. The Association became Local 353.

Throughout the 1960s and early 1970s the relationship between management and Local 353 was generally excellent. Leaders on both sides had been working together for many years. As an outgrowth of the previous Association/City relationship, both sides tried to find integrative solutions to problems that arose. This period of cooperation instead of confrontation was fostered in large part by favourable economic circumstances. Both the city's tax base and the public's demand for municipal services were increasing due to generally high income levels and low unemployment. During the 1960-1973 period Northville's overall municipal employment more than doubled. In addition, both the union and the city officials could point with pride to the fact that Northville's wage/benefit package was as good as any municipality in the Province. Most contracts were reached without resorting to arbitration.

Recent Experience   About 1975, the relationship between Local 353 and the City began to change. One major difference was the slowdown in the economy combined with high rates of inflation. Perhaps as response to this the public mood shifted toward government restraint. In addition to arguments that all levels of governments were wasting money on needless programs, many expressed the view that public employee unions were extorting high wage settlements from governments. Certainly, bitter postal and teacher strikes helped to mobilize public opinion against *all* public sector unions.

These phenomena have hurt the city and the union in two ways. As a provincial capital, much of the local economy depends on provincial employment levels. The Province has responded to cries of excessive government spending by cutting all department budgets. As a result, provincial government employment has gone from about a 3% annual increase in 1970-75 to a 1% annual decrease at present. The city tax base has levelled off as a result (and is actually decreasing in real terms). Combined with shrinking sources of revenue is the municipality's own desire to increase efficiency and spend less. In the wake of Proposition 13, municipal politicians are loathe to raise property rates. One of the city's policies was to contract out garbage collection two years ago. Fifty members of Local 353 were displaced although almost all were able to transfer to other jobs in the municipality (or to the private sanitation company, although some were forced to accept lower wages/benefit packages). Generally, the public responded favourably to the privatization of garbage collection. The municipality has claimed a saving of $250,000* per year with no reduction in service. For Local 353, the entire contracting out exercise was a signal of their declining job security.

The Previous Round of Negotiations   During the last bargaining round, the economic and political pressures on both parties led to a further deterioration in relations.

The outside workers negotiated first and set the pattern for the inside workers. The major concerns of the union were tightening up job security provisions, improving vacation benefits, introduction of jointly sponsored job evaluation and obtaining a wage increase that would keep pace with the cost of living. Generally speaking, Local 353 felt that their demands were moderate and in keeping with the previous spirit of cooperation.

Management, from its perspective, was also being reasonable, given the financial squeeze. They felt the only way that Local 353 would be able to keep its wages up was to give management more flexibility to manage efficiently. They took the view, not uncommon to managers nowadays, that the entire contract is up for review and therefore management can negotiate *out* existing clauses. In particular, the city's negotiators wanted to remove the article on terminal allowances from the existing agreement and insert the following phrase (underlined) to the preamble of the contract:

> Whereas it is the intent and purpose of this Agreement to recognize the community of interest between the Employer and the Union, in promoting the utmost cooperation between the Employer and its employees, consistent with the rights of both parties, *and in the interest of providing an efficient and economic service to the tax-payers and citizens of the municipality.*

Negotiators for Local 353 were appalled by management's demands. They believed that the tradition of the existing contract being the floor from which the union could negotiate further improvements would be continued. They made it clear to management during negotiations that they would not move an inch on accepting "takeaways."

Negotiations went on for almost three months and some concessions on monetary issues were made by both sides. When an impasse was reached over non-monetary issues, negotiators for Local 353 told management that any previous agreements on specific articles were made on the assumption of an acceptable overall package, and were therefore null and void. The Arbitration Board was left with a host of issues to deal with.

---

* This represents a saving of about 2.5% of the total annual sanitation budget.

Selections from the submissions of the parties further illustrate the degree of confrontation between the parties. Management argued that a "militant attitude by perhaps 2% of the membership" had led to the rejection of the city's final offer* and "had created an unreasonable situation which must have been difficult for the negotiating team." Management went on to accuse the union of reneging on their past agreements by submitting monetary and non-monetary issues to the Arbitration Board. They ended their submission as follows: "An action taken by a very small group within the union doomed responsible negotiation."

In their rebuttal to the city, Local 353 said:

> The employers suffer from the view that the union's primary responsibility is to adjust to the needs of the Employer. Therefore, if the union does not submit to the Employer's demand, the union is perceived as irresponsible... To put it as bluntly as possible, if the union had given serious consideration to takeaways sought by the Employer, the union would have been accepting a total violation of existing contractural rights we had struggled for in the past. The onus of responsibility must be placed with the employers who have chosen to make a mockery of accepted industrial relations practices by submitting proposals which will create total dissatisfaction among employees...

They went on to refute management's contention that the union was divided. At a subsequent membership meeting attended by 400+ members of Local 353, over 90% reconfirmed the decision to proceed to arbitration. Finally, the union addressed management's desired addition to the preamble about providing efficient and economic service to the taxpayers.

> In the name of efficiency and economy, the Employers have reorganized departments, declaring positions redundant without necessarily making provision for the placement of incumbents, some with as many as over thirty years of faithful service.

> Efficiency and economy with regard to the human element, which results in employees being treated like instruments to be disposed of when they are no longer useful, has a debilitating effect on all other employees as well. If employees must constantly be concerned about their job security, if they don't know that their commitment to the Employer is reciprocal, then undoubtedly, the efficiency will suffer and the service provided will not be as economic as it might be.

> Another management tool employed under the guise of "efficiency and economy" is the right to contract out services provided by employees of the municipality. To suggest that the contracting out of services results in a decrease in costs or the introduction of a more efficient operation is highly questionable. In fact, it may be argued that the Employers abandon their responsibility to the citizens of the area by relinquishing direct control over municipal services to others — i.e., private contractors. The only certain impact of contracting out is that there will be different faces on the unemployment line.

---

* The membership meeting of Local 353 which rejected the city's offer took place on the evening of a severe snow-storm.

Two months later the Arbitration Board made its ruling. The Board went along with the improvements recommended by the union for the vacation schedule (the qualification for 4 weeks paid vacation was reduced from 15 to 10 years of service). The ruling on the scale increase was 1% below the annual increase in the cost of living as measured by the change in the National Consumer Price Index over the previous 12 months (what the management had offered). Many other groups in both the public and private sector were settling for wage increases below the C.P.I. increase.

Not surprisingly, the Arbitration Board "ducked" a number of the non-monetary issues saying that the issue was too important and complex to be imposed on the parties. The Board ruled against the union demand for a jointly-sponsored job evaluation program. Both parties were encouraged to be prepared to negotiate this issue at the next round of bargaining. The Board agreed with the union, in principle, on the employer's responsibility to provide retraining for employees displaced as a result of contracting out but was unwilling to require management to retrain employees for one year as the union had demanded.

Finally, the Board made it clear to the union that management's desire to negotiate clauses *out* of bargaining is no longer a process by which only management bargains and only the union collects. That issue of principle aside, the Board felt that management had not made a convincing case for the limitation of terminal allowances or the addition of their phrase to the preamble of the contract. Both cases reverted to the previous agreement.

One month later, the inside workers unit of Local 353* and the municipality reached an agreement on a new contract which was clearly patterned on the arbitration award for the outside workers.

In summary, last year's negotiations demonstrated that the adversary system has replaced the previous era of cooperation. Within this context, both sides are no doubt reevaluating their commitment to arbitration. As it stands, both sides must formally agree to continue arbitration (in lieu of strikes and/or lockouts) at the beginning of each round of negotiations. Such agreement may not be pro-forma this time.

As was the case last round, the outside workers will bargain first and likely set the pattern for the office workers' contract. The issues for both sides will probably include those unresolved by the Arbitration Board. In its news-letter, Local 353 has made it clear that job evaluation** was a high priority once again: "If a lesson is to be drawn from the previous attempts to intro-duce a job evaluation program it is that the Union must be provided with the right to participate in the development and maintenance of the plan. Only recently, the Employer has used job evaluation officers in order to unilater-ally develop a job evaluation program. We cannot trust the Employer to initiate an unbiased program."

---

* There are currently 800 inside (office) workers in the bargaining unit.

** Job evaluation: a formal scheme for ranking jobs or classes of jobs intended to determine their relative values when pay levels are set.

Neither the financial picture of the city nor the media image of public sector employers have changed over the year. As such the union is still concerned about job security and management still wants greater flexibility.

The rank and file are quite aware that real wages went down. Wage rates are clearly going to be an issue this time around. Other membership issues have surfaced, including flexible hours, voluntary overtime and greater employer contributions to health plans.*

The negotiating team for Local 353 have all worked together for the last three bargaining rounds. The municipality's team will have some unfamiliar faces. The Head of Personnel was hired since the last bargaining round and will be leading the negotiations for the first time. The Chief Administrative Officer, the man who was responsible for contracting out garbage collection, will be negotiating for only the second time. Finally, the Union has been notified that the Chairman of the City Council Finance Committee (and potential mayoralty aspirant) will be present as an "observer."

The Relationship Between Local 353 and the National Union (C.U.M.W.)

C.U.M.W. currently represents 250,000 employees in about 1,000 locals across Canada. It has a reputation for being an extremely democratic union based on a very decentralized structure. The locus of decision making has always been with the local union. Generally, the national will provide technical and legal assistance to its locals if and when it is asked. In fact, some locals would argue they have too much independence (i.e. they could use more leadership).

Within this context, the relations between C.U.M.W. and Local 353 are special in nature. First of all, many Local 353 members, particularly the "oldtimers," feel a strong loyalty to the older "Northville Municipal Service Association" and find the concept of unionism a bit hard to take. The desire for autonomy from C.U.M.W. shows up in some peculiar ways. For instance, the sign on Local 353's headquarters still says, The Northville Municipal Service Association, with no reference to C.U.M.W.

By coincidence, the regional headquarters for C.U.M.W. are also located in Northville.**As a result, Local 353 has never had a problem getting help when it was needed. C.U.M.W. has generally provided one of their staff as a member of the negotiating team. C.U.M.W. for its part does have some special interest in Local 353's negotiations. Local 353 is the only municipal bargaining unit in C.U.M.W. which has arbitration instead of the right to strike. Some C.U.M.W. officials view this as a sign of weakness, almost an embarrassment. In its public statements, C.U.M.W. is always in favour of extending the right to strike to all employees (including many of their own

---

* Some aspects of the contract are acknowledged by both sides as working well. The grievance/arbitration procedures and the pension plan are two examples.

** C.U.M.W. services its locals on a regional basis. The five regions are Atlantic, Quebec, Ontario, Prairies, and B.C.-Territories.

bargaining units like Ontario hospital workers who are prohibited from striking by law). Nonetheless, the C.U.M.W. is keenly interested in the outcome of the upcoming negotiations and arbitration if necessary. Given the current low media image of public employees and the public backlash about government spending in general, some C.U.M.W. leaders are privately of the view that arbitrators may generate better contract settlements than strikes.

Bargaining Teams

(Detailed role profiles will be distributed by the Instructor)

For the City of Northville:
1. Councillor and Chairman of the City Council Finance Committee.
2. Director of Personnel, the chief negotiator for the City team.
3. Chief Administrative Officer.
4. Director of the Department of Physical Environment.
5. Assistant Director of Personnel in charge of Compensations and Benefits.
6. Chief, Road Maintenance Division, Department of Physical Environment.

For Local 353 of C.U.M.W.:
1. President, Local 353.
2. Business Agent, Local 353.
3. Regional Representative, C.U.M.W., Chief Negotiator for Union.
4. Treasurer, Local 353.
5. Shop Steward, Snow Removal.
6. Research Associate, C.U.M.W.

INDEX TO THE COLLECTIVE AGREEMENT BETWEEN CITY OF NORTHVILLE AND LOCAL 353

COLLECTIVE AGREEMENT

This Agreement made in duplicate this day of _____

— BETWEEN —

THE CORPORATION OF THE CITY OF NORTHVILLE

(herein called "The Employer")

of the first part

— AND —

Local 353

CANADIAN UNION OF MUNICIPAL WORKERS (C.U.M.W.)

(herein called "The Union")

of the second part

Whereas it is the intent and purpose of this Agreement to recognize the community of interest between the Employer and the Union, in promoting the utmost cooperation between the employer and its employees, consistent with the rights of both parties.

And whereas it is the further intent of this Agreement to foster a friendly spirit which shall prevail at all times between the Employer and its employees and to this end this Agreement is signed in good faith by the two parties. And whereas this Agreement is designed to set out clearly the rates of pay, hours of work and conditions of employment to be observed by the Employer and the Union.

NOW THEREFORE THIS AGREEMENT WITNESSETH

ARTICLE 1
SCOPE

1.1 This Agreement shall apply to all operational (non-office) employees listed in Appendix I of this Agreement, except those excluded on managerial or confidential grounds.

ARTICLE 2
RESPONSIBILITY OF THE EMPLOYER

2.1 The Employer recognizes the Union as the sole collective bargaining agent for all employees coming within the scope of this Agreement.

2.2 The Employer agrees not to interfere with the rights of its employees designated with the scope of the Agreement, and there shall be no discrimination, interference, restraint and coercion by the Employer, or any of its representatives against any employee because of Union Membership.

2.3 The Employer agrees that during the life of this Agreement and during the period of negotiation of any revisions to this Agreement, or of a new agreement including the period of arbitration, there shall be no lockout.

2.4 The Employer agrees that there shall be no discrimination against any person in the employing or continuing to employ because of race, creed, colour, ancestry, age, sex, marital status, political and religious affiliation, or place of residence.

2.5 The Employer recognizes and accepts the provisions of this Agreement as binding upon itself and upon each of its authorized representatives and pledges that it and each of its duly authorized representatives will observe the provisions of this Agreement.

2.6 The Employer agrees to recognize the Business Agents of the Union.

ARTICLE 3
RESPONSIBILITY OF THE UNION

3.1 The Union agrees that it will not intimidate or coerce employees into membership in the Union.

3.2 The Union agrees that memberships solicitation and other Union activity not pertaining to this Agreement, will not take place during working hours or on the premises of the Employer or on any work project the Employer may be engaged in.

3.3 The Union agrees that during the life of this Agreement and during the period of negotiation of any revision to this Agreement, or of any new agreement including the period of arbitration, there shall be no strike or other cessation of work.

3.4 The Union agrees that there shall be no discrimination against any person in the employing or continuing to employ because of race, creed, colour, ancestry, age, sex, marital status, political and religious affiliation, or places of residence.

3.5 The Union recognizes and accepts the provisions of this Agreement as binding upon itself, each of its duly authorized officers, representatives and employees represented by the Union, will observe the provisions of this Agreement.

3.6 The Union recognizes that, subject to the provisions of this Agreement, it is the function of the Employer:
  (i)   to maintain order, discipline and efficiency;
  (ii) to classify positions;
  (iii) to hire, transfer and promote;
  (iv) to suspend, discharge or otherwise discipline employees for proper cause subject to the right of the employee concerned to lodge a grievance under the orderly procedure outlined in Article 14.

ARTICLE 4
HOURS OF WORK

4.1   **REPORTING**
      Employees shall report for duty at the place directed by the person in charge and shall go to and from such place on their own time within the limits of the Corporation of the City of Northville.

4.2   **Standard Hours of Work**
      The standard hours of work operative during the term of this Agreement shall be as follows:

4.2.1 **Wage Employees**
      A 5 day week, Monday to Friday, 8 hours per day between the hours of 7 a.m. and 5 p.m. with a maximum of one hour for lunch. It is recognized that Saturday may be scheduled by the Employer as a regular working day, part of the 5 day week. (See Section 5.3.5).

4.2.2 **Regular (Permanent) Shift Employees**
      A 5 day week, 8 hours per day, providing for two consecutive days off and normally a one hour lunch period. A regular shift shall be defined as part of a 24 or 16 hour operation and not part of a 24 hour rotating shift schedule.

4.2.3 **Rotating Shift Employees**
      An average of 40 hours per week on a 4 to 6 week cycle as the case may be. Rotating shift shall be defined as a period of 8 hours, part of a 24 hour operation. The hours of starting and finishing of each shift shall be determined by the Head of the Department in consultation with the employees. Normally an employee on a rotating shift will alternate through day, afternoon and night shifts as laid down in the Shift Schedule. Alternate arrangements in relation to the length of the cycle may be made by mutual agreement between the Employer and the Union.

4.2.4 (a) Employees shall be permitted a paid 10 minute rest period in both the first half and second half of a shift.
      (b) The employer shall provide, where appropriate, a paid 5 minute wash-up period at the end of the first half and second half of a shift.

4.2.5 (a) The parties to this Agreement recognize that the Employer may be required to alter the hours of work in relation to various operations and if such is the case, the provisions of Article 5 shall apply.
      (b) Where the Employer wishes to introduce a new shift operation, which shall require the starting and quitting times to be other than those specified in the Collective Agreement, the Employer will notify and discuss the new shifts with the Union.

4.2.6 Daily working hours referred to in this Article are to be worked consecutively.

ARTICLE 5
PREMIUMS

5.1 OVERTIME

5.1.1 (a) No employee shall work overtime unless authorized by the Head of the Department or a person delegated by the Head. Overtime shall be defined as time worked before or after a normal work day or normal work week as well as time worked in excess of the normal hours of work.

(b) No employee shall be required to work in excess of sixteen (16) hours in any twenty-four (24) hour period, or to exceed thirty-two (32) Overtime hours in any bi-weekly pay period. It is recognized, however, that the limitation of thirty-two (32) Overtime hours may be exceeded in those situations where it is deemed that an emergency exists which requires the employee to exceed the Overtime limit.

5.1.2 All wage employees who are required to work overtime hours (as defined in 5.1.1 (a)) shall be paid for such hours at the rate of one and one-half ($1\frac{1}{2}$) times their regular hourly rate of pay.

5.1.3 Any employee receiving a premium who works overtime shall be paid at a rate of one and one-half times the total of his normal rate and his premium.

5.1.4 Any employee who is required to work on a statutory holiday shall be paid one day's pay at his regular rate for the statutory holiday, and for such hours as he works, at time and one-half.

5.1.5 A regular forty (40) hour shift employee whose day off falls on a statutory holiday shall receive an additional eight (8) hours pay while the employee who is working shall receive two and one-half times the regular rate of pay.

5.1.6 All employees may elect to bank Overtime to a maximum in one year of seventy-five (75) hours straight time (50 hours worked at time and one-half) for the purpose of having time off in lieu of Overtime. Overtime will be paid in accordance with the Overtime provisions if the employee has not elected time off in lieu. Requests to bank Overtime hours must be made to the employee's immediate supervisor and must be dated and signed.

5.2 ON CALL

5.2.1. The period of On Call shall be construed as being from 5 p.m. to 7 a.m. the following morning. On Saturday the period of On Call shall be 7 a.m. Saturday to 7 a.m. Sunday, and on Sunday the period of On Call shall be from 7 a.m. Sunday to 7 a.m. Monday. In the case of a statutory holiday or declared holiday the period of On Call shall be as on Sunday, that is from 7 a.m. of the morning of the holiday until 7 a.m. on the following day.

5.2.2 Any employee placed On Call from Monday through Friday shall be entitled to receive two hours pay at straight time rates for each period of On Call and if called shall be paid at time and one-half his regular rate plus any shift bonus applicable. The minimum payment for any call out shall be one hour in terms of the pay to be received.

5.2.3 An employee placed On Call on Saturday or Sunday shall be entitled to receive three hours pay at straight time rates for the period of On Call. This arrangement will also apply in the case of statutory holidays. If the employee is called he shall be entitled to receive payment for the hours worked at the rate of time and one-half his rate, including any shift or other premium. The minimum payment shall be for one hour in terms of the pay to be received.

5.3   **PREMIUM PAY**

5.3.1 **Rotating Shift Employees**
Any employee of the rotating shift schedule required to work on a rotating shift basis, will receive a premium of 7% of the regular rate of pay for his classification for all shifts.

5.3.2 Rotating shift employees who are granted their request that they not rotate through day, afternoon and night shifts shall not receive the 7% premium.

5.3.3 **Premium for Hours Worked Between 7 p.m. and 7 a.m.**
Where the Employer requires any employee to work hours other than what has been defined under Hours of Work, the employee shall be paid the 7% premium for all regular hours worked provided that 50% or more of those regular hours fall between 7 p.m. and 7 a.m.

5.3.4 **Regular (permanent) Shift Employees.**
Employees who are granted their request that they not work the shift as requested by the Employer, shall not receive the 7% premium.

5.3.5. **Work on Saturday and Sunday**
All hours which fall within an employee's regular work hours or work week which fall on Saturday and/or Sunday shall be subject to a 7% premium.

5.3.6 (a) **Posting of Shift**
The Employer agrees that, where possible, a schedule reflecting the changed hours of work for any employee shall:
(i) Be posted at least one week (5 working days) prior to the commencement of this shift.
(ii) Be five consecutive days, Monday through Friday. Monday through Friday for this purpose shall be defined as Monday commencing at 7 a.m. and finishing on Saturday at 7 a.m.

(b) **Change of Posted Shift**
(i) Where an employee's shift has been changed and the notice of change of shift is less than one week, the Employer shall pay 4 hours at straight time rates of the employee's regular salary in lieu of notice.
(ii) An employee required to work a changed shift or who is ordered by the employer to return to his regular day shift shall, for the balance of that week, receive or continue to receive 7% premium pay.

5.4   **REPORTING PAY**

5.4.1 In the event of an employee reporting for work in the ordinary course of his employment and not being able to perform his regular work because of inclement weather, he shall be provided with work to the end of the half shift or pay in lieu thereof.

ARTICLE 6
LEAVE

6.1   **VACATION LEAVE**

6.1.1 Vacation leave shall be earned and granted to all employees at the following rates:
(a) Two (2) weeks per year, which is earned at the rate of five-sixths ($5/6$) working days for each completed month of continuous service, if the employee has completed less than two (2) years of continuous employment.

(b) Three (3) weeks per year, which is earned at the rate of one and one-quarter ($1^{1}/4$) working days for each completed month of continuous service, if the employee has completed two (2) but less than ten (10) years of continuous employment.

(c) Four (4) weeks per year, which is earned at the rate of one and two-thirds ($1^{2}/3$) working days for each completed month of continuous service, if the employee has completed ten (10) but less than eighteen (18) years of continuous employment.

(d) Five (5) weeks per year which is earned at the rate of $2^{1}/2$ working days for each completed month of continuous service if the employee has completed eighteen (18) years of continuous employment.

(e) An employee earns but is not entitled to receive vacation leave with pay during his probationary period.

(f) A weekly pay for employees shall be the basic hours worked per week multiplied by the employee's standard rate per hour but shall not include any overtime rates. Employees not completing their probationary period are entitled to 4% vacation pay.

(g) After the first year of continuous employment an employee may be granted vacation leave in excess of the earned credits to the extent of credits that would accumulate to the end of that year.

(h) Vacation leave shall be taken at a time mutually agreed upon by the employee and his department.

(i) If, in any year the Employer has been unable to grant all of the vacation leave earned by the employee in that year, the unused portion of vacation leave shall be carried over into the following year.

(j) Employees are not permitted to carry over more vacation leave into the following year than the number of days of leave earned by them in that year.

(k) Employees who have vacation leave to their credit must obtain written authorization from the Head of their Department to carry over their leave to the following year.

(l) If an employee has taken more leave than he has earned at the time when the employee's services are terminated for a reason other than lay-off or death, the salary overpayment resulting from the use of unearned vacation leave shall be recovered from the employee by the Employer.

(m) When the employment of an employee terminates for any reason and the employee has earned, but unused, vacation leave, the employee or the estate of the deceased employee shall be paid an amount equal to the product obtained by multiplying the number of days of earned but unused vacation leave by the daily rate of pay applicable to the employee immediately prior to the termination of employment. When any employee retires, he shall be deemed to have earned vacation leave for the full year in which he retires.

6.2   SICK LEAVE

6.2.1   (i) Any probationary employee shall, on account of sickness, be entitled to one and one-half ($1^{1}/2$) days leave of absence with full pay for each completed month of service, which leave shall be known as "sick leave" and shall be cumulative.

(ii) Employees who are entitled to leave of absence on account of sickness may obtain it on production, through the Head of their Department to the Director of Personnel Services, of satisfactory application for sick leave. Each employee who is absent for a period of more than five consecutive working days shall file with his application a satisfactory certificate from a qualified medical practitioner. Each employee shall be allowed, if qualified, to apply for sick leave up to five consecutive working days without a doctor's certificate provided that the total number of such uncertified days in any calendar year shall not exceed ten (10).

(iii) Employees, including employees absent as a result of an industrial accident, will be required to produce any medical certificate necessary within the first 10 days of absence. It will be necessary to renew such certificate(s) every 20 days thereafter, unless the Director of Personnel Services is satisfied with the initial certificate indicating the total period of absence and probable date of return to work.

(iv) If it should appear to the Director of Personnel Services that any employee is making too frequent applications for sick leave, or that the correctness of a certificate is questionable, the matter shall be referred to the Medical Officer for investigation and report.

(v) Any employee who has completed his probationary period shall immediately have to his credit accumulated sick leave.

6.2.2 (i) Where a long-term employee, as a result of extended illness, has exhausted his sick leave credits and the case is recommended by the Medical Officer, Director of Personnel Services and President of the Union, such credits may be extended as a result of individual employees transferring credits from their accumulated balance. Such transfers must be at least three days and may not be greater than 20 days.

(ii) Any employee with more than five (5) years of service who has exhausted his sick leave credits may be allowed to anticipate an extension of his sick leave credits to a maximum of 15 days. On his return to duty the employee shall reduce the amount of the extension by his normal monthly accumulation of one and one-half days. Should the employee's employment be terminated before he has fully repaid this extension of sick leave, any overdrawn sick leave shall be recovered from the employee from any money coming to him as a result of the termination of his employment.

6.3 SPECIAL LEAVE

Special leave is a provision which is designed to enable an employee to be absent from his employment with full pay for the following reasons:

(i) Professional appointments such as medical, dental, legal and optical.

(ii) The unexpected or sudden illness of the employee's spouse or child which prevents the employee from reporting to duty.

(iii) Emergency situations which prevent the employee from reporting to duty.

Special leave is to be utilized solely for the purpose as specified in (i), (ii), and (iii) above.

To qualify for special leave the employee must have —

(a) completed the probationary period as specified in this Agreement,

(b) notified his department at least 48 hours in advance of the date and required time off.

In the event of an emergency situation (b) above shall be waived.

Special leave is limited to a maximum of three (3) days per annum, non-cumulative, and may be taken in quarter, half or full days. Time required in excess of one (1) day may be extended by the Head of the employee's Department.

Application beyond the one day will be considered on an individual basis and authorization shall be solely at the discretion of the Employer.

Employees who have taken special leave may be required to produce satisfactory evidence.

6.4 BEREAVEMENT/PARENTAL LEAVE

6.4.1 Bereavement Leave

(a) The Employer shall grant leave of absence with full pay, not to exceed three (3) working days (one of which will be the day of the funeral), to any employee on the following basis:

death of husband, wife, child, mother, father, or person standing in loco parentis, sister, brother, father-in-law, mother-in-law, brother-in-law, sister-in-law, grandchild.

For the purposes of definition, brother-in-law and sister-in-law shall be the brother or sister of the employee's spouse or the spouse of the employee's brother or sister.

One day leave of absence with full pay shall be granted to any employee to attend the funeral of the employee's grandparent. Grandparent is to be defined as the father or mother of the employee's father or mother.

6.4.1 (b) For extension of the clauses mentioned as required or in special cases or where any employee's total allowance of bereavement leave will be in excess of five days in the current calendar year, application shall be made to the Director of Personnel Services.

6.4.2 Parental Leave

(a) An employee with more than 12 months and 11 weeks seniority upon written request to the Department Head, shall be granted parental leave of absence without pay for a period of up to seventeen (17) weeks. This leave shall only be used for adoption or birth of an employee's child.

(b) It is understood and agreed that an employee is not covered by the provisions of paid sick leave as outlined in Section 6.2 of this Agreement.

(c) While on Parental Leave of Absence without pay:

(i) the employee shall retain seniority held to the commencement of the leave but shall not accumulate further seniority during the period of leave,

(ii) the employee's benefits shall be maintained, provided the employee makes the necessary arrangements to pay 100% of the cost of benefits in which the employee continues to be enrolled during the period of leave.

(d) The employee shall be entitled to return to his/her job upon the completion of this Parental Leave, in the same manner as provided by the Employment Standards Act for a woman on maternity leave under this legislation.

6.5 **LEAVE OF ABSENCE TO ATTEND UNION CONVENTION**

The Employer agrees to grant leave of absence without pay to accredited union delegates to conventions of the following organizations: Canadian Labour Congress, Canadian Union of Municipal Workers.

6.6 (a) **Union Business**

The Employer agrees to grant reasonable leave of absence with pay to duly elected or appointed representatives of the union for the purpose of transacting business which the Union deems necessary. Such leave of absence shall not exceed thirty (30) working days in any calendar year.

(b) It is also agreed that the Union will reimburse the Employer following such absences for the time spent by the employees in Union business.

6.7 **LEAVE OF ABSENCE WITHOUT PAY**

(a) Employees who desire leave of absence without pay shall make application to the municipality through the Head of the employee's Department.

(b) Under special circumstances, one employee who is elected or selected for a full-time position with the Union or any body with which the Union is affiliated may apply to the Employer for leave of absence without loss of seniority, and, while the granting of such leave and its duration are at the sole discretion of the Employer, such leave will not be unreasonably withheld.

(c) For the period during which any employee has been granted leave of absence without pay in excess of 20 continuous working days within the calendar year, his benefits including vacation leave, sick leave, leave for statutory holidays, bereavement/maternity leave, seniority and all other benefits shall be suspended or adjusted on the basis of the period of his total absence within the year. When the employee returns to full time employment with pay he shall be entitled to resume his benefits at the level at which they were at the time when he absented himself on leave without pay.

6.8 **TERMINAL ALLOWANCE**

(a) On termination, other than discharge for just cause, an employee who has five (5) or more years of continuous employment shall be entitled to a terminal allowance equal to the product obtained by multiplying one half the number of days of unused sick leave credits on termination of employment by the employee's daily rate of pay to a maximum of one hundred and thirty (130) days' pay.

(b) On termination of employment by reason of death or retirement, an employee or the estate of the employee shall be entitled to a terminal allowance equal to the product obtained by multiplying the number of days of unused sick leave credits on termination of employment by the employee's daily rate of pay to a maximum of one hundred and thirty (130) days' pay.

6.9 **RETIREMENT LEAVE**

(a) The effective date of retirement of an employee is the first day of the month following the month in which the employee has reached sixty-five years of age.

(b) An employee who is entitled to a Terminal Allowance in accordance with the provisions of paragraph (b) of Section 6.8 may apply to City Council for permission to advance his last day of active employment prior to his effective date of retirement by the number of days of Terminal Allowance to which he is entitled and these days shall be called Retirement Leave.

(c) The retiring employee's position shall be considered vacated on the effective date of retirement or on the date the employee starts retirement leave.

6.10   STATUTORY HOLIDAYS

(a) The following days shall be statutory and declared holidays:

NEW YEAR'S DAY	LABOUR DAY
GOOD FRIDAY	THANKSGIVING DAY
EASTER MONDAY	REMEMBRANCE DAY
VICTORIA DAY	CHRISTMAS DAY
DOMINION DAY	BOXING DAY
CIVIC HOLIDAY (August)	

(b) In addition to those set out in the preceding sub-paragraph, any day proclaimed by the Governor General in Council or the Lieutenant Governor in Council for the Province shall be a statutory holiday.

(c) Employees who have worked the day previous to and the day subsequent to the above-mentioned holidays, and those on authorized leave with pay or authorized leave of absence without pay of less than 5 days duration shall be entitled to the above-mentioned statutory holidays with no reduction in their normal pay.

(d) With the exception of Remembrance Day, any holiday falling on a Saturday or Sunday shall be celebrated on the following Monday. When Christmas and Boxing Day fall on a Saturday and Sunday, or when Christmas falls on Sunday, Christmas and Boxing Day shall be celebrated on the following Monday and Tuesday.

6.12   JURY/WITNESS/COURT

6.12.1   Jury and Witness Duty Leave

An employee who is called upon to

(i)   serve on a jury or

(ii)   attend as a witness by subpoena or summons or by providing proof satisfactory to the Employer of being required to attend as a witness in any proceeding held in or under the authority of any court in Canada, or before any legislative committee authorized to compel the attendance of witnesses before it or any person or body of persons authorized by law to compel the attendance of witnesses before it shall be allowed leave of absence with full pay.

6.12.2   Court Duty

An employee on authorized vacation leave who is required to testify or is subpoenaed as a witness to give evidence on behalf of the Employer shall have his vacation leave entitlement restored for the period of time required to attend court or any legal proceeding and will, in addition for the hours so required to attend, receive twice his regular or normal salary.

6.13 **TIME OFF FOR VOTING**

Every employee who is a qualified elector in a municipal or provincial or federal election shall, for the purpose of casting his vote on an election day, be excused from his regular duties for a period sufficient to allow him four (4) consecutive hours immediately prior to the closing of the polls.

ARTICLE 7
WORKERS' COMPENSATION

7.1 Every employee who is absent from duty as a result of personal illness or injury arising from his employment within the meaning of the Workers' Compensation Act, will be provided with medical care and treatment as provided in the Act and shall comply with Section 6.2.1 (iii) of this Agreement.

7.2 Every employee who is absent from duty as a result of personal illness or injury arising out of and in the course of his employment (within the meaning of the Workers' Compensation Act) and, who has not completed his probationary period as provided for in this Agreement, shall receive compensation from the Employer to the level provided under the Workers' Compensation Act effective from the date of disability. Where a claim has been disallowed by the Workers' Compensation Board all payments made by the Employer will be recovered from the employee's sick leave credits.

7.3 In addition, every employee who has completed his probationary period, and who suffers a personal injury arising out of and in the course of his employment (within the meaning of the Workers' Compensation Act) shall be entitled to the following:

   (a) Payment of salary or earnings by the Employer to the maximum allowable under the Workers' Compensation Act and the Employer will also pay to the employee, where applicable, the difference between the maximum allowable under the Act and the actual amount equal to 75% of the employee's salary or regular wage.

   (b) In addition, the Employer will pay on behalf of the employee the total payment or premium for the following plans:
   (i) Pension
   (ii) Medical plans as specified in the Agreement
   (iii) Life Insurance
   (iv) Long term disability
   provided that in any calendar month the employee is absent 5 or more working days.

   (c) When the employee returns to full and regular duties, he shall be returned to a position equal to the one which he held prior to his compensable injury and the benefits specified in (a) and (b) above shall cease. When the employee is able to return to modified duties, the benefits specified in (a) and (b) above shall cease.

7.4 In the event that an employee is able to return to light or modified duties as determined by the Workers' Compensation Board of the Province, the Employer shall attempt to provide such work and the employee shall continue to receive the hourly rate of pay or bi-weekly salary he was receiving prior to the date of his accident.

7.5 Any employee who returns to modified or light duties shall be assessed on an on-going basis by the Workers' Compensation Board of the Province. In the event such assessments determine that the employee is able to return to full and regular duties, 7.3(c) above shall apply. In the event the employee's condition is assessed as deteriorating, the Employer shall provide rehabilitation as recommended by the Workers' Compensation Board for employment with the Employer or other employers. In this case, the Employer will make a reasonable effort to offer the employee on-going alternate employment. In any case, when the employee returns to light or modified duties, the Employer shall be guided by the assessment of the Workers' Compensation Board of the Province.

7.6 The Union recognizes that reassignment of a permanently partially disabled employee to alternate employment, may necessitate a change of classification and pay.

7.7 It is recognized that where the employee has been reassigned or offered, and accepts alternate employment with the Employer, the employee shall be entitled to any lump sum payment or permanent award payable as determined by the Workers' Compensation Board, and such payments will not reduce the wage or salary the employee will be receiving.

ARTICLE 8

8.1 SUPERANNUATION

(a) Any employee who has completed 244 days during a period of 52 weeks shall have his or her superannuation governed by the provisions of the basic plan of the Municipal Employees Retirement System of the Province.

(b) The Employer agrees that it will not make any unilateral revisions to the provision of benefits under the Municipal Employees Retirement System. Any changes or revisions shall only be made with the concurrence of the Union.

ARTICLE 9
PROBATIONARY PERIOD

9.1 New employees shall be on a probationary period not exceeding six (6) consecutive calendar months and, no disputes as to the termination or rejection of such employees shall be considered under the Grievance or Arbitration procedures as outlined in this Agreement.

ARTICLE 10
SENIORITY

10.1 Seniority, as referred to in this Agreement, shall mean the length of continuous service of an employee within the Bargaining Unit.

10.2 Seniority shall commence from the first day of continuous employment provided that the employee has completed the probationary period.

10.3 Seniority shall accumulate under the following circumstances:
  (a) when the employee is on the active payroll of the Employer;
  (b) when the employee is off the payroll due to an authorized lay-off of not more than 120 working days;
  (c) when the employee is off the payroll due to an accident and when the employee is receiving compensation under the Workers' Compensation Act, and when the employee has not accepted employment with another employer;
  (d) when the employee is off the payroll on any leave of absence authorized by the Employer and/or under the provisions of this Agreement;
  (e) as outlined in Article 6.4.2(b)(i).

10.4 An employee shall lose his seniority when he —
  (a) voluntarily resigns or leaves the employment of the Employer or is absent from work without authorization for a period in excess of five working days, in which case it shall be deemed to be a voluntary termination;
  (b) is discharged and not reinstated;
  (c) is off the payroll for a continuous period of more than 120 working days as a result of a lay-off;
  (d) fails to report to work within three working days after having been notified of a recall to work following a lay off unless the employee has a reason acceptable to the Employer;
  (e) fails to return to work upon termination of authorized leave of absence unless the employee has a reason acceptable to the Employer. Such failure shall be considered as a voluntary termination.

10.5 In the event an employee, covered by this Agreement, is transferred to a position outside the scope of this Agreement and at a later period, returns to a position within the scope of this Agreement, he shall retain the seniority which he held at the time of transfer but shall not accumulate any additional seniority for the period during which he held a position outside the scope of this Collective Agreement.

10.6 **SENIORITY LISTS**

The Employer shall supply a seniority list to the Union on a monthly basis.

ARTICLE 11

11.1 **PROMOTIONS & TRANSFERS**
  (a) All vacancies and new positions of a permanent nature within the Bargaining Unit, and the position of Foremen shall be posted for a period of not less than five working days throughout the Employer's premises.
  (b) All applications of employees within the Department in which the position is available shall be given first preference.
  (c) Appointment shall be made of the applicant having the greatest seniority and the required qualifications, academic or otherwise for the position available, and in the case of a tradesman, demonstrated ability to carry out the work of the Employer and competence in the trade. The employee's absenteeism, past record and ability to perform the work of the Employer, shall be considered.

11.2 The Employer shall notify unsuccessful inservice candidates of or post the name of the successful inservice candidates in all competitions.

11.3 All job vacancy notices shall contain the following information: Job title, qualifications, required knowledge and education skills, shift, salary range or wage rate.

ARTICLE 12
LAY-OFF AND RECALL

12.1 For the purpose of this Article, a lay-off shall be defined as a temporary cessation of work instituted by the Employer because of lack of work, during which the employee is not paid.

12.2 Any employee being laid-off, who has standing to his credit an entitlement to vacation leave or time off in lieu of overtime may elect to take either during the period of lay-off but his recall to work shall be governed by the regulation set forth in this section.

12.3 The Employer will notify employees one week prior to a lay-off provided that the employee has completed his probationary period. An employee who has not completed the probationary period, will not be entitled to notice of lay-off under the terms of this Agreement.

12.4 No new employee will be hired until those employees who have been laid-off have been given an opportunity of re-employment subject to the conditions of recall set forth in this Agreement.

12.5 SENIORITY RIGHTS — LAY-OFF AND RECALL

12.5.1 In the event of a lay-off, an employee shall be given the opportunity to revert to a classification equal to or less than the classification he held within his Department. In the wage schedule, a classification shall be equal to or less than another classification if the hourly rates of pay are equal or less than those paid in the other classification.

12.5.2 In the event that he reverts to a classification within Group 1 of the Wage Schedule, he may exercise his seniority rights on a Bargaining Unit wide basis.

12.5.3 If the employee fails to exercise his seniority rights as outlined in 12.5.1 or 12.5.2, he shall be subject to recall in the classification he held prior to the lay-off.

12.6 Recalls to work following such lay-offs shall be in accordance with seniority provided that the employee has the required knowledge and ability to perform the work available.

12.7 It is the responsibility of every employee to notify the Employer promptly of any change of address or telephone number. If an employee fails to make this notification to the Employer, the Employer shall not be responsible for the failure of notice of recall to reach the employee.

ARTICLE 13
SHOP STEWARD RECOGNITION

13.1 In order to provide for an orderly and speedy procedure for the settling of grievances, the Employer agrees to recognize as steward any employee appointed by the Union, who has acquired at least one year of seniority under the terms of this Agreement, and the Union shall notify the Employer in writing of the names of such stewards at the time of their appointment. The Employer shall not be required to recognize any stewards until it has been so notified.

13.2 The Union recognizes that each steward is employed to perform full-time work for the Employer and, wherever possible, the processing of Grievances and other activities on behalf of the Union shall be performed outside the stewards' regular working hours. Therefore, no steward shall leave his work to perform these functions without the prior consent of the foreman, supervisor or person in charge and such permission shall not be unreasonably withheld.

13.3 Generally speaking, there shall be one steward appointed for every 75 employees.

ARTICLE 14
GRIEVANCE PROCEDURE

(a) For the purposes of this Agreement, a grievance is a complaint which has been reduced to writing respecting the meaning and/or application of the provisions of this Agreement and all matters pertaining thereto. A grievance may concern a difference arising between an employee and the Employer or the Union and the Employer.

(b) The parties to this Agreement share a desire to adjust employee complaints as quickly as possible. An employee shall discuss his complaint with his immediate supervisor within 5 days of the occurrence giving rise to the complaint so as to afford the supervisor an opportunity to resolve the complaint. The employee may be accompanied by a representative of the Union when the complaint is being discussed with the supervisor.

(c) It is agreed that an employee shall not file a grievance until he has discussed his complaint with his supervisor in accordance with paragraph (b).

(d) When an employee has presented his complaint to his supervisor and the complaint has not been resolved to his satisfaction within three (3) days of the meeting, he may file a grievance with the Union Grievance Committee. The grievance must be signed and dated by the employee within fifteen (15) days of the day on which he was notified or became aware of the incident, giving rise to the grievance or within ten (10) days of the receipt by him of his supervisor's reply to his complaint, whichever shall last occur.

(e) Where an employee has filed a grievance with the Union Grievance Committee, the Union may, within ten (10) days from the date thereof, present the grievance to the employee's Department Head, or designate. The Department Head or designate shall meet with the grievor and the Union representative within five (5) days from the meeting, and render his decision in writing.

    (f)   If the Department Head or designate
- (i)   fails to meet the grievor and the Union representative, or
- (ii)   fails to render his decision to the grievor and the Union representative within the times prescribed in paragraph (g), or
- (iii) the decision is not acceptable to the grievor and the Union representative,

the Union Grievance Committee may forward a copy of the grievance to the Director of Personnel Services within fifteen (15) days from the day on which the grievance was presented to the Department Head or designate.

    (g)   The Director of Personnel Services or his designate shall within seven (7) days after the service of the copy of the grievance upon him, meet with the Union Grievance Committee and the Department Head or designate of the employee's department, and shall within five (5) days after the meeting with the Union Grievance Committee, notify the said Committee in writing of his decision with regard to the grievance.

    (h)   In the event that the decision of the Director of Personnel Services is not acceptable to the Union Grievance Committee, the Committee may notify the Director of Personnel Services within ten (10) days of the receipt by it of the decision of the Director of Personnel Services that it desires to submit the grievance to arbitration for final disposition in accordance with the procedure for Arbitration of Grievances contained in this Agreement.

    (i)   In the event that the Director of Personnel Services is unable to resolve a matter referred by the Employer to the Union Grievance Committee, the Director of Personnel Services may notify the Chairman of the Union Grievance Committee within ten (10) days of the receipt by the Director of Personnel Services of the decision of the Chairman of the Union Grievance Committee that the Employer desires to submit the grievance to arbitration for final disposition, in accordance with the procedure for Arbitration of Grievances contained in this Agreement.

    (j)   Where the grievance relates to the discharge of an employee, the grievance procedure shall start with the Director of Personnel Services in accordance with the provisions of paragraph (g).

    (k)   Where the grievance is initiated by either the Union or by the Employer, the procedure shall start with the Director of Personnel Services in accordance with the provisions of paragraph (g).

    (l)   At any stage in the grievance procedure an employee may be present and shall be represented by the Union in the presentation of a complaint or grievance.

    (m) The time limits expressed in this Article are working days and may be extended by mutual agreement between the Union and the Director of Personnel Services.

ARTICLE 15
ARBITRATION PROCEDURE — GRIEVANCES

15.1   Any dispute or grievance concerning the interpretation or alleged violation of this Agreement, including any question as to whether a matter is arbitrable, which having passed through the grievance procedure outlined in the previous Article still remains unresolved, may be submitted to arbitration. Either party to the Agreement desirous of exercising this provision shall give notice of intention to the other party and at the same time appoint its member to the Board of Arbitration. The other party shall, within a period of seven (7) days, appoint its member to the Board of Arbitration. The two members thus appointed shall confer jointly in an endeavour to select a third member who shall be the Chairman of the Board.

If, within ten (10) days, the two members have not reached agreement, the matter shall be referred to the Minister of Labour of the Province who shall appoint a Chairman. The decision of the Board of Arbitration shall be final and binding on both parties to the Agreement as well as upon the employee or employees involved in the dispute. The Board of Arbitration shall not have any power to alter or change any provision in this Agreement or to substitute any new provision for an existing provision, nor to render any decision inconsistent with the terms and content of this Agreement.

15.2   Each party shall bear the expenses of its own nominee and shall bear equally the expense of the Chairman and all other expenses of the arbitration.

15.3   In the case of an employee who has been found to be unjustly suspended or discharged, he shall be reinstated and have all rights and benefits restored. The penalty, if any, shall be at the discretion of the Board of Arbitration.

ARTICLE 16
UNION SECURITY

16.1   All new employees shall, as a condition of continued employment, become and remain members in good standing in the Union within 30 days of employment.

16.2   The Employer shall deduct from the pay cheque of present members of the Union and all future employees represented by the Union, all normal dues chargeable by the Union and shall remit the same to the Treasurer of the Union once a month. "Normal dues" shall not include entrance fees or special assessments levied by the Union.

16.3   The Employer shall supply a dues check-off list to the Union on a monthly basis.

ARTICLE 17
INSURANCE

17.1   **Health Medical**
The employer shall pay 100% of the cost to each employee for membership in the following plans:
   (i)   Provincial Health Insurance Plan
   (ii) Extended Health Care Services Plan
The cost of membership shall be computed on the basis of providing coverage in the Health Plan for the employee and for the dependents of a married employee.

17.2 **Life Insurance**

The Employer shall pay 100% of the cost of membership in the Group Life Insurance Plan. All employees shall be provided with life insurance coverage in the amount of one and one-half ($1^1/2$) times the employee's basic annual wages to the nearest $500.00. Eligibility for participation shall be after the completion of 122 days in any six month period.

17.3 **Long Term Disability Insurance**

The Employer agrees to pay $66^2/3$% of the premium cost to each employee for membership in a Long Term Disability Insurance Plan which will provide for 60% of the Employee's salary commencing six (6) months after his initial date of disability.

Eligibility for participation shall be after the completion of 122 days in any 6-month period.

17.4 During the period that an employee is a member of the plan or plans introduced as aforesaid, the Employer shall deduct from the employee's pay the employee's share of the cost of membership.

ARTICLE 18
WAGES

18.1 The wages to be paid to employees covered by this Agreement shall be in accordance with the official schedule of wages included in Appendix 2.

ARTICLE 19
SAFETY COMMITTEE

19.1 The Employer and the Union shall establish a joint Safety Commitee in an endeavour to reduce the incidence of industrial accidents.

ARTICLE 20
JOB SECURITY RESPECTING CONTRACTING OUT

20.1 Contracting Out will be defined as the carrying out of work by a firm or a private contractor, which work was formerly done by the Employer itself utilizing its own regular staff and work crews.

20.2 It is recognized that certain services have in the past been contracted out and that the municipality shall continue this practice without reference to the procedures discussed herein.

20.3 If the municipality wishes to contract out any service which will result in the reduction of permanent employees on the payroll of the municipality, the following shall occur:

(a) The Employer shall give notice to the Union, three months in advance of the date the Employer expects to contract out the service.

(b) The Union can concur with the arrangement or prepare an alternate proposal. The Head of the Department shall meet with the Union within 10 days of the notification for the purpose of discussing the proposed matter of contracting out. Information with respect to contracting out shall be made available to the Union at this time.

(c) Where the Union and departmental management do not reach agreement, both parties will present their case at a public meeting to the City Council whose decision will be final and binding.

(d) There shall be no recourse to grievance or arbitration procedures as specified in the Collective Agreement.

20.4 The Employer shall retain complete responsibility and the right to determine the methods by which municipal services are provided. However, in the event that an employee of three or more years of continuous service is displaced from his job as a result of contracting out of work or services, the Employer shall take one or a combination of the following actions:

(a) Relocate the employee in another job in his area of competence if such is available within the service of the Employer.

(b) If (a) is not possible, but a position is available in which the employee could be retrained within a period of six (6) months, the Employer will assume the responsibility of retraining the employee.

(c) For all employees who are within five years of normal retirement age and who have ten (10) or more years of continuous service with the Employer, the Employer will attempt to work out an early retirement that would be mutually acceptable to the employee and the Employer. In discussing the early retirement arrangements, the Union is to be involved.

(d) If none of the foregoing action is possible, and it is necessary to terminate the employment of the employee, it is agreed to provide the employee with six (6) months notice of termination and provide the employee with a separation settlement equal to one week's pay for each completed year of continuous service.

ARTICLE 21
TECHNOLOGICAL CHANGE

21.1. Where the introduction of technological change or new methods of operation will displace (or result in the lay-off of) any employee, the employer shall notify the Union of its intention to implement such technological change or new method of operation and will discuss its implications with the Union before putting such technological change or new method of operation in place. The Employer will make every effort to retrain or provide alternative employment for such employees.

ARTICLE 22
ACTING PAY

22.1 When in accordance with a written instruction from his Department Head, an employee temporarily performs the full duties of a position in a classification having a higher salary range than the one the employee presently holds, the employee shall be paid acting pay providing:

(a) the period of acting continues in excess of twenty-five (25) consecutive working days, in which case the employee shall be entitled to acting pay from the day he commenced to perform the duties,

(b) the wage is at least two (2) groups higher than the employee's present classification.

22.2 Entitlement shall be from the day the employee commenced to perform the duties and continuing for the period he so acts.

22.3 The provisions in respect of acting pay shall not derogate from the provisions in respect of vacancies and new positions.

ARTICLE 23

23.1 **Protective Clothing and Footwear**
(a) The Employer shall continue its present policy regarding the issuance of protective clothing.
(b) Employees who are required by the Employer to wear protective footwear shall be supplied with protective footwear by February of each year.

23.2 **Feminine Gender or Plural**
Wherever the singular or masculine is used in this Agreement it shall be considered as if the plural or feminine has been used wherever the context so requires.

ARTICLE 24
DURATION OF AGREEMENT

24.1 This Agreement shall remain in force and effect from the first day of _____ for 12 months until the last day of _____ and thereafter from year to year.

24.2 Should either party to the Agreement wish to seek amendments to or modifications of the Agreement or to terminate the Agreement and negotiate a new Agreement, it shall give notice to the other party not later than 60 days before the contract termination of its intention.

24.3 Within thirty days of the receipt of this notice the parties shall meet for the purpose of considering the proposed amendments or terms of a new agreement.

ARTICLE 25
ARBITRATION RESPECTING AMENDMENTS TO THE
AGREEMENT OR TERMS OF A NEW AGREEMENT

25.1 If by 90 days following notification of the desire to seek amendments or a new agreement the parties have failed to reach a satisfactory agreement, the parties may mutually agree to request the Minister of Labour of the Province to provide the services of an Officer of Conciliation. Failing this or in the event that no agreement is reached either party may demand that matters still in disagreement be submitted to arbitration and shall give notice in writing to the other party detailing the points still at issue.

25.2 The Board of Arbitration shall consist of three members to be appointed within thirty (30) days of the demand for arbitration and shall consist of one (1) member appointed by the Employer and one (1) member appointed by the Union who within seven (7) days of their appointment shall meet together for the purpose of selecting the third member who shall act as Chairman.

25.3 In the event of disagreement and a selection not being made within seven (7) days after the date on which the two members first meet, either of the members may on not less than two days' notice in writing to the other member, apply to the Minister of Labour of the Province to appoint the Chairman.

25.4 The decision of the Board of Arbitration shall be final and binding on both parties.

25.5 The parties shall each bear the expense of its own nominee, and shall bear equally the expense of the Chairman and all other expenses of the arbitration.

APPENDIX 1

	WAGE CLASSIFICATION/RATES PER HOUR		Number of Employees in Group
Group 01	Caretaker or Janitor Concrete Spreader Gas Pump Attendant General Labourer Guide Constable Hydrant Maintenanceman Protective Painter (unskilled) Rink Caretaker I Traffic Maintenanceman I Watchman	$_____	155
Group 02	Asphalt Smoother Asphalt Mixerman Driller and Breakerman Formsetter Gardener General Plant Helper Landscape Equipment Operators Pipe Caulker Playground Maintenanceman I Rink Caretaker II Sewer Maintenanceman I Traffic Maintenanceman II Treeman I	$_____	145
Group 03	Asphalt Raker Concrete Finisher Handyman Junior Pipelayer	$_____	155

Rink Caretaker III
Serviceman
Sewer Maintenanceman II
Traffic Maintenanceman III
Traffic Sign Painter I
Treeman II
Parks Crew Leader
Event Attendant

Group 04 Asphalt Crew Leader $_____   145
Asphalt Heavy Equipment Operator
Assistant Grounds Foreman
Chlorinator Maintenanceman
Construction Inspector
Greenskeeper
Meter Installer I
Parks Crew Leader (L.P.A.)
Senior Treeman
Service Installer and Repairman
Sewer Maintenanceman III
Sidewalk Crew Leader
Snow Removal Equipment Operator
Truck Drivers
Ward Assistant
Contract Security Inspector I

Group 05 Construction Inspection $_____   65
Supervisor I
Meter Installer II
Meter Tester and Repairman
Playground Maintenanceman II
Senior Pipelayer
Service Installer and Repairman II
Stationary Engineer (4th Class)
Traffic Sign Painter II
Grader Operators

Group 06 Construction Inspection $_____   55
Supervisor II
Maintenance Engineer
Sub-Foreman
Contract Security Inspector II
Painter I
Brick/Blocklayer

Group 07 Construction Inspection $_____   50
Supervisor III
Roadways and Maintenance
Inspectors
Stationary Engineer (3rd Class)
Contract Security Inspector III

Group 08	Welder I Carpenter I Painter II Mechanic I Plumber I Body Repairman/Painter I Brick/Blocklayer II	$_____	65
Group 09	Welder II Electrician I Carpenter II Machinist I Mechanic II Plumber II Body Repairman/Painter II	$_____	45
Group 10	Electrician II Welder/Fitter Machinist II	$_____	20

TOTAL   900 EMPLOYEES

APPENDIX 2

Group Wage Rates
Hourly Wage ($)

Group 01:	_____
Group 02:	_____
Group 03:	_____
Group 04:	_____
Group 05:	_____
Group 06:	_____
Group 07:	_____
Group 08:	_____
Group 09:	_____
Group 10:	_____
Weighted Average Wage:	_____

Existing wage rates for each group will be provided by the Instructor.

SUPPORTING DATA

1. **Overtime Leave and Other Usage During the Past Year**

a.	Overtime	10,000 hours*
b.	Sick Leave	12,000 days*
c.	Special Leave	1,500 days*
d.	Premium Pay Entitlement	100 workers/day*
e.	On Call	50 workers/week**
f.	Attrition	3% of workers per year*

   * Usage was spread roughly proportionately across all ten levels.

   ** All workers come from Groups 4 and 5.

2. **Demographic Breakdown of Bargaining Unit**
   a. Marital Status — 800 married; 100 single
   b. Sex — 800 male; 100 female
   c. Length of Service — 100   0-5 years

100	0-5 years
350	5-10 years
150	10-15 years
200	15-20 years
100	20+ years

3. **Current Health Care Plan Costs (Employer + Employee)**
   Monthly Premiums
   a. Life Insurance Plan *$.49 per $1,000 of annual salary per employee*
   b. Long-Term Disability *$.95 per $1,000 of annual salary per employee*
   c. Extended Health Care Services Plan   *single — $8.60*
                                                   family — $25.80
   d. O.H.I.P.   *single — $29.75*
                                               married — $59.50

4. **Unemployment Insurance — Employer contribution 12.46 per week per employee.**

   At this time dental plans are not included in the contract. There is a wide range of plans available. Depending on the amount of coverage provided, monthly premiums range from:

            single — $10.85-$23.20
            family — $23.28-$51.69

   These premiums represent partial or total reimbursement of current Provincial Dentists' Association fee schedule payments.

Pension costs for the Municipal Employees Retirement System total 14% of the straight wage payroll. Of this, 7% is paid by the employer and 7% by the employee. This amount also covers Canada Pension payments.

COSTING FORMULA

1. Annual Cost of a 1 cent per hour across the board wage increase:
   (40 hours) × (52 weeks) × (900 workers) × ($.01) =

2. Annual Cost of a 1% wage increase:
   (.01) × (40 hours) × (52 weeks) × (900 workers) × (mean wage) =

3. Annual Cost of one additional statutory holiday:
   (900 workers) × (8 hours) × (mean wage) =

4. Annual Cost of one additional week of vacation leave to *all* workers:
   (5 days) × (annual cost of one additional statutory holiday) =

5. Annual Cost of a one hour reduction in hours worked per week, with no change in weekly wages:
   (1 hour) × (900 workers) × (52 weeks) × (mean wage) =

6. Annual Cost of a one-day increase in special leave, sick leave, etc.:
   (1 day) × (number of workers on leave) × (8 hours) × (mean wage) =

appendix four

Arbitration

A Dispute Over New Classifications — The Tri-Co Broadcasting Case*

In the Matter of an Arbitration
Between:
Tri-Co Broadcasting Ltd.,
And:
National Association of Broadcast Employees and Technicians

Award

The undersigned was appointed, pursuant to a letter of appointment dated June 27, 1983, by the Minister of Labour as a Sole Arbitrator for the purpose of resolving the within dispute. The arbitration is pursuant to Part V of The Canada Labour Code. A hearing was arranged for October 19th, 1983. At the conclusion of the evidence and argument my Decision was reserved.

The Grievance

The grievance was filed under a Collective Agreement between Tri-Co Broadcasting Ltd. AM & FM Radio, Cornwall, Ontario (Tri-Co) and the National Association of Broadcast Employees and Technicians (NABET). The agreement . . . covers the period September 1, 1980 to August 31, 1982.

The grievance . . . is dated July 14th, 1982, and reads as follows:

Date of Occurence: Ongoing since Feb/82
Nature of Grievance:

The Company unilaterally expanded the number of classifications of excluded persons described in the CLRB certificate dated December 2, 1973 and outlined in Article 2.2.

The Union has repeatedly suggested that the Company should seek a change from the CLRB but after months of stalling have refused to take any action to solve the dispute.

---

* Permission to use this case was granted by Labour Canada. Minor deletions were made by the author for the purposes of this book and all names have been changed to prevent embarrassment to the individuals involved.

This grievance is being filed under Article 6.2 and furthermore the Union would suggest that adequate discussion has taken place and that the matter should proceed to Arbitration. — Step 4.

Settlement Desired:

Retroactive to the date of the unilateral action, the Company shall put Mr. Howard Hughes back in the bargaining unit subject to all benefits and provisions of the contract including dues check-off.

Preliminary Matters

At the outset Tri-Co indicated that some issue might be taken with the timing of the delivery of the grievance and its submission to arbitration. However, during the course of the hearing, this issue was described by Counsel for the employer as "not being seriously pressed." Accordingly, I have not treated timeliness as one of the issues before me. The parties acknowledged my jurisdiction at the opening of the hearing.

It is clear that the complaint of the Union in this grievance relates to a purported unilateral expansion of the number of positions excluded from the bargaining unit. At the hearing the Union conceded that the employer had a perfect right to promote Mr. Howard Hughes out of the bargaining unit and into a managerial position and that this step taken by the employer was not directly related to the issue of expansion of the number of excluded positions. Thus no question of returning Mr. Hughes, as an individual, to the bargaining unit arises. In the circumstances the Union amended its request for relief in the grievance by inviting me to issue a declaration with respect to two issues:

Whether or not the employer in fact unilaterally expanded the number of classifications of excluded persons contemplated by the Collective Agreement, and
Whether the employer could do so legally.

The disposition of this grievance by me is confined therefore to the matter of the declarations requested.

Mr. Hughes, who was present at the hearing, was invited, in view of the fact that his position was referred to in the grievance, to seek status before the tribunal. He declined and thus took no independent part in the proceedings. As a precaution Mr. Robert Blackburn, a former occupant of a position at issue, who was also at the hearing, was asked whether he wished to be accorded status and he also declined and took no independent part in the proceedings.

The Facts

By letter dated January 28, 1982 ... Mr. Robert Blackburn, over the title "Operations Manager" wrote to the representative of the Union advising him that Mr. Howard Hughes had been appointed to the post of Program Director of Radio Station CJSS. This document was accompanied by a memorandum from the Operations Manager to all staff at the station advising of the same appointment.

To understand the significance of this event in the context of the filing of the grievance some history is required. Tri-Co is a Company which operates two separate radio stations through the same corporate vehicle in the City of Cornwall, Ontario. It has an AM facility which has been operating for several years on a 24 hour a day basis using the call sign CJSS. In addition, for some years it has been licensed to operate an FM facility which it has done under the call letters CFLG. Until 1978 CFLG was operating on a 6 hour a day basis as an introductory exercise, in accordance with the requirements of the [CRTC]. My impression of the evidence is that, during the period of time that the FM station was operating at less than full capacity, the staffing was reduced over that which developed once FM became a 24 hour a day on-air station.

The Union was certified on December 2nd, 1975. The description of the bargaining unit as found in Article 2.2 of the Collective Agreement has not changed since then. It reads as follows:

> All employees of Tri-Co Broadcasting Limited, Cornwall, Ontario, excluding the President, Vice-President/General Manager, Program Director, salesmen and secretary to the President (bookkeeper) (Emphasis added).

At the time of certification there was only one Program Director who was, for all practical purposes, the Program Director for CJSS (AM) because this was the major business undertaking of Tri-Co. The office was occupied by one John Wayne. In August of the year 1978, the management team consisted of Mr. John Gordon, President, Mr. Thomas Henderson, Vice-President/General Manager, and Mr. Wayne, Program Director. These were the positions occupied and also the line of authority, that is to say, the Vice-President/General Manager was responsible to the President, the Program Director to the Vice-President/General Manager etc.

On September 5, 1978, CFLG (FM) went to a full-time 24-hour-a-day service. This required some reorganization and addition of staff. While the realignment of people was described in evidence there was some lack of clarity as to the rationale in every case. It is clear that the need was to marry programming as opposed to marketing skills to the various positions in question. According to Mr. Henderson, who gave evidence on behalf of the Employer, this involved moving Mr. John Wayne up to Operations Manager with added responsibility over his continuing responsibility as Program Director. Effectively, he remained Program Director at CJSS (AM) and had added responsibilities in the FM operation. He secured additional assistance from one Terry Brood, a member of the bargaining unit who was Music Director. The "Operations Manager" position was created in July 1978 for this purpose and Wayne was the first to occupy it. Mr. Samuel Gompers, the Union Representative, said that the first time he heard of this "new position" was in January, 1982.

In early 1981 John Wayne left Tri-Co. At that time Mr. Robert Blackburn was appointed Operations Manager, and also Program Director at CFLG (FM). In January 1982 Mr. Hughes was appointed Program Director at CJSS (AM). In January of 1982, therefore, middle management consisted of either an Operations Manager and one Program Director, two Program Directors, or two Program Directors, one of whom also functioned as the Operations Manager. The significant fact is that the office of Operations Manager is not identified as one of the exclusions in the definition of the bargaining unit.

It is clear that as each successive person viz; Wayne, Blackburn and Hughes were appointed to their positions, dues were stopped since they were leaving the bargaining unit and joining the management team.

As above indicated, the position of Operations Manager was created by the President of the Company in July of 1978. The two incumbents have been Mr. Wayne and presently Mr. Blackburn. Mr. Blackburn's duties include programming in the FM operation and, as Operations Manager, coordinating the complete AM/FM operation from an administrative standpoint. He stands, from a hierarchical point of view, between Mr. Henderson, as Vice-President/General Manager, and Mr. Hughes as Program Director. It would appear to be clear that, for the moment at least, there are two Program Directors and one Operations Manager, but only two people.

Decision

Certain things are clear and beyond dispute. In the first place the Union does not challenge Management's authority to promote people out of the bargaining unit into managerial positions, provided such positions are within the exclusions set out in Article 2.2. Further there is no dispute that at the time that the individuals in question were promoted to the management team their dues were stopped as they had clearly been removed from the bargaining unit.

It is perhaps not without significance that in cross-examination Mr. Hughes said that when Mr. Blackburn took over Mr. Wayne's position in 1981, he only took over the Program Director's role, and not the Operations Manager's role. This would lead one to the conclusion that after Waldruff's departure there was no Operations Manager, and that the true state of affairs was that the promotion of Hughes was to fill the vacancy created by Mr. Blackburn who was in fact being appointed Operations Manager.

The Union argues that when the post of Operations Manager was created there were additional responsibilities associated with the position which went beyond those conventionally borne by a Program Director. It was also pointed out that when Mr. Hughes was appointed Program Director there was then an added managerial person over the situation which pertained at the time of certification. Mr. Porter, in behalf of Tri-Co, describes this added managerial person as a Program Director and urges that the certificate contemplates more than one Program Director. Mr. Gompers suggests that this is not the case and says that, in fact, the added person is an Operations Manager.

The exclusions outlined in Article 2.2 refer to a "Program Director". In my opinion it is unnecessary to deal with the question of whether or not this description entitles the employer to add Program Directors from time to time as the operations expand or whether this exclusion from the bargaining unit is confined to a single Program Director.

The real issue is whether or not there really is a new and separate position, that of Operations Manager. In my opinion there is and I draw this conclusion from two circumstances. The first is that there is indeed an office entitled "Operations Manager." In fact when the Union was advised of the appointment of Mr. Hughes to the position of the Program Director the letter of advice was signed by the Operations Manager, not by another Program Director. Further, and perhaps more important, it is clear that Mr. Blackburn and Mr. Hughes do not share the same position of responsibility. The Program Director reports to the Operations Manager, the Operations Manager reports to the Vice-President/General Manager, and the latter reports to the President. This is a sequential arrangement of authority which is inconsistent with the conclusion that Mr. Blackburn and Mr. Hughes occupy essentially the same position. While Mr. Blackburn may be performing the functions of a Program Director, it is clear that he is also occupying another office, that of Operations Manager. Little imagination is required to see that in future as the business expands, it is likely that a Program Director (or some such person) would be appointed for CJSS/FM, and Mr. Blackburn's activities would be confined entirely to his role as Operations Manager. This flows logically from the manner in which the managerial hierarchy has been developed to date and would be consistent with the lines of authority. Managerial exclusions could, over time, expand by creating a new position and superimposing it upon an existing excluded position "for the time being".

I therefore conclude that Tri-Co has created a new managerial position with new responsibilities which it regards as being excluded from the bargaining unit, the position being Operations Manager. It is a position which stands between Program Director and Vice-President/General Manager. This answers the first question posed in the grievance, whether or not management has unilaterally expanded the number of classifications of excluded persons. The answer is that it has. It matters not who the "persons" are that are occupying the positions. The issue is whether the positions, in number, have changed over those set out in the exclusion. They clearly have.

There can be no doubt of the practical entitlement of management to proceed as it sees fit in the best interests of the Company in accordance with its management rights as set out in Article 3 of the Collective Agreement. No criticism can be leveled at the Corporation for creating this management position. Indeed the fact of its creation, and its character as a senior management position, has been conceded by the Union in documentation filed before the Canada Labour Relations Board. The legal issue however is whether or not there can be effective creation of such a position without the intervention and approval of the Board. Mr. Gompers, on behalf of the Union, says that the Board must approve any changes in the bargaining unit on the application of the employer and that this has not been done in the present case. Mr. Porter essentially argues that there is no need to secure approval of the Board because no new position has been created, both Mr. Blackburn and Mr. Hughes are said to be Program Directors. I have already disposed of this question. My understanding of Mr. Porter's position is that he is in agreement that if a new position is created (a fact which he does not admit has occurred) it cannot be unilaterally imposed. The Canada Labour Relations Board must approve it by appropriate application to alter the certificate. This has not been done in the present case.

A number of authorities were cited in support of the jurisdiction of the Board in this area. No useful purpose would be served in reviewing them in detail, suffice to say that in the British Columbia Telephone Moffatt et al case,* the Board, after referring to Section 119 of the Code, dealt with this general subject. Section 119 reads as follows:

> The Board may review, rescind, amend, alter or vary any Order or Decision made by it, and may rehear any application before making an Order in respect of the application.

The Order in question of course is the certificate dated December 2nd, 1975 as referred to in Article 2.2 of the Collective Agreement.

In the B.C. Telephone case, the [CLRB] observed as follows with respect to its jurisdiction:

> The practice of describing bargaining units by listed classifications is one that was followed for several years by this and provincial boards. Because of the problem that resulted from that mode of describing bargaining units, most labour relations boards have abandoned that approach where possible and described bargaining units in terms of "all employees" excepting certain listed classifications. The practical effect of this "all employee" description of bargaining units is that the onus is on the employer to establish that new classifications created by the employer should be excluded from the bargaining unit. Failing acceptance of that proposition by the union, the remedy for the employer is to bring the matter to the board. (Emphasis added).

The rationale underlying the Board's supervisory role is to prevent the erosion of the unit by the unilateral creation by management of managerial positions and staffing the same with persons within the unit. This of course is not to say that a legitimate reorganization of management's team including the creation of new managerial positions, will not have the full approval of the Board, but it is to say that it is a matter for the Board and not for the unilateral action of management. This it seems to me is true, even if the managerial character of the position is conceded by the Union. Approval is nonetheless required. This jurisdiction is jealously guarded by the Board as appears from the fact that it will insist on being the instrumentality for change even if the parties consent to management's action.

In answer to the second question therefore the unilateral action of management in creating the position of Operations Manager, in the absence of the approval of the change by the Canada Labour Relations Board, is illegal and of no force and effect.

---

* Telecommunications Workers' Union and British Columbia Telephone Company and Telecommunications Employees Managerial and Professional Organization and Paul L. Moffatt et al and Association of Professional Engineers 1978 CLR BR387 Dec. 14.

Conclusion

In allowing the grievance therefore I declare that indeed Tri-Co created a new position, that of Operations Manager, a position not theretofore contemplated by the exclusions set out in the certificate as reproduced in Article 2.2 of the Collective Agreement and that, absent the approval of the Canada Labour Relations Board, it had no authority to do so.

Questions

1 Were the two questions posed by the arbitrator the only major issues in the case?

2 What do you think the arbitrator had in mind in inviting Mr. Hughes and Mr. Blackburn to seek status before the arbitration tribunal? Do you think it was necessary to seek status? Elaborate.

3 Do you agree with the arbitrator's decision that a new position had been created?

4 If you do agree, do you agree with his conclusion that the position is illegal and of no force and effect? Elaborate.

5 Do you agree that, even if the union agreed with management on the appropriateness of the position and its exclusion, management would still have to seek approval from the CLRB? Elaborate.

6 Could the parties agree on the exclusion and include it as part of the collective agreement without changing the certificate issued by the Board when the union was certified? Elaborate.

7 Why should an issue which is submitted to arbitration appear to be a matter for a labour relations board? Elaborate.

8 If the arbitrator's award is correct, do you think that there are many illegal exclusions among the many bargaining relationships established by the CLRB? Elaborate.

9 What are the implications of this decision, if it is correct, for the workload of the CLRB? Elaborate.

A Dispute Over Manning Requirements —
The Maritime Employers' Association Case*

In the Matter of an Arbitration
Between:
The International Longshoremen's Association,
Local 273, hereinafter referred to
as the "Union"
And:
The Maritime Employers' Association
(Saint John, New Brunswick)
acting for and on behalf of
Ceres Stevedoring Co. Ltd.,
hereinafter referred to
as the "Company"
Hearing: at Saint John, New Brunswick,
on April 22, 1981.

Decision

This case involves the question of whether extra men must be hired by the Company when the work which is being done by a foreman and his gang on the job involves the moving of containers out of one hatch into another hatch of the same ship.

The Facts

The evidence is that members of the Union have the primary duty of loading and unloading ships that dock in the Port of Saint John. They are employed by the various stevedoring companies that do business within the Port. The method of hiring most of the Company's employees is that the Company names its foremen twice each year from among the membership in the Union. The foreman, in turn, is responsible to select 12 members from the Union to make up his gang. It is then his responsibility to make sure that the men in his gang have the skills to do the tasks for which the Company may be hired. It is also the foreman's responsibility to make sure that the men in his gang are available for work when they are called out. The basic work gang for the Union in the Port is a foreman and 12 men. A notice by the Company (or any member of the MEA) that men are needed is given to the Union by naming the foreman and indicating the wharf and work for which the Company requires men. If extra men are needed the extra number is noted on the call out to the Union.

---

* Permission to use this case was granted by Labour Canada. Minor deletions were made by the author for the purposes of this book and all names changed to prevent embarrassment to the individuals involved.

On the shifts in question (on January 16 and January 17, 1981) the gang for which Fraser Cameron was the foreman had been called out to work on the loading of newsprint into the #4 hold (or hatch) of the M.V. Visha Pallov. That operation was being carried on by placing 5 men in the ship's hold to handle the cargo as it was lowered into the hold and stowed, 3 men on the deck of the ship to operate the cranes and to give directions to the crane operator, and 4 men on the wharf, or pier, to feed the cargo from the shed to the area alongside the ship. It is customary in such an operation that 2 of the men on the pier and 2 in the hold operate fork-lifts, or other similar machines, to carry the cargo so that the operation will run smoothly, efficiently and safely.

Mr. Cameron was ordered to bring his wharf crew of 4 men on board the ship and have them work in the #3 hold. The order was given to move containers from the forward section of #3 hold in one continuous movement into the after section of #4 hold. The containers were lifted by using two of the ship's cranes (which were "married" to work in tandem) up out of #3 hold over the top deck, and down into #4 hold, without putting the containers onto the pier.

The Union protested that the operation should not have been done so as to split Mr. Cameron's gang to work on two hatches. They suggested that this was a violation of the Collective Agreement in that Article 7.01-B.3 (see Appendix "A") prohibits splitting a gang between hatches and that not less than 5 men be in the hold. The Union submits that in the past the normal method would have been for the containers to be lifted from the #3 hold onto the pier from where they would be taken into a storage shed. Then the containers would be taken by men from a second gang to a position abreast of the #4 hold from whence the ship's crane would lift them up and into the #4 hold. There would be one gang, of 12 men each, working on each of the holds (or hatches).

It is the Union's submission that all members of a gang remain with its foreman in that it is not split up between holds. In addition, they all move from one hold to another when the foreman moves.

There was evidence that cargo is not shifted from one hold to another on the same ship in one continuous movement in a situation where only one gang is used . . . in 2 holds. There was additional evidence that on the "Barbour" ships one gang does shift containers from one hold to another so as to maintain the ship's trim in the water.

The alleged violation took place on the evening shift of January 16 from 7:30 to 11:00 P.M. and from 8:00 A.M. to 10:00 A.M. on January 17, 1981. The Union claims that a foreman and 12 men should have been compensated for the lost time when the extra gang was not called out.

Argument for the Union

Mr. Brown suggested that the loading and unloading spoken of in 7:01-B.3 includes the shifting of cargo from one hatch to another. That is clearly in the evidence in this case.

Article 6.11 decrees that the basic gang is to consist of one foreman and 12 men. The onus is on the foreman, and the Union, to make sure that a normal complement of men is selected for each gang, Article 6:10(b). Under Article 7:02(a) the men in each basic gang are required to be flexible and interchangeable in all the work that is required to be done. In fact in Article 7:02(a) loading or unloading a ship includes shifting cargo from ship to ship, hatch to hatch, as well as, ship to and from shed. That is the only article where the concept of hatch to hatch is mentioned in the Collective Agreement.

Reference in Article 2:02(b)(7) concerns shifting cargo in the hold, not from one hatch to another. The work function of shifting from hatch to hatch is included within the recognition article 2:02(b) in "(1) discharging/loading of cargo vessels."

It was the submission of Counsel that the concept that a gang stays together (under Article 7:01-B.3) is reinforced in Article 7:02(b) where it is said that extra men may be shifted from gang to gang.

Further Article 7:01-B.3(c) requires that at least 5 men be in a hold. Article 13.08 requires 3 men to be on deck working the ship's gear for each hatch.

It was submitted that the Union's position is the only way that the Collective Agreement can be read. Mr. Brown requested that the grievance be allowed and the corrective action be ordered.

Argument for the Employer

It was the submission of Counsel for the Company that there is no violation of Article 7:01-B.3 in that the gang in the instant case was not split between 2 operations. There was just a single flow of material or cargo from one hold to the other. The similarities between the normal movement of cargo from ship to shore are quite evident. A gang is not said to be "split" just because 5 men may be working in a hold, 3 on deck and 4 on a pier.

The Cameron gang was not taking cargo from the pier to 2 hatches.

Article 2:02(b) in defining the local's work jurisdiction does distinguish between loading and unloading as longshoremen's work and shifting cargo in the hold. The very concept of loading signifies that a vessel becomes heavier and in unloading it becomes lighter.

Mr. Christopher, counsel for the company, suggested that the impugned Article 7:01-B deals solely with manning a gang when it is loading or unloading a ship at a pier. Each of the 12 subdivisions of Article 7:01-B refers to a separate operation, loading or unloading ships. And, it is clear in the instant case that the Cameron gang was shifting cargo not loading or unloading it; therefore, there can be no breach of 7:01-B.3 for what was done here.

Instead, the Article that covers this situation is 7:01-C. It was work other than loading/unloading of a cargo vessel. It was not the work of the basic gang under 7:01-B. Accordingly, the rules that pertain to a basic 12-man gang are irrelevant. Rather, it was up to the management of the Company to determine the number of men required in this operation. Article 7:01-C covers those situations that are described elsewhere in the Collective Agreement. Shifting cargo from one hatch to another is not described in 7:01-B.

Mr. Christopher also referred to Article 14:00(n), at page 43; where the concept of loading and unloading cargo is separated from shifting or restowed cargo. There it is clear that the payments to the Union's Pension and Welfare Fund is based on cargo movement onto and from a ship. No payment is made for cargo that is merely shifted.

Company counsel requested that the grievance be dismissed.

Reasons for Decision and Conclusion

Collective Agreement between Maritime Employers' Association and General Longshore Workers of the Port of Saint John, N.B. Local 273, International Longshoremen's Association Effective from September 29, 1978 to June 30, 1981

Article II — Recognition

2:02(a) It is agreed that at container terminal operations, the loading/unloading of containers to/from railcars, the receiving and delivery of cargo to/from truck tailgate including any related terminal work shall be performed by members of the Union.

2:02(b) It is agreed that the following work, when under the control of the employer shall be performed by members of the Union unless another Union is certified and recognized:
1 discharging/loading of cargo vessels;
7 shifting cargo on deck, in the hold or in the shed.

6:10(b) Each foreman of a gang shall select the normal complement of his gang from among the Union membership and shall at all times be responsible for his gang and have his men available for work when called.

6:11(a) The basic gang shall consist of a foreman and 12 men.

(b) Where extra men are required in compliance with manning provisions of Article VII and/or employed, they shall be considered as additions to the basic gang or work unit set forth therein.

7:01 — Manning and Deployment
B. The following manning and deployment provisions shall apply for all work performed in the loading or unloading of a cargo vessel when alongside the pier:
3. When loading/unloading heavy lifts, units, pieces, packages, bundles, pre-slung and non-manhandled cargo, not less than a foreman and twelve men. It is understood that (a) the twelve men will not be split between hatches; (b) not more than four of the twelve men will be required to operate . . . trucks at any one time; (c) during the actual loading/unloading of cargo in the hold, not less than five men will be in the hold.

10. When loading or unloading containers at other than a container terminal operation, not less than a foreman and twelve (12) men.

C. For work other than the loading/unloading of a cargo vessel, the number of men required shall be determined by Management, except that on a container terminal operation a foreman is to be employed when men are employed on the terminal.

7:02 (a) The men in the basic gang shall be flexible and interchangeable to the extent that during any work period they will perform any and all work as directed by Management in connection with the loading/unloading of the ship, which is the place of rest to the hold and vice versa, except as otherwise provided for in Section 7:02(d) below. It is understood that this shall include shifting from hatch to hatch, from ship to ship, and ship to/from shed within a Company, except as otherwise provided for in Section 7:02(d) below.

7:02 (b) Extras or men employed in addition to the basic gang shall work under the same conditions as Paragraph (a), and may be shifted from gang to gang.

Article X — Violation of Agreement
10:01 Should working conditions as set out in the present Agreement be violated by either party to this Agreement or by any person represented by either party, the party affected by such violation may submit a grievance according to Article XI. In such cases, the Arbitrator has the authority to order reimbursement of any payment made or loss suffered by Management, or loss suffered by any employee as a result of said violation.

Article XIII — General

13:08 Any ship loading or discharging using ship's gear (i.e. winches or cranes), three (3) men to be employed on each working hatch, year round.

Health, Welfare and Pension Plans
14:00 (n)

(ii) It is clearly understood that transhipments are paid for only once and that shifted or restowed cargo is exempt.

Questions

1 Paragraphs 3 and 4 in the case describe the work to be done. Do you find any inconsistency in what was requested and what was actually done? Are there clauses which cover this situation? If so, identify them.

2 What do you make of the union's argument that the containers should have been unloaded and put into storage by one gang of 12, and later taken from storage and loaned by a gang of 12? Elaborate.

3 Since the gang in question was called out to work on loading newsprint into the #4 hold (or hatch), did the company have the right, as it maintains, under Section 7:01-C to use the gang to move containers from one hold to another in light of the wording of Clause 7:01-B(a)? Elaborate.

4 If you had been the arbitrator in this case, would you have supported the company's position or the union's position? Give the rationale for your decision.

5 Assume that you supported the union's position which claimed that "a foreman and 12 men should have been compensated for the time lost when the extra gang was not called out". To whom and for what period of time would compensation be made? Give the rationale for your award.

Misuse of an Organization's Financial System — The CBC Case*

Between:
Canadian Broadcasting Corporation
And:
Canadian Union of Public Employees
Grievance of Alfred Keating

The grievor, Mr. A. Keating, was discharged by the CBC for "abusing [his] position of trust" as a Set Designer "by using . . . Instaccount purchase orders to secure money for personal use" (letter of dismissal, Jan. 15, 1979).

There is no substantial dispute as to the facts. As a Set Designer, the grievor was required to procure props to dress sets for television productions. When appropriate props were not available from CBC stores, they were purchased outright or rented for the duration of the production. In order to facilitate procurement, the grievor, and other employees, were provided with serially-numbered purchase orders (called "Instaccount" vouchers) which guaranteed payment to the merchant supplying the props of the amount shown, up to a total value of $300 per order.

The merchant would submit an invoice for the goods to the CBC, either showing the Instaccount number or attaching a copy of the voucher. These invoices would be verified by the CBC Accounts Payable department against the voucher copy submitted by the employee. In the event no voucher had yet been submitted, the invoice would be sent along to the employee (identified by his holding of the relevant numbered voucher) for verification, and then returned to Accounts Payable for payment.

* Permission to use this case was granted by Labour Canada. Minor deletions were made by the author for the purposes of this book and all names changed to prevent embarrassment to the individuals involved.

The grievor, in brief, arranged by use of his Instaccount, to lease a number of musical instruments, which he subsequently pawned. On several occasions, he prolonged the lease of these instruments by further Instaccount transactions. Finally, in circumstances related below, he redeemed the pawned instruments and paid the rental charges. No loss was actually incurred by the CBC, but this course of action was, nonetheless, serious misconduct warranting serious disciplinary action. The only issue of consequence is whether the misconduct was so extreme as to warrant discharge, or whether there were circumstances which would make a lesser penalty appropriate.

1   The analysis must begin with a consideration of why the misconduct was so extremely serious. Employees permitted to use Instaccount are undoubtedly in a position of trust. They are enabled to pledge the credit of the CBC and are, of course, thereby the custodians of its commercial reputation. If merchants cannot be sure whether they are dealing with the CBC or one of its employees, acting in his personal capacity, the whole Instaccount system may be undermined. Moreover, while as matters turned out, the grievor did pay for all transactions in question (except one legitimately chargeable to the CBC), he was able to do so only because he received two sizeable last-minute loans from a sympathetic supervisor and from his girlfriend. Since he could not, as he testified, borrow from either his bank or his credit union, due to an already excessive burden of debt, it is clear that he was very lucky to be able to pay what he owed. In the circumstances, this means that the CBC was very lucky not to have been saddled with debts by the grievor for his own purposes. Thus it can be seen that the grievor risked both financial and reputational [sic] injury to his employer.

Moreover, his acts were incompatible with the discharge of his fiduciary responsibilities, and approached the border of criminality, if they did not actually cross it. There can be no doubt — he admitted as much — that Mr. Keating would not have been able to obtain the lease of the musical instruments, and the several extensions of the lease period, without elaborate personal identification and a sizeable deposit, if he had not used Instaccount vouchers. But a person in a position of trust is not permitted to make personal gain from that position, whether or not he does so at the expense of the person whose interests he is supposed to serve. Thus, apart from financial loss or reputation [sic] damage to the CBC, the grievor breached his duty to it. And, moreover, he did so by an act which was clearly wrongful vis-à-vis the merchants who leased him the instruments. A person who leases the goods of another is under an obligation to return them; he acquires only possession of, and not property in, the goods. Yet by pawning the goods, the grievor put himself in the position of being possibly unable to return them; indeed, for some part of the period, the grievor was in precisely that position. Next, the grievor represented to the merchants that they were dealing with the CBC, when he intended that they should deal with him personally. He thus obtained the rental by a false pretense. And finally, in pawning the goods, Mr. Keating implicitly or explicitly represented to the pawnbroker that they were his to pawn; they obviously were not. Clearly, it is no part of my function to determine which of these acts, if any, amounted to criminal conduct. Quite apart from the question of the grievor's guilty intention, or lack thereof, it is possible that one or more technical aspects of the relevant crimes were absent. But to accept that conduct may not have transgressed the boundaries of the criminal law is not to concede that it was acceptable in the industrial relation sense. It was not. Each of the matters mentioned betrayed a substantial ignorance of, or indifference to, the obligations of an employee in a position of trust.

2 Is discharge the only possible response to employee misconduct involving such a breach of trust?

Counsel for both parties submitted extensive, but of course not binding, arbitral authority on this point. I have examined all authorities cited, and I believe that the following summary accurately reflects their significance. The older cases generally (but not inevitably) treated theft or dishonesty as an offence which warranted automatic discharge; more recent cases, especially those decided by arbitrators subscribing to the theory of "corrective discipline," do not treat dishonesty as per se grounds for discharge; and, various mitigating factors have been identified as justifying the substitution of a lesser penalty for discharge in such cases. Such factors include:

1 *bona fide* confusion or mistake by the grievor as to whether he was entitled to do the act complained of;
2 the grievor's inability, due to drunkenness or emotional problems, to appreciate the wrongfulness of his act;
3 the impulsive or non-premeditated nature of the act;
4 the relatively trivial nature of the harm done;
5 the frank acknowledgement of his misconduct by the grievor;
6 the existence of a sympathetic, personal motive for dishonesty, such as family need, rather than hardened criminality;
7 the past record of the grievor;
8 the grievor's future prospects for likely good behaviour; and
9 the economic impact of discharge in view of the grievor's age, personal circumstances, etc.

But these factors, while helpful, are not components of a mathematical equation whose computation will yield an easy solution. Rather, they are but special circumstances of general considerations which bear upon the employee's future prospects for acceptable behaviour, which is the essence of the whole corrective approach to discipline. How well or badly the grievor had behaved in the past is some indication of his likely future behaviour. How aggravated or trivial was the offence is some clue to the risks the employer is being asked to run if the grievor is reinstated in employment. And how seriously the discharge will affect the grievor is at least one (but not the only) measure of whether a reasonable balance is struck between the other two considerations.

3   I accept the reasoning of those arbitrators who hold that breach of trust should not be automatic grounds for discharge. How, then, should I assess Mr. Keating's conduct?

First, it is said that the grievor had redeemed the pawned instruments and paid all rental charges, prior to being confronted by the CBC with this misconduct. If, indeed, he had voluntarily brought his misconduct to an end, the quality of the offence would not have been altered, but such an act might be evidence of contrition going to the question of self-awareness, and hence of his future prospects. In fact, it was virtually admitted that the grievor did what he did because he was warned by his supervisor that an investigation was imminent. In such circumstances "voluntary" rectification of misconduct neither alters the basic nature of the wrong nor diminishes the penalty.

Second, it is said that the grievor did not appreciate the wrongfulness of his conduct, although it may be properly characterized (in the words of union counsel) as "naive, foolish, stupid, or ill-conceived."

This allegedly missing element of guilty intention may be dealt with in one of two ways. The absence of guilty intention may be rejected as inconsistent with any sensible interpretation of the facts; this, in effect, was the CBC's primary position. Or the grievor's naivete may be treated as evidence of insufficient understanding to warrant his continuation in an employment situation requiring keen awareness of his trust responsibility. Both responses, in my view, are equally plausible, and both have the effect of underlining the seriousness of the offence, rather than the contrary.

As to the facts, it is hard to accept that the grievor believed that he had a "colour of right" to act as he did, or that he acted under the innocent misapprehension that what he was doing was permissible. He knew he had to conceal these transactions from the CBC; that is why he never submitted his Instaccount vouchers. He knew he was misleading the merchants; he conceded expressly that they were relying on Instaccount rather than himself in giving him possession of the instruments in the first place. And he knew he was misleading the pawnbrokers; that is why he took instruments to two different pawnshops rather than arouse suspicion by trying to pawn two instruments in a single visit to one establishment.

As to the fitness of the grievor to continue to occupy a position of trust, if his version of the facts is believed, his equities are not strong. I have already sketched out the several respects in which the grievor proved himself unworthy of trust responsibilities, by conduct which was wrong vis-à-vis three separate "victims" — the CBC, the merchants, and the pawnbrokers. It is conceivable that a wrong done to any one of these could be described as a lapse of judgment. But repeated wrongs done to all three over a period of several weeks, and as part of an integrated scheme, betray, at least, more than passing insensitivity to basic precepts of honesty.

I, therefore, decline to relieve the grievor of the consequences of his conduct on the basis that he did not believe it to be wrongful.

Third, and most important from the grievor's point of view, is his apparent attempt to ensure that no financial loss was incurred by the CBC. It is relatively clear that the grievor knew that he could intercept all invoices before they were approved for payment by the Accounts Payable department. This he was able to do, and did, by not submitting his Instaccount vouchers, thus forcing all invoices to be sent to him for verification, and by not in fact verifying any such invoices, thus preventing payment from being made.

The grievor also apparently cancelled two of his Instaccount vouchers by marking them "Cancel. Pay Cash on return. Personal." No such marking appeared on the two corresponding invoices submitted by the merchants to whom, however, he had given only Instaccount numbers, and not copies of the vouchers themselves. These two invoices were both addressed to "CBC c/o Alfred Keating" which, perhaps, lends some slight credence to his claim that he had declared his intention to pay for them personally. All other invoices relating to the grievor's personal transactions were similarly addressed, except for one. That one was issued in respect of a transaction which, it is conceded, was initially entered into by the grievor for the CBC and only subsequently converted into a transaction for himself. And, finally, the grievor gave uncontradicted evidence that he had orally advised the merchants involved on several occasions that he would be paying their accounts personally.

The effect of this evidence, however, is equivocal. Even interpreted in the light most favourable to the grievor, it can be read as a scheme on his part to prevent the CBC from discovering that he was using the Instaccount system to his own advantage, and to ensure that no payments were made by the CBC on behalf of himself. It does not convincingly exculpate him from the charge that he was misleading both the merchants who leased him the instruments, and the pawnbrokers who advanced him money. However the invoices were addressed (presumably at the grievor's direction), these facts remain clear: the goods were rented against Instaccount numbers; the invoices were addressed to the CBC, while the grievor's name appears only as that of a reference, not a primary contracting party; and the merchants were looking to the CBC for payment, rather than the grievor.

In all of this, there is the sole redeeming consideration that the grievor intercepted all invoices and thereby prevented the CBC's direct financial loss. But that does not change the basically improper and serious nature and quality of the grievor's conduct. As I have said, even without loss to the CBC, it verged on criminality.

I turn finally to evidence submitted on behalf of the grievor to indicate that he acted "bizarrely," atypically, and in such a way that there is no reason to anticipate any such conduct in the future.

The grievor testified that the motive for his behaviour was the desire to buy Christmas presents, and an expensive ring (worth over $500) for his girlfriend. Because he was already carrying a burden of debt over $12,000, partly as the result of old gambling obligations, he could not borrow money for these concededly altruistic purposes. He, therefore, decided to obtain the money by means of the scheme described above, but at the same time to redeem the pawns and pay the rental charges by earning money driving a taxicab during a period of his annual leave taken just prior to Christmas. The scheme failed; he could not earn enough as a cabdriver; and he had to extend the rental period because he could not redeem the pawned instruments.

I was not given extensive details of the grievor's earlier financial difficulties. However, Mr. Keating did say that he had previously gotten into difficulty by spending more than he earned, and that he was now obliged to pay about $650 per month in respect of his debts, in effect all he was making. In light of his past experience and present obligations, it would seem that the decision which led the grievor into his present difficulty — especially the purchase of an expensive ring — was not at all atypical. Rather, it was part of a continuing history of financial management.

It is true that the grievor conceded at the hearing that his conduct was "foolish," and that he answered "yes, sir" when union counsel asked him whether he had learned from this present experience (although he did not explain what he had learned). But there is nothing in these two, brief statements which would justify the conclusion that the grievor is unlikely to encounter similar financial pressures in the future, or deal with them more sensibly.

Finally, the grievor's work record of some eight years' duration was placed in evidence. It shows him to have been good at his job of set decoration, and it is free from any recorded notation of misconduct. There is no suggestion at all that the grievor has been guilty of breach of trust in the past. In certain circumstances, such a record might argue for a diminished penalty on the grounds that the grievor could be expected, on the basis of past behaviour, to correct the current problem. But such a prediction is difficult to make in the present case because the grievor's financial pressures have not abated; indeed, they have probably increased because he has earned virtually nothing since his discharge, while incurring additional debts of $1,000, and, probably accumulating additional debt charges to be added to his former burden of $12,000.

Questions

1 If you had been the arbitrator in this case, what decision would you have handed down? Be concise and logically consistent in your reply.

2 What is your assessment of the nine factors suggested as mitigating factors, particularly item 9?

3 What do you think the arbitrator meant by the "theory of 'corrective discipline'"?

4 Does the evidence about the grievor's behaviour suggest that he has any redeeming features? Elaborate.

5 To what extent does a worker's work record "compensate" for the kind of behaviour exhibited by Mr. Keating?

6 Do you see any hope in Mr. Keating changing his behaviour to become a responsible worker? Elaborate.

7 How far does an employer's obligation go in situations such as this?

The Effect of Criminal Conviction on Employment — The B.C. Telephone Co. Case*

In the Matter of an Arbitration
Between:
Telecommunications Workers Union
And:
British Columbia Telephone Company
Re: Grievance of A.S. Gallant

There is little in issue factually in this case. The union questions the propriety of the dismissal of Mr. Gallant from his job by the employer on 20 June, 1978. Mr. Gallant is 26 years of age, married. He had been employed since 15 October, 1975, as an installer repairman. His total service was approximately 4 years. It is of some relevance to note that a strike prevailed between 20 November 1977 and 14 February, 1978.

Mr. Gallant's difficulties began, in a sense, when he essayed to traffic in drugs in the Courtenay area on 18 November 1977 (M.D.A.), 3 December, 1977 (cocaine), 4 December, 1977 (cannabis) and 20 December (conspiring to traffic in cocaine) in Victoria and on 6 March, 1978 (driving with blood alcohol over the maximum permitted).

These activities led to his trial and conviction on the driving offence on 2 June, 1978, which produced a fine and a suspension of his licence to drive, and to his trial and conviction for the Courtenay drug offences on 15, 16, 19 June 1978, resulting in a sentence of 90 days to be served intermittently of which in fact he served 60 days, and to his trial and conviction in Victoria in April 1979 for the Victoria offence which resulted in a sentence of 30 days, of which he in fact served 20 days.

Filed as an exhibit was an item from the Comox Valley paper of 22 August, 1978, which described his conviction by a jury for the Courtenay drug cases, the judge's observations relative to the matter and to the fact adverted to by his counsel that he was employed by B.C. Tel and faced loss of that employment. It may be noted that the board was constituted on 22 November 1978 and first met on 9 March at which time the matter was by consent, adjourned *sine die* because of the necessity of disposition of the Victoria drug charge then outstanding.

Mr. Gallant's supervisor, Mr. Gillis, testified to calling Gallant in when the strike was over, discussing the pending charges of which he had read in the press, expressing concern about the "public image" of a telephone installer repairman in the circumstances and transferring Gallant to an "inside"

---

* Permission to use this case was granted by Labour Canada. Minor deletions were made by the author for the purposes of this book and all names changed to prevent embarrassment to the individuals involved.

job minimizing his public contact. In his view it was a sort of "created" job which in his mind would continue pending disposition of the charges against Mr. Gallant. He had also read of Mr. Gallant's driving charge in the press and was concerned about his licence because he was occasionally required to operate a vehicle in what Mr. Gillis called the "makeshift" job.

When Mr. Gallant was convicted of the Courtenay drug charges and so advised Mr. Gillis, the latter discussed the matter with the personnel department of the employer. There had been apparently some intimation to him that the pending Victoria drug charge might result in a lengthy sentence of imprisonment. In any event considering that Gallant had been convicted of the serious offence of trafficking in so-called "hard drugs" to the prejudice of his and his employer's image in the Courtenay community, the loss of his licence to drive (necessary for his job), a question about his access to Canadian Forces Base Comox by reason of his conviction and the pending criminal prosecution, it was determined to fire him.

Mr. Gallant's stance is that he was a good and competent employee, that he "fell" into these activities which were not in fact profitable and emphasized that though there were separate charges, all arose out of one foolish involvement.

Counsel "zeroed in" on the "Craig" case. In it an employee of B.C. Tel had been convicted of conspiracy to traffic in a large amount of marijuana. He was initially sentenced to a fine of $500.00 and one day's imprisonment. On appeal this was raised to two years less a day. In addition in the course of investigation, tools and materials, the property of the employer of a value of about $300.00 were recovered from Craig's home. He was dismissed from employment on 3 November 1976. Craig was apparently in custody for only six days following the C of A decision and then given a work release. Craig grieved his dismissal and the arbitrator (Professor T.) directed his reinstatement on 7 July, 1978, without compensation.

Employer's counsel says the Craig decision is distinguishable or wrong or both. Union's counsel says the Craig case was right, that Gallant's conduct is not as "bad" as Craig's and hence his dismissal was improper.

It may be invidious but nevertheless useful to make a comparison of the two cases. Craig had a good record of 11 years' service with the company, supporting a wife and three children. He was convicted of conspiracy to traffic in a large amount of marijuana which resulted in a sentence of two years less a day — actual incarceration amounting to 6 days.

Gallant had a good record 4 years with the company and supported a wife. He was convicted of three counts of trafficking (Mar., M.D.A., cocaine) and one of conspiring to traffic in cocaine resulting in a total sentence of 120 days of which he was incarcerated for 80 days on an intermittent basis. These several convictions arose out of basically one involvement. In addition he was convicted of impaired driving resulting in a fine and licence suspension. Professor T. noted that the fact of Craig's being an employee of the company was not publicized, though he suffered "public humiliation." The press in reporting Mr. Gallant's conviction and the judge's comments did advert to his being an employee of the company.

Professor T. adverted at some length to the circumstances of the recovery of tools and materials belonging to the Company from Craig's home. Professor T. went at some length into the prevalence of practices whereby employees contrary to rules might possess and use company tools and equipment for private purposes and concluded that the Company had not met the burden of proof of theft he reckoned applicable in cases of this kind. Although he was obviously troubled by

> the installation of the extension telephone and the unexplained possession of chimes, screws, plugs and tool boxes,

he nevertheless concluded,

> When seen in the context of the grievor's long and commendable employment record, the theft and misappropriation of the items referred to earlier (which are of small monetary value) do not warrant a penalty of discharge.

In our view, with respect, this conduct by Craig puts him in a much graver situation than Mr. Gallant on a comparative basis. The question of value of items has to be considered in perspective. At the bottom line, the bulk of what the company sells is the rental of telephone service to individuals. The improper installation of an extension phone is theft of its basic product.

As to the issue of the comparative publicity between the two cases, we are not sure but that the reporting of the sentencing judge's remarks did not, in a sense, ameliorate any adverse effect the company sensed from the disclosure by his counsel (as reported) of his employment relationship with the employer.

Derived from earlier cases, Professor T. set out criteria for judging whether discharge for conduct outside the workplace is justified. These are:

1 The conduct of the grievor harms the Company's reputation or conduct.
2 The grievor's behaviour renders him unable to perform his duties satisfactorily.
3 The grievor's behaviour leads to a refusal, reluctance or inability of the other employees to work with him.
4 The grievor has been guilty of a serious breach of the Criminal Code and thus rendering his conduct injurious to the general reputation of the Company and its employees.
5 The grievor's conduct places difficulty in the way of the Company properly carrying out its function of efficiently managing its works and efficiently directing its working forces, adding that it was not necessary to prove all of these factors in order to sustain discharge.

• • •

Questions

1 How serious is a criminal conviction on future employment of a worker? Elaborate.
2 What do you think of the criteria discussed by Professor T. regarding conduct outside the workplace with respect to the justification for discharge? Elaborate.

3 How would you assess Gallant's behaviour against these criteria? Elaborate.

4 By the time the case was heard, the grievor's driving licence had been reinstated. Would this have any effect on your decision? Elaborate.

5 Does the decision in the Craig case have any binding influence on your decision? Elaborate.

6 If you had been chairperson of the arbitration board, what decision would you have handed down? Be concise and logically consistent in your reply.

A Dispute Over Overtime Compensation — The Scott and Skinner Case*

The Public Service Staff Relations Act
Before the Public Service Staff Relations Board
Between:
Marie T. Scott
and Pauline M. Skinner,
Grievors
and
Treasury Board
(National Defence),
Employer
Heard at Halifax, Nova Scotia, October 12, 1988.

Decision

Marie Scott is employed as an English language teacher, classification ED-LAT-01, at the Fleet School, Department of National Defence, Halifax, Nova Scotia. She continued to be covered by the terms and conditions of employment contained in the collective agreement between Treasury Board and the Public Service Alliance of Canada for the Education (all employees) Group (Code 209/82) to the extent that they had not been altered by an arbitral award rendered on May 16, 1986 (Board File 185-2-300). She grieves that the employer has violated the collective agreement at clause B1.06 by requiring her to teach 2.5 hours in excess of the 40 hours of teaching over a two consecutive week period stipulated in that clause. She requests that she be compensated for this excess of 2.5 hours teaching as Extra Professional Services under article 31 of the collective agreement. It was agreed that this hearing address the grievance of Marie Scott only but that the decision rendered would apply as well to the grievance of Pauline Skinner, where the

---

* Permission to use this case was granted by the Public Service Staff Relations Board.

facts are identical but the number of excess hours of teaching is claimed to be 35 minutes.

Appendix B applies "to employees certified in the language Teaching Sub-Group". Clause B1.06 states:

> The normal daily hours of work shall be scheduled between 8:00 a.m. and 5:00 p.m. and shall include not more than four (4) hours of teaching per day, as determined by the Employer with the exception where an employee may be required to provide classroom teaching or to spend other time with students up to six (6) hours, provided that two (2) days of teaching which include more than four (4) hours shall never be consecutive during the same week and that the week does not exceed twenty-four (24) hours.
>
> The work shall be scheduled over two (2) consecutive weeks and the total number of hours of teaching shall in no way exceed forty (40) hours during that period.

Ms. Scott testified that just prior to March 25, 1987, she assumed responsibility for teaching English to a group of six military personnel who had recently failed their English language tests. These persons were reassigned to the classroom where Ms. Scott was to help them improve in the areas of their weaknesses, particularly in the areas of speaking, listening, reading and writing. Four of the six needed improvement in speaking and reading. The students were demoralized after failing the language test and showed it by staying in barracks rather than going out amongst the predominately English speaking population of Halifax. Ms. Scott had recently taken a course at Dalhousie University in motivating students and she decided to use some of the techniques learned with these students. Field trips would be the answer she figured, where the students would be first taught certain things in the classroom and then go out amongst the people of Halifax and practice what they had learned in class by conversing in English with waiters and waitresses in restaurants, visiting museums and discussing in English the exhibits, visiting libraries to learn of resource material to assist them, etc. She had brought her plan to the attention of her supervisor, Bernice Doucet, and had obtained the latter's permission to proceed in accordance with her plan. Therefore, on March 25, 1987, after a short period of classroom work, she left with her students on the field trip and spent most of the day in what she considered to be a successful day of teaching, returning to the classroom towards the very end of the day. She recorded on her time sheet that she had that day spent 6.5 hours teaching. On Friday, March 27, 1987, in the morning, she informed her employer that she had by then put in 40 hours of teaching over a two-week period and requested that she be relieved of further teaching on that day and be allowed instead to complete her day of work preparing for the classes which she would teach on the following Monday. Her 37½ hour work week would be completed by the end of the work day on Friday, March 27, 1987.

She was refused permission to cease teaching at the time she requested on Friday, March 27, and was told to complete her four hours of teaching for that day. It was at this moment that Ms. Scott realized that her field trip would not be recognized in its entirety as teaching. She claims that on March 25, 1987, she had taught 2.5 hours in excess of the normal maximum four hours per day which she should under clause B1.06 be required to teach and that she should be compensated for this extra teaching time, which brought her past 40 hours teaching over a two-week period, as if it was overtime and she should be paid overtime in keeping with the provisions of article 31.

Bernice Doucet, Ms. Scott's supervisor, testified that she had in fact authorized her to proceed on the field trip in question. She considered that this method of teaching, as outlined to her by Ms. Scott and more fully described in a report filed as exhibit E-8, would be effective in the face of the low morale of the students. The students needed to learn English both for their work aboard ship, where they could communicate with co-workers, and in order to prepare themselves for life amongst the predominately English speaking population of Halifax. She considered that this particular field trip was actual teaching of students and a good method of teaching to follow, in the circumstances. In the past, some field trips had been authorized. The difference, however, with the instant situation was that in the past the teachers did not make anything of the fact that those field trips which constituted teaching brought them past the 40 hour limit of teaching over a two-week period stipulated in clause B1.06. There never was a claim before for compensation in such a situation. Now, for the first time, two teachers who were involved in field trips, Marie Scott and Pauline Skinner, had objected to being required to go past the 40 hour teaching limitation over a two-week period when the authorized field trips were not recognized hour for hour. They demanded compensation. Since these claims, the employer has ceased authorizing field trips as a method of teaching, even though they were in the past recommended as an effective method of teaching.

Argument for the Grievors

Counsel for the grievors stated that the two issues involved in this case are, firstly, whether the work which Ms. Scott performed during her field trip on March 25, 1987, constituted "teaching", as envisaged by clause B1.06 and, if so, whether the employer can be required to compensate her for the extra work involved on that day, 2.5 hours, at overtime rates under clause 31 of the collective agreement because she had thus taught more than 40 hours over a two-week period. She pointed to Ms. Scott's job description and the work she performed on the day in question and argued that by any definition it constituted "teaching" as contemplated by clause B1.06 and "teaching" authorized by the employer. In addition, Ms. Scott was "required" to do the "teaching", as Clause B1.06 stipulates. The teaching she did on that day together with the teaching she did on Friday brought her past, by 2.5 hours, the 40 hours of teaching which the employer was permitted by clause B1.06 to require her to perform. There was thus a violation of the collective agreement.

Counsel for the grievors stated that the compensation which the employer should be required to pay to Ms. Scott is provided for in article 31 of the collective agreement. The additional teaching performed by Ms. Scott should be compensated just as if it were extra professional services. Counsel suggested that, on the other hand, should I find that article 31 is not applicable in the instant case, then I should determine what kind of compensation is payable to Ms. Scott. Should I find that there is no extra compensation payable to her then the bargaining agent can take this state of affairs into account during the next round of negotiations for the renewal of the collective agreement.

Argument for the Employer

Counsel for the employer argued that in the instant case I am being asked by Ms. Scott to disregard the collective agreement at clause B1.06 and to amend the collective agreement to provide for compensation for a violation of the collective agreement, if I should find that there was a violation. To begin with, he argued, clause B1.06 provides that any work by a language teacher must be "determined" to be teaching by the employer in advance of it being done and, additionally, the employee must be "required" to perform this "teaching" by the employer. Here, the work performed by Ms. Scott might, in a simple dictionary definition approach, be considered to have been "teaching". However, under the collective agreement, the right to "determine" what constitutes "teaching" is reserved to the employer. In its two directives, filed by counsel as exhibits E-3 and E-4, the employer has determined that field trips, or socio-cultural activities as they are recognized, do not constitute "teaching". Additionally, the employer did not "require" Ms. Scott to perform any work which constitutes "teaching" when on the field trip on March 25, 1987.

Counsel for the employer argued, finally, that there is no provision in the collective agreement for providing additional compensation to Ms. Scott for having, if I should so hold, performed "teaching" duties in excess of the maximum four hours permitted on any given day, in this case on March 25, 1987. Article 31 deals with compensation for extra professional services, that is, overtime beyond an employee's normal hours of work. In this case Ms. Scott's normal hours of work were $7\frac{1}{2}$ per day or $37\frac{1}{2}$ hours per week. Ms. Scott had not worked beyond $7\frac{1}{2}$ hours on March 25, 1987, nor beyond $37\frac{1}{2}$ hours the week in question. She was thus not entitled to overtime. Counsel added that this was not a case where I should award damages in favour of Ms. Scott, should I find that the collective agreement does not provide for compensation in the event of a violation. Ms. Scott was compensated for the additional hours of "teaching" on March 25, 1987, at her regular rate of pay, if I should find that the field trip constituted "teaching", so she has not suffered any damages. What she is asking for in this grievance is simply a punitive measure against the employer in the form of additional compensation to which she is not entitled under the collective agreement.

Reasons for Decision

The facts, as brought out in testimony by Ms. Scott and her supervisor, Bernice Doucet, clearly establish that the 6.5 hours of work performed by her during the field trip on March 25, 1987, constitute "teaching" and were "required" by the employer. This is a form of teaching which was highly recommended by the employer prior to March 25, 1987. On that day, Ms. Scott, for the very first time, claimed that because the field trip, which constituted teaching, was longer than the normal maximum four hours of teaching which the employer could require her to perform on any given day, she would seek time off from teaching on a subsequent day equivalent to the time she had taught in excess of four hours on March 25, 1987. When this was refused, she grieved against having been required to work 2.5 hours in excess of the maximum forty (40) hours of teaching over a two-week period stipulated in the collective agreement at clause B1.06 and requested compensation at overtime rates under article 31 of the collective agreement.

However, having found that the field trip on March 25, 1987, constituted "teaching" which was "required" by the employer, what compensation, if any, is Ms. Scott entitled to for having been required to teach more than 40 hours over a two-week period which clause B1.06 establishes. Ms. Scott claims compensation under article 31, dealing with extra professional services, which reads at clause 31.02 as follows:

> 31.02 In this Article, "extra professional services" means work performed by an employee beyond his normal hours of work or on a designated holiday or on a day of rest.

Questions

1 If you had been the adjudicator in this case, would you have awarded the requested compensation to Scott and Skinner? If so, in what form and under which clause in the collective agreement? Elaborate fully.

2 Do you see any implications in the award that you would hand down? Elaborate fully.

Alcohol and Drug Abuse — The Bell Canada Case*

IN THE MATTER OF AN ARBITRATION
BETWEEN:
Bell Canada
("the Company")
AND:
Communications Workers of Canada
("the Union")
AND IN THE MATTER OF A GRIEVANCE OF:
Helen Barry
A hearing in this matter was held in Toronto on January 25, 1984.

Award

This is a grievance against discharge. The grievor, Ms. Helen Barry, also grieves a letter of warning dated August 3, 1982. Both the warning and the discharge relate to the grievor's rate of innocent absenteeism. It is on that basis that the grievor was discharged pursuant to the following letter dated January 31, 1983:

> Helen Barry
>
> Your health problems continue to prevent you from fulfilling your obligation to be at work on a regular and consistent basis. This situation was reviewed in our letter dated 1982 08 03.
>
> We regret, that in view of the circumstances, your employment with Bell Canada will terminate effective Monday, 1983 01 31.
>
> "Velma Haire"
> Manager Operator Services
> Intercept

The foregoing letter of termination followed the earlier warning letter dated August 3, 1982 which is as follows:

> Miss Helen Barry
>
> This letter confirms our discussion of 1982 08 03 concerning your complete absence record. As you are aware, we do consider it to be excessive. Your absence record demonstrates that you are unable to report for work on a regular and consistent basis. If this performance continues, we will be obligated to terminate your employment with Bell Canada.
>
> "Velma Haire"
> Manager Operator Services Intercept/SOST
> 6 Fl. 15 Asquith Avenue,
> Toronto, Ontario.

---

* Permission to use this case was granted by Labour Canada. Minor deletions were made by the author for the purposes of this book and all names changed to prevent embarrassment to the individuals involved.

The grievor maintains that both the warning letter and her termination were without just cause, contrary to the provisions of the collective agreement. She seeks reinstatement without loss of seniority and with full compensation for wages and benefits lost.

The facts are not disputed. The evidence establishes that the grievor is afflicted both by alcoholism and the abuse of prescription drugs. These difficulties caused the grievor chronic absenteeism throughout the entire period of her employment with the Company. The grievor was first employed as an operator for the period of one year in 1969. She voluntarily left the Company at that time to return to school. She was subsequently rehired as an operator in the centralized intercept office of the Company on Asquith Street in Toronto on September 14, 1981. The evidence of Ms. Velma Haire, manager of Operator Services at the time of the grievor's employment, establishes beyond any doubt that Ms. Barry recorded an excessive and unacceptable rate of absenteeism. While the grievor's record was adduced in evidence in some detail, it suffices to say that the Board is satisfied, on the unchallenged evidence before it, that the grievor's rate of absence between the time of her re-employment and the letter of warning of August 3, 1982 was approximately 45 to 50 per cent of her scheduled work time. We are satisfied that that rate of absence was far in excess of the average of other employees in the same division of the Company's operations and that the grievor's recurring and intermittent absences caused substantial inconvenience and disruption to the normal operations of her department.

The evidence also establishes that on a number of occasions the grievor received verbal counselling from Ms. Haire with respect to the rate and causes of her attendance problems. The evidence establishes that Ms. Haire met with the grievor in January, February and May of 1982 with a view both to impressing upon her the seriousness of her ongoing absenteeism and to offering any assistance, including medical assistance, which might help to correct her problem. While Ms. Haire had grounds to suspect that alcohol might be at the root of Ms. Barry's attendance problems, she had no firm evidence to confirm that suspicion. The grievor generally justified her absences in terms of short-term illnesses and family problems, offering explanations which her supervisor was not in a position to challenge. On November 4, 1982 Ms. Haire met with the grievor following another period of absence. Without confronting her or suggesting the nature of her problem, her supervisor did emphasize that, as an employee, she could take advantage of the Company's benefit plan which included some measure of wage protection during an extended leave of absence for illness, including mental illness, alcoholism and drug addiction. The grievor did not pursue that suggestion, and made no further inquiries either of the Company or her Union with respect to the possibility of treatment with the support of the Company's benefits plan.

The grievor's medical absences were monitored by the Company's medical health physician, Dr. Roberta Hall. In the normal course, documentation provided by the grievor in relation to her absences was forwarded to Dr. Hall. The documents were in the nature of confidential memoranda from her own physician which established that she was medically unfit for work and under a doctor's care. Although the Company's physician had as many as six interviews with the grievor relating to her medical absences and her ongoing ability to work, she did not treat Ms. Barry or give her any medical examination. In the course of her encounters with the grievor, Dr. Hall developed a concern that she might be abusing herself chemically. On several occasions she wrote reports to the grievor's supervisors, based on the medical records before her, indicating that in her view there was little or no basis to expect improvement in Ms. Barry's rate of attendance in the future. On four occasions Ms. Haire requested that Dr. Hall do an employee health assessment with respect to the grievor's future employability. Each time the report returned to Ms. Haire expressed a pessimistic prognosis for her future attendance. However, the evidence of Dr. Hall, and a memorandum which she wrote to Ms. Haire, establish that she did not view the grievor's situation as hopeless. In a memorandum dated December 16, 1982 Dr. Hall noted that in light of the grievor's age (30 years) and good physical condition it would be within her ability to end the problems giving rise to her absences, and that she could correct her attendance pattern in a period of three to six months. Unfortunately, Ms. Barry's attendance pattern was not corrected. The grievor continued to believe that she could solve her own problem without medical assistance or outside help. In the result, her attendance problems continued, and indeed worsened, until the point of her termination.

Evidence was adduced respecting the grievor's change of attitude and her efforts at medical rehabilitation after her discharge. By her own account, following her termination, the grievor's abuse of alcohol increased and was further complicated by her continuing intake of prescription drugs, including a compound of codeine and barbiturates, a sedative and valium. Her own concern increased when she began to have progressively longer memory black-outs; in the earlier stages these were as short as five minutes and eventually lasted as long as a half-day in which she would have no recollection of what she had done. According to the grievor's evidence she first acknowledged that she was an alcoholic and drug-dependent in the spring of 1983. In June of that year she approached her family physician, Dr. Joseph Tillman, and asked for medical help for her alcohol and drug dependency. Dr. Tillman referred her to the Donwood Institute where she was admitted for seven weeks of treatment on July 15, 1983.

A letter from Dr. J. Cohen, co-ordinator of medical services at the Donwood Institute, was adduced in evidence by agreement. It establishes that the grievor was diagnosed as having no substantial medical or psychiatric problems other than her alcohol and drug dependency. During her treatment she participated in an educational program of lectures and discussion groups and in group therapy. According to Dr. Cohen's letter, Ms. Barry took good advantage of her seven weeks' treatment and made appropriate gains during that time. She appeared positively motivated at the time of her discharge. She was then given a prescription for 50 mgs. Tempacil to be taken twice a day and was scheduled to participate in the Institute's two-year "continuing health services program" for continuing support during her recovery.

Her record of progress and attendance in that program has been less than perfect. She suffered relapses in September, October and November of 1983, although she did re-attend at the Institute on two occasions in December of 1983 and January of 1984 respectively, at which times she is described as appearing "well and chemically clear." Dr. Cohen's letter indicates that maintaining regular contact at the Donwood Institute would provide the grievor with the support necessary to work toward a complete recovery from her illness. Dr. Tillman also indicates, in a letter filed by the agreement of the parties, that the grievor has responded well and is now taking Antabuse, and that he sees "a good progress."

Substantial argument was addressed to the issue of the admissibility and weight to be given to evidence respecting the facts of the grievor's condition as they evolved after her discharge. Counsel for the Company argued that the correct arbitral authority in this regard looks to the date of termination as the appropriate time to determine whether the prognosis for the grievor's attendance was such as to justify her termination. In his submission subsequent events cannot be admitted to alter the merits of the grievor's case or to establish that the Company did not have just cause for her termination. In support of that proposition, reference was made to a number of cases: *Re Corporation of the City of Sudbury and Canadian Union of Public Employees, Local 207* (1981), 2 L.A.C. (3d) 161 (P. Picher), and two unreported decisions involving the parties to this grievance, *Bell Canada and Communications Workers of Canada*, a decision of a board of arbitration chaired by Mr. H. Frumkin, dated August 6, 1982 (Dion grievance) and a subsequent award between the same parties issued by a board of arbitration chaired by Mr. André Rousseau, dated November 4, 1982 (Veillet grievance).

Counsel for the Union argued that a board of arbitration is entitled to take into account circumstances arising after the discharge of an employee for innocent absenteeism, particularly as they may have a bearing on the discretion of the arbitrator to fashion a remedy with regard to the future employment of the grievor. Counsel for the Union referred the Board to *Re Canada Post Corporation and Canadian Union of Postal Workers* (1982), 6 L.A.C. (3d) 385 (Burkett) and another case involving the parties to the instant matter, *Re Bell Canada and Communications Workers of Canada* (1983), 10 L.A.C. (3d) 285 (Shime). The decision of the board chaired by Mr. Shime, which was apparently unanimous, plainly rejects the approach taken by arbitrators Rousseau and Frumkin in the cases noted above. In that case, as in the instant case, the grievor was an alcoholic who did not recognize or admit his problem until his dismissal. Between the time of his discharge and the arbitration of his grievance, the employee received treatment, joined Alcoholics Anonymous and became a complete abstainer. Relying in part on the authority of the Divisional Court of Ontario in *Re The Queen in right of Ontario and Grievance Settlement Board* (1980), 107 D.L.R. (3d) 599, and also based upon the provisions of article 15.06 of the collective agreement, which allow the board of arbitration "to modify the penalty in a just and reasonable manner," the board found that it could rely on facts and events occurring subsequent to the grievor's dismissal in considering a modification of the penalty. Taking into account the grievor's work record, his seniority and his rehabilitative steps, the board then reinstated the grievor, without compensation, subject to a number of conditions relating to continued rehabilitative treatment and his record of employment in the next two years.

It is generally accepted that an employer may terminate with justification when it is shown that an employee has a blameless shortcoming which undermines his or her employment relationship and where it is reasonably probable that the conditions giving rise to that shortcoming are not likely to improve. Blameless absenteeism, including absenteeism for alcoholism, can therefore entitle an employer to end the employment relationship if it is established that the employee has been and will continue to be incapable of regular attendance at work. [See *Re U.A.W., Local 458 and Massey-Ferguson Industries Ltd.* (1972), 24 L.A.C. 344 (Shime); *Re U.A.W. and Massey-Ferguson Ltd.* (1969), 20 L.A.C. 370 (Weiler); *Re Atlas Steels Co. and Canadian Steelworkers' Union, Atlas Division* (1975), 8 L.A.C. (2d) 350 (Weatherill); *Re National Auto Radiator Manufacturing Co. Ltd. and U.A.W.*, Local 195 (1976), 11 L.A.C. (2d) (Brandt); *Re Niagara Structural Steel (St. Catharines) Ltd. and U.S.W., Local 7012* (1978), 18 L.A.C. (2d) (O'Shea); *Re City of Sudbury and C.U.P.E., Local 207* (supra); *Re Crousse-Hinds Canada Ltd. and U.A.W.* (1981), 3 L.A.C. (3d) 230 (Brown), and *Re American Standard, Division of Wabco-Standard Ltd. and Int'l Brotherhood of Pottery & Allied Workers* (1977), 14 L.A.C. (2d) (Burkett).]

The evidence in the instant case establishes that the Company has an enlightened policy with respect to the treatment of employees suffering from alcohol and drug dependencies. Among the materials filed in evidence is a notice distributed by the Company's personnel headquarters establishing a generous and sophisticated plan "for identifying and treating those employees with a health problem caused by alcohol or drug abuse." Without relating the details of that plan, it specifically acknowledges that alcohol and drug abuse are to be treated as an involuntary illness. The plan reflects an offer of assistance to the afflicted employee involving five components: identification, confrontation, referral, treatment and rehabilitation. Unfortunately, in the instant case, the best efforts of Ms. Haire and Dr. Hall did not succeed in bringing the grievor to the critical acknowledgement of her own drug dependence. If the grievor had recognized her own problem, and bearing in mind that the refusal to recognize alcoholism is itself part of the illness, Ms. Barry would in all likelihood have had the advantage of a leave of absence with medical benefits to help her overcome her problem, as well as the ongoing support of her employer in working toward her rehabilitation. We make that observation in full awareness of the similar comment by the unanimous board chaired by Mr. Shime, noted above, at p.287. In that instance the board reinstated the grievor.

• • •

Questions

1 What is meant by "innocent absenteeism"?
2 Do you think that the "Manager Operator Services" was forceful enough in dealing with the grievor?
3 Do you think that the Company's physician was assertive enough with the grievor?
4 What do you make of the conflicting awards by arbitrators in the other cases cited?
5 How far does an organization's responsibility go in cases such as this one? Elaborate.
6 Do you think that cases such as this should become the subject of an arbitration case when a worker has been discharged and has been away from the company for such an extended period of time? Elaborate.
7 If you had been the chairperson of the arbitration board, what award would you have handed down in this case? Give the rationale for your award.

A Case of Alleged Insubordination — The Paul Potvin Case*

Public Service Staff Relations Act
Before the Public Service Staff Relations Board
Between:
Paul Potvin, Grievor,
And:
Treasury Board (Department of Veterans' Affairs), Employer.

Decision

This decision concerns a grievance referred to adjudication by Paul Potvin, an orderly, HS-PHS-5, employed at the Ste-Anne-de-Bellevue Hospital.

The grievance reads as follows:

> On May 25, 1983, I received a letter dated May 25, 1983 and signed by Ms. Audette Meursault, Assistant Director of Nursing, informing me that I was being suspended for three days. . . . I consider this decision unfair, arbitrary, discriminatory and unfounded. . . . This action is contrary to article I of my collective agreement. [unofficial translation]

* Permission to use this case was granted by the Public Service Staff Relations Board. Minor deletions were made by the author for the purposes of this book and all names changed to prevent embarrassment to the individuals involved.

The grievor requests the following corrective action:

1 That the employer delay implementation of the decision to suspend me until the final resolution of this grievance, as a demonstration of its good faith.
2 That the employer rescind the decision it announced in its letter of May 25, 1983 and that no other measures be imposed.
3 That the employer reinstate me in my duties, retroactively.
4 That the employer reimburse me fully for the pay I lost, retroactively and with no loss of benefits.
5 That all documents relating to this matter be removed from my personal file and destroyed in my presence and/or in the presence of my union representative, that these documents not be replaced with any other documents, and that no further use be made of such documents.
6 That the employer issue me a letter of apology exonerating me of all blame or suspicion.
7 That I receive the assurance that no reprisals will be taken against me for filing this grievance.
8 That the employer hold consultations at each and every level of the grievance procedure, subject to any mutual agreement to dispense with one or more levels.
9 That I be present during these consultations, at the employer's expense.
10 That the employer comply with article I of my collective agreement. [unofficial translation]

Evidence

Mss. France Joly, Sylvie-Anne Poirier, and Audette Meursault, and Mr. Berthelot Belanger testified for the employer and filed the following exhibits:

Exhibit 1: Letter of May 25, 1983, signed by Ms. Audette Meursault, suspending the grievor without pay on June 1, 2 and 3, 1983 for insubordination.
Exhibit 2: (filed jointly) Letters of March 22, 1982, May 20, 1982, August 3, 1982, August 6, 1981, February 24, 1982, November 25, 1982, December 7, 1982 and March 17, 1983, constituting the grievor's personal file.

I ordered the witnesses excluded. The grievor did not present any evidence and his representative argued that the employer had not proved the misconduct alleged against the grievor.

Ms. France Joly testified that she has worked at the Ste-Anne-de-Bellevue Hospital for six years. She is a nursing team leader. She works with the grievor, an orderly, whose job it is to provide basic care to the patients at the Hospital. She explained that a team comprises one or two nurses and a number of orderlies. The nurse asks the orderly to provide the care that the patients require. The team leader decides what duties the nurses perform and how many orderlies are needed. The duties are then allocated among the team members.

On May 19, 1983, the team consisted of three nurses and a single orderly, the grievor. Ms. Joly was the grievor's immediate supervisor that day and the grievor was responsible to Ms. Sylvie-Anne Poirier and Ms. Boisvert. Mr. Potvin and the witness worked from 7:30 a.m. until 3:30 p.m. They were entitled to half an hour for lunch, but this half-hour was not always taken at the same time; it varied, depending on the department's needs. In principle, the first lunch break was at 11:15 a.m. The second was around 12:00 noon or 12:10 p.m., depending on how long it took to prepare the patients' lunches. On May 19, Ms. Joly had 34 patients under her care. The majority were bedridden, confused and ambulatory to varying degrees. Mr. Potvin and Ms. Poirier had seated a patient by the name of Sim on the toilet. Mr. Sim was difficult to handle, nervous, hesitant and very stiff, was not co-operating and was confused. He weighed about 150 pounds. He was in the bathroom for some fifteen or twenty minutes.

Ms. Joly explained that it was not part of the nurses' duties to put a patient like Mr. Sim into bed. She knew the technique, but did not do this work routinely, and when she did, she was assisted by an orderly. On May 19, around 11:15 a.m., the witness was some thirty feet away from the grievor. She heard Ms. Poirier twice call out "Paul, Paul." Ms. Poirier was 10 to 15 feet away from Ms. Joly and behind the grievor who was in front of the elevator, opposite Ms. Joly. The witness then said in a rather loud voice, "Paul, come and help us put Mr. Sim to bed." Mr. Potvin answered, "I'm down for the first lunch hour; I'm going down," to which Ms. Joly replied, "I'm asking you to put off your lunch and come help us put Mr. Sim to bed right now." Mr. Potvin replied, "All you had to do was schedule two orderlies. I'm going to lunch." The grievor then took the elevator and went downstairs.

The witness testified that the three nurses (Sylvie-Anne Poirier, Lyne Boleyn and France Joly) had to put Mr. Sim into bed, and that they had problems doing so. It took five minutes. They had to get him up from the toilet, wipe him, bring him to the bed and put him into it. Once Mr. Sim was in bed, Ms. Joly telephoned Mr. Belanger, the Co-ordinator, around 11:20 a.m. to inform him of the incident. Around noon, Mr. Belanger called her back to ask whether Mr. Potvin was back from lunch and asked her to tell him to report to the personnel office. When Mr. Potvin returned from lunch at noon, she told him she was going to make a report to Mr. Berthelot Belanger, Co-ordinator, on his refusal and attitude. The grievor replied, "Make a report. Anyway, I'm sick. I'm going home." Mr. Potvin went to the personnel office and was away some 30 to 50 minutes.

Sylvie-Anne Poirier testified that she has been a nurse and team leader at the Ste-Anne-de-Bellevue Hospital for six years. She was in charge of a nursing team that included an orderly. On May 19, 1983, she was working with the grievor. Ms. Joly was a fellow nurse. She testified that, on May 19, around 10:50 or 10:55 a.m., she and Mr. Potvin had seated patient Sim on the toilet. Mr. Sim's limbs were stiff and he was a difficult patient. He weighed about 140 pounds.

She described the incident as follows. Mr. Potvin informed nurses France Joly, Lyne Boleyn and Sylvie-Anne Poirier that he was going to lunch. He said, "I'm going to lunch," and no one objected. However, Sylvie-Anne Poirier, who is a quiet person, suddenly exclaimed, "Oh my God, Mr. Sim is still in the bathroom!" and she immediately called out in a normal tone of voice, "Paul, Paul," but the grievor did not answer. She stated that Mr. Potvin may not have heard her. Ms. Joly, who was at the nurses' station, ten feet away from Mr. Potvin, turned around and saw the grievor in front of the elevator. She then asked him to help and said to him, "Will you delay your lunch a little?" Mr. Potvin replied, "You should have scheduled more order- lies. If the elevator had come earlier, I would be gone now," and he got into the elevator. Ms. Joly told him she was going to make a report on the incident and he replied, "Make a report. Anyway, I'm booking off sick. All you had to do was schedule two orderlies."

Nurses France Joly, Lyne Boleyn and Sylvie-Anne Poirier put patient Sim back to bed. France Joly then telephoned Mr. Belanger and Mr. Potvin returned from lunch around noon. Ms. Poirier testified that she did not discuss the incident with Ms. Joly in any detail because the lunch hour was a very busy time. Ms. Joly said that she was going to make a written report, which she did. The witness also made a report.

Berthelot Belanger testified that he has worked at the Ste-Anne-de- Bellevue Hospital since October 1982. He was co-ordinator of six work units. He was responsible for scheduling, leave applications, patient care and work assignments. He testified that, on May 19, 1983, around 11:25 a.m., he received a first call from Ms. Joly who explained to him that Mr. Potvin had just left. She had asked the grievor repeatedly to help her, but Mr. Potvin took the elevator. Ms. Joly added that she had approached the grievor to make sure that he had heard her. Ms. Joly told Mr. Belanger that she had said to Mr. Potvin, "Will you put off your lunch a few minutes?", to which Mr. Potvin had replied, "If the elevator had come earlier, I would be gone now."

Ms. Joly explained to Mr. Belanger that she needed help with Mr. Sim. Mr. Belanger recalled that Ms. Joly spoke to Mr. Potvin more than once. The first time, she said to him, "Will you come here and help us?" The second time she said, "Will you put off your lunch hour a few minutes?" Ms. Joly also told the witness that another nurse had also asked Mr. Potvin to help her.

Mr. Belanger discussed the incident with the three nurses involved and noted down the most important facts in a report. He also asked the nurses to make a written report.

Around noon, he called unit 8B back to ask whether Mr. Potvin had returned from lunch and to ask him to come and see him. At noon, the grievor came to the personnel office, and during the afternoon of May 19, he came to the witness's office to discuss the incident in 8B.

Mr. Belanger asked the grievor three specific questions:

Why did you leave the unit?, to which Mr. Potvin replied that it was 11:15 a.m., his lunchtime, and he was leaving anyway.

Did you hear the nurses' words? and Mr. Belanger repeated the nurses' words: "Will you put off your lunch? Come and help us get Mr. Sim up right away." Mr. Potvin did not remember the exact words the nurses used.

Did you understand what the nurses said? Mr. Potvin simply replied, "Yes."

Mr. Belanger then stated that he explained to the grievor that this situation was intolerable and constituted insubordination. The grievor replied that the employer was responsible for assigning the necessary personnel and that he did not want to miss his lunch break to which he was entitled. Mr. Belanger was angered by this incident. He tried to make the grievor understand the consequences of his action in terms of his responsibilities and those of the unit.

Mr. Belanger consulted the staff relations officer, Charles Larocque, his immediate supervisor, and Ms. Audette Meursault regarding the appropriate disciplinary action for this incident.

Audette Meursault has been assistant director of nursing at the Ste-Anne-de-Bellevue Hospital for two years. She wrote the disciplinary letter of May 25, 1983 (Exhibit 1) which imposed a three-day suspension served on June 1, 2 and 3, 1983. She testified that she studied the reports on the incident from the nurses (Mss. Joly, Poirier and Boleyn) and from Mr. Belanger, the co-ordinator, as well as the grievor's disciplinary record (Exhibit 2), and concluded that he deserved a three-day suspension. He had job responsibilities that consisted in doing the work assigned by the nurses to ensure the care and comfort of the patients. Ms. Meursault testified that the grievor had received a two-day suspension earlier for a similar offence. Ms. Meursault also took into consideration the nature of the assistance requested, the fact that the patient was on the toilet, the kind of patient, and the fact that the patient's care and comfort took precedence. Employee Potvin had no valid reason to refuse to assist the nurse when she asked for help.

The witness did not discuss the incident with the grievor. She left this matter to the nurses and the co-ordinator. She could not say with certainty that she had discussed the incident with Ms. Poirier and Ms. Joly, but said that she probably saw them. She did discuss the incident with Mr. Belanger.

Arguments

Ms. Roy, counsel for the employer, argued that the grievor's insubordination was serious. She added that the employer proved its allegation according to the balance of probabilities. The evidence established that an order was given, even if the witnesses did not agree on the exact words used by Ms. Joly. It was also clear that the grievor did not obey the order and that he went to have his lunch instead of helping the nurses, as was his duty. He was therefore guilty of insubordination. Ms. Roy cited *Varzeliotis* (166-2-9721) to illustrate the principles that apply in cases of insubordination.

Mr. Potvin worked in a hospital where there was no set lunch hour. This hospital was responsible for the health and care of veterans and it was essential that the obligations to the patients be fulfilled. For this reason, the grievor's insubordination was very serious. Ms. Roy cited *Reiner Busse* (166-2-9535) in which a three-day suspension was imposed, *Collective Agreement Arbitration in Canada* by Palmer, at pages 11 and 12, and *Terrence S. Arnfinson* (166-2-13851), in which Mr. Arnfinson displayed an attitude similar to Mr.

Potvin. Mr. Arnfinson had said, "I will be back when I get my laundry done." This attitude therefore constituted insubordination.

Ms. Roy argued that the grievor could easily have obeyed the order, and in support of this argument, she cited *Re International Nickel Co. of Canada Ltd. and United Steelworkers,* 6 L.A.C. (2d) 172. In *Re United Steelworkers and Lake Ontario Steel Co. Ltd.* 19 L.A.C. 103, where the lunch break was also at issue, it was held that the employer could reasonably interrupt an employee's lunch break. In the present case, the employer asked the grievor to perform a necessary duty that would not have taken much time. The employer's request was reasonable.

Citing *Gareau* (166-2-11454) and *Varzeliotis,* (supra), Ms. Roy argued that I should not reduce the three-day suspension because it would deter Mr. Potvin from any further such behaviour.

Mr. Dupuis argued that there was no evidence to substantiate the employer's allegation and referred in this regard to the disciplinary letter that imposed the three-day suspension (Exhibit E-1). The letter stated that Ms. Meursault reported Ms. Joly's statements. The onus of proof was on the employer who must prove that the grievor refused to obey an order. Mr. Dupuis wondered whether Ms. Joly really made the remarks attributed to her in the disciplinary letter. Did Ms. Joly ask Mr. Potvin to delay his lunch a few minutes and help her move a patient? The letter stated that Ms. Joly made her request in a direct manner and, furthermore, that she spoke the following words to him in a clear and polite tone of voice: "Put off your lunch a few minutes and come and help us lift Mr. Sim off the toilet and put him into bed right away." Mr. Dupuis argued that the statements attributed to Ms. Joly were a distortion of the truth and of the actual words she used.

Mr. Dupuis cited the three principles that apply in cases of insubordination as described in Canadian Labour Arbitration, by Brown and Beatty, and in "Les Mesures disciplinaires . . .", by Claude Daout, who stated at page 323 of his work that the order must be clear, unequivocal, and clearly understood by the employee. The order must be given by a person in authority, during working hours.

Reviewing the evidence, Mr. Dupuis noted that the grievor asked the three nurses on his team for permission to go to lunch. They did not object. When Ms. Poirier realized that Mr. Sim was still in the bathroom, she uttered an exclamation and called out "Paul, Paul." Could this exclamation be considered an order? Moreover, Ms. Poirier testified that she heard Ms. Joly say to the grievor, "Will you put off your lunch hour?" This question was a request. It was not a command. The question was not therefore an order. Ms. Poirier further testified that Ms. Joly added, "Will you help us?" Again, this question was not a command, and even if one wanted to argue that Mr. Potvin clearly understood the question, it was not an order. Mr. Dupuis argued that precedent established that the employer must prove that an order was given. However, in this case, the words used were "Will you," and one must ask whether this expression was an order or merely a request that could be refused. In *Emile R. Andre* (166-2-12239), Mrs. Falardeau-Ramsay showed how this expression could be distorted. The question "Will you" was not an order. The testimony of the employer's witnesses regarding whether Mr. Potvin actually received an order was contradictory and confused.

Mr. Dupuis argued that the employer did not adduce any *prima facie* evidence. Since the letter of May 25, 1983 (Exhibit 1) did not establish the truth about the incident, and since there was no insubordination, the grievor did not have to answer the allegation.

On this point, Mr. Dupuis cited *Adam Butcher* (166-2-13507), a decision rendered by Leon Mitchell, Q.C., in which the grievor did not testify and in which the adjudicator held that the onus was on the employer to establish the facts as they happened. Mr. Dupuis argued that the employer did not prove that the grievor was guilty of the misconduct alleged against him, and in support of this argument, he cited *Gareau*, (supra), at page 23. Moreover, the fact that Mr. Potvin sought permission to go to lunch showed that he was not insubordinate or disrespectful. Furthermore, no proof was adduced that Mr. Potvin's alleged misconduct affected the Hospital's productivity. For these reasons, Mr. Dupuis asked that the three-day suspension be rescinded, that the disciplinary letter be removed from the grievor's file and destroyed, and that all the benefits denied Mr. Potvin as a result of this three-day suspension be restored to him. If a penalty was warranted, Mr. Dupuis asked that the three-day suspension be reduced to a reprimand, as decided in *Emile Andre*, supra.

In reply, Ms. Roy argued that the employer, with whom the burden of proof rested in this case, had proved insubordination. The evidence revealed that the incident described by the witnesses was not a figment of their imagination or a "distortion," as the grievor's representative claimed. There was uncontradicted evidence that Mr. Potvin told Mr. Belanger that he understood what was being asked of him. Mr. Dupuis' claim that Mr. Potvin sought permission to go to lunch was not valid. The grievor merely said that he was going to lunch and this statement was not a request for permission. Moreover, there was no evidence that he was granted permission. On the contrary, Ms. Joly testified that she in no way gave Mr. Potvin permission to leave the workplace.

• • •

Questions

1 What is the major issue involved in this case? Elaborate.

2 For whom do you think the environment in which this case took place made it easier to prove a point — the grievor or the employer? Elaborate.

3 Do you think that the nurses needed to make such a fuss over putting a 140-pound man into bed? Why did they do so?

4 If you had been counsel for the grievor, what approach would you have taken during the arbitration proceedings? Elaborate.

5 If you had been the arbitrator, what award would you have handed down? Give the full rationale in support of your award.

Dismissal for Mishandling Funds, and a Proposal for Reinstatement by the Grievor's Union — The Allan Ryan Case*

IN THE MATTER OF AN ARBITRATION
BETWEEN:
AIR CANADA
(Employer)
and
CANADIAN AIR LINE EMPLOYEES ASSOCIATION
(Union)
and
IN THE MATTER OF A GRIEVANCE OF
Mr. Allan Ryan
(Grievor)

Before:	Mr. M.C. Thompson	Union Nominee
	Mr. G. Milley	Employer Nominee
	Mr. C. Gordon Simmons	Chairman

Representing the
Employer: Mr. George Mitchell, Q.C.
Union: Mr. Harold Caley

A hearing into this matter was held in St. John's, Newfoundland on March 28, 1981.

By letter dated December 6, 1979, signed by Mr. P.J. Maddigan, Airport Manager for Air Canada at St. John's Airport, the grievor was "suspended pending discharge" for allegedly failing to account for cash funds paid to the grievor by passengers of Air Canada. The grievor has admitted the allegations and was dismissed. He seeks reinstatement on the following conditions:

1 He seeks no compensation during the period when his employment had been severed.
2 He seeks to be transferred from the position of passenger agent to one of reservations agent where he agrees to remain until such time as the employer is satisfied that he can be transferred elsewhere.
3 The record of this incident is to remain on the grievor's personnel record notwithstanding any provision to the contrary in any collective agreement which purports or may purport to wipe out offences of employees after a certain period of time has elapsed.

---

* Permission to use this case was granted by Labour Canada. Minor deletions were made by the author for the purposes of this book and all names changed to prevent embarrassment to the individuals involved.

4 If it is ever again established that the grievor has committed such an offence in the future, either admitted or proved, the grievor agrees that he will not be entitled to again argue that the penalty be modified.

The above conditions of reinstatement were advanced by counsel for the union who informed the board that both the grievor and union have agreed to adhere to the above conditions. Accordingly, the union seeks reinstatement as above but without any break in seniority or service.

The second condition requires further explanation. The board was informed that reservations agents do not handle money and they encounter customers solely by telephone. Therefore, the grievor could be employed without placing undue concern on the employer.

The facts are not in dispute. The grievor has been an employee of Air Canada since October 15, 1963. He has been employed as a passenger agent and as a reservations agent in St. John's, both downtown and at the airport. In 1979 he was employed as a passenger agent at the St. John's airport. In this position he had face to face contact with the travelling public. As such, he received money from passengers in payment of air fares and excess baggage. On two occasions he failed to account to Air Canada for payments for excess baggage. These amounts were $8.50 and $10.00 respectively and the occasions were November 18, 1979 and December 2, 1979. The grievor admitted to the offences when questioned by the R.C.M.P. and he was subsequently convicted in Provincial Court on March 27, 1980. The court awarded a "conditional discharge" providing the grievor keep the peace and be of good behaviour for a period of one year.

The grievor testified that he could not understand why he had done "such a stupid thing". He is married and owns his own home which is mortgage free. He informed the board that he has no outstanding debts.

During the course of the evidence it was learned that certain cash shortages had been occurring at the airport during the summer of 1979. One day in September, 1979, the grievor experienced a $200 cash shortage. For some reason he decided to make up the shortage out of his own pocket although he was aware that company policy did not require him to do so. He admitted under cross-examination that his motive in taking the $18.50 may have been a desire to obtain repayment of the $200.00.

The grievor stated that he has undergone psychiatric treatment in an effort to learn why he took the money. He also stated that he has felt ashamed and for a long time after the incident could not face his friends in church or elsewhere.

On the day of his conviction in Provincial Court, he was contacted by a local travel agency and was offered a position, which he accepted, and where he is presently employed.

Mr. Caley, counsel for the union, led evidence to show that the grievor had been a good employee during the past fifteen years. Indeed, a Mr. Jack Fardy testified that he had offered to accept the grievor into his department when he heard of the matter. Mr. Fardy retired from Air Canada on February 28, 1981 as reservations and sales office Manager after twenty-five years of employment with Air Canada. The employer decided not to accept Mr. Fardy's offer.

Counsel for both parties submitted a number of arbitration decisions in support of their respective positions. Mr. Caley also relied on article 17.05 which reads:

> The arbitrator or arbitration board shall have the authority to render any decision that they consider just and equitable.

Moreover, he referred us to the *Canada Labour Code* R.S.C. 1970 c. L-1 as amended 1977-78, c. 27 s. 55, s. 157 which enables an arbitration board to substitute a penalty which is "just and reasonable in the circumstances".

Mr. Caley cited twenty-four arbitration decisions in support of his position that the grievor ought to be reinstated. He placed considerable reliance on Arbitrator Adams' comments in *Phillips Cables Ltd. & Int'l Electrical Workers* 6 L.A.C. (2d) 35 wherein he commented that while deterrence is extremely important, consideration ought to be given to mitigating factors to determine whether or not an employee can be salvaged. Mr. Adams then proceeded to quote from *The Steel Equipment Co. Ltd.*, (14 L.A.C. 356) and list the ten points outlined in that decision. Mr. Caley also relied on *Fiberglas Canada Limited and Amalgamated Clothing and Textile Workers*, an unreported decision of G.J. Brandt, February 21, 1980 where he states at pp 17 and 18,

> A reading of this more recent line of authority would tend to indicate that arbitrators no longer take at face value the claim that an employee who has committed an act of theft or dishonesty is, by virtue of that fact alone, incapable of rehabilitation or of restoring the element of trust that must exist between himself and his employer. It is that view which seems to have lain at the base of some of the earlier cases where discharge for theft was almost always upheld except in very extreme cases. It now appears to be the case that arbitrators are willing to examine closely the facts of each particular case of theft with a view to determining whether or not there may be some circumstances which would justify a reinstatement.
>
> In general the kinds of mitigating factors which are looked at are the value of the goods stolen, the grievor's work record and the length of seniority. It is difficult to see why the value of the property stolen should have any bearing on this issue. An act of theft is an act of theft and, absent other considerations, should be viewed seriously. (However, where it can be demonstrated that an employee's work record and seniority have, in the past, given no cause for concern as to his satisfactory nature as an employee and, where it would appear that the act in question was an isolated one, there would appear to be good reason for concluding that such an employee stands a good prospect of re-establishing himself as a credible and trustworthy employee in the eyes of his employer).

Mr. Mitchell, counsel for the employer, also supplied the board with a number of prior arbitration decisions in support of his position that the grievor ought not be reinstated. He attempted to distinguish the cases cited by the union on the basis that they involved petty theft consisting of items that had very little value. More importantly, he urged the board to take cognizance of the fact that they almost invariably did not involve employees who held positions of trust and considerable responsibility. Moreover, this was not an isolated incident. Rather, it was premeditated. The grievor had taken the money on two separate occasions which revealed a determined and continuing state of mind to steal from the employer.

Mr. Mitchell pressed the grievor during cross-examination on the issue of whether or not the grievor had ever taken money at other times than the two known ones. A good deal of discussion centered around a letter from the grievor's psychiatrist (part of exhibit 4) which reads in part "During the year prior to my seeing him there were apparently shortages and Mr. Sparkes readily admitted that some of this money at least he had taken". The grievor explained that the letter was handed to the employer in a sealed envelope and he did not have an opportunity to read it beforehand. In his view the doctor was mistaken or had misconstrued what the grievor had told him. He further explained that he would have gone back to the doctor to have the letter reworded had he known its contents. In any event, Mr. Mitchell pursued the theme that the grievor's actions had not been a spur of the moment happening but instead had been a planned undertaking. Accordingly, as he held a position of trust and responsibility the employer was fully justified in dismissing him because he had broken that trust. Finally, he argued that there does not exist any mitigating circumstances. The grievor is presently employed elsewhere. He has no debts and has not suffered except in a personal fashion for his wrongdoing.

The board is of the opinion that the employer had just cause in dismissing the grievor. We agree with Mr. Mitchell that the grievor occupied a position of trust whereby he handled money belonging to the employer. When he misappropriated the employer's money to himself he broke that trust which gave the employer the necessary just cause to dismiss him. Furthermore, the position which he occupied gave him plenty of opportunity to misappropriate funds which is difficult if not impossible for the employer to oversee. In this connection the grievor is placed in a similar situation as the grievor in another arbitration case which involved the same employer (but a different union — the International Association of Machinists and Aerospace Workers). The grievor in the case was named Sowerby and the award was dated October 2, 1979.

In that decision the present chairman stated:

> What about the nature of the employee's job. He receives very little direct supervision. He travels around the airport in one of the employer's vehicles transporting company property. He must be trusted completely by the employer to properly carry out his duties without concern that he will misappropriate property. Has the grievor misplaced that trust to the extent that the employment relationship should be severed? In view of the grievor's admitted awareness of the employer's policy concerning theft before he committed the offence and the seriousness that the employer places on theft of its property, I am driven to the conclusion that the employer had just cause in dismissing the grievor.

The dismissal was upheld in that case. It was found that the theft was not a spur of the moment thing and that because of the nature of the grievor's duties he could not be closely supervised and therefore the employer would be required to continue to place a great deal of trust in him. In those circumstances the chairman in the instant situation refused to disturb the decision of the employer.

The instant situation is similar to the Sowerby award in many respects. Both grievors were aware of the employer's policy that theft from the employer means dismissal. Sowerby had a previously unblemished record. The grievor in the instant situation received a written reprimand in September, 1975 when he boarded two contingent passengers on an aircraft who had lower priority than other contingent passengers. Both grievors have been found to have committed premeditated acts of theft. The grievor in the instant case has sixteen years of service whereas Mr. Sowerby had approximately six.

Unlike the Sowerby case the union has proposed several conditions to the grievor's reinstatement. Ought such a proposal be given serious consideration?

• • •

Questions

1 Do you think that Mr. Ryan has already suffered enough for the theft that he has committed?

2 If you were chairing the arbitration board in this case, would you consider seriously the proposition put forward by the grievor's union? Elaborate.

3 If you were chairing the arbitration board, would you reinstate Mr. Ryan on the conditions suggested by his union? Elaborate fully.

4 Assume that you reinstated Mr. Ryan on the terms suggested in the case, would you add any additional conditions to his reinstatement? Elaborate.

5 Assume that you reinstated Mr. Ryan on the terms suggested in the case and further assume that five years from the date of your award an opportunity for promotion presented itself. Would Mr. Ryan be eligible for consideration for promotion? Elaborate fully.

6 Again assume that you reinstated Mr. Ryan. Would you wish to add any further stipulations to deal with situations such as the one suggested in question five above? Elaborate fully.

Alleged Falsification of a Time Card —
The J. Ward Case*

In the Matter of an Arbitration
Between:
Western Airlines, hereafter referred to as the "Employer"
And:
Brotherhood of Railway and Airline Clerks, Canada
(on behalf of J. Ward and hereafter referred to as the "Union")

This proceeding occurred pursuant to Section 36 of the Collective Agreement between the parties. The parties agreed that the Board was properly constituted to hear the case and that the issue before the Board was as follows:

> Was the termination of [the employment of] the grievor, J. Ward, for just cause? If not, what shall be the remedy?

Specifically, the offence for which the grievor was discharged was the alleged falsification of his time card August 28, 1978. The parties agreed to waive the time limits for issuing an award in the collective agreement.

Evidence presented by the Employer indicated that the Grievor arrived late at his work station, the passenger check-in counter in the Vancouver International Airport August 28. His supervisor, Mr. Goodwin, testified that Mr. Ward's starting time that day was 8:00 a.m., and that he arrived between 8:20 and 8:25. Mr. Waugh, who was in operations August 28, saw the Grievor enter the building at 8:10 a.m.; a few minutes later Mr. Ward entered the operations office, and the two talked for 7 or 8 minutes. Because Mr. Ward arrived late, passengers were not checked in at the normal rate. The flight scheduled to depart at 8:50 a.m. was late, although other factors may have caused the delay. Delayed departures are not uncommon in August.

Later that morning, when he was in the operations area, Mr. Goodwin checked Mr. Ward's time card. The card had the single digit "8" in the box for punching in August 28. The time clock normally imprints one or more digits for the hour, followed by a decimal, a digit to indicate tenths of an hour, plus one or more letters corresponding to the day of the week. Mr. Waugh also testified that the time card contained only an "8" later that morning. He notified Mr. Gordon, the Assistant Manager for the station, who made a photocopy of the card, date stamped the copy, and returned the card to its normal position. The next day Mr. Gordon examined the time card and found it contained the notation "8.AM" for August 28, i.e. showing that Mr. Ward had punched in at 8:00 a.m. There was no mark on the card for

---

* Permission to use this case was granted by Labour Canada. Minor deletions were made by the author for the purposes of this book and all names changed to prevent embarrassment to the individuals involved.

punching out that day. Again he made a copy of the card and dated the copy. Examples of both copies were presented to the Board as evidence. On August 29 Mr. Gordon commenced disciplinary action that ended in the Grievor's discharge. According to Mr. Gordon, the Employer regards falsification of time cards as a grave matter. The Employer's publication "You and Your Job," distributed to employees, warns that altering a time card is "a serious offense and is considered cause for dismissal." An excerpt from the publication, plus a management bulletin containing similar language, were posted in the operations area in June 1978. There were marks opposite Mr. Ward's name on the briefing sheet which might have been his initials, indicating that he had read the notice.

The parties recently negotiated their first collective agreement for the Vancouver station, and this case was the first example of an employee having been charged with falsification of a time card. Management witnesses could recall no such incidents prior to certification of the Union. Problems with time cards improperly filled in have arisen from time to time.

The Union based its case on Mr. Ward's testimony, the burden of proof on the Employer, and management's failure to comply with provisions of the grievance procedure.

Mr. Ward stated he arrived on time August 28 and punched in at 8:00 a.m., changed into his uniform in the locker room, and proceeded to his work station. He admitted that he might have arrived at his work station five or ten minutes late. He completed his shift, but forgot to punch out at the end of the day. Mr. Ward denied altering the time card in any way. When he received a disciplinary letter August 29, Mr. Gordon refused to elaborate on the specifics of the charge against him. The letter referred to "falsification of company records — your time card," and the Grievor assumed it referred to his failure to punch out on August 28. On August 29 or soon thereafter, the Union representative assisting him with his grievance explained the specific offense with which he was charged.

The Union pointed to Section 33B of the Collective Agreement which states: "an employee charged with an offense . . . shall be furnished with a letter . . . stating the precise charge against him. . . ." According to the Union, the Employer's letter of August 29 failed to meet this requirement, thereby denying the Grievor natural justice in the disciplinary hearing that followed.

In analyzing this case, the Union's procedural argument is an appropriate starting point. The contract requires statement of a "precise charge" against an employee in the Employer's letter. The letter referred to "falsification" of a time card. To have amplified on that statement might have required several paragraphs, given the problem of describing the time card before and after the alleged alteration of the original entry. Such amplification would have contained primarily the facts of the incident leading to the charge. Moreover, the Employer supplied the Union with the full facts of the case shortly after the letter was issued. By the Union's admission, the purpose of Section 33B is to ensure than an employee knows the charges against him when preparing his defense. Mr. Ward had the relevant facts of the charges well before the hearing. Therefore, we rule that the Employer fulfilled the requirements of Section 33B.

The Union also asserted that the Employer had to establish the basic facts on which the action was based. In this category of case, where an employee's morality has been attacked, guilt must be demonstrated beyond reasonable doubt. The Union claim raises the issue of the standard of proof, inevitably a question to be addressed in a case of alleged misconduct. The general principle applied is summarized by Brown and Beatty, *Canadian Labour Arbitration* at pp.289-291. In general, arbitrators require the employer to prove its case on "the balance of probabilities." They note, "at one time where the alleged misconduct might have involved a criminal offense, some arbitrators required the employer to prove beyond a reasonable doubt, that is clearly no longer the prevailing principle" (Ibid. at p. 290). Some arbitrators hold that the balance of probabilities is the appropriate standard, though many others demand a higher standard, but still less than the criminal burden of proof. In the latter case, the standard required is more stringent the more serious the alleged misconduct. "Thus, it is said that an allegation of criminal misconduct must be proven by 'clear evidence' or a standard of 'reasonable probability'" (Ibid. at p. 291).

In this case, criminal conduct was not alleged. Many of the decisions cited by Brown and Beatty as justifying a standard of proof substantially higher than the civil burden dealt with employee theft of company property, or similar offenses. Although the Employer asserted that the Grievor's intent was dishonest, there was no allegation of material or monetary loss. Therefore, the appropriate standard of proof in this case is the balance of probabilities.

Using this standard, we find that the Grievor did falsify his time card. The Employer presented documentary evidence that someone altered the time card, an assertion the Union admitted. Both Mr. Goodwin and Mr. Waugh gave testimony consistent with Mr. Ward arriving at his work station between 8:20 and 8:25. Because of their jobs, both witnesses must be aware of the time of day, so their evidence has special weight. We prefer their testimony to that of Mr. Ward when he claimed to have arrived at the time clock by 8:00. While the case against Mr. Ward is circumstantial, his own account of the events of August 28 was confused. We find no other probable explanation for the changes in the time card except action by Mr. Ward.

This finding raises the question of the appropriate penalty. Counsel for each party submitted copies of past arbitration awards by employees of the Employer involving falsification of time cards. All of the cases were from the United States. Clearly, prior decisions within the Employer deserve careful consideration by this Board. But the incident occurred in Canada, and this proceeding was governed by the Canada Labour Code, so due consideration must be given to Canadian practice.

A review of the cases heard elsewhere in the Employer's system reveals that discharges for falsification of time cards is not the norm. In four cases

(Rockey, Letourneau, Anderson, and Orcutt) the arbitrator ruled that the Employer had not demonstrated guilt beyond a reasonable doubt, and the grievors were found guilty of some infraction that warranted discipline. In two cases (Farias and McSwain), discharges were upheld in light of the grievor's past record. In the Farias case, the arbitrator stated,

> While this referee would find it difficult to support discharges solely on the issue of questionable falsification of a time card, when it is related to a clear attempt to avoid potential discharge for absence and tardiness and when there is no question the employee did falsify his time card, then just cause for discharge would seem to be well established.

In the McSwain case, the grievor's discharge was upheld partly because of three previous offenses.

The Employer's experience seems typical in American arbitral jurisprudence. In a thoroughly researched decision, involving falsification of a time card, Arbitrator Williams in *Park'N Fly of Texas and International Association of Machinists* (1975) 64 L.A. 1009 at 1013, wrote, "It is clear that arbitrators generally uphold discipline in cases similar to the subject one, but tend to consider discharge, demotion, etc. as too severe." In *National Airlines and International Association of Machinists* (1973) 61 L.D. 681 (Cushman), the arbitrator upheld the discharge of an employee who falsified his time card for 1 hour 45 minutes in light of his very poor work record.

Few similar cases seem to have been decided in Canada. Falsification of time cards is typically related to piece rates, so the offense implies an attempt to secure payment for work not performed. Such cases raise issues of theft and criminal conduct mentioned earlier, but which are absent here (See *United Automobile Workers, Local 127 and Ontario Steel Products Ltd.* (1962) 13 LAC 197 (Beardall). In one case an employee signed his time sheet for a full shift, even though the arbitrator concluded he had arrived late, and the award sustained the penalty of demotion. (*International Chemical Workers, Local 721 and Brockville Chemical Industries* (1971) 23 LAC 336 (Shime).)

In assessing a penalty for such an offense, several criteria seem appropriate. Dishonesty by an employee of any variety is a serious offense and should not be treated lightly. The Employer had taken reasonable action to ensure employees knew the gravity of the offense. But the degree of trust in an employee's job should be considered. The employee's work record, seniority, and possible motive are also important. Finally the magnitude of the offense should be considered.

In this case, the Grievor's job does not involve an unusual amount of trust. His arrival and departure are subject to monitoring. He has approximately 2.5 years of seniority, with no record of previous disciplinary action of any type. Beyond concealing his negligent arrival, he had no motive to deceive the Employer. Finally, his offense did not entail a claim for a substantial amount of money, perhaps $2.00.

· · ·

Questions

1 What procedural rules did the arbitration board dispose of in the first paragraph of the case?
2 In your view, did the charge "falsification of company records—your time card" meet the requirement of Section 33B of the collective agreement?
3 What standard of proof was the employer required to provide? Elaborate.
4 Would you as the arbitrator, uphold the discharge in this case or would you change the penalty? Be specific and logical in your answer.

Determining Overtime Pay Aboard Ship — The Paton Case*

The Public Service Staff Relations Act
Before the Public Service Staff Relations Board
Between:
David W. Paton, Grievor
And:
Treasury Board (Fisheries and Oceans), Employer

Decision

Mr. David Paton is employed with the Department of Fisheries and Oceans as a Chemistry Technologist, and is classified as an EG-ESS-6. Mr. Paton's normal worksite is the Institute of Ocean Sciences in Sydney, British Columbia; where his usual hours of work are from 8:30 to 4:30, Monday through Friday. From time to time, Mr. Paton is required to work aboard sea-going vessels. It was one of these assignments beginning on October 18, 1987, which gave rise to the grievance which is the subject of this reference to adjudication.

Upon being advised that he was to engage in a field trip aboard the C.S.S. JOHN P. TULLY, Mr. Paton advised his supervisor that he intended to, in effect, challenge the employer's practice of not paying employees in his bargaining unit for time spent aboard ship when they are not performing duties specified by the employer. In response, Mr. Jeff Thompson, his immediate supervisor, presented him with a memo (Exhibit G-3) entitled "Duties Aboard the C.S.S. TULLY, October 19-24, 1987." As the title indicates, the

---

* Permission to use this case was granted by the Public Service Staff Relations Board. Minor deletions were made by the author for the purposes of this book and all names changed to prevent embarrassment to the individuals involved.

immediate purpose of the memo was to "define your duties and overtime requirements for the period noted above." It is evident that the longer term purpose of the memorandum was to clearly set out the employer's position in what both parties expected would be a test case concerning the interpretation and application of clause 22.09 of the Engineering and Scientific Support Collective Agreement (Code 405/86, expiring December 21, 1987). To this end, the memorandum also states the following, under the subtitle "Hours of Work:"

> While in the Operations area, you will be required to work a normal 7.5 h day, beginning normally at 0800 h. Overtime may be required to complete dissections on October 22 and 23. You are authorized to utilize the following overtime.
>
> Operations area: 25 hrs. (extended time, based on 100 percent taken as cash)
> 19 hours (based on 75 percent cash; 25 percent CTO)
> Saturday, Oct. 24: 18 hrs. (at 1½ times (x) 12 hrs)
> (Travel status begins approx. 1200, terminates 2000)
> Total overtime at 100 percent cash = 43 hrs.
> At 75 percent cash = 37 hrs.

Clause 22.09 of the collective agreement provides as follows:

> 22.09 Each fifteen (15) minute period of overtime shall be compensated for at the following rates:
> (a) time and one-half (1½), except as provided for in clause 22.09 (b);
> (b) double (2) time for all hours of overtime worked in excess of seven and one-half (7½) consecutive hours of overtime in any contiguous period, and for all hours worked on the second or subsequent day of rest. Second or subsequent day of rest means the second or subsequent day in an unbroken series of consecutive and contiguous calendar days of rest.

The grievor duly reported for work on the C.S.S. TULLY on October 18, 1987 and performed a number of functions and assignments in accordance with the usual duties of a chemistry technologist aboard ship. At the request of Mr. Thompson, as stated in the memo noted above, Mr. Paton prepared a log (Exhibit G-5) outlining in detail his activities from Sunday, October 18 when he left his residence to travel to the TULLY until the following Sunday, October 25 when he returned to his residence. Mr. Paton also submitted a form entitled "Extra Duty Pay and Shift Work Report" (Exhibit G-4) which constituted his claim for overtime and is in fact the essential subject matter of this grievance. The disputed hours of work are in respect of the balance of the day (that is, the full 24 hour period), except for his normal 7½ hour shift. While the grievor has not been paid for any of the overtime which he had claimed for, the employer had agreed at the first level of the grievance procedure that the grievor was entitled to overtime pay in respect of certain hours claimed for 18/12/87, and 24/10/87, as well as all hours claimed for 25/10/87.

The grievor stated that what is in dispute here was the payment of overtime of 7½ hours following his normal hours of work at the rate of time and one half, and 8½ hours at double time following the first overtime. In respect of October 24, 1987, the employer accepts that the grievor was entitled to two hours at double time. However, in keeping with his principal submission, it is Mr. Paton's contention that he is entitled to ten hours at double time.

In his testimony, the grievor outlined his activities during the period in question, none of which are not in dispute. On Monday, October 19, the ship got underway with the grievor on board; the grievor spent a half-hour from midnight of that day securing his equipment (it should be noted that the employer's representative acknowledges that this period of time should be compensated at overtime rates of time and one half). The grievor had no specific duties to perform for the balance of that day.

On Tuesday, October 20, the ship continued to be in transit; the grievor had no prescribed duties at that time; however, he would check periodically to ensure that the equipment was secure.

On Wednesday, October 21, the ship reached the Operations area at 8:30 a.m.; at 10:00 a.m. the grievor, on his own initiative, assisted crew members of other ships that were in the area; the grievor stated that this was not part of his assigned duties.

On October 22, aside from his assigned duties, the grievor spent approximately three hours assisting other persons in the area who are not employed by the Department of Fisheries and Oceans; this task was not part of the grievor's assigned duties. On Friday, October 23, the grievor performed his assigned duties, in addition to which he did some "voluntary work" assisting other personnel. On Saturday, October 24, the grievor was supposed to be picked up by charter plane and taken to Prince Rupert. The grievor testified that the plane was delayed and did not arrive until 16:30 hrs. He then left on the charter plane, arriving at Prince Rupert at 17:30 hrs. From there he checked in at a hotel at 18:00 hrs.

There is no dispute by the employer as to the overtime claimed for Sunday, October 25.

The grievor described the conditions to which he was subject during his spare time on board ship. He indicated that his spare time activities were limited by his confinement on the ship, as well as being subject to the rules posted by the Master of the ship, which are referred to as the ship's Standing Orders. According to the grievor, these orders dictate who can associate with whom on board ship. He also stated that the rules stipulate when certain activities could be conducted, for example when the staff could watch television.

In cross-examination, Mr. Paton identified Exhibit E-1, a job description for his position effective December 22, 1987. The grievor acknowledged that the duties described therein fairly represented his responsibilities at the relevant period of time. His attention was directed to page 5, paragraph 6 which referred to the carrying out of field surveys on board ships.

The grievor responded that at the time of the period of his stay on board the TULLY, he was president of his union local. He noted also that he had told his immediate supervisor, Mr. Thompson, that he was familiar with the PSSRB decision in *Falconer* and wanted to test the effect of the case. Mr. Paton stated that Mr. Thompson said he disagreed with Mr. Paton's interpretation of the effect of this decision, and as a consequence Mr. Thompson had prepared Exhibit B-3, the memorandum outlining his assigned duties aboard the TULLY.

Mr. Paton acknowledged in cross-examination that he did not do any assigned work beyond his normal 7½ hour shift on any of the days in question. He stated that any other work activities which he performed were for the purpose of keeping himself busy in order to avoid boredom. He stated that the TULLY is a 230 foot vessel, and that he shared a cabin with another scientist. The cabin had no television and he could not obtain radio reception. There was a video cassette recorder in the lounge with cassettes; however, the captain imposed certain restrictions as to when the VCR could be utilized. He also acknowledged that there was a library and a modest gymnasium on board, with a sauna.

The employer called no evidence.

Argument

On behalf of the grievor, Ms. Rossignol submitted that the main issue in this matter is what constitutes work. In order to claim overtime pursuant to clause 22.09 of the pertinent agreement, it must be established that the employee had worked. To make this determination, it is necessary to look at all the relevant facts including the purpose of the mission, which in this instance was to conduct certain experiments. In her submission, all the time spent by the grievor on this trip was part of his mission. Accordingly, under clause 22.09 each fifteen minute period of overtime is compensable, the first 7½ hours at straight time, the next 7½ hours at time and one half, and the balance of the day is compensable at double time. Reference was made to the Board decision in *Falconer et al* (Board file 166-2-15281, 15336), which decision was upheld by the Federal Court of Appeal, Court file no. A-417-86. Ms. Rossignol noted that the *Falconer* decision involved the same provisions in an agreement governing the same bargaining unit. Neither the instant agreement nor the agreement in the *Falconer* decision had a provision respecting rest time. She noted that in *Falconer*, the grievors had spare time while on board ship when they could relax, but they were of course unable to leave the work site. Accordingly, former Chairman Brown concluded that all their time aboard ship constituted work time, and consequently, it was compensable at overtime rates. The essence of this decision was that when an employee is authorized to go aboard ship for an extended period of time, this constitutes authorized hours of work and therefore the employer is obliged to pay for all hours spent on board ship. An identical decision of the Board in *O'Leary and Humphreys* (Board file no. 166-2-15199) was also upheld by the Court of Appeal, Court file no. A-416-86.

Ms. Rossignol also referred to the *Duggan* decision (Board file no. 166-2-15033) in which the adjudicator interpreted the identical language in the PM collective agreement, and concluded that all time necessary to complete an assigned task constituted work. The Federal Court of Appeal relied on the *Duggan* decision in overturning the *Apesland* decision, the Court concluding that "the character of the entire trip was determined by its purpose" (Court file no. A-669-87). Finally, she cited the decision of *Kerr et al v. Canada* [1985] 59

N.R. 313 where according to Ms. Rossignol, the Court found that where an employee is "captive," that is, cannot leave the work site, then that period of time is considered as work, pursuant to the provisions of the agreement in that case which is again similar to the agreement in the instant case.

Counsel for the employer submitted that the grievor is seeking premium pay in respect of periods of time when he is not performing duties on behalf of the employer. He maintained that in essence the grievor's position is that when the parties entered into a negotiated agreement, it was agreed that employees would be paid round the clock when they are aboard ship. However, the collective agreement makes it clear that the parties did not intend that premium pay should be paid for time not worked while on board ship. Thus clause M-2.01 (O) which defines "overtime" in the Master Agreement between the Public Service Alliance and the Employer refers to "authorized work." In this instance, the memorandum from Mr. Thompson specifically provided what work is authorized and no other overtime work was expressly or impliedly authorized.

Article 28 of the master agreement which deals with travelling time provides for specific compensation for employees who are required to travel. Article M-28.05 excludes the application of Article 28 when an employee is on, for example, a ship. Thus, Article 28.05(b) refers to compensation for "pay for actual hours worked." That is, where an employee is required to perform a tour of duty on a vessel, he gets paid for his normal working day or "actual hours worked" where he puts in overtime. In Mr. Newman's submission, this requires that the employee be compensated for assigned work only, and not for all time spent on a vessel. Mr. Newman maintains that the *Falconer* and *O'Leary* decisions never addressed this particular aspect. By virtue of Article M-28, the parties set out a complete code of remuneration in respect of such situations which the grievor had found himself in. The grievor knew what his hours of work would be in advance and he knew what were the parameters of any overtime work. This situation has been addressed definitively in the master agreement and under the provisions of that agreement, the grievor is not entitled to the overtime which he is claiming.

Mr. Newman further maintained that the Court of Appeal in the *Falconer* decision relied on the facts of that particular case. The Court did not endorse Mr. Brown's interpretation of Article 22.09 in general terms. He also submitted that the *Falconer* and *O'Leary* cases are distinguishable on their facts. He referred to page 7 of the *Falconer* decision where reference is made to the fact that the grievor "felt" he had to leave it (that is, his equipment) in case he was called upon during the night to do some further readings." In Mr. Newman's view, this demonstrates that the grievors were in effect psychologically "captive" by their work, in contrast to Mr. Paton who did not have to be concerned about performing his assigned duties during his rest periods. He also referred to page 9 of this decision which refers to the base standing orders which appear to have at least impliedly authorized the employees to consider themselves as being at work while on the vessel. Based on these facts, it was open to Chairman Brown to find that there was an understanding that the employees may consider themselves at work while on the vessel.

Mr. Newman noted that in the *Kerr* decision (supra), the Court emphasized that there was specific contract language that authorized the payment of overtime in the circumstances described therein. Furthermore, in that case the employees were on call and were again, psychologically at least, subject to the employer's authority. He attempted to distinguish the decision of the Court of Appeal in *Apesland* (supra) on the basis that in that case the travel was intimately bound up with the work to be performed, that is the escort duty; such is not the case here.

In support of his position, Mr. Newman cited *Slaney and Williams* (Board file no. 166-2-17761 and 17762) where the grievance was upheld by the adjudicator because the grievors could be called upon to work on a twelve-hour a day basis. Likewise, in the Board decision in *Isnor and Moors* (Board file no. 166-2-16622), the Board found in favour of the grievor because "they had to be available, ready and fit to work (p. 12)."

In conclusion, Mr. Newman submitted that the case law had to be reviewed in light of their particular facts. He submitted that it is apparent, in that light, that they do not stand for the proposition that once an employee is aboard ship, he is entitled to pay for 24 hours a day. A person is no more captive on a ship than in, for example, Prince Rupert; an employee is only captive when he is called upon by the employer to perform duties.

In reply, Ms. Rossignol stated that *Isnor and Moors* decision is of no relevance to the instant case, the adjudicator in that decision having specifically noted that, unlike the EG agreement, there was a specific provision for compensation for unworked hours while aboard vessels. Ms. Rossignol also submitted that travel time, as understood in the master agreement, refers to circumstances where, for example, an employee is leaving home to proceed to a ship; when an employee is actually on a ship for a specific purpose, this is not travel time. As in *Apesland*, travel on board ship is an integral part in the employee's duties, and therefore is considered as time worked. Accordingly, Article 28.05(b) does not apply since the employee is considered to be working. She further submitted that the facts in *Falconer* are not particularly unusual. It is clear in that case that the adjudicator came to the factual conclusion that the grievors were not on call but could relax on board ship, the same situation which pertains here.

Reasons For Decision

There is no dispute as to the facts in this case. The grievor was directed to report to a vessel and perform certain duties while on board this vessel. The grievor has admitted that the tasks which he was specifically assigned to do had been completed during his normal working shift of $7^1/2$ hour's duration. It is also clear that the grievor was not in a position to leave the vessel during the period in question, and as a result, his range of activities was necessarily limited, even during those hours when he was not performing the tasks to which he was assigned.

• • •

Questions

1 This case, which is referred to as a test case, may also be given another title. What is the other title?

2 Why do you suppose that Mr. Thompson gave Mr. Paton a memo regarding "Hours of Work"?

3 If it were general practice for managers to issue "hours of work" memos for various situations, what kinds of problems might this lead to? Elaborate. Would you expect to find consistency or inconsistencies in such memos? Elaborate.

4 Clause 22.09 of the collective agreement under which Mr. Paton works specifies what constitutes overtime pay. Do you agree with Mr. Newman, counsel for the employer, that the Master Agreement between the Public Service Alliance and the Employer refers to situations such as those in which Mr. Paton finds himself? Elaborate.

5 If you were the adjudicator in this case, would you award Mr. Paton overtime pay as prescribed by Mr. Thompson or would you award time and a half for the first 7½ hours of overtime and double time for the balance of the day as requested by Mr. Paton? Elaborate.

6 Do you feel that you would have the authority to prescribe some other remedy? Elaborate.

7 What do you suggest should be done to clarify what seems to be an ambiguous situation for granting overtime to persons in situations such as that of Mr. Paton? Elaborate.

Indecisiveness in Applying a Disciplinary Penalty — The T. Smith Case*

Public Service Staff Relations Act
Before the Public Service Staff Relations Board
Between:
T. Smith, Grievor,
And:
Treasury Board (Post Office Department), Employer

Mr. T. Smith filed a grievance under date of September 16, 1978 reading:

> I grieve that I am being disciplined without just cause, resulting in my being suspended. Commencing August 28, 1978. Corrective Action Requested: Full redress.

* Permission to use this case was granted by the Public Service Staff Relations Board. Minor deletions were made by the author for the purposes of this book and all names changed to prevent embarrassment to the individuals involved.

The grounds relied upon by the employer for the suspension of the grievor are set out in a letter of September 1, 1978 and signed by the Postmaster A. Jones.

> The purpose of this letter is to advise you that you are being suspended from duty for a period of twenty (20) working days from 6:35 A.M. August 28th, 1978 to 3:05 P.M. September 25th, 1978.
>
> The reason for this suspension is your act of major misconduct on Friday, August 18th, 1978 in that you did physically assault P.O. Sup 1, J. McGough in the Letter Carrier Section.
>
> I have had the opportunity to review the facts and the situation again as well as revised thinking on corrective discipline in this Region. In view of this I have decided that this suspension of twenty (20) days is appropriate.
>
> Further, the intention of this revised suspension is to impress upon you the serious nature of these actions. You chose not to exercise the options open to you when you observed the supervisor activity that you disagreed with. Instead, you chose to physically abuse the supervisor. Such actions cannot and will not be tolerated.
>
> Any further occurrences will result in recommendation to discharge you from the service. You have the right to the grievance process.

Mr. Smith has been employed in the Sarnia Post Office for a period of 18 years and is presently classified as a Letter Carrier (PO-3). He is also president of the Sarnia Local of the Letter Carriers' Union of Canada.

Counsel for the employer called as witnesses J. McGough, a Cell Supervisor (Supervisor 1); P. Jay, a Letter Carrier Coordinator, (Supervisor 3); and T. McKenzie (Operations Supervisor, Days). In addition, counsel called but did not examine J. Burke, a Letter Carrier, who on August 18 was an Acting Supervisor. Mr. Burke was made available for cross-examination by the representative of the grievor but no cross-examination was undertaken.

The representative of the grievor called T. Smith and a witness, W. Clarke, also a Letter Carrier (PO-5). Notwithstanding my having made an order for the exclusion of witnesses at the outset of the hearing, Mr. Clarke did remain in the room during much of Mr. McGough's testimony. His ability to testify was challenged by counsel for the employer. I permitted Mr. Clarke to testify but advised the parties that the weight to be attached to his testimony could be affected by his conduct. As will be noted later, Clarke's testimony was not material to my decision.

At approximately 8:35 a.m. on August 18, 1978, Mr. McGough together with Mr. Burke were at a relay bundle rack (identified as a C 22 rack), situated temporarily in the centre aisle of the letter carrier section of the Sarnia Post Office. Mr. McGough was opening a relay bundle bag on a lower shelf of the C 22 rack when the grievor, in a loud voice spiced with some profanity, challenged Mr. McGough's authority to open relay bags of a letter carrier not under his supervision (Note: but under Mr. Burke's). Following an exchange of opinions, the grievor placed his right hand on the C 22 rack and his right foot on top of the bag, apparently in an attempt to prevent Mr. McGough from continuing his examination. Mr. McGough, in pulling the string that closed the relay bag, jerked the bag out from under the grievor's foot. There is serious disagreement as to what then transpired. The grievor would have me believe that he was momentarily off balance and reached at Mr. McGough for support. Mr. McGough was convinced that the grievor was able to retain his balance and then deliberately seized him. They are, however, in agreement that the grievor did place his arms around Mr. McGough's shoulders and "pushed/pulled" him against the C 22 rack. Mr. McGough may have suffered some contusions as a result of the incident.

The evidence indicates that the grievor was guilty of misconduct in that he was abusive in his remarks and insubordinate in his conduct. On the balance of probabilities I must conclude that the evidence of Mr. McGough as to what occurred with respect to the alleged physical abuse appears more reasonable than the testimony of the grievor. However, I must point out that my decision does not turn on my finding on the conflict of evidence.

Immediately following the incident, in the words of Mr. McGough, "things came to a stop." Asked how he would account for the incident, Mr. McGough testified in cross-examination that "I was the most surprised man in the world."

Mr. Jay, the senior plant supervisor, appeared upon the scene at that point. He testified that he had been in his office when he heard the commotion and had identified the grievor's voice. Upon his arrival he saw Mr. McGough and the grievor facing each other. He demanded, "What the hell is going on" and Mr. McGough replied, "I don't have to take that kind of abuse. I want that man out of the plant." The grievor then interjected to say he wanted Mr. Jay to tell Mr. McGough that it was against procedure for Mr. McGough to touch the relay bags.

Mr. Jay testified that he then told the grievor to "shut up," that he would not tolerate his profane language. The grievor quietened down and Mr. Jay decided to "take the situation from the work floor." He asked the grievor to accompany him to his office and the two left the scene.

In his office Mr. Jay talked with the grievor. The grievor was subdued but still convinced that supervisors could not check relay bags. Mr. Jay stated that he cautioned the grievor as to his "ranting and raving" and suggested to him that he grieve if he felt supervisors could not examine relay bags. Mr. Jay then stated that he told the grievor that, in order to permit him to perform his duties for the day, he would first have to apologize to Mr. McGough. The grievor agreed to apologize.

Mr. McGough, in his evidence, stated that the grievor returned after approximately 15 minutes, with Mr. Jay behind him. The grievor apologized, stating he was sorry "it" had happened. Mr. McGough accepted the apology, the two men shook hands and Mr. McGough said to the grievor, "Okay, Tom, go on and get your work done." Mr. McGough testified that he had looked at Mr. Jay as the two men had approached and had concluded from the look on Mr. Jay's face that "that was what he wanted me to do."

It may be observed that there was no effort on Mr. Jay's part to secure any explanation from Mr. McGough as to what had transpired. For reasons best know to Mr. Jay himself, he elected to make the decision without communicating with Mr. McGough. He was well aware of the latter's conviction that he did not have to take abuse from the grievor and that he wanted the employee out of the plant. Mr. Jay testified that in matters of discipline a supervisor could suspend an employee for the balance of a shift. In that context, Mr. McGough's statement can only be interpreted as meaning that he had wanted the grievor suspended for the balance of the shift.

The grievor's testimony corroborated that of Mr. Jay as to what transpired although he attributed to Mr. McGough more profane language than "man" and "abuse" in Mr. McGough's initial reply to Mr. Jay.

On August 24 the grievor was handed, at his workplace and in the presence of Mr. Jay, a letter from the Postmaster, A. Jones, (Exhibit 8) reading as follows:

> The purpose of this letter is to advise you that you are being suspended from duty for a period of 6 months, from 6:35 AM August 28, 1978 to February 22, 1979, 3:05 PM.
>
> The reason for this suspension is your act of major misconduct on Friday, August 18, 1978, in that you did physically assault P.O. SUP 1, J. McGough in the Letter Carrier Section.
>
> The intention of this suspension is to impress upon you the seriousness of your present conduct. A further occurrence or breach of conduct can result in further disciplinary action, up to and including Discharge [sic].

On September 1, 1978, the grievor received a further letter (Exhibit 11) by registered mail, reading:

> This is to advise you that I hereby withdraw my letter to you of August 24th, 1978 and it will be removed from your personal file.
>
> I will be advising you further on this matter perhaps.

Later on the same day, he was called into the plant to receive the second letter of the same date which led to the filing of the grievance.

According to Mr. Jay, the six-month suspension was withdrawn the same afternoon as it was issued and "pending further investigation" by a review committee including Mr. Jones. That committee had interviewed the grievor and Mr. Jay, as well as others, before determining that a suspension of 20 days was the appropriate discipline. Such testimony is somewhat difficult to reconcile with the exhibits, but little turns on this feature of the evidence. It may be pointed out, moreover, that Mr. Jones has passed away since the issuance of the letter and, consequently, was not available to clarify the matter.

• • •

Questions

1 What do you think of the phrasing of the issues to be adjudicated? Elaborate.
2 How would you assess the Sarnia Post Office's manner of handling this case? Elaborate.
3 Does the Sarnia Post Office have any "policy" in dealing with discipline cases?
4 What do you make of the incident that precipitated this grievance? Elaborate.

5 Should Smith, the grievor and president of the local union, have handled the incident in a different way? Elaborate.

6 Did Mr. Jay do an adequate job in assessing the seriousness of the incident? Elaborate.

7 If you had been the adjudicator, what would you have done when Clarke refused to leave the room?

8 If you had been the adjudicator, what award would you have handed down? Be concise and logical in your reply.

Fighting and the Use of a Knife — The McKay Case*

In the Matter of an Arbitration
Between:
Canadian National Railway Company
And:
Division No. 4, Railway Employees' Department A.F. of L. — C.I.O.
And in the Matter of the Grievance of A. McKay
[The case was heard by a single arbitrator]
A hearing in this matter was held at Montreal on June 13, 1979.

Award

Joint Statement of Issue

On 6 October 1978 Electrician A. McKay was working the 1600 to 2400 hours shift in the passenger car paint shop at Transcona Main Shops. At approximately 2115 hours an altercation occurred involving Mr. McKay and Carman Apprentice R. Jacot.

During the altercation Mr. Ward drew a utility knife from his tool pouch and Mr. Jacot was cut on the little finger of his left hand.

An investigation was conducted and the electrician was discharged for his part in the altercation.

The International Brotherhood of Electrical Workers appealed the company's decision requesting that Mr. Ward be reinstated in his former position and that the discipline assessed be similar to that assessed the other persons involved in the incident.

The company declined the appeal.

---

* Permission to use this case was granted by Labour Canada. Minor deletions were made by the author for purposes of this book and all names changed to prevent embarrassment to the individuals involved.

From the statement of all the employees concerned, it is clear that there was a fight between the grievor and another employee, and that as a result the other employee was injured (his hand was cut) by the grievor's utility knife. What is not clear is the degree of responsibility of the various persons involved.

The grievor did participate in a fight and for that (except in clear cases of self-defence) some discipline would be warranted. He did, as well, draw from his pocket (and from the pouch protecting the blade) his utility knife. The use of any weapon, or the use of a tool as a weapon (even if its blade was very short) is obviously wrong, and for that too the grievor would be subject to discipline. I do not consider that the grievor was deliberately attacked by another employee or employees, so that he was in reasonable fear of serious injury. I do not consider, then, that there was that degree of justification which would excuse resort to such a weapon in the circumstances. Thus, for his participation in the fight, and especially for his use of a knife, I consider that the grievor would be liable to severe discipline.

It is necessary, however, in assessing the penalty imposed on the grievor to consider all the circumstances of the incident, as well as the grievor's disciplinary record. In this case the grievor, an electrician, had relatively short seniority, but had a clear disciplinary record and was regarded as a good employee. He was considered by his supervisor to be cooperative and of a good disposition. It appears that he immigrated to Canada from the Philippines a few years ago, and is of relatively slight build.

On the evening in question the grievor had been speaking to his wife on the telephone, mounted on a pillar just outside a foreman's office, with respect to their sick child. Several other employees, Carmen and Carman Apprentices, were nearby, and one of them was anxious to use the telephone. The group considered that the grievor had been too long on the telephone and began to make noise, sing songs and, it seems, beat on a garbage can. While the evidence is conflicting on the point, it seems most likely that one of the employees, Mr. Jacot, actually threw a garbage can against the pillar on which the telephone was mounted. The grievor thought, perhaps not entirely without reason, that it was aimed at him, although I doubt that it really was.

Finally, the grievor hung up the telephone and some conversation took place between him and Mr. Jacot. Mr. Jacot, a Carman Apprentice, is a younger man than the grievor and is taller and heavier. The accounts of the matter differ, but it appears to me that the most probable account of what occurred is that Mr. Jacot taunted the grievor and invited him to fight. I have no doubt, from the material before me, that whatever the particular incidents may have been, Mr. Jacot was the overall aggressor, and that the grievor's conduct was provoked by the actions of the younger man and by the taunts of his companions. That the grievor was in fact frightened is, I think, the case, although obviously his reaction to the situation was an improper one.

As to the severity of the penalty imposed on the grievor, it is to be noted that there were six persons involved, to some extent, in the incident: the grievor on one hand and five other employees. Of those five, two would appear not to have been substantially implicated, and were not disciplined. Two others were assessed ten and twenty demerits, respectively, for unnecessary harassment of a fellow employee. These penalties would appear to reflect the involvement of the employees concerned. The fifth member of the group which was harassing the grievor was Mr. Jacot, who was assessed thirty demerits and was suspended for ten days. That is a substantial penalty and was, it would appear, merited. None of the penalties just described were appealed and they are not before me for determination.

· · ·

Questions

1 Do you think that the "Joint Statement of Issue" is well presented? Elaborate.
2 What is your assessment of the actions of the "aggressors" and their possible impact on Mr. McKay?
3 Under what specific situations might the use of a knife be permitted? Elaborate.
4 Do you agree with the disciplinary measures given to the other employees? Explain.
5 If you were the arbitrator, would you uphold the company's decision? Elaborate and be as concise and logically consistent as possible.

The Alleged Use of Alcohol Making an Employee Unfit for Work — The D. Curtis Case*

In the Matter of an Arbitration
Between:
Charterways Transportation Limited, Air Terminal Transport Division
(Hereinafter referred to as the Company)
And:
Fuel, Bus, Limousine, Petroleum Drivers and Allied Employees,
Local Union No. 352 (Hereinafter referred to as the Union)
And in the Matter of the Grievance of D. Curtis
[The case was heard by an arbitration board]

* Permission to use this case was granted by Labour Canada. Minor deletions were made by the author for the purposes of this book and all names changed to prevent embarrassment to the individuals involved.

Award

The matter before the board arises out of a grievance (Ex. 2) dated March 17, 1980 concerning the grievor's discharge on March 6, 1980. The parties agreed that the matter was arbitrable and that the board had jurisdiction to deal with the grievance.

The grievor was discharged following an incident which took place on the Company's premises on or about March 5, 1980. The board heard a great deal of evidence concerning the events of March 5th, but there appears to be relatively little dispute about the significant occurrences; therefore, the evidence will be summarized without specific reference to the witnesses who tendered it.

The grievor was scheduled to work on March 5, 1980 from 5:30 p.m. to 2:30 a.m., and had worked the same shift on March 4th. At all material times he was employed as a bus driver by the Company at its Toronto airport operation. On March 5th the grievor also performed some work for Mr. G. Fortier who was engaged in some work on behalf of a trustee in bankruptcy for a Quebec firm. The grievor began work for Mr. Fortier early that morning around 7:30 or so, and finished around 4:00 p.m. The work he performed involved getting a truck started and moved to the Avion Motor Hotel where Mr. Fortier was storing the vehicle. The work was not what one would regard as strenuous, but it did involve the grievor in standing outside for long periods of time while waiting for a tow truck to assist in starting the truck.

Around 4:00 p.m. the grievor met Mr. Fortier at the Avion Hotel and was paid his money for the work involved. Mr. Fortier bought the grievor one drink (a single) and the grievor left glass in hand. Mr. Fortier next saw the grievor some time later, offered him another drink, and was told by the grievor that he had already had another one.

After leaving Mr. Fortier, the grievor apparently joined several of his fellow employees, who had gone to the hotel for a drink and a game of darts after work. The grievor spent enough time with them to play a game of darts and have another drink, probably a double vodka. At around 5:30 p.m. the grievor said that he had to go to work and was told by at least two of his fellow employees at the table that he should not report for work because he was in no fit state to work. They apparently reached this conclusion because they believed the grievor to be unsteady on his feet.

The grievor ignored this warning, left the Hotel, got something to eat at a nearby restaurant and drove to the Company's yard. He punched in around 6:20 p.m. He was observed then by Mr. Ross who was, at all material times, employed as a security guard by the Company. Mr. Ross concluded that the grievor was intoxicated because he was unsteady on his feet, flushed, bleary-eyed, and his speech was slurred.

Sometime before 7:00 p.m. the grievor fell asleep in a chair in the office. Mr. Ross said that at that time, and for some time thereafter, the cleaners were in the office working, but that the grievor was not awakened by any of this noise.

Mr. Ross called the dispatcher at the airport, Mr. Maloney, to inform him that the grievor was in no fit condition to drive and to report on what had happened. Mr. Maloney reported this to Mr. Langley, a supervisor, who drove over to the Company's office and found the grievor "passed out" in a chair in the starter's office. Mr. Langley attempted to awaken the grievor but without success.

Shortly after Mr. Langley's arrival, Mr. West, who was then the operations manager, arrived. He said that the grievor did not wake up even though the phones were ringing in the office and the cleaners were cleaning. Mr. West arranged for the Union steward, Mr. Hyde, to come to the office. Following Mr. Hyde's arrival, Mr. West made some unsuccessful attempts to awaken the grievor by calling his name in a loud voice. Finally, after about the fourth attempt, the grievor woke up.

The preponderance of evidence suggests that he was disoriented and unsteady on his feet. By this time he had been asleep for about an hour or so, despite the activity in the office and the attempts to awaken him.

After the grievor awoke he denied he had anything to drink at all that evening, and also claimed that he had just returned to Toronto after having driven to Trois Rivieres and back. There are various accounts about the grievor's appearance and the presence, or absence, of alcohol on his breath. There is no doubt however that the grievor was, at all times, unfit to drive that night, and that he misled the Union Steward and the Company representatives with his account of his previous activities that day.

The grievor's past record was introduced by the Company. The record shows three disciplinary actions taken by the Company in the two years immediately preceding the incident in question. In October, 1978 the grievor was suspended for two days for punching out early without informing the dispatcher; in November, 1978 he was warned about the number of "book-offs" without reason which he had taken, and in October, 1979 he was warned for negligently causing damage to the Company's gas pump.

The uncontradicted evidence of Mr. Stroud, the general manager, was that the incident of March 5th was regarded as very serious, and that the grievor's record was a very minor consideration. Mr. Stroud also said that before the grievor was discharged, representatives of the Company and the Union met in the grievor's presence, and that the grievor continued to deny that he had consumed any alcohol at all that day. Mr. Stroud said that he also expressed a concern that the grievor had an alcohol problem, but the grievor denied having such a problem.

Evidence was also led about an incident involving another driver named Kelly who had been given a thirty-day suspension shortly before the incident involving the grievor. Mr. Kelly also had reported for work in an unfit condition and was not allowed to drive. Upon learning that he would not be able to drive, Mr. Kelly apparently became quite upset; however, the next day, when he met with Mr. Stroud, Mr. Kelly admitted to having had a couple of drinks, but explained that at the time he was also on medication which had affected him along with the alcohol. Mr. Kelly submitted that he had been foolish, said that it would never happen again and apologized. Mr. Kelly had no disciplinary record at all.

Mr. Stroud explained that he had originally intended to suspend Mr. Kelly for three months, but, after hearing his explanation about the medication and in view of all of the other factors involved, he agreed to reduce the suspension to thirty days. The suspension was accepted by Mr. Kelly.

There is no doubt, indeed it is admitted by the Union, that the grievor reported for work in an unfit condition, and that the Company has just cause to discipline him on that account. It is difficult to determine exactly whether the sole cause for his being so unfit was alcohol or fatigue. It is likely that both contributed to his condition, and it is abundantly clear that he exercised extremely bad judgment both in consuming alcohol when he was fatigued and in reporting for work after he had done this. The Company is in the business of transporting people on public roads, and any accident caused by one of its drivers while driving in an unfit condition could endanger lives as well as property. The Company was unquestionably right when it refused to let the grievor drive that night.

Before dealing with the ultimate disposition of this case, the matters raised in argument concerning the grievor's record and the Kelly case should be dealt with. Article 13.23(a) of the collective agreement deals with the use which can be made of the past disciplinary record.

> . . . . previous offences shall not be taken into consideration except insofar as they relate to the offence under review.

It seems from this that the parties may well have agreed to limit what may be referred to as the "culminating incident doctrine." Accepting that the Company is precluded from relying on the grievor's past record to justify the discharge because no past offences dealt with the use of alcohol or with reporting to work while unfit, the Union's case is not advanced significantly here. As I understood Mr. Stroud, he looked at the grievor's record to determine if there was anything there to help him (i.e., whether it was clear) rather than to determine the appropriate level of penalty. Even agreeing that the record cannot be relied on to help support the discharge, it can surely be looked at by the Company to determine whether it provides a justification for some other penalty short of discharge. The fact that the grievor's record was looked at does not, in these circumstances, provide a reason for varying the penalty.

There are definite parallels between this case and the Kelly situation. Both involve employees who had about five years' seniority at the time, and who reported for work in an unfit condition due, at least in part, to the consumption of alcohol. Mr. Kelly, however, admitted everything to Mr. Stroud, explained what had occurred, and apologized for his actions. The grievor lied about his alcohol consumption, and persisted in this even after confronted with Mr. Stroud's knowledge that other employees had seen him drinking. The grievor also lied concerning his activities on the day and tried to give the impression that fatigue was the sole cause for the incident. It stands to reason that those should be regarded as significant differences between this situation and the treatment given Mr. Kelly. On the other hand, it is significant that Mr. Kelly was not discharged nor was discharge considered in his case, even though both his case and the grievor's concern employees reporting for work in an unfit state due in part, at least, to the consumption of alcohol. Also, in neither case did the employee drive a Company vehicle while unfit to do so.

One must agree completely with the Company's submission that, given the nature of its business and the fact that public safety is at stake, this matter must be regarded extremely seriously and any penalty should reflect the seriousness of the grievor's actions. The similarities with the Kelly case are such that it is difficult to justify discharge without some past record of reporting in an unfit state or alcohol-related misconduct. It is particularly important in this regard that discharge was not considered in the Kelly case, even before the Company learned about the medication he was taking, and before Mr. Kelly's apology.

A significant difference between the two cases, in the Company's view, appeared to be that the grievor was suspected of having a problem with alcohol despite his denials to Mr. Stroud. It is impossible to doubt the sincerity of Mr. Stroud's belief that the grievor has a problem and his wish that the grievor seek some sort of medical assessment; however, on the basis of the evidence presented, it is difficult to determine the basis for Mr. Stroud's conclusion. If one could be persuaded on balance that the grievor may have such a problem, then it would be reasonable to compel him to have a competent medical assessment of his situation. On the other hand, once the allegation has been made and the belief is sincerely held by the Company's officers, the grievor must face the situation that if he is reinstated this cloud of suspicion may remain and may affect his future relationship with his employer. Accordingly, the best way of dealing with this situation may well be to construct a remedy whereby the grievor has the choice of whether to seek a medical assessment; but, that if he so chooses to put the Company's apprehension to rest, then that decision should be taken into account in the penalty.

· · ·

Questions

1 What was the first thing the arbitrator did to ensure his award would not be appealed to a court on procedural grounds? Elaborate.
2 What do you think of the condition of the grievor on the night in question and the roles of all of the people involved to witness his condition?
3 What was the employee's past record and what relevance does it have for this case? Elaborate.

4 Is the general manager in a position to make a judgment as to whether the grievor has an alcohol problem? Elaborate.

5 What impact, if any, would management's decision in the Kelly case have on the present one? Elaborate. Will the apparent fact that Mr. Kelly told the "truth" and Mr. Curtis "lied" make any difference in the disposition of the two cases? Elaborate.

6 What impact does article 13.23(a) have on Mr. Curtis' past record in this case?

7 Do you think that Mr. Curtis should be put in the position of having a choice as to whether or not he should seek medical assessment? Elaborate.

8 If you were the arbitrator in this case, what award would you hand down? Be concise and logically consistent in your reply.

9 Could you envisage a situation under which you would want to be seized of the matter for a specified period of time? Elaborate.

A Select Bibliography

Aaron, B., J. R. Grodin, and J. L. Stern, eds. *Public-Sector Bargaining*. Industrial Relations Research Series. Washington: Bureau of National Affairs, Inc., 1979.

Abella, M. A. *Nationalism, Communism and Canadian Labour*. Toronto: University of Toronto Press, 1979.

Anderson, J., M. Gunderson, and A. Ponak. *Union Management Relations in Canada*, 2nd ed. Don Mills: Addison-Wesley Publishers, 1989.

Arthurs, H. W., D. D. Carter, and H. J. Glasbeek, *Labour Law and Industrial Relations in Canada*. London: Kluwer, 1981. Toronto: Butterworths, 1981.

Auld, D. A. L., L. N. Christofides, R. Swidinsky, and D. A. Wilton. *The Determinants of Negotiated Wage Settlements in Canada (1966-1975): A Microeconomic Analysis*. Ottawa: Anti-Inflation Board, Supply and Services Canada, 1979.

Bacharach, S. B., and E. J. Lawler. *Bargaining: Power, Tactics and Outcomes*. San Francisco: Jossey-Bass Publishers, 1981.

Barbash, J. "Collective Bargaining and the Theory of Conflict." Vol.XVIII, No. 1, *British Journal of Industrial Relations*. March 1980, pp.82-90.

Barbash, J., and K. Barbash. *Theories and Concepts in Comparative Industrial Relations*. Columbia, S.C.: University of South Carolina Press, 1989.

Barrett, B., E. Rhodes, and J. Beishon, eds. *Industrial Relations and the Wider Society*. London: Collier Macmillan/The Open University Press, 1975.

Boivin, J., and G. Guilbault. *Les relations paternelles-syndicales au Québec*. Chicoutimi: Gaëtan Morin, 1982.

Brown, D. J. M., and D. M. Beatty. *Canadian Labour Arbitration*, 2nd. ed. Aurora: Canada Law Book Limited, 1984.

Canadian Industrial Relations. Report of the Task Force on Labour Relations, Chairman H. D. Woods. Ottawa: Privy Council Office, December 1968.

Chamberlain, N. W., and J. W. Kuhn. *Collective Bargaining*, 2nd. ed. New York: McGraw-Hill Book Company, 1965.

Cousineau, J. M., and R. Lacroix, *Wage Determination in Major Collective Agreements in the Private and Public Sectors*. Ottawa: Economic Council of Canada, 1977.

Crispo, John. *International Unionism: A Study in Canadian-American Relations*. Toronto: McGraw-Hill Ryerson Limited, 1967.

_____ *Industrial Democracy in Western Europe: A North American Perspective*. Toronto: McGraw-Hill Ryerson Limited, 1978.

Downie, B. M. *The Behavioural, Economic and Institutional Effect of Compulsory Interest Arbitration.* Economic Council of Canada Discussion Paper 147. Ottawa: December 1979.

Finkelman, J., and S. B. Goldenberg. *Collective Bargaining in the Public Sector: The Federal Experience in Canada.* Montreal: Institute for Research on Public Policy, 1983. 2 vols.

Forsey, E. *Trade Unions in Canada: 1812-1902.* Toronto: University of Toronto Press, 1982.

Freeman, R. B., and J. L. Medoss. *What do Unions Do?* New York: Basic Books, Inc., Publishers, 1984.

Gunderson, M., ed. *Collective Bargaining in the Essential and Public Service Sectors.* Toronto: University of Toronto Press, 1975.

Gunderson, M., and W. C. Riddell. *Labour Market Economics: Theory Evidence and Policy in Canada,* 2nd ed. Toronto: McGraw-Hill Ryerson, 1988.

Healy, J. J., ed. *Creative Collective Bargaining.* Englewood Cliffs: Prentice-Hall Inc., 1965. *Industrial Relations,* Vol. 19, No. 3. California: Fall 1980.

Hébert, G., H. C. Jain, and N. M. Meltz, eds. *The State of the Art in Industrial Relations.* Kingston: Queen's University, Industrial Relations Centre and Toronto: University of Toronto, Centre for Industrial Relations, 1988.

Hébert, G., H. C. Jain, and N. M. Meltz, sous la direction de. *L'Etat de la Discipline en Relations Industrielles au Canada.* Montréal: Université de Montréal, Ecole de Relations Industrielles, Juin 1988, Monographie 19.

Jamieson, S. M. *Industrial Relations in Canada,* 2nd ed. Toronto: Macmillan of Canada, 1973.

Industrial Conflict in Canada. Economic Council of Canada Discussion Paper 142. Ottawa: December 1979. Juris, A., M. Thompson, and W. Daniels, eds. *Industrial Relations in a Decade of Change.* Industrial Relations Research Association Series. Madison: 1985.

Kochan, T. A. *Collective Bargaining and Industrial Relations.* Homewood: Richard D. Irwin, 1980.

Kochan, T. A., ed. *Challenges and Choices Facing American Labor.* Cambridge, Mass.: The MIT Press, 1986.

Kochan, T. A., H. C. Katz, and R. B. McKersie. *The Transformation of American Industrial Relations.* New York: Basic Books, 1986.

Kumar, P., *Canadian Industrial Relations Information — Sources, Technical Notes and Glossary.* Kingston: Queen's University Industrial Relations Centre, 1979.

Labour Law under the Charter. Kingston: Queen's Law Journal and Industrial Relations Centre, 1988. Proceedings of a conference sponsored by Industrial Relations Centre/School of Industrial Relations and Faculty of Law, 24-26 September, 1987.

Logan, H. A. *Trade Unions in Canada.* Toronto: Macmillan of Canada, 1948.

Miller, R. U., and F. Isbester, eds. *Canadian Labour in Transition.* Scarborough: Prentice-Hall Canada Inc., 1971.

Ostry, S., and M. A. Zaidi. *Labour Economics in Canada,* 3rd ed. Toronto: Macmillan of Canada, 1979.

Palmer, E. E. *Collective Agreement Arbitration in Canada,* 2nd ed. Toronto: Butterworths, 1983.

Peach, D. A. and B. Kuechle. *The Practice of Industrial Relations,* 2nd ed. Toronto: McGraw-Hill Ryerson Limited, 1985.

Phillips, G. E. *Labour Relations and the Collective Bargaining Cycle,* 2nd ed. Toronto: Butterworths, 1981.

Porter, J. *The Vertical Mosaic: An Analysis of Social Class and Power in Canada.* Toronto: University of Toronto Press, 1965.

Relations industrielles/Industrial Relations. Laval: quarterly.

Reynolds, L. G., S. H. Masters, and C. H. Moser, eds. *Readings in Labour Economics and Labour Relations,* 2nd ed. Englewood Cliffs: Prentice-Hall Inc., 1978.

Riddell, W. C., *Canadian Labor Relations.* Toronto: University of Toronto Press, 1986.

——————————, Researcher Coordinator. *Adapting to Change: Labour Market Adjustment in Canada.* Toronto: University of Toronto Press, 1986.

——————————, Research Coordinator. *Labour-Management Cooperation in Canada.* Toronto: University of Toronto Press, 1986.

——————————, Research Coordinator. *Work and Pay: The Canadian Labour Market.* Toronto: University of Toronto Press, 1985.

Rose, J. B. *Public Policy, Bargaining Structure and the Construction Industry.* Toronto: Butterworths, 1980.

Rowan, R. R. ed. *Readings in Labour Economics and Labour Relations,* 4th ed. Homewood: Richard D. Irwin, Inc., 1980.

Sen, J., and S. Hameed. *Theories of Industrial Relations.* Littleton, Mass.: Copley Publishing Group, 1988.

Sethi, A. S., ed. *Collective Bargaining in Canada.* Scarborough, Ont.: Nelson Canada, 1989.

Stevens, C. M. *Strategy and Collective Bargaining Negotiation.* New York: McGraw-Hill Book Company, 1965.

Swan, K. P., and K. E. Swinton, eds. *Studies in Labour Law.* Toronto: Butterworths, 1983.

Thompson, M., and G. Swimmer, eds. *Conflict or Compromise: The Future of Public Sector Industrial Relations.* Montreal: The Institute for Research on Public Policy, 1984.

Tremblay, L. M. *Le syndicalisme québecois: Idéologies de la CSN et de la FTQ.* Montréal: Les presses de l'Université de Montréal, 1972.

Walton, R. E., and R. B. McKersie. *A Behavioural Theory of Labour Negotiations.* New York: McGraw-Hill Book Company, 1965.

Weiler, P. *Reconcilable Differences.* Toronto: The Carswell Co. Ltd. 1980.

Willes, J. A. *Contemporary Canadian Labour Relations.* Toronto: McGraw-Hill Ryerson Limited, 1984.

Wood, W. D., and P. Kumar. *The Current Industrial Relations Scene in Canada.* Kingston: Queen's University Industrial Relations Centre, annually.

Woods, H. D. *Labour Policy in Canada,* 2nd ed. Toronto: Macmillan of Canada, 1973.

Glossary of Industrial Relations Terms*

Accreditation: The process used to certify an organization of employers as the bargaining agent for a unit of employers. (*Accréditation syndicale*) The parallel term for employee organizations is "certification". (*Certification*)

Adversary System: The industrial relations system seen as consisting of two necessarily opposing forces, labour and management. This viewpoint ignores the co-operative elements of the relationship. (*Régime d'antagonisme*)

Affiliation: The establishment of an organic bond between two or more organizations. In an affiliation, the organization maintains its essential character and continues to enjoy a relative autonomy within the limits established by the purpose of the affiliation. (*Affiliation*)

Affirmative Action Plan: A written program to actively eliminate employment standards and practices that tend to discriminate on the grounds of race, creed, sex or national origin. (*Programme d'action positive*)

Agreement: (See **Collective Agreement**)

Appeal: A procedure by which a party dissatisfied with a decision, award or ruling may refer the matter to a higher authority for review. (*Appel*)

Apprentice: A worker who enters into agreement with an employer to learn a skilled trade through a special training period combining practical training with related off-the-job technical instruction. Apprenticeship is sometimes regulated by statute (designated trades). (*Apprenti/ie*)

Arbitration: The procedure by which a board or a single arbitrator, acting under the authority of both parties to a dispute, hears both sides of the controversy and issues an award, usually accompanied by a written decision, which is ordinarily binding on both parties. Arbitrators are usually appointed by the parties concerned, but under special circumstances, they are appointed by the Minister of Labour. (*Arbitrage*) **Compulsory arbitration** is that required by law and is the usual procedure for settling contract interpretation disputes. (*L'arbitrage obligatoire*) The term **voluntary arbitration** indicates that the parties to a dispute agree to arbitration in the absence of statutory compulsion. (*L'arbitrage facultatif*)

*Quoted from Labour Canada, *Glossary of Industrial Relations Terms* (Ottawa: Supply and Services Canada, 1984).

Arbitrator: Third party chosen to hear a case or group of cases which are submitted for arbitration. *(Arbitre)*

Assembly-line Work: A manufacturing procedure in which many workers successively perform an operation or task while the item under production is moved along a conveyor system timed to move in accordance with the time allotted for each distinct function to be performed. *(Production à la chaîne)*

Automation: Automation is usually characterized by two major principles: (1) mechanization, i.e., machines are self-regulated so as to meet predetermined requirements (a simple example of self-regulation can be found in the operation of a thermostatically controlled furnace); (2) continuous process, i.e., production facilities are linked together, thereby integrating several separate elements of a productive process into a unified whole. There are three basic kinds of automated process: (1) assembly-line automation, characteristic of the automobile industry; (2) extensive use of computers, as found in many modern offices and businesses; (3) utilization of complex electronic equipment as controls in the manufacturing and processing of products, such as in the refining industry. *(Automatisation)*

Award: In labour-management arbitration, the final decision of an arbitrator, binding on both parties to the dispute. *(Sentence arbitrale)*

Bargaining Agent: The organization that is the exclusive representative of a group of workers or employers in the process of collective bargaining. *(Agent négociateur)*

Bargaining Unit: A group of employees in a firm, plant, or industry that has been recognized by the employer and certified by a labour relations board as appropriate to be represented by a union for purposes of collective bargaining. In a craft union, this could be all members of a trade, such as all tool and die makers in a plant; in an industrial union, the bargaining unit may include all production workers in a plant or all plants in a company. *(Unité de négociation)*

Base Rate: The lowest rate of pay, expressed in hourly terms, for the lowest paid qualified worker classification in the bargaining unit. Not to be confused with **basic rate** which is the straight-time rate of pay per hour, job or unit, excluding premiums, incentive bonuses, etc. *(Taux de base)*

Blue-collar Workers: Term used to describe manual workers, i.e. production and maintenance workers. In recent years, the percentage of blue-collar workers in the labour force has declined considerably. *(Cols bleus)*

Boycott: An organized refusal on the part of employees and their union to deal with an employer, with the objective of winning concessions. Primary boycotts usually take the form of putting pressure on consumers not to buy the goods of an employer who is directly involved in a dispute. In the dress industry, for example, the International Ladies' Garment Workers' Union frequently boycotts the sale of non-union made dresses. Secondary boycotts are those in which pressure is exerted on employers who are not directly involved in a dispute, e.g., workers of Company A refuse to buy or handle goods of Company B, which is engaged in a labour dispute. *(Boycottage)*

Broader-based or Centralized Bargaining: A type of bargaining that aims to reduce the degree of fragmentation in the collective bargaining process and the potential conflict that can result, by combining employers on the one hand and/or unions on the other to form negotiating coalitions, thereby reducing the potential for sequential work stoppages in the same industry/company as various contracts terminate. *(Négociation sectorielle)*

Bumping: Exercise of seniority rights by workers to displace less senior union employees when business conditions require temporary layoffs or the discontinuance of departments. *(Supplantation, déplacement)*

Business Agent: A full-time union officer of a local union who handles grievances, helps enforce agreements, and performs other tasks in the day-to-day operation of a union. *(Agent d'affaires)*

Business Council on National Issues: A consultative body formed in 1970, consisting of the chief executive officers of 150 leading Canadian corporations, which meets with governments, labour unions and other interest groups to develop policy recommendations on economic and social issues. A major area of interest to the council is its task force on employment and labour relations.

Call-back Pay: Compensation, often at higher wage rates, for workers called back on the job after completing their regular shift. Contract provisions usually provide for a minimum number of hours of pay, regardless of the number of hours actually worked. *(Indemnité de rappel)*

Call-in Pay: Guaranteed hours of pay (ranging from two to eight hours) to a worker who reports for work and finds there is insufficient work for him or her to do. Provisions for call-in pay are usually spelled out in collective agreements. *(Indemnité de convocation au travail)*

Canada Labour Code: Legislation applicable to employers whose operations fall within federal jurisdiction and to their employees. The Canada Labour Code consists of Part III (Labour Standards); Part IV (Safety of Employees); and Part I (Industrial Relations). *(Code canadien du travail)*

Canada Labour Relations Board: A board whose powers and duties under the industrial relations provisions of the Canada Labour Code include the determination of appropriate bargaining units, the certification or decertification of trade unions, decisions as to unfair labour practices or failure to bargain in good faith, etc. The board is composed of a chairman, at least one vice-chairman and not less than four nor more than eight members. (See also Labour Relations Board) *(Conseil canadien des relations du travail)*

Canadian Chamber of Commerce: A national body representing business interests, which seeks to influence federal legislation by presentation of briefs; it disseminates commercial information and attempts to foster understanding and sympathy for the problems businessmen encounter. *(Chambre de commerce du Canada)*

Canadian Labour Congress (CLC): Canada's national labour body, formed in 1956 from the merger of the Trades and Labour Congress and the Canadian Congress of Labour, and representing more than half of organized labour in the country. *(Congrés du Travail du Canada (CTC))*

Canadian Manufacturers' Association: A large organization of manufacturers in every type of industry, founded in 1871, incorporated 1902, it serves as a spokesman for interests of the Canadian manufacturing industry. *(Association des manufacturiers canadiens)*

Centrale des syndicats démocratiques (CSD): A federation of Québec unions founded in 1972 by unions that broke away from the Confédération des syndicats nationaux (CSN). *(Centrale des syndicats démocratiques (CSD))*

Certification: Official designation by a labour relations board or similar government agency of a union as sole and exclusive bargaining agent, following proof of majority support among employees in a bargaining unit. *(Accréditation syndicale)*

Certified Union: A union designed by a labour relations board as the exclusive bargaining agent of a group of workers. *(Syndicat accrédité)*

Checkoff: A clause in a collective agreement authorizing an employer to deduct union dues and, sometimes, other assessments, and transmit these funds to the union. There are four main types; the first three apply to union members only: (1) Voluntary revocable; (2) Voluntary irrevocable; (3) Compulsory; (4) Rand Formula - dues deducted from both union and non-union employees. *(Précompte, retenue, prélèvement)*

Closed Shop: A provision in a collective agreement whereby all employees in a bargaining unit must be union members in good standing before being hired, and new employees must be hired through the union. *(Atelier fermé)*

Code of Ethical Practices: A declaration of principle adopted by the Canadian Labour Congress, requiring unions to try to ensure maximum attendance at meetings and general participation by membership. Under this code no one engaging in corrupt practices may hold office in the union or in the CLC. *(Code d'éthique)*

Co-determination: A process whereby decisions are made jointly by management and workers (or their representatives). These joint decisions may be made at various levels within a company — at the board level, for example, through the appointment of worker directors, or at shop-floor level by establishing some form of labour-management committee or even by utilizing existing collective bargaining machinery. *(Cogestion)*

COLA Clause: Literally a "cost of living adjustment" (or allowance) clause. A clause built into a collective agreement which links wage or salary increases to changes in the cost of living during the life of the contract. Also termed an "escalator clause." *Clause d'échelle mobile de salaires)*

Collective Agreement: An agreement in writing between an employer and the union representing his/her employees which contains provisions respecting conditions of employment, rates of pay, hours of work, and the rights and obligations of the parties to the agreement. Ordinarily the agreement is for a definite period such as one, two, or three years, usually not less than twelve months. Under some conditions, amendments are made to agreements by mutual consent during the term of the agreement in order to deal with special circumstances. *(Convention collective)*

Collective Bargaining: Method of determining wages, hours and other conditions of employment through direct negotiations between the union and employer. Normally the result of collective bargaining is a written contract that covers all employees in the bargaining unit, both union members and non-members, for a specified period of time. More recently the term has been broadened to include the day-to-day activities involved in giving effect to or carrying out the terms of a collective agreement. *(Négociation collective)* **Bargaining in good faith** refers to the requirement that the two parties meet and confer at reasonable times with minds open to persuasion with a view to reaching agreement on new contract terms. Good faith bargaining does not imply that either party is required to reach agreement on any proposal. *(Négociation de bonne foi)* The term collective bargaining is frequently prefaced with expressions such as company-wide, industry-wide or multi-employer, which serve to specify more precisely the form of bargaining. Thus **company-wide collective bargaining** *(Négociation à l'échelle de la firme)* refers to bargaining that takes place between a company with many plants and (typically) a single union representing employees of a particular craft or skill. The terms and conditions arrived at are generally uniform throughout the company. **Industry-wide bargaining** *(Négociation de branche)* refers to situations in which the terms and conditions of employment agreed to by labour and management cover an entire industry. **Multi-employer**

bargaining *(Négociation multi-employeurs)* covers those situations in which bargaining takes place between a union and a group or association of employers (hence it is also termed "association bargaining"). Quite often, in fact, much so-called industry-wide bargaining is actually multi-employer bargaining, since there are relatively few industries in which collective bargaining is conducted in a genuinely industry-wide context.

Combines Investigation Act: A federal government act providing for the investigation and repression of trade combinations operating in restraint of trade and to the detriment of the public. *(Loi relative aux enquêtes sur les coalitions)*

Company Union: An employee organization, usually of a single company, that is dominated or strongly influenced by management. Company unions were wide-spread in the 1920s and early '30s. The Labour Relations Acts of the 1940s declared that such employer domination is an unfair labour practice, and company unions have since been on the decline. *(Syndicat de boutique)*

Compensation: Recompense to employees for lost wages due to delays, injury on the job, etc. **Workers' compensation** *(indemnisation des accidents du travail)* is paid to workers temporarily or permanently disabled by an accident in the workplace. Total compensation may refer to all forms of payment for work done, i.e., wages plus pensions and fringe benefits. *(Indemnité)*

Conciliation and Mediation: A process that attempts to resolve labour disputes by compromise or voluntary agreement. By contrast with arbitration, the mediator, conciliator, or conciliation commissioner does not bring in a binding award, and the parties are free to accept or reject the recommendation. The conciliator is often a government official whose report contains recommendations and is made public. Conciliation is a prerequisite to legal strike/lockout action. The mediator is usually a private individual appointed as a last resort after conciliation has failed to prevent or put an end to a strike. **Preventive mediation** *(médiation préventive)* is intervention by a neutral third party during the closed period of a collective agreement to assist in resolving contentious problems, before they reach the bargaining table. *(Conciliation et médiation)*

Confederation of Canadian Unions (CCU): Federation of unions dedicated to a Canadian union movement independent of the internationals. Founded in 1969 by B.C. pulp and paper and aluminum workers, it has affiliated unions in the five provinces west of Québec. *(Confédération des syndicats canadiens (CSC))*

Confederation of National Trade Unions (CNTU): A Quebec-based central labour body. *(Confédération des syndicats nationaux (CSN))*

Consumer Price Index: A Statistics Canada monthly statistical indicator which follows changes in retail prices of selected consumer items in major Canadian cities. The index and its monthly fluctuations are employed in calculating COLA payments (cost of living allowance) in collective agreements. *(Indice des prix à la consommation)*

Contract: A collective agreement. (See **Collective Agreement.**) *(Contrat)*

Contracting out: The use by employers of workers outside their own work force to perform tasks previously performed by the employers' own employees. *(Concession)*

Cooling-off Period: A required period of delay (fixed by federal or provincial law) following legal notice of a pending labour dispute, during which there can be neither strike nor lockout. It follows upon the unsatisfactory conclusion of compulsory conciliation attempts. Wages and conditions of work are usually frozen under conditions set by the previous contract. Every effort is made during this time to settle the dispute. *(Délai de réflexion)*

Cost of Living: Relationship of the retail cost of consumer goods and services to the purchasing power of wages. *(Coût de la vie)*

Craft: A manual occupation that requires extensive training and a high degree of skill, such as carpentry, plumbing, linotype operation. *(Métier)*

Craft Union: A union that limits its members to a particular craft. Most craft unions today, however, have broadened their jurisdiction to include many occupations and skills that are not closely related to the originally designated craft. *(Syndicat de métier)*

Cyclical Unemployment: Unemployment caused by fluctuations in the economy, i.e., loss of jobs due to a downward trend in the business cycle. Cyclical unemployment is of far greater magnitude than seasonal, technological or frictional unemployment. *(Chômage cyclique)*

Decertification: The procedure for removing a union's official recognition as exclusive bargaining representative. *(Révocation d'accréditation syndicale)*

Discrimination (at work): Unequal treatment of persons, whether through hiring or employment rules or through variation of the conditions of employment, because of sex, age, marital status, race, creed, union membership, or other activities. In many cases discrimination is an unfair labour practice under federal or provincial laws. *(Discrimination au travail)*

Dismissal Pay: (See **Severance Pay.**)

Dispute Resolution System: The process and procedures for applying third-party assistance to collective bargaining parties to reach an agreement on the matter(s) in dispute. The notion of dispute resolution includes both legislative and non-legislative elements. There is a range of possible stages in the dispute resolution process, and various mechanisms (both voluntary and compulsory) can be used to this end. *(Méthode de règlement de conflit)*

Earnings: Compensation for services rendered or time worked. *(Gains)*

Economic Council of Canada: An economic research and policy advisory agency created by an Act of Parliament in 1963. Its members represented business, labour, agriculture, and other interests until 1976, when labour representatives withdrew to protest the government's anti-inflation program. *(Conseil économique du Canada)*

Employee: A person working in an industry or enterprise who is entitled to wages for labour or services performed. Not included are persons employed in certain professions or who exercise managerial functions. *(Employé)*

Employer: A person or firm having control over the employment of workers and the payment of their wages. *(Employeur)*

Equal Pay for Equal Work: The principle that wage rates should be based on the job, rather than upon the sex, race, etc., of the worker, or upon other factors not related to his/her ability to perform. *(À travail égal, salaire égal)*

Equal Pay for Work of Equal Value: The principle that workers who are performing work of equal value must receive the same pay for work in the same establishment. Equal value is determined by an analysis of the composite skill, effort, and responsibility required in the performance of such work and the conditions under which the work is performed. *(Égalité de rémunération pour un travail de valeur égale)*

Essential Industries: Industries which render such important and necessarily uninterrupted service to the general public as to warrant special regulation to prevent the stoppage of their operations by labour disputes. *(Service d'intérêt public)*

Exclusivity: The right acquired by an employee organization to be the sole representative of the bargaining unit. Exclusive representation is usually provided by labour relations statutes, although some statutes governing public employee labour relations provide alternatives such as proportional representation. Proportional representation accords bargaining rights to be one or more organizations in direct relation to the number of members in the bargaining unit who belong to or vote for the organization. *(Exclusivité)*

Expedited Arbitration: Used independently or in conjunction with the term "industry arbitration," it encompasses systems used in specific industries whereby a "permanent" arbitrator or panel of arbitrators is selected to hear grievances arising under one or more collective agreements over a period of time, as well as any procedures or mechanisms designed to expedite the grievance arbitration process. *(Arbitrage accéléré)*

Fact-finding: A formal/informal dispute resolution procedure for investigating and reporting on the facts of a situation, such as a work stoppage affecting the public. *(Enquête factuelle)*

Fair Employment Practices: The practice of employers or unions of offering workers equal employment opportunities regardless of race, national or ethnic origin, colour, religion, age, sex, marital status, conviction for which a pardon has been granted, or physical handicap. *(Pratique loyale en matière d'emploi)*

Featherbedding: The practice of extending work through the limitation of production, the amount of work to be performed or other make-work arrangements. Many such practices have come about as a consequence of workers being laid off through mechanization or technological change, which has led unions to seek some method of retaining workers even though there may be no work for them to perform. *(Sinécure ouvière)*

Federal Jurisdiction: Authority of the federal government exercised over employees or employers in any enterprise of an interprovincial, national or international nature, such as air transport, broadcasting, banks, pipelines, railways, highway transport, shipping, and grain elevators. Generally speaking, all other enterprises fall within the jurisdiction of provincial or territorial governments. *(Compétence fédérale)*

Federation of Labour: An allied group of unions in one or several industries, covering a geographical area, such as a district, province or country. An example of a national federation is the Canadian Labour Congress (CLC)/*Congrès du Travail du Canada (CTC)*. National federations may join to form confederations or international federations such as the International Confederation of Free Trade Unions (ICFTU). *(Fédération des travailleurs)*

Final Offer Selection: A form of arbitration used in the United States and more recently in Canada, usually after a predetermined period of unsuccessful negotiation. Both sides put forward final offers, one of which an arbitrator or board of arbitrators must choose. *(Arbitrage des propositions finales)*

Flexible Work-week or Flextime: A system which provides workers with some freedom in deciding when they start and finish work, subject to the requirement that they are present during certain "core" hours and fulfill a minimum attendance requirement each day. *(Horaire variable de travail)*

Foreman: A supervisory employee, usually classed as a part of management. A working foreman or leadman is one who regularly performs production work or other work unrelated to supervisory duties. *(Contremaître)*

Free Riders: Non-union employees who share in whatever benefits result from union activities without sharing union expenses, or union members who are 'delinquent' in paying their dues. *(Resquilleurs)*

Freeze: Government action restricting wage, salary and price increases in order to stabilize the economy. *(Blocage)*

Frictional Unemployment: Unemployment due to time lost in changing jobs rather than a lack of job opportunities. Frictional unemployment would not be reduced significantly even if there were an increased demand for workers, but might be reduced by improving the information available to job seekers about vacancies. *(Chômage frictionnel)*

Fringe Benefits: Non-wage benefits such as paid vacations, pensions, health and welfare provisions, life insurance, etc., the cost of which is borne in whole or in part by the employer. Such benefits have accounted for an increasing percentage of worker income and labour costs in recent years and have thus become an important aspect of collective bargaining. *(Avantages sociaux)*

Garnishment: Attachment of an employee's wages in the hands of the employer to pay a creditor. *(Saisie du salaire)*

General Strike: A general strike is a cessation of work by all union members in a geographical area, usually as a political protest. *(Grève générale)*

Grievance: A statement of dissatisfaction, usually by an individual but sometimes by the union or management, concerning interpretation of a collective bargaining agreement or traditional work practices. The grievance machinery (i.e., the method of dealing with individual grievances) is nearly always spelled out in the contract. If a grievance cannot be handled at the shop level (where most of them are settled), and the grievance arises out of an interpretation of the contract, it must be resolved by arbitration. *(Grief)*

Guaranteed Wage Plan: A system under which an employer (a) contributes to a fund used to pay additional wages during slack periods or (b) contractually guarantees a specified number of days of work during a specific period. *(Régime de salaire garanti)*

Handicapped Workers: Workers whose earning capacity is impaired by age, physical or mental deficiency, or injury. To encourage their employment, they are sometimes given special treatment in labour statutes, for example, by permitting employment at subminimum rates. *(Travailleur handicapé)*

Harmony Pledge (Co-operation Clause): A clause in a union contract in which the employer and the union agree to co-operate on some specific subject. *(Clause de coopération)*

Hazardous Occupations: Jobs which are classified as dangerous by provincial or federal laws, and in which employment of minors is restricted or forbidden. Federal legislation provides workers with the right to refuse work that is considered hazardous to health or safety. *(Emploi dangereux)*

Hiring Hall: An office, usually run by the union, or jointly by employers and union, for referring workers to jobs or for the actual hiring operation. *(Bureau d'embauchage)*

Holidays: Days established by law or custom for which workers receive pay while absent from work. Statutory holidays *(congé statutaire)* are established by law. When the customary day falls on a weekend a moveable holiday *(congé mobile)* may be substituted for it on another day. *(Jours fériés)*

Hot Cargo: Merchandise shipped from a struck plant or by an employer on a union boycott list. *(Produit boycotté)*

Idle Time: Nonproductive time resulting from waiting for work, machinery or other breakdowns, and the like. *(Temps inoccupé)*

Illegal Strike: A strike called in violation of the law. Strikes are generally illegal when they occur as a result of a dispute over the interpretation of a collective agreement currently in force, when they occur before conciliation procedures have been complied with, or when certification proceedings are under way. *(Grève illégale)*

Independent Union: A labour organization which is not affiliated with and remains independent of any federation. *(Syndicat autonome)*

Individual Bargaining: The right of individual members of a unit for which an exclusive representative has been designated for collective bargaining purposes to present, as individuals, grievances that are not contrary to the existing union contract. *(Négociation individuelle)*

Industrial Conflict: A general term used to describe the broad areas of disagreement and difficulty between labour and management (though the government may also be involved). The strike is the most common and most visible manifestation of conflict. It may also take the form of peaceful bargaining and grievance handling, boycotts, political action and restriction of output, industrial sabotage, absenteeism or labour turnover. Several of these forms, such as restriction of output, absenteeism and turnover, may take place on an individual as well as on an organized basis, and as such they constitute alternatives to collective action. *(Conflit de travail)*

Industrial Democracy: The involvement of workers (or their representatives) in decision making within industry. The machinery of industrial democracy may involve such devices as joint labour-management committees, works councils or worker representatives in the boardroom. The development of collective bargaining is viewed by many as providing the machinery through which industrial democracy may be developed. (See also **Quality of Working Life** and **Worker Participation**.) *(Démocratie industrielle)*

Industrial Health: A branch of public health which concerns itself with the health and well-being of workers. A body of rules and practices has evolved, designed to eliminate hazards and industrial fatigue in the workplace. *(Hygiène industrielle)*

Industrial Relations: A broad term that may refer to relations between unions and management, unions themselves, management and government, unions and government, or between employers and unorganized employees. Within this definition, specific attention may be directed toward industrial conflict or its regulation through the formulation of work rules or agreements. *(Relations industrielles)*

Industrial Union: A union organized on the basis of product, i.e., along industrial lines; in contrast to a craft union organized along skill lines. *(Syndicat industriel)*

Industry-wide Bargaining: Collective bargaining that takes place on an industry-wide basis; terms and conditions of employment agreed upon cover all or a major portion of the organized employees in the industry. *(Négociation de branche)*

Initiation Fees: Fees that must be paid by new members of a union or by former employees who have left the union and wish to return. Initiation fees serve several purposes: (1) a source of revenue; (2) an equity payment by new members to compensate for the efforts older members have made in building the union; (3) a device to restrict membership (if initiation fees are very high) in those unions desiring to remain small in order to protect job opportunities. *(Droits d'adhésion)*

Injunction: A court order restraining an employer or union from committing or engaging in certain acts. An ex parte injunction is one in which the application for an injunction is made in the absence of the party affected. *(Injonction)*

Interest Dispute: A dispute arising from the negotiation of a new collective agreement or the revision of an existing agreement on expiry. *(Conflit d'intérêts)*

International Confederation of Free Trade Unions (ICFTU): An international trade union body, formed in 1949, composed of a large number of national central labour bodies such as the Canadian Labour Congress/Congre's du Travail du Canada. It represents 50 million members in 96 non-communist countries. *(Confédération internationale des syndicats libres (CISL))*

International Labour Office: The secretariat of the **International Labour Organization,** which administers and co-ordinates the activities of the ILO. *(Bureau international du travail)*

International Labour Organization (ILO): A tripartite world body representing labour, management and government. Since 1946 one of the specialized agencies of the United Nations. It disseminates labour information to workers of all countries and sets minimum international labour standards, called "conventions," offered to member nations for ratification. Its headquarters are in Geneva, Switzerland. *(Organisation internationale du travail OIT))*

International Union: An international union is a union with members in both Canada and the United States. *(Syndicat international)*

Job Classification: A system designed to create a hierarchy of jobs based on such factors as skill, responsibility or experience, time and effort. The determination of the value of each job in relation to other jobs in the workplace, based on the material and content of the job and such factors as education, skill, experience and responsibility. Often used for the purpose of arriving at a system of wage differentials between jobs or classes of jobs *(Classification des emplois)*

Job Description: A description of the nature of a particular job, its relation to other jobs, the working conditions, the degree of responsibility and the other qualifications called for. *(Description des tâches)*

Job Enrichment: The attempt to make jobs more rewarding and less monotonous for the individual worker. Procedures used may include job enlargement (including more responsibilities on the job), or job rotation (allowing the worker to move from one job to another at specific intervals). (See also **Quality of Working Life** . . . *Valorisation du travail)*

Job Rotation: Used as a means to provide variety and experience for employees while creating back-up potential for performance of individual jobs. *(Rotation d'emplois)*

Job Security: A worker's sense of having continuity of employment resulting from the possession of special skills, seniority, or protection provided in a collective agreement against unforeseen technological change. *(Sécurité d'emploi)*

Job Training: A procedure whereby workers, while working, learn how to perform particular jobs. (See also "**Apprentice.**") *(Formation professionnelle)*

Joint Bargaining: Two or more unions joining forces to negotiate an agreement with a single employer. *(Front commun)*

Journeyman: A craft or skilled worker who has completed apprenticeship training and been admitted to full membership in his or her craft. Examples: journeyman plumber, journeyman carpenter. *(Compagnon)*

Jurisdiction (Union): The area of jobs, skills, occupations and industries within which a union organizes and engages in collective bargaining. International unions often assert exclusive claim to particular areas of employment. Jurisdiction has always been a problem in organized labour, since two or more unions often claim the same jurisdiction. The CLC has attempted to cope with the problem by having affiliated unions sign no-raiding agreements, in which member unions agree not to trespass on one another's jurisdiction. These agreements, however, have not been completely observed. In the case of local unions, jurisdiction refers to a region within which the local union exercises authority. *(Compétence syndicale)*

Jurisdictional Dispute — Inter-union Dispute: A conflict between two or more unions over the right of their membership to perform certain types of work. If the conflict develops into a work stoppage, it is called a jurisdictional strike. *(Conflit de compétence syndicale/ Conflit intersyndical)*

Labour Canada: The federal government department responsible for disseminating information on labour-related issues and administering labour legislation within federal jurisdiction. The department's aims are to promote stable industrial relations and establish appropriate labour standards and occupational safety and health in the federal jurisdiction, to promote labour-management co-operation throughout Canada, and to co-ordinate the Canadian contribution to the improvement of labour conditions throughout the world. The government of each province has a department of labour to administer labour laws in its jurisdiction. *(Travail Canada)*

Labour College of Canada: Bilingual institution of higher education for trade union members, operated jointly by the Canadian Labour Congress, McGill University and the Université de Montréal for the purpose of providing a training ground for future trade union leaders. *(Collège canadien des travailleurs)*

Labour Council: An organization formed by a labour federation at the city level. It is organized and functions in the same manner as a provincial federation but within a city. Finances are often obtained through a per capita tax on affiliates. *(Conseil du travail)*

Labour Education: Education by unions of union members or officials in industrial relations subjects. *(Education syndicale)*

Labour Federation: An association of unions which, while retaining their autonomy, co-operate to achieve common goals. *(Fédération du travail)*

Labour Force: All persons 15 and over who are either employed, temporarily idle, or unemployed and seeking employment. *(Population active)*

Labour Law: That part of the law which treats persons in their capacity as workers or employers; the governing of labour relations, labour and employer organizations, employment practices and conditions in the workplace. *(Droit du travail)*

Labour-Management Committee: Any committee having representation from both management and labour; discussion subjects may include safety and health, productivity, quality of working life, training, etc. *(Comité syndical-patronal)*

Labour Relations Board: A board, usually provided for under the provincial labour relations acts, which is responsible for certification of trade unions, the inclusion of dispute-settling provisions in collective agreements and investigation of complaints of bad faith in collective bargaining. (See also **Canada Labour Relations Board.**) *(Commission des relations du travail)*

Labour Turnover: Rate at which workers move into and out of employment, usually expressed as a percentage based on the number of employees leaving a plant or industry during a certain time over the average number of employees in the plant or industry during the same period. *(Roulement de la main-d'oeuvre)*

Layoff: Temporary, prolonged, or final separation from employment as a result of a lack of work. *(Mise à pied)*

Leave of Absence: Paid or unpaid time away from work, with employer's permission, to meet family or civic responsibilities. Common forms of leave include maternity leave *(congé de maternité)*, bereavement or funeral leave *(congé pour décès)*, and leave for jury duty *(congé de service judiciaire)*. *(Absence autorisée)*

Line Employee: An employee whose duties are directly related to the production and distribution of the company's products or services. *(Exécutant)*

Local Union: The unit of labour organization formed in a particular locality, through which members participate directly in the affairs of their organization, such as the election of local officers, the financial and other business matters of a local, relations with their employer(s), and the collection of members' dues. *(Section locale d'un syndicat)*

Lockout: The closing of a place of employment, a suspension of work, or a refusal by an employer to continue to employ a number of his employees, undertaken with a view to compelling them to agree to conditions of employment on his terms or to refrain from exercising their existing rights and privileges. *(Lock-out)*

Maintenance of Membership: A provision in a collective agreement stating that no worker need join the union as a condition of employment, but that all workers who voluntarily join must maintain their membership for the duration of the agreement as a condition of continued employment. (See **Union Security.**) *(Maintien de l'adhésion syndicale)*

Management Rights: These encompass those aspects of the employer's operations that do not require discussion with or concurrence by the union, or rights reserved to management which are not subject to collective bargaining. Such rights may include matters of hiring, production, manufacturing and sales. The resistance of many managers to innovations such as industrial democracy may frequently be traced to concern over the erosion of management prerogatives that such innovations sometimes entail. *(Prérogatives de l'employeur)*

Master Agreement: A collective bargaining agreement which serves as the pattern for major terms and conditions for an entire industry or segment thereof. Local terms may be negotiated in addition to the terms set forth in the master contract. *(Convention collective cadre)*

Mediation: (See **Conciliation and Mediation.**) *(Médiation)*

Mediation-Arbitration (Med-Arb): A dispute resolution procedure where the mediator is armed with the power to settle unresolved issues by binding arbitration in the event they are not settled through mediation. In such cases, the right to strike or lock out is waived by the parties. *(Médiation-arbitrage)*

Minimum Wage: The rate of pay established by statute or by minimum wage order as the lowest wage that may be paid, whether for a particular type of work, to a particular class of workers, or to any worker. *(Salaire minimum)*

Modified Union Shop: A place of work in which non-union workers already employed need not join the union, but all new employees must join, and those already members must remain in the union. (See **Union Security Clauses, Union Shop**.) *(Atelier syndical modifié)*

Monopoly: Control of a commodity or service in a particular market which enables the one having control to raise the price substantially above that fixed by free competition. *(Monopole)*

Moonlighting: The holding by a single individual of more than one paid job at the same time. *(Travail noir ou Double emploi)*

Multinational Bargaining: Bargaining between an international union or union federation and a company whose operations are international in scope. These companies, known as multinationals, pose many unique problems for organized labour. In particular, their international status gives them scope for transferring production from one country to another on a temporary or permanent basis in order to use non-union employees or break a strike. *(Négociation avec une entreprise multinationale)*

National Union: A union whose membership and locals are confined within one country. *(Syndicat national)*

Nepotism: The practice of giving promotions, basic employment, higher earnings, and other benefits to employees who are relatives of management. *(Népotisme)*

Open Shop: A shop in which union membership is not required as a condition of securing or retaining employment. *(Atelier ouvert)*

Organized Labour: Consists of all unions and workers' organizations whose principal objects are the regulation of relations between workers and employers and the protection of the interests of workers; the union movement as a whole. *(Mouvement syndicat)*

Overtime: Hours worked in excess of the maximum regular number of hours fixed by statute, union contract, or custom. Clock overtime is a premium, paid for work during specified regular working hours, required by collective agreement. *(Temps supplémentaire)*

Paid Educational Leave: Leave for educational purposes granted to a worker and paid for by the employer or government. *(Congé-éducation payé)*

Part-time Employee: An employee who works fewer than the normally scheduled weekly or monthly hours of work established for persons doing similar work. There are different kinds of part-time work. For example, an employee may work regular hours that are less than full-time, or may be "on call" and work for a firm occasionally, as needed. *(Employé à temps partiel)*

Pattern Bargaining: A procedure in collective bargaining whereby a union seeks to obtain equal or identical terms from other employers as in an agreement already obtained from an important company. *(Négociation type)*

Pension Plan: An arrangement to provide definite sums of money for payment to employees following retirement. A final-earnings plan is a pension based upon length of service and average earnings for a stated period just before retirement. A contributory plan is financed by both the employer and the employees. *(Régime de pension)*

Per Capita Tax: Regular payments by a local to its national international union, labour council or federation, or by a union to its central labour body. It is based on the number of members. *(Capitation, taxe par tête)*

Picket Line: A group of workers (pickets) posted at plant entrances and gates, or marching near the entrances and gates, to inform employees of the existence of a labour dispute and to persuade and influence them not to enter the premises or do business with the employer.

Picketing: Patrolling near the employer's place of business by union members - pickets - to publicize the existence of a labour dispute, persuade workers to join a strike or join the union, discourage customers from buying or using the employer's goods or services, etc. *(Piquetage)*

Piece Rate: A predetermined amount paid to an employee for each unit of output. *(Salaire à la pièce)*

Premium Pay: A wage rate higher than straight time, payable for overtime work, work on holidays or scheduled days off, etc., or for work under extraordinary conditions such as dangerous, dirty or unpleasant work. *(Prime)*

Preventive Mediation: (See **Conciliation and Mediation**.)

Probationary Period: The initial period of employment during which a worker is on trial and may be discharged with or without cause. *(Stage)*

Productivity: Output per unit of input; a measure of efficiency. *(Productivité)*

Profit-sharing Plan: An arrangement under which employees receive a percentage of the employer's profits in addition to their wages. A cash payment plan is one under which the employees' share of the profits is paid immediately in cash. A deferred payment plan is one under which the employer deposits the employees' portion of the profits with a trustee to be paid to them at some time in the future, depending upon conditions specified in the trust. Under some schemes, profits are distributed in the form of shares. Also sometimes called gain sharing. *(Participation aux bénéfices)*

Quality Circle: A voluntary group of production workers in a workplace who meet, often with management authorization or assistance, to attempt to resolve problems affecting quality control, production and productivity. *(Cercle de qualité)*

Quality of Working Life: A process designed to assist employers, unions, and employees in implementing joint problem-solving approaches to improve the quality of working life within organizations in the interests of improved labour-management relations, organization effectiveness and employee work satisfaction. *(Qualité de la vie au travail)*

Raiding: An attempt by one union to induce members of another union to defect and join its ranks. (See **Jurisdiction (Union)**.) *(Maraudage)*

Rand Formula: A provision of a collective agreement stating that non-union employees in the bargaining unit must pay the union a sum equal to union fees as a condition of continuing employment Non-union workers are not, however, required to join the union. *(Formule Rand)*

Rank and File: Individual union members who have no special status either as officers or shop stewards in the plant. *(Base syndicale, syndiqués de la base)*

Ratification: Formal approval of a newly negotiated agreement by vote of the union members affected, as well as by employers or employer associations. *(Ratification)*

Real Wages: The actual purchasing power of wages. Often computed by dividing money wages by the cost-of-living index. Example: if money wages increase from $1.00 to $1.25 an hour, but the cost-of-living also increases by 25 per cent, real wages having remained constant. It is by looking at the changes in real wages that changes in living standards can be observed. (See also **COLA Clause**.) *(Salaire réel)*

Recognition: Employer acceptance of a union as the exclusive bargaining representative for the employees in the bargaining unit. (See also **Certification**.) *(Reconnaissance)*

Redundancy Pay: (See **Severance Pay**.)

Reopener: A provision in a collective agreement which permits either side to reopen the contract at a specified time, or under special circumstances, prior to its expiration, in order to bargain on stated subjects such as wage increases, pensions, health and welfare schemes, etc. *(Clause de réouverture)*

Representation Vote: A vote ordered by a Labour Relations Board to determine whether employees in an appropriate bargaining unit wish to have a particular union represent them as their bargaining agent. *(Vote de représentation)*

Residual Rights: Those rights not spelled out in a collective agreement, generally considered to be management rights. *(Droits résiduaires)*

Rest Period: Specified short period, sometimes required by law, during which workers are allowed to cease work, usually on company time. *(Période de repos)*

Retirement: Permanent withdrawal from the labour force. **Delayed retirement** is withdrawal after the normal retirement date, usually with the consent or at the request of the employer. **Disability retirement** is withdrawal before the normal retirement age because of physical incapacity. **Early retirement** is withdrawal before the normal retirement date. *(Retraite)*

Retraining: The establishment of programs and training activities to educate employees in new skills or knowledge made necessary by changing technology, work rotation, reassignment, etc. *(Recyclage)*

Rights Dispute: A dispute arising from the interpretation or application of one or more of the provisions of an existing collective agreement. *(Conflit de droits)*

Right-to-Work: The right of an employee to refrain from joining a union and to keep his job without union membership or activity. *(Droit au travail)*

Safety and Health Committee: A committee composed of workers and management set up for the purpose of promoting a greater concern for improvement of safety and health in the workplace. *(Comité de sécurité et d'hygiène)*

Scab: (See **Strikebreakers**.)

Scanlon Plan: An incentive plan developed by Joseph Scanlon, one-time research director of the United Steelworkers and later on staff at the Massachusetts Institute of Technology. The plan is designed to achieve greater production through increased efficiency with the opportunity for the accrued savings achieved to be distributed among the workers. *(Système Scanlon)*

Seasonal Unemployment: Unemployment that is due to the seasonal nature of the work. Agricultural workers, lumber workers and some construction workers are unemployed for a part of each year because of weather conditions. *(Chômage saisonnier)*

Semi-skilled Labour: Workers who have acquired some proficiency at particular jobs but whose activities do not come within any of the traditional skilled crafts. *(Manoueuvre spécialisé)*

Seniority: An employee's standing in the plant, based on length of continuous employment. Employees with the greatest seniority are usually the last to be laid off (see **Layoff and Bumping**) and are often given certain advantages in the matters of promotion and selection of holiday periods based on seniority. *(Ancienneté)*

Severance Pay, Dismissal Pay, Redundancy Pay: A lump-sum payment by an employer to a worker whose employment is permanently ended, usually for reasons beyond the worker's control. Such payments are in addition to any back wages due to the worker. *(Indemnité de fin d'emploi)*

Shift: The stated daily working period for a group of employees, e.g., 8 a.m. to 4 p.m., 4 p.m. to midnight, midnight to 8 a.m. (see **Split Shift.**) *(Poste, quart, équipe)*

Shift Differential: Added pay for work performed at other than regular daytime hours. *(Prime de poste)*

Shop Committee: A committee of employees elected by fellow workers to represent them in considering grievances and related matters. *(Comité d'atelier)*

Shop Steward: (See **Union Steward**.) *(Délégué d'atelier)*

Sick Leave: Time off allowed for absence because of illness. *(Congé de maladie)*

Slowdown: A deliberate lessening of work effort without an actual strike, in order to force concessions from the employer. (See also **Work to Rule**.) *(Grève perlée)*

Speed-up: A union term describing situations in which workers are required to increase production without a compensating increase in wages. (See also **Stretch-out**) *(Cadence accélérée)*

Split Shift: Division of an employee's daily working time into two or more working periods, to meet peak needs. *(Poste fractionné)*

Staff: (1) Employees of an organization. (2) Workers with administrative duties. *(Personnel)*

Standard of Living: Conditions under which a person or group of persons lives at a particular time in a particular locality, considered in relation to expenses and income. *(Niveau de vie)*

Straw-boss: A sub-foreman. *(Sous-contremaître)*

Stretch-out: A union term describing a situation in which workers are required to assume additional work duties, such as tending more machines, without additional compensation. (See also **Speed-up**.) *(Surcharge)*

Strike: A cessation of work or a refusal to work or to continue work by employees in combination or in accordance with a common understanding for the purpose of compelling an employer to agree to terms or conditions of employment. Strikes usually occur as a last resort when collective bargaining and all other means have failed to obtain the employees' demands. Except in special cases, strikes are legal only when a collective agreement is not in force. A **Rotating or Hit-and-Run Strike** is a strike organized in such a way that only part of the employees stop work at any given time, each group taking its turn. A **Sympathy Strike** is a strike by workers not directly involved in a labour dispute; an attempt to show labour solidarity and bring pressure on an employer in a labour dispute. A **Wildcat Strike** is a strike that violates the collective agreement and is not authorized by the union. *(Grève)*

Strike Benefits: Union payments, usually a small proportion of regular income, to workers during a strike. Many unions do not supply monetary aid but distribute groceries and other types of aid to needy families of strikers. *(Indemnité de grève)*

Strikebreakers: Persons who continue to work during a strike or who accept employment to replace workers on strike. By filling strikers' jobs, they may weaken or break the strike. Also known as scabs. *(Briseur de grève, jaune)*

Strike Fund: Funds held by international, national, or local unions for allocation during a strike to cover costs of benefits, legal fees, publicity, and the like. Some national and international unions assess each member a small amount each month to build the fund. Other unions use the national's or international's general fund. The amount of the fund often determines the staying power of the workers and, consequently, the success or failure of the strike. Strike funds are often designated in union financial statements as "emergency", "reserve" or "special" funds. *(Caisse de grève)*

Strike Notice: Formal announcement by a group of workers to their employer or to an appropriate government agency that on a certain date they will go on strike. *(Avis de grève)*

Strike Vote: A vote conducted among employees in a bargaining unit on the question of whether they should go on strike. *(Vote de grève)*

Struck-Work Clause: A clause in a collective bargaining agreement which permits employees to refuse to perform work farmed out by a strike-bound plant. *(Clause de refus de travail)*

Successor Rights: The rights, privileges, and duties of a union or employer that succeeds another by reason of a merger, sale, amalgamation, or transfer of jurisdiction. *(Obligation du successeur)*

Supervisor: An employee having certain management rights, such as the right to hire or fire or to recommend such action. *(Surveillant)*

Supplemental Unemployment Benefit (SUB) Plans: Private plans providing compensation for wage loss to laid-off workers, usually in addition to public unemployment insurance payments. *(Régimes d'indemnités complémentaires de chômage)*

Sweat Shop: A factory where wage rates and sanitation, safety and working conditions do not meet accepted standards. *(Atelier de pressurage)*

Sweetheart Contract: Term of derision for an agreement negotiated by an employer and a company-dominated union granting terms and conditions of employment more favourable to the contracting union than the employer would be willing to grant to a rival non-dominated labour organization, the usual purpose being to keep the rival out. *(Accord de compérage)*

Take-home Pay: The net paycheck after tax and other deductions have been made. *(Salaire net)*

Technological Change: Technical progress in industrial methods, for example, the introduction of labour-saving machinery or new production techniques. Such change can result in manpower reductions. (See **Automation**.) *(Changement technologique)*

Technological Unemployment: Unemployment that results from the introduction of labour-saving machinery. *(Chômage technique)*

Time-and-a-half: Wage payment at one and one-half times the employee's regular rate of pay or of the statutory minimum rate of pay for all hours worked in excess of a specified number per day or week. *(Taux majoré de moitié)*

Time Card: The record sheet on which, either manually or mechanically, a worker's attendance is reported. *(Fiche de présence)*

Time Clock: Clock with a mechanism to indicate on a paycard, by punch hole or other means, the time of arrival and departure of employees. *(Horloge de pointage, horloge poinçon)*

Trade Union: (See **Union**.) *(Syndicat)*

Tripartitism (Tripartism): Consultation between representatives of labour, management and government to consider issues of mutual interest. *(Tripartisme)*

Trusteeship: (See **Union Trusteeship**.) *(Tutelle)*

Unemployed: Persons who do not have work. The official definition, for unemployment insurance purposes, described the unemployed as those persons who during the reference week: (a) were without work, had actively looked for work in the past four weeks (ending with reference week), and were available for work; (b) had not actively looked for work in the past four weeks but had been on layoff for twenty-six weeks or less and were available for work; (c) had not actively looked for work in the past four weeks but had a new job to start in four weeks or less from reference week, and were available for work. *(Chômeur)*

Unemployment Insurance: A federal program whereby eligible unemployed persons receive cash benefits for a specified period of time. These benefits are paid out of funds derived from employer, employee and government contributions. *(Assurance-chômage)*

Unfair Labour Practice: A practice on the part of either union or management that violates provisions of federal or provincial labour law. *(Pratique déloyale de travail)*

Unfair Labour Practice Proceeding: A proceeding before a labour relations board to determine whether an employer or a union has committed unfair labour practices as charged. *(Procédure en matière de pratiques déloyales de travail)*

Union: The unit of labour organization which organizes and charters locals in the industries or trades as defined in its constitution, sets general policy for its locals, assists them in the conduct of their affairs, and is the medium for co-ordinating their activities. Finances are obtained from the locals through per capita dues. Unions usually hold regular conventions of delegates from the locals at which general policy is set and at which officers are elected. A union may be affiliated with a larger labour organization (e.g., congress, federation, labour council). *(Syndicat)*

Union Dues: Periodic payments by union members for the financial support of their union. *(Cotisations syndicales)*

Union Label; Bug: A tag, imprint or design affixed to a product to show it was made by union labour. *(Étiquette syndicale)*

Union Local: (See **Local Union**.) *(Syndicat local)*

Union Organizer: A person who solicits workers to join a union. *(Recruteur syndical)*

Union Scale: A rate of pay set by a union contract as the minimum rate for a job, whether or not paid to a union member. *(Tarif syndical)*

Union Security Clauses: Provisions in collective agreements designed to protect the institutional authority of the union. Examples of union security clauses are: **closed shop**, an agreement between union and employer that the employer may hire only union members and retain only union members in the shop; **preferential hiring**, an agreement that an employer, in hiring new workers, will give preference to union members; **union shop**, an agreement that the employer may hire anyone he wants, but all workers must join the union within a specified time after being hired and retain membership as a condition of continuing employment; **maintenance of membership**, a provision that no worker must join as a condition of employment, but all workers who voluntary join must maintain their membership for the duration of the contract in order to keep their jobs. (See also **Checkoff, Closed shop, Maintenance of Membership, Rand Formula, Union Shop, Modified Union Shop**.) *(Clause de sécurité syndicale)*

Union Shop: A place of work where every worker covered by the collective agreement must become and remain a member of the union. New workers need not be union members to be hired, but must join after a certain number of days. (See **Union Security Clauses, Modified Union Shop**.) *(Atelier syndical)*

Union Steward: Union member ordinarily elected to represent workers in a particular shop or department. His or her functions may include collecting dues, soliciting for new members, announcing meetings, receiving, investigating, and attempting the adjustment of grievances, and education. *(Délégué syndical)*

Union Trusteeship: Describes a situation in which a national or international union suspends the normal operations of a union local and takes over control of the local's assets and the administration of its internal affairs. The constitutions of many international unions authorize international officers to establish trusteeships over local unions in order to prevent corruption, mismanagement and other abuses. *(Tutelle syndicale)*

Unjust Dismissal: Dismissal of an employee in an arbitrary or unjust fashion, contrary to statute or in contravention of a collective agreement. *(Congédiement injuste)*

Unorganized Workers: Workers who do not belong to any union. *(Travailleurs non syndiqués)*

Vacation: Paid leave for a relatively extended period. Employers are required by law to give employees paid annual vacations, the length of time being dependent on length of services and provisions of the collective agreement. *(Vacances)*

Voluntary Recognition: A voluntary agreement (not involving the formal certification process) between an employer and a trade union to recognize the trade union as the exclusive bargaining agent of the employees in a defined bargaining unit. *(Reconnaissance volontaire)*

Wage and Price Controls: Government effort to restrain wage and price increases, usually through the establishment of some form of review or control agency (e.g., Anti-Inflation Board). *(Contrôle des salaires et des prix)*

Wage Determination: The practices and procedures used to fix wage rates in collective bargaining. *(Fixation des salaries)*

Wage Differentials: Variations among wage rates due to a variety of factors — job content, location, skill, industry, company, sex, etc. Unions are frequently concerned with eliminating wage differentials not based on the degree of effort or skill required in a job but considered discriminatory. *(Différence de salaire)*

Wage Parity: Equality of wages between workers in the same occupation but in different geographical areas; for workers in the same sector, e.g., the public sector, but in different occupations, e.g., policemen and firemen; or for workers in the same occupation but in different companies or countries. *(Parité)*

Walkout: A spontaneous, co-ordinated work stoppage. *(Débrayage)*

White-collar Workers: Term used to describe non-manual workers, e.g. office, clerical, sales, supervisory, professional and technical workers. To be contrasted with blue-collar workers, e.g., maintenance and production workers. *(Cols blancs)*

Wider-based Bargaining: (See **Broader-based Bargaining**.)

Wildcat Strike: A spontaneous and short-lived work stoppage, not authorized by the union. It is usually a reaction to a specific problem in the workplace, rather than a planned strike action. *(Grève sauvage)*

Work Restriction: Limitation ordinarily placed by unions on the types or amounts of work that union members can do. *(Frienage de la production)*

Work Rules: Rules regulating on-the-job conditions of work, usually incorporated in the collective agreement. Example (1) limiting production work of supervisory personnel; (2) limiting the assignment of work outside an employee's classification; (3) requiring a minimum number of workers on a job; (4) limiting the use of labour-saving methods and equipment. *(Règles du travail)*

Work Sharing: Plan by which available work is distributed as evenly as possible among all workers when production slackens, or by which working time is generally reduced to prevent layoffs. Under the Canada Employment and Immigration Commission's Work Sharing Program, in effect since 1982, unemployment insurance benefits help compensate workers for the reduction in wages caused by such an arrangement. Under the same program, workers affected by work sharing may take part in appropriate vocational training. *(Partage du travail)*

Work Stoppage: A cessation of work resulting from a strike or lockout. *(Arrêt de travail)*

Work to Rule: A practice where workers obey to the letter all laws and rules pertaining to their work, thereby effecting a slowdown. The practice also frequently involves a refusal to perform duties which, though related, are not explicitly included in the job description. (See also **Slowdown**.) *(Grève du zèle)*

Worker Directions: Representation of employee interests by persons, usually union officials, on the board of directors of a corporation. Practised in a number of European countries, notably West Germany. *(Administrateur (travailleurs))*

Worker Participation: The opportunity for workers to share, either directly or indirectly through elected representatives, in the decision-making process. Various degrees of participation may be identified according to the amount of influence that workers are allowed to exert. Thus, **communication** refers to the simple conveyance of information to workers either before or after decisions have been made. **Consultation** involves sounding out workers' opinions, usually before decisions are made. **Co-determination** refers to a system under which workers are able to participate in a joint decision-making process. Participation is often used as a synonym for industrial democracy. *(Participation ouvrière)*

Workers' Compensation: Compensation payable by employers collectively for injuries sustained by employees in the course of their employment. Each province has a worker's compensation act. *(Indemnisation des accidents du travail)*

Working Conditions: Conditions pertaining to the worker's job environment, such as hours of work, safety, paid holidays and vacations, rest periods, free clothing or uniforms, possibilities of advancement, etc. Many of these are included in the collective agreement and subject to collective bargaining. *(Conditions de travail)*

Index